# THE AUTHORS

Christopher Pass, BSc (Econ), M Phil, PhD is a reader, and Bryan Lowes, BSc, M Phil, PhD, ACMA is a senior lecturer, at the Management Centre, University of Bradford. Andrew Pendleton, MA, PhD and Leslie Chadwick MBA, FCCA are lecturers at the Management Centre. Their teaching and research in business studies is complemented by their varied work as consultants to a number of companies and public organizations.

Christopher Pass and Bryan Lowes are authors of the *Collins Dictionary of Economics*.

# COLLINS

## DICTIONARY OF

# BUSINESS

# COLLINS

## DICTIONARY OF

# BUSINESS

### SECOND EDITION

*Christopher Pass, Bryan Lowes,*
*Andrew Pendleton and Leslie Chadwick*

HarperCollins*Publishers*

HarperCollinsPublishers
P.O. Box, Glasgow G4 0NB

First published 1991
Second edition 1995

Reprint 9 8 7 6

© 1991, 1995 C Pass, B Lowes, A Pendleton, L Chadwick

ISBN 0 00 470803 2

Printed in Great Britain

# Preface

This dictionary, now updated, contains material especially suitable for students reading specialist business studies courses at schools, universities and polytechnics and for students undertaking a business studies course as part of a broader-based economics and commerce degree or professional qualification. It will also be useful to people working in industry, commerce and public service who may need to familiarize themselves with a particular concept or practice.

Entries have been selected and structured to reflect the following considerations: (1) the various strategies and policies which firms and other organizations can pursue in order to achieve their objectives; (2) the 'nuts and bolts' of business practice, that is, the various concepts, techniques and methods used in the functional areas of business: marketing, finance, production, personnel, etc.; (3) the industrial and economic environment of business, that is, the various factors which impinge *directly* on the operations of business (for example, market structure and competitive influences) and those which have a more general and *indirect* impact (for example, government economic policy and international trade influences).

It is, of course, difficult to draw a precise dividing line between business-orientated material and other subject matter. Accordingly, readers are recommended to consult other volumes in this series (in particular, the *Collins Dictionary of Economics* and *Collins Dictionary of Computing*) should they fail to find a particular entry in this dictionary.

To cater for a wide-ranging readership with varying degrees of knowledge requirements, the entries have been structured, where appropriate, to provide a basic definition followed by an explanation of a particular concept, which leads through cross-references to related terms.

Cross-references are denoted both in the text and at the end of entries by SMALL CAPITAL LETTERS.

# ACKNOWLEDGEMENTS

We should like to thank Monica Thorp for her invaluable editorial advice and work in preparing the book for publication; and Sylvia Ashdown, Gill Sharpley, Sylvia Bentley and Lorna Pickersgill for their painstaking and efficient typing of the manuscript.

# A

**ABC analysis** or **Pareto analysis** a means of classifying items such as sales, stock, etc., in which items are ranked according to their relative importance to the firm. For example, products may be ranked according to their sales value, as in Fig. 1, with sales items plotted cumulatively on the horizontal axis and sales cumulated on the vertical axis to show a Pareto curve. Using this curve it is possible to place items into three classes: A items, often the first 10% of items, which may account for up to 60% of sales value; B items, often the second 30% accounting for perhaps 30% of sales value; and finally C items. Having classified items in this manner it is possible to develop STOCK CONTROL procedures which are appropriate for each class of item.

Fig. 1. **ABC analysis.** The Pareto curve.

In retailing, for example, products could be ranked according to their profit margins and the speed at which they sell, for example a high margin, fast-moving product could be ranked A and at the other extreme a low margin, slow-moving product could be ranked C. The rankings can assist management to decide the frequency with which the items will be monitored, for example A items daily, B items weekly and C items monthly. See PARETO DISTRIBUTION.

**'above-the-line' promotion** a form of promotion, especially ADVERTISING, where an ADVERTISING AGENCY is paid a commission by a MEDIA firm such as a newspaper or commercial television company for buying space or time.

'BELOW-THE-LINE' promotions such as POINT OF SALE DISPLAYS and demonstrations, by contrast, do not involve the payment of a commission. See PROMOTIONAL MIX.

**absenteeism 1.** the level of unsanctioned absences from work in an organization.
**2.** chronic unsanctioned absence from work by individuals.

Absence from work may be sanctioned by managers in advance for certain reasons (for example for a forthcoming visit to the dentist), or may be sanctioned subsequently (for example for illness – see SICK PAY). The difficulty arises where there are no acceptable reasons for absence or where managers believe the excuses tendered to be untrue. In theory, DISCIPLINARY PROCEDURES can be activated but it can be difficult to prove that employees were absent without due cause. Managers could visit absentees at home to establish the facts but this can be time-consuming and counter-productive since it can indicate to committed employees that they are not trusted. Whilst punishing absence can be difficult, measures can be taken to encourage attendance, such as extra pay (see ATTENDANCE BONUS). A high level of absenteeism is often seen as an indicator of the quality of a workforce but it can equally be an indicator of poor working conditions. Improvement of the latter may also reduce absenteeism.

**absolute advantage** the possession by a country of certain advantages (lower labour costs, plentiful supplies of raw materials) which enable it to produce some products more cheaply than other countries. However, the country may find it more economical not to produce all of these products for itself, but instead specialize in those products in which it has the greatest relative or 'comparative advantage', exporting these products in exchange for imports of products in which its comparative advantage is lower. See INTERNATIONAL TRADE.

**absorption** the sharing of indirect costs or OVERHEADS to units of product by means of COST RATES. Provided that actual overheads do not exceed BUDGET and that actual output is the same as budgeted output, then the overhead cost rate should allow total product cost to be determined, and a selling price set which will recover the overhead costs involved in producing and selling the product. See STANDARD COST, OVERHEAD COST VARIANCE.

**absorption costing** a system of product COSTING which assigns materials and labour, and OVERHEAD costs to units of product manufactured (as in STANDARD COSTS). Fixed overhead costs are assigned to products by means of an appropriate COST RATE which divides planned overhead costs by planned output. Fig. 2 shows an illustration of absorption costing.

With absorption costing, fixed overhead costs are included in the value of work in progress and finished goods stock. By contrast, with MARGINAL COSTING systems fixed overhead costs are charged as a single block against revenues in the period when they are incurred, and work in progress and finished goods stocks are valued at direct materials and labour cost only.

| | TOTAL £ | Tables £ | Chairs £ | Stools £ |
|---|---|---|---|---|
| Sales | 500 | 200 | 200 | 100 |
| Material cost | 250 | 100 | 75 | 75 |
| Wages | 100 | 35 | 50 | 15 |
| Overheads (100% wgs) | 100 | 35 | 50 | 15 |
| TOTAL COST | 450 | 170 | 175 | 105 |
| PROFIT (LOSS) | 50 | 30 | 25 | (5) |

Fig. 2. **Absorption costing.** Table showing an example.

**ACAS** see ADVISORY, CONCILIATION AND ARBITRATION SERVICE.

**ACCA** see CHARTERED ASSOCIATION OF CERTIFIED ACCOUNTANTS.

**accelerated depreciation** a DEPRECIATION method which charges a higher proportion of the HISTORIC COST of an ASSET against profits during the early years of its life than is charged in the later years of its life, for example the *reducing balance* method of depreciation. It is often argued that an accelerated depreciation method is more appropriate since it levies higher depreciation charges in the early years of an asset's life when

3

maintenance and repair charges are modest, while charging less for depreciation in the later years of the asset's life when maintenance and repair charges are higher.

**acceptable quality level (AQL)** the highest proportion of rejects from a sample of raw materials, work in progress or finished goods which will be tolerated by a business. See ACCEPTANCE SAMPLING, QUALITY CONTROL.

**acceptance** see CONTRACT.

**acceptance sampling** a process in which a sample is taken from a batch of raw materials, work in progress or finished goods to be inspected and tested so as to ensure a pre-determined QUALITY standard is consistently achieved. The whole batch will then be accepted or rejected according to whether or not the sample is of an ACCEPTABLE QUALITY LEVEL. This saves the business from having to carry out 100% INSPECTION and testing of the goods involved. For example, a manufacturer taking delivery of 100 identical components from a supplier might inspect and test 10 components (10%) and specify that if more than 2 components (20% of the sample) fail to meet the required specification, then the whole batch will be rejected. In order to specify the performance of a particular sampling plan or evaluate alternative sampling plans, managers can develop OPERATING CHARACTERISTIC CURVES which show the relationship between percentage defects in batches of raw materials or components and the probability of their acceptance.

With JUST-IN-TIME production systems, a company or department may reduce its own acceptance sampling and place the onus of providing fault-free raw materials or components on its supplier. See TOTAL QUALITY MANAGEMENT, QUALITY CONTROL.

**accepting house** a division of a MERCHANT BANK or similar organization that 'accepts' (guarantees to honour) a BILL OF EXCHANGE, should a borrower default on the loan, in return for an agreed fee. By 'accepting' the bill the accepting house makes the bill more negotiable and so enables the bill to be discounted at more favourable interest rates.

**Accepting Houses Committee** an organization which represents the interests of UK ACCEPTING HOUSES.

**account 1.** a LEDGER record in which is entered details of all financial transactions relating to an individual supplier (in the creditors' ledger), or customer (in the debtors' ledger), or particular asset or liability (in the assets ledger), or type of expense or receipt (in the nominal ledgers). See DOUBLE ENTRY ACCOUNTS, ACCOUNTING.

**2.** a BANK or BUILDING SOCIETY'S record of its dealings with a particular customer which itemizes the customer's business with the bank such as deposits of cash and cheques and withdrawals of funds.

**accountability** an employee's RESPONSIBILITY for the exercise of certain duties and the requirement to report to his superiors on his performance of them. In recent years, many managers have attempted to strengthen lines of accountability so as to achieve improvements in the job performance of their subordinates. One approach to this has been the creation of PROFIT CENTRES. The profit performance of these subunits of the organization can be closely monitored by organizational leaders, thereby increasing the accountability of those working in the profit centres. In so far as creation of profit centres involves a measure of decentralization of decision-making, decentralization of responsibility and AUTHORITY can be coupled with increased accountability. See MANAGEMENT, ORGANIZATION.

**account executive** an employee of an ADVERTISING AGENCY who is responsible for looking after the interests of a particular client's ACCOUNT with the agency.

**accounting** the process of recording a firm's financial transactions in appropriate book-keeping records and of summarizing this information in the form of accounting reports, using acknowledged methods and conventions. FINANCIAL ACCOUNTING is geared to the preparation of summary reports for the shareholders or owners of the business, while MANAGEMENT ACCOUNTING is geared to the preparation of more detailed reports for managers. Fig. 3 (overleaf) shows a typical data-recording sequence.

**accounting exposure** see EXCHANGE RATE EXPOSURE.

**accounting period** the time period over which a firm prepares its PROFIT-AND-LOSS ACCOUNT and at the end of which it draws up its BALANCE SHEET. JOINT-STOCK COMPANIES are required by law to prepare ANNUAL REPORTS AND ACCOUNTS for the shareholders. Many firms now prepare quarterly, monthly or even weekly trading accounts to give managers prompt feedback about performance.

**accounting principles** or **policies** the principles which must

Fig. 3. **Accounting.** A typical data-recording sequence.

LLYFRGELL COLEG MENAI LIBRARY

be followed in preparing accounting records and summarizing them in financial statements:

(a) the *going concern* principle suggests that all financial reports be prepared to reflect the business's expected continuation as a going concern which will trade in the future, rather than being a one-off venture or a business which is likely to cease trading imminently and have its assets sold off;

(b) the *accruals* principle suggests that all revenues and expenses should be taken into account when they become due rather than when they are actually received or paid. In this way revenues and profits are *matched* with the associated expenses incurred in earning them;

(c) the *consistency* principle suggests that all accounting information should be consistently based between one year and the next, to aid comparisons of performance over time. This means, for example, that a business should not readily switch from one DEPRECIATION method to another from year to year;

(d) the *prudence* or *conservatism* principle suggests that revenues and profits should never be anticipated in the accounts of a business, but should only be included in the PROFIT-AND-LOSS ACCOUNT when such revenues and profits are reasonably certain. This means, for example, that companies would take account only of sales made, not of orders taken, and even then might make provision for some customers who have bought goods not paying up. Companies would also take a fairly conservative view of the value of assets such as stock in following this principle, adjusting the book value of stocks down to their realizable market value when market values fall. The prudence principle aims to ensure that a business's profits and assets are not overstated nor its liabilities understated;

(e) the *materiality* principle suggests that only data which are significant enough to be relevant need be disclosed, minor items being ignored in accounting reports;

(f) the *objectivity* principle suggests a need to establish rules for recording and summarizing financial transactions which avoid the exercise of personal judgement by the person doing the recording and summarizing. Thus accountants usually account for ASSETS on the basis of their HISTORIC COST, since historic cost provides an objective basis, rather than estimating the changing market value of assets.

In preparing financial accounts for shareholders, joint-stock companies are required to disclose the specific accounting policies (based on the above principles) which they have used in valuing stocks, calculating depreciation and the like.

**accounting ratio** a means of placing a firm's accounting results in context by expressing the figures as ratios or percentages of other figures in order to appraise their 'bigness' or 'smallness'. Examples include RETURN ON CAPITAL EMPLOYED and STOCK TURNOVER RATIO. Fig. 4 shows the main ratios used and the relationship between them.

**accounting return** a criterion used in INVESTMENT APPRAISAL to evaluate the desirability of an INVESTMENT project. Accounting return involves calculating the anticipated return on an investment in terms of the average yearly accounting profit expected from the project, expressed as a percentage of the capital invested. Fig. 5 shows a typical calculation for a proposed machine purchase, which in this case promises an accounting return of 36% per year. If a firm's target rate of return for new investment projects was, say, 30% plus, then this particular project would be undertaken.

Whether or not the calculated return is realized depends upon how accurate the future estimates of sales volume, selling prices, materials costs, machine life, etc. turn out to be. Since all investments involve assessments of future revenues and costs they are all subject to a degree of uncertainty. This problem, in part, can be handled by undertaking a sensitivity analysis, making not one but three estimates from each item of project cost or revenue ('optimistic', 'most likely', 'pessimistic') to indicate the range of possible outcomes.

**accounting standards** see STATEMENTS OF RECOMMENDED PRACTICE.

**Accounting Standards Board** the UK body which formulates accounting standards or STATEMENTS OF RECOMMENDED PRACTICE and ensures that companies comply with these standards in drawing up their ACCOUNTS.

**account payee** a means of indicating on a CHEQUE that the money should only be paid into the bank or building society account of the payee.

**account period** a designated trading period for the buying and selling of FINANCIAL SECURITIES on the STOCK MARKET. Until 1994 trading on the UK Stock Market took place within a series of end-on fortnightly account periods with all purchases

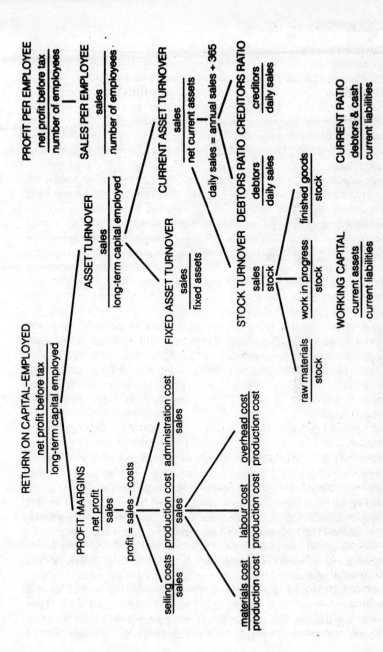

Fig. 4. **Accounting ratio.** The ratio pyramid.

9

# ACCOUNTS

|  | Year 1<br>£ | Year 2<br>£ | Yearly Average<br>£ |
|---|---|---|---|
| unit sales | 3,000 | 2,000 | 2,500 |
| price | ×3 | ×3 | ×3 |
| revenue | 9,000 | 6,000 | 7,500 |
| materials, labour and overhead costs | 4,000 | 3,000 | 3,500 |
| gross profit | 5,000 | 3,000 | 4,000 |
| depreciation | 2,200 | 2,200 | 2,200 |
| Profit | 2,800 | 800 | 1,800 |

accounting return = $\frac{£1,800}{£5,000}$ × 100 = 36% per year

Fig. 5. Accounting return. Example: machine: cost £5,000, estimated life 2 years, residual value £600, depreciation $\frac{£5,000 - 600}{2}$ = £2,200 per year.

and sales struck during a particular account period being paid for or settled six working days after the end of the account period – the 'settlement' day or 'account' day.

In 1994 this system was replaced by a 'rolling settlement' system in which settlement takes place ten working days after a deal has been struck. Thus, *every* working day is a settlement day.

Settlement was cut to five days in 1995. See TALISMAN, CREST.

**accounts** the financial statements of a business prepared from a system of recorded financial transactions. Public limited JOINT-STOCK COMPANIES are required to publish their year-end financial statements, which must comprise at least a PROFIT-AND-LOSS ACCOUNT and BALANCE SHEET, to enable SHAREHOLDERS to assess their company's financial performance during the period. AUDITORS also require a set of year-end accounts to enable them to undertake appropriate tests of the LEDGER records and submit their opinion on the accuracy of the company's reported results to shareholders. Nonincorporated bodies such as sole proprietors and partnerships are not subject to such rigorous legislation but most prepare appropriate financial statements to submit to the INLAND REVENUE as a basis for tax assessments.

**accounts payable** see CREDITORS.

**accounts receivable** see DEBTORS.

**accreditation of experiential learning** the award of credit for a period of relevant work experience or similar to gain admission to or exemption from some part of an educational or TRAINING course. The principle underlying it is that the technical skills ('competences') and conceptual understanding likely to have been gained during this time is broadly equivalent to that which would have been obtained from a specified programme of education or training. Some method of assessment might be used as part of the accreditation process. This type of accreditation is linked to the attempt to establish national standards of competence found in the NATIONAL VOCATIONAL QUALIFICATION initiative.

**accreditation of prior learning** the award of credit for a course of study or TRAINING previously undertaken to give exemption from some part of an educational or training course currently being taken. It facilitates greater flexibility in the provision of training and education, and is therefore thought likely to encourage take-up of vocational training and education. Accreditation of prior learning is likely to be facilitated by the attempts to set national standards of training and education in the NATIONAL VOCATIONAL QUALIFICATION initiative.

**accrual** an expense which is outstanding at the end of a trading period and which needs to be included in the accounting results for the period. For example, an unpaid INVOICE for car repairs would be included in the expenses of the trading period in calculating profits, since the repair costs relate to that period; the unpaid bill is counted as a liability of the firm at the period end, and afterwards until it is paid, and is added to CURRENT LIABILITIES in the firm's BALANCE SHEET. See PREPAYMENT.

**accruals principle of accounting** the principle that all a firm's costs and revenues should be counted in the company's accounts from the date when the expenses are legally incurred and when the revenues are receivable, not when the expenses are actually paid or the cash received. Organizations such as local drama groups which require less formal accounts may settle for RECEIPTS AND PAYMENTS ACCOUNTS which deviate from the accruals principle in the interests of simplicity; though even here *income and expenditure accounts* which follow the accruals principle are more common.

**accumulated profit** see RETAINED PROFIT.

**achievement test** see PSYCHOLOGICAL TEST.

**acid test ratio** see CURRENT RATIO.

**Acquired Rights Directive** see TRANSFER OF UNDERTAKINGS (PROTECTION OF EMPLOYMENT) REGULATIONS.

**acquisition** see TAKEOVER.

**action learning** see MANAGEMENT DEVELOPMENT.

**action programme** a STRATEGY for achieving prompt results, which sets deadlines for meeting targets. For instance, a company targeting a new MARKET SEGMENT will draw up an action plan specifying which market segment is being aimed at and how the company is going to market the product (in terms of price, special offers, methods of selling, etc.), thus establishing sales and market share targets.

**activity chart** or **process chart** or **flowchart** a means of recording all the work tasks performed by a person and/or machine at a 'work station'. Activity charts break down work tasks into five main categories: operation (altering materials, assembly, etc.); transportation (moving materials, components or products); inspection (checking for defects); delay (hold-ups in production caused by lack of materials, machine breakdowns, etc.); storage (items placed in stock).

Fig. 6 shows the symbols which are conventionally used to depict these activities:

| | |
|---|---|
| ● | operation |
| → | transportation |
| ▥ | inspection |
| ◗ | delay |
| ▼ | storage |

Fig. 6. **Activity chart symbols**

Activity charts are used in METHOD STUDY to record the methods used to perform work tasks as a basis for improving these methods by reducing delays, minimizing materials handling and combining operations. They are also used to assist in the planning of FACTORY LAYOUTS and in PRODUCTION SCHEDUL-

ING by depicting the sequence of work tasks involved.

Where several machines or operatives are deployed alongside each other in a work station, *multiple activity charts* may be used to depict their interactions.

**activity-based costing** a system of product costing which seeks to break down the divide between FIXED COSTS and VARIABLE COSTS by looking at the total cost to the business of making a product. All costs are related to *cost drivers* – the factors which influence the cost of a product.

Activity costing is suggested as an alternative to STANDARD COSTING, which analyses labour costs in detail and tends to share out overheads between products by reference to the *direct* labour hours involved in making different products. However, in automated factories, where labour is a relatively unimportant part of the total product cost, such detailed analysis of labour may not be justified and direct labour costs may be an inappropriate basis for analysing overheads. For such automated plants activity costing may be preferable, focusing as it does on the forces driving the costs of being in business.

**activity sampling** or **work sampling** a means of studying the work of managers, staff and indirect factory workers (see INDIRECT LABOUR). Activity sampling involves noting at predetermined time intervals, say every five minutes, what activity or work a particular individual or group of employees is engaged in. From these observations it is then possible to calculate the percentage of their time which the individual or group of workers is spending upon various tasks. Activity sampling information can be used to assess the proportions of productive and non-productive time and to help managers and workers to use their time more efficiently.

See METHOD STUDY.

**actuary** a statistician employed by an INSURANCE COMPANY to calculate insurance risks and premiums.

**added value** see VALUE ADDED.

**ad-hocracy** those ORGANIZATIONS in which work roles and routines tend not to be specialized or standardized. Job content is not closely or formally defined. Thus individuals' tasks can be adapted as required to meet current exigencies. An important feature of this type of organization is that employees determine among themselves who does what when new tasks arise. Hence organizations of this sort can normally respond flexibly to new situations. However, a negative feature of organizations of this sort is the lack of strategy to guide the organization; this results in the absence of clearly-defined or consistent policies to ensure achievement of organizational goals. See MECHANISTIC AND ORGANISMIC.

**administered price** a PRICE for a product which is set and controlled by an individual supplier, a group of suppliers or the government, as opposed to being determined by the free interplay of market forces. A monopoly supplier or firms operating a price-fixing CARTEL may administer product prices in order to secure high profits. Governments may likewise administer product prices, using PRICE CONTROL systems to support particular sectional interests or, more generally, as a means of controlling inflation (see PRICES AND INCOMES POLICY). Additionally, under a FIXED EXCHANGE RATE system, governments are committed to maintaining a fixed price (exchange rate) for the country's currency against other currencies.

**administration** see MANAGEMENT.

**administrator** see INSOLVENCY.

**ADR** see AMERICAN DEPOSITORY RECEIPT.

**ADST** see EMPLOYEE SHARE OWNERSHIP, PROFIT SHARING.

**ad valorem tax** a TAX which is levied as a percentage of the price or value of a unit of OUTPUT. See VALUE ADDED TAX. Compare SPECIFIC TAX.

**advance corporation tax** see CORPORATION TAX.

**advertisement** a written or visual presentation in the MEDIA of a BRAND of good or service supplied by a firm (or some other organization, for example the government), which is aimed at encouraging either prospective buyers to purchase the product, or greater usage of a facility, or to provide the population with public safety information. See ADVERTISING, ADVERTISING CAMPAIGN, ADVERTISING COPY, ADVERTISING EFFECTIVENESS TEST, REINFORCEMENT ADVERTISING, ADVERTISING STANDARDS AUTHORITY, CONTROL OF MISLEADING ADVERTISEMENTS REGULATION 1988.

**advertising** a means by which a seller of a BRAND of good or service attempts to increase his sales by communicating with BUYERS, informing them of the nature and attributes of his brand and persuading them to buy it in preference to competitors' brands. Advertising comprises part of a firm's PROMOTIONAL MIX and is undertaken in a variety of ways, including the use of mass MEDIA channels such as television, national newspapers and magazines, posters, etc., and more targeted approaches through 'special interest' magazines and trade journals, and regional and local newspapers.

Although some advertising is largely concerned with providing buyers with information about the product, the majority of advertising is 'persuasive' in orientation. Persuasive advertising aims to encourage consumers to purchase products, and the skill of advertising copywriters lies in designing ADVERTISEMENTS which are visually attractive and which appeal to deep-seated consumer motivations, both physical and psychological. If advertisements appeal sufficiently to consumer motives they will encourage repeat buying of the product, thereby establishing BRAND LOYALTY and increasing or maintaining the firm's MARKET SHARE.

The selection of the advertising medium will depend upon the MARKET or market segment which is being targeted (see MARKET SEGMENTATION) and the relative costs and effectiveness of using different media. For example, in respect of specialized INDUSTRIAL BUYERS advertisements may be placed in appropriate trade/professional journals. On the other hand, if large numbers of final consumers are being targeted, it may be more cost-effective to use the mass media which, although more expensive in absolute terms, actually costs less per potential customer reached.

Advertising is an important part of a firm's MARKETING MIX which seeks to differentiate its brand of product from competitors' offerings. See ADVERTISING COPY, ADVERTISING COVERAGE, ADVERTISING EFFECTIVENESS TEST, ADVERTISING FREQUENCY, DIRECT MARKETING, PRODUCT DIFFERENTIATION, COMPETITIVE ADVANTAGE, ADVERTISING CAMPAIGN, ADVERTISING OBJECTIVE, BUYER BEHAVIOUR, PRODUCT IMAGE, ADVERTISING STANDARDS AUTHORITY, CONTROL OF MISLEADING ADVERTISEMENTS REGULATIONS 1988.

**advertising agency** a business which specializes in providing various MARKETING services for firms and other organizations, particularly ADVERTISING services. Advertising agents devise, programme and manage specific ADVERTISING CAMPAIGNS on behalf of clients as well as undertaking more general MARKET RESEARCH, product and market analyses, SALES PROMOTION planning and public relations activities. See ADVERTISING COPY.

## ADVERTISING CAMPAIGN

**advertising campaign** a planned series of ADVERTISEMENTS aimed at increasing the sales of a particular BRAND of good or service. Such campaigns usually include a set of linked advertisements stressing a common promotional theme and this same theme will be deployed across several advertising MEDIA. A campaign might run over a short period of time, or over a number of years if it proves successful. See ADVERTISING EFFECTIVENESS TEST.

**advertising copy** the specific wording and/or visual presentation of an ADVERTISEMENT of a BRAND of good or service, which highlights the 'theme' or 'message' the advertisement is intended to convey to prospective BUYERS or users of that product. Advertising copy may be pitched to appeal to consumers in general or targeted to attract the attention of a particular type of buyer (see MARKET SEGMENTATION).

Advertising copy can take a variety of forms, but ADVERTISING AGENCIES and other writers and producers of advertising material must be mindful that an advertisement should not be misleading, untruthful or in bad taste.

See ADVERTISING STANDARDS AUTHORITY, ADVERTISING EFFECTIVENESS TEST, MOTIVATIONAL RESEARCH.

**advertising coverage** the number of prospective buyers of a BRAND of good or service reached by an ADVERTISEMENT of that product. This will depend largely on the choice of MEDIA (commercial television, newspapers, etc.) selected for the advertisement and the frequency with which the advertisement appears. See ADVERTISING, ADVERTISING FREQUENCY, ADVERTISING CAMPAIGN.

**advertising effectiveness test** a means of measuring the impact or likely impact of an ADVERTISEMENT or an ADVERTISING CAMPAIGN on the sales of a product. Such tests fall into two basic categories:

(a) *pre-testing* in which particular advertisements are tried out on a representative sample of buyers or potential buyers (see TEST MARKETING) to decide, in advance, which one of them is likely to make the biggest impact on prospective buyers. Methods used for this purpose include the *sales conviction test* and the *blind product test*. In the former case established buyers of the product are asked which of a number of advertisements would induce them to buy the product, while in the latter case respondents are given ADVERTISING COPY and asked to select from a number of unidentified products the one which best 'fits' the advertisement;

(b) *post-testing* which aims to measure the impact of the advertisements currently used by the firm. Various *recognition tests* can be used for this purpose, including asking readers of a newspaper or viewers of commercial television where the advertisement has been placed whether they have read or seen the advertisement in question. Deeper probing of the impression an advertisement may have made can be done by the *unaided recall test* where respondents are asked to comment from memory on particular details of the advertisement.

**advertising frequency** the number of times an ADVERTISEMENT appears in the MEDIA (commercial television, newspapers, etc.). Advertising frequency can be extended by increasing over a specific time period the number of times the advertisement appears in the firm's existing choice of media, or by placing the advertisement in a wider range of media. A high advertising frequency is often required to launch a NEW PRODUCT onto the market and is also important in supporting existing BRANDS over time, encouraging repeat purchasing and maintaining BRAND LOYALTY.

**advertising message** a communication designed to influence BUYER BEHAVIOUR. See ADVERTISING COPY.

**advertising objective** the goal of ADVERTISING which can be stated in qualitative terms such as increasing consumers' awareness of a particular BRAND of good or service or the company itself. Alternatively, the objective may be operationalized as a specific target such as increasing the SALES/ MARKET SHARE of a product by x% over a one-year period.

**Advertising Standards Authority (ASA)** a body which regulates (on a 'voluntary' basis) the UK ADVERTISING industry. The ASA administers the British Code of Advertising Practice which aims to ensure that ADVERTISEMENTS provide a fair, honest and unambiguous representation of the products they promote, including the wording of, and impressions conveyed by, ADVERTISING COPY. The ASA gives guidance to advertisers on whether a proposed advertisement would be regarded as acceptable, and deals with complaints from the general public about cases of allegedly untruthful, misleading or offensive advertisements.

**Advisory, Conciliation and Arbitration Service (ACAS)**

an independent service set up in 1975, financed by the government and used to resolve collective and individual INDUSTRIAL DISPUTES in the UK. It is able to provide CONCILIATION to bring the parties together and to provide ARBITRATION and MEDIATION where it is deemed desirable. ACAS also provides advisory services to employers, employees and trade unions on work and employment issues. So far these have been provided free of charge but there is speculation that ACAS will be required to charge for these services in the near future. ACAS had a duty to promote COLLECTIVE BARGAINING since its inception but this was abolished by the TRADE UNION REFORM AND EMPLOYMENT RIGHTS ACT 1993. See CENTRAL ARBITRATION COMMITTEE, INDUSTRIAL TRIBUNAL.

**AEEU** see AMALGAMATED ENGINEERING AND ELECTRICAL UNION.

**AFBD** see SECURITIES AND FUTURES AUTHORITY.

**after-sales service** back-up services and facilities provided by the suppliers of goods and services to their customers. After-sales service can include free maintenance and repairs, a telephone service for dealing with customers' queries, and an express parts delivery service. An after-sales service is an important part of the MARKETING MIX, serving to enhance customer loyalty and provide valuable feedback about its goods and services. See CUSTOMER SERVICES, GUARANTEE.

**AG** see AKTIENGESELLSCHAFT.

**age analysis profile for debtors** a summary analysis of outstanding DEBTOR balances in the debtors LEDGER classified according to how long these debts have been outstanding. For example, the age analysis profile might distinguish between debts which are less than one month old; those which are two months old; those which are three months old (stale debts); those which are four months old (doubtful as to repayment); and five months or older (mostly bad debts to be written off as irrecoverable). Preparation of periodic age analysis profiles which monitor the proportions of total outstanding debt falling into each age category can provide useful data for CREDIT CONTROL purposes. See CREDIT PERIOD, DEBTORS RATIO.

**Agency status** a UK civil service function which operates at arm's length from the civil service. Agencies developed in the wake of the 'Next Steps' report in the late 1980s which argued that the service provision function of the civil service (e.g. payment of unemployment benefit) should be separated from the policy-formulation part and become the responsibility of executive agencies.

See NEW PUBLIC MANAGEMENT.

**agenda** a list of items of business scheduled for discussion at a meeting.

**agent** a person or company employed by another person or company (called the PRINCIPAL) for the purpose of arranging CONTRACTS between the principal and third parties. An agent generally has authority to act within broad limits in conducting business on behalf of his or her principal and has a basic duty to carry out the tasks involved with due skill and diligence.

An agent or broker acts as an intermediary in bringing together buyers and sellers of a good or service, receiving a flat or sliding scale commission or fee related to the nature and comprehensiveness of the work undertaken and/or value of the transaction involved. Agents and agencies are encountered in one way or another in most economic activities and play an important role in the smooth functioning of the market mechanism. A *stockbroker*, for example, acts on behalf of clients wishing to buy and sell financial securities; an *estate agent* acts as an intermediary between buyers and sellers of houses, offices, etc.; while an *insurance broker* negotiates insurance cover on behalf of clients with an insurance company. A *recruitment agency* performs the services of advertising for, interviewing and selecting employees on behalf of a company; an *advertising agency* acts on behalf of a manufacturer in selling his product, introducing the product to wholesalers and retailers as well as performing various support services to promote the product.

**aggregated rebate** or **overriding discount** a business practice whereby a supplier offers distributors/retailers a discount on their *total* purchases over a specified time period (usually one year) rather than on individual orders. The operation of aggregated rebates, by encouraging dealers/retailers to place the whole or a substantial part of their regular orders with one supplier, may help the supplier increase his sales and protect market share. However, if undertaken by a DOMINANT FIRM, the practice may serve to limit competition in a market by depriving rival suppliers of distribution outlets. See OFFICE OF FAIR TRADING, QUANTITY DISCOUNT, BULK BUYING.

**AGM** see ANNUAL GENERAL MEETING.

**agricultural policy** a policy which is concerned with both supporting the agricultural industry by the subsidization of farm incomes and prices, and providing cash grants and other financial aids designed to promote large-scale capital-intensive farming.

Price support and income support systems are used to 'top-up' farming revenues (see Fig. 7). In the former case, the government sets 'support prices' or 'intervention prices' for specified agricultural products such as wheat and beef, standing ready to purchase any output which is not sold in the market. This system forms the basis of the *Common Agricultural Policy* of the EUROPEAN UNION/COMMUNITY. The problem with this system is that if support prices are set in excess of market-clearing prices (see EQUILIBRIUM MARKET PRICE) it encourages wasteful overproduction, with the government then having to stockpile surplus output. The income support system, by contrast, allows the prices of agricultural products to be determined by market forces. If these prices yield farmers insufficient income the government will then pay farmers a 'deficiency payment' to bring their incomes up to some agreed minimum level.

**aims** see BUSINESS OBJECTIVES.

**AITC** see ASSOCIATION OF INVESTMENT TRUST COMPANIES.

**Aktiengesellschaft (AG)** the German equivalent of a British public limited company. See JOINT-STOCK COMPANY.

**alienation** the separation of people from their essential qualities as human beings in capitalist societies. Karl Marx (1818–83), who first developed the concept, believed that 'free conscious activity' was the hallmark of human activity. Work in modern capitalist society, which involves the worker producing goods and services for the profit of an employer and in a manner dictated by the employer, separates (i.e. alienates) people from their essence. In effect an individual's labour power is reduced to a commodity to be bought and sold. Job dissatisfaction may well result, but the possibility arises that alienation from 'true' human desires is so deep that individuals have no standard against which to compare their lot and hence may nevertheless experience job satisfaction. Since alienation, as defined here, has no clear discernible relationship with JOB SATISFACTION, many critics have argued that its use in

Fig. 7. **Agricultural policy.** *Subsidization of agriculture*
Equilibrium market price = OA
*Price support:* support price = OB paid by consumers; government buys up the unsold output CD; total cost to the government = area CDEQ
*income support:* market price = OA paid by consumers; government sets SHADOW PRICE, say OB, and pays farmers a deficiency payment equal to DF per unit of output; total cost to the government = area ABDF.

the analysis of work attitudes and behaviour is decidely limited.

A closer link between alienation and job satisfaction has been provided by American sociologist Robert Blauner (1929– ). He defined alienation as a 'fragmentation in man's consciousness', experienced as dissatisfaction. The dimensions of this are a sense of powerlessness (i.e. inability to control what happens at work), a feeling of meaninglessness (i.e. the job tasks seem pointless), a sense of isolation from others, and a feeling of self-estrangement (i.e. that one's creativity is stifled). In Blauner's view, technology is the most important determinant of alienation.

In assembly-line work (see FORDISM) alienation reaches its peak. By contrast, more recent process technology, in which the worker oversees a range of operations rather than being subjugated to the machine, is associated with lower levels of alienation. The logic of Blauner's account, in contrast to that of Marx, is that alienation can be reduced by managerial policies to modify the nature of workers' tasks (see JOB DESIGN AND REDESIGN) and to integrate workers into a work community (see HUMAN RELATIONS). See ANOMIE.

**all-current method** see FOREIGN CURRENCY TRANSLATION.

**allocation 1.** the breakdown of COSTS (and REVENUES) between different products, functions or company departments where it is possible to attribute costs (and revenues) directly to the departments where the cost (revenue) arises. For example, in analysing costs, the depreciation OVERHEADS of factory departments can be allocated precisely between the production departments where the specific fixed assets are located. Such allocations help in tracing responsibility for costs to the managers responsible, as well as assessing the profitability of different departments or products. Fig. 8 shows a typical departmental revenue/cost breakdown where some costs are precisely allocated while others are apportioned on an equitable basis. See BUDGETING, STANDARD COST.

**2.** the process of assigning or 'earmarking' materials which are in STOCK in order to fulfil specified product orders. The stock of materials that has not been currently allocated is referred to as the 'free balance', which is available for allocation to future orders.

**allotment** the allocation of shares by directors of a company to intending shareholders who have made applications for new shares. In the event of a new SHARE ISSUE being oversubscribed (i.e. more applications for shares than the number being issued), then the company must use some formula to allocate shares among applicants. Often this involves granting applicants for small blocks of shares the full number of shares applied for, while applicants for large blocks of shares may be granted only a proportion of the numbers they applied for, or, in the event of a ballot, receive none at all if unsuccessful.

**allowances 1.** the additional time which is added to the 'basic time' allowed for the completion of a particular work task in order to calculate a 'standard time' for that task. These include:

(a) Relaxation allowances, which are made to take account of the mental and physical needs of workers, who require rest periods;

(b) contingency allowances which are made to cover the unforeseen circumstances such as the extra work caused by defective machines or substandard materials;

| EXPENSE | TOTAL £ | BASIS OF ALLOCATION | FRAME SHOP £ | UPHOLSTERY SECTION £ |
|---|---|---|---|---|
| *DIRECT COSTS* | | | | |
| Direct Materials | 350,000 | Actual | 200,000 | 150,000 |
| Direct Labour | 174,000 | Actual | 74,000 | 100,000 |
| Prime Cost | 524,000 | | 274,000 | 250,000 |
| | | | | |
| *PRODUCTION OVERHEADS* | | | | |
| Factory Rent and Rates | 10,800 | Floor area | 5,000 | 5,800 |
| Power and Light | 10,750 | Metered Consumption | 5,750 | 5,000 |
| General Labour | 21,850 | Actual | 10,000 | 11,850 |
| Depreciation | 23,300 | Plant Installed | 12,300 | 11,000 |
| Works Management | 5,000 | Time Occupied Estimate | 2,000 | 3,000 |
| | 71,700 | | 35,050 | 36,650 |

Fig. 8. **Allocation**. Budgeted production costs: departmental analysis.

(c) interference allowances which are made to take account of nonproductive or IDLE TIME caused by delays in materials, machine breakdowns and machine SET-UP TIMES. See WORK MEASUREMENT.

**2.** the additional raw materials or components which are added to the basic materials allowed for the completion of a particular product or subassembly in a PRODUCT SPECIFICATION, to allow for cutting losses and anticipated wastage of materials.

**3.** Tax allowances. See INCOME TAX ALLOWANCE, CAPITAL ALLOWANCE, CORPORATION TAX.

**allowed time** the maximum amount of time which an employee should take to perform a specific production task. Allowed times tend to be used in INCENTIVE BONUS SCHEMES as the basis for computing bonus payments. If the allowed time is exceeded no bonus is payable. However, if the actual time taken to perform the particular task is less than the allowed time, a bonus would be payable based upon the amount of time saved. See WORK MEASUREMENT.

**alpha stock** the STOCKS and SHARES (generally of large well-established companies) listed on the STOCK MARKET which are highly regarded by investors.

**Alternative Investment Market** see UNLISTED SECURITIES MARKET.

**Amalgamated Engineering and Electrical Union (AEEU)** the fourth largest TRADE UNION in the UK, with just under 800,000 members. It was formed in 1992 by a merger of the Amalgamated Engineering Union and the Electrical, Electronics, Telecommunication and Plumbing Union.

**amalgamation** see MERGER.

**American Depository Receipt (ADR)** a certificate of ownership issued to an individual or company investor by a US bank which holds (on deposit) the investor's or company's STOCKS and SHARES. The ADR serves as proof of the ownership of the securities held by the bank and can be used as a negotiable instrument.

American Depository Receipts have been used extensively by UK companies wishing to encourage investment by US institutional investors. Such companies lodge a proportion of their shares with a US bank, which then issues depository shares which can be traded on the US stock market.

**amortization** see DEPRECIATION, definition 1.

**analytical estimating** see WORK MEASUREMENT.

**ancillary operation** an operation in which material or plant is being cleaned, prepared or put away, where the work performed does not result in added value to the material or plant. For example, the time spent setting up or cleaning a machine contributes to the smooth running of the production presses even though it does not contribute directly to the manufacture of the product. See MAINTENANCE, SET-UP TIME.

**annual general meeting (AGM)** the yearly meeting of SHAREHOLDERS which JOINT-STOCK COMPANIES are required by law to convene, in order to allow shareholders to discuss their company's ANNUAL REPORT AND ACCOUNTS, elect directors and agree the DIVIDEND payouts suggested by directors. In practice, annual general meetings are usually poorly attended by shareholders and only rarely do directors fail to be re-elected on the strength of PROXY votes cast in favour of the directors.

*Extraordinary* or *special* general meetings may also be called by directors or shareholders to deal with major changes in, say, the firm's capital structure. See BOARD OF DIRECTORS.

**annual hours** the contractual requirement that employees work a number of hours over the year rather than a standard number of hours each week. This means that the length of the working day can be varied day by day to fit in with production requirements ('flexible rostering'). Alternatively, at certain times of the year employees work very short days whilst at other times they work long days. This can be advantageous to employers when product demand is seasonal in nature and storage of the product is either difficult or impossible (for example where a service is provided). Thus annual hours facilitate the synchronization of labour utilization with production requirements, thereby potentially improving labour productivity. A common feature of annual hours contracts is that the right to determine daily working hours is largely reserved to the employer (compare with FLEXITIME system). So far it is a rare form of WORK ORGANIZATION in the UK.

**annual report and accounts** a yearly report by the directors of a JOINT-STOCK COMPANY to the SHAREHOLDERS. It includes a copy of the company's BALANCE SHEET and a summary PROFIT-AND-LOSS ACCOUNT for the current and immediately-prior year, along with other information which directors are required by law to disclose to shareholders. Large joint-stock companies must also include a SOURCES AND USES OF FUNDS STATEMENT. A copy of the annual report and accounts is sent to every shareholder prior to the company's ANNUAL GENERAL MEETING.

**annual return** a document which must be completed by the COMPANY SECRETARY and DIRECTORS of a JOINT-STOCK COMPANY after its ANNUAL GENERAL MEETING and forwarded to the COMPANY REGISTRAR. The annual return includes details about company directors, MORTGAGES and charges, the updated SHARE REGISTER and the ANNUAL REPORT AND ACCOUNTS. Annual returns can be inspected by members of the public on payment of a fee.

**annuity** a series of equal payments at fixed intervals deriving from an original lump-sum INVESTMENT.

**annuity table** a table that shows the effect of compound interest on an annually invested sum. Specifically, the table shows what the investment of the same amount of money on an annual basis at a fixed rate of interest for a certain number of years will accumulate to. For example, if £250 is invested at 10% at the end of each of the next 6 years, using the annuity table (which shows a figure of 7.716), it would accumulate to £250 × 7.716 = £1,929.

**anomie** a state of normlessness (i.e. a sense of confusion and loss about values and personal objectives) which French sociologist Emile Durkheim (1858–1917) believed could arise from the disruption of community caused by growing specialization in the division of labour. It could be expressed in job dissatisfaction and 'deviant' behaviour at work. The solution was to create a sense of community appropriate to the new division of labour. See ALIENATION, HUMAN RELATIONS, JOB SATISFACTION.

**answering machine** see VOICE MESSAGING.

**anti-competitive practice** a practice employed by a firm which has the effect of restricting or eliminating competition in a market. Practices which may potentially adversely affect the position of a firm's rivals, suppliers or distributors include EXCLUSIVE DEALING, REFUSAL TO SUPPLY, FULL LINE FORCING, TIE-IN SALES and AGGREGATED REBATES. These practices are likely to be particularly restrictive if employed by a DOMINANT FIRM as a means of buttressing its market position against competitive encroachment. The COMPETITION ACT, 1980, gives the OFFICE OF FAIR TRADING powers to investigate and, where appropriate, prohibit offending practices. See COMPETITION POLICY.

**anti-dumping duty** a special TAX levied by a country on a product which is imported from some other country and which is deemed to have been 'dumped', that is, sold by a foreign firm in that country at a price below that which is charged in the firm's own domestic market. See DUMPING for further discussion, LOCAL CONTENT RULE.

**anti-trust policy** the US version of COMPETITION POLICY.

**AOQL** see AVERAGE OUTGOING QUALITY LEVEL.

**application money** the amount payable per share on application for a new SHARE ISSUE.

**apportionment** the breakdown of COSTS (and REVENUES) between different products, functions or company departments, where it is not possible to attribute costs (and revenues) directly to the departments where the cost or revenue concerned arises. For example, it is generally impossible to allocate rent and rates OVERHEADS exactly between departments in a factory and they can only be apportioned on some equitable basis such as the respective floor areas of departments.

Such apportionments can help in assessing the profitability of different departments or products. See BUDGETING, STANDARD COST, ALLOCATION.

**appraisal** see PERFORMANCE APPRAISAL.

**appraisal costs** see QUALITY COSTS.

**appreciation** or **capital appreciation 1.** an increase in the price of an ASSET. Assets held for long periods, such as factory buildings, offices or houses, are most likely to appreciate in value because of the effects of INFLATION and increasing site values, though the value of short-term assets like STOCKS can also appreciate. Where assets appreciate their REPLACEMENT COST will exceed their HISTORIC COST and such assets may need to be revalued periodically to keep their book values in line with their market values.

See DEPRECIATION, definition 1, INFLATION ACCOUNTING, REVALUATION PROVISION.

**2.** an increase in the EXCHANGE RATE of a currency against other currencies under a FLOATING EXCHANGE RATE SYSTEM, reflecting an increase in market demand for that currency combined with a decrease in market demand for other countries' currencies. The effect of an appreciation is to make imports (in the local currency) cheaper, thereby increasing import demand, and EXPORTS (in the local currency) more expensive, thereby reducing export demand, ultimately working towards keeping a country's BALANCE OF PAYMENTS in equilibrium on a more or less continuous basis.

Appreciations, like REVALUATIONS, can adversely affect the profitability and market position of domestic firms by making imports more price competitive in the home market and, similarly, reducing their price competitiveness in export markets.

See REVALUATION, definition 2, for further discussion. Contrast with DEPRECIATION, definition 2, EXCHANGE RATE EXPOSURE.

**apprenticeship** see TRAINING.

**appropriation account** see PROFIT-AND-LOSS APPROPRIATION ACCOUNT.

**approved all-employee savings related share option scheme** see EMPLOYEE SHARE OWNERSHIP.

**approved deferred share trusts (ADST)** see EMPLOYEE SHARE OWNERSHIP, PROFIT SHARING.

**approved discretionary share options schemes** see EMPLOYEE SHARE OWNERSHIP.

**APR** the 'annualized percentage rate of INTEREST' charged on a LOAN. The APR rate will depend on the total 'charge for credit' applied by the lender and will be influenced by such factors as the general level of INTEREST RATES, and the nature and duration of the loan.

Where lenders relate total interest charges on INSTALMENT CREDIT loans to the *original* amount borrowed, this can give a misleading impression of the interest rate being charged, for as borrowers make monthly or weekly repayments on the loan they are reducing the amount borrowed, and interest charges should be related to the lower *average* amount owed. For example, if someone borrows £1,000 for one year with a total credit charge of £200 the 'simple interest' charge on the original loan is 20%. However, if the loan terms provide for monthly repayments of £100, then at the end of the *first* month the borrower would have repaid a proportion of the original £1,000 borrowed and by the end of the *second* month would have repaid a further proportion of the original loan, etc. In effect, therefore, the borrower does *not* borrow £1,000 for one whole year but much less than this over the year *on average* as he or she repays parts of the outstanding loan. If the total credit charge of £200 were related to this much smaller *average* amount borrowed to show the 'annualized' percentage rate' then this credit charge would be nearer 40% than the 20% quoted.

To make clear to the borrower the *actual* charge for credit and the 'true' rate of interest the CONSUMER CREDIT ACT 1974 requires lenders to publish both rates to potential borrowers.

**aptitude test** see PSYCHOLOGICAL TEST.

**AQL** see ACCEPTABLE QUALITY LEVEL.

**arbitrage** the buying and selling of PRODUCTS, FINANCIAL SECURITIES or FOREIGN CURRENCIES between two or more markets in order to take profitable advantage of any differences in the prices quoted in those markets.

If the price of the *same* product is different, as between two markets, a dealer, by simultaneously buying in the lower-priced market and reselling in the higher-priced market, stands to make a profit on the transaction (allowing for dealing expenses). Arbitrage thus serves to narrow or eliminate price differentials between markets, with buying in the lower-priced market causing prices to rise there, and selling in the higher-priced market causing prices to fall.

See SPOT MARKET, ARBITRAGEUR, SPECULATION, COVERED INTEREST ARBITRAGE.

**arbitrageur** a person or firm which purchases SHARES in a company and other FINANCIAL SECURITIES in the hope of making a windfall profit. Arbitrageurs deliberately put a company into 'play'; that is, by making strategic share purchases in the company the arbitrageur fuels SPECULATION that a TAKEOVER BID is in the offing, causing the company's share price to rise. The arbitrageur then sells off his stake at a suitable profit. See ARBITRAGE.

**arbitration** a procedure for settling INDUSTRIAL DISPUTES in which a neutral third party (arbitrator) makes an award which is usually binding on all parties to the dispute. Arbitration is usually used as a last resort when it has been impossible to reach agreement under normal procedures. Some PROCEDURAL AGREEMENTS, especially those forming part of a NO STRIKE AGREEMENT, include an automatic reference to arbitration if agreement cannot be reached during COLLECTIVE BARGAINING. The benefit of arbitration is that it facilitates a compromise solution to a dispute in a way which allows both parties to save face. The arbitrator in effect finds a middle way.

A relatively novel form of arbitration in Britain is *pendulum* arbitration (also known as 'flip-flop' or 'last-offer' arbitration), in which the arbitrator has to decide for one case in its entirety rather than 'splitting the difference'. The benefits of this are said to be that it encourages more reasonable bargaining behaviour and that it precludes potentially unworkable compromises. Some of the Japanese companies which have recently opened factories in the UK have included this form of arbitration in their NO STRIKE AGREEMENTS/SINGLE UNION DEALS.

See also JAPANIZATION, ADVISORY, CONCILIATION AND ARBITRATION SERVICE, CENTRAL ARBITRATION COMMITTEE.

**arms-length price** the PRICE at which unrelated sellers and buyers agree to transact a product or asset.

**articles of association** the legal constitution of a JOINT-STOCK COMPANY which governs the internal relationship between the company and its members or SHAREHOLDERS. The articles govern the rights and duties of the membership and aspects of administration of the company. They will contain, for instance, the powers of the directors, the conduct of meetings, the dividend and voting rights assigned to separate classes of shareholders, and other miscellaneous rules and regulations. See MEMORANDUM OF ASSOCIATION.

**ASA** see ADVERTISING STANDARDS AUTHORITY.

**ASCII (American Standard Code for Information Interchange)** a system for coding individual numbers, letters and punctuation marks which is widely used in COMPUTERS.

**'A' shares** see NONVOTING SHARES.

**ask price** see BID PRICE.

**assembly chart** see MATERIALS FLOW MANAGEMENT.

**assembly drawings** see MATERIALS FLOW MANAGEMENT.

**assembly line** see PRODUCTION LINE, PRODUCT-FOCUSED LAYOUT.

**assented shares** SHARES in a company which a shareholder has agreed to sell to a takeover bidder for the company. If in the interim the shareholder sells his shares in the market, any purchaser is automatically committed to accept the bid.

**assessment centre** see RECRUITMENT AND SELECTION, PSYCHOLOGICAL TEST.

**asset** an item or property which is owned by a business or individual and which has a money value. Assets are of two main types: (a) physical assets such as plant and equipment, land, consumer durables (cars, etc.); (b) financial assets such as currency, bank deposits, stocks and shares. Alternatively, assets can be classified into FIXED ASSETS (those intended for long-term use by a business); and CURRENT ASSETS (those intended to be turned over, in trading, as raw materials are converted into finished goods, then sold to generate cash). See INVESTMENT, LIQUIDITY, BALANCE SHEET, LIABILITY.

**asset register** a LEDGER record which notes the HISTORIC COST of each physical asset owned by a business, any DEPRECIATION charged on that asset to date and its NET BOOK VALUE. Such information is summarized periodically in the FIXED ASSETS section of the BALANCE SHEET.

**asset-stripper** a predator firm which takes control of another firm (see TAKEOVER) with a view to selling off that firm's ASSETS, wholly or in part, for financial gain rather than continuing the firm as an ongoing business.

The classical recipe for asset-stripping arises when the realizable MARKET VALUE of the firm's assets is much greater than what it would cost the predator to buy the firm; i.e., where there is a marked discrepancy between the asset-backing per share of the target firm and the price per share required to take the firm over. This discrepancy usually results from a combination of two factors:

(a) gross under-valuation of the firm's assets in the BALANCE SHEET;

(b) mismanagement or bad luck resulting in low profits or losses, both of which serve to depress the firm's share price.

**asset structure** the proportions of various types of ASSET held by a firm as shown in the BALANCE SHEET. For example, a large manufacturing company or public utility is likely to have proportionately large FIXED ASSETS, while retail companies are likely to have proportionately large CURRENT ASSETS, such as DEBTORS and STOCK. A firm's asset structure helps to determine the way in which finance is raised, in particular the balance of long-term LOANS and short-term DEBT. See CAPITAL GEARING.

**asset turnover, asset utilization** or **sales-to-capital-employed ratio** a measure of a firm's ASSET turnover, which expresses the firm's sales revenue as a ratio of its size to measure the amount of sales revenue generated by each pound's worth of assets employed in the business. Often total assets are taken as the basis for comparison with sales, though sometimes long-term capital employed is used instead, taking a narrower definition of assets. The asset turnover ratio is often regarded as an important test of business efficiency. Asset turnover has a significant impact upon a firm's RETURN ON CAPITAL EMPLOYED.

**asset utilization** SEE ASSET TURNOVER.

**asset value per share** or **break-up value** the total value of a firm's tangible book ASSETS less all short- and long-term LIABILITIES as shown in the BALANCE SHEET. The net assets figure is divided by the number of ORDINARY SHARES the company has, to show approximately how much asset value supports each share. In the case of a LIQUIDATION it would be of some use to the SHAREHOLDERS in estimating how much they may reasonably expect to receive from the sale of the firm or of its assets. Book values of assets may be a reasonable estimate of their value to the firm as a going concern, but upon break-up they tend to be worth considerably less depending upon the alternative uses to which they can be put.

## ASSISTED AREA

See also ASSET-STRIPPER, SHARE CAPITAL.

**assisted area** a region of economic decline designated under UK REGIONAL POLICY as in need of industrial regeneration. Financial assistance in the form of REGIONAL SELECTIVE ASSISTANCE and REGIONAL ENTERPRISE GRANTS are available in 'development areas' and regional selective assistance is available in 'intermediate areas', to manufacturing and service businesses prepared to undertake new investment in these areas.

**associated company** or **related company** a JOINT-STOCK COMPANY in which another company, the HOLDING COMPANY, has a significant but not controlling shareholding (specifically 20% or more of the voting shares but not more than 50%). In such a situation the investing company can exert influence on the commercial and financial policy decisions of the associated company, though in principle the associated company remains independent under its own management, producing its own annual accounts, and is not a SUBSIDIARY COMPANY of the holding company.

If the second company held 50% or more of the first company's shares then the first company's assets and profits would be *consolidated* with those of the second, and the two companies would be regarded as part of the same group of firms. Where the second company holds 20% or more of the first company's shares then it must note in its own accounts information about the profits, capital and reserves of the first company in which it is heavily invested. If the second company holds less than 20% of the first company's shares it may still exercise influence over that company, though it is not obliged to disclose details of its shareholding. See CONSOLIDATED ACCOUNTS.

**Association of British Insurers** a TRADE ASSOCIATION which represents the collective interests of INSURANCE COMPANIES and INSURANCE BROKERS in the UK.

**Association of Futures Brokers and Dealers (AFBD)** see SECURITIES AND FUTURES AUTHORITY.

**Association of Investment Trust Companies (AITC)** the TRADE ASSOCIATION which represents the collective interests of INVESTMENT TRUST COMPANIES in the UK.

**assurance** a contractual saving arrangement whereby a person pays premiums at regular intervals to an INSURANCE COMPANY in return for a sum of money to be received at a later date.

With *life* assurance a lump sum payment and/or annuity becomes due to the dependants of the person assured. With *endowment* assurance a lump sum payment and/or annuity is payable to the person assured at an agreed future date.

**Aston School** see CONTINGENCY THEORY.

**attack strategy** the specific manoeuvres a business adopts to establish COMPETITIVE ADVANTAGE over rival suppliers. Such an attack may be designed to eliminate a competitor or reduce his MARKET SHARE. In order to formulate an attack strategy a MARKET CHALLENGER must define clearly his own marketing objective and identify those businesses or MARKET SEGMENTS where his rivals are vulnerable.

**attainment test** see PSYCHOLOGICAL TEST.

**attendance bonus** a payment made to employees by their employer as part of their wage to reward satisfactory attendance at work. Although many would argue that such payments should not be necessary because satisfactory attendance is usually a condition of the CONTRACT OF EMPLOYMENT, it can be a useful means of discouraging ABSENTEEISM.

**attitude survey** see SURVEY.

**auction** a form of SALE which is used to sell a product by inviting competitive bidding. Prospective buyers are convened to view the items to be sold, which may be limited to a particular type of product (used cars, for instance) or varied (the entire contents of a house, for example). The items will then be sold to the highest bidder, subject in some cases to a prearranged reserve 'minimum' price being offered.

**audit 1.** the legal requirement for a JOINT-STOCK COMPANY to have its BALANCE SHEET and PROFIT-AND-LOSS ACCOUNT (the financial statements) and underlying accounting system and records examined by a qualified AUDITOR, so as to enable an opinion to be formed as to whether such financial statements show a TRUE AND FAIR VIEW of the company's state of affairs and that they comply with the relevant statutes. Auditing involves inspecting documentary evidence of transactions such as INVOICES, STATEMENTS and DELIVERY NOTES to ensure that the DOUBLE-ENTRY accounting entries are complete and authentic.

Where the auditor is satisfied that the financial statements show a 'true and fair view' he will report this to the SHAREHOLDERS in the ANNUAL REPORT AND ACCOUNTS. However, if he is not satisfied that the financial statements show a 'true and fair view' or he is unhappy about any explanations given by the managers, then he may make a 'qualified report' to the shareholders expressing his precise misgivings.

2. internal audits of accounting procedures, marketing activities, production operations, quality control systems, and safety may be undertaken to monitor and review the efficiency and effectiveness with which these various activities are undertaken. In addition, a company may undertake a *value-for-money* audit, to evaluate whether the organization is operating effectively.

**Auditing Practices Board** the UK body which is responsible for the work of AUDITORS and which issues guidelines on auditing practice.

**auditor** a professional accountant appointed to check the accuracy of a JOINT-STOCK COMPANY'S LEDGER accounts and ANNUAL REPORT AND ACCOUNTS, and to present an independent report to SHAREHOLDERS on whether the accounts present a *true and fair view* of the company's affairs.

**audit trail** a trail of primary documents such as INVOICES, and LEDGER entries, for example sales ledger records, which are used to identify how ACCOUNTING records have been kept. By selecting a sample of primary documents and ledger entries an AUDITOR can check the completeness and accuracy of a firm's accounting system.

**authority** the capacity to give commands which are accepted as legitimate by others. In the modern ORGANIZATION the manager's authority to give instructions to subordinates is drawn primarily from his formal position as a manager, and the set of rights and obligations formally associated with the post, rather than from the manager's individual leadership qualities. However, both sources of authority can be important. Managers whose personal standing with their subordinates is low may find that their authority is not fully accepted. Equally, some managers claim that they are given insufficient powers to exercise their authority fully.

Modern analysis of authority relationships owes much to German sociologist Max Weber (1864–1920). He discerned three forms of authority:

(a) *traditional authority*, where people obey those who occupy religious or monarchical positions;

(b) *charismatic authority*, where people obey those who have special inspirational personal qualities;

(c) rational–legal authority, where individuals obey laws or rules which have been devised as a result of the application of reason to achieve certain objectives.

In Weber's view the last is the distinctive form of authority in modern industrial societies, and is exemplified in the workings of the modern ORGANIZATION or BUREAUCRACY.

**authorization** the granting of permission by a senior manager to a subordinate to undertake a particular task. For example, the chief executive could empower his purchasing officer to buy raw materials and authorize his production manager to buy machinery. The authorization process attempts to make sure that subordinates know the extent of their DELEGATED AUTHORITY.

**authorized depository** a UK agent such as a stockbroker or commercial bank, which holds foreign STOCKS and SHARES on behalf of its owners, and which is authorized to conduct such business by the Bank of England.

**authorized share capital** or **registered share capital** the maximum amount of SHARE CAPITAL which a JOINT-STOCK COMPANY can issue at any time. This amount is authorized by the company's ARTICLES OF ASSOCIATION, is disclosed in the BALANCE SHEET and may be altered by SHAREHOLDERS at the company ANNUAL GENERAL MEETING. The ISSUED SHARE CAPITAL cannot exceed the authorized amount, though not all the authorized capital need be issued.

**automatic vending** a means of retailing products to consumers via vending machines. Vending machines augment conventional point-of-sale retailing (shops and stores) and provide a comparatively inexpensive and convenient way of making products available. Automatic vending has been employed extensively in selling, for instance, food and beverages, stamps and latterly money. See RETAIL OUTLET.

**automation** the use of mechanical or electrical machines such as robots to undertake frequently-repeated PRODUCTION processes to make them self-regulating, thus avoiding human intervention in these processes. Automation often involves high initial capital investment but, by reducing labour costs, cuts VARIABLE COST per unit.

Automation can be applied to mass production,

# AVERAGE

PRODUCTION-LINE operations which are performed in a fixed sequence with high volumes but in a relatively inflexible way, where changes in the process to accommodate product changes are difficult and costly to implement (fixed automation). Automation can also be applied to lower volume BATCH PRODUCTION type operations, allowing in this case for greater flexibility in accommodating product changes by reprogramming the numerically-controlled machine's/robot's instructions to facilitate rapid changeovers (flexible or programmable automation). See FLEXIBLE MANUFACTURING SYSTEM.

**average** or **mean** a method of representing the middle of a set of numbers by a single number, i.e. the sum of the set of numbers divided by the quantity of numbers in the set. For example, if five people had weekly incomes of £100, £100, £150, £250 and £400, then the average income of the group would be:

$$£\frac{100 + 100 + 150 + 250 + 400}{5} = £\frac{1000}{5} = £200$$

See also MEDIAN, MODE, WEIGHTED AVERAGE.

**average collection period** see DEBTORS RATIO.

**average cost** the unit cost of a product (total cost divided by number of units produced). Average total cost (ATC) can be split up into average FIXED COST (AFC) and average VARIABLE COST (AVC). AFC declines continuously as output rises, as a given total amount of fixed cost is 'spread' over a greater number of units. For example, with fixed costs of £1,000 per year and annual output of 1000 units, fixed costs per unit would be £1, but if annual output rose to 2000 units the fixed cost per unit would fall to 50p. Unit variable cost (AVC) tends to remain constant over the output range.

**average deviation** a measure of variation within a group of numerical observations, i.e. the average of the deviations of the observations from the group AVERAGE. For example, if five products had prices of £5, £4, £3, £2 and £1 then the mean price is:

$$£\frac{5 + 4 + 3 + 2 + 1}{5} = £\frac{15}{5} = £3$$

and the distances by which the various prices depart from the mean price is:

$$
\left.
\begin{array}{rcl}
£5 - 3 & = & £2 \\
£4 - 3 & = & £1 \\
£3 - 3 & = & £0 \\
£2 - 3 & = & -£1 \\
£1 - 3 & = & -£2 \\
\hline
& & £0
\end{array}
\right\}
$$

Unfortunately, the sum of these deviations is always zero because in using an average for a group of observations, the positive deviations from the average will always exactly match the negative deviations from the average. To get around this problem and concentrate upon the magnitude of the deviations rather than their signs, the absolute values of the deviations can be considered, ignoring their signs. The sum of the absolute values of the deviations in the example above is £6 and the average of the absolute deviations is therefore $£6/5 = £1.2$. If the observations are grouped closely around the average then their dispersion is small and the average of the absolute deviations will be small; if the observations are spread over a considerable distance from the main then their dispersion is large and the average of the absolute deviations will be large. Compare STANDARD DEVIATION.

**average outgoing quality level (AOQL)** the lowest quality which will be accepted by INSPECTION when inspection/testing a sample from a batch of raw materials, work in progress or finished goods. See ACCEPTABLE QUALITY LEVEL, ACCEPTANCE SAMPLING, QUALITY CONTROL.

# B

**backlog** a build-up of customer orders which a firm has agreed to deliver at specified future dates. Backlogging is one means by which a firm can 'even out' demand in relation to its production capacity, allowing delivery lead times to increase during peaks in demand and shorten during slack periods. Backlogs of orders can provide an alternative to STOCKHOLDING or OVERTIME working, and varying the backlog may be the only way of dealing with demand fluctuations in some service industries. See PRODUCTION SCHEDULING.

**back-to-back loan or parallel loan** an arrangement under which two companies in different countries borrow each other's currency and agree to repay the loans at a specified future date. At the expiry date of the loans each company receives the full amount of its loan in its domestic currency without risk of losses from exchange-rate changes. In this way back-to-back loans serve to minimize EXCHANGE RATE EXPOSURE.

**backward integration** see VERTICAL INTEGRATION.

**bad debt** an accounting term for money owed to a company by customers or borrowers which is highly unlikely to be paid because, for example, a customer has become insolvent (see INSOLVENCY). Such bad debts are written off against the PROFITS of the trading period as a business cost. See CREDIT CONTROL, DEBTORS RATIO, DOUBTFUL DEBTS.

**balance of payments** a record of a country's trade and financial transactions with the rest of the world over a particular period of time, usually one year. Fig. 9 shows the UK's balance of payments account for 1996. The account is divided into two main sections, the current account and the investment and other capital transactions account. The current account shows the country's day-to-day dealings in goods and services, together with various short-run income flows such as profit, dividend, and interest payments and receipts. The current account is split into two main components:

(a) the BALANCE OF TRADE in goods, i.e. sterling receipts from the EXPORTS of UK goods, and foreign currency payments for IMPORTS of overseas goods (referred to as 'visible' trade, as flows of goods are measured by the CUSTOMS AND EXCISE authorities as they physically enter or leave the country);

(b) sterling receipts from the provision (export) of UK services and from the repatriation of profits, dividends and interest on UK-owned foreign assets, and foreign currency payments for the provision (import) of services by foreign businesses and from the repatriation abroad of profits, dividends and interest on foreign-owned UK assets (referred to as 'invisible' trade since such transactions can only be measured indirectly).

The investment and other capital transactions account embraces a number of capital items including:

(a) the purchase of overseas physical assets (the establishment of a new factory or acquisition of a company);

(b) the purchase of financial assets (stocks and shares, government bonds, etc.) by UK individuals, companies, financial institutions and the government;

(c) the purchase of UK physical and financial assets by foreigners;

(d) banking and money market transactions in financial instruments and lending and borrowing in sterling and foreign currencies;

(e) various intergovernment transfers, for example UK payments to, and receipts from the European Union, and

(f) the provision of economic aid to less developed countries. Included also in the capital transactions account are movements in the UK's stock of INTERNATIONAL RESERVES of gold and FOREIGN EXCHANGE, an overall balance of payments deficit being financed by a fall in the reserves (and/or increased borrowing), and a surplus leading to an addition to the reserve position (and/or increased lending).

Broadly speaking, governments aim to maintain a balance of payments equilibrium over a run of years, avoiding in particular a build-up of deficits. The external payments position of the country often acts as a major constraint on the government's ECONOMIC POLICIES and in consequence the general economic climate in which businesses operate. For

# BALANCE OF PAYMENTS

## CURRENT ACCOUNT

£ million

**Visible balance** [1]

| | |
|---|---:|
| Food, beverages and tobacco | −5348 |
| Basic materials | −3724 |
| Oil, lubricants | 4879 |
| Manufacturers | −8079 |
| Other items | 193 |

−12598

**Invisible balance** [2]

| | |
|---|---:|
| Services balance | 7142 |
| Interest, profit and dividends balance | 9652 |
| Transfers balance (mainly government European Union payments) | −4631 |

12163

**Current balance**      −435

## TRANSACTIONS IN UK EXTERNAL ASSETS AND LIABILITIES (INVESTMENT AND OTHER CAPITAL TRANSACTIONS)

| | |
|---|---:|
| UK external assets (increase) | −219293 |
| UK external liabilities (increase) | 217095 |

**Net transactions**      −2198

*Notes*
(1) Visible trade – flows of goods which are recorded by the customs and excise authorities as they enter or leave the country.
(2) Invisible trade – transactions that are recorded by the Bank of England from company and bank foreign currency receipts and payments data.

Fig.9. **Balance of payments**. UK balance of payments, 1996.
(Source: UK balance of payments, ONS, 1997.)

example, balance of payments deficits are usually rectified by a combination of domestic DEFLATION and DEVALUATION/ DEPRECIATION of the country's EXCHANGE RATE, which can pose difficulties for domestic firms as well as providing opportunities for the more enterprising of them. Deflationary measures which reduce domestic demand may limit sales potential in the home market, but by damping down INFLATION can make a firm's exports more competitive and thus increase its overseas sales. A devaluation can be even more helpful since it works to increase the prices of foreign products in the home market, and by lowering export prices serves, like deflation, to make exports more price competitive.

See FIXED EXCHANGE RATE SYSTEM, FLOATING EXCHANGE RATE SYSTEM, INTERNATIONAL TRADE, FOREIGN EXCHANGE MARKET, FOREIGN EXCHANGE CONTROLS.

**balance of trade** a financial record of a country's trade in goods, specifically manufactures, intermediate goods and raw materials, with the rest of the world over a particular period of time, usually one year. Conventionally, the 'balance of trade' excludes trade in services, so that in order to get an overall picture of the country's trading position it is necessary to look at the current account of the BALANCE OF PAYMENTS.

A *trade gap* occurs when payments for imports of goods exceed receipts from the exports of goods, but such a deficit is not a problem provided it is offset by surpluses earned on services and capital transactions.

**balance sheet** an accounting statement of a firm's ASSETS and LIABILITIES on the last day of a trading period. The balance sheet lists the assets which the firm owns and sets against these the balancing obligations or claims of those groups of people who provided the funds to acquire the assets. Assets take the form of FIXED ASSETS and CURRENT ASSETS, while obligations take the form of SHAREHOLDERS' CAPITAL EMPLOYED, long-term loans and CURRENT LIABILITIES. The balance sheet is compiled by summarizing information derived from the LEDGER accounts and provides a condensed financial snapshot of a company's state of affairs.

A simple balance sheet is illustrated in Fig. 10. Assets include fixed assets (such as equipment and buildings) and current assets (stocks, debtors and cash); liabilities include money owed to the bank and suppliers of raw materials and components. The difference between current assets and current liabilities is referred to as the net current assets or WORKING CAPITAL. Working capital plus fixed assets equals NET ASSETS employed or NET WORTH. This is equal to LONG-TERM CAPITAL of the company and represents monies subscribed by SHARE-HOLDERS (the owners of the company), together with any profits retained in the business. Thus, fixed assets + (current assets − current liabilities) = long-term capital ('net worth').

**Baltic Mercantile and Shipping Exchange** a London-based MARKET which is concerned with arranging FREIGHT facilities

# BANK

| ASSETS EMPLOYED | | | |
|---|---|---|---|
| | £ | £ | £ |
| *Fixed assets* | | | |
| Equipment | 500,000 | | |
| Factory | 300,000 | | |
| | | | 800,000 |
| *Current assets* | | | |
| Stock | 600,000 | | |
| Debtors | 175,000 | | |
| Cash | 25,000 | | |
| | | 800,000 | |
| *Current liabilities* | | | |
| Trade creditors | 300,000 | | |
| Bank overdraft | 200,000 | | |
| | | 500,000 | |
| *Net current assets* | | | 300,000 |
| *Net assets employed* | | | 1,100,000 |
| FINANCED BY: | | | |
| Ordinary shareholders capital | | | 900,000 |
| Retained profits | | | 200,000 |
| | | | 1,100,000 |

Fig. 10. **Balance sheet.** Balance sheet of Y Co as at 31 December 19xx.

for cargo consignments moved by sea and air, and which also acts as a retail commodity exchange for dealings in cereals. See CORN EXCHANGE, COMMODITY MARKET.

**bank** a deposit-taking institution which is licensed by the monetary authorities of a country (the Bank of England in the UK) to act as a repository for money deposited by persons, companies and institutions, and which undertakes to repay such deposits either immediately on demand or subject to due notice being given. Banks perform various services for their customers (money transmission, investment advice, etc.) and lend out money deposited with them in the form of loans and overdrafts or use their funds to purchase financial securities, in order to operate at a profit. There are many types of banks, including COMMERCIAL BANKS, MERCHANT BANKS, SAVINGS BANKS and INVESTMENT BANKS. See BANKING SYSTEM, CENTRAL BANK.

**bank advance** see BANK LOAN.

**banking system** a network of COMMERCIAL BANKS and other more specialized BANKS (INVESTMENT BANKS, SAVINGS BANKS,

MERCHANT BANKS) which accept deposits and savings from the general public, firms and other institutions, and which provide money transmission and other financial services for customers, operate loan and credit facilities for borrowers and invest in corporate and government securities. The banking system is part of a wider FINANCIAL SYSTEM and exerts a major influence on the functioning of the 'money economy' of a country. Bank deposits occupy a central position in the country's MONEY SUPPLY and hence the banking system is closely regulated by the monetary authorities. See CENTRAL BANK, CLEARING HOUSE SYSTEM.

**bank loan** or **bank advance** the advance of a specified sum of money to an individual or business (the borrower) by a COMMERCIAL BANK, SAVINGS BANK, etc. (the lender). A bank loan is a form of CREDIT which is extended for a specified period of time, usually on fixed-interest terms related to the base rate of interest, with the principal being repaid either on a regular instalment basis or in full on the appointed redemption date. Depending upon the nature of the loan and the degree of risk involved, a bank loan may be unsecured or secured, the latter requiring the borrower to deposit with the bank an approved form of COLLATERAL SECURITY (for example the property deeds to his house). In the case of businesses, bank loans are usually renegotiated shortly before expiring, thus providing the borrower with a 'revolving' line of credit used mainly to finance WORKING CAPITAL requirements. See OVERDRAFT, INTEREST RATE.

**Bank of England** the CENTRAL BANK of the United Kingdom.

**bank reconciliation** the process of reconciling an individual's or business's CASH ACCOUNT records of receipts and payments with the BANK STATEMENT record of receipts and payments. These two need not coincide exactly since cheques drawn and received but not yet banked do not appear on the bank statement until a later date.

**bankruptcy** see INSOLVENCY.

**bank statement** a periodic record of an individual's or business's transactions with a BANK (or BUILDING SOCIETY) which itemizes on the one hand cash deposits and cheques paid in, and on the other hand cash withdrawals and cheques drawn and presented against the account.

A company's bank statement needs to be reconciled periodically against the firm's own CASH ACCOUNT to verify the accuracy of its cash account. See BANK RECONCILIATION.

**bar chart** or **histogram** a graphical presentation of data in which the absolute and relative size of each category in a total is portrayed by means of the height of the 'bar' or block representing that category.

**bar code** an alpha or alpha-numeric code, converted into a series of lines and spaces which are marked on products. Bar coding and the use of bar code scanners enables a firm to obtain accurate data quickly on its STOCK position to help with planning its reordering of goods; and can be used to adjust the prices of goods more easily than by replacing price tags. See EPOS.

**bar-code reader** a device which reads bar codes using a light scanner, widely used in supermarket checkouts.

**bargain 1.** the sale of a product at a cut price as a means of promoting sales of the product. See SALES PROMOTION.
**2.** the sale or purchase of a FINANCIAL SECURITY on the STOCK MARKET.

**bargaining depth** see COLLECTIVE BARGAINING.

**bargaining level** see COLLECTIVE BARGAINING.

**bargaining scope** see COLLECTIVE BARGAINING.

**bargaining structure** see COLLECTIVE BARGAINING.

**bargaining unit** see COLLECTIVE BARGAINING.

**barriers to entry** obstacles in the way of firms attempting to enter a MARKET, which operate to give established firms particular advantages over newcomers. There are a number of potential barriers to entry, including:

(a) ECONOMIES OF SCALE – where unit costs of production (marketing, distribution and research and development) decline with the volume produced, the minimum efficient scale of operation may require entry on a large scale; otherwise entrants would be put at a relative cost disadvantage;

(b) PRODUCT DIFFERENTIATION – entrants with 'unknown' and 'untried' products may be unable to win a viable share of the market because of customer loyalty to existing brands built up by established firms through cumulative investment in advertising and sales promotion;

(c) capital requirements – the cost of financing investment in plant and product differentiation, and meeting initial operating losses, may be prohibitively high;

(d) vertical restrictions – key raw materials, component sources and distribution channels – may be controlled by established firms, thereby limiting access to inputs and market outlets. See VERTICAL INTEGRATION;

(e) absolute cost disadvantages – entrants, for example, may be denied access to 'best state-of-the-art technology' because of PATENT rights accruing to established firms, and thus be forced to adopt inferior, higher cost methods of production, etc.

One, or some combination, of the above factors may pose particular problems for a small scale, GREENFIELD type of entrant. However, they may be of little consequence to a large conglomerate firm possessing ample financial resources, and which chooses to effect entry by MERGER with, or TAKEOVER of, an established producer. Moreover, the basic assumption of much entry theory that established firms invariably possess advantages over potential entrants must also be challenged. In a dynamic market situation entrants may be in a position to introduce new technology ahead of existing firms, or develop innovative new products, thereby giving them COMPETITIVE ADVANTAGES over established firms.

See MARKET ENTRY, MARKET STRUCTURE, DIVERSIFICATION, BRAND PROLIFERATION, MARKET SYSTEM, MOBILITY BARRIER.

**barriers to exit** obstacles in the way of a firm contemplating leaving a market which serve to keep the firm in the market despite falling sales and profitability. There are a number of potential exit barriers including:

(a) whether the firm owns the assets used to make the product, or leases them;

(b) the age of the firm's assets used to serve the particular market and the extent to which they have been depreciated. Where DEPRECIATION charges on old assets are low then operating costs will be lower, and this may encourage the firm to remain in the market despite low prices. On the other hand, with fully-depreciated assets the firm would suffer little capital loss in writing off these assets and exiting the market;

(c) the nature of the firm's assets. Specifically, if the assets are special purpose and so difficult to redeploy to other uses;

(d) the extent to which the firm's plant and equipment is re-saleable in second-hand markets;

(e) whether the firm needs to make any additional investment in order to remain competitive;

(f) the extent of market excess capacity, and thus related price and profit levels;

(g) the extent of shared production and distribution facilities. For example, where a multiproduct firm's plant produces a number of different products rather than just one, then a decision to drop one product could affect the cost and availability of other products;

(h) the extent of VERTICAL INTEGRATION. A vertically-integrated petrochemical firms, for example, may find it difficult to drop one product without affecting downstream operations which use that product as a raw material, or upstream operations which rely upon the product as a use for their intermediate material;

(i) the spread of a firm's product range. A single product firm would be reluctant to cease making its product, for then the firm would cease trading, whilst a diversified firm would find it easier to exit from one particular market since it has many others available. See DIVERSIFICATION.

Barriers to exit determine the ease with which firms can leave declining markets, and thus affect both the profitability of firms and the smooth functioning of markets.

See BUSINESS STRATEGY, ENDGAME STRATEGY, PRODUCT LIFE CYCLE, MARKET SYSTEM.

**BARS** see BEHAVIOURALLY-ANCHORED RATING SCALE.

**barter** an exchange mechanism for buying and selling goods and services which involves the physical 'swapping' of one product for another. Generally, barter is a cumbersome and inefficient means of organizing exchanges in an economy, since a large amount of time is wasted in seeking out and finding compatible 'swap' partners (i.e. each selling what the other wants to buy), and then haggling over an appropriate exchange rate (for example how many tomatoes equal a sewing machine?). All these difficulties can be overcome by the use of MONEY as a common denominator to conclude transactions and 'price' individual products.

For all its disadvantages, barter (or COUNTERTRADE as it is often referred to) is still widely used in the context of INTERNATIONAL TRADE. Firms which are unable to obtain the necessary foreign currencies they require to finance a trade deal (because the government operates FOREIGN EXCHANGE CONTROLS or because the country has simply run out of currencies due to a balance of payment deficit), often enter into a bilateral 'swap' deal with firms in other countries arranging a suitable product exchange.

**base rate** see INTEREST RATE.

**base stock system** see STOCK CONTROL.

**BASIC (Beginners All-Purpose Symbolic Instruction Code)** a simple COMPUTER programming language widely used by nonspecialists for programming computers.

**basic time** the time that it should take an operative with the appropriate level of skill to complete a task. However, it should be noted that this ignores any ALLOWANCES designed to compensate for contingencies, interferences and relaxation. See WORK MEASUREMENT, STANDARD TIME.

**basing point price system** see GEOGRAPHICAL PRICING.

**batch production** a method of organizing PRODUCTION whereby a number of identical components or products are passed through one or more production operations or processes as a 'batch'. Batch-production systems are used to make components or products in comparatively small quantities using 'general purpose' machines on an intermittent basis. See BATCH SIZE, PROCESS-FOCUSED LAYOUT, PRODUCTION SCHEDULING, SET-UP TIME, SET-UP COSTS.

**batch size** the number of items which constitute a 'batch' in BATCH PRODUCTION. The use of very large batch sizes, whilst having the advantage of minimizing the total costs associated with setting up the production facilities, has the disadvantage of incurring high stock-holding costs. On the other hand, the manufacture of many small batches of items, whilst keeping average stock levels down and thus reducing stock-holding costs, increases total SET-UP COSTS since more set ups are required for the production of a given total quantity of items in a given time. Some compromise must therefore be reached which has the effect of minimizing total stock-holding and setting-up costs.

The economic batch quantity which minimizes total costs can be calculated in similar fashion to the economic order quantity in the STOCKHOLDING MODEL.

**bath tub curve** see FAILURE RATE CURVE.

**bear** a person who sells a financial security (stock, share, foreign currency, etc.) in expectation that its market price is likely to fall. See SPECULATION. Compare BULL.

**bearer bonds** FINANCIAL SECURITIES which are not registered under the name of a particular holder but whose possession serves as proof of ownership. Such securities are popular in the US financial system but fairly rare in the UK, where the names of holders of STOCKS and SHARES are recorded in a company's SHARE REGISTER.

**bear market** a situation in which the prices of FINANCIAL SECURITIES (stocks, shares, etc.) or COMMODITIES (tin, wheat, etc.) tend to fall as a result of persistent selling and only limited buying. See SPECULATION. Compare BULL MARKET.

**beauty contest** a competition between TRADE UNIONS to gain recognition by an employer for COLLECTIVE BARGAINING and/or representational purposes. Often these contests will take place before a factory or office has actually opened and before any employees have been hired. In this process the unions involved are essentially selling themselves to management rather than to any prospective members. Beauty contests have caused controversy in union circles because they may be seen to involve undue collaboration with management and because they lead to unions violating the traditional 'spheres of influence' of other unions. See BRIDLINGTON RULES.

**bed and breakfast** the process of selling SHARES at the end of a trading day on the STOCK MARKET and buying them back at the beginning of the following day's trading. This is done primarily to establish on a formal basis the amount of profit or loss made on these shares over the period when they are held, in order to calculate CAPITAL GAINS TAX.

**behaviourally-anchored rating scale (BARS)** a scale of behaviour patterns against which observed behaviour can be compared as a tool for analysing an individual's behaviour at work or elsewhere. To construct a BARS, various patterns of behaviour associated with a particular activity or aspect of work performance are compiled on a scale. These patterns are derived from earlier observation of behaviour or from behaviour patterns identified by analysis of CRITICAL INCIDENTS. The scale can thus be said to be 'anchored' in real behaviour. The behaviour of particular individuals can then be rated on this scale. The advantage of BARS is that they facilitate a fairly objective rating of behaviour since individual behaviour can be compared systematically against real behaviour patterns of other people. However, construction of these scales can be time-consuming and expensive because to be reliable they need to be based on a large population. An important use of rating scales of this type is in PERFORMANCE APPRAISAL. See OCCUPATIONAL PSYCHOLOGY.

**behavioural observation scale (BOS)** a scale upon which observed behaviour can be graded. For example, the degree to which an individual consults with his colleagues can be graded from 'never' through to 'always'. This method of rating behaviour can be used where behaviour is observed as part of RECRUITMENT AND SELECTION and where behaviour is a subject of PERFORMANCE APPRAISAL. Such scales are easy to compile but observation of behaviour may be difficult (it may not be possible to scrutinize all relevant behaviour), and it can be difficult to exclude the observer's subjective opinion of the nature of the behaviour observed.

**behaviour reinforcement** see OCCUPATIONAL PSYCHOLOGY.

**below-the-line** an accounting term describing items (other than dividends and retained profit) which appear below the net profit figure in the PROFIT-AND-LOSS ACCOUNT. These would normally include items relating to previous trading periods or extraordinary nonrecurring items, for example losses associated with the reorganization of a company division involving significant sales of assets. Below-the-line items are deducted directly from the company's RESERVES rather than being charged against the profits of the trading period, to avoid affecting the trading profit with one-off, non-trading revenues or costs.

**'below-the-line' promotion** see 'ABOVE-THE-LINE' PROMOTION.

**benchmarking** the practice whereby a firm studies the 'best' production and marketing processes used by immediate competitors and firms from other similar industries so as to identify possible ways for the firm to improve its own methods. Benchmarking usually involves a number of steps: selection of critical processes that may need improvement; in-depth study of other firms who perform these processes particularly well; adaptations of the processes identified so as to facilitate their implementation by the firm.

**beneficial owner** the ultimate owner of a FINANCIAL SECURITY rather than any NOMINEE who may have been appointed to hold legally the financial security on behalf of the beneficial owner.

**beta coefficient** a measure of the responsiveness of the expected return on a particular FINANCIAL SECURITY relative to movements in the average expected return on all other securities in the market. The Financial Times all-share index or the Dow-Jones index are usually taken as proxy measurements for general market movements. In the CAPITAL-ASSET PRICING MODEL, the beta coefficient (ß) is taken as a measure of the market (or non-diversifiable) RISK of a particular security. The beta coefficient links the return on the security and the average market return. The average market risk of all securities is where ß = 1, that is, a 10% increase in market return is reflected as a 10% increase in the return of, say, security A. If the return on, say, security B, is 20%, but there is only a 10% increase in market return, this security has a ß = 2 which indicates a risk greater than the market. If security C has a ß = 0.5, this indicates a security less risky than the market in general. See EFFICIENT-MARKETS HYPOTHESIS.

**bid 1.** an offer by one company to purchase all or the majority of the SHARES of another company as a means of effecting a TAKEOVER. The bid price offered by the predator for the voting shares in the victim company must generally exceed the current market price of those shares, the difference being a premium which the predator must pay for control of the company. However, on occasions, the market price of the shares may subsequently rise to exceed the initial bid price where investors either feel that the bid price undervalues the company, or where investors anticipate, for example, the possibility of a second party making a higher bid. The offer price could be paid solely in cash, or in a mix of cash and shares in the acquirer's own company, or solely in terms of the acquirer's shares (called a paper bid). In order to finance a takeover bid, a predator company may raise loans. See TAKEOVER BID (leveraged bid).
**2.** an offer to purchase an item (for example, a house or antique vase) which has been put up for sale at a specified price or is to be sold subject to receipt of 'other prices'. The latter may occur at an AUCTION where a number of would-be buyers each put in a bid for an item, the final sale going to the highest bidder unless a predetermined 'reserve' has been set but not reached.

**bid price** the price at which a dealer in a FINANCIAL SECURITY (such as a STOCK or SHARE), FOREIGN CURRENCY or COMMODITY (tin, wheat, etc.) is prepared to buy a security, currency or commodity. Such dealers usually cite two prices to potential customers, the smaller bid price, and a higher *offer price* or 'ask price' at which they are prepared to sell a security, etc. The difference between the bid and offer price (referred to as the 'spread') represents the dealer's profit margin on the transaction. See MARKET MAKER, MIDDLE PRICE.

**big bang** see STOCK MARKET.

**bilateral netting** see MULTILATERAL NETTING.

**bill–discounting rate** see INTEREST RATE.

**bill of exchange** a FINANCIAL SECURITY which is used to extend business CREDIT for a limited time period. The lender draws up a bill of exchange for a specified sum of money payable at a given future date, usually three months hence, and the borrower signifies his agreement to pay the amount involved by signing (i.e. accepting) the bill. In addition, a borrower will often arrange for a bill to be guaranteed by an ACCEPTING HOUSE, which in return for a fee will agree to repay the debt should the borrower be unable to do so. Most bills are in fact 'discounted' (i.e. bought from the drawer) by a DISCOUNT HOUSE for an amount less than the face value of the bill (the difference between the two sums being the interest charged). The bill may then be held until maturity or sold at a lower price ('rediscounted') to another discount house, or, more commonly, on-sold to the COMMERCIAL BANKS. See DISCOUNT, DISCOUNT MARKET, REDISCOUNTING, INTEREST RATE.

**bill of lading** a document used to ship internationally traded goods that gives the holder (the consignee) the right to take possession of the goods. The bill of lading gives details of the goods shipped, the identification marks and numbers on crates, etc., the name of the ship, ports of embarkation and destination, rate of freight, etc. Bills of lading are drawn up by shipowners, the original being sent to the consignee with copies being retained by the captain of the ship and the FREIGHT FORWARDER. See EXPORTING.

**bill of materials** see PRODUCT SPECIFICATION.

**bin card** a STORES record card of quantities of a particular material or component received, quantities issued and the balance of the material in store. These balances can be checked against the actual quantities in stock by STOCKTAKING.

**birth rate** see POPULATION.

**bit** a digit which takes the value zero or one and which can therefore be represented electronically by an off/on switch in a COMPUTER. Computers use groups of bits to represent numbers or letters for storage, transmission and processing of numerical or alphabetical data. Specifically, computers use various off/on permutations of eight bits to represent all numbers, letters and punctuation characters. Most computers use multiples of eight bits to handle data in this way and various eight-bit, sixteen-bit and thirty-two bit machines are available, the larger ones generally being able to process data faster.

**black-coated worker** see WORKER.

**black economy** activities which are performed in an ECONOMY which go unrecorded and hence do not appear in a country's official NATIONAL INCOME ACCOUNTS. Such activities include, for example, work which is undertaken for a friend 'as a favour' without payment, or the unpaid services of a housewife. In addition one person may provide goods or services to another in return for 'payment in kind' rather than cash. Where two people agree to exchange products in this way no transaction will be recorded, making it difficult to trace the income each derives from the transaction and subject it to INCOME TAX.

**blacking** a form of INDUSTRIAL ACTION in which workers in one organization refuse to handle goods or services either bought from or intended for sale to another organization which is engaged in an INDUSTRIAL DISPUTE with its workforce; this is a way of providing support to the workforce in dispute. See SECONDARY ACTION.

**black knight** see TAKEOVER BID.

**blackleg** a worker who reports for work normally whilst the majority of his or her colleagues are on STRIKE.

**black market** an unofficial or 'under-the-counter' MARKET trading in a product which the government has declared to be illegal (for example narcotic drugs), or on the sale of which the government has imposed controls thus limiting its availability.

**blind product test** see ADVERTISING EFFECTIVENESS TESTS.

**blocked currency** a currency that is not freely convertible into other currencies because of FOREIGN EXCHANGE CONTROLS operated by the government of the country concerned. In these circumstances nonresidents may be unable to transfer money held in their bank accounts out of the country without the permission of the monetary authorities.

**'blue-chip' company** a large well-established JOINT-STOCK COMPANY, with considerable assets whose SHARES investors regard as a low-risk investment.

**blue-collar worker** see WORKER.

**board of directors** the group responsible to the SHAREHOLDERS for running a JOINT-STOCK COMPANY. Often boards of directors are composed of full-time, salaried company executives (the executive directors) and part-time, nonexecutive directors. The board of directors meets periodically under the company chairman to decide on major policy matters within the company and the appointment of key managers. DIRECTORS are elected annually at the company ANNUAL GENERAL MEETING.

In recent years the responsibilities of British directors have been increased under the terms of the Insolvency Act and they may be held personally liable for company debts incurred if they knowingly and recklessly trade after the company is insolvent (see INSOLVENCY).

In certain European countries, like Germany, there are two-tier boards of directors with a supervisory board composed of representatives of shareholders, employees, etc., which appoints a management board to deal with the detailed management of the company.

See FIFTH DIRECTIVE.

**BOGOF** see BUY ONE GET ONE FREE.

**bond** a FINANCIAL SECURITY issued by a company or by the government as a means of borrowing long-term funds. Bonds are typically issued for a set number of years (often 10 years plus), being repayable on maturity. They are issued in units of a fixed (nominal) face value and bear a fixed (nominal) rate of interest. Purchasers of bonds include private individuals, commercial banks and institutional investors (pension funds, etc.) who hold them as a form of portfolio investment.

Once issued, bonds can be bought and sold on the STOCK MARKET. Bond prices tend to fluctuate at prices below their face value, reflecting buying and selling strengths, but are closely linked to prevailing market interest rates so as to remain attractive to potential buyers. For example, a £100 bond with a nominal 5% interest rate returning £5 per year would have to be priced at £50 if current market interest rates were 10% so that a buyer could earn an effective return of £5/£50 = 10% on his investment.

In addition to their role as a means of borrowing money, the sale and purchase of bonds is used by the monetary authorities to control the MONEY SUPPLY.

See MONETARY POLICY. See also EUROCURRENCY MARKET, GILT-EDGED SECURITY.

**bonded goods** products on which CUSTOMS DUTY or EXCISE DUTY have not yet been paid. They are stored in a 'bonded warehouse' and duty is paid to the CUSTOMS AND EXCISE authorities when goods are released from the warehouse for EXPORT or domestic sale.

**bonus payment** a form of incentive payment made to individual employees of a firm or groups of employees who exceed specified output or sales targets. Bonus payments are usually paid in cash (monthly or annually) but could also take the form of an allocation of shares in the company (see GOLDEN HANDCUFF).

See PERFORMANCE-RELATED PAY, INCENTIVE BONUS SCHEME, GROUP INCENTIVE BONUS SCHEME.

**bonus shares** additional SHARES issued to existing SHAREHOLDERS in a JOINT-STOCK COMPANY without further payment on their part. See CAPITALIZATION ISSUE.

**book-keeping** see ACCOUNTING.

**books of prime entry** the JOURNALS or DAY BOOKS in which information about business transactions are first recorded. The books of prime entry include the purchases and sales day books, and the cash book. See LEDGER, ACCOUNTING.

**book value** the money amount of an ASSET as stated in a company's LEDGER accounts and BALANCE SHEET. FIXED ASSETS are often stated at NET BOOK VALUE (original cost less cumulative DEPRECIATION), while CURRENT ASSETS are stated at original cost or market value, whichever is the lower.

**boom** see BUSINESS CYCLE.

**borrower** a person, company or institution who obtains MONEY or some other asset (for example machinery, property) in the form of a LOAN, MORTGAGE or LEASING arrangement from a LENDER in order to finance consumption and investment. See DEBT, FINANCIAL SYSTEM, COLLATERAL SECURITY.

**BOS** see BEHAVIOURAL OBSERVATION SCALE.

**Boston matrix** a framework for highlighting and analysing PRODUCT DEVELOPMENT policy and associated CASH FLOW implications in a firm, used by corporate planners in formulating BUSINESS STRATEGY.

Fig. 11 shows the matrix which depicts market growth rate on one axis and the product's market share on the other; the matrix indicates that the higher the product's growth rate, the greater will be the capital investment required and hence cash used, while the greater the product's market share, the greater will be the profit earned and hence cash generated. The four market growth/share segments relate to four product types:

(a) cash cows – products, usually in the mature phase of the PRODUCT LIFE CYCLE, which have a low growth rate, so that they require little new investment to support them, and a high market share yielding a high profit return. Cash cows are the firm's primary source of internal funds for financing the introduction and development of new products;

(b) stars – products which have a high growth rate and need a considerable amount of new investment to keep up with market demand, and a high market share often yielding sufficient cash to make their operations self-financing. Star products are usually relatively new products in the growth phase of the product life cycle that it is hoped, with proper handling, will become the firm's cash cows of the future;

(c) problem children – products which have a high growth rate and so require heavy injections of capital to support them, and a low market share providing only a modest profit return if at all. Such products are a cash drain but they have 'star' potential if their market shares can be improved;

(d) dogs – products which have both a low growth rate and a low market share and which seemingly lack potential for future development. Such products are prime candidates for

|  |  | MARKET SHARE | |
|---|---|---|---|
|  |  | High | Low |
| MARKET GROWTH RATE | High | Star | Problem Child |
|  | Low | Cash Cow | Dog |

Fig. 11. **Boston matrix.** The matrix identifies cash generators and cash users.

DIVESTMENT if a suitable buyer can be found.

The Boston matrix can be used in conjunction with the PRODUCT-MARKET MATRIX to assist the firm in planning for a suitable 'balanced' portfolio of mature, growth and newly-launched products so as to sustain the growth of the firm's profits over time. See COMPETITIVE ADVANTAGE.

**BOT** see BUILD, OPERATE, TRANSFER PROJECT.

**bottleneck** see PRODUCTION-LINE BALANCING.

**bottom line** an accounting term denoting the NET PROFIT from a business operation after all costs have been paid. In financial accounting terms, profit would be sales revenue less all the costs of production, marketing, finance, etc., and frequently after taxation charges for the period. However, profit would generally be stated before the payment of dividends or appropriation to RESERVES.

**bought day book** see JOURNAL or DAY BOOK, ACCOUNTING.

**bought journal** see JOURNAL or DAY BOOK, ACCOUNTING.

**bought ledger** see LEDGER, ACCOUNTING.

**Bourse** the French STOCK MARKET.

**boycott 1.** the withholding of supplies of products to a trader by a producer because the trader is, for example, in breach of CONTRACT or the trader is selling the products as LOSS LEADERS. See REFUSAL TO SUPPLY.
**2.** the cessation of INTERNATIONAL TRADE, wholly or in part, with a particular country by other countries. See EMBARGO.

**brainstorming** a technique for generating ideas in which members of a group express ideas as they think of them. The object is to compile a list of ideas which can subsequently be considered and evaluated in greater depth. It is often recommended as a means of stimulating creativity when a group is experiencing difficulties in generating new ideas or solutions to apparently intractable problems. However, it is uncertain whether the ideas so generated are of any greater value than those arising in more conventional discussions. See DELPHI TECHNIQUE.

**brand** a name, term, sign, symbol or design used to identify a supplier's GOOD or SERVICE and to distinguish it from similar products offered by competitors. A brand may be given legal protection through the use of TRADEMARKS and COPYRIGHT. See BRANDING.

**brand extension** or **brand transference** the use of an existing

BRAND for new or modified products. Brand extension seeks to capitalize on consumer awareness of and loyalty towards a firm's established brands in order to gain rapid consumer approval and acceptance of the new or modified product.

Where a modified product simply serves another segment of the same market the term brand extension is generally used (see MARKET SEGMENTATION). The term brand transference is used where an established brand name is associated with a new product serving a different market. For instance, the manufacturer of a well-known vacuum cleaner might use that brand name to launch a new product in some other market, for example washing machines. See MARKET POSITIONING.

**brand image** the perceptions and beliefs held by consumers about a particular BRAND of GOOD or SERVICE which reinforce BRAND LOYALTY and encourage repeat purchases. The image may have been cultivated by media ADVERTISING, SALES PROMOTION and word-of-mouth recommendation by existing consumers.

**branding** a means of helping consumers to identify a particular supplier's BRAND of GOOD or SERVICE, and to create and maintain consumer confidence in the performance of the brand. This is achieved by ensuring consistent brand quality and reinforcing this by appropriate ADVERTISING and SALES PROMOTION in order to foster consumer goodwill. Once the supplier has created significant BRAND LOYALTY this enables him to exert greater control over the advertising, sales promotion and distribution of the brand, and may well enable him to command a premium price over competitors' offerings. A well-established brand has considerable value in giving a supplier COMPETITIVE ADVANTAGE over rival suppliers and such brands can have a significant impact upon the valuation of a business. See BRAND VALUATION.

**brand loyalty** the extent to which consumers buy a particular BRAND of a product in preference to similar brands. Consumers may be totally loyal to a single brand but more usually will switch irregularly between two or more brands. Brand loyalty will depend largely upon consumer satisfaction with the intrinsic qualities and attributes of the brand but may also be swayed by persuasive ADVERTISING and SALES PROMOTION.

Strong brand loyalty serves to protect and increase the firm's MARKET SHARE vis-à-vis competitors, and may afford opportunities to charge a premium price for the brand.

See BRANDING, BRAND SWITCHING, COMPETITIVE ADVANTAGE.

**brand manager** see PRODUCT MANAGER.

**brand mark** the symbol, design or distinctive colouring or lettering used to identify a particular BRAND, for example the jaguar symbol used by Jaguar cars or the lion used by Peugeot cars.

**brand name** the name used to identify a particular BRAND. This can consist of a newly created word or phrase, or a conventional word or phrase adapted to have a particular meaning. The skill of advertising copywriters lies in creating or finding words which have a broad-ranging and powerful appeal, and which are meaningful and pronounceable in several languages. Once created, brand names can be given legal protection against unauthorized use by registering them as TRADEMARKS. See BRAND EXTENSION, GLOBAL BRAND.

**brand positioning and repositioning** the matching of a particular BRAND with a selected MARKET SEGMENT(S) which offers good sales potential. This will involve developing a new brand with characteristics which match the identified product characteristics of the segment. Alternatively, an existing brand whose market segment is declining or which is experiencing intense competition may be adapted to target alternative market segments. For example, a company which manufactures shampoo or talcum powder for babies may attempt to market those products to adults. See MARKET SEGMENTATION, MARKET POSITIONING.

**brand preference** the selection of a particular BRAND over other brands by a consumer. See BRAND LOYALTY.

**brand proliferation** the availability in a market of an extensive number of similar brands reflecting the MARKET SEGMENTATION policies of suppliers and the need to offer a comprehensive range of brands to compete against rivals. By offering a number of brands, suppliers may be able to expand their sales. However, they have to be mindful of the extra production and marketing costs this involves and the particular danger of 'cannibalizing' their own sales (i.e. an increase in the sales of one particular brand may be largely at the expense of their other brands rather than taking away sales from rivals' brands). From a wider public interest perspective, brand proliferation is sometimes considered objectionable by the

COMPETITION POLICY authorities, because, while ostensibly serving to increase consumer choice, the 'saturation' of a market by established firms' brands may result in 'excessive' advertising and act as a BARRIER TO ENTRY to new firms. See PRODUCT DIFFERENTIATION, PRODUCT RANGE, PRODUCT VARIETY.

**brand repositioning** see BRAND POSITIONING.

**brand switching** the decision by consumers to substitute alternative BRANDS for the ones they currently consume. This may be a response to dissatisfaction with their existing brand, the attractions of newly-available brands or consumers' search for variety. Brand switching may be induced by ADVERTISING and SALES PROMOTION designed to overcome BRAND LOYALTY to existing brands.

**brand transference** see BRAND EXTENSION.

**brand value** the money value attached to an established BRAND name by consumer goods companies. The valuation attached to a brand name reflects past advertising by the company to create public awareness of the brand and gives the brand a value to the company and to a potential takeover bidder. Valuation of brands and their incorporation in a company's accounts serves to create an INTANGIBLE FIXED ASSET. See GOODWILL.

**breakaway union** a TRADE UNION formed by disaffected members of another union who feel that their particular interests are given insufficient weight in union decision making. Such unions rarely have much impact because managements are often reluctant to recognize an additional union for COLLECTIVE BARGAINING purposes (the Union of Democratic Mineworkers in the UK coal industry is an important exception).

**breakeven** the short-run rate of output and sales at which a supplier generates just enough revenue to cover his fixed and variable costs, earning neither a PROFIT nor a LOSS. If the selling price of a product exceeds its unit VARIABLE COST then each unit of product sold will earn a CONTRIBUTION towards FIXED COSTS and profits. Once sufficient units are being sold so that their total contributions cover the supplier's fixed costs then the company breaks even. If less than the breakeven sales volume is achieved then total contributions will not meet fixed costs and the supplier will make a loss. If the sales volume achieved exceeds the breakeven volume, total contributions will cover the fixed costs and leave a surplus which constitutes profit. See Fig. 12.

Differences in cost structures can have a significant effect upon companies' breakeven points. For example, a company with low levels of automation and so little capital equipment (for example Rolls Royce cars) would have low fixed depreciation costs but high direct labour costs. With high unit direct costs relative to selling prices such a firm would have a low unit contribution but low fixed costs, so would break even at a low sales volume, though profits would climb only slowly beyond the breakeven point because of low unit contribution. By contrast, a highly automated plant would have high fixed depreciation costs, but with low unit direct labour costs, would have a higher unit contribution. Firms with such plants (for example Ford) would not break even until a much higher sales volume was achieved, but thereafter profits would increase rapidly with larger unit contributions. See MARGINAL COSTING.

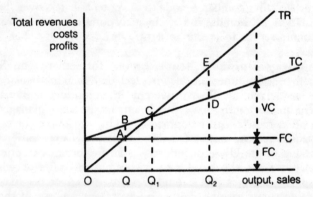

Fig. 12. **Break-even.** A supplier's typical short-run costs and revenues. Fixed costs do not vary with output and so are shown as the horizontal line FC. Total cost comprises both fixed costs and total variable costs and is shown by line TC. Total revenue rises as output and sales are expanded and is depicted by line TR. At low levels of output such as Q total costs exceed total revenues and the supplier makes a loss equal to AB. At high levels of output such as $Q_2$ revenues exceed costs and the supplier makes a profit equal to DE. At output $Q_1$ total revenues exactly match total costs (at C) and the supplier breaks even.

**breakeven pricing** see COST-BASED PRICING.

**breaking bulk** an activity performed by intermediaries in a DISTRIBUTION CHANNEL which involves the buying-in of products in large quantities and on-selling them in much smaller quantities.

See WHOLESALER.

**break-up value** the value of a business's ASSETS when sold off separately, as opposed to selling the business as a going concern.

**bridging loan** a form of short-term LOAN that is used by a borrower as a continuing source of funds to 'bridge' the period until the borrower obtains a medium or long-term loan to replace it. Bridging loans are used in particular in the housing market to finance the purchase of a new house while arranging long-term MORTGAGE finance and awaiting the proceeds from the sale of any existing property.

**Bridlington Rules** a code of practice operated by the TRADES UNION CONGRESS (TUC) to regulate inter-union competition for members in the UK, so called because they were agreed by the TUC at its Congress in Bridlington (in 1939). Where a TRADE UNION believes that its 'sphere of influence' has been encroached upon by another it may take the issue to a disputes committee of the TUC for resolution.

**Brisch system** a coding/classification system used to identify the characteristics of a part or component which is to be used in the manufacture of a product.

**British Institute of Management** see INSTITUTE OF MANAGEMENT.

**British Standard** see BS5750.

**British Standards Institution (BSI)** an organization which produces national standards for products and processes at the request of particular industries. The BSI generally seeks to produce national standards which are consistent with the international standards established by the International Standardization Organization (ISO).

In designing products and processes firms must generally meet the QUALITY, performance and safety standards laid down by the BSI if their products are to be acceptable to consumers. Products which meet these specifications are entitled to bear the BSI's 'kite' mark.

See BS5750.

# BRITISH TECHNOLOGY GROUP

**British Technology Group (BTG)** a UK government-owned organization which assists in the development of inventions made both in the private and public sectors (government and university/polytechnic research laboratories). The BTG (formed by the merger in 1981 of the National Research and Development Council and the National Enterprise Board) works in tandem with private sector VENTURE CAPITAL specialists in providing start-up finance for projects unable, because of the high risks involved, to attract conventional finance. See RESEARCH AND DEVELOPMENT.

**British Venture Capital Association** see VENTURE CAPITAL.

**broker** a business such as a stockbroker, insurance broker, commodity broker, which acts as a market intermediary in bringing together buyers and sellers of a financial asset, financial service or commodity.

See AGENT, TRADER/DEALER, STOCK MARKET, COMMODITY MARKET, INSURANCE.

**BS5750** a QUALITY standard drawn up by the BRITISH STANDARDS INSTITUTION. To obtain BS5750 certification a supplier is required to establish, document and maintain an effective and economical quality system to ensure and demonstrate that materials, products or services conform to the specified requirements.

**BSI** see BRITISH STANDARDS INSTITUTION.

**BTG** see BRITISH TECHNOLOGY GROUP.

**budget 1.** a firm's predetermined plan (expressed in quantitative or financial terms) for a given future period. The *sales budget* is generally compiled with the aid of sales forecasts and shows quantities and values of planned sales broken down by product group, area and type of customer. The linked *selling costs budget* shows planned salesforce and advertising costs; while the *distribution costs budget* shows planned distribution activity measured in packages handled, tonnage, etc. and associated warehousing and transport costs. Once the sales budget is complete then the consequences of planned sales can be spelled out in the production budget, after making allowance for any planned changes in finished goods stock. The *production budget* specifies the quantities of various goods to be produced and the planned DIRECT MATERIALS, DIRECT LABOUR and factory OVERHEADS associated with

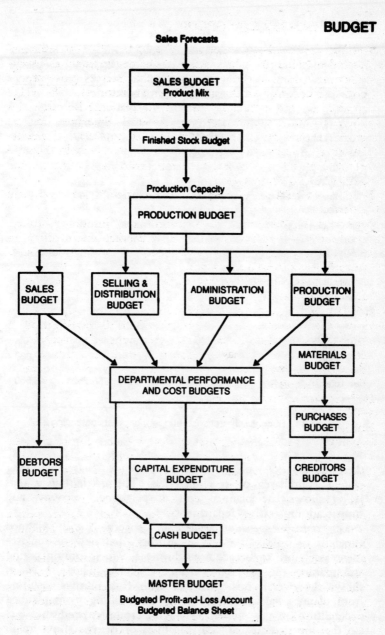

Fig. 13. **Budget**. Development of budgets.

# BUDGET

| | TOTAL £ | Sales Manager £ | Production Manager £ | Secretary/ Accountant £ |
|---|---|---|---|---|
| Sales Net | 826,000 | 826,000 | | |
| Less Direct Costs: | | | | |
| Direct Materials | 366,000 | | 366,000 | |
| Direct Labour | 147,550 | | 147,550 | |
| GROSS MARGIN | 312,450 | | | |
| Production Overheads: | | | | |
| Indirect Wages | 44,400 | | 44,400 | |
| Maintenance | 2,000 | | 2,000 | |
| Depreciation | 9,350 | | 9,350 | |
| Selling Overheads: | | | | |
| Salaries | 47,150 | 47,150 | | |
| Advertising | 31,000 | 31,000 | | |
| Transport | 21,250 | 21,250 | | |
| Administration Overheads: | | | | |
| Salaries | 15,850 | | | 15,850 |
| Rent and rates | 21,000 | | | 21,000 |
| Postage/telephone | 7,500 | | | 7,500 |
| Other Costs: | | | | |
| Training | 1,500 | 300 | 1,000 | 200 |
| Finance charges | 2,000 | | | 2,000 |
| Sub Total | 203,000 | 99,700 | 56,750 | 46,550 |
| NET PROFIT | 109,450 | | | |

Fig. 14. **Budget.** Operational budget for year beginning 1 January 19xx.

these production plans, with a *purchases budget* showing planned purchases of raw materials. The *administration costs budget* shows the planned cost of personnel, accounts and similar administrative departments.

The *capital expenditure budget* is concerned with planned expenditure on FIXED ASSETS, itemizing what new or replacement assets are to be acquired during the forthcoming period and making the necessary finance available. The *cash budget* shows the overall cash position, with cash inflows resulting from planned sales and cash outflows resulting from planned expenditure on raw materials, wages, capital expenditure, etc. (so that any anticipated cash surpluses or deficits show up in good time to deal with them). Finally the *master budget* aggregates all the former budgets to produce a budgeted PROFIT-AND-LOSS ACCOUNT and a budgeted BALANCE SHEET, showing what profit will be earned and what the year-end position will be, provided that actual operations go according to plan. Fig. 13 shows the steps involved in developing a budget while Fig. 14 shows a simple company budget. See BUDGETING, BUDGETARY CONTROL.

2. a statement of the government's financial position which is used for planning the government's economic and social welfare programmes and as part of FISCAL POLICY in managing the level and distribution of spending in the economy. Government revenue comes primarily from receipts from various taxes such as income tax and value added tax (see DIRECT TAX, INDIRECT TAX), NATIONAL INSURANCE CONTRIBUTIONS, and miscellaneous sales, including the proceeds from selling off State industries. See Fig. 15. Government expenditure is directed towards a variety of current and capital commitments. A large

|  |  | £ million |
|---|---|---|
| *Current receipts* | | **275,407** |
| of which | | |
| Taxes on Income (Income Tax, Corporation Tax etc.) | (94,685) | |
| Taxes on expenditure (VAT, Excise duty on Petrol, cigarettes etc.) | (108,484) | |
| National Insurance | (46,270) | |
| *Current expenditure* | | **295,535** |
| of which: | | |
| Spending on provision of goods and services | (152,079) | |
| Transfer payments (unemployment benefit, old-age pensions etc.) | (98,611) | |
| Debt interest | (27,159) | |
| *Capital receipts* | | **3,228** |
| Taxes on capital etc. | | |
| *Capital expenditure* | | **18,140** |
| Nationalized industries' investment etc. | | |
| **Overall Budget Deficit** | | **−35,040** |

Fig. 15. **Budget**. Budget (government), 1996.
(Source: UK National Accounts, 1997.)

proportion of current spending is taken up by social welfare payments (social security and unemployment benefits, old age pensions etc.) and the payment of wages and salaries to central and local authority employees in the Health Service, schools etc. National defence payments also take up a sizeable part of current spending. Capital spending is undertaken on various projects, including investment in infrastructure (roads, schools, hospitals and other public works) and the nationalized industries.

Taxation and government expenditure changes are used by the government to influence the total amount of spending in the economy. For example, if the authorities consider it necessary to reduce total spending, they can aim for a budget surplus, increasing taxes and cutting government expenditure. Alternatively, if a stimulus to the economy is needed, the government can run a budget deficit, cutting taxes and increasing government spending.

See PUBLIC SECTOR BORROWING REQUIREMENT.

**budgetary control** a system for controlling COSTS and REVENUES by comparing actual results with BUDGET estimates and then taking corrective action where necessary. See COMPARISON STATEMENT.

Budgetary control involves two mains stages:

(a) *preparation of the budget* prior to the start of the budget period, forecasting and planning activities for that future period;

(b) *control* by taking action based upon an evaluation of actual performance during the budget period in the light of the plans and standards developed in the budget.

**budget deficit (government)** the excess of government expenditure over taxation and other receipts. See BUDGET SURPLUS (GOVERNMENT).

**budgeting** the process of preparing BUDGETS and exercising BUDGETARY CONTROL. Budgeting encourages forward thinking by managers; serves to help coordinate different functions and departments in the firm; defines the responsibilities of individual managers; provides a framework for delegating responsibility; and provides incentives by setting standards of achievement. Budgeting also provides an instrument for control by pointing out where corrective action is required and a basis for modifying plans where necessary. Finally budgeting enables managers to practise MANAGEMENT BY EXCEPTION concentrating only on important deviations from plans.

**budget surplus (government)** the excess of taxation and other receipts over government expenditure. See BUDGET DEFICIT (GOVERNMENT).

**buffer stock 1.** a reserve of a particular COMMODITY or product held by some appointed body (often a government agency) which is used as part of a support mechanism to stabilize its price at some agreed level. If current production exceeds current demand, surplus output is bought up and held in reserve (otherwise excess supply would force the price down). Similarly, if current production cannot meet current demand then stock is released onto the market (otherwise excess demand would force prices up). Buffer stocks are used, for example, in connection with the operation of an INTERNATIONAL COMMODITY AGREEMENT, and employed to support agricultural produce prices in the EUROPEAN COMMUNITY.

**2.** see STOCK CONTROL.

**building society** a financial institution which offers a variety of savings accounts to attract deposits, mainly from the general public, and which specializes in the provision of long-term MORTGAGE loans used to purchase property. In recent years, many of the larger UK building societies have moved into the estate agency business. Additionally, they have entered into arrangements with other financial institutions whereby they are enabled to provide their depositors with limited banking facilities (the use of cheque books and credit cards, for instance) and other financial services, a development which has been given added impetus by the BUILDING SOCIETY ACT 1986. See ESTATE AGENT.

**Building Society Act 1986** a UK Act which consolidated earlier legislation in respect of the legal framework governing the activities of BUILDING SOCIETIES and, importantly, extended their powers to provide a range of financial services beyond that of providing principally MORTGAGE loans. In effect, the Act has opened the door to societies to engage in the provision of an extensive package of financial services for their clients in competition with the COMMERCIAL BANKS and other financial institutions, including money transmission facilities (via cheque books and cheque cards), foreign exchange (via travellers cheques and foreign currencies), and buying and selling of shares and other securities, the management of UNIT TRUST schemes for pensions and PERSONAL EQUITY PLANS, arranging all kinds of INSURANCE, and the provision of estate agency facilities, surveying and valuation services.

The Act established an authority, the Building Societies Commission, to regulate the sector, replacing the Registrar of Friendly Societies in this capacity. In the past the larger building societies have expanded their mortgage business by merger with, and takeover of, other building societies while retaining their 'friendly society' status (i.e. being owned by their subscribing members). In addition to widening the scope of their business, the 1986 Act also permits building societies to increase their capital resources and growth potential by incorporating themselves as JOINT-STOCK COMPANIES, issuing shares to the investing public and securing a listing on the stock exchange.

**build, operate, transfer project (BOT)** a 'one-off' major construction project such as the building of a petrochemical complex in a country, in which the government is involved in contracting a foreign firm (or firms) not only to design and construct the facility, but also to finance it and run it on completion for a number of years. During this time the firm will expect to recoup its investment on the project before eventually transferring it to the government. See TURNKEY PROJECT.

**bulk buying** the purchase of raw materials, components and finished products in large quantities, which enables a BUYER to take advantage of DISCOUNTS off suppliers' LIST PRICES. A supplier may offer a price discount to encourage the placement of large orders as a means of obtaining extra sales. In many cases, however, the initiative lies with buyers, with powerful retailing and wholesaling groups exacting favourable price concessions from suppliers by playing one supplier off against another. See RETAILER, WHOLESALER, CHAIN STORE.

**bulk discount** see QUANTITY DISCOUNT, BULK BUYING.

**bulletin board** a COMPUTER accessory which enables users to post, read and reply to electronic messages transmitted through a computer network.

**bull** a person who buys a financial security (stock, share, foreign currency, etc.) in expectation that its market price is likely to rise. See SPECULATION. Compare BEAR.

**bullion** precious metals such as GOLD, silver, platinum, etc., which are traded commercially in the form of bars and coins for investment purposes, and which are used to produce jewellery and as industrial base metals.

**bullion market** a MARKET established for the buying and selling of precious metals such as GOLD and silver, and of gold and silver coins such as 'Krugerrands' and 'Sovereigns'. The London Bullion Market is a leading centre for such transactions.

**bull market** a situation in which the prices of FINANCIAL SECURITIES (stocks, shares, etc.) or COMMODITIES (tin, wheat, etc.) tend to rise as a result of persistent buying and only limited selling. See SPECULATION. Compare BEAR MARKET.

**Bullock Report** the report of the Committee of Inquiry on Industrial Democracy, chaired by Sir Alan Bullock and published in 1977. The Committee was created in response to growing interest in the UK in the 1970s in INDUSTRIAL DEMOCRACY, among both TRADE UNIONS and the population at large. Some of the former were becoming aware that important managerial decisions impinging on INDUSTRIAL RELATIONS were difficult to influence through conventional COLLECTIVE BARGAINING. More generally, people were coming to expect a greater say in decision-making at work. Pressure for greater industrial democracy also came from the European Community which the UK had recently joined. In particular the draft FIFTH DIRECTIVE proposed that WORKER DIRECTORS be placed on company boards. The report recommended that company BOARDS OF DIRECTORS be restructured to include equal numbers of representatives of the workforce and of shareholder representatives, plus a third group of independent members (known as the 2x + y formula). Faced with employer hostility and trade union uncertainty about the proposals, the then government proposed that Bullock's recommendations be put on a voluntary rather than a statutory basis. This lack of enthusiasm for Bullock resulted in the demise of the scheme. In the 1980s attention shifted from this form of indirect employee involvement in strategic decisions to more direct, individualistic EMPLOYEE PARTICIPATION and EMPLOYEE INVOLVEMENT in task-related decisions. However in the 1990s there was a renewed interest in worker representation at the strategic level, largely because of proposals emanating from the institutions of the EUROPEAN UNION. Although the UK derogated from the SOCIAL CHAPTER it is believed that EUROPEAN WORKS COUNCILS will need to be introduced in many large UK companies and large European companies with plants in the UK.

**bureaucracy** a structured ORGANIZATION formed to achieve specified goals. The term is commonly used in a pejorative sense to refer to those organizations which appear to have an excessive number of levels in the HIERARCHY, where job roles are narrow and sharply defined and where rules are rigidly adhered to, whatever the circumstances.

As developed by German sociologist Max Weber (1864–1920), however, the term is used to apply to all organizations which include the following features: clearly defined jobs; a hierarchy; a set of rules to govern operations; employees who are appointed (not elected) to posts which constitute their main occupation; and a system of promotion. In Weber's view personal emotions should not enter into the running of the bureaucracy. Weber viewed the bureaucratic organization as a distinctive feature of the modern world. In contrast to traditional societies, the bureaucracy involved a clear separation of home and work life.

In his writing on bureaucracy Weber pioneered the analytical device of the 'ideal type' as a means of identifying the essential features of a phenomenon. The features outlined above constitute the essential features that are present to a greater or lesser extent in bureaucracies. The notion of ideal type has no evaluation or prescriptive connotations.

Subsequent research has questioned Weber's contention that the bureaucracy is a highly efficient form of organization. The emphasis on following the rules can deflect employees' attention from the efficient or effective production of goods and services (see GOAL DISPLACEMENT).

American sociologist Alvin Gouldner (1920–80) identified three types of bureaucracy in terms of the function and observance of rules:

(a) *mock bureaucracy*, where rules are imposed from outside the organization, e.g. by legislation, and where all or most employees, including managers, evade or ignore them;

(b) *representative bureaucracy*, where rules are supported by all organization members, and hence are willingly obeyed;

(c) *punishment-centred bureaucracy*, where rules are enforced by one group upon another in the organization, using punishments to achieve compliance. This approach can lead to CONFLICT.

**burn-in period** see FAILURE RATE CURVE.

**business** or **firm** a producer or distributor of GOODS or SERVICES. The economic form of a business consists of:

(a) a *horizontal business*, a business which specializes in a single activity, for example the production of bread. See HORIZONTAL INTEGRATION;

(b) a *vertical business*, a business which combines two or more successively-related vertical activities, for example flour milling and bread production. See VERTICAL INTEGRATION;

(c) a *conglomerate or diversified business*, a business that is engaged in a number of unrelated production activities, for example bread production and the supply of financial services. See DIVERSIFICATION.

A business can take a number of 'legal' forms:

(a) *a sole proprietorship*, a business owned and controlled by a single person;

(b) *a partnership*, a business owned and controlled by two or more persons who are parties to a partnership agreement;

(c) a JOINT-STOCK COMPANY, a business owned by a group of SHAREHOLDERS and whose capital is divided up into a number of shares;

(d) *a cooperative*, a business owned and controlled by a group of workers. See WORKERS' COOPERATIVE.

**business cycle** fluctuations in the level of business activity in an economy brought about by changes in demand conditions, particularly increases and decreases in investment spending. The business cycle is characterized by four phases, with the economy moving upwards from 'depression' through 'recovery' to 'boom' and back through 'recession' to depression once again. The *depression* stage of the cycle is characterized by a very low level of demand relative to supply capacity, accompanied by low levels of output, unsold stock and high unemployment. As demand picks up in the *recovery* stage, stock levels fall and output and employment increases. *Boom* conditions are characterized by full-capacity levels of output and employment, but with a tendency for the economy to 'overheat', producing inflationary pressures. The ending of a boom is followed by a period of *recession*, with falling demand leading to modest falls in output and employment at first but then accelerating into *depression* as demand continues to fall. In practice, however, governments attempt to use anticyclical FISCAL POLICY and MONETARY POLICY to stabilize the economy, aiming in general to keep total demand in balance with the supply capabilities of the economy, thus avoiding undesirable output- and employment-losses as well as containing inflation. See ECONOMIC POLICY.

**business establishment** SEE BUSINESS PREMISES.

**business ethics** moral guidelines for the conduct of business based on notions of what is right, wrong and fair. Most business people rely upon their own consciences in making business decisions, falling back upon their own moral and religious backgrounds for guidance. However, business people are also affected by their superiors and immediate colleagues when making business decisions and may feel pressurized to behave unethically when seeking to make profits. Over recent years many firms and industries have attempted to develop codes of conduct which can be used to guide managers when making decisions.

**Business Expansion Scheme** a facility offering income tax relief on equity investments in unquoted companies which was replaced in 1994 by the ENTERPRISE INVESTMENT SCHEME.

**business objectives** the goals which a firm sets for itself in respect of profit returns, sales and assets growth, etc., which in turn determine the strategic and operational policies it adopts.

The firm may pursue a single objective or multiple objectives; objectives may be operationalized in 'maximization' or 'satisfactory' target level terms; the time frame in which objectives are pursued may be short term or long term. Thus, it can be seen that objective-setting can be a complex matter. Critical factors affecting the setting of objectives include *who* controls decision-making in the firm, and the various constraints – institutional, financial and environmental, etc. – impinging upon this process.

Economic theories of the firm emphasize that firms which are *owner*-controlled will tend to pursue single period or multi-period profit maximization; likewise, theories of finance suggest that the operational goal of the firm will be to max-imize the value of the firm (shareholders' wealth) over the long term. Firms which are *management*-controlled will tend to pursue objectives such as multi-period sales revenue maximiza-tion and asset growth maximization. In this latter case, although shareholders are the owners of the firm, there is a de facto 'divorce of ownership from control' enabling the appointed representatives of the shareholders, namely members of the Board of Directors, to make the key decisions affecting the firm's business. In general, shareholdings are too fragmented and shareholders, as 'outsiders', are too remote from the seat of power to be able to exercise control over the business, thus leaving the incumbent managers relatively free to run the company as they see fit. Obviously shareholders' interests cannot be ignored (i.e. directors can be removed at the ANNUAL GENERAL MEETING (AGM) if the firm is badly managed and dividends are not paid). However, within this constraint managers will be able to set objectives which en-hance their own interests; sales revenue maximization and asset growth maximization objectives, it is argued, result in 'bigger' firms – big firms pay higher salaries to managers and accord them power and status.

An alternative framework to the largely normative max-imization view of objective setting is provided by the 'organizational' or 'behavioural' schools, which argue that the decision-making process at work in most firms tends to produce objectives couched in 'satisfactory' terms – objectives tend to reflect organizational bargaining between the various divisions of the firm (marketing, production, finance, etc.), re-sulting in the specification of objectives generally 'acceptable' (i.e. satisfactory) to all participants rather than optimal for one group alone. Maximization is ruled out in any case by the organizational school as being unattainable in a business envir-onment which is highly uncertain, so that the degree of preci-sion and 'perfect knowledge' that is required to achieve optimization is simply not to be found. In practice, examina-tion of directors' statements at AGMs reveals a strong concern in most companies with increasing EARNINGS PER SHARE as a measure of corporate 'success'. This is, of course, a profit-related yardstick which nonetheless requires the firm to increase its sales and asset base over time in order to provide a sustainable platform for profit growth.

See BUSINESS STRATEGY, STRATEGY, MISSION STATEMENT.

**business park** see SCIENCE PARK.

**business plan** a detailed statement of the objectives, proposed operations, resource requirements, financial forecasts etc. of a completely new business or an established business which is being developed further. It is particularly important to draw up such a plan not only to ensure that the owners/managers of the business themselves understand clearly what is required to make a success of the venture but also that external parties, in particular providers of capital and loan facilities, can evaluate the viability of what is being attempted.

There is no set formula for a business plan but typical elements would include:

    * name, address, products and objectives of the business; what product is to be supplied

    * market analysis – customer needs, competitors, size of market etc. and proposed marketing/competitive strategy

    * operations analysis – production, purchasing, selling etc.

    * financial analysis – profit and loss forecasts, cash flow forecasts, capital expenditure requirements

    * management information/business controls – recording procedures, monitoring progress.

See BUSINESS STRATEGY.

**business policy** see BUSINESS STRATEGY.

**business premises** or **establishment** a building which is used to produce a good or provide a service. The main types of business premises are: FACTORY, OFFICE, retail or work SHOP or STORE, WAREHOUSE. See UNIFORM BUSINESS RATE.

**business process re-engineering (BPR)** an approach to management which emphasizes the need to organize business operations in a multi-functional way rather than the conventional 'compartmentalized' way built round separate functions such as production and marketing.

Under the traditional functional-focused approach, employees tend to identify with 'their' own function rather than with the firm as a whole. Given, however, the growing complexity of modern business and the need to adapt to change quickly to remain competitive, BPR requires firms to take a holistic view of their operations stressing that everything which affects outcomes – processes, people, technology, etc. – must be effectively co-ordinated *across* departmental boundaries. Thus the 'focus' of the business is clearly based on satisfying external customer needs as competitively as possible and internal processes are 're-engineered' as appropriate to meet this objective. See DE-LAYERING.

**business strategy, business policy, corporate strategy** or **strategic management** the formulation of a unified body of strategic plans by a firm in order to achieve its BUSINESS OBJECTIVES. Business STRATEGY interlocks all aspects of a firm's production activities from the top downwards, including:

(a) objective setting: determining the general goals of the firm (for example increasing the rate of return on capital employed, or increasing earnings per share, etc.);

(b) STRATEGIC DIRECTION: deciding what business activities the firm should operate in, and where: for example continue its existing activities, DIVEST some of them and/or DIVERSIFY into new product markets (see PRODUCT MARKET MATRIX, BOSTON MATRIX); remain a national supplier or globalize its operations (see MULTINATIONAL ENTERPRISE);

(c) choice of growth mode: deciding for each particular area of activity the most appropriate means of expanding its business interests; for example ORGANIC GROWTH or EXTERNAL GROWTH via MERGERS, TAKEOVERS and JOINT VENTURES;

(d) COMPETITIVE STRATEGY: deciding, on the basis of an evaluation of the firm's own competitive strengths and weaknesses vis-à-vis those of its rivals (see SWOT ANALYSIS) and the requirements of customers, the best means of establishing a position of COMPETITIVE ADVANTAGE (lower price, innovative products, etc.) over rival suppliers;

(e) functional responsibilities: ensuring an efficient and co-ordinated effort from the various operational divisions of the firm: MARKETING, PRODUCTION, etc. through appropriate management and organizational structures and management control and reward systems.

See BUSINESS PLAN, HORIZONTAL INTEGRATION, VERTICAL INTEGRATION, DIVERSIFICATION, DIVESTMENT, ENDGAME STRATEGY, TURNROUND, MANAGEMENT BUY-OUT, MANAGEMENT BUY-IN, MARKET ENTRY, MARKET STRUCTURE, MARKET CONDUCT, MARKET PERFORMANCE, STRATEGIC GROUP, FRANCHISE, BARRIERS TO EXIT, BARRIERS TO ENTRY, CORE SKILL, CORPORATE RESTRUCTURING, BUSINESS PROCESS RE-ENGINEERING.

## BUSINESS UNIONISM

**business unionism** see TRADE UNION.

**buyback** see COUNTERTRADE.

**buyer** a purchaser of a GOOD, SERVICE or FINANCIAL SECURITY. A broad distinction can be made between purchasers of goods and services such as raw materials, components, plant and equipment which are used to produce other products (referred to as 'industrial buyers') and purchasers of products for personal consumption (referred to as 'consumers').

The distinction between the two groups is important in terms of the application of appropriate MARKETING STRATEGIES. In general, industrial buyers, mainly purchasing/procurement officers, are involved in the purchase of 'functional' inputs to the production process, usually in large quantities and often involving the outlay of thousands of pounds. Their particular concern is to obtain input supplies which are of an appropriate quality and possess the technical attributes necessary to ensure that the production process goes ahead smoothly and efficiently. In selling to industrial buyers, personal contacts, the provision of technical advice and back-up services are important. Buyers of consumer goods, by contrast, typically buy a much wider range of products, mainly in small quantities. Purchases are made to satisfy some physical or psychological need of the consumer. Thus, it is important for marketers to understand the basis of these needs and to produce and promote BRANDS which satisfy identifiable consumer demands. In this context, ADVERTISING and SALES PROMOTION are important tools for shaping consumers' perceptions of a brand and establishing BRAND LOYALTY. See BUYER BEHAVIOUR.

**buyer behaviour** the purchasing decisions of BUYERS as shaped by their functional and psychological motivations and needs. A broad distinction can be made between industrial buyers and consumers in general. Industrial buyers purchase products purely on the basis of functional or technical requirements: the producer of a motor car, for instance may seek to buy suitable components such as tyres, batteries, etc. for incorporation into a particular car model. Consumers too buy many products on the basis of some functional or physical requirement, for example a consumer may decide to purchase a motor car as a means of personal transport. However, a consumer's decision to buy a product such as a car is also influenced by his or her personality and the image of him or herself it is desired to project to others ('extrovert', 'sporty', 'affluent', etc.).

It is thus important for producers of consumer goods to understand the psychological impulses of prospective buyers of their products as well as their practical needs. This requires careful MARKET RESEARCH into the motivation and perception of buyers aimed at matching products with identified customer needs, and the deployment of appropriate MARKETING MIX strategies (product quality, pricing, advertising, etc.) designed to maximize sales potential.

See PRE-PURCHASE BEHAVIOUR, POST-PURCHASE BEHAVIOUR, PRODUCT IMAGE, PSYCHOLOGICAL PRICING, ADVERTISING, LIFE STYLE, MOTIVATIONAL RESEARCH.

**buyer concentration** see MARKET CONCENTRATION.

**buyer's market** a MARKET situation characterized by the temporary excess supply of a GOOD or SERVICE often leading to cut-throat price competition. In such markets BUYERS are advantageously placed to obtain price concessions. Compare SELLER'S MARKET.

**buying intentions survey** an investigation designed to discover BUYERS' future plans in respect of purchasing a particular GOOD or SERVICE. Such a survey is undertaken to enable a firm to produce more realistic forecasts of the anticipated future demand for their product. Surveys are generally carried out by interviewers or direct mail questionnaires. See SALES FORECASTING.

**buy one get one free (BOGOF)** an EMPLOYEE SHARE OWNERSHIP SCHEME in the UK where for each share in their company purchased by an employee he or she is given one free. The latter is free of income tax if given under the provisions of recent legislation on share ownership and PROFIT SHARING.

**by-product** a product which results from a common production process but which is secondary to the main product being produced from that process. The refining of crude oil to produce petrol, for example, also produces by-products such as tar and creosote. See BY-PRODUCT PRICING, PROCESS PRODUCTION.

**by-product pricing** the PRICING of the various BY-PRODUCTS emerging from a common production process. The PRICE of each by-product should, if possible, cover its cost. However, the precise individual cost of each by-product is very difficult to determine given the *common* process costs involved. As a consequence by-products are often priced according to what the market will bear. See PROCESS COSTING.

**byte** a group of eight bits (zeros/ones) used to represent a single number or letter in a COMPUTER. The capacity of a computer is often measured in terms of thousands of bytes (K), for example 640K; or millions of bytes, for example 20 megabytes.

# C

**CACA** see CHARTERED ASSOCIATION OF CERTIFIED ACCOUNTANTS.

**CAD** see COMPUTER-AIDED DESIGN.

**CAE (computer-aided engineering)**, see COMPUTER-AIDED DESIGN.

**c&f** see COST AND FREIGHT.

**cafeteria benefits** a PAY system where employees are able to design their own remuneration package selecting from a menu of pay and fringe benefit items up to a value stipulated by the employer. Full cafeteria systems are rare but it is more common for employees to have a degree of choice over their FRINGE BENEFITS. For example, some firms allow employees to take a cash alternative to a company car. The advantage of cafeteria pay systems is that they can reduce LABOUR TURNOVER by aligning reward packages with individual preferences but the downside is that they can be complex and time consuming to administer.

**called-up capital** the amount of issued share capital which shareholders have been called upon to subscribe to date, where a JOINT-STOCK COMPANY issues shares with phased payment terms. For example, a company may issue £1 shares with 50p payable immediately upon application by intending shareholders, a further 25p upon ALLOTMENT of the shares to shareholders and the final 25p three months later. Here the called-up capital at the time of allotment of shares would be 75p times the number of shares allotted. Called-up capital is usually equal to PAID-UP CAPITAL unless there are any calls in arrears – shares on which subsequent instalments are owing. See SHARE ISSUE.

**call option** see OPTION.

**call reports** reports completed by sales representatives after visiting customers and potential customers as a basis for compiling MARKETING INTELLIGENCE and monitoring representatives' performance. The reports may include information about new customers, reasons why particular customers have been lost and creditworthiness of buyers. See CALLS.

**calls** visits by SALES REPRESENTATIVES to customers and potential customers as a means of securing SALES and maintaining customer contact. Calls provide a useful opportunity for sales persons to inform customers about the firm's product offerings and promotions. Additionally, calls may be used to obtain data about customer needs for SALES FORECASTING and NEW PRODUCT DEVELOPMENT purposes. See CALL REPORTS.

**CAM** see COMPUTER-AIDED MANUFACTURING.

**campaign** see ADVERTISING CAMPAIGN.

**capacity** the maximum amount of output that a firm is physically capable of producing, at a point in time, given the fullest and most efficient use of its existing plant or plants. Over time, a firm may adjust its capacity to meet changes in demand and the competitive situation facing it, investing in new plant or extending existing plant to meet an increase in demand, or closing down plant, permanently or temporarily ('MOTHBALLING'), to meet a situation of OVERCAPACITY.

When preparing a PRODUCTION BUDGET, it is necessary to ensure that the firm has sufficient production capacity to meet planned output levels. A firm's capacity or the capacity of industry in general may be limited by the availability of capital equipment and labour.

The maximum rate of output which the firm can produce will depend upon the capacity of its individual factories which in turn depends upon the capacity of various departments and work stations within each factory. See INPUT-OUTPUT CONTROL, PRODUCTION SCHEDULING, PRODUCTION-LINE BALANCING.

See CAPACITY UTILIZATION, LIMITING FACTOR, RATIONALIZATION, INDIVISIBILITIES.

**capacity utilization** the proportion of a firm's available CAPACITY which is currently being employed in producing out-

# CAPITAL

put. This depends to a great extent on the state of demand and a firm's competitive abilities. A fall in demand, or a failure to win orders against competition, may force a firm to operate at below BREAKEVEN levels of capacity utilization. See INDIVISIBILITIES, BUSINESS CYCLE, MACHINE UTILIZATION.

**capital 1.** the funds invested in a BUSINESS in order to acquire the ASSETS which the business needs to trade. Capital can consist of SHARE CAPITAL subscribed by SHAREHOLDERS or LOAN CAPITAL provided by lenders.
**2.** GOODS such as plant, machinery and equipment which are used to produce other goods and services.
See CAPITAL STOCK, INVESTMENT.

**capital accumulation** see CAPITAL FORMATION.

**capital allowances** standard allowances, for TAXATION purposes, against expenditure on FIXED ASSETS by a firm in lieu of DEPRECIATION. A business may choose its own rates of depreciation for fixed assets which may differ from the statutory capital allowances. Capital allowances may also be varied by the government to encourage or discourage capital INVESTMENT. See DEPRECIATION, CORPORATION TAX.

**capital appreciation** see APPRECIATION.

**capital-asset pricing model** a share-price valuation model in which the major factors of short-term share-price determination are explained. The capital-asset pricing model provides a method of computing the return on a FINANCIAL SECURITY which specifically identifies and measures the risk factor within a PORTFOLIO holding. The expected rate of return on a particular investment has two components:

(a) the risk-free percentage return which could be obtained from, say, a gilt-edged, government financial security;

(b) the risk return associated with the investment.

(Risk itself can be split into market or nondiversifiable risk and specific or diversifiable risk.) This relationship between risk and return is shown in Fig. 16.

The total expected return on an investment is $Or_m$, but risk only attaches to non gilt-edged securities which is why the capital market line intercepts the vertical axis at $r_f$. The capital market line shows how, in a competitive market, the additional risk premium varies in direct proportion to б, known as the BETA COEFFICIENT. At point M in the figure there is perfect correlation between movements in the market generally, as detailed by an all-share index, and a particular investment. Therefore $\beta=1$ at point M. Where there is no risk, as in Treasury bills, $\beta=0$. $\beta$ is a measure of market risk because investors have it within their power to diversify away specific risk to almost zero by holding a broad portfolio of shares. It is possible to estimate the beta coefficient of a security from published information.

See also EFFICIENT MARKETS HYPOTHESIS, PORTFOLIO THEORY.

Fig. 16. **Capital-asset pricing model.** This identifies the market risk factor for the expected rate of investment.

**capital budgeting** the process of planning and controlling CAPITAL expenditure within a firm. Capital budgeting involves the search for suitable investment opportunities; evaluating particular investment projects; raising LONG-TERM CAPITAL to finance investments; assessing the COST OF CAPITAL; applying suitable expenditure controls to ensure that investment outlays conform with the expenditures authorized; and ensuring that adequate cash is available when required for investments. See INVESTMENT APPRAISAL, BUDGETING.

**capital employed** the total funds invested in a business made up of SHAREHOLDERS' funds and long-term LOAN CAPITAL. It is equivalent in value to the company's NET ASSETS in its BALANCE SHEET. See SHAREHOLDER'S CAPITAL EMPLOYED, LONG-TERM CAPITAL EMPLOYED.

**capital expenditure** expenditure on the acquisition or improvement of FIXED ASSETS that is subsequently written off against profits over several ACCOUNTING PERIODS. Contrast with REVENUE EXPENDITURE. See INVESTMENT, CAPITAL BUDGETING.

**capital export** see EXPORT, BALANCE OF PAYMENTS.

**capital formation** or **capital accumulation 1.** the process of increasing the internally available CAPITAL of a business by retaining earnings to add to RESERVES.
**2.** the process of adding to the net physical CAPITAL STOCK of an economy as a means of increasing the economy's capacity to produce goods and services. INVESTMENT by businesses in new plant and equipment is one important source of capital formation, as is investment by the government in INFRASTRUCTURE (roads, railways, etc.).

**capital gain** the surplus realized when an ASSET (house, SHARE, etc.) is sold at a higher price than was originally paid for it. However, because of INFLATION it is important to distinguish between NOMINAL VALUES and REAL VALUES. Thus what appears to be a large nominal gain may, after allowing for the effects of inflation, turn out to be a very small real gain. Furthermore, in an ongoing business, provision has to be made for the REPLACEMENT COST of assets, which can be much higher than the HISTORIC COST of these assets being sold. See CAPITAL GAINS TAX, CAPITAL LOSS, REVALUATION PROVISION, APPRECIATION, definition 1.

**capital gains tax** a TAX on the surplus obtained from the sale of an ASSET for more than was originally paid for it. Because capital gains tax is generally levied on the nominal CAPITAL GAIN, in a period of rapid INFLATION it can seriously over-tax companies whose real gains (after allowing for the high REPLACEMENT COST of assets) are considerably smaller than their nominal gain.

In the UK, capital gains up to a maximum of £6,500 per year are exempt. Chargeable capital gains above £6,500 per year are subject to capital gains tax on a sliding scale of 24% and 40%.

**capital gearing** or **leverage** the proportion of fixed-interest LOAN CAPITAL to SHARE CAPITAL employed in financing a company. Where a company raises most of the funds required by issuing shares and uses very few fixed-interest loans it has a low capital gearing; where a company raises most of the funds needed from fixed-interest loans and few funds from SHAREHOLDERS it is highly geared.

Capital gearing is important to company shareholders because fixed-interest charges on loans have the effect of gearing up or down the eventual residual return to shareholders from trading profits. When the trading return on total funds invested exceeds the interest rate on loans, any residual surplus accrues to shareholders, enhancing their return. On the other hand, when the average return on total funds invested is less than interest rates, then interest still has to be paid and this has the effect of reducing the residual return to shareholders. For example, compare two companies, one financed solely from share capital (*ungeared*) and another which raises half of its capital from fixed-interest loans on which it must pay 10% interest (*highgeared*). Fig. 17 (overleaf) shows how returns to shareholders vary more widely when highgeared.

The extent to which a company can employ fixed-interest capital as a source of long-term funds depends to a large extent upon the stability of its profits over time. For example, large retailing companies whose profits tend to vary little from year to year tend to be more highly geared than, say, mining companies whose profit record is more volatile.

**capital good** see GOOD.

**capital import** see IMPORT, BALANCE OF PAYMENTS, CAPITAL INFLOW.

**capital inflow** a movement of funds into a particular country, the HOST COUNTRY, from one or more foreign countries, the source countries. The host country may attract capital inflows for a variety of reasons, including:

(a) Investment by MULTINATIONAL ENTERPRISES in physical assets such as the establishment of a local manufacturing plant or the acquisition of a local firm;

(b) Portfolio investment in financial securities (equities and bonds etc. issued in the host country by overseas residents and financial institutions, pension funds, insurance companies etc.);

(c) Host government borrowing from international banks or from other governments to finance a BALANCE OF PAYMENTS deficit, borrowing by individuals and companies from international banks and inter-company transfers to finance current consumption and investment;

(d) Short-term deposits with money market and banking institutions in the host country relating to interest rate differentials between countries and/or speculation in the hope that a

# CAPITALIST ECONOMY

| | Firm A: ungeared £ | Firm B: highgeared £ |
|---|---|---|
| Ordinary Shares | 1,000 | 500 |
| Fixed-interest loans | – | 500 |
| Total capital employed | 1,000 | 1,000 |

*Year 1 trading profit = 30% on total capital employed*

| | | |
|---|---|---|
| Trading profit | 300 | 300 |
| Less loan interest (at 10%) | – | 50 |
| Net profit | 300 | 250 |
| Return to shareholders | $\dfrac{300}{1,000}$ = 30% | $\dfrac{250}{500}$ = 50% |

*Year 2 trading profit = 7% on total capital employed*

| | | |
|---|---|---|
| Trading profit | 70 | 70 |
| Less loan interest (at 10%) | – | 50 |
| Net profit | 70 | 20 |
| Return to shareholders | $\dfrac{70}{1,000}$ = 7% | $\dfrac{20}{500}$ = 4% |

Fig. 17. **Capital gearing**. Table comparing the effects of ungeared and highgeared capital on returns to shareholders.

country's EXCHANGE RATE may appreciate, thereby producing a CAPITAL GAIN.

By contrast, a CAPITAL OUTFLOW is the outward movement of funds from one country to other countries for the kinds of reasons listed above. See FOREIGN INVESTMENT.

**capitalist economy** see ECONOMY.

**capital intensiveness** the extent to which capital (plant, equipment, etc.) is used in the PRODUCTION of goods and services. Where capital is relatively cheap and labour is comparatively expensive, then firms will be inclined to use large amounts of capital in their production processes and automate (see AUTOMATION) their production.

See CAPITAL LABOUR RATIO.

Compare LABOUR INTENSIVENESS.

**capitalization issue** or **scrip issue,** the issue by a JOINT-STOCK COMPANY of additional SHARES to existing SHAREHOLDERS without any further payment being required. Capitalization issues are usually made when a company has ploughed back profits over several years and so has accumulated substantial RESERVES, or has revalued its fixed assets and accumulated capital reserves. If the company wishes to capitalize the reserves it can do so by creating extra shares to match the reserves, and issues them as BONUS SHARES to existing shareholders in proportion to their existing shareholdings. In the USA the term *stock dividend* is used to describe this same process. See also RETAINED PROFIT.

**capitalization rate** the rate at which the STOCK MARKET capitalizes the current earnings of a company. It is calculated by dividing a company's earnings per ordinary share by the current market price per ordinary share in order to arrive at the EARNINGS YIELD.

**capitalizing** the process of converting an expense into an equivalent capital sum, carrying forward that expense as a FIXED ASSET in the BALANCE SHEET of a firm rather than writing off that expense as a current cost. Capitalization is applied to expenditure on assets that have been acquired for use in the business for periods in excess of a year and which are not for resale, for example motor vehicles, plant, machinery, equipment, land and buildings, patents, goodwill, trademarks, brands etc.

**capital labour ratio** the proportion of CAPITAL to LABOUR inputs in a company. This can be measured by means of a number of accounting ratios. One measure is total assets per pound of employee remuneration: the higher the ratio (the more capital per pound of labour cost), the greater the degree of capital intensity. Alternatively, we could take FIXED ASSETS per employee, or more narrowly plant and machinery per employee, as an index of the degree of mechanization in a firm. Where a company employs a high proportion of part-time workers, numbers employed may need to be adjusted to full-time equivalent numbers to assist comparability. Alternatively, assets may be expressed as a proportion of total employee remuneration.

**capital loss** the deficit realized when an ASSET (house, SHARE, etc.) is sold at a lower price than was originally paid for it. Compare CAPITAL GAIN.

**capital market** see STOCK MARKET.

**capital outflow** a movement of funds out of a particular country into one or more foreign countries, representing, on the one hand, investments by individuals, companies and institutions and by government in foreign physical assets and financial securities, and on the other hand, the provision of borrowing facilities and loans to foreigners. See CAPITAL INFLOW, FOREIGN INVESTMENT, BALANCE OF PAYMENTS.

**capital rationing** a situation where a firm selects an annual capital budget which is less than the amount required to undertake all INVESTMENTS promising a rate of return in excess of the cost of capital. For example, if a firm requires a minimum 20% return on any investment then *all* of the appropriate investment opportunities available to the firm which promise a return of 20% or more may involve a total expenditure of, say, £10 million. However, if the firm decides that it is willing to spend only £6 million, then it must rank investment opportunities in descending order of rate of return, undertaking those with the highest promised return and rejecting others even though the latter opportunities promise a return greater than the 20% cost of capital. The firm is said to be in a situation of capital rationing because it is investing less than the amount dictated by usual profit maximizing criteria. See CAPITAL BUDGETING, INVESTMENT APPRAISAL.

**capital reserves** see RESERVES.

**capital servicing cost** interest paid on long-term and medium-term loan capital, and on overdrafts.

**capital stock** the total amount of capital GOODS (plant, offices, machinery and equipment) currently available to a firm or an economy with which to produce goods and services. The firm's/economy's capital stock requires maintaining by INVESTMENT to replace worn out or obsolete capital items (see DEPRECIATION) but more importantly, the size of the capital stock can be increased over time by new investment. Capital formation or accumulation plays a crucial role in expanding the firm's/economy's productive capacity and hence its ability to sustain a high rate of business growth and ECONOMIC GROWTH.

**capital structure** the composition of a JOINT-STOCK COMPANY'S long-term capital which reflects the source of that capital, for example SHARE CAPITAL and long-term LOAN CAPITAL. See CAPITAL GEARING.

**capital transfer tax** see INHERITANCE TAX.

**CAPP (computer-aided process planning)**, see COMPUTER-

AIDED DESIGN.

**captive product** a product which needs to be bought on a continuing basis once a main product has been bought in order to operate the main product; for example films for a camera. See CAPTIVE PRODUCT PRICING.

**captive product pricing** the PRICING of a CAPTIVE PRODUCT. When a supplier's main product and captive product are unique (i.e. there is no interchangeability with competing products), the supplier may choose to charge a low price for the main product to encourage people to buy it, with the objective of thereafter making the bulk of his profits from continuing sales of captive products.

**career break** an interruption to an individual's career for the purpose of childcare or achievement of personal goals outside work. Some organizations now allow staff to take career breaks of several years' duration without loss of seniority or occupational position. It can be a way of reducing LABOUR TURNOVER and tackling DISCRIMINATION against female employees.

**cargo** see FREIGHT.

**cartel** a form of COLLUSION between a group of suppliers aimed at suppressing competition between themselves, wholly or in part. Cartels can take a number of forms. For example, suppliers may set up a sole selling agency which buys up their individual output at an agreed price and arranges for the marketing of these products on a coordinated basis. Another form is where suppliers operate an agreement (see RESTRICTIVE TRADE AGREEMENT) which sets uniform selling prices for their products, thereby suppressing price competition, but with suppliers then competing for market share through PRODUCT DIFFERENTIATION strategies. A more comprehensive version of a cartel is the application not only of common selling prices and joint marketing, but also of restrictions on production involving the assignment of specific output quotas to individual suppliers, and the making of coordinated capacity adjustments, thereby either removing over-capacity or extending capacity on a coordinated basis.

Cartels are usually established either to exploit the joint marketing power of suppliers to extract MONOPOLY profits, or as a means of preventing cutthroat competition from forcing firms to operate at a loss, often resorted to in times of depressed demand (a so-called 'crisis cartel').

A number of factors are crucial to the successful operation of a cartel, in particular the participation of all significant suppliers of the product and their full compliance with the policies of the cartel. Nonparticipation of some key suppliers and 'cheating' by cartel members, together with the ability of buyers to switch to substitute products, may well serve to undermine a cartel's ability to control prices. In many countries, most notably the US and European Community, cartels concerned with price fixing, market sharing and restrictions on production and capacity are prohibited by law.

See COMPETITION POLICY, ORGANIZATION OF PETROLEUM EXPORTING COUNTRIES (OPEC).

**case law** see COMMON LAW.

**cash** see CURRENCY.

**cash account** or **cash book** a LEDGER account which records all of a company's cash incomings and outgoings. See ACCOUNTING.

**cash and carry** a form of wholesaling which requires customers (predominantly RETAILERS) to pay cash for products bought and to collect these products themselves from a warehouse. By eliminating the costs involved in offering credit terms and a delivery service, such WHOLESALERS are able to offer products at highly-competitive prices. See DISTRIBUTION CHANNEL.

**cash book** see CASH ACCOUNT.

**cash budget** an accounting statement which analyses expected cash receipts and payments over forthcoming trading periods with a view to anticipating any potential cash shortages or surpluses before they arise and thus allow appropriate remedial action to be taken. This action could take the form of tightened CREDIT CONTROL to get cash in from customers more quickly, or arranging short-term loans in advance to cover an expected cash shortage, or plans to invest profitably any expected cash surplus. Fig. 18 shows a typical cash budget. See BUDGET, BUDGETING, BUDGETARY CONTROL.

**cash card** see COMMERCIAL BANK.

**cash discount** a reduction in the total amount of money owed by a customer to a supplier in return for prompt payment. Cash discounts are offered by suppliers as a means of persuading customers to pay for their CREDIT purchases more quickly

| | January £ | February £ | March £ | etc. |
|---|---|---|---|---|
| Opening Balance | 3,000 | (2,000) | 4,000 | |
| add Inflows | | | | |
| cash sales | 5,000 | 6,000 | 5,500 | |
| collections on credit sales | 15,000 | 17,000 | 16,000 | |
| sale of short-term investments | — | 4,000 | — | |
| Total inflows | 20,000 | 27,000 | 21,500 | |
| Less Outflows | | | | |
| payments to materials suppliers | 6,000 | 5,000 | 7,000 | |
| payments of wages | 8,000 | 8,500 | 9,500 | |
| interest and dividend payments | 4,500 | 500 | 500 | |
| expenditure on plant and equipment | 6,500 | 7,000 | 2,000 | |
| Total outflows | 25,000 | 21,000 | 19,000 | |
| Excess of Inflows over Outflows (Outflows over Inflows) | (5,000) | 6,000 | 2,500 | |
| Closing Balance | (2,000) | 4,000 | 6,500 | |

Fig. 18. Cash budget. A typical example.

and thereby improve the supplier's CASH FLOW.

**cash flow** the money coming into a business from sales and other receipts and going out of the businesses in the form of cash payments to suppliers, workers, etc. Cash receipts and cash payments in a trading period are not necessarily the same as the accounting revenues and cost applicable to that same period, because customers need not pay cash for goods sold until some time afterwards while the firm may not pay for materials and services used until afterwards. Fig. 19 (overleaf) shows the main causes of disparities between cash flow and profit. See SOURCES AND USES OF FUNDS STATEMENT.

**cash flow exposure** see EXCHANGE RATE EXPOSURE.

**cash on delivery (COD)** an arrangement whereby goods previously ordered are paid for when delivered.

**cash settlement** purchases of FINANCIAL SECURITIES which have to be paid for immediately rather than being settled after the end of the stock exchange ACCOUNT PERIOD.

**catalogue shopping** a North American term for MAIL ORDER.

**catalogue showroom** a means of retailing products from premises displaying catalogues from which consumers purchase

## CATEGORY DISCOUNTER

| | BUY | SELL | PROFIT £ | CASH FLOW £ | Difference |
|---|---|---|---|---|---|
| cash purchase cash sale | 10 units (cash) −£50 | 10 units (cash) +£100 | 50 | 50 (−50+100) | |
| cash purchase credit sale | 10 units (cash) −£50 | 10 units (credit) +£0 | 50 | −50 (−50+0) | Debtors £100 |
| credit purchase cash sale | 10 units (credit) −£0 | 10 units (cash) +£100 | 50 | 100 (−0+100) | Creditors £50 |
| purchases exceed sales | 12 units (cash) −£60 | 10 units (cash) +£100 | 50 | 40 (−60+100) | Stock £10 |

Fig. 19. **Cash flow.** A trader sells 10 units at £10 each which cost £5 each.

Sales: 10×£10=£100
cost: 10× £5= £50
profit: 10× £5= £50

products for immediate collection and payment. See RETAILER, RETAIL OUTLET. Contrast with MAIL ORDER.

**category discounter** a RETAILER or WHOLESALER which sells an extensive range of a *particular* product category at low, 'discounted' prices on a SELF SERVICE basis. Toys-R-Us is a prominent discounter of toy products.

See DISTRIBUTION CHANNEL, DISCOUNT STORE.

**cause and effect analysis** a technique used in the control of QUALITY in which all possible causes of defective production are investigated. Its purpose is to detect causes of defects and to take any necessary corrective action to prevent a recurrence of the problem.

See FISHBONE CHART.

**caveat emptor** 'let the buyer beware': a situation where a supplier of a good or service is under no legal obligation to inform buyers of any defects or deficiencies in the products supplied. It is thus the responsibility of buyers to determine for themselves whether or not the product is satisfactory. Compare CAVEAT VENDOR.

**caveat vendor** 'let the seller beware': a situation where a supplier of a good or service is legally obliged to inform

buyers of any defects in the product. Compare CAVEAT
EMPTOR.

**CBI** see CONFEDERATION OF BRITISH INDUSTRY.

**CCT** see COMPETITIVE TENDERING.

**celebrity message** a form of ADVERTISING in which a well-
known sports or media person is used to endorse a product.

**cell** an independent team of operatives who work together in a
GROUP TECHNOLOGY (GT) production environment.

**census** a survey carried out by a government department to
obtain economic and social data which can be used in the formulation of social and industrial policies. In the UK a *production census* is conducted yearly to provide information on industrial production, employment, exports, capital investment
etc.; a *population census* is carried out every ten years to obtain
data on demographic trends.

**Central Arbitration Committee** a UK body with power to
arbitrate in cases where employers contest the legal right of
TRADE UNIONS to receive information relevant to COLLECTIVE
BARGAINING and where unions claim that pay structures are dis-
criminatory. See ARBITRATION, DISCLOSURE OF INFORMATION, DIS-
CRIMINATION.

**central bank** a country's leading BANK which acts as banker to
the government and the BANKING SYSTEM and acts as the
authority responsible for implementing the government's MON-
ETARY POLICY. Central banks such as the Bank of England in
the UK handle the government's financial accounts in conjunction with the TREASURY, taking in receipts from taxation and
the sale of government assets, and making disbursements to
the various government departments to fund their activities.
The central bank acts as the government's broker in its
borrowing and lending operations, issuing and dealing in
government BONDS and TREASURY BILLS to underpin its year to
year budgetary position and management of the country's
NATIONAL DEBT.

The Bank of England and its satellite, the Royal Mint, are
responsible for issuing the country's basic stock of money –
LEGAL TENDER consisting of bank notes and coins (see MONEY
SUPPLY). The central bank occupies a key role in the management of the money supply, influencing the level of bank
deposits and credit creation by the financial institutions,
particularly COMMERCIAL BANKS, as well as the structure of

# CENTRALIZATION

INTEREST RATES in the economy, through buying and selling operations in the market for short- and long-dated financial securities. See DISCOUNT MARKET, STOCK MARKET.

The central bank is also responsible for managing the country's EXCHANGE RATE and holding the country's stock of INTERNATIONAL RESERVES to be used in the financing of balance of payments deficits. The Bank of England operates an 'Exchange Equalization Account' which it uses to intervene in the FOREIGN EXCHANGE MARKET, buying and selling currencies to 'fix' the exchange rate at a particular level or ensure that it falls (depreciates) or rises (appreciates) in an 'orderly' manner.

**centralization** the vertical dimension of ORGANIZATION structure. Organizations are centralized when important decisions are largely taken by managers at the top of the organization. There is a persistent tension between DECENTRALIZATION and centralisation organizations. Centralization of decisions is useful to provide central direction to the organization. However, it can mean that the organization cannot respond quickly to PRODUCT MARKET developments. Also, if lower level managers are precluded from making important decisions it can have negative effects on their job satisfaction. See ORGANIZATIONAL ANALYSIS.

**centrally-planned economy** see ECONOMY.

**Central Processing Unit** see CPU.

**Central Statistical Office (CSO)** – now called the Office for National Statistics – the UK government department which collects and publishes statistics concerning the economy, such as the National Income 'blue book'.

**certainty equivalent** see DECISION TREE.

**certificate** a document signifying ownership of a FINANCIAL SECURITY (STOCK, SHARE, etc.). In the UK such certificates are issued in the name of the person or company recorded in the company's register of SHAREHOLDERS as the owner of these shares, new certificates being issued to buyers when shares are sold. In countries like the USA where BEARER BONDS are used, stock certificates merely note the number of stocks or shares represented and do not include the name of the owner, the holder of the certificate being presumed to be the owner.

**certificate of deposit** a FINANCIAL SECURITY issued by BANKS, BUILDING SOCIETIES and other financial institutions as a means of borrowing money for periods ranging from one month to five years. Once issued, certificates of deposit may be bought and sold on the MONEY MARKET and are redeemable on their maturity for their face value plus accrued interest.

**certificate of incorporation** a certificate issued by the RE-GISTRAR OF COMPANIES to a new JOINT-STOCK COMPANY whose MEMORANDUM OF ASSOCIATION and ARTICLES OF ASSOCIATION are acceptable to the Registrar. A company starts its legal existence from the date of its incorporation and thereafter is able to enter into CONTRACTS in its own name.

**certificate of origin** a document used to authenticate the country of origin of internationally traded goods. Most trading countries are prepared to accept certificates of origin issued by government departments of their trade partners or their appointees (CHAMBERS OF COMMERCE in the UK). However, complications as to their precise country of origin often arise in the case of goods which are assembled in one country using components which are in the main imported from other countries. See LOCAL CONTENT RULE, EXPORTING.

**certification 1.** a means of recording the details of a transaction in SHARES involving noting on the TRANSFER DEED that the SHARE CERTIFICATE has been placed with the company or its representative. Certification is necessary where a seller is not selling all of his shareholding or where a block of shares are bought by more than one person to enable new share certificates to be issued which reflect the new ownership of the shares.

**2.** a status granted by a manufacturer to a supplier which is able to demonstrate that it is able to achieve consistent QUALITY in the materials or components it supplies. The materials or components supplied by a certified supplier can be used directly by the manufacturer without the need for INSPECTION of these items. See QUALITY CONTROL.

**Certification Officer** the UK officer responsible for overseeing the accounts of TRADE UNIONS and EMPLOYERS' ASSOCIATIONS, and ensuring that unions observe the statutory procedures relating to POLITICAL FUNDS, mergers between unions, and ballots to elect union executive members.

**chain of command** the line of command flowing down from the top of an ORGANIZATION to the bottom. In theory, the chief executive issues commands to his or her subordinates which are then relayed down to those they have AUTHORITY over. In practice, those in the chain of command often do not follow such commands, either because they do not have the resources to meet them or because they believe them to be incorrect or otherwise inappropriate. See UNITY OF COMMAND, LINE AND STAFF, HIERARCHY.

**chain store** a multibranch retail business. All types of RETAILER, ranging from SPECIALIST SHOPS to SUPERMARKETS can be organized to take advantage of the growth and competitive opportunities deriving from large-scale operations. Unlike single-shop concerns, chain stores, by operating a network of stores each located strategically in catchment areas serving large populations, are in a position to expand their sales potential. Moreover, by selling the same general range of products in all of their stores and utilizing a central buying system, chain stores are able to secure BULK BUYING price discounts from manufacturers. In addition, the larger chain stores have found it advantageous to establish their 'OWN LABEL' BRANDS as a means of maximizing the group's sales potential. See DISTRIBUTION CHANNEL.

**chairperson 1.** a person who organizes and runs a committee, drawing up the agenda for each committee meeting, ensuring the orderly conduct of the meeting and approving the minutes or records of the meeting.
**2.** a person who organizes and runs the BOARD OF DIRECTORS of a JOINT STOCK COMPANY. See DIRECTOR.

**Chamber of Commerce** an organization which operates primarily to serve the needs of the business community in an industrial city or area. Chambers of Commerce provide a forum for local businessmen and traders to discuss matters of mutual interest and provide a range of services to their members, especially small businesses, including, for example in the UK, information on business opportunities locally and nationally and, in conjunction with the DEPARTMENT OF TRADE AND INDUSTRY, export advisory services, export market intelligence, participation in overseas visits and trade fairs, and the issue of CERTIFICATES OF ORIGIN. In recent years, a particular concern of many chambers has been the provision of training facilities and centres, run either independently or in conjunction with the government's recently-established TRAINING AND EDUCATION COUNCILS. At the national level the movement is represented by the Association of British Chambers of

Commerce. See EXPORTING, TRAINING..

**changeover cost** see SET-UP COST.

**channel of distribution** see DISTRIBUTION CHANNEL.

**chargeable gain** see CAPITAL GAINS TAX.

**charismatic authority** see AUTHORITY.

**Chartered Association of Certified Accountants (CACA** or more usually **ACCA)** a large UK body of accountants, some of whose members operate in professional practice (auditing, taxation, etc.), whilst others work in industry.

**Chartered Institute of Management Accountants (CIMA)** a large UK body of professional accountants whose members work primarily in industry undertaking MANAGEMENT ACCOUNTING work.

**Chartermark** see CITIZENS' CHARTER.

**chartism** the monitoring of price movements of financial securities such as STOCKS and SHARES and FOREIGN CURRENCIES as a means of indicating appropriate buying and selling positions. For instance, by plotting a particular share's price on a graph it may be possible to discern distinct patterns of upward and downward price movements over a run of weeks or months, which may then serve as a guide to the buying and selling of that share on a profitable basis, i.e. buy when the price is low, sell when the price is high. Because of future uncertainties, however, it is not possible to forecast consistently the high or low of a share price. Accordingly, some chartists employ 'mechanistic' buy and sell rules: thus, a share may be sold once it has fallen (cumulatively) 5% or 10% from its peak price, and likewise bought once it has risen (cumulatively) 5% or 10% above its lowest price. See SHARE PRICE INDEX, STOCK MARKET, FOREIGN EXCHANGE MARKET.

**check-off agreement** an agreement between EMPLOYER and TRADE UNION, enabling the employer to deduct the union membership subscription ('union dues') from employee's pay (with their consent) and pass them to the union as a lump sum. This was a more efficient method of collecting membership fees than the traditional method whereby shop stewards or officials collected union dues in cash from each member each week. Unions are now required by the TRADE UNION REFORM AND EMPLOYMENT RIGHTS ACT 1993 to seek written authorization for check-off from employees every three years. This is viewed as having serious implications for trade union finances and in response many unions are now encouraging their members to pay their subscription by direct debit. See CLOSED SHOP.

**cheque** a means of transferring or withdrawing money from a BANK or BUILDING SOCIETY current account. In the former case, the drawer of a cheque creates a written instruction to his bank or building society to transfer funds to some other person's or company's bank or building society account (the 'payee'). In the latter case, money may be withdrawn in cash by a person or company writing out a cheque payable to themselves. Cheques may be 'open' in which case they can be used to draw cash, or 'crossed' with two parallel lines, in which case they cannot be presented for cash but must be paid into the account of the payee. See COMMERCIAL BANK.

**cheque card** see COMMERCIAL BANK.

**chief executive** the person who has overall responsibility for the MANAGEMENT of a firm. In a JOINT-STOCK COMPANY the chief executive is usually the full-time managing director or the full-time executive chairman appointed by the BOARD OF DIRECTORS.

**chinese wall** the segregation of the related activities of a financial institution in order to protect the interests of its clients. For example, a stock market firm could be responsible for 'making a market' in a particular share (see MARKET MAKER), while at the same time offering investment advice to clients to purchase this share, bringing with it the danger that the advice given will not be impartial.

**CIM** see COMPUTER-INTEGRATED MANUFACTURING.

**CIMA** see CHARTERED INSTITUTE OF MANAGEMENT ACCOUNTANTS.

**cif** see COST, INSURANCE AND FREIGHT.

**circles** see QUALITY CIRCLES.

**circulating capital** another way of describing WORKING CAPITAL which stresses how stock, debtors and cash circulate continuously through the business, as raw materials stocks are converted into finished goods stocks, sold to customers who become debtors, then are converted back to cash as the debtors pay, making funds available to buy yet more raw materials stock and so on.

**Citizens' Charter** an initiative launched by the UK government in 1991 to promote high-quality service delivery in the public services. The Charter sets out the government's view on what citizens should expect to get from public services. Public sector organizations are now encouraged to set public targets for service delivery e.g. that 90% of trains should arrive on time, and to communicate to the public the extent to which these targets are achieved. Those organizations judged by a government committee to have set and achieved targets which bring about significant improvements to services may be awarded a *Chartermark*. The philosophy behind the Charter is that public services do not experience the market pressures faced by commercial organizations and hence some mechanism like the Citizens' Charter is necessary to ensure responsiveness to consumers. See NEW PUBLIC MANAGEMENT.

**City code on takeovers and mergers** a regulatory system operated voluntarily by interested parties to the UK STOCK MARKET that lays down rules of good conduct governing the tactics and procedures used in TAKEOVERS and MERGERS. The general purpose of the code is to ensure that all SHAREHOLDERS (both the shareholders of the firm planning the takeover and those of the target firm) are treated equitably. For example, a potential bidder who has been acquiring shares in the open market is required to make a formal bid for all outstanding shares at a price not less than the highest price paid in the market over the previous 12 months, once his holding exceeds 30%. There are various other rules covering such areas as the accumulation of shares by several buyers acting together (see TAKEOVER BID), and the possible misuse of privileged information (see INSIDER DEALING). The City code is administered by the City panel on Takeovers and Mergers, which is responsible for formulating rules of practice and for investigating suspected cases of malpractice.

**civil law** legal arrangements whereby the State acts as an impartial judge of a dispute between two parties, the *plaintiff*, who sues and the *defendant*; the plaintiff usually requires *damages* which are a form of monetary compensation paid to him by the defendant. Civil law can be invoked for breach of CONTRACT or behaviour which constitutes a TORT and if the plaintiff wins his case he will receive damages to compensate him financially for the harm done to him by the defendant. As an alternative to damages the court may instead grant an injunction ordering the defendant to stop doing the act which is harming the plaintiff. Civil law judgements are enforced by the threat of imprisonment for contempt of court.

**CKD (completely knocked down)** a kit supplied either for self-assembly by a final customer (for example, a do-it-yourself kitchen flat pack) or for assembly by a firm as part of a manufacturing operation.

**classical management theory** the body of theory mainly associated with French mining engineer and manager Henri Fayol (1841–1925) but also with English army Colonel Lyndall Urwick (1891–1983). Common to all members of this school was an attempt to extrapolate from their practical experiences in management roles in large organizations a set of rules about how to manage effectively and efficiently. Fayol defined MANAGEMENT in terms of forecasting, planning, organizing, commanding, coordinating and controlling. To this end, management should function according to a set of principles which were valid whatever the ORGANIZATION'S environment and goals. These included the principle of UNITY OF COMMAND, a clear HIERARCHY and JOB SPECIALIZATION. Fayol's analysis could be viewed as the first attempt to generate a theory of management and can be seen as a prescriptive version of Weber's ideal type of BUREAUCRACY. Compare CONTINGENCY THEORY.

**clearing bank** see COMMERCIAL BANK.

**clearing house system** a centralized mechanism for settling indebtedness between financial institutions involved in money transmission and dealers in commodities and financial securities. In the case of UK commercial banking, for example, the London Clearing House collates all of the many thousands of cheques drawn, transfers bank deposits from one bank to another, cross-cancels them, and calculates the net balances owing or receivable for each bank. The COMMERCIAL BANKS' balances at the Bank of England are then debited or credited as appropriate. A similar 'clearing' function is performed in the commodities and financial securities market by, for example, the International Commodities Clearing House and the London Financial Futures Exchange and TAURUS. See FINANCIAL SERVICES ACT 1986, FINANCIAL SYSTEM, BANKING SYSTEM, COMMODITY MARKET, STOCK MARKET, FORWARD MARKET.

**clerical work measurement** a technique for measuring and controlling clerical work. It involves setting targets or standards for clerical activities such as filing and typing against which actual clerical outputs can be assessed. See STANDARD TIME, WORK MEASUREMENT.

**client** a BUYER of a professional SERVICE.

**clientele effect** the description applied in looking at a company's DIVIDEND policy which states that different shareholders invest in the shares of a company for different reasons. For example, some investors may favour a company with a high or a low dividend payout, those who favour the low payout being more interested in CAPITAL GAINS. In practice, therefore, to make a major change to a company's dividend policy could upset certain shareholders because the reason why they invested, e.g. a high percentage payout, no longer holds true.

**clock card** a document on which an employee records the precise time at which he or she arrives to start work and departs at the end of the work period. Such time records are used to check on employees' punctuality and to calculate wages due where employees are paid on a time basis. See FLEXITIME.

**close company** a JOINT-STOCK COMPANY which is under the control of five or fewer larger SHAREHOLDERS or directors.

**closed shop** a requirement that all employees in a given workplace or organization be members of a specified TRADE UNION. There are two types of closed shop:

(a) *pre-entry closed shop*, where union membership is necessary to gain employment;

(b) *post-entry closed shop*, where union membership is necessary once employment has commenced.

The pre-entry closed shop, found in parts of the printing and food wholesaling industries, is often unilaterally imposed by unions, whereas the post-entry closed shop has often been formally recognized in Union Membership Agreements with managements. Many managers have found the post-entry closed shop advantageous since it helps to ensure that union representatives speak for all employees. However, it can be viewed as an infringement of individual rights, especially when employees are dismissed for refusing to join a union. Employment laws in the early 1980s stipulated that where an employee is dismissed it is an UNFAIR DISMISSAL if the employee objects to union membership on grounds of conscience or if the closed shop has not been validated by an employee ballot within the last five years. The EMPLOYMENT ACT 1988 made dismissal on the grounds of refusing to join a union automatically unfair. The EMPLOYMENT ACT 1990 made it unlawful to refuse employment on the grounds of non-union (or union) membership. See EMPLOYMENT ACT 1980, EMPLOYMENT ACT 1982, CONTRACT OF EMPLOYMENT.

**closed union** see TRADE UNION.

**closing off** the process of listing all the balances in the LEDGERS and CASH ACCOUNT of a firm after the TRIAL BALANCE, PROFIT AND LOSS ACCOUNT and BALANCE SHEET have been completed. It ensures that all the balances have been carried forward to the next accounting period before any more transactions are recorded or posted. See ACCOUNTING.

**closing price** the price of a STOCK or SHARE ruling at the close of the day's trading on the STOCK MARKET.

**closing rate method** see FOREIGN CURRENCY TRANSLATION.

**COBOL (Common Business Orientated Language)** a COMPUTER programming language used for business applications.

**CoCom** see COORDINATING COMMITTEE ON MULTILATERAL EXPORT CONTROLS.

**COD** see CASH ON DELIVERY.

**code of practice** a set of guidelines used to encourage desirable patterns of behaviour but which generally lack any formal sanctions to punish inappropriate behaviour. Often codes of practice are developed as an alternative to legal regulation. For instance, companies engaged in food production might develop a code of practice between them to define hygiene standards, possibly to forestall government action in this area. Critics of this voluntaristic approach to regulation argue that they provide insufficient deterrents to wrong-doing. However, codes of practice are sometimes developed by official agencies and whilst not legally binding they are taken into account by courts in any legal action in the area covered by the code. For instance, employer adherence to the guidelines in the ADVISORY. CONCILIATION AND ARBITRATION SERVICE'S code of practice on DISCIPLINARY PROCEDURES is often an issue in UNFAIR DISMISSAL cases. Where the employer fails to follow the code the tribunal may award against the employer.

**co-determination** the German form of INDUSTRIAL DEMOCRACY in which all companies with more than 2000 employees are required to have an equal number of employee and shareholder representatives on the upper tier of a two-tier board of directors. However, full parity representation is not achieved (except in the coal and steel industries) because the chairperson, nominated by the shareholders, has a casting vote. In enterprises of 500–2000 employees one-third of the seats on the supervisory board are reserved for employee representatives. Employee representatives are nominated by the Works Council, elected by all employees in the company. These Councils have the legal right to co-determine with management methods and changes in WORK organization, hours of work, payments by results, HEALTH AND SAFETY regulations and discipline. To support them in this activity Works Councils have the right to DISCLOSURE OF INFORMATION from management. The Works Council system is formally separate from TRADE UNION representation but in practice union representatives are often deeply involved in the Works Council system. See BULLOCK REPORT, FIFTH DIRECTIVE, WORKER DIRECTOR.

**coding system** a numerical or alpha-numerical referencing system which is used to identify specific factor inputs and costs within a business. Code numbers (reference numbers) can be used for many purposes, for instance to identify STOCK items and for the allocation of costs to COST CENTRES.

**coinage** metal coins made of brass, nickels etc., issued by a country's CENTRAL BANK which constitute the 'low value' or 'small change' component of the MONEY SUPPLY. See CURRENCY.

**cold calling** a method of selling products which involves a business making unsolicited approaches to potential customers by door-to-door DIRECT SELLING, TELEPHONE SELLING or DIRECT MAIL.

**collateral security** an ASSET which a BORROWER is required to deposit with, or pledge to, a LENDER as a condition of obtaining a LOAN, which can be sold off if the loan is not repaid. For example, a bank may require a borrower to hand over the title deeds to his house as collateral for a BANK LOAN, or a company may issue DEBENTURE stock as a means of obtaining loan capital, which is secured by a charge on the company's business assets.

**collective agreement** see COLLECTIVE BARGAINING, MULTI-EMPLOYER AGREEMENT.

**collective bargaining** NEGOTIATION between employers or managers and representatives of the workforce to determine rates of pay (see WAGE), conditions of employment, etc. The desired outcome of collective bargaining is a collective agreement between the parties. In the UK these agreements have no legal force (see VOLUNTARISM) and, except where they incorporate statutory requirements, there are no legal sanctions that can be used if one party chooses to break the agreement. It is now customary in the UK for collective bargaining over pay rates to take place annually, though some employers have recently sought collective agreements of a longer duration. Collective bargaining usually takes place in accordance with procedures which are themselves generally established through bargaining (see PROCEDURAL AGREEMENT). Although there are no conclusive figures, it is reliably estimated that currently under 50% of the employed labour force in the UK have their pay and conditions determined by collective bargaining.

Contrasts can be drawn between two fundamentally different approaches to collective bargaining. *Distributive bargaining* is where one side's gain is seen as the other's loss. The money to be distributed as a result of this bargaining process is essentially seen as a 'cake' of a fixed size. This sort of bargaining is inevitably adversarial as each side seeks to minimize the concessions it makes to the other. In *integrative bargaining*, by contrast, the parties seek ways of increasing the size of cake. For instance, the money available for wage increases could be enlarged by agreeing changes to working practices. This approach therefore tends to be more cooperative in character.

In the UK, integrative bargaining is more widely known as productivity bargaining. This involves employers offering to improve pay or conditions of employment in return for the relaxation by the workforce and trade union of DEMARCATION LINES, 'RESTRICTIVE LABOUR PRACTICES' and other restraints on the efficient utilization of labour (see LABOUR FLEXIBILITY). It became popular in the 1960s in part because it provided a legitimate means of awarding pay increases in excess of those stipulated in PRICES AND INCOMES POLICY. Productivity bargaining enjoyed renewed popularity in the 1980s because of the imperative for many firms to secure improvements in productivity. An alternative approach known as *concession bargaining* also occurred in the 1980s. Whereas productivity bargaining trades extra payments for changes in working practices, this form involves no offer of payment, management arguing instead that unemployment will result if changes are not agreed. It can, therefore, involve a more confrontational approach and can be viewed as a form of distributive bargaining.

To compare patterns of collective bargaining between firms, various dimensions of collective bargaining are used in INDUSTRIAL RELATIONS analysis:

(a) *extent of bargaining*: the proportion of employees who are covered by collective agreements;

(b) *bargaining depth*: the extent to which workforce representatives are involved in the administration of agreements achieved through collective bargaining;

(c) *bargaining scope*: the range of issues which are subject to bargaining;

(d) *bargaining level*: the level of an industry at which bargaining takes place (see below);

(e) *bargaining unit*: the occupations which are covered by an agreement. There may be one bargaining unit – covering an entire workforce in a plant or industry – or separate units for different categories of employee.

These dimensions taken together are said to form the *bargaining structure*.

Industrial relations research in the UK has been especially concerned with the level of bargaining over pay. Three levels are most important:

(a) *industry-wide or multi-employer bargaining*: where representatives of all or most employers in a particular industry and TRADE UNION negotiate pay rates for employees in that industry. See EMPLOYERS' ASSOCIATION, MULTI-EMPLOYER AGREEMENT;

(b) *company or single employer bargaining*: where head office managers in a firm and either SHOP STEWARDS or trade union officials negotiate pay rates for employees at all locations of the company;

(c) *plant, decentralized or workplace bargaining*: where shop stewards bargain on behalf of employees at a particular plant or workplace with managers at that plant.

Broadly speaking, there has been a trend in UK manufacturing industry away from industry-wide bargaining to company and plant bargaining. In the public sector, 'industry' or company bargaining are the dominant forms. It is difficult to generalize about private services; all three forms of bargaining can be found, though collective bargaining is less widespread than in other sectors.

In practice the structure of bargaining in the UK is highly complex. Collective bargaining on behalf of a given set of employees may occur at more than one level. Some issues may be determined in industry-wide bargaining, others by plant bargaining, whilst particular issues may be subject to negotiations at more than one level. Where collective bargaining breaks down, the parties may refer the issue to a third party for ARBITRATION. If this is not done it is possible that a STRIKE or some other form of INDUSTRIAL ACTION could occur. See SINGLE TABLE BARGAINING.

**collective labour law** see LABOUR LAW.

**Collective Redundancies Directive** see REDUNDANCY.

**collectivism** the philosophy that society is composed of groups or classes of people, each with its own interests, and that social CONFLICT stems largely from conflicts of interest between them. To achieve general wellbeing, policy makers should seek to balance group interests. Political action to advance the claims of disadvantaged groups and to regulate the actions of individuals is generally viewed as desirable by those subscribing to this philosophy. TRADE UNIONS are often viewed as vehicles of collectivism in that they represent and advance group interests. Critics of this philosophy argue that it subsumes the unique interests of each individual. See INDIVIDUALISM.

**collusion** the deliberate suppression of competition between themselves by a group of rival suppliers. Collusion may be confined to a single area of business activity, for example prices, or cover a wider range of limitations including co-ordinated marketing, production and capacity adjustments. Collusion may be practised through formalized arrangements specifying obligations (either in writing or orally) and institutional mechanisms for coordinating behaviour, as in a CARTEL or RESTRICTIVE TRADE AGREEMENT, or operated by more informal means through, for example, an INFORMATION AGREEMENT or CONCERTED PRACTICE.

The purpose of collusion may be to monopolize jointly the supply of a product in order to extract MONOPOLY profits, or it may be a defensive response to poor trading conditions, seeking to prevent prices from dropping to uneconomic levels. Because, however, of its generally adverse effects on market efficiency (cushioning inefficient, high-cost suppliers), and because it deprives buyers of the benefits of competition (particularly lower prices), collusion is either prohibited outright by COMPETITION POLICY or permitted, as in the UK, to continue only in exceptional circumstances. See OFFICE OF FAIR TRADING, RESTRICTIVE PRACTICES COURT, MARKET CONDUCT.

**combine committee** a committee of TRADE UNION representatives, usually SHOP STEWARDS, drawn from a number of plants in a company with the objective of coordinating pressure (for example to improve pay) on the management of the company. Combine committees are rarely effective in the long term because it is often difficult to identify all the plants in a company and because the interests of workers between plants are often divergent (especially where there is plant-level COLLECTIVE BARGAINING).

**commercial bank** or **clearing bank** a BANK which accepts deposits of money from persons and businesses and provides them with a payments transmission service and various saving and loan facilities.

Commercial banking in the UK is conducted on the basis of an interlocking branch network system, which caters for local and regional needs as well as allowing the major banks such as Barclays, Lloyds, NatWest and the Midland to cover the national market. Increasingly, the leading banks have globalized their operations to provide traditional banking services to international companies as well as diversifying (see DIVERSIFICATION) into a range of related financial services such as the provision of MORTGAGES, INSURANCE and UNIT TRUST investment.

Bank deposits are of two types:

(a) *sight deposits*, or *current account* deposits, which are withdrawable on demand and which are used by depositors to finance day-to-day personal and business transactions as well as to pay regular commitments such as instalment credit repayments. Most banks now pay interest on outstanding current account balances;

(b) *time deposits*, or *deposit accounts*, which are usually withdrawable subject to some notice being given to the bank and which are held as a form of personal and corporate saving and to finance irregular, 'one-off' payments. Interest is payable on deposit accounts, normally at rates above those paid on current accounts, in order to encourage clients to deposit money for longer periods of time, thereby providing the bank with a more stable financial base.

Customers requiring to draw on their bank deposits may do so in a number of ways; direct cash withdrawals are still popular and have been augmented by the use of *cheque/cash cards* for greater convenience (i.e. cheque/cash cards can be used to draw cash from a dispensing machine outside normal business hours). However, the greater proportion of banking transactions are undertaken by *cheque* and CREDIT CARD payments and by such facilities as *standing orders* and *direct debits*. Some of these services, like cheque payments for customers in current account surplus, are provided free, while for others a small charge is made. Payment by cheque is the commonest form of non-cash payment involving the drawer detailing the person or business to receive payment and authorizing his bank to make payment by signing the cheque, with the recipient then depositing the cheque with his own bank. Cheques are 'cleared' through an inter-bank CLEARING HOUSE SYSTEM with customers' accounts being debited and credited as appropriate. Credit cards enable a client of the bank to make a number of individual purchases of goods and services on CREDIT over a particular period of time which are then settled by a single debit to the person's current account, or, alternatively, paid off on a loan basis (see below).

Under a standing order arrangement, a depositor instructs his bank to pay from his account a regular fixed sum of money into the account of a person or firm he is indebted to, again involving the respective debiting and crediting of the two accounts concerned. In the case of a direct debit, the customer authorizes the person or firm to whom he is indebted to arrange with his bank for the required regular payment to be transferred from the account.

Commercial banks have the dual objective of being able to meet money withdrawals on demand and of putting their resources to profitable use (i.e. they are in business to make profits for their shareholders). This influences the structure of their asset holdings. A proportion of the banks' funds are held in a highly liquid form (till money, 'call money' with the DIS-

COUNT MARKET, BILLS OF EXCHANGE and TREASURY BILLS) to cover short-term needs. The remaining funds are deployed in areas yielding a higher return, specifically portfolio investment, in particular government BONDS and corporate fixed interest securities such as DEBENTURES and, to a much greater extent, in the provision of *bank loans (bank advances)* to personal and corporate borrowers. Loans are used by personal borrowers to finance the purchase of a variety of products, while they are a major source of WORKING CAPITAL finance for businesses, covering the purchase of short-term assets such as the materials and components and the financing of work in progress and the stockholding of final products. Loans may be for a specified amount and made available for fixed periods of time at agreed rates of interest, or take the form of an *overdraft* facility where the person or firm can borrow as much as they require up to a prearranged total amount and is charged interest on outstanding balances. In recent years, the banks have introduced more flexible and varied loan arrangements for clients of suitable creditworthiness, which enables them to borrow money on a more or less continuous basis without the formality of having to make separate loan applications.

See MONEY SUPPLY, BANKING SYSTEM, CENTRAL BANK, MONETARY POLICY, LOAN GUARANTEE SCHEME, VENTURE CAPITAL, THREE I'S, SHARE PURCHASE/SALE.

**commission 1.** a payment to an AGENT or employee for performing particular services on behalf of a buyer or seller of a product, for example the sale of a financial security by a stockbroker (paid by the client); the sale of a car by a salesperson (paid by the garage owners). Commissions may be paid on a fixed or sliding scale basis related to the value of the transaction involved.

**2.** a body which acts as an official regulatory or administrative authority with respect to a specified activity. For example, the MONOPOLIES AND MERGERS COMMISSION hears cases of monopolies, mergers and anticompetitive practices referred to it by the Office of Fair Trading under UK competition policy. The European Commission is the main body responsible for the day-to-day administration of the affairs of the EUROPEAN COMMUNITY.

**Commission des Opérations de Bourse** the French STOCK MARKET.

## COMMISSIONE NAZIONALE PER LA SOCIETA A LA BORSA

**Commissione Nazionale per la Società a la Borsa** the Italian STOCK MARKET.

**Commissioner for the Rights of Trade Union Members** see EMPLOYMENT ACT 1988.

**Commission for Racial Equality** see DISCRIMINATION.

**commodity** any economic GOOD but in commercial circles more specifically agricultural produce and minerals such as wheat, tea, copper, iron ore, etc. See COMMODITY MARKET, INTERNATIONAL COMMODITY AGREEMENT.

**commodity broker** see COMMODITY MARKET.

**commodity market** a MARKET for the buying and selling of agricultural produce and minerals such as coffee and tin. Commodity business is conducted through various international commodity exchanges, some of the more prominent ones being based in London, for example the London Metal Exchange and the London International Financial Futures Exchange. Commodity markets provide an organizational framework for the establishment of market prices and 'clearing' deals between buyers and sellers (see CLEARING HOUSE SYSTEM). Commodity dealers and brokers act as intermediaries between buyers and sellers wishing to conclude immediate spot transactions (see SPOT MARKET) or to buy or sell forward (see FORWARD MARKET). See BALTIC MERCANTILE AND SHIPPING EXCHANGE, CORN EXCHANGE.

**commodity-type product** a good or service which is highly standardized so that the offerings of competing suppliers are perceived by buyers as being virtually identical. Such products offer little scope for PRODUCT DIFFERENTIATION and are mainly sold on price. See PRODUCT LIFE-CYCLE.

**Common Agricultural Policy** see EUROPEAN COMMUNITY, AGRICULTURAL POLICY.

**Common Business Orientated Language** see COBOL.

**common law** or **case law** laws based upon the outcome of previous court cases which serve as a precedent in guiding the judgment of present court cases. Where important legal principles are involved in a particular court case, the plaintiff or defendant may appeal against the judgment of a court to a higher court such as the High Court and then the House of Lords in the UK and finally the European Court of Justice. Compare STATUTE LAW.

**common market** see FREE TRADE BLOC, EUROPEAN COMMUNITY.

EUROPEAN UNION.

**common ownership** a form of employee ownership where equity is held collectively by the workforce. Individual employees do not own equity and when they leave the organization their ownership rights cease. See EMPLOYEE SHARE OWNERSHIP PLAN, WORKERS' COOPERATIVE.

**common stock** a North American term for ORDINARY SHARES.

**communication** the exchange of information in an ORGANIZATION. For organizations to work effectively, it is vital that information be communicated to those who need it. For example, the pay department would not be able to function properly if it were not notified of employees' hours of work. In this sense organizations can be conceived of as systems for exchanging information. Withholding information, i.e. failure to communicate, can be an effective means of exerting power over others in the organization. If a manager is not fully aware of what is going on in the organization he or she may be unable to influence decisions or events.

Often the effective transmission of information is impeded. As a piece of information is passed from top to bottom of an organization it may be modified by the misinterpretation or bias of each individual involved, so that by the time the information reaches its final destination it has a very different content. Effective communication can also be time-consuming, and hence arduous to perform. However, the effort can be worthwhile since those employees who feel they are not fully informed about matters relevant to their job may become demotivated and dissatisfied. As a result performance suffers. There is also evidence that individuals are more likely to respect bosses who they feel keep them informed.

It is often said that poor INDUSTRIAL RELATIONS are the result of a failure to communicate. This may be so on occasions but often industrial relations problems and disputes arise from a genuine divergence of interests which improvements in communication would not resolve. Nevertheless, in the 1980s many organizations placed much greater emphasis on communications with their employees than before, on the grounds that the more employees knew about their organizations the more they were likely to perform and behave in ways conducive to the good of the organization. Thus the traditional methods of communication such as company newspapers were supplemented by videos, personalized letters and TEAM BRIEFING. These methods often bypassed trade unions as channels of communication because it was felt that unions, often unwittingly, distorted information. An inherent weakness of many communications programmes of this sort is that they are premised on what top managers want employees to know rather than what employees themselves want, whilst the mechanisms used often inhibit or preclude meaningful *exchange* of information. In other words it is essentially one-way communication. Managers have often attempted to gauge workforce opinion by the use of attitude surveys. However, employees often feel that these are a poor substitute for genuine listening by management.

In addition to these 'behavioural' aspects of communication the *process* or 'technology' of internal and external communication has changed dramatically in the last decade. For example, conventional telephone systems (based on fixed-wired handsets) have been increasingly augmented by the cordless (mobile) telephone and accessories such as VOICE MESSAGING. Moreover, many businesses have integrated their PC (personal computer) networks and telecommunications to take advantage of value-added network services such as ELECTRONIC MAIL, VIDEO CONFERENCING and ELECTRONIC DATA INTERCHANGE. These developments, while enhancing the immediacy and effectiveness of communications, have also facilitated flexibility and mobility, allowing staff to reduce their dependency on being physically present at an office in order to conduct business.

See CONSULTATION, EMPLOYEE INVOLVEMENT, EMPLOYEE PARTICIPATION, INDUSTRIAL DEMOCRACY, COMMUNITY CHARTER OF FUNDAMENTAL SOCIAL RIGHTS, DISCLOSURE OF INFORMATION, INFORMATION MANAGEMENT, INFORMATION HIGHWAY, BUSINESS PROCESS RE-ENGINEERING.

**communications mix** see PROMOTIONAL MIX.

**community action** see TRAINING.

**community charge** see LOCAL TAX.

**Companies Acts** see COMPANY LAW.

**Companies House** see REGISTRAR OF COMPANIES.

**company** see JOINT-STOCK COMPANY.

**company bargaining** see COLLECTIVE BARGAINING.

**company council** an institution composed of top managers and employee representatives which discusses company strategy and policies. Usually these organs perform an advisory and consultative rather than decision-making function, but in some of the Japanese companies in the UK they provide the forum for COLLECTIVE BARGAINING over pay. See CONSULTATION, JAPANIZATION, INDUSTRIAL DEMOCRACY, PARTICIPATION.

**Company Directors Disqualification Act 1986** see INSOLVENCY.

**company formation** the process of forming a JOINT-STOCK COMPANY, which involves a number of steps:

    (a) drawing up a MEMORANDUM OF ASSOCIATION;

    (b) preparation of ARTICLES OF ASSOCIATION;

    (c) application to the REGISTRAR OF COMPANIES for a CERTIFICATE OF INCORPORATION;

    (d) issuing SHARE CAPITAL;

    (e) commencing trading.

**company image** commonly held beliefs and impressions about a firm as a supplier of products, an employer and member of the community. Companies seek to promote positive public perceptions of themselves as progressive and enlightened organizations, caring for their employees and the environment and looking after the interests of consumers, because of the beneficial impact of good image upon, for example, company recruitment and sales. See PUBLIC RELATIONS, CORPORATE IDENTITY.

**company law** a body of legislation providing for the regulation of JOINT-STOCK COMPANIES. British company law encouraged the development of joint-stock companies by establishing the principle of LIMITED LIABILITY and provides for the protection of SHAREHOLDERS' interests by controlling the formation and financing of companies. The major provisions of UK company law are contained in the 1948, 1967, 1976, 1981, 1985 and 1989 Companies Acts. See ARTICLES OF ASSOCIATION, MEMORANDUM OF ASSOCIATION.

**company registrar** the officer of a JOINT-STOCK COMPANY who is responsible for maintaining an up-to-date SHARE REGISTER and for issuing new SHARE CERTIFICATES and cancelling old share certificates as shares are bought and sold on the STOCK MARKET.

    Many companies, however, have chosen to sub-contract these tasks to specialist institutions, often departments of commercial banks.

## COMPANY SECRETARY

The role of the company registrar identified above should not be confused with that of the role of the government's REGISTRAR OF COMPANIES, who is responsible for supervising *all* joint-stock companies.

**company secretary** an officer of a JOINT-STOCK COMPANY with responsibility for maintaining the company's SHARE REGISTER, for notifying shareholders of ANNUAL GENERAL MEETINGS and for preparing the company's ANNUAL RETURN.

**Company Securities (Insider Dealing) Act 1985** see IN-SIDER DEALING.

**company union** a TRADE UNION which is in effect run by the management of a company and which is intended to defuse employee grievances or wage demands. As such it cannot be considered to be a genuine union, and would therefore find it difficult to secure a certificate of independence from the CERTIFICATION OFFICER, and hence would be denied the benefits unions usually obtain as FRIENDLY SOCIETIES. See STAFF ASSOCIA-TION.

**comparability** an approach to PAY determination in which levels or increases in pay are sought or offered which maintain a relationship to those for other industries or occupations. The notion of the *going rate* is a form of comparability in that workers seek pay increases which are similar to those being achieved or sought by others. See JOB EVALUATION, PAY DIFFER-ENTIAL.

**comparative advantage** the competitive advantages (lower costs and prices, innovative products, etc.) possessed by one country over other countries in certain internationally traded GOODS and SERVICES. See INTERNATIONAL TRADE.

**comparison statement** a management accounting statement which sets out budgeted revenues and costs alongside actual revenues and costs in order to facilitate comparisons between the two. Fig. 20 shows a typical comparison statement. See BUDGET, BUDGETARY CONTROL, STANDARD COST.

**compatibility** the extent to which COMPUTER HARDWARE or SOFTWARE is compatible with the user's existing hardware or software, that is, capable of running existing programs on new machines or alongside existing programs.

**compensation deal** see COUNTERTRADE.

**competency** see CORE SKILL, NATIONAL VOCATIONAL QUALIFICA-TION.

| | Month ended 30 April 19xx | | | | | |
|---|---|---|---|---|---|---|
| PRODUCTION MANAGER | This month | | | 4 months to date | | |
| | Budget £ | Actual £ | Variance £ | Budget £ | Actual £ | Variance £ |
| Value of production | 65,750 | 68,725 | +2,975 | 270,000 | 291,000 | +21,000 |
| *Expenditure:* | | | | | | |
| Direct Wages | 11,550 | 11,975 | − 425 | 45,700 | 47,500 | − 1,800 |
| Direct Materials | 22,450 | 23,147 | − 697 | 81,350 | 92,177 | −10,827 |
| PRIME COST | 34,000 | 35,122 | −1,122 | 127,050 | 139,677 | −12,627 |
| *Production Overheads:* | | | | | | |
| Indirect Wages | 2,711 | 2,588 | + 123 | 10,794 | 10,774 | + 20 |
| Maintenance | 200 | 176 | + 24 | 800 | 680 | + 120 |
| Depreciation | 650 | 650 | | 2,600 | 2,600 | |
| Training | 100 | 125 | − 25 | 400 | 125 | + 275 |
| TOTAL PRODUCTION OVERHEADS: | 3,661 | 3,539 | + 122 | 14,594 | 14,179 | + 415 |

Fig. 20. **Comparison statement.** A typical example.

**competition** the process of active rivalry between the sellers of a particular product as they seek to win and retain buyer demand for their offerings. Competition can take a number of forms including price cutting, ADVERTISING and SALES PROMOTION, quality variations, packaging and design, and market segmentation (see MARKETING MIX). The nature and intensity of competitive relationships in a market, in turn, depends on various factors such as product and buyer characteristics, the extent of market concentration, and cost and demand considerations (see MARKET STRUCTURE, MARKET CONDUCT). For example, where products are standardized, competition is usually focused on price, whereas in markets where buyers demand a wide range of product variety and quality mixes, PRODUCT DIFFERENTIATION competition tends to be emphasized. In markets characterized by high levels of seller concentration, suppliers tend wherever possible to substitute product differentiation competition for price competition because of the mutually ruinous consequences of price wars. Moreover, in some instances, mutual interest considerations may well lead suppliers to control competition so as to promote orderly and profitable trading conditions by, for example, establishing price-fixing CARTELS.

Business strategy and marketing analysts are especially concerned with identifying and exploiting product and buyer characteristics as a means of establishing COMPETITIVE ADVANT-AGES over rival suppliers. From a wider public interest angle, the nature and strength of competition has an important effect on MARKET PERFORMANCE and hence is of particular relevance to the application of COMPETITION POLICIES.

**Competition Act 1980** an Act which extended UK COMPETI-TION POLICY by providing for the investigation of potentially ANTI-COMPETITIVE PRACTICES such as EXCLUSIVE DEALING, REFUSAL TO SUPPLY, etc. on an individual 'one-off' basis rather than as part of a wider-ranging monopoly investigation. Under the Act, anti-competitive practices are examined in the first in-stance by the OFFICE OF FAIR TRADING which may itself order the discontinuance of an offending practice, or may refer it to the MONOPOLIES AND MERGERS COMMISSION for further investigation and report.

**competition-based pricing** pricing methods which determine the PRICE of a product primarily on the basis of the prices charged by competitors.

In markets where products are highly standardized (i.e. COMMODITY-TYPE PRODUCTS), customers are likely to see competing brands as close substitutes for one another, so that any price differences would cause switching to the lower-priced brand. In such markets a seller has little pricing latitude and must set the price at the going rate as determined by supply and demand. With few manufacturers supplying the product (i.e. OLIGOPOLY), any one firm will be acutely aware of the harmful effects on its market share and sales volume of a price which is even slightly higher than those of its competitors and will therefore tend to charge an identical price to competitors.

Where suppliers are required to put in a *sealed price bid* or *tender* to supply, for example, components to a manufacturer, or build a complete factory or ship, competitive conditions may be paramount. A firm must guess the likely sealed bid prices of its competitors for the work and in the light of its own cost conditions make an appropriate price bid.

See COST-BASED PRICING, DEMAND-BASED PRICING.

**competition laws** a body of legislation providing for the con-trol of MONOPOLIES, MERGERS and TAKEOVERS, RESTRICTIVE TRADE AGREEMENTS and ANTI-COMPETITIVE PRACTICES. UK competition law is contained in a number of statutes, including the FAIR TRADING ACT 1973, COMPETITION ACT 1980, RESTRICTIVE TRADE PRACTICES ACTS 1956, 1968, 1976 and RESALE PRICES ACTS 1964, 1976. These laws are administered by the OFFICE OF FAIR TRADING.

In the European Union/Community, competition law is enshrined in Articles 85 and 86 of the Treaty of Rome, and is administered by the European Commission's Competition-Directorate. See COMPETITION POLICY.

**competition policy** a policy concerned with the regulation of MONOPOLIES, MERGERS and TAKEOVERS, RESTRICTIVE TRADE AGREEMENTS, RESALE PRICES and ANTI-COMPETITIVE PRACTICES. Competition policy, by promoting greater competition in markets, aims to secure an efficient use of economic resources and the enhancement of consumer welfare; specifically, least-cost supply, 'fair' prices and profit levels, technological advance and product improvement.

Competition policy is implemented mainly through the control of MARKET STRUCTURE and MARKET CONDUCT but also, on occasions, through the direct control of MARKET PERFORMANCE itself (by, for example, the use of PRICE CONTROLS to limit industry profit levels, see RATE OF RETURN REGULATION).

There are two basic approaches to the control of market structure and conduct: the nondiscretionary approach and the discretionary approach. The nondiscretionary approach lays down 'acceptable' standards of structure and conduct and prohibits outright any transgression of these standards. Typical ingredients of this approach include:

(a) the stipulation of maximum permitted market share limits (say, no more than 20% of the market) in order to limit the degree of MARKET CONCENTRATION and thus prevent the emergence of a monopoly supplier. Under this stipulation any proposed mergers or takeover which would take the combined group's market share above the permitted limit would be automatically prohibited;

(b) the outright prohibition of all forms of 'shared monopoly' (CARTELS, RESTRICTIVE TRADE AGREEMENTS) involving price-fixing, market sharing, etc.;

(c) the outright prohibition of specific practices designed to limit competition, for example EXCLUSIVE DEALING, RESALE PRICE MAINTENANCE, etc.

Thus the nondiscretionary approach attempts to promote

competitive conditions by a direct attack on the possession and exercise of monopoly power as such.

By contrast, the discretionary approach takes a more pragmatic line, recognizing that often high levels of market concentration and certain agreements between firms may serve to improve economic efficiency rather than impair it. It is the essence of the discretionary approach that each situation be judged on its own merits rather than be automatically condemned. Thus, under the discretionary approach, mergers, restrictive agreements and practices of the kind noted above are evaluated in terms of their possible benefits and detriments, and only prohibited if they are found to be, on balance, detrimental. See COMPETITION POLICY (UK), COMPETITION POLICY (EUROPEAN UNION/COMMUNITY), INDUSTRIAL POLICY.

**competition policy (European Union/Community)** covers three main areas of application:

(a) CARTELS: Articles 85(1) and (2) of the Treaty of Rome prohibit cartel agreements and CONCERTED PRACTICES (i.e. formal and informal collusion) between firms involving price fixing, limitations on production, technical developments and investment, and market sharing whose effect is to restrict competition and trade within the European Union (EU). Certain other agreements (for example, those providing for joint technical research and specialization of production) may be exempted from the general prohibition contained in Articles 85(1) and (2) provided they do not restrict inter-state competition and trade;

(b) MONOPOLIES/DOMINANT FIRMS: Article 86 of the Treaty of Rome prohibits the abuse of a dominant position in the supply of a particular product if this serves to restrict competition and trade within the EU. What constitutes abusive behaviour is similar to that applied in the UK, namely actions which are unfair or unreasonable towards customers (for example PRICE DISCRIMINATION between EU markets), retailers (for example REFUSAL TO SUPPLY) and other suppliers (for example selective price cuts to eliminate competitors). Firms found guilty by the European Commission of illegal cartelization and the abuse of a dominant position can be fined up to 10% of their annual sales turnover;

(c) MERGERS: the Commission can investigate mergers involving companies with a combined worldwide turnover of over

ECU 5 billion (£3.7 bn) if the aggregate EU-wide turnover of the companies concerned is greater than ECU 250 million. Again, the main aim is to prevent mergers likely to affect competition and trade adversely within the EU.

**competition policy (UK)** covers five main areas of application:

(a) MONOPOLIES: a monopoly position is defined as a situation where one firm supplies at least one quarter of a specified good or service (DOMINANT FIRM, MONOPOLY) or where two or more suppliers pursue policies which restrict competition between them (COMPLEX MONOPOLY). The OFFICE OF FAIR TRADING (OFT) is responsible for referral of selected goods and services monopolies (both private and public sector) to the MONOPOLIES AND MERGERS COMMISSION (MMC) for investigation and report and the implementation (where appropriate) of the MMC's recommendations. Monopoly positions are evaluated by the MMC in terms of whether or not they operate in the 'public interest';

(b) MERGERS and TAKEOVERS: mergers and takeovers fall within the ambit of the legislation if they create or intensify a monopoly position (defined by the one quarter market share rule) or where the value of assets taken over exceeds £70 million. The OFT is responsible, in conjunction with the Secretary of State for Industry, for the referral of selected mergers to the MMC for investigation and report and the implementation (where appropriate) of the MMC's recommendations. Again, the criterion of the 'public interest' is used to assess whether or not a particular merger or takeover is to be allowed to proceed or to be vetoed;

(c) RESTRICTIVE TRADE AGREEMENTS: under the legislation parties to restrictive trade agreements are compulsorily required to register such agreements with the OFT. This applies to (i) all goods and services agreements which contain restrictions (i.e. anti-competitive provisions) relating to prices charged, terms and conditions, qualities and descriptions, processes, areas and persons to be supplied; and (ii) INFORMATION AGREEMENTS (goods only) relating to prices and terms and conditions. The OFT is responsible for the referral of agreements to the RESTRICTIVE PRACTICES COURT (RPC) for investigation and report, and the implementation of the recommendations of the Court. Restrictive agreements are presumed to operate against the public interest and are invariably prohibited unless the parties to them can gain exemption by satisfying the Court that, on balance, they confer net economic benefit;

(d) RESALE PRICE MAINTENANCE (RPM): manufacturers' stipulation of the resale prices of their products is generally prohibited in the UK, although under the RESALE PRICES ACTS it is possible for a manufacturer to obtain exemption by satisfying the RPC that, on balance RPM confers net economic benefit. The OFT is responsible for monitoring manufacturers' policies towards retail prices and can take action against suspected cases of manufacturers attempting (illegally) to enforce RPM. Manufacturers can, however, take action against retailers who use their products as LOSS LEADERS;

(e) ANTI-COMPETITIVE PRACTICES: various trade practices such as EXCLUSIVE DEALING, REFUSAL TO SUPPLY, FULL-LINE FORCING, etc. may be investigated both by the OFT itself and (if necessary) by the MMC, and prohibited if they are found to be unduly restrictive of competition.

**competitive advantage** the possession by a firm of various ASSETS and attributes (low cost plants, innovative brands, ownership of raw material supplies, etc.) which give it a competitive edge over rival suppliers. To succeed against competitors in winning customers on a viable (profitable) and sustainable (long-run) basis, a firm must, depending on the nature of the market, be cost-effective and/or able to offer products which customers regard as preferable to the products offered by rival suppliers. The former enables a firm to meet and beat competitors on price, while the latter reflects the firm's ability to establish PRODUCT DIFFERENTIATION advantages over competitors.

Cost advantages over competitors are of two major types:

(a) absolute cost advantages, that is, lower costs than competitors at *all* levels of output deriving from, for example, the use of superior production technology or from VERTICAL INTEGRATION of input supply and assembly operations;

(b) relative cost advantages, that is, cost advantages related to the scale of output accruing through the exploitation of ECONOMIES OF SCALE in production and marketing and through cumulative EXPERIENCE CURVE effects. Over time, investment in plant renewal, modernization and process innovation (either through in-house research and development or the early adoption of new technology developed elsewhere) is essential to maintain cost advantages.

Product differentiation advantages derive from:

(a) a variety of physical product properties and attributes (notably the ability to offer products which are regarded by customers as having unique qualities or as being functionally better than competitors' products);

(b) the particular nuances and psychological images built into the firm's product by associated advertising and sales promotion. Again, given the dynamic nature of markets, particularly PRODUCT LIFE CYCLE considerations, competitive advantage in this area needs to be sustained by an active programme of new product innovation and upgrading of existing lines. See SWOT ANALYSIS, COMPETITIVE STRATEGY, BUSINESS STRATEGY.

**competitive strategy** the formulation of strategic plans by a firm aimed at ensuring that the firm is able to meet and beat its competitors in supplying a particular product. Competitive strategy constitutes an integral part of overall BUSINESS STRATEGY formulation (deciding *which* markets to operate in etc.), since no matter how few or many product markets the firm chooses to be in, its corporate prosperity depends fundamentally on how well it succeeds in the individual product markets making up its business. A main concern of competitive strategy is to identify:

(a) the competitive strengths and weaknesses of one's own firm and of rival firms (see SWOT ANALYSIS);

(b) the nature and strength of the various forces driving competition in a market (see Fig. 21). The key to a successful competitive strategy is then

(c) to understand fully what product attributes are demanded by buyers (whether it be low prices or product sophistication) with a view to

(d) establishing, operationally, a position of COMPETITIVE ADVANTAGE which makes the firm less vulnerable to attack from established competitors and potential new entrants, and to erosion from the direction of buyers, suppliers and substitute products.

There are three generic strategies for competitive success (Fig. 22): cost leadership, product differentiation and 'focus'. Low costs, particularly in commodity-type markets, help the

Fig. 21. **Competitive strategy.** Forces driving competition in a market.

firm not only to survive price competition should it break out, but, importantly, enable it to assume the role of market leader in establishing price levels which ensure high and stable levels of market profitability. The sources of cost–effectiveness are varied, including the exploitation of ECONOMIES OF SCALE, investment in best state–of–the–art technology and preferential access to raw materials or distribution channels. By adopting a PRODUCT DIFFERENTIATION strategy a firm seeks to be unique in its market in a way that is valued by its potential customers. Product differentiation possibilities vary from market to market but are associated with the potential for distinguishing products by their physical properties and attributes and the experience of satisfaction – real and psychological – imparted by the product to consumers. General cost leadership and differentiation strategies seek to establish a COMPETITIVE ADVANTAGE over rival suppliers across the whole market. By contrast, 'focus' strategies aim to build competitive advantages in narrower segments of a market, but again either in terms of cost or, more usually, differentiation characteristics, with 'niche' suppliers primarily catering for speciality product demands. See MARKET STRUCTURE, MARKET CONDUCT, MARKET PERFORMANCE, STRATEGIC GROUP.

**competitive tendering** the system of awarding contracts in the public services to the lowest cost tender. The novelty of competitive tendering in the UK is that private sector firms

Fig. 22. **Competitive strategy**. Three generic strategies.

are invited to submit tenders to provide services previously run directly by public sector organizations e.g. local authority refuse-collection. The assumption underlying this is that competition for contracts will drive down costs and encourage efficiency. Competitive tendering has been encouraged since the early 1980s, ('voluntary competitive tendering' or VCT) but increasingly public sector authorities have been forced by legislation to put services out to tender ('compulsory competitive tendering' or CCT). Where competitive tendering is compulsory, those parts of the public sector organization which have hitherto provided the service are required to operate at 'arm's length' from the parent authority and to submit a bid to run the service. In most cases contracts have been awarded to the 'in-house' organization. Where they are awarded to an external organization it is common for most of the public sector workforce to be transferred to the contractor.

See ENABLING AUTHORITY, NEW PUBLIC MANAGEMENT, PURCHASER-PROVIDER SPLIT.

**competitor** a business rival of a firm supplying a particular GOOD or SERVICE which offers buyers an identical or similar product. Where customers regard a rival's products as being close substitutes then the rival's marketing strategies are likely to have a significant effect on the firm's own market position. See COMPETITION, COMPETITIVE ADVANTAGE, COMPETITIVE STRATEGY, PRODUCT DIFFERENTIATION.

**competitor analysis** the process whereby a firm studies the production and marketing practices used by its immediate competitors so that the firm can gauge its own strengths and weaknesses in relation to its main competitors.

See SWOT ANALYSIS.

**completion date** the date by which a particular project is scheduled to be finished. In civil engineering projects completion dates are often formally written into the contract terms between the supplier and customer, with financial penalties for late completion and bonuses for early completion.

See NETWORK ANALYSIS.

**complex monopoly** a situation defined by UK COMPETITION POLICY as one in which two or more suppliers of a particular product restrict competition between themselves. Complex monopoly is in essence an OLIGOPOLY situation where the firms concerned, although pursuing individual (i.e. noncollusive) policies, nonetheless behave in a uniform manner and produce a result which is noncompetitive (i.e. similar to COLLUSION). The problem is that it is often difficult to distinguish between competitive and noncompetitive situations. For example, if firms charge identical prices, is this reflective of competition (i.e. prices which are brought together *because* of competition) or a deliberate suppression of competition?

**component** or **part** an item such as a gearbox, steering wheel, etc. which is used in the assembly of another component or final product (such as a motorcar).

**compound interest** see INTEREST.

**comprehensive agreement** see MULTI-EMPLOYER AGREEMENT.

**compressed hours** a method used to reduce the number of days worked each week or month by extending the number of hours worked each day. For instance, employees on a 40 hour week might work four days each week of 10 hours duration. See also ANNUAL HOURS, FLEXITIME, SHIFT WORK.

**compulsory competitive tendering** see COMPETITIVE TENDERING.

**computer** an electronic/electromechanical device which accepts alphabetical and numerical data in a predefined form, stores and processes this data according to the instructions contained in a COMPUTER PROGRAM, and presents the analysed data in an organized form. Fig. 23 shows the main items of computer HARDWARE, with input devices like KEYBOARDS, and magnetic tape readers; the CPU (central processing unit) which manipulates data; DISK DRIVES which provide additional data storage capacity; and output devices like PRINTERS and VISUAL

Fig. 23. Computer. The main items of hardware.

**PROGRAM AND DATA**

customer orders

mouse

magnetic tape reader

modem

keyboard

keyboard

**INPUT DEVICES**

**DATA MANIPULATION ACCORDING TO PROGRAM**

sales ledger
stock records
orders outstanding

external memory (Winchester)

**CENTRAL PROCESSING UNIT (CPU)**

**INFORMATION OUTPUT**

invoices
despatch
notes

monitor (visual display unit)

hello

printer

**OUTPUT DEVICES**

# COMPUTER-AIDED DESIGN

DISPLAY UNITS. The figure shows how a number of computers may be linked in a LOCAL AREA NETWORK, in this case to process customer orders, maintain the sales LEDGER and issue INVOICES.

Big 'mainframe' computers are used to handle large data bases. For example, the Driver and Vehicle Licensing Agency in Swansea holds over 60 million records on its mainframe computer. Increasingly, however, with the development of faster, more powerful and more cost-effective microprocessors the mainframe computer has been replaced by the desktop 'personal computer' (PC) in routine office data-processing operations (DOWNSIZING), with PCs being linked together in LOCAL AREA NETWORKS, enabling them to share data. A further development has been the introduction of small portable computers typified by the 'notebook' personal computer which can be carried in a brief-case.

Computers have dramatically improved the productivity of DATA PROCESSING in business, facilitating the keeping of ACCOUNTING ledger records like sales ledger, purchases ledger and payroll and personal records by small numbers of clerical staff. In addition, software packages like SPREADSHEETS and WORD PROCESSORS have improved the presentation and analysis of management information, helping to improve decision-making.

See FLEXIBLE MANUFACTURING SYSTEM, PRODUCTION-LINE, ELECTRONIC MAIL SYSTEM, COMPUTER-AIDED DESIGN, COMPUTER-AIDED MANUFACTURING, INFORMATION MANAGEMENT, BULLETIN BOARD, MODEM, INTERNET.

**computer–aided design (CAD)** the use of COMPUTERS in the design of new components or products and in the re-design of existing products. Unlike hand drawings, CAD design specifications can be shown on a visual display unit and redrawn to produce different versions of the components or product. CAD can also be linked to computer-aided process planning (CAPP) to determine the best methods by which to manufacture a product. Moreover, a component or product can be subjected to various tests of strength, performance, etc. using computer-aided engineering (CAE) software without having to build prototypes; thus changes in product design can be made quickly and cheaply (see NEW PRODUCT DEVELOPMENT). CAD is particularly useful in designing and classifying components and products used in GROUP TECHNOLOGY production and in FLEXIBLE MANUFACTURING SYSTEMS. See COMPUTER-AIDED MANUFACTURING.

**computer-aided engineering** see COMPUTER-AIDED DESIGN.

**computer-aided manufacturing (CAM)** the use of COMPUTERS to impart operating instructions to NUMERICALLY-CONTROLLED MACHINES and ROBOTS employed in PRODUCTION systems (mass production, batch production, group technology and flexible manufacturing systems). CAM enables PRODUCTION SCHEDULING to be completed more efficiently and quickly, particularly in rescheduling production to accommodate new or redesigned components or products. CAM systems are especially effective when linked to COMPUTER-AIDED DESIGN (CAD), for with CAD/CAM computer software packages it is possible to provide design specifications and parts lists for components or products *directly* to the machines that will produce these items.

**computer-aided process planning** see COMPUTER-AIDED DESIGN.

**computer-integrated manufacturing (CIM)** the use of COMPUTERS to integrate all facets of PRODUCTION planning and control, including product design, factory layout planning, production scheduling and stock control. See COMPUTER-AIDED DESIGN, COMPUTER-AIDED MANUFACTURING.

**computer program** a set of instructions set out in a clear and logical sequence which tells a processor within a COMPUTER how to perform a particular task. Computer programs are often written in 'high-level' program languages like BASIC (beginners all-purpose symbolic instruction code) or COBOL (common business-orientated language), but must then be converted into MACHINE CODE for use in a computer.

**concentrated marketing strategy** a MARKETING STRATEGY for a product which is based on the use of a MARKETING MIX format (pricing, advertising messages, sales promotion) aimed at *one* particular group of customers in the market. This approach thus focuses exclusively on one MARKET SEGMENT, rather than several market segments (DIFFERENTIATED MARKETING STRATEGY) or the whole market (UNDIFFERENTIATED MARKETING STRATEGY).

A concentrated marketing approach is particularly suited to a smaller firm with limited financial and marketing resources or a specialist producer, and could be used by a new entrant to the market as a means of establishing a toe-hold in the market before undertaking further expansion (see MARKET PENE-TRATION). By concentrating its resources narrowly, a firm may well be in a better position to boost its sales but, on the debit side, may fail to capitalize on the sales potential of other segments. Worse still, dependency on one segment leaves the firm unduly exposed to a fall in demand in that segment.

**concentration ratio** a measure of the extent to which the supply of a particular GOOD or SERVICE is controlled by a specific number of producers (see MARKET CONCENTRATION). A typical concentration ratio (see Fig. 24) shows the proportion of total domestic market sales of a product by *domestic* producers accounted for by the largest five or ten of these producers.

Concentration ratios are often used in MARKET analysis and in the application of COMPETITION POLICY as proxies to indicate the degree of competition or monopolization present in a market, but their focus is too limited to capture the full nuances of market forces. For example, a concentration ratio may *overstate* the degree of monopolization of a market because it does not include imports of the product (IMPORT PENETRATION may be substantial and based on price-cutting

Number of domestic firms cumulated from largest size.
5-firm concentration ratio = 85%

Fig. 24. **Concentration ratio**. A typical example.

strategies), and because it makes no allowance for the effects of high concentration on the buying side of the market (large buyers may pressurize suppliers into discount competition). By the same token, the degree of monopolization may be *understated* because although in structural terms the market may exhibit relatively low levels of concentration, the leading suppliers may be parties to a price-fixing and market-sharing CARTEL.

**concept testing** testing a new product concept with a sample of target consumers to assess the product's likely customer acceptability. Concept testing is used at a very early stage of NEW PRODUCT DEVELOPMENT in order to eliminate products which are unlikely to succeed and to pinpoint products whose potential warrants further research and development work.

**concerted practice** a situation where rival firms, without being party to a formal CARTEL agreement, nonetheless informally coordinate their behaviour in respect of prices, output levels, etc., thereby eliminating competition between themselves. See COMPETITION POLICY (EC), COLLUSION.

**concert party** see TAKEOVER BID.

**concession bargaining** see COLLECTIVE BARGAINING.

**conciliation** a form of intervention in collective and individual INDUSTRIAL DISPUTES in which a third party assists the disputants in resolving their differences. The primary role of the conciliator is to encourage the parties to settle the dispute themselves through continued NEGOTIATION, rather than to cast judgment on the disputants' claims (ARBITRATION) or to bring forward the conciliator's own proposals for a settlement (MEDIATION). In the UK, conciliation services are provided officially by the ADVISORY, CONCILIATION AND ARBITRATION SERVICE (ACAS). Conciliation in collective disputes is typically resorted to when agreed procedures for resolving differences have been exhausted and a STRIKE could well occur. Individual conciliation may take place where an employee claims that his or her employer has treated him or her unlawfully. In the UK all such claims that are lodged with INDUSTRIAL TRIBUNALS are automatically referred to ACAS to determine whether conciliation may render a formal hearing unnecessary. See INDUSTRIAL DISPUTE, UNFAIR DISMISSAL, DISCRIMINATION, COLLECTIVE BARGAINING.

**concurrent engineering** an approach to innovation management which emphasizes the need to involve a firm's research and development, production and marketing departments at the outset in NEW PRODUCT DEVELOPMENT. Simultaneous inputs into the development process avoid the potential 'gaps' and delays which can emerge if this is done on a discontinuous basis, as when, for example, R&D may come up with a new product concept but production is unable to produce it without considerable modifications.

Thus, concurrent engineering can both speed up, and reduce the expense of, bringing new products to the market. See TIME MANAGEMENT 2.

**condition-based maintenance** a PREVENTIVE MAINTENANCE system in which a firm's plant, machinery or equipment is inspected at frequent intervals to assess maintenance needs. With this type of system the condition of components is monitored and they are replaced when they reach a certain state in order to avoid breakdowns. See INSPECTION.

**condition of employment** see CONTRACT OF EMPLOYMENT.

**condition of entry** the degree of ease or difficulty facing firms in entering a market. In most markets there are various BARRIERS TO ENTRY which operate to give established firms some advantage over newcomers and which, in the extreme, may preclude entry altogether. See MARKET ENTRY.

**Confederation of British Industry (CBI)** a UK organization which represents the collective interests of employers. The CBI is run by a centrally–elected committee, a secretariat, and a network of regional and local branches which provide a forum for company executives to meet and discuss affairs of mutual concern, and act as a means of disseminating information on the government's industrial policy, European Union/Community directives on employers' obligations, etc.

A major objective of the CBI is to promote industrial enterprise and efficiency, thereby helping the country to increase its wealth and create employment.

**confidence interval** the range of values within which it is possible to assert (with a suitable PROBABILITY) that the true population AVERAGE will lie. With a 95% confidence interval there is a 0.95 probability that this interval contains the true average of the population. Confidence intervals are used in statistical QUALITY CONTROL to suggest the limits of variation in the size or other characteristic of a product which is acceptable in SAMPLES of a product being tested. For example, if a component is intended to measure 100 mm across then the testers might accept all components measuring between 96 mm and 104 mm across and reject the whole batch if components of more than 5% of the sample components are larger or smaller than these confidence limits. See NORMAL CURVE.

**conflict** a disagreement or divergence of interests which may result in one party taking action against another. Conflict can occur at the inter-personal, group or societal level and may involve collective or individual action. It may arise out of simple dislike of another person or out of opposed collective interests. Marxists argue that conflict is endemic to capitalist society. In their view capitalism has created two classes of people, the proletariat (i.e. paid employees) and the bourgeoisie (i.e. entrepreneurs and their supporters), whose interests are diametrically opposed. This opposition of interests in the employment sphere leads to various forms of conflict including sabotage and STRIKES. In Marx's view this conflict would lead to the overthrow of capitalism. That this has not happened in most advanced industrial societies has been attributed to various factors, including rising living standards and the institutionalization of conflict. This is the development of DISPUTES PROCEDURES and mechanisms for COLLECTIVE BARGAINING which have provided TRADE UNIONS and managers with the means to resolve many manifestations of conflict. Putting a grievance into procedure (i.e. passing it to a joint management–union committee for discussion and resolution) tends to take the heat out of an issue, thereby lowering overt conflict. Although industrial conflict has not led to revolution in countries such as the UK, radical observers argue that there is nevertheless still a fundamental conflict of interests at work and that this is manifested in less overt or more indirect forms of conflict, such as ABSENTEEISM and LABOUR TURNOVER, which do not necessarily appear to be explicitly directed against the other party.

As against the Marxist view of two diametrically opposed interests in society, PLURALISM suggests that there is a plurality of interests, possibly organized in interest groups, in any society or organization. Although on occasions these interests may conflict, pluralists would dispute that such conflicts are an expression of a fundamental cleavage. Instead conflict tends to arise over specific distributional issues, such as the size of an annual pay increase, and the composition of interest groups varies according to the issue at stake. Indeed some pluralists would go further and assert that there is a basic identity of interests underneath these specific differences. Pluralists argue that conflict can be beneficial in so far as its expression ('giving voice') can both reduce the intensity of conflict and provide the impetus to design procedures for resolving differences.

Pluralism has been an influential approach in political science, in the study of INDUSTRIAL RELATIONS, and in ORGANIZATIONAL ANALYSIS. In industrial relations pluralists argue that TRADE UNIONS are the expression of distinct employee interests and that recognition of them by managers enables the creation of mechanisms for conflict resolution and hence for managers to regain or maintain control of work. Pluralism has been a less explicit approach in the study of organizations but has nevertheless informed much of the recent work in this area. For instance, writers have showed that whilst all in the organization may subscribe to the organization's broad goals, various departments may acquire specific and divergent interests relating to their contribution to these goals. These interests are expressed in the decision-making process, making it as much a political as a rational or technical process. Although an influential approach, pluralism has been criticized for its assumption that the power of interest groups is more or less equal and that there are no fundamental structural bases to power differences in organizations and society.

See INDUSTRIAL DISPUTE, INDUSTRIAL ACTION, MANAGEMENT STYLE.

**conformance** the extent to which a product meets the standard of QUALITY which was designed into the product. See QUALITY CONTROL.

**conglomerate integration** see DIVERSIFICATION.

**conjoint analysis** a MARKET RESEARCH technique which involves potential buyers in assigning ordinal rankings to attributes possessed by varieties of a particular product.

In assessing television sets, for instance, conjoint analysis would rate particular BRANDS on the characteristics of sound quality, picture quality and layout of controls (see Fig. 25). A 'conjunctive buyer' would distinguish between the alternative brands by requiring minimum performance standards for every attribute, rejecting brands which fail to meet these standards. For example, a consumer might set minimum standards of 5 for picture and sound quality and 3 for layout of controls, in which case brands A and C would be rejected in favour of brand B.

By contrast, a 'disjunctive buyer' would select a brand by setting minimum attribute levels for only certain highly-regarded characteristics and would be indifferent about other attributes.

Conjoint analysis is used to develop product brands which contain combinations of attributes in proportions which appeal to the mass of consumers or to particular MARKET SEGMENTS.

| Brand | Sound Quality | Picture Quality | Layout of Controls |
|-------|---------------|-----------------|--------------------|
| A | 4 | 4 | 3 |
| B | 5 | 5 | 3 |
| C | 3 | 4 | 4 |

Fig. 25. **Conjoint analysis.** Rating scores for television set.

**conjunctive buyer** see CONJOINT ANALYSIS.

**conservatism** or **prudence** see ACCOUNTING PRINCIPLES.

**consideration 1.** something of value which is offered by a party to a CONTRACT in exchange for something of value received. Consideration usually takes the form of a monetary payment in exchange for GOODS or SERVICES received, but could involve, for example, the direct exchange of one product for another (as in BARTER).
**2.** the sum of money paid by an investor to purchase SHARES, STOCKS, etc., or the proceeds from selling such securities before allowing for stockbroker's commission and other transfer expenses.

**consignment** an arrangement between an exporter and an importer of a product under which the exporter only receives payment for the product after it has been transported to, and sold by, the importer. Where exporters sell GOODS on consignment they may experience significant delays in being paid and must make appropriate funding arrangements to maintain their cash flow. See EXPORTING, EXPORT CREDIT GUARANTEE DEPARTMENT.

**consistency** see ACCOUNTING PRINCIPLES.

**consol** a FINANCIAL SECURITY issued by the government as a means of raising money. Consols are issued at a fixed price and bear a nominal fixed INTEREST RATE. Unlike other securities issued by the government such as TREASURY BILLS and BONDS, consols are irredeemable, i.e. they do not carry a specified redemption date. However, consols can be bought and sold on the STOCK MARKET at variable prices reflecting the forces of supply and demand for them.

**consolidated accounts** the aggregate accounts of a group of companies. A consolidated BALANCE SHEET is compiled by adding the ASSETS and LIABILITIES of all companies in the group, after making allowance for any amounts that companies in the group owe to one another. A consolidated PROFIT-AND-LOSS ACCOUNT is prepared by adding the SALES REVENUES and COSTS of all companies in the group, after deducting the effects of any sales between companies within the group. The claims of any MINORITY INTERESTS in group assets and profits must also be allowed for.

Preparation of consolidated accounts for a MULTINATIONAL ENTERPRISE with subsidiary companies in several countries is complicated by the need to translate the accounts of these subsidiaries, expressed in terms of their local currencies, into the domestic currency of the parent company (see FOREIGN CURRENCY TRANSLATION, EXCHANGE RATE EXPOSURE).

See HOLDING COMPANY.

**consortium** a group of independent companies or financial institutions which agree to work together jointly on some undertaking, for example the construction of an electricity power plant or the provision of a range of financial services, each contributing some particular resource input or expertise. In recent years, many TAKEOVERS of companies have been arranged on a consortium basis, with a view to breaking up the target company and sharing out its assets between the individual participants in the consortium.

See CONTRACTOR.

**constant failure rate** see FAILURE RATE CURVE.

**constructive dismissal** see UNFAIR DISMISSAL.

**consultation** the process in which managers inform and seek the views of others before finally deciding what course of action to take. It may take place with interested parties outside the organization, for example local authorities, or with those inside. In INDUSTRIAL RELATIONS, joint consultation is where managers consult with employee representatives. It differs from COLLECTIVE BARGAINING in that managers do not usually seek formal agreement and in theory NEGOTIATION does not occur. Instead, representatives are there to listen to management plans and to express their views on them. However, since these views may be forcefully expressed and may be backed up by substantial power resources, managers may have to modify or even abandon their plans as a result. Thus the difference between consultation and collective bargaining may therefore be more apparent than real, and may hinge on the procedural distinction that disagreements during consultation cannot normally be carried forward to the next stage of a GRIEVANCE PROCEDURE.

Consultation may occur in a variety of bodies – joint consultative committee, works committee, etc. – and may involve workplace trade union representatives (SHOP STEWARDS) or representatives elected by all employees separately from union channels of representation. In the latter case, the consultative body is often known as the Works Council, after the German name for such institutions (see CO-DETERMINATION).

Traditionally, consultation has been viewed as dealing with minor welfare issues ('tea 'n' toilets') though major rationalizations can be the subject of consultation. However, it is a common complaint that employees are either not consulted at all over such important issues or else consultation is left to such a late stage that it is impossible to modify managerial plans. In recent years some companies, e.g. some of the Japanese firms in the UK, have extended consultation to cover issues relating to company strategy, whilst legislation has stipulated that information should be disclosed to unions and their representatives relating to REDUNDANCY. Equally, there has been a shift in some organizations from formal joint consultation with employee representatives to direct COMMUNICATION with individual employees. Currently the EUROPEAN WORKS COUNCIL directive of the European Commission is requiring that large European firms with plants in more than one member state establish works councils composed of employee representatives from all parts of the company for the purpose of consultation on key issues of company strategy.

## CONSUMER

See JAPANIZATION, DISCLOSURE OF INFORMATION, EMPLOYEE INVOLVEMENT, EMPLOYEE PARTICIPATION.

**consumer** a BUYER of a final GOOD or SERVICE which is purchased to satisfy a personal consumption need. See BUYER BEHAVIOUR.

**consumer adoption** the acceptance and purchasing of NEW PRODUCTS or BRANDS by CONSUMERS. The rate at which consumers adopt a new product will determine whether or not it is withdrawn from the market or continues to be sold. A very high proportion of new products launched are rejected by consumers and only a minority gain rapid consumer acceptance. Consumer acceptance of a particular brand of a good determines the extent to which the consumer will continue to purchase that brand in preference to competitors' brands. See BRAND LOYALTY, TEST MARKETING.

**consumer behaviour** see BUYER BEHAVIOUR.

**Consumer Credit Act 1974** a UK Act which provides for the licensing of persons and businesses engaged in the provision of consumer CREDIT (specifically moneylenders, pawnbrokers and INSTALMENT CREDIT traders – but not banks which are covered by separate legislation), and the regulation of DEBTOR-CREDITOR contracts. The former requirement is designed to ensure that only 'fit and proper' persons are allowed to provide consumer finance, and the latter gives borrowers certain rights in respect of withdrawal from an agreement, to complete payments ahead of time and to terminate the agreement. The Act contains important provisions protecting creditors from extortionate rates of interest. The Act is administered by the OFFICE OF FAIR TRADING in conjunction with the DEPARTMENT OF TRADE AND INDUSTRY. See CONSUMER PROTECTION, APR.

**consumer durables** CONSUMER GOODS such as television sets, motorcars and microwave ovens which yield satisfaction to consumers over relatively long periods of time rather than immediately. Consumer durables tend to be purchased infrequently by a consumer, and are generally expensive items which are often purchased on CREDIT terms. Compare CONSUMER NONDURABLES. See GOOD.

**consumer goods** products such as television sets, bread and clothing, which are purchased by CONSUMERS for their own personal consumption. See GOOD, CONSUMER DURABLES, CON-

SUMER NONDURABLES.

**consumerism** an organized movement to protect the interests of CONSUMERS by forcing companies to behave in a more socially responsible manner. The movement developed in response to the increasing technical complexity of products, the growing power of big businesses and environmental pollution. In many countries there are now consumer bodies, such as the Consumer Association in the UK, which provide product-testing facilities and publish comparative information on products through magazines such as *Which*. See GREEN CONSUMER.

**consumer loyalty** see BRAND LOYALTY.

**consumer nondurables** CONSUMER GOODS such as coffee, beefburgers and hair shampoos which yield satisfaction to consumers at the time of immediate use. Such GOODS are purchased frequently and are generally low-priced items. Compare CONSUMER DURABLES.

**consumer orientation** a business philosophy of a company which emphasizes the provision of GOODS and SERVICES that have been specially designed to satisfy the needs of its customers. A CONSUMER or customer orientation involves the identification of customer needs with a view to developing products which satisfy these needs (see NEW PRODUCT DEVELOPMENT).

Once a firm has chosen to operate in a particular MARKET it needs to identify the needs of customers including, where appropriate, the needs of specific subgroups of customers (see MARKET SEGMENTATION).

A consumer orientation strategy thus requires a firm to understand the attitudes, wants and behaviour of a target group of consumers (see MARKETING RESEARCH, BUYER BEHAVIOUR). Having defined consumer wants, a firm can then develop products with characteristics which satisfy these wants and develop an appropriate MARKETING MIX to market them.

Contrast with PRODUCTION ORIENTATION. See MARKETING CONCEPT.

**consumer panel** see MARKETING INTELLIGENCE.

**consumer preference** product attributes which CONSUMERS seek and which will lead them to choose one BRAND of a product in preference to other similar brands. Information about consumer preferences may be obtained from MARKETING

RESEARCH techniques like interviews or postal questionnaires. PRODUCT DEVELOPMENT can then be geared to designing products which match consumer preferences, offering the appropriate blend of product characteristics to suit the demands of the market as a whole or of particular market segments (see MARKET SEGMENTATION).

**consumer products** see SELLER.

**consumer protection** a generic term used to describe various pieces of legislation whose objective is to protect CONSUMERS from unscrupulous, unfair and intrusive trade practices and unsafe products. In the UK the main Acts concerning consumer protection in force at the present time are: the WEIGHTS AND MEASURES ACT 1963; the TRADE DESCRIPTIONS ACTS 1968 and 1972; the UNSOLICITED GOODS AND SERVICES ACT 1971 and 1975; the FAIR TRADING ACT 1973; the CONSUMER CREDIT ACT 1974; the CONSUMER SAFETY ACT 1978; the PRICE MARKING (BARGAIN OFFERS) ORDER 1979, SALE OF GOODS ACT 1979; SALE OF GOODS AND SERVICES ACT 1982; ESTATE AGENCY ACT 1979; CONTROL OF MISLEADING ADVERTISEMENTS REGULATIONS 1988; CONSUMER PROTECTION ACT 1987. See OFFICE OF FAIR TRADING, DEPARTMENT OF TRADE AND INDUSTRY. See also CONSUMERISM.

**Consumer Protection Act 1987** a UK Act which extends existing powers to protect consumers in the areas of consumer safety (the Act makes it a criminal offence to supply unsafe goods) and misleading price indications (the Act makes deceptive price advertising an offence and requires price promises to be kept). In addition, the Act introduces new powers for consumers to obtain damages against suppliers whose products prove defective.

See CONSUMER SAFETY ACT 1978; TRADE DESCRIPTIONS ACT 1968; CONSUMER PROTECTION.

**Consumer Safety Act 1978** a UK Act which empowers the Secretary of State for Trade and Industry to make regulations in respect of a product so as to prevent or reduce the risk of personal injury or death. This Act subsumes the Consumer Protection Acts 1961 and 1971 and the regulations previously made under these Acts covering, for example, gas and electric fires, electric blankets, cooking utensils and perambulators. See CONSUMER PROTECTION ACT 1987.

**Consumers' Association** see CONSUMERISM.

**consumer segmentation** an approach to marketing which involves grouping together potential BUYERS of a product on the basis of similarities in their buying characteristics. This enables a firm to match the attributes of its products with that of identified buyer characteristics when selecting MARKET SEGMENTS to target. See MARKET SEGMENTATION.

**consumer survey** see MARKETING RESEARCH.

**consumer wants** the desire of CONSUMERS to have particular NEEDS satisfied by the consumption of GOODS and SERVICES. See BUYER BEHAVIOUR.

**contango 1.** an additional payment made by an investor or speculator who has purchased or sold a SHARE, STOCK etc. on the UK STOCK MARKET in return for being permitted to carry over the settlement of the share transaction from one ACCOUNT PERIOD to the next.
**2.** a condition in a FORWARD MARKET where the most distant delivery months trade at a premium to the near term delivery months.

**continental shift** see SHIFT WORK.

**contingency allowance** see ALLOWANCES.

**contingency plan** tactics which would be adopted in the event of a firm's original plans being thwarted. It is important for a BUSINESS to establish contingency plans so that they have a fall-back position. If, for example, a key component supplier is unable to deliver on time, the firm should have alternative suppliers lined up to avoid excessive disruption to its own production process.

**contingency theory** an approach to ORGANIZATIONAL ANALYSIS which emphasizes that the character and structure of ORGANIZATIONS can take a number of forms, and may be related to the technology in use or the organization's environment. Organizational features can be said to be contingent on such factors.

The idea of contingency is now so widely accepted in the study of organizations, and views premised on it so diverse that it is more accurate to speak of a contingency approach rather than one theory as such. The contingency approach is notable for rejecting the notion that there is one best way of structuring organizations (see CLASSICAL MANAGEMENT THEORY, SCIENTIFIC MANAGEMENT).

The contingency approach initially became popular in the 1960s. British industrial sociologist Joan Woodward (1916–71) found that technology (in itself determined by what product the firm was making) was associated with certain structural characteristics. For instance, the more advanced the technology, the longer the CHAIN OF COMMAND. Woodward argued that there was a particular form of organizational structure appropriate to each technical situation. Other writers emphasized the importance of environment. American writers Paul Lawrence (1922– ) and Jay Lorsch (1932– ) suggested that the greater the degree of environmental uncertainty and complexity, the greater the need for differentiation of management functions within the organization, but also the need for integrative devices to pull the organization together. Like Woodward they argued that there was an appropriate organizational form for each type of environment. A number of British writers also traced the relationship between environment and organizational form (see MECHANISTIC AND ORGANISMIC).

The most important investigation of these issues in the UK was conducted by the 'Aston School' (members of the Industrial Administration Research Unit at Aston University, including Derek Pugh (1930– ) and David Hickson (1931– )) in the 1960s. This project found that the structuring of organizational activities (e.g. specialization of job roles and departments) was correlated not with technology but with the size of the organization, whilst the degree of centralization of decision-making was correlated with the degree of dependence upon other organizations, such as suppliers.

Whilst most writers on organizations now adopt a contingency approach, views differ on how far certain factors, such as environment, determine organizational form and how far top managers can make a strategic choice to model their organizations in certain ways by taking account of such factors.

**contingent liability** a liability which may or may not occur depending upon an uncertain event, for example, the outcome of a court case in which damages are being claimed against a firm.

**continuation day** the first day of the UK STOCK MARKET ACCOUNT PERIOD.

**continuous production** see MASS PRODUCTION.

**continuous review system of stock control** see FIXED

QUANTITY REORDER SYSTEM.

**continuous stock-taking** see STOCK CONTROL.

**contract** a legally enforceable agreement between two or more parties. A contract involves obligations on the part of the contractors which may be expressed verbally or in writing. Formation of a contract involves one party making an *offer* to the other party which must then be *accepted* by the latter party. For example, one firm may offer to supply a PRODUCT to another company at a given future date and on specified terms. In return, the latter company would agree to pay a specified sum of money as *consideration* for the product to be supplied. Both parties would then be legally bound to honour their agreement to sell and to buy the product. In the event of either party failing to comply with the terms of the contract the other party could seek damages for breach of contract through the courts.

**contract costing** see COSTING.

**contracting-out 1.** the nonparticipation in some specific scheme operated by a company or government in favour of an alternative arrangement; for example, in the UK, an employee may opt out of his employer's company PENSION scheme, choosing instead to invest in a personal pension plan.

**2.** the placement of some or all of a firm's input requirements (raw materials, components, services) with independent suppliers. Whether or not a firm provides these resources itself through backward vertical integration or relies on outside suppliers will depend on a number of financial, technical and strategic considerations (see MAKE OR BUY DECISION).

**3.** the putting-out to private firms of contracts for the provision of services to a public institution. The term 'contracting-out' has assumed a particular significance in the government's current privatization programme, referring specifically to a situation in which a publicly owned service such as the National Health Service employs private sector firms to supply, for example, laundry, cleaning and catering services. The logic for this is that it is more cost-effective for these services to be bought in under conditions of competitive tendering by specialist firms enjoying economies of scale than for them to be provided by hospital staff. (See NATIONALIZATION VERSUS PRIVATIZATION).

**contract note** a document issued by a STOCKBROKER to a client, which confirms details of a purchase or sale of STOCKS and SHARES on behalf of the client.

**contract of employment** an agreement whereby a worker undertakes to work for an employer in return for a wage or salary. In the UK, employees have been entitled since 1964 to a written statement of the main elements of the contract, such as rates of pay and hours of work, known as the terms and conditions of employment. It is usual for a brief JOB DESCRIPTION to be included in this statement. However, this document is not necessarily the full contract: the requirements stipulated in a separate company rule book and the agreements reached through COLLECTIVE BARGAINING also form part of the contract.

The contract both provides rights and imposes obligations on each party to it. The employer has the broad right to direct the work of the employee: what to do and how to do it. If the employee fails to carry out his or her allotted duties satisfactorily the employer can terminate the contract. Similarly, if the employee breaches the contract by going on STRIKE the contract can be terminated. However, the scope for employer action is limited to some degree by the employee's right not to be unfairly dismissed (see UNFAIR DISMISSAL). The employer must have a valid reason for sacking the employee and have carried out the termination in accordance with an acceptable DISCIPLINARY PROCEDURE. In the case of official INDUSTRIAL DISPUTES, all employees breaching their contracts must be dismissed if the dismissal is to be deemed fair. However, the EMPLOYMENT ACT 1990 permits selective dismissal of strikers when industrial action is unofficial.

Since the 1970s employee rights have been expanded by legislative action. For instance, employees now have the right not to be discriminated against on the grounds of sex or race (see DISCRIMINATION). In the 1980s the UK government placed some limitations on these rights (e.g. by extending the qualifying period for protection against unfair dismissal) as part of its policy of reducing employment regulation. However, legislation of the EUROPEAN COMMUNITY counteracted this trend to a certain extent and appears likely to lead to further expansion of employee rights in the coming years. See IMPLIED TERMS; PERSONAL CONTRACT.

**contract of sale** a CONTRACT under which the SELLER of a product transfers or agrees to transfer the product to the BUYER of the product for a money consideration. Contracts of sale contain various terms or conditions on which the product is to be supplied including, typically, product descriptions, qualities, quantities, delivery dates and prices. Remedies for breach of contract can be sought through the Courts. See SALE OF GOODS ACTS 1979, 1982.

**contractor** a person or firm which enters into a legal CONTRACT with another person or firm to supply GOODS or SERVICES. For example, in the building industry a housebuilder may employ contractors to undertake the plumbing and electrical work involved in the construction of houses, rather than do this work himself. The plumbing and electrical contractors would provide, for the contract price, all piping, wire, etc. needed, plus the specialist workers to install them. In turn, the plumber may enter into an agreement with a *subcontractor* to install the timeclocks and electrical controls for the central heating system. Complex projects requiring a large number of specialist inputs are frequently undertaken on a CONSORTIUM basis.

**contribution** the difference between SALES REVENUE and VARIABLE COSTS. If total contributions are just large enough to cover FIXED COSTS then the producer BREAKS EVEN; if contributions are less than fixed costs the producer makes a LOSS; while if contributions exceed fixed costs then the producer makes a PROFIT. Fig. 26 (overleaf) shows how contributions provide a fund out of which total fixed costs must be paid before any profit is made. See MARGINAL COSTING.

**contribution per £ of sales** see PROFIT-VOLUME RATIO.

**control** the process of ensuring that activities are carried out as intended. Control involves monitoring aspects of performance and taking corrective action where necessary. For instance, control of expenditure involves regular monitoring of expenditure figures, comparison of these with budget targets, and decisions to cut or increase expenditure where any discrepancy is believed to be harmful. Without control an ORGANIZATION cannot function: employees would go their own way (possibly with the best of intentions) and the organization would fragment, making COORDINATION impossible. Control can, therefore, be viewed as a central component of MANAGE-

# CONTROL CHART

| Outputs (units per annum) | 700 £ | 800 £ | 900 £ | 1,000 £ | 1,100 £ |
|---|---|---|---|---|---|
| Sales Revenue (at price £20) less Variable Cost | 14,000 | 16,000 | 18,000 | 20,000 | 22,000 |
| (£10 per unit) | 7,000 | 8,000 | 9,000 | 10,000 | 11,000 |
| Contribution (£10 per unit) | 7,000 | 8,000 | 9,000 | 10,000 | 11,000 |
| less Fixed Costs | 9,000 | 9,000 | 9,000 | 9,000 | 9,000 |
| Profit (Loss) | (2,000) | (1,000) | NIL | 1,000 | 2,000 |
| *Note* Total Cost | 16,000 | 17,000 | 18,000 | 19,000 | 20,000 |
| Unit Total Cost | 22.86 | 21.25 | 20.00 | 19.00 | 18.18 |

Fig. 26. **Contribution**. Output and sales of chairs.

MENT.

Some writers in the SOCIOLOGY OF WORK have argued that, since (in their view) employers' and employees' interests are opposed, control of labour is the main task of management. Without it, workers would behave in a way which is detrimental to managerial goals. Research has shown, however, that many managers attach more importance to other managerial functions (such as budgeting), whilst it is questionable whether employees would necessarily act in the way suggested.

See ORGANIZATIONAL ANALYSIS.

**control chart, quality control chart, process chart** or **P (percent defective control chart)** a diagram used to plot variations in the size or other characteristic of a component or PRODUCT made by a machine and/or operative. Such charts are compiled by taking samples of items produced and measuring their sizes or characteristics. Where variations are small and fall within predefined normal or acceptable limits marked on the control chart, no action is necessary. However, where machine faults, worn tools or defective materials cause larger variations than the control limits then the cause of this variation must be investigated and immediate corrective action taken to avoid any further production of defective items. See QUALITY CONTROL.

Fig. 27 shows a typical control chart which depicts variations in the size of a machine component, and the upper and lower control limits at which the process would require

Fig. 27. Control chart.

correction.

**control costs** the costs to a firm of avoiding making defective products. Control costs fall into two main categories. First *prevention costs*, which are the costs of pre-production activities aimed at preventing defects. Prevention costs include costs of preparing quality manuals and procedures, training, process planning and collecting data about product quality.

Second, *appraisal costs*, which are the costs of eliminating defects after they occur but before products reach the customer. These costs include final goods inspection, inspection during the production process, and laboratory testing.

See QUALITY COSTS, QUALITY CONTROL.

**control limits** see CONTROL CHART.

**Control of Misleading Advertisements Regulations 1988** a UK regulatory framework which gives the OFFICE OF FAIR TRADING powers to protect the general buying public from deceptive ADVERTISEMENTS. An advertisement is misleading if it deceives people by, for example, making a false statement of fact or concealing or omitting important facts about the product.

See CONSUMER PROTECTION.

**convenience goods** PRODUCTS such as newspapers which CONSUMERS buy at frequent intervals with little comparison or buying effort. Contrast with SHOPPING GOODS.

**convenor** a senior SHOP STEWARD responsible, in negotiations and discussions with management, for representing the views and policies of the shop stewards' committee in a work place.

**convertibility** the extent to which a financial security such as a FOREIGN CURRENCY or CONVERTIBLE LOAN can be exchanged for some other currency or financial ASSET. The full convertibility of foreign currencies plays an important part in fostering INTERNATIONAL TRADE and FOREIGN INVESTMENT. See FOREIGN EXCHANGE CONTROLS.

**convertible currency** a currency which can be converted into another currency without special permission from the FOREIGN EXCHANGE CONTROL authorities.

**convertible loans** long-term LOANS to a JOINT-STOCK COMPANY which may be converted at the option of the lender into ORDINARY SHARES at a predetermined share price.

**conveyance** a document which transfers the legal ownership of land and buildings from one person/business to another person/business.

**conveyor** equipment which is used to transport raw materials, work in progress and finished GOODS around a factory. Conveyors assist the smooth flow of materials/PRODUCTS and are used extensively in PRODUCTION-LINE/ASSEMBLY-LINE operations.

**cooperative** see WORKERS' COOPERATIVE, RETAIL COOPERATIVE.

**coordinated marketing** see MARKETING STRATEGY.

**Coordinating Committee on Multilateral Export Controls (CoCom)** an organization whose members include the UK, Germany and other members of NATO plus Japan and Australia, which regulates the export of militarily sensitive products (mainly high technology items like defence equipment, computers and telecommunications systems) to Eastern Europe. As a result of the recent improvement in East–West political relations, a large number of previously banned items can now be freely traded. See EMBARGO.

**coordination** the process of combining together the work of ORGANIZATION members and departments to achieve the desired end-product or goals of the organization. Coordination is necessary at two levels:

(a) the bringing together of production tasks to achieve production goals with the minimum of waste, buffer stocks, etc.;

(b) the coordination of all organizational functions to achieve effective and efficient operations and the maintenance of the organization as a viable entity.

Coordination of a complex range of activities is fraught

with problems, and it is a central issue in the design and running of organizations. Some organizations seek to achieve coordination by formulating a range of rules and procedures to guide and govern the work of employees and departments. Others prefer to rely on the skills, knowledge and commitment of their employees to interpret what forms of coordination are necessary (see MECHANISTIC AND ORGANISMIC, CULTURE). Most organizations adopt a combination of the two. In all organizations, however, the need for coordination is embodied in the formal structure. Some adopt a FUNCTIONAL STRUCTURE, some a PRODUCT-BASED STRUCTURE, whilst others adopt a MATRIX STRUCTURE explicitly to tackle problems of coordination.

**co-ownership** see WORKERS' COOPERATIVE.

**copycat product** see MARKET POSITIONING.

**copyright** the legal ownership by persons or businesses of certain kinds of material, in particular original literary, dramatic, musical and artistic work; sound recordings, films, broadcasts and cable programmes; the typographical arrangement or layout of a published edition; and computer programs. In the UK, the COPYRIGHT, DESIGNS AND PATENTS ACT 1988 gives legal rights to the creators of copyright material so that they can control the various ways in which their work may be exploited. Copyright protection is automatic and there is no registration or other formality. The 1988 Act gives copyright owners protection against unauthorized copying of such material in most cases for a period of 50 years. If copyright is infringed, the copyright owner (or assignee or licencee) may seek an injunction through the courts preventing further abuses, with offenders liable to pay unlimited damages/fines and prison sentences in extreme cases. See BRAND.

**Copyright, Designs and Patents Act 1988** a UK Act which provides for the establishment and protection of the legal ownership rights of persons and businesses in respect of various classes of 'intellectual property', in particular COPYRIGHTS, PERFORMERS RIGHTS, DESIGN RIGHTS (including registered designs) and PATENTS. The Act amends and restates various earlier statutes, including the Copyright Act 1956, the Registered Designs Act 1949, the Performers' Protection Acts 1958–72 and the Patents Act 1977.

The Act is administered in part by the PATENTS OFFICE, with

cases of unauthorized copying, patent infringements, etc. being handled by the courts.

**core business** a division of a conglomerate firm which is considered to be central to the firm's corporate success insofar as it embodies the firm's CORE SKILLS and competencies and generates the bulk of its sales revenue and profits. See DIVERSIFICATION, DIVESTMENT.

By contrast, a non-core business is one which makes only a relatively small contribution to the firm's overall activities. However, the dividing-line between core and non-core businesses can be elastic when viewed over time. For example, BAT Industries' main core business continues to be tobacco products but since 1983 it has developed through acquisitions a large insurance division which it now regards also as a core business.

**core product-benefit** the most important attribute of a product in the judgment of a *particular* buyer when considering the purchase of a PRODUCT. Thus one buyer of a motor-car might look specifically for style, another for comfort, and yet another for speed, so that each is seeking a different version of it. By identifying groups of consumers who are seeking the same core product-benefit, it is possible to undertake appropriate PRODUCT DIFFERENTIATION strategies. See CONJOINT ANALYSIS.

**core skill or competency** the particular, often unique, abilities possessed by a firm in supplying a product which provides the basis for the firm's on-going COMPETITIVE ADVANTAGES over rival suppliers. Such skills may reside, for example, in the firm's research and development or marketing capabilities. Essentially they embody the expertise of the firm's incumbent staff, accumulated know-how and intellectual property rights (PATENTS).

From a strategic perspective, the possession of core skills suggests that firms should concentrate on what they do best (that is, 'stick to the knitting') rather than be tempted to diversify (see DIVERSIFICATION) into areas they know little about or dissipate their energies by trying to do too many things. See CORE BUSINESS.

**core workforce** see LABOUR FLEXIBILITY.

**cornering the market** an attempt to buy up all the supplies of a particular commodity in order to exploit the market by charging high prices.

**Corn Exchange** a London-based wholesale commodity exchange which undertakes dealings in cereals, seeds, fertilizers and animal feedstuffs. See BALTIC MERCANTILE AND SHIPPING EXCHANGE, COMMODITY MARKET.

**corporate governance** the arrangements which are made to ensure that the DIRECTORS and senior managers of a public company exercise their power responsibly in running the company in the interest of shareholders and the broader community. Such arrangements need to incorporate suitable 'checks and balances' upon the power of the chief executive, for example, by splitting the rôles of chairman and managing director, strengthening the power of board audit committees and providing a greater rôle for non-executive directors. In the UK the issue of corporate governance was highlighted by the report of the Cadbury Committee in 1992.

**corporate identity** a specially designed symbol or printed heading used by a company to make it more easily recognized by the general public. Such symbols or headings are used on company letterheads, business cards, invoices, advertisements and signs. See COMPANY IMAGE.

**corporate raider** see ARBITRAGEUR.

**corporate restructuring 1.** a change in a firm's STRATEGIC DIRECTION involving, for example, its expansion into new business activities (see DIVERSIFICATION) and its withdrawal from some existing activities (see DIVESTMENT).

**2.** a change in a firm's internal ORGANIZATION involving, for example, the replacement of a highly centralized decision-making structure by one based on individual STRATEGIC BUSINESS UNITS. See ORGANIZATIONAL STRUCTURE, BUSINESS PROCESS RE-ENGINEERING.

**corporate strategy** see BUSINESS STRATEGY.

**corporate venturing** a situation where a major company takes a minority stake in a new or relatively new company and injects cash into that company. However, corporate venturing may go much further than the provision of finance, and may involve a cross-fertilization of skills, talents, know-how and expertise which may be of benefit to both parties involved. See VENTURE CAPITAL.

**corporation** a North American term for a JOINT-STOCK COMPANY.

**corporation tax** a DIRECT TAX levied by the government on the PROFITS accruing to businesses. A company's corporation tax is loosely based upon its profit for the accounting period as determined in the company's PROFIT-AND-LOSS ACCOUNT. However, since firms use different methods for calculating DEPRECIATION of FIXED ASSETS to charge against revenues and so arrive at different PROFIT figures, the UK government establishes a standard scale of CAPITAL ALLOWANCES which all firms must apply to their fixed assets when computing *taxable profit*. These capital allowances take the form of an annual *writing down allowance*, currently 4% per year of the initial cost of industrial buildings; and 25% per year on plant and machinery.

When a company pays dividends or makes other distributions of profit to shareholders, then it must also make a payment of *advance corporation tax* to the government, currently equal to one third of the dividend paid. This is an advance payment of corporation tax and can be offset by the company against its liability to *mainstream corporation tax* when this liability is assessed at the year end.

Shareholders receiving a dividend are also treated as receiving a *tax credit* equal, at current rates, to one third of the dividend received. This tax credit is added to the dividend received to establish the shareholders' total taxable income. This *imputation system*, whereby the tax paid on distributed profits by the company is credited to the shareholders, avoids double-taxing the shareholders both on their company's profits and on their dividend distributions.

In the UK the general corporation tax rate is 31% of taxable profits but there is also a 'smaller companies' corporation tax rate of 21% for companies whose taxable profits are less than £300,000 per annum (as at 1997/8).

The level of corporation tax is important to a firm insofar as it determines the amount of after-tax profit which is available to it to pay out DIVIDENDS to shareholders or to reinvest in the business (see RETAINED PROFITS).

See INLAND REVENUE.

**corporatism** see TRIPARTISM.

**correlation** a statistical term that describes the degree of association between two VARIABLES such as sales and income. When two variables tend to change together then they are said to be correlated, and the extent to which they are correlated is measured by means of the CORRELATION COEFFICIENT.

**correlation coefficient** a measure of the strength of the association between two VARIABLES. Where two variables are completely unrelated then their correlation coefficient (r) will be zero; where two variables are perfectly related then their correlation would be one. A high correlation coefficient between two variables merely indicates that the two generally vary together – it does not imply that changes in one variable cause changes in the other.

Where high values of one variable are associated with high values of the other, then they are said to be *positively correlated*. Where high values of one variable are associated with low values of the other, then they are said to be *negatively correlated*. Thus correlation coefficients can range from +1 for perfect positive association to –1 for perfect negative association, with zero representing the case where there is no association between the two.

**cost** the expenditure upon resources incurred by a firm in producing and selling its output. Each cost is a charge against revenues and profits for the use or consumption of resources during a trading period. Costs can be classified along functional lines, distinguishing between production, selling, distribution, administration and financing costs. Alternatively costs can be classified as either direct costs (usually raw materials and direct labour) or indirect costs (overheads). Costs may also be classified as variable costs and fixed costs, depending on whether they vary with the level of output or activity. In addition, costs may be analysed by product. Finally costs may be classified by location (division, subsidiary, company, department, etc.).

Classification and analysis of costs is necessary for three main business purposes:

(a) for *product costing*;
(b) for *management control*;
(c) for *decision making*.

Identification and classification of these costs is the core of MANAGEMENT ACCOUNTING. Fig. 28 (overleaf) shows the build up of major cost elements.

See PRODUCTION COST, SELLING COST.

**cost accounting** see MANAGEMENT ACCOUNTING.

**cost and freight (c&f)** a term used to denote the respective

## COST-BASED PRICING

Fig. 28. **Cost.** Major elements of cost.

contractual obligations of sellers and buyers of a GOOD which is exported. Under a c&f contract, the seller pays the cost of transporting the good to the port of shipment, the loading charges and the freight charges to the port of destination. From then on the buyer bears the cost of unloading and transporting the good to its final destination. The buyer pays *all* the insurance costs incurred.

See COST, INSURANCE AND FREIGHT, FREE ON BOARD, EXPORTING.

**cost-based pricing** pricing methods which determine the PRICE of a product on the basis of its production, distribution and marketing COSTS. Three cost-based pricing methods may be distinguished:

(a) *full-cost* or *mark-up* or *average cost pricing* of a product is determined by adding a percentage profit mark-up to average or unit total cost, unit total cost being composed of average or unit variable cost and average or unit fixed cost (both of which can be determined from MANAGEMENT ACCOUNTING records). Fig. 29 shows an example of full-cost pricing based on an estimated sales/production volume of 1000 units per month. Unit variable cost (costs which vary with the level of output, such as raw materials and direct labour) are £2. Total fixed costs (costs which do not vary with output, such as depreciation and factory rent) are £1000 per month so that average fixed cost at a volume of 1000 units are £1. Unit total cost is the sum of average variable cost and average fixed cost, and managers decide on the percentage profit markup (here 50%) to add to total cost to arrive at a selling price (here £4.50). At this price, revenue would be £4.50×1000 units or £4,500 per month and profits £1.50×1000 units or £1,500 per month, provided that 1000 units per month can be sold at this price;

| Sales/production volume | 1,000 units per month £ |
|---|---|
| unit variable cost | 2.00 |
| unit fixed cost (FC÷volume) | 1.00 |
| unit total cost | 3.00 |
| profit markup (50%) | 1.50 |
| selling price | 4.50 |
| resulting total revenue £4.50 × 1,000 = £4,500 per month | |
| resulting total profit  £1.50 × 1,000 = £1,500 per month | |

Fig. 29. **Cost-based pricing.** Full cost or markup pricing example.

(b) *cost-plus pricing* is very similar to full–cost or mark–up pricing, in so far as the price of a product is determined by adding a percentage profit mark–up to the product's unit total cost. Indeed the terms are often used interchangeably. However, cost-plus pricing is used more specifically to refer to an agreed price between a purchaser and the seller, where the price is based on actual costs incurred plus a fixed percentage of actual cost or a fixed amount of profit per unit. Such pricing methods are often used for large capital projects or high technology contracts where the length of time of construction or changing technical specifications lead to a high degree of uncertainty about the final price;

(c) *breakeven* or *target-profit* or *marginal cost* pricing of a product is based upon the CONTRIBUTION needed for the product to BREAK EVEN or provide a predetermined target profit. Fig. 30 shows an example of breakeven pricing based on an estimated sales/production volume of 1,000 units per month and total fixed costs (depreciation, rent, etc.) of £1,000 per month. Unit contribution is simply the difference between selling price and unit variable cost or marginal cost. Unit contribution, when multiplied by sales/production volume gives total contribution, and this total contribution should provide sufficient money to cover fixed costs (to break even) or fixed costs and target profit. Fig. 30 shows the unit contribution required in each case. To calculate selling price it is necessary to add unit contribution to unit variable cost or marginal cost as shown in Fig. 30.

All three pricing methods are cost-based and to this extent appear to ignore demand. However, demand and competition cannot be ignored in setting prices. For instance, in full-cost and breakeven pricing, estimates of sales volume are necessary to calculate average fixed cost and required unit contribution respectively. Yet in both cases the price charged will affect sales volume. In practice, managers take account of demand or competition, so that in using full-cost pricing they tend to vary the percentage mark-up over time to reflect fluctuations in demand, and to use different percentage mark-ups for different products to reflect differences in the intensity of competition.

See DEMAND-BASED PRICING, COMPETITION-BASED PRICING.

| Sales/production volume | 1,000 units per month |
| --- | --- |
| | £ |
| fixed cost | 1,000 per month |
| target profit | 1,500 per month |
| unit contribution to break-even = $\dfrac{£1,000}{1,000 \text{ units}}$ =£1.00 | |
| Selling price to break-even | |
| | £ |
| unit variable cost | 2.00 |
| unit contribution | 1.00 |
| selling price | 3.00 |
| unit contribution to achieve target profit = $\dfrac{£1,000+1,500}{1,000 \text{ units}}$ =£2.50 | |
| Selling price to achieve target profit | |
| | £ |
| unit variable cost | 2.00 |
| unit contribution | 2.50 |
| selling price | 4.50 |

Fig. 30. **Cost-based pricing.** Break-even or marginal cost pricing example.

**cost-benefit analysis** a technique for enumerating and evaluating the total social costs and social benefits associated with an economic project. Cost-benefit analysis is generally used by public agencies when evaluating large-scale public INVESTMENT projects such as major new motorways or rail lines, in order to assess the welfare or net social benefits which will accrue to the nation from these projects. This generally involves the sponsoring bodies taking a broader and longer-term view of a project than would a commercial organization concentrating on project profitability alone.

**cost centre** a group of machines, a factory department or some other organizational subunit of a firm under the control of a manager, for which costs can be ascertained and used for purposes of COST CONTROL. See STANDARD COST, PROFIT CENTRE, REVENUE CENTRE.

**cost code** a series of alphabetical or numerical symbols each of which represents a particular labour, material or overhead cost item. Cost codes facilitate the classification and recording of costs for cost control purposes.

**cost control** the task of controlling all items of expenditure by regular and frequent comparison of actual costs with pre-determined budgeted or standard costs, identifying the causes of deviations of actual cost from standard, and taking corrective action to minimize such deviations. With regard to materials cost, deviations from planned materials usage can occur through excessive usage of raw materials for the output achieved or defective production leading to high scrap rates. With regard to labour cost, deviations from planned labour hours can occur, for example, through idle time caused by production bottlenecks. With regard to overheads, deviations from planned production–overheads per unit of product can occur because expenditure on overhead items exceeds budget or because actual output was less than planned.

See MATERIALS COST VARIANCE, LABOUR COST VARIANCE, STANDARD COST, PRODUCTION MANAGEMENT, PRODUCTION CONTROL, BUDGETARY CONTROL, VARIANCE ANALYSIS.

**costing** the process of ascertaining the cost of a PRODUCT, COMPONENT or SERVICE. With historical costing, costs are ascertained after they have been incurred, though most businesses seek to gauge future costs through STANDARD COSTING.

*Product* costing seeks to determine the cost of each job or batch of products in order to assess the cost per unit. *Contract* costing is used to determine the construction costs of a large-scale building or civil engineering contract. *Process* costing is used where liquid or gaseous materials such as oil pass through several refining/heating processes to produce products such as petrol and by-products such as tar, and seeks to determine the costs of products by dividing output volume by materials and processing costs.

**cost, insurance and freight (c.i.f)** a term used to denote the respective contractual obligations of sellers and buyers of a good which is exported. Under a c.i.f. contract, the seller pays the cost of transporting the good to the port of shipment, the loading charges, and the freight charges to the port of destination, plus all insurance cover up to this point. From then on the buyer bears the cost of unloading, transporting, and insuring the good to its final destination. See COST AND FREIGHT, FREE ON BOARD, EXPORTING.

**cost of capital** the cost to a firm of the LONG-TERM CAPITAL used to finance its business activities. The average cost of capital to a firm which uses several sources of long-term funds (for example LOANS, SHARE CAPITAL (EQUITY)) to finance its investments will depend upon the individual cost of each separate source of capital (for example INTEREST on loans), weighted in accordance with the proportions of each source used. See CAPITAL GEARING.

**cost of goods sold** see COST OF SALES.

**cost of living** the general level of prices of GOODS and SERVICES in an economy as measured by a representative PRICE-INDEX. An increase in the prices of products (INFLATION) increases, by definition, the general cost of living, but provided wage increases, etc. keep pace with inflation or incomes are fully INDEX-LINKED, people's living standards will remain unchanged. See STANDARD OF LIVING.

**cost of sales** or **cost of goods sold** the relevant COST that is compared with SALES REVENUE in order to determine GROSS PROFIT in the PROFIT-AND-LOSS ACCOUNT. Where a trading company has STOCKS of finished goods, the cost of goods sold is not the same as purchases of finished goods. Rather, purchases of goods must be added to stock at the start of the trading period to determine the goods available for sale, then the stocks left at the end of the trading period must be deducted from this to determine the cost of the goods which have been sold during the period. See STOCK VALUATION.

**cost of sales adjustment** the difference between the COST OF SALES calculated on an HISTORIC COST and on a current cost or replacement cost basis. See INFLATION ACCOUNTING.

**cost-plus pricing** see COST-BASED PRICING.

**cost price** a PRICE for a product which just covers its production and distribution COSTS with no PROFIT MARGIN added.

**cost-push inflation** see INFLATION.

**cost rate** or **recovery rate** a means of charging OVERHEADS to products. By relating budgeted overhead costs to budgeted output, it is possible to calculate an overhead rate per unit of product to add to the standard DIRECT COST (direct materials cost and direct labour cost) of a product in order to determine its production cost. Alternatively, production overheads can be charged as a percentage on the direct labour cost of a product; or a percentage on the direct materials cost of the product; or on the basis of the direct labour hours to make the product (at a rate per direct labour hour); or on the basis of the machine hours needed to make the product (at a rate per machine hour).

Once the production cost of a product has been determined by adding production overheads, then a further addition must be made to cover selling, distribution and administration overheads. These can be allowed for by means of other cost rates, such as by adding an appropriate percentage to the production cost of the product. The addition of overhead cost rates to the standard direct cost of products serves to establish their total cost, and facilitates their ABSORPTION through selling prices.

See BUDGET, STANDARD COST.

**counselling** see OCCUPATIONAL PSYCHOLOGY.

**counterpurchase** see COUNTERTRADE.

**countertrade** the direct or indirect exchange of goods for other goods in INTERNATIONAL TRADE. Countertrade is generally resorted to when particular FOREIGN CURRENCIES are in short supply, or when countries apply FOREIGN EXCHANGE CONTROLS.

There are various forms of countertrade, including:

(a) BARTER – the direct exchange of product for product;

(b) *compensation deal* – where the seller from the exporting country receives part payment in his own currency and the remainder in goods supplied by the buyer;

(c) *buyback* – where the seller of plant and equipment from the exporting country agrees to accept some of the goods produced by that plant and equipment in the importing country as part payment;

(d) *counterpurchase* – where the seller from the exporting country receives part payment for the goods in his own currency and the remainder in the local currency of the buyer, the latter then being used to purchase other products in the buyer's country.

See EXPORTING.

**countervailing duty** a special TAX levied by a country on a product imported from another country which is considered to have been 'dumped', that is, sold by a foreign firm in that country at a price below that which the firm charges for it in its own domestic market. See DUMPING for further discussion.

**coupon 1.** a voucher used as a means of promoting the sale of a product which is offered to buyers of the product to be redeemed for cash, gifts or other goods. Coupons can be mailed direct to households, printed in newspapers and magazines, incorporated into the packaging of the product, or distributed in a shop. See SALES PROMOTION.

**2.** a detachable slip which forms part of a SHARE CERTIFICATE or BOND and which is presented in order to claim the owner's entitlement to dividends or interest paid out on the security.

**covenant** a written agreement by a person to pay a given sum of money to some other person or organization for a specified period of time. Where a covenant arrangement allows a donor relief from income tax on any sums paid over, the covenant provides a tax-efficient means of making financial provision for a relative or charity.

**cover** see DIVIDEND COVER, INTEREST COVER.

**covered interest arbitrage** the borrowing and investing of foreign currencies to take advantage of differences in INTEREST RATES between countries. For example, a company could borrow an amount of one currency (say, the UK pound (£)), convert this into another currency (say, the US dollar ($)) and invest the proceeds in the USA. Concurrently, the company would sell $s for £s in the FORWARD MARKET for delivery at a future specified date. The company would earn a profit on such a transaction if the rate of return on its investment in the USA was greater than the combined expenses of interest payments on the amount of £s borrowed and the costs of concluding the forward exchange contract. Covered interest ARBITRAGE takes advantage of (and in the process eliminates) any temporary discrepancies between relative interest rates in two countries and the forward exchange rate of the two countries' currencies. See INTERNATIONAL FISHER EFFECT.

**covering** a means of protecting the domestic currency value of the future proceeds of an international trade transaction, usually by buying or selling the proceeds of the transaction in the FORWARD MARKET for foreign currencies.

**cover note** a document issued by an INSURANCE COMPANY to cover temporarily the period between the acceptance of an insurance risk and the issue of a detailed insurance policy to the client.

**CPU (Central Processing Unit)** the 'brain' of a COMPUTER which stores and processes data.

**craft union** SEE TRADE UNION.

**crash** any breakdown or malfunction of a COMPUTER.

**creative accounting** the use of discretion in the application of ACCOUNTING PRINCIPLES so as to report profit and asset figures which are flattering to the company. By subtle use of different DEPRECIATION methods for fixed assets, or different STOCK VALUATION methods, or techniques like OFF-BALANCE SHEET FINANCING, a company's senior managers can 'massage' or 'window-dress' the profits for any trading period to impress shareholders. Such interpretations are legal, if somewhat dubious. Although the professional accounting bodies have issued STATEMENTS OF RECOMMENDED PRACTICE (SORPs) to try to curtail the scope for arbitrariness in the application of accounting principles when measuring business income, considerable latitude still exists in the interpretation of accounting data and the reporting of accounting results.

**credit 1.** *n.* a financial facility which enables a person or business to borrow MONEY to purchase (i.e. take immediate possession of) products, raw materials and components, etc. and to pay for them over an extended time period. Credit facilities come in a variety of forms including BANK LOANS and OVERDRAFTS, INSTALMENT CREDIT, CREDIT CARDS and TRADE CREDIT. Interest charges on credit may be fixed or variable according to the type of facilities offered or, in some cases, loans may be interest free as a means of stimulating business. See CREDIT CONTROL, MONETARY POLICY, EXPORTING, LETTER OF CREDIT, BILL OF EXCHANGE, CONSUMER CREDIT ACT 1974, INTEREST

RATE.

**2.** *v.* to acknowledge (in DOUBLE-ENTRY ACCOUNTS) the receipt of services rendered to a firm. This is done by making an accounting entry which records the value of goods or services received by the company in the company's account of the supplier of the goods or services. A credit entry in a company's double entry accounts represents either a decrease in the company's assets or an increase in its liabilities.

See DEBIT.

**credit card** a card issued by a financial institution (mainly COMMERCIAL BANKS and BUILDING SOCIETIES), which can be used generally to purchase goods and services on CREDIT up to an agreed limit, or, for example, by a retail group for in-house purchases only. Credit cards are a convenient way of making purchases and many issuers provide the facility interest-free, provided clients pay off the outstanding balance in full when due. In the UK, retailers pay the credit card companies, on average, around 2% commission to participate in the credit card schemes and may pass on this charge to customers who pay for products by credit card rather than cash.

**credit control 1.** the control exercised by a firm over its TRADE DEBTORS to ensure that customers pay their DEBTS on time and to minimize the risk of BAD DEBTS. Credit control involves: assessing the creditworthiness of new and established customers to determine borrowing limits and terms; encouraging prompt payment by offering cash discounts and monitoring and recording payments due; the recovering of bad debts. Effective credit control minimizes the funds which a firm has tied up in debtors, so improving profitability and LIQUIDITY. See FACTORING, DEBTORS RATIO, WORKING CAPITAL RATIO.

**2.** the regulation of borrowing from the COMMERCIAL BANKS, FINANCE HOUSES, etc. by the monetary authorities in order to exercise control over the level of spending in the economy. See MONETARY POLICY.

**credit note** a document issued by a supplier to a customer giving the customer CREDIT for any products returned by the customer for which payment has already been received.

**creditors (accounts payable)** the money owed to individuals or firms because they have supplied goods, services or raw materials for which they have not yet been paid (trade creditors), or because they have made LOANS. Amounts falling due for payment within one year are counted as part of a company's CURRENT LIABILITIES in its BALANCE SHEET, while amounts falling due after more than one year appear as part of long-term liabilities.

Some creditors, called secured creditors, are offered collateral or security for their loans by means of a fixed charge on a specific asset owned by a debtor, which they could legally claim in the event of default on the loan. Other secured creditors are offered security by means of a 'floating charge' on the debtors' assets, which would offer them priority in claiming the proceeds from the sale of these assets in the event of default. Unsecured creditors such as trade creditors have less security in the event of default.

See DEBTORS (ACCOUNTS RECEIVABLE), CREDIT, CREDITORS RATIO.

**creditors ledger** see LEDGER, ACCOUNTING.

**creditors ratio** an accounting measure of a firm's average period of CREDIT taken from suppliers, which expresses the amount owed by the firm to period-end CREDITORS as a ratio of its average daily purchases (or sales). The resulting figure shows how many days on average the firm took to pay its creditors. Compare DEBTORS RATIO.

**credit period** the average number of days' (or weeks') CREDIT granted to customers by a company, or the average time it takes for the company to collect its debts. See CREDIT CONTROL, AGE ANALYSIS PROFILE FOR DEBTORS.

**credit rating** an assessment of the creditworthiness of a firm or an individual, which indicates the amount of CREDIT they can reasonably be allowed by a supplier.

The creditworthiness of a company can often be assessed on the basis of information derived from the company's past annual report and accounts, and from confidential details provided by the company's bank. Additionally, there are a number of specialized credit rating companies, such as Dunn and Bradstreet in the UK, who provide information about the creditworthiness of companies in return for a fee.

The creditworthiness of individual customers is more difficult to assess and is often based on some hard information such as court bankruptcy proceedings and default information on hire purchase agreements, together with circumstantial information such as the postal areas in which a potential debtor lives (indicating a suburb or inner city estate, for example). Firms specialize in collecting and processing such data and provide credit ratings in return for a fee. Under the terms of the UK CONSUMER CREDIT ACT, an individual has a right to inspect any credit record kept about them by such a firm.

Suppliers use credit ratings as a means of determining the maximum amount of credit to allow a customer as part of their CREDIT CONTROL procedures.

**credit squeeze** an attempt by the monetary authorities to reduce the amount of CREDIT granted by financial institutions to consumers and businesses, in order to reduce the level of spending in the economy. A credit squeeze forces up INTEREST RATES, affecting businesses by reducing consumer demand and raising the cost of financing stockholding and investment.

**creditworthiness** see CREDIT CONTROL.

**Crest** a paperless settlement system which was introduced in 1996 to cut the costs and speed up the completion of dealings on the UK STOCK MARKET. Under Crest, STOCK and SHARE transactions are recorded electronically, in contrast to the existing parallel system (TALISMAN) which involves the issue of settlement papers and share certificates. However, as with Talisman, investors will still receive a contract note from their broker to confirm their purchase or sale.

**criminal law** a body of rules which the State imposes upon individuals for the protection of other individuals and to restrain antisocial behaviour. Criminal law covers such crimes as theft and fraud. Prosecution of the accused is at the instance of the State and could result in imprisonment or fines as a punishment if the accused is found guilty.

**critical function structure** an ORGANIZATION structure in which one management function is considered so important that it is organized separately to some extent from the rest of the organization. For example, in retailing the overall structure is often the geographical variant of the PRODUCT-BASED STRUCTURE, with DECENTRALIZATION of AUTHORITY to an area or regional manager; however, standardized merchandising is considered so critical to the organization's success that this function is centralized on a functional basis (see Fig. 31).

**critical incident technique** an examination of a series of important incidents in an employee's work performance so as to isolate the factors which determine effectiveness. Usually

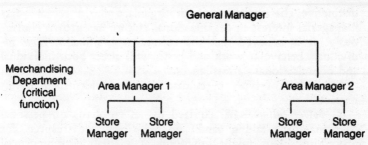

Fig. 31. **Critical function structure.** A typical example.

the employees will be asked to suggest these critical incidents themselves and to indicate what influenced their effectiveness, or lack of it, in each case. This method can be used in PERFORMANCE APPRAISAL, especially when a key objective is improving work performance. Its benefits are that it encourages individuals to consider their own performance, and in so far as they propose the issues to be considered it can make appraisal a fairly open and nonthreatening process.

**critical path analysis** see NETWORK ANALYSIS.

**cross chart** see RELATIONSHIP CHART.

**cross-elasticity of demand** see ELASTICITY OF DEMAND.

**cross-licence** see LICENCE.

**cross rate** the EXCHANGE RATE between two foreign currencies derived from the exchange rate of each of these currencies in terms of a common third currency. For example, the exchange rate between the UK pound and the German Deutschmark would be calculated by reference to the exchange rate of each of these currencies against, say, the US dollar.

**cross-subsidization** see SUBSIDY.

**CSO** see CENTRAL STATISTICAL OFFICE.

**cultural values** the perceptions, beliefs and standards which people acquire from the society in which they grew up. Differences in cultural values both *between* countries and between ethnic groups *within* a country (subcultures) are often important in designing a company's MARKET SEGMENTATION strategies.

**culture** the norms and shared attitudes that pervade an ORGANIZATION. It may be expressed in symbols, rituals and the language used by organization members. It thus constitutes the distinctive characteristics of an organization. In recent years managerial interest in organizational culture has grown enormously. It is believed that the culture will influence how individuals behave at work and hence will affect both individual and organizational performances.

A number of types of culture have been identified in this respect:

(a) *power culture*, characterized by an emphasis on personal charisma, risk-taking and a low level of respect for procedures. This might be found in a small entrepreneurial organization, where power tends to be concentrated in the entrepreneur;

(b) *rôle culture*, characterized by well-defined procedures and job roles, and an emphasis on conformity. This might be found in an established BUREAUCRACY for example government administration;

(c) *task culture*, characterized by an emphasis on problem solving by expert teams. Groups are formed to deal with particular problems. Once the task is completed the group may be disbanded. Here the culture is one which attaches importance to expertise, though in fact expertise may be less developed in organizations of this sort than in role culture organizations, where job roles are more specialized. Task culture places a much greater emphasis on flexibility and creativity than does role culture;

(d) *person-oriented culture*, characterized by an emphasis on meeting the needs of individuals in the organization. This is often found in small, 'alternative' organizations. It may also characterize small organizations composed mainly of PROFESSIONALS, such as small consultancy companies, where it is deemed important that individuals be given some freedom to shape their jobs so that they can pursue particular professional or other 'acceptable' outside interests (for example, being a local councillor).

A concern of many managers in recent years has been that the prevailing culture of their organization is inappropriate, or even obstructive, to a desired change in objectives. For instance, a rôle culture, where jobs are specialized and well-defined, could obstruct creativity and hence prevent an organization from becoming more entrepreneurial. As a result much attention recently has been devoted to changing cultures.

It is doubtful, however, whether managers can actually achieve dramatic cultural change in the short term. Culture is influenced by a complex of factors, such as the character and background of the workforce, many of which are to some extent independent of managerial action.

See MANAGEMENT STYLE, MECHANISTIC AND ORGANISMIC.

**cum-dividend 1.** *adj.* (of a particular SHARE) including the right to receive the DIVIDEND which attaches to a SHARE.

**2.** *adv.* with dividend. If shares are purchased on the STOCK MARKET, 'cum-div', the purchaser would be entitled to the dividend accruing to those shares when the dividend is next paid. Compare EX-DIVIDEND.

**cumulative preference share** see PREFERENCE SHARE.

**currency** or **cash** the coins and bank notes which constitute the physical component of a country's MONEY SUPPLY, i.e. coins and notes have a physical identity, whereas the other assets comprising the money supply, such as bank deposits, are book-keeping entries and have no tangible life of their own. See LEGAL TENDER, FOREIGN CURRENCY.

**currency matching** the financial management practice within multinational companies of matching their foreign currency holdings with equal foreign currency borrowings in order to minimize their exposure to losses from exchange rate changes. See EXCHANGE RATE EXPOSURE.

**currency swap** see SWAP.

**currency translation** the translation of the financial accounts of foreign subsidiaries, which are expressed in terms of local currencies, into the currency of the parent company so that they can be included in the CONSOLIDATED ACCOUNTS. Thus a UK MULTINATIONAL ENTERPRISE with a US subsidiary would need to translate the accounts of the subsidiary expressed in dollars into sterling in order to consolidate them with its UK accounts. The most common method of translation is the *closing rate method* which translates all ASSETS, LIABILITIES, REVENUES and COSTS at the currency exchange rate ruling at the end-date of the ACCOUNTING PERIOD.

**current account 1.** an individual's or company's account kept at a COMMERCIAL BANK or BUILDING SOCIETY into which the customer can deposit cash or cheques and from which he or she can draw cheques or make withdrawals on a day-to-day basis.

# CURRENT ASSETS

**2.** a financial record of a country's trade in GOODS and SERVICES with the rest of the world (see BALANCE OF PAYMENTS).

**current assets** ASSETS such as STOCKS, money owed by DEBTORS, and cash, which are held for short-term conversion within a firm as raw materials are bought, made up, sold as finished goods and eventually paid for. See FIXED ASSETS, WORKING CAPITAL, WORKING CAPITAL RATIO.

**current cost accounting** see INFLATION ACCOUNTING.

**current liabilities** all obligations to pay out cash at some date in the near future, including amounts which a firm owes to trade CREDITORS and BANK LOANS/OVERDRAFTS. See WORKING CAPITAL, WORKING CAPITAL RATIO.

**current/noncurrent method** see FOREIGN CURRENCY TRANSLATION.

**current purchasing power accounting** see INFLATION ACCOUNTING.

**current ratio** or **acid-test ratio** an accounting measure of a firm's ability to pay its short-term liabilities out of its quickly-realizable CURRENT ASSETS, which expresses the firm's liquid current assets (DEBTORS plus cash) as a ratio of CURRENT LIABILITIES. Sometimes called the 'quick ratio', this is a more stringent test of liquidity than the WORKING CAPITAL RATIO, because it excludes STOCK from CURRENT ASSETS on the grounds that STOCKS cannot be as readily convertible into cash to meet short-term debts as can DEBTORS where the goods or services have already been sold and only collecting the money remains.

**current yield** see YIELD.

**custom and practice** a way of doing things that receives its justification from the claim that 'things have always been done like this' rather than from any specific rule. In INDUSTRIAL RELATIONS it generally refers to working practices which are operated by workforces and TRADE UNIONS and which are implicitly condoned by management, but have not been explicitly sanctioned in a formal agreement. The buying-out of such practices is often the subject of productivity initiatives tabled by managements during COLLECTIVE BARGAINING. See RESTRICTIVE LABOUR PRACTICE.

**customer** a BUYER of a good or service from a BUSINESS. See also INTERNAL CUSTOMER.

**customer centred** see CONSUMER ORIENTATION.

**customer resistance** consumers' unwillingness to buy a product or BRAND because of their misgivings about it. Their objections could be based on some dislike of the product's functional attributes, their view about its price and value to them, or antipathy towards the product's image. See SELLING.

**customer service** the marketing and technical functions within a firm, which deal direct with customers. Customer services can involve offering pre-sales services, such as providing advice to customers on their product needs; and AFTER-SALES SERVICES, such as repair and maintenance back-up and the replacement of faulty products or parts. Customer services are an important part of the MARKETING MIX, serving to attract new customers and reinforcing BRAND LOYALTY among existing customers. See GUARANTEE.

**customer target** the MARKET SEGMENT or segments identified by the firm as offering considerable sales potential and on which the firm focuses its marketing efforts. See MARKET SEGMENTATION.

**customization** the adaption of a good or service to meet the particular requirements of a specific customer or group of customers. Extreme customization involves the design and production of a different product for each customer, which tends to be expensive. In order to achieve cost savings associated with ECONOMIES OF SCALE firms may prefer to produce a limited range of standardized products (see STANDARDIZATION). As a compromise firms often seek to produce a single standardized product which can then be varied slightly through customization to meet broadly the requirements of different groups of buyers.

See MARKET SEGMENTATION, PRODUCT RANGE.

**Customs and Excise** a UK government department responsible for the administration and collection of REVENUES from VALUE ADDED TAX, EXCISE DUTIES and CUSTOMS DUTIES. The department is responsible for policing and enforcing the revenue laws and restrictions and prohibitions on the IMPORT and EXPORT of certain goods, as well as for the control of smuggling. Customs and Excise also provides statistical details of taxes raised and the volume and value of UK overseas trade; these are used by the Treasury or the Central Statistical Office in compiling budget and balance of payments returns. See IMPORTING, EXPORTING.

## CUSTOMS DUTY

**customs duty** a form of EXPENDITURE TAX which is levied by the government on foreign products imported into the country. Customs duties are used mainly to raise revenue for the government, although they can serve, like TARIFFS, to reduce domestic spending on imports. See IMPORT, CUSTOMS AND EXCISE.

**customs union** see FREE TRADE BLOC.

**cut-off date** the date, coinciding with the end of an accounting period, after which goods received from suppliers or sold to customers will not enter the accounting records for that accounting period but will be recorded at the start of the next accounting period. This date is of particular importance to the stocktaking at the period end and to the measurement of sales, purchases and profit.

**cut-off rate** the minimum rate of return used in INVESTMENT APPRAISAL for the purpose of deciding if an investment project is to go ahead. A predetermined arbitrary cut-off rate may be used in place of the COST OF CAPITAL as the DISCOUNT RATE. Different cut-off rates may be employed for projects with different degrees of riskiness. See DISCOUNTED CASH FLOW.

**cut-throat competition** see PRICE WAR.

**cycle time** the time which is required at each work station (machine or operative) to complete the workload allocated to it. Cycle times are important in PRODUCTION LINE or ASSEMBLY-LINE balancing to ensure the smooth flow of raw materials, components and work in progress from work station to work station, thereby avoiding bottlenecks and idle periods.

**cyclical ordering system** see FIXED INTERVAL REORDER SYSTEM.

**cyclical unemployment** see UNEMPLOYMENT, BUSINESS CYCLE.

**cyclical variation** see SALES FORECASTING.

# D

**DAGMAR (Defining Advertising Goals for Measured Advertising Response)** a marketing model which suggests that there are a number of stages of consumer response to products, namely unawareness; awareness; comprehension; conviction and action. The model can help in devising advertising and promotion strategies which persuade potential customers to buy a product.

**damages** money awarded by a court to a plaintiff who has suffered loss at the hands of the defendant as a result of breach of CONTRACT or a TORT committed by the defendant.

**databank** a collection of information on a specific topic, such as consumer purchases, which is added to over time.

**database** a COMPUTER software package which enables data to be created and stored, to be retrieved and analysed later. Databases can, for example, store names and addresses of potential or past customers which can be used to produce mailing lists for SALES PROMOTIONS.

**data processing** the organization and processing of information in a business. The use of COMPUTERS to store data (see DATA STORAGE) and to undertake routine data processing activities such as recording purchases, sales, payroll etc. can save time, improve recording accuracy and reduce staffing costs. See INFORMATION MANAGEMENT, LOCAL AREA NETWORK.

**data storage** the storing of business documentation. This can involve the accumulation of physical 'paper mountains' with attendant problems of space availability, extra staff and retrieval. However, many firms now use COMPUTER-based electronic systems such as *document image processing* (DIP). DIP compresses a document into a series of digits which is indexed and stored on a disk file; scanners search and retrieve information held on disk, reproducing items by laser printout.

See INFORMATION MANAGEMENT.

**dawn raid** a situation in which a potential TAKEOVER bidder for a company buys a substantial shareholding in the target company at current market prices, often through intermediaries (to disguise the identity of the bidder). This shareholding can then be used as a platform for a full takeover bid for all the shares at a stated offer price. In the UK, company law provisions on DISCLOSURE OF SHAREHOLDINGS, requiring shareholders with more than 3% of the shares in a public company to declare such shareholdings to the directors of that company, have made it more difficult to mount a dawn raid. See TAKE-OVER BID, CITY CODE ON TAKEOVERS AND MERGERS.

**day book** see JOURNAL.

**DE** see DEPARTMENT OF EMPLOYMENT.

**dead stock** raw materials, work in progress or finished goods which have not been used for a considerable time. Businesses need to employ careful STOCK CONTROLS, monitoring the usage rate of STOCK items in order to avoid tying up WORKING CAPITAL in high levels of redundant stock.

**dealer** see TRADER.

**death duty** see INHERITANCE TAX.

**death rate** see POPULATION.

**debentures** a means of financing companies through fixed-interest LOANS secured against company ASSETS. In some cases the company may offer a specific asset such as a particular machine as security for the loan (fixed charge); in other cases lenders are offered security by means of a general claim against all company assets in the event of default (floating charge). Most debentures are redeemable by the borrower at a future specified date, say 10 or 15 years from the date of issue. Some debentures, however, are irredeemable and never have to be repaid, the lender continuing to be rewarded through interest payments forever. See LOAN CAPITAL.

**debit 1.** *n.* a means of charging (in DOUBLE-ENTRY ACCOUNTS) for services rendered by a firm. This is done by making an accounting entry which records the value of GOODS or SERVICES supplied by the company in the company's account of the customer for these goods and services. A debit entry in a company's DOUBLE-ENTRY ACCOUNTS represents either an increase in the company's assets or a decrease in its LIABILITIES.

**2.** *v.* to enter the value of goods or services supplied to a customer in the supplying company's account of that customer. See CREDIT, definition 2.

**debit note** a document issued by a supplier to a customer charging the customer for any additional products supplied to the customer for which payment has not been received.

**debt** an amount of money owed by one person, company, etc. to another. Debts result from borrowing money to purchase a product, service or financial asset (e.g. INSTALMENT CREDIT). Debt contracts provide for the eventual repayment of the sum borrowed and include INTEREST charges for the duration of the LOAN. See DEBTORS, BORROWER.

**debt collection** see CREDIT CONTROL.

**debt control** see LOAN CAPITAL.

**debt finance** see LOAN CAPITAL.

**debtors (accounts receivable)** the money owed by individuals or firms because they have bought goods, services or raw materials for which they have not yet paid (trade DEBTORS), or because they have borrowed money. See CREDITORS (ACCOUNTS PAYABLE), DEBT, DEBTORS RATIO, CREDIT CONTROL, WORKING CAPITAL, BAD DEBT.

**debtors ledger** see LEDGER, ACCOUNTING.

**debtors ratio, average collection period** or **debtor days ratio** an accounting measure of a firm's average collection period for DEBTS, which expresses the amount owed by firm's period-end DEBTORS as a ratio of its average daily sales. The resulting figure shows the average period that customers took to pay their debts, expressed in days. See CREDITORS RATIO, CREDIT CONTROL, BAD DEBT, FACTORING.

**debt servicing** the cost of meeting INTEREST payments and regular contractual repayments of principal on a LOAN, along with any administration charges borne by the BORROWER.

**debug** to identify and remove errors from a COMPUTER program.

**'decency threshold'** see LOW PAY.

**decentralization** the relocation of managerial AUTHORITY and RESPONSIBILITY to a lower level in the ORGANIZATION. A restructuring of a FUNCTIONAL STRUCTURE to a PRODUCT-BASED STRUCTURE will generally involve some degree of decentralization, especially regarding operational (but not strategic) matters. In the 1980s many organizations attempted to decentralize further, shifting some decision-making to STRATEGIC BUSINESS UNITS and PROFIT CENTRES. The rationale was that decentralization would increase the motivation of lower-level managers and enable the organization to respond faster to product market developments. See CENTRALIZATION, ORGANIZATIONAL ANALYSIS.

**decentralized bargaining** see COLLECTIVE BARGAINING.

**deciles** the numerical values that divide a group of numerical observations into 10 parts, each containing an equal number of observations. Deciles are frequently applied to data arranged in decreasing numerical order. Consequently one-tenth of the observations will exceed the first decile, two-tenths will exceed the second decile, etc. Compare QUARTILES, PERCENTILES.

**decision making** see ORGANIZATIONAL ANALYSIS, 'GARBAGE-CAN' MODEL OF DECISION MAKING, DISJOINTED INCREMENTALISM.

**decision support system** a procedure which is concerned with getting appropriate information to managers as and when they need it and which aids the manager in making decisions. Decision support systems are generally based upon interactive COMPUTER networks which can help the manager to solve problems and to gauge the effects of alternative outcomes of a decision.

See INFORMATION MANAGEMENT.

**decision tree** an aid to decision making in uncertain conditions, that sets out alternative courses of action and the financial consequences of each alternative, and assigns subjective probabilities to the likelihood of future events occurring. For example, a firm thinking of opening a new factory the success of which will depend upon consumer spending (and thus the state of the economy) would have a decision tree like Fig. 32.

In order to make a decision, the manager needs a decision criterion to enable him to choose which he regards as the best of the alternatives and, since these choices involve an element of risk, we therefore need to know something about his attitudes to risk. If the manager were neutral in his attitude to risk then we could calculate the *certainty equivalent* of the 'open factory' alternative using the expected money value criterion, which takes the financial consequence of each outcome and weights it by the probability of its occurrence, thus:

$$0.5 \times + £80,000 = + £40,000$$
$$0.5 \times - £30,000 = - £15,000$$
$$+ £25,000$$

which being greater than the £0 for certain of not opening the factory would justify going ahead with the factory project.

However, if the manager were averse to risk then he might not regard the expected money value criterion as being appropriate, for he might require a risk premium to induce him to take the risk. Application of a more cautious certainty equivalent criterion would reduce the certainty equivalent of the 'open factory' branch and might even tip the decision against going ahead on the grounds of the 'downside risk' of losing £30,000.

See UNCERTAINTY AND RISK.

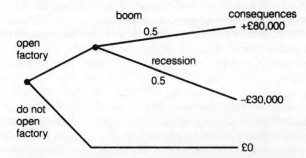

Fig. 32. **Decision tree.** The businessman has two options: to open a new factory to boost production capacity or not to open a new factory; and he has to consider two states of nature or events which can occur: economic boom or recession. The businessman must assess the likelihood of each of these events occurring and, in this case, based on his knowledge and experience, he estimates that there is a one-in-two chance of a boom and a 0.5 probability of a recession. Finally, the businessman estimates the financial consequences as a £80,000 profit for the new factory if there is a boom, and a £30,000 loss if there is a recession.

**decline phase** see PRODUCT LIFE CYCLE.

**declining industry strategy** see ENDGAME STRATEGY.

**defective work** work in progress or finished goods which fail to pass INSPECTION because they do not conform to the standards laid down. Defective work may arise because of poor workmanship, poor supervision, poor materials or poor machine maintenance. See QUALITY CONTROL.

**deferred tax** a PROVISION which a company may make to reflect the difference between CORPORATION TAX actually payable (based on CAPITAL ALLOWANCES), and the tax which would have been payable if the charge had been based solely on accounting profits (reflecting DEPRECIATION rates applied).

**deficiency payment** see AGRICULTURAL POLICY.

**deflation** a fall in the rate of growth of the general level of prices in an economy, or an absolute reduction in the general level of prices (see PRICE INDEX). The authorities may seek to deflate the economy in order to combat INFLATION and eliminate a BALANCE OF PAYMENTS deficit by using restrictive monetary and fiscal measures, i.e. increasing interest rates and taxes to cut spending. See ECONOMIC POLICY, MONETARY POLICY, FISCAL POLICY, PRICES AND INCOMES POLICY.

**de-industrialization** a sustained fall in the proportion of national output accounted for by the industrial (manufacturing, construction, etc.) sector of the economy. See STRUCTURE OF INDUSTRY.

**de-layering** the removal of tiers in an ORGANIZATION's HIERARCHY. This is often implemented to shorten lines of communication and to increase the speed of decision-making. It often forms part of an attempt at DECENTRALIZATION and has been associated with moves to shift authority away from hierarchically organized functional departments to multi-function process teams, as in BUSINESS PROCESS RE-ENGINEERING. Currently a fashionable term, many view it as a euphemism for measures aimed at contraction and labour-shedding. Middle managers are particularly susceptible to REDUNDANCY as a result of de-layering. See DOWNSIZING, SCALAR CONCEPT.

**delegation** the passing of certain duties or decisions by a manager or SUPERVISOR to a subordinate whilst still retaining overall AUTHORITY for them. Delegation can increase a subordinate's JOB SATISFACTION whilst reducing the workload of a manager. See MANAGEMENT.

**delivered price system** see GEOGRAPHICAL PRICING.

**delivery cost** see STOCKHOLDING MODEL.

**delivery date** the agreed date by which a supplier will deliver GOODS or SERVICES ordered by a customer. This date is often specified as part of the terms of a CONTRACT OF SALE and the CONTRACT may specify financial penalties for late delivery. Meeting delivery dates is an important element in the MARKET-

ING MIX for winning and retaining customers. See 'JUST-IN-TIME' (JIT) SYSTEM.

**delivery note** a document sent by a supplier to a customer at the time when products are supplied, itemizing the physical quantities of product supplied. Thereafter an INVOICE is usually sent to the customer showing the money value of products supplied. Compare STATEMENT OF ACCOUNT.

**Delors plan** see EUROPEAN MONETARY SYSTEM.

**Delphi technique** an approach to generating new ideas or problem-solving amongst a GROUP or team. Each member or interested party submits his or her recommendations or views on the issue under review to a central contact point. All ideas generated in this way are then circulated to all those participating in the process, who then have the opportunity to submit comments on them. This process is repeated until a consensus emerges. Although time consuming, it can be an effective approach to the management of change since it enables all interested parties to express their views, generates consensus and, by incorporating all in the decision-making process, tends to generate commitment to the final outcome. See TECHNOLOGICAL FORECASTING.

**demand** the amount of a product which is purchased at a particular price at a particular point in time. A *demand curve* is a line showing the relationship between the price of a product and the quantity demanded per time period over a range of possible prices. Demand curves are usually downward-sloping, indicating that as the price of the product falls, more is demanded. The extent to which the demand for a product will increase as price falls (and the extent to which demand will drop if the price rises) depends on the product's price-ELASTICITY OF DEMAND. The demand for a product, however, is determined also by a variety of non-price factors. A *demand function* attempts to incorporate *all* the factors that have a statistically significant influence on demand; for example, consumers' incomes, the prices of substitute products, advertising, etc. Demand curves will shift if any of these factors change over time.

In practice, firms are unable to derive definitive demand curves because of incomplete information. For this reason many firms use a COST-BASED PRICING formula for determining prices, but allow for the influence of demand by varying the profit mark-up (see DEMAND-BASED PRICING, COMPETITION-BASED PRICING).

There are various methods a firm can use to 'forecast' demand, including time series analysis, barometric indicators and econometric models.

See SALES FORECASTING.

**demand-based pricing** pricing methods which determine the PRICE of a product primarily on the basis of intensity of demand rather than on costs of production and distribution. There are several facets of demand which are relevant to pricing:

(a) Firms may vary their prices over time as demand for their products changes as a result of BUSINESS CYCLES, charging higher prices when demand is strong and shading down prices in conditions of weak demand. More specifically, particular products will be subject to variations in demand over their PRODUCT LIFE CYCLE with implications for pricing. High skimming prices may be charged for a novel product in the early launch phase of its life cycle when demand is price-inelastic, with lower prices and larger promotion expenditures in the later, growth phase of its life cycle;

(b) Firms may also practise price discrimination, varying prices between types of customers, the location of customers, the time of purchase and versions of a product. Customer-based pricing recognizes the different bargaining power of potential buyers and seeks to capitalize on this by charging whatever price particular customers are prepared to pay. For example, in pricing theatre tickets special low prices may be charged to low income, price-sensitive consumers (for example, students and pensioners), and price discounts may be offered on block bookings. In addition, prices may be scaled for theatre seats in different parts of the theatre, with higher prices for the stalls and lower prices for the upper circle. Furthermore, different prices may be charged on different days or at different times of the day, with higher prices for week-end evening performances and lower prices for mid-week afternoon matinée performances. Finally, prices can be varied according to the version of a product, with different prices for a particular model of car, for example, according to whether the customer specifies fabric or leather seats.

See COST-BASED PRICING, COMPETITION-BASED PRICING, ELASTICITY

OF DEMAND.

**demand curve** see EQUILIBRIUM MARKET PRICE.

**demand forecasting** see SALES FORECASTING.

**demand-pull inflation** see INFLATION.

**demarcation line** the boundary between those tasks workers are permitted to do and those which they are not, as established by their TRADE UNION or by themselves collectively. Characteristically, demarcation lines develop in workplaces where there are several unions representing different occupational groups: their function is to establish which unions' members can work on which job, and hence to ensure that the unions do not damage each others' interests. They are usually policed by SHOP STEWARDS. Demarcation lines have been criticized for their potentially damaging impact on efficiency and LABOUR FLEXIBILITY, especially where tasks either side of the line are very similar. See RESTRICTIVE LABOUR PRACTICE.

**de-merger** the break-up of a company, originally formed through a MERGER, into two (or more) separate companies. This is most easily achieved when the original businesses comprising the merger have continued to be run as separate divisions of the enlarged group. In this case, for example, the A-B company could be split into separate quoted companies, A and B, with the company's existing shareholders being given shares in *both* companies. Thus, unlike a DIVESTMENT (the sale of a division to outside interests) or a MANAGEMENT BUY-OUT (the sale of a division to its existing management), initially at least the companies continue to be owned by their existing shareholders.

A de-merger may occur because the merged company has failed to perform up to expectations because of internal conflicts of management, or result from a rethink of the company's BUSINESS STRATEGY favouring a concentration on 'core' businesses.

**demographic segmentation** the division of a market into SOCIOECONOMIC GROUPS according to demographic variables like age, sex, occupation, education and family size. See MARKET SEGMENTATION.

**demography** the analysis of human POPULATIONS according to their total size, birth rates, death rates and migration; the age and sex distribution of populations and their geographical and occupational distributions; racial and religious profiles, etc.

## DENATIONALIZATION

Firms need to monitor changes in the demographic environment because these changes can have a significant impact on the demand for particular CONSUMER GOODS and SERVICES. For instance, the increase in the proportions of elderly citizens in the total population in most industrialized countries over recent decades has created new market opportunities for companies in such areas as health care and leisure products; while declining birth rates have reduced the demand for children's clothing and toys.

See SOCIOECONOMIC GROUP.

**denationalization** see NATIONALIZATION VERSUS PRIVATIZATION.

**department** a grouping of similar or closely related JOB roles into a discrete section within an ORGANIZATION, for example, the finance department. Departments may be confined to one level of the HIERARCHY or, as in FUNCTIONAL STRUCTURED organizations, extend over several levels and contain their own hierarchy. Grouping of tasks in this way is generally necessary to facilitate the integration and CO-ORDINATION of activities, but there is the danger that departments will prioritize internal objectives over those of the organization as a whole. See BUREAUCRACY.

**departmental load** the amount of work which is allocated to a production department during a specified period of time. The loading will take into account delivery promises and the availability of plant and personnel. In scheduling production it is important to avoid any department becoming over-loaded. See PRODUCTION SCHEDULING.

**departmental location** the siting of a department within a firm. In the case of manufacturing, departments need to be located so that production can flow smoothly from one department to another over minimum distances and with a minimum of rehandling. Service departments such as materials stores and maintenance should likewise be sited in close proximity to the main production areas.

**Department of Employment (DE)** the UK government department responsible for helping people seeking work to find a job, and likewise employers with job vacancies to find suitable employees. To this end the DE operates a network of employment exchanges each serving a local area as well as running the unemployment benefits scheme for those unable to find employment. The DE is also responsible for overseeing various TRAINING schemes aimed at improving work SKILLS, such as the *youth training* scheme.

**Department of Health** the UK government department responsible for administering the National Health Service.

**Department of Social Security (DSS)** the UK government department responsible for administering the government's social welfare programmes. The DSS collects NATIONAL INSURANCE CONTRIBUTIONS which, together with other monies, are used to fund SOCIAL SECURITY BENEFIT such as unemployment benefit, child allowances, old-age pensions, etc.

**Department of the Environment (DOE)** the UK Government department responsible for controlling environmental POLLUTION and for the regulation of local authorities.

**Department of Trade and Industry (DTI)** the UK Government office which is primarily responsible for implementing and administering the Government's industrial and trade policies. A particular concern at the DTI is the promotion of greater efficiency through an INDUSTRIAL POLICY programme, which includes support for new business start-ups, consultancy services for small firms, research and development, and technology transfer. In the past, the DTI has been required by governments to involve itself in the rationalization of declining industries and support for 'failing' firms, but now the emphasis is very much on fostering greater enterprise by business itself, with a minimum of direct State intervention.

The DTI is responsible for the operation of REGIONAL POLICY, vetting applications for regional selective assistance by firms investing in the 'assisted areas' and enterprise zones. The DTI works closely with the OFFICE OF FAIR TRADING in matters affecting COMPETITION POLICY in general, and MERGER and TAKEOVER investigations in particular; the DTI regulates the formation of companies and their conduct through the REGISTRAR OF COMPANIES, and is responsible for issuing licences to deposit-taking institutions and authorizing dealers in stocks and shares, etc. (see FINANCIAL SERVICES ACT 1986). Finally, the DTI plays a prominent part in the running of the UK's overseas trade affairs, representing the country's interests at international (GENERAL AGREEMENT ON TARIFFS AND TRADE) and regional (EUROPEAN UNION/COMMUNITY) levels. The DTI is important in the promotion of exports through the Export Market Information Centre, British Overseas Trade Board and related back-up facilities and services, including the EXPORT CREDIT GUARANTEE DEPARTMENT (see EXPORTING).

See CONSUMER CREDIT ACT 1974, LOAN GUARANTEE SCHEME, PRICES ACT 1974, PRICE MARKING (BARGAIN OFFERS) ORDER 1979, TRADE DESCRIPTIONS ACT 1965, TECHNOLOGY TRANSFER.

**Department of Transport (DOT)** the UK Government department responsible for road, rail and sea transport.

**department store** a RETAILER which sells a great variety of products, the term 'department' denoting the fact that a typical store will be divided up into a large number of sections each offering a particular kind of merchandise: the food department, the footwear department, the toys and games department, etc. Department stores may be under single-shop ownership or run as a multiple CHAIN STORE business.

Department stores compete mainly by offering customers convenience ('everything under one roof'), personal service and good quality products rather than on the basis of SELF SERVICE and cut prices. The larger department stores are able to boost their profitability by obtaining BULK-BUYING discounts from manufacturers as well as by promoting their OWN LABEL BRANDS.

See DISTRIBUTION CHANNEL.

**deposit account** see COMMERCIAL BANK.

**depot 1.** a business premise which is used to warehouse (i.e. store) goods in transit as part of a physical DISTRIBUTION CHANNEL engaged in the movement of goods from their place of manufacture to WHOLESALERS and RETAILERS of the product.
**2.** a business premise which is used to provide a central parking facility for fleet operators of lorries, vans, coaches and buses who are engaged in the distribution of goods and the provision of travel services.

**depreciation** or **amortization 1.** the fall in the value of an ASSET during the course of its working life. The condition of plant and equipment used in production deteriorates over time and these items will eventually have to be replaced. Accordingly, a firm needs to make financial provision for the depreciation of its assets.

Depreciation is an accounting means of dividing up the HISTORIC COST of a FIXED ASSET over a number of accounting periods which correspond with the asset's estimated life. The depreciation charged against the revenue of successive time periods in the PROFIT-AND-LOSS ACCOUNT serves to spread the original cost of a fixed asset yielding benefit to the firm over several trading periods. In the period–end BALANCE SHEET such an asset would be included at its net book value (cost less cumulative depreciation deducted to date). This depreciation charge does not attempt to calculate the reducing market value of fixed assets, so that balance sheets do not show realization values.

Different formulas used to calculate depreciation can lead to variations in the balance sheet value of a fixed asset and in the charge against GROSS PROFIT for depreciation. The second formula in Fig. 33 gives a large depreciation charge in the early periods of the fixed asset's life and a small charge in the later years (accelerated depreciation). In the interests of consistency, firms generally do not change the depreciation formula used for their fixed assets but stick to the same formula indefinitely.

All these depreciation formulas base the depreciation charge on the historic cost of fixed assets. However, during a period of INFLATION it is likely that the REPLACEMENT COST of an asset is likely to be higher than its original cost. Therefore, prudent companies need to make PROVISION for higher replacement costs in the form of a REVALUATION RESERVE.

See INFLATION ACCOUNTING, CAPITAL CONSUMPTION, APPRECIATION, CREATIVE ACCOUNTING.

**2.** a decrease in the EXCHANGE RATE of a currency against other currencies under a FLOATING EXCHANGE RATE SYSTEM, reflecting a fall in market demand for that currency combined with a rise in market demand for other countries' currencies. The effect of a depreciation is to make imports (in the local currency) more expensive and exports (in the local currency) cheaper, thereby assisting in the removal of a BALANCE OF PAYMENTS deficit by acting to reduce import demand for goods and services and increasing export demand.

Depreciations, like DEVALUATION, provide firms with an opportunity to expand sales and boost profitability by improving their price competitiveness in both home and export markets.

See DEVALUATION for further discussion. Contrast with APPRECIATION, definition 2. See EXCHANGE RATE EXPOSURE.

# DEPRECIATION ADJUSTMENT

*Straight-line method*

| | Opening book value | Depreciation (£24,000 ÷ 3) | Closing book value |
|---|---|---|---|
| | £ | £ | £ |
| Year 1 | 24,000 | 8,000 | 16,000 |
| Year 2 | 16,000 | 8,000 | 8,000 |
| Year 3 | 8,000 | 8,000 | — |

The *straight-line method* divides the original cost of a fixed asset (£24,000) by its estimated life (three years), giving equal depreciation charges each trading period.

*Reducing-balance or diminishing-balance method*

| | Opening book value | Depreciation (50%) | Closing book value |
|---|---|---|---|
| | £ | £ | £ |
| Year 1 | 24,000 | 12,000 | 12,000 |
| Year 2 | 12,000 | 6,000 | 6,000 |
| Year 3 | 6,000 | 3,000 | 3,000 |

The *reducing-balance method* writes off, each trading period, a fixed percentage of the net book value of the fixed asset at the beginning of the period.

Fig. 33. **Depreciation.** Two methods of calculating depreciation.

**depreciation adjustment** SCC INFLATION ACCOUNTING.

**depression** see BUSINESS CYCLE.

**deregulation** the removal of controls over a particular economic activity which have been imposed by the government or some other regulatory body, for example an industry trade association. Deregulation may be initiated either because the controls are no longer seen as necessary (for example the ending of PRICE CONTROLS to combat inflation); or because they are over-restrictive, preventing companies from taking advantage of business opportunities (for example the ending of most FOREIGN EXCHANGE CONTROLS by the UK in 1979 designed to liberalize overseas physical and portfolio investment).

Deregulation has assumed particular significance in the context of recent initiatives by the UK government to stimulate greater competition by, for example, allowing private companies to compete for business in areas (such as local bus services) hitherto confined to central government or local authority operators. The Government has also initiated programmes of deregulation in the employment protection field, because it believes that extensive regulation imposes an unwelcome burden on business, stifling flexibility and inhibiting the action of market forces.

Conversely, government initiatives can be seen to have promoted regulation in so far as they have imposed rules on how trade unions should conduct their affairs (see TRADE UNION ACT 1984). Also, paradoxically, the privatization of nationalized industries has in some cases led to greater regulation of their activities, because public pressure has necessitated the creation of regulatory agencies to ensure that private monopoly status is not abused at consumers' expense.

See NATIONALIZATION VERSUS PRIVATIZATION, EMPLOYMENT ACT 1989.

**derivative** a financial instrument such as an OPTION or SWAP whose value is derived from some other financial asset (for example, a STOCK or SHARE) or indices (for example, a price index for a commodity such as cocoa). Derivatives are traded on the FORWARD MARKETS and are used by businesses and dealers to 'hedge' against future movements in share, commodity etc. prices and by speculators seeking to secure windfall profits.

**de-seasonalize** see SALES FORECASTING.

**design** the process of translating a product idea into a product which can be produced and marketed on a commercial basis. Though design is a creative process it has economic consequences insofar as a product's shape, configuration and performance affect its marketability and its cost of production. In order to achieve high product variety without involving an excessive variety of components, designers often use common, interchangeable parts and design products on a modular basis.

In order to remain competitive, firms need continously to review the design of their products in the light of new developments in materials and processes. The technique of VALUE ANALAYSIS is used to identify possible sources of cost savings without impairing a product's performance.

See COMPUTER AIDED DESIGN, NEW PRODUCT DEVELOPMENT.

## DESIGN RIGHTS

**design rights** the legal ownership by persons or businesses of original designs of the shape or configuration of industrial products. In the UK, the COPYRIGHT, DESIGNS AND PATENTS ACT 1988 gives protection to the creators of industrial designs against unauthorized copying for a period of 10 years after the first marketing of the product. Design right protection is automatic and there are no registration requirements. Design right is an exclusive right for five years after first marketing and then becomes subject to licences of right for the remaining five years. If a design right is infringed, the design right owner (or licensee) may seek an injunction from the courts preventing further abuses, with offenders liable to pay damages/fines.

Under the Registered Design Act 1949, designs judged to be original *solely* by their outward appearance (i.e. by 'eye appeal' and not by their functioning) can be registered with the Designs Registry, a branch of the PATENT OFFICE. This facility has been continued by the 1988 Act which increased the term of protection for registered designs from a maximum of 15 years to 25 years.

**desk research** SEE MARKETING INTELLIGENCE.

**de-unionization** the termination by management of COLLECTIVE BARGAINING and representational rights of TRADE UNIONS in an organization. If managers decide to de-unionize, they will need to withdraw unions' rights to represent aggrieved employees in disputes with management and to cease to negotiate pay and conditions with them. Instead, management will unilaterally determine rates of pay and the relevant terms of the CONTRACT OF EMPLOYMENT. To achieve de-unionization, managers may also need to engineer the dismissal of key union activists.

The rationale for de-unionization is that union action leads to wages being artificially high (i.e. higher than the 'true' market rate) and inhibits LABOUR FLEXIBILITY (by generating RESTRICTIVE LABOUR PRACTICES). However, some labour economists claim that unions bring efficiency benefits. By 'giving voice' to employee grievances they defuse them and, by forcing wages up they provide an incentive to firms to invest in labour-saving technology. Firms also often find it easier to negotiate with employee representatives rather than directly with each individual employee.

De-unionization strategies have been rare in recent years in the UK, though in the 1980s some employers sought to terminate collective bargaining over managerial pay and replace it with a performance-based system of pay determination (see MERIT PAY). Even where organizations de-recognize unions it does not necessarily end union activity. Trade unions may continue to recruit employees into union membership. If a sizeable proportion of the organization's employees remain or become union members, managers may find it difficult to sustain the non-union recognition policy, even though there is no longer a statutory procedure for achieving union recognition in the UK.

See MANAGEMENT STYLE.

**devaluation** an administered reduction in the EXCHANGE RATE of a currency against other currencies under a FIXED EXCHANGE RATE SYSTEM; for example, the lowering of the UK pound (£) against the US dollar ($) from one fixed or 'pegged' level to a lower level, say from £1 = $3 to £1 = $2. Devaluations are resorted to by governments to assist in the removal of a BALANCE OF PAYMENTS deficit. The effect of a devaluation is to make imports (in the local currency) more expensive, thereby reducing import demand, and exports cheaper (in the local currency), thereby acting as a stimulus to export demand. Whether or not a devaluation 'works' in achieving balance of payments equilibrium, however, depends on a number of factors, including the sensitivity of import and export demand to price changes (see ELASTICITY OF DEMAND); the availability of resources to expand export volumes and replace imports; and, critically over the longer term, the control of inflation to ensure that domestic price rises are kept in line with or below other countries' inflation rates.

Devaluations can affect the business climate in a number of ways, but in particular provide firms with an opportunity to expand sales and boost profitability. A devaluation increases import prices, which makes imports less competitive against domestic products and encourages domestic buyers to switch to locally-produced substitutes. Likewise, a fall in export prices is likely to cause overseas customers to increase their demand for the country's exported products in preference to locally produced items and to the exports of other overseas producers. If the pound, as in our example above, is devalued by one-third, then this would allow UK exporters to reduce their prices by a similar amount, thus increasing their price competitiveness in the US market. Alternatively, they may choose not to reduce their prices by the full amount of the devaluation in order to increase unit profit margins and provide additional funds for advertising and sales promotion, etc.

Contrast with REVALUATION, definition 2.

**developed country** an economically advanced country whose economy is characterized by large industrial and service sectors and high levels of GROSS NATIONAL PRODUCT and PER CAPITA INCOME. See STRUCTURE OF INDUSTRY.

**developing country, newly industrializing country (NIC)** or **emerging country** a country characterized by low levels of GROSS NATIONAL PRODUCT and PER CAPITA INCOME, which is typically reliant on the production of a limited range of agricultural and mineral products to sustain its economy. The term 'developing' indicates that, as seen by most such countries, the way to improve their economic fortunes is for them to diversify the industrial base of the economy by, in particular, establishing new manufacturing industries and by adopting the MARKET SYSTEM. See STRUCTURE OF INDUSTRY, DUMPING, ECONOMIC AID, WORLD BANK, UNITED NATIONS CONFERENCE ON TRADE AND DEVELOPMENT.

**development** see NEW PRODUCT DEVELOPMENT, RESEARCH AND DEVELOPMENT, MANAGEMENT DEVELOPMENT.

**development area** a region of economic decline designated under UK REGIONAL POLICY as in need of industrial regeneration. Financial assistance in the form of REGIONAL SELECTIVE ASSISTANCE and REGIONAL ENTERPRISE GRANTS are available to manufacturing and service businesses prepared to undertake new investments in the area.

**development corporation** an organization whose general remit is to foster the industrial regeneration of a small area or region currently suffering economic decline. Development corporations are variously funded by local authorities, local business interests and the government, and provide finance for general projects designed to improve the environment, as well as give financial assistance and other support to manufacturing and service businesses. See REGIONAL POLICY (UK).

**differentiated marketing strategy** a MARKETING STRATEGY for a product which is based on the use of a *variety* of MARKETING MIX formats (different prices, advertising messages, retail outlets, etc.) each aimed at a particular group of customers in the market, i.e. MARKET SEGMENT. Contrasted with an UNDIFFERENTIATED MARKETING STRATEGY, which applies the same marketing mix formula right across the market, the differentiated approach attempts to customize its marketing mix for each particular segment in order to maximize its appeal to the buyers constituting those segments.

This approach is best suited to a market in which the product being sold is capable of being differentiated either by physical variations of the product itself or by its psychological appeal (see PRODUCT DIFFERENTIATION), and where buyers demand a substantial amount of product variety. In these cases, differentiated marketing is usually much more successful than an across the board approach in boosting sales. However, the targeted approach may prove to be unduly costly in terms of both higher production costs (for example, with smaller production runs a firm may be unable to lower costs through exploiting economies of scale) and marketing costs (for example, the need to finance a number of separate ADVERTISING and SALES PROMOTION budgets).

See CONCENTRATED MARKETING STRATEGY, INTERNATIONAL MARKETING, MARKET SEGMENTATION.

**differentiation** see DIFFERENTIATED MARKETING STRATEGY, PRODUCT DIFFERENTIATION.

**diffusion process** the spread of a NEW PRODUCT (or process) through society. Initially, new products tend to be purchased by a small number of *pioneering customers* (see PRODUCT LIFE CYCLE) and then by *early adopters* who begin to purchase the product soon after it has been introduced. In due course the product may become a mass market item with a widespead demand.

**dilution 1.** the decrease in control and EARNINGS PER SHARE experienced by existing shareholders in a JOINT-STOCK COMPANY when SHARE ISSUES are made which attract new shareholders. Dilution is a particular problem in fast-growing, family-controlled companies where the need to raise new capital may dilute the founding family's shareholdings to below 50%, causing them to lose potential control of the company.

# DIMINISHING BALANCE DEPRECIATION

In the past, companies have sought to avoid dilution whilst continuing to raise capital by issuing NON-VOTING SHARES; but these are nowadays disapproved of by most STOCK MARKETS.

2. the weakening of the monopoly of skills of a particular occupational group by the recruitment of less-skilled workers to perform the same work. See SKILL.

**diminishing balance depreciation** see DEPRECIATION.

**direct cost** or **prime cost** the sum of the DIRECT MATERIALS cost and the DIRECT LABOUR cost of a product. Direct costs tend to vary proportionately with the level of output. See COST.

**direct debit** see COMMERCIAL BANK.

**direct exporting** see EXPORTING.

**direct investment** see INVESTMENT.

**directional matrix** a tool used to assist in formulating a firm's STRATEGIC DIRECTION and 'positioning' (that is, deciding what markets and market segments the firm should operate in). A directional matrix juxtaposes 'market attractiveness' (growth rate, profitability, structure, etc.) alongside the firm's corporate strengths (financial resources, core skills, product uniqueness) so as to maximize the firm's profit potential.

**directive** a 'request' by the monetary authorities that the COMMERCIAL BANKS and other financial institutions should limit the amount of LOANS and OVERDRAFTS they make available, in order to control spending in the economy. See MONETARY POLICY for further details.

**direct labour 1.** that part of the labour force in a firm which is directly concerned with the manufacture of a good or the provision of a service. Direct labour cost depends on the hours of labour worked by factory operatives engaged directly in making a product. Provided that wage rates remain constant then direct labour cost will tend to vary exactly with output. See VARIABLE COST, STANDARD COST.

2. workers employed directly by local or central government to perform tasks rather than such tasks being contracted out to private-sector companies.

See CONTRACTING-OUT, INDIRECT LABOUR.

**direct-mail** a form of DIRECT MARKETING which involves posting information about a firm's GOODS and SERVICES direct to prospective/existing customers. This type of marketing offers a more targeted approach than conventional forms of advertising which employ mass MEDIA (commercial television, etc.). Potential customers can be identified in terms of various socioeconomic criteria and added to a mailing list which becomes the basis for a targeted mailing shot. See SOCIO-ECONOMIC GROUP, MARKET SEGMENTATION.

**direct marketing** forms of MARKETING a product that lead the customer to make an active response to the selling stimuli, rather than merely passively absorb ADVERTISING messages. Direct marketing's principal aim is to sell the good or service which is on offer. Forms of direct marketing include: MAIL ORDER, DIRECT MAIL, DIRECT SELLING, TELEPHONE SELLING, TELEVISION MARKETING and ELECTRONIC SHOPPING.

**direct materials** raw materials which are incorporated in a product. Provided that materials prices remain constant, then direct materials cost will tend to vary exactly with output. See INDIRECT MATERIALS, VARIABLE COST.

**director** an official of a JOINT-STOCK COMPANY elected by the SHAREHOLDERS at the company's ANNUAL GENERAL MEETING and charged with certain powers and responsibilities to run the company on behalf of the shareholders. Each company will have a number of directors who constitute the BOARD OF DIRECTORS and the directors will meet regularly to determine company policy. The board generally elects one of their number to act as *chairman* of the BOARD OF DIRECTORS and may also elect one of their number to serve as *managing director* with responsibility for the day to day management of the company. Some directors will be *executive* directors and will hold senior salaried management posts in the company; others may be *non-executive* directors who are not primarily employed by the company but may be bankers or executives employed by other companies, contributing their expertise at board meetings in return for directors' fees.

**directors' report** a report by the directors of a JOINT-STOCK COMPANY to the SHAREHOLDERS which appears alongside the published annual accounts of the company to form the ANNUAL REPORT AND ACCOUNTS. Company law requires the directors to produce an annual report and specifies the information which it should contain; it also requires the AUDIT of any financial information given in the report.

**direct quotation** see EXCHANGE RATE.

**direct selling** a form of DIRECT MARKETING which involves face-to-face contact between seller and buyer. This takes place either when buyers visit the seller's SHOP or STORE (see RE-TAILER), or when the seller makes door-to-door calls on customers, or through party plan type selling.

Door-to-door selling is made to both domestic and industrial consumers. The SALES REPRESENTATIVE will either deliver immediately from stocks carried in his own vehicle or take an order for the GOODS and SERVICES.

Party plan type selling is aimed at groups of domestic buyers who are brought together by a common contact or friend, who is recruited by the seller and offered financial inducements to host the party of buyers, direct selling being undertaken by the firm's sales personnel.

**direct tax** a TAX imposed by the government on the income and wealth of persons and businesses in order to raise revenue, redistribute income and wealth, and as an instrument of FISCAL POLICY in managing the economy. The main forms of direct tax in the UK are INCOME TAX, CORPORATION TAX and INHERITANCE TAX. See BUDGET DEFICIT/SURPLUS (GOVERNMENT).

**dirty float** see FLOATING EXCHANGE RATE SYSTEM.

**disability quota** see DISCRIMINATION.

**disciplinary procedure** a set of rules governing the way managers should conduct investigations into infringements of company rules or unsatisfactory performance by employees. Generally, disciplinary procedures require that employees be formally notified of the charge against them, have an opportunity to defend themselves (accompanied by a friend or TRADE UNION representative), be formally notified of any punishments, and have a right of appeal. If an employee is dismissed, failure to abide by such a procedure can lay a company open to a charge of UNFAIR DISMISSAL. See GRIEVANCE PROCEDURE.

**disclosure of information** any release of information from one party to another. Usually it refers to release of management information relevant to COLLECTIVE BARGAINING and potentially useful to trade union negotiators. In the UK, managers are statutorily required to release information, if requested, to union representatives; otherwise, collective bargaining would be impeded. However, managers are allowed to withhold certain categories of information, for example that which would be commercially damaging if released, and are entitled to withhold original documentation from scrutiny. The mechanisms for unions to challenge withholding of information on these grounds are cumbersome and in fact rarely used.

Employers are statutorily required to consult trade unions when it has been decided to make a number of employees redundant. 30 days' notice is required if 10–100 employees in any establishment are to be made redundant, 90 days if over 100. Management is required to state formally the reason for redundancy, how many employees will be made redundant and what methods will be used to select employees for redundancy.

See REDUNDANCY, CONSULTATION, COMMUNICATION, VREDELING DIRECTIVE.

**disclosure of shareholdings** the requirement in the UK under current COMPANY LAW for an investor owning more than 3% of the SHARES of a public JOINT-STOCK COMPANY to declare ownership of these shares to the directors of that company. Where several blocks of shares held by NOMINEE shareholders on behalf of a BENEFICIAL OWNER *collectively* amount to more than 3%, then the identity of the beneficial owner must be declared to the directors of the company. Disclosure provisions make it more difficult for someone to mount a DAWN RAID on a public company.

**discount 1.** a deduction from the published LIST PRICE of a product by a supplier to a customer. The discount could be offered in respect of bulk purchases (*trade discount*) or for prompt payment in cash (*cash discount*). Discounts may be given when stores offer goods at special low prices as, for example, during a sale period, or on a more permanent basis by DISCOUNT STORES.

**2.** the purchase of a BOND, TREASURY BILL or BILL OF EXCHANGE for less than its nominal value. Bills and bonds are redeemable at a specific future date at their face values. The original buyer will purchase the bill or bond for less than its nominal value (at a discount). The discount between the price which he pays and the nominal value of the bill or bond represents interest received on the loan made against the security of the bill or bond, which will depend largely on the length of time before maturity. For example, if a bond with a nominal value of £1,000 redeemable in one year's time was bought for £900, then the £100 discount on redemption value represents an interest rate of (£100/900) 11.1% on the loan.

**3.** the sale of new STOCKS and SHARES at a reduced price. In the UK this involves the issue of a new share at a price below its nominal value. Where shares have no nominal value it involves the sale of new shares at below their current market price.

**4.** the rating of a particular company's shares at a price below the average market price of the shares of other companies operating in the same sector, the discount reflecting investors' general view that this company is likely to perform less well than the others.

**5.** the amount by which a foreign currency's spot exchange rate stands below its official par value in a FIXED EXCHANGE RATE SYSTEM which allows some degree of short-term fluctuation either side of the par value.

**discounted cash flow** a method used in INVESTMENT APPRAISAL to evaluate the desirability of an INVESTMENT project. Discounted cash flow is the CASH FLOW associated with an investment project that is adjusted to allow for the timing of the cash flow and the potential interest on the funds involved. Such an allowance for timing is important because most investment projects have their main costs or cash outflows in the first year or so, while their revenues or cash inflows are spread over future years.

For example, if the INTEREST RATE was 10% a company could invest £100 now and have it accumulate at compound interest to £110 at the end of one year and £121 at the end of two years. So £100 in the hands of the company now is worth the same as £110 in one year's time, or £121 receivable in two years' time, that is, it has a *present value* of £100.

The *net present value* investment criterion uses this principle to calculate the present value of the estimated stream of future cash outflows associated with an investment project, and the present value of the estimated stream of future cash inflows from the project, and to compare the two. If the present value of the cash inflows from the project exceeds the present value of outflows when both are discounted at, say, 10%, then the net present value is positive (see Fig. 34 A). If the firm's cost of capital (based on market interest rate) was 10% then it would be worthwhile for the company to undertake this project, because it will earn a return in excess of its financing costs.

A  *Net Present Value* at discount rate 10%

| Year | Cash flows | Present Value Index at 10% | Present value of cash flows (at 10%) |
|------|-----------|----------------------------|--------------------------------------|
|      | £         |                            | £                                    |
| now | −5,000 | 1.000 | −5,000 |
| end year 1 | +5,000 | 0.909 | +4,545 |
| end year 2 | +3,000 | 0.826 | +2,478 |
|      | +3,400 |  NPV    =   | +2,023 |

B  *Internal Rate of Return*

| Year | Cash Flows | Present Value Index at 42% | Present Value of Cash Flows (at 42%) | Present Value Index at 43% | Present Value of Cash Flows (at 43%) |
|------|-----------|----------------------------|--------------------------------------|----------------------------|--------------------------------------|
|      | £         |                            | £                                    |                            | £                                    |
| now | −5,000 | 1.0000 | −5,000 | 1.0000 | −5,000 |
| end year 1 | +5,000 | 0.7042 | +3,521 | 0.6993 | +3,496 |
| end year 2 | +3,000 | 0.4959 | +1,488 | 0.4890 | +1,467 |
|      |  | NPV   = | +9 | NPV   = | −37 |

Fig. 34. Discounted cash flow. Examples of two investment criteria for a machine: cost £5,000, estimated life 2 years, cash receipts/inflows £5,000 (year 1), £3,000 (year 2).

The *internal rate of return* investment criterion seeks to calculate the percentage internal rate of return which will equate the present value of the stream of cash outflows associated with an investment project, with the present value of the stream of cash inflows from the project, so as to give a zero net present value. For example, in Fig. 34 B, the calculated internal rate of return is just over 42%, this being the rate at which net present value is zero.

This calculated internal rate of return can then be compared with the firm's cost of capital which is usually based on market rates. If the calculated internal rate of return (here 42%) exceeds the cost of capital (say 10%) then the project is worthwhile; otherwise not.

Whether or not the machine has a positive net present value,

191

or an internal rate of return which exceeds the cost of capital, depends upon how accurate the future estimates of sales volumes, selling prices, materials costs, etc. turn out to be. Since all investments involve assessments of future revenues and costs they are all subject to a degree of uncertainty. This problem can to some extent be handled by undertaking sensitivity analysis, and by making not one but three estimates for each item of project cost or revenue ('optimistic', 'most likely', 'pessimistic') to indicate the range of possible outcomes.

**discount house** a financial institution (unique to the UK financial system) which specializes in the buying and selling of commercial BILLS OF EXCHANGE and government TREASURY BILLS. See DISCOUNT MARKET.

**discount market** a market engaged in the buying and selling of short-dated BILLS OF EXCHANGE and TREASURY BILLS. Such transactions are conducted through a number of DISCOUNT HOUSES which use money borrowed primarily from the COMMERCIAL BANKS (usually on a revolving day-to-day basis) to purchase bills (i.e. to 'discount' them) which they then hold until maturity or sell to each other ('re-discount') or more commonly on-sell to the commercial banks. When the discount houses find themselves temporarily unable to cover their purchase commitments by borrowing from the commercial banks, it is possible for them to obtain additional funds from the Bank of England in its capacity as the 'lender of last resort'. See ACCEPTING HOUSE.

**discount rate** the INTEREST RATE at which future cash inflows and cash outflows associated with an INVESTMENT project are discounted in order to allow for the timing of these cash flows. The discount rate used by firms in evaluating the desirability of investments is frequently based upon the average COST OF CAPITAL to the firm. See DISCOUNTED CASH FLOW.

**discount store** a RETAILER which sells a relatively limited range of products at low, 'discounted' prices (that is, prices substantially below manufacturers' RECOMMENDED RETAIL PRICES and the prices charged by other types of retailer) on a SELF SERVICE basis.

Discount stores may be under single-shop ownership or run as a multiple CHAIN STORE business. In the latter case the bigger chains are usually able to obtain substantial price concessions by BULK BUYING direct from manufacturers.

See DISTRIBUTION CHANNEL, CATEGORY DISCOUNTER, WAREHOUSE CLUB.

**discount tables** see PRESENT VALUE TABLES.

**discrimination** inequitable treatment of employees of which the main forms are:

(a) *sex discrimination*, where men and women are treated differently by their employer;

(b) *race discrimination*, where people are treated differently according to their colour, nationality, race or ethnic origins.

Discrimination can be said to be morally unacceptable in that it infringes peoples' rights and is also counterproductive in that it can result in people's talents being under-utilized. Since the late 1960s legislation has been aimed at tackling the more overt forms of discrimination at work in the UK. The *Equal Pay Act 1970* established the right for men and women to be paid the same rate of pay for performing the *same* job or a job rated as *equivalent*. It was widely believed, however, that employees could circumvent the intentions of this legislation by segregating men's and women's jobs. That the average female wage is only 75% of the average male wage tends to support this contention. In 1983, however, UK law was amended to establish the right to *equal pay* for work of *equal value* (in line with the European Commission directive on equal pay). Thus, a woman doing a job which is shown to be of equal value to a different job done by a man has a right to the rate of pay of the latter. Aggrieved individuals may pursue their claim to an INDUSTRIAL TRIBUNAL, whereupon the techniques of JOB EVALUATION will be used to assess the claim.

The *Sex Discrimination Act 1975* made discrimination on grounds of sex or marital status in RECRUITMENT AND SELECTION, TRAINING and employment benefits unlawful. The 1975 Act also established the Equal Opportunities Commission with a remit to:

(a) work towards the elimination of sex discrimination in employment, education and consumer services;

(b) promote equality of opportunity;

(c) monitor the effectiveness of the Sex Discrimination and Equal Pay Acts. As well as direct discrimination, indirect discrimination, for example framing a job advertisement in a way which intentionally excludes women, is unlawful. Initially small firms and private household employers were exempt, but the *Sex Discrimination Act 1986* (passed in response to a European Court ruling) removed this exemption.

The *Race Relations Act 1976* is similar to the Sex Discrimination Act 1975 in making both direct and indirect discrimination in employment on grounds of colour, race, nationality or ethnic origins unlawful. As with claims of sex discrimination, aggrieved individuals can pursue a claim to an industrial tribunal. This legislation also created the Commission for Racial Equality to:

(a) work towards the elimination of racial discrimination in employment, education and consumer service;

(b) promote equality of opportunity;

(c) monitor the effectiveness of the 1976 Act.

As well as sex and race discrimination there is the problem of discrimination against *disabled people*. Discrimination occurs when disabled individuals are denied, by virtue of their disability, access to jobs which they are capable of performing. Employers are encouraged to employ people with disabilities by a *quota system*: firms of more than 20 employees should have 3% of the workforce drawn from people with registered disabilities. However, the quota system is widely believed to be ineffective as there are few effective sanctions that can be brought to bear against those employers who choose to disregard them.

Whilst legislation has largely curbed the more blatant forms of sex and race discrimination, it cannot be said to have achieved equality of opportunity. Only a minority of top managerial positions are held by women or black people. To encourage the recruitment and advancement of these people, many organizations have recently styled themselves as 'equal opportunities employers'. What this means in practice varies and many are sceptical of employers' claims in this respect. It is generally believed that to be meaningful such claims need to be supported by explicit equal opportunities policies in the area of recruitment, selection, training, etc., coupled with monitoring procedures to permit assessment of their impact. As part of this, data will need to be collected on the proportion of recruits, trainees, and those promoted, who are drawn from disadvantaged groups (for example ethnic monitoring). In addition DISCIPLINARY PROCEDURES and GRIEVANCE PROCEDURES will probably require amendment so as to discourage discriminatory behaviour and to provide channels of redress for those who feel they have been discriminated against. See GLASS CEILING.

**discriminatory pricing** see DEMAND-BASED PRICING, PRICE DISCRIMINATION.

**diseconomies of scale** see ECONOMIES OF SCALE.

**disjointed incrementalism** a pattern of decision making in organizations, identified by American political scientist Charles Lindblom (1917–  ), in which decisions are taken step by step as a problem unfolds. The various incremental stages of decision making are not closely integrated with the preceding stages. Although this differs sharply from the rational-deductive ideal of decision making (where a problem is fully identified at the outset, all relevant information is collected and finally a set of rational procedures is used to choose the appropriate course of action), Lindblom believed it was a sensible strategy for decision makers. This is because the human capacity to absorb information is limited, perfect information is unavailable anyway, and it is difficult to determine at the outset what information is relevant. See ORGANIZATIONAL ANALYSIS, 'GARBAGE-CAN' MODEL OF DECISION MAKING.

**disjunctive buyer** see CONJOINT ANALYSIS.

**disk drive** a mechanical device in a COMPUTER which records and retrieves data from a rotating magnetic or vinyl disk.

**Disk Operating System** see DOS.

**dismissal** the termination of an employee's employment with an organization due to unsatisfactory work performance or breach of CONTRACT OF EMPLOYMENT. The term *firing* is sometimes used to refer to dismissal. See UNFAIR DISMISSAL.

**dispatch 1.** the sending out of finished goods for distribution and sale. Such finished goods can be dispatched from STOCK or as particular customers' orders are manufactured.

**2.** the selection of JOBS or batches of a product to be completed in a PRODUCTION schedule. Various *dispatch rules* can be used to select which particular job should be completed next from a queue of jobs awaiting completion, such as 'first come first served', 'random selection', 'minimum processing time' (starting with the job which has the shortest machine processing time) etc.

**displays** information presented visually to assist operatives in the control and operation of machinery and equipment. For example, the displays may consist of different coloured lights or data on a VISUAL DISPLAY UNIT (VDU).

**disposable income** the amount of INCOME which a person has available after paying INCOME TAX, NATIONAL INSURANCE CONTRIBUTIONS and PENSION contributions. The amount of a person's disposable income has an important effect on the ability to buy products.

**disputes procedure** a set of rules stipulating the procedures to be followed where two (or more) parties are in dispute with each other, with the aim of resolving the difference without recourse to open conflict. Such a procedure may be used to deal with disputes between employers and TRADE UNIONS concerning pay and conditions of employment. Where these matters are the subject of COLLECTIVE BARGAINING within the firm, the procedure will normally form part of the PROCEDURAL AGREEMENT governing relations between management and unions. Where, however, they are dealt with externally (by industry-wide bargaining), the disputes procedure will probably be operated by the EMPLOYERS' ASSOCIATION of which the company is a member. When a dispute arises the company hands it over to the association for resolution. See GRIEVANCE PROCEDURE.

**distribution** the process of storing and moving products to customers, often through intermediaries such as WHOLESALERS and RETAILERS. The task of *physical distribution management* involves moving specified quantities of products to places where customers can conveniently buy them, in time to replenish stocks, and in good condition. The objective is to maximize the availability of the product whilst minimizing the cost of distribution. Distribution is often described as one of the FOUR P'S of marketing as it is concerned with getting products to the correct *place* where they can be bought. Thus, distribution will include the selection of appropriate DISTRIBUTION CHANNELS in order to bring a firm's products to its selected markets. However, where a business employs an *integrated distribution system*, distribution will include inventory, warehousing, materials handling, transport and order processing. See MARKETING LOGISTICS, JUST-IN-TIME (JIT) SYSTEM, DISTRIBUTION RESOURCE PLANNING; FOUR P'S OF MARKETING.

**distribution centre** a WAREHOUSE or DEPOT which carries

sufficient stock to serve the needs of a particular area.

**distribution channel** the route used in the physical distribution of a PRODUCT from the MANUFACTURER to the ultimate buyer of that product.

*Functionally*, a typical distribution channel consists of three basic interrelated operations:

(a) manufacturing (making the product);

(b) wholesaling (the holding of large STOCKS and 'breaking-bulk' into retail packs);

(c) retailing (the sale of the product to the final buyer) (see WHOLESALER, RETAILER).

*Organizationally*, these functions may be undertaken by firms which specialize at a particular stage in the chain or they may be combined wholly or partially, and undertaken by the one firm as an integrated operation (see VERTICAL INTEGRATION). The attractions of 'INTERNALIZING' the distribution function include the avoidance of TRANSACTION COSTS involved in dealing through the market, better control and coordination of the movement of products, various advantages over competitors (see FORECLOSURE, PRICE SQUEEZE) and the more effective MARKETING of products.

1. Manufacturing (M) → wholesaling (W) → retailing (R) → buyers

2. M → $\boxed{\text{WR}}$ → buyers

3. $\boxed{\text{MW}}$ → R → buyers

4. $\boxed{\text{MWR}}$ → buyers

→ = independent function

☐ = intregrated function

Fig. 35. **Distribution channel**. Examples of typical channels of distribution.

Thus, depending upon the traditions of the trade, the nature of the product and the characteristics of the market being served, and the relative costs and marketing effectiveness of using different channel intermediaries, a number of distributive channel configurations may be identified, as Fig. 35 illustrates. Line 1 shows a conventional channel structure with the products being moved on an arms-length basis, that is, through independent intermediaries at each separate stage. Alternatively (line 2), a retailer such as a SUPERMARKET chain

## DISTRIBUTION CHANNEL

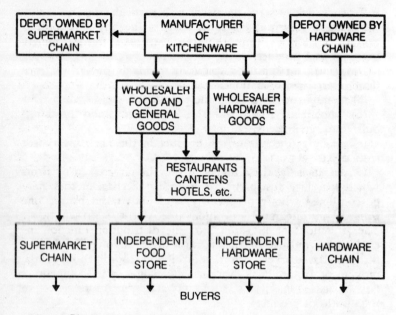

Fig. 36. **Distribution channel.** Some distribution channels for kitchenware.

may buy in bulk direct from manufacturers and undertake the wholesaling function itself as an integrated wholesaling-retailing operation; a manufacturer may combine the production and wholesaling functions (line 3), on-selling to independent retailers or, alternatively, combine all three operations (line 4), selling direct to final buyers.

Additionally, at some stage in a channel, SALES AGENTS, whose primary function is to generate new business contacts, may be employed. Typically, agents do not take title to the goods but are employed by, for example, a manufacturer to obtain new wholesale customers or a wholesaler seeking new retail accounts. For many products, distributive arrangements are multi-dimensional with a variety of modes employed depending upon which MARKET or MARKET SEGMENTS are being targeted (see Fig. 36).

See VERTICAL MARKETING SYSTEM, SELECTIVE DISTRIBUTION, EXCLUSIVE DISTRIBUTION.

**distribution of income** the division of a country's GROSS NATIONAL PRODUCT (national income) among the multitude of people making up its POPULATION. In most countries, income (wages and salaries, rent, dividends, profit) is unequally divided; this reflects differences in people's natural abilities, educational attainments, special skills, but most importantly differences in the ownership of WEALTH assets such as businesses, houses, stocks and shares, etc. In many countries, however, governments operate progressive TAXATION systems and SOCIAL SECURITY programmes designed to redistribute income and so assist the poorer members of society. Thus, as Fig. 37 shows for the UK in 1995, the poorest 20% of the population received only 2% of total original income, but after taxation and state benefits they received 10% of total final income.

| Quintile groups of households | Original income % | Final income % |
|---|---|---|
| Bottom fifth | 2 | 10 |
| Second fifth | 7 | 13 |
| Third fifth | 16 | 17 |
| Fourth fifth | 27 | 23 |
| Top fifth | 48 | 37 |
| | 100 | 100 |

Fig. 37. **Distribution of income.** The personal distribution of original and final income in the UK, 1995. Final income = original income less taxes paid, plus state spending on education, health, security benefits.
(Source: Social Trends 1997.)

**distribution ratio** a measure of the proportion of NET PROFIT which a company distributes to SHAREHOLDERS instead of ploughing it back into the business. Specifically, the distribution ratio expresses DIVIDENDS as a percentage of net profit after tax and interest. Thus, for example, if a company pays out one-quarter of its profits as dividends, then the distribution ratio is 25%. The distribution ratio is the opposite of the RETENTIONS RATIO and the mirror image of the DIVIDEND COVER ratio. See RESERVES, RETAINED PROFIT.

**distribution resource planning (DRP)** a computer-based PRODUCTION planning system which integrates a firm's PRODUC-

TION SCHEDULES, product DISTRIBUTION system and customers' orders, in order both to minimize stockholding costs and to improve customer service by reducing delivery times. See STOCKHOLDING MODEL, DELIVERY DATE, PRODUCTION MANAGEMENT.

**distributive bargaining** see COLLECTIVE BARGAINING.

**distributor** a business such as a RETAILER or WHOLESALER which acts as an intermediary in a DISTRIBUTION CHANNEL. Distributors take title to goods (that is, purchase goods) which they then on-sell to customers.

**diversifiable risk** see CAPITAL-ASSET PRICING MODEL.

**diversification** or **conglomerate integration** the expansion of a firm into a range of different product areas which leads to its operating in a number of markets rather than a single market. Diversification may be 'concentric' or 'pure', the former involving some carry over of production or marketing functions (for example, two firms which utilize a common technological base – razor blades and garden spades both produced from stainless steel and sold through the same outlets – supermarkets), while in the latter case the products are entirely unrelated (for example cars and cement). Diversification may take the form of ORGANIC (INTERNAL) GROWTH, or firms may choose to expand by EXTERNAL GROWTH, merging with or taking over established firms. Concentric diversification via internal growth often arises as a result of new discoveries and applications made by the firm's RESEARCH AND DEVELOPMENT activities as an extension of its existing technological expertise. For example, many producers of basic chemicals have extended their businesses into areas of chemical derivatives, such as paint and pharmaceuticals. In the case of pure diversification, mergers and takeovers often offer the best prospects of a successful entry into a new area.

The main attraction of diversification as a growth strategy compared with HORIZONTAL INTEGRATION (expansion in the firm's existing markets) and VERTICAL INTEGRATION (expansion into different supply levels, but again within an existing market), is the ability to spread risks and broaden the firm's profit-earning potential. Specifically, a one-market firm is vulnerable not only to erratic, cyclical profit returns resulting from the business cycle, but worse still, its very survival may be threatened by a declining customer base as the firm's product moves into the final stages of the PRODUCT LIFE-CYCLE.

Diversification is thus the main way the firm can reduce its exposure to business risk and fluctuating profitability, while reorientating its activities away from mature and declining markets into new areas offering sustained growth and profit opportunities.

Diversification can produce both pro- and anti-competitive effects and for this reason may attract the attentions of the competition policy authorities. Diversifying firms can redeploy profits earned in other areas of their businesses in order to finance entry into new markets, thereby increasing competition in the entered market; on the other hand, 'cross subsidization' may be used in a predatory manner to undercut competitors' prices and drive them out of business. In the UK, conglomerate mergers and takeovers involving assets in excess of £70 million may be referred by the OFFICE OF FAIR TRADING to the MONOPOLIES AND MERGERS COMMISSION for investigation, to determine whether or not they should be allowed to proceed.

See BUSINESS STRATEGY, PRODUCT MARKET MATRIX, STRATEGIC BUSINESS UNIT, INTERNALIZATION, SYNERGY, CORE SKILL, CORE BUSINESS.

**divestment** the closure or sale by a firm of one or more of its operating units (for example a production plant) or a whole business division. In the former case, divestment usually occurs in order to rationalize production and/or to concentrate the firm's output in a more modern plant. In contrast, the divestment of a whole business division represents a more fundamental strategic decision on the part of the firm. Divestment in this case may reflect a number of considerations, including a desire to pull out of an unprofitable, loss-making activity deemed to be incapable of TURNROUND; the wish to shed peripheral businesses in order to release cash and managerial resources which, in opportunity cost terms, could be more effectively redeployed in the firm's other activities; a major rethink of a firm's strategic position involving a retrenchment back to 'core' businesses; and finally, a wish to avoid the opposition of the COMPETITION POLICY authorities, particularly in cases of MERGERS and TAKEOVER.

Divestment by one firm often presents an opportunity for some other firm to diversify (see DIVERSIFICATION), in turn, into new business areas, or for former competitors to increase

## DIVIDEND

their market shares.

See ENDGAME STRATEGY, BUSINESS STRATEGY, BOSTON MATRIX, DE-MERGER, MANAGEMENT BUY-OUT, JOINT VENTURE, PRODUCT MARKET MATRIX, PRODUCT RATIONALIZATION, CORE BUSINESS.

**dividend** a payment made by a JOINT-STOCK COMPANY to its SHAREHOLDERS for providing SHARE CAPITAL. Dividends are a distribution of the after-tax PROFITS of the company, and are paid in proportion to the number of shares held. Generally the directors of a company will decide to pay out only a proportion of after-tax profit as dividends, reinvesting the remaining profits in the business (see RETAINED PROFIT).

The DIRECTORS may pay an *interim dividend* during the accounting period then recommend a final rate of dividend per share for approval by shareholders at the ANNUAL GENERAL MEETING, this *final dividend* being paid after the AGM. In the UK dividends are paid net of income tax, though shareholders receive a tax credit for the amount of tax deducted by the company from their dividends, which must be added to the net dividends received to establish the shareholder's gross taxable dividend income (see CORPORATION TAX).

**dividend cover** or **times covered** a measure of the extent to which a firm's earnings (profit after tax and interest) cover DIVIDEND paid, which expresses PROFITS as a multiple of dividends paid. Thus, for example, if a company pays out one quarter of its profit as dividends, then the dividend cover ratio is four. The dividend ratio is the mirror image of the DISTRIBUTION RATIO.

**dividend yield** the DIVIDEND paid by a JOINT-STOCK COMPANY for a given ACCOUNTING PERIOD expressed as a percentage of the current market price per share. For example, if Company X declared a dividend of £1 per ORDINARY SHARE for the 12 month accounting period ending 31 December, and the current market price of one ordinary share in Company X was £5, the dividend yield would be:

$$\frac{\text{Dividend per share}}{\text{Price per share}} \times 100 = \frac{£1}{£5} \times 100 = 20\%$$

**division** see PRODUCT-BASED STRUCTURE.

**divisionalization** see PRODUCT-BASED STRUCTURE.

**division of labour** see SPECIALIZATION.

**document image processing (DIP)** see DATA STORAGE.

**DOE** see DEPARTMENT OF THE ENVIRONMENT.

**Do-It-Yourself store** a RETAILER which sells mainly home-improvement and repair equipment and materials (paint, wallpaper, patio doors, etc.) and garden accessories. DIY stores may be under single-shop ownership or run as a multiple CHAIN STORE business.

They compete principally by offering customers both convenience, by stocking an extensive range of products under the one roof, and competitive prices. The bigger DIY chains are able to obtain significant price discounts by BULK BUYING manufacturers' brands and have found it advantageous also to establish their OWN-LABEL BRANDS. See DISTRIBUTION CHANNEL, SELF-SERVICE.

**dollar ($)** the domestic currency of the USA. In addition the dollar is used extensively as an INTERNATIONAL RESERVE asset, a key currency in the EUROCURRENCY MARKET and is used to finance the international oil business.

**domestic labour** work performed by household members for the benefit of the household (for example child rearing). It has been argued that since domestic labour ultimately benefits employers by preparing and sustaining a LABOUR FORCE, those performing it should be paid a WAGE.

**dominant firm** a firm that accounts for a substantial proportion of the total supply of a particular product. Such a firm not only has a high absolute market share, but also often a (relative) market share which is considerably greater than its nearest rival. In consequence, a dominant firm may be in a position to exercise market (monopoly) power to the detriment of both consumers and rival suppliers.

Under UK COMPETITION POLICY, a dominant firm is defined as a firm which supplies 25% or more of a specified GOOD or SERVICE.

**Donovan Commission** the Royal Commission on Trades Unions and Employers' Associations which reported in 1968 into the state of INDUSTRIAL RELATIONS in the UK. The Commission's main finding was that informal, uncontrolled bargaining had developed at shop-floor level alongside the existing formal system of industry-wide bargaining, leading to spiralling pay claims, unofficial STRIKES, etc. The solution proposed was the rationalization and formalization of work-place industrial relations. Employee representatives were to be given a formal rôle in new procedures governing discipline, grievance and pay determination. Though it is questionable how far the Report provided the impetus, many UK employers have embarked upon this policy over the last 25 years. However, more recently a growing number of employers (especially those establishing new firms) have not been following the Donovan prescription. See COLLECTIVE BARGAINING, EMPLOYERS' ASSOCIATION, MULTI-EMPLOYER AGREEMENTS, TRADE UNION.

**DOS (Disk Operating System)** a COMPUTER program which enables a computer to record and retrieve data from a rotating magnetic or vinyl disk. The most widely-used disk operating system is MSDOS, which is used on computers that are compatible with the IBM personal computer.

**DOT** see DEPARTMENT OF TRANSPORT.

**'dotted-line relationship'** see ORGANIZATION CHART.

**double-day shifts** see SHIFT WORK.

**double-entry accounts** the ACCOUNTING records of a firm's day-to-day financial transactions with outside parties which record both aspects of each transaction, namely, what is 'given' and what is received in return. By making a double entry in the accounts the firm can record both aspects of the exchange, for example the exchange of cash for raw materials purchased, or the exchange for cash of GOODS or SERVICES sold. See LEDGER, DEBIT, CREDIT.

**double taxation** the TAXATION of INCOMES and PROFITS in both the country where they arise, and again where these incomes and profits are remitted to the income earner's home country. Such double taxation can be a significant deterrent to international labour and capital movements. For this reason many countries have negotiated double taxation agreements which limit taxation liability to the country in which the income is earned. Compare UNITARY TAXATION, WITHHOLDING TAX.

**doubtful debts** amounts owed to a company by customers or borrowers which may possibly not be paid because the customers or borrowers are in financial difficulties. In anticipation that many doubtful debts will eventually become BAD DEBTS, a company may make a PROVISION against profits for some doubtful debts. See CREDIT CONTROL.

**Dow-Jones Index** see SHARE PRICE INDEX.

**downgrading** the re-classification of a product as sub-standard or second quality. See QUALITY CONTROL, TOTAL QUALITY MANAGEMENT.

**downside risk** the risk of experiencing losses associated with an investment project and the magnitude of these losses. Managers' attitudes towards UNCERTAINTY will influence their assessment of the desirability of a project which has substantial downside risk.

**downsizing 1.** the use of PERSONAL COMPUTERS in a business in place of large mainframe computers. The introduction of smaller, faster and more cost-effective microprocessors has made it possible for tasks which formerly could only be performed by mainframe computers to be carried out at the personal workstation level, allowing a greater devolution of DATA PROCESSING down to the 'desk top'.
**2.** a currently fashionable term for policies aimed at organizational contraction, usually leading to REDUNDANCY for some employees. The oft-stated rationale for downsizing is that a smaller, more flexible ORGANIZATION will be able to respond better to market forces. Cost reduction, however, is probably an equally important motive. See DELAYERING, RIGHTSIZING.

**downstream integration** see VERTICAL INTEGRATION.

**downtime** time when a machine or COMPUTER is not operating correctly owing to machine failure or because the machine is being set up for the next work task (SET-UP TIME). Downtime in a factory can cause considerable loss of output and disruption to production schedules, and the aim of PREVENTIVE MAINTENANCE is to minimize such downtime. See IDLE TIME.

**drawing office** the department of a manufacturer's business responsible for producing the technical drawings of products, components and plant lay-out. See COMPUTER-AIDED DESIGN, COMPUTER-AIDED MANUFACTURING.

**DSS** see DEPARTMENT OF SOCIAL SECURITY.

**DTI** see DEPARTMENT OF TRADE AND INDUSTRY.

**dual capacity** the right of firms in the STOCK MARKET to operate both as MARKET MAKERS, buying and selling SHARES on their own account, and as STOCKBROKERS, acting on behalf of clients. See SINGLE CAPACITY.

**dual commitment** the commitment of an individual to two apparently opposed ORGANIZATIONS. Specifically it refers to employee commitment to both the employing organization and a trade union. In theory employees seem likely to be committed to one or the other but some research findings indicate that those most committed to their trade union are also the most committed to their organization, thereby refuting one of the key tenets of the unitarist perspective on INDUSTRIAL RELATIONS (see MANAGEMENT STYLE). See also ORGANIZATIONAL COMMITMENT.

**duality** the dual aspect of each business transaction, in which something is given by a firm and something is received in return, for example, goods for cash in a cash sale. Both aspects of a transaction are recorded in DOUBLE ENTRY ACCOUNTS. See ACCOUNTING.

**dumping** the sale of a product by a firm in an EXPORT MARKET at a price *below* that charged in its own domestic market. Firms may choose to lower their overseas sales prices in order, for example, to dispose of surplus output, or as part of a MARKET PENETRATION PRICING strategy aimed at building the firm's market share in export markets over the longer term. Whatever the firm's motivation, such a pricing practice constitutes 'unfair' INTERNATIONAL TRADE under GENERAL AGREEMENT ON TARIFFS AND TRADE conventions, and member countries are entitled to protect their domestic producers against dumping by applying ANTI-DUMPING DUTIES, or COUNTERVAILING DUTIES on offending products. Disputes between countries frequently arise, however, because of the different possible ways of calculating the domestic price; for example, it could be based either on the producer's ex-factory price, or on the final retail price which not only includes the producer's marketing expenses but also independent distributors' and retailers' costs and mark-ups. The picture is further complicated by the fact that MULTINATIONAL ENTERPRISES often source their inputs, and supply exports, to a market, from a number of different countries, thus making it difficult to identify a definitive domestic price. See LOCAL CONTENT RULE, PROTECTIONISM.

**durability** the ability of a product or component to perform its required function under its stated conditions of use until its performance deteriorates below an acceptable level.

**durable goods** see CONSUMER DURABLES.

**dysfunction** any consequence of an activity which inhibits the achievement of the desired objective. In the study of

ORGANIZATIONS, dysfunctions refer to those aspects of organizations which are essential to the organization's proper functioning but at the same time detract from organizational performance. For instance, a justifiable emphasis on following the correct procedures can also stifle the flexibility that is often needed in work situations. See GOAL DISPLACEMENT.

# E

**early adopter** see DIFFUSION PROCESS.

**early failure rate** see FAILURE RATE CURVE.

**earned income** that part of a person's income earned from employment or self-employment (WAGES, SALARIES, FEES, COMMISSIONS and PROFITS). By contrast unearned income derives from the ownership of assets (interest and dividends from investment, rents from property, etc.) or can take the form of unemployment benefits, old age pensions, etc.

**earnings** see INCOME.

**earnings per share** NET PROFIT after tax accruing to the ordinary shareholders in a JOINT-STOCK COMPANY, divided by the number of ORDINARY SHARES. Comparison of earnings per share with DIVIDEND per share indicates the proportion of earnings paid out as dividends and the proportion retained in the business.

**earnings yield** NET PROFIT after tax per ordinary share (EARNINGS PER SHARE) of a JOINT-STOCK COMPANY for a given ACCOUNTING PERIOD, expressed as a percentage of the current market price per share. For example, if profit after tax was £2 per share and the market price per share was £5 then the earnings yield would be 40%. Earnings yield is the mirror image of the PRICE-EARNINGS RATIO.

Earnings yield depends upon DIVIDEND YIELD and DIVIDEND COVER. For example, if dividend yield was 20% and the dividend was covered twice over then the earnings yield would be 20% × 2 or 40%.

**EBCDIC (Extended Binary Coded Decimal Interchange**

**Code)** a system for coding individual numbers, letters and punctuation marks which is widely used in computing.

**EC** see EUROPEAN COMMUNITY.

**ECGD** see EXPORT CREDIT GUARANTEE DEPARTMENT.

**econometrics** the application of statistical techniques in the analysis of economic data. Econometrics is used extensively in establishing statistical relationships between, for example, levels of national income and consumption in the economy, as a basis for formulating government ECONOMIC POLICY, and is used by firms to forecast demand for their products. See SALES FORECASTING, REGRESSION ANALYSIS.

**economic aid** the provision of LOANS, grants, technology and skilled personnel by the WORLD BANK, individual countries and private institutions to countries requiring economic assistance, mainly the less developed countries. Unconditional grants and the transfer of technology and capital goods free of charge are especially useful to recipients. Conditional grants or 'tied aid' is seen to be beneficial both ways, i.e. such aid requires recipients to spend the money on goods and services supplied by private firms in the donor country. Loan aid, of course, has to be repaid and interest charges may reflect market rates, or may be provided on a 'soft' loan basis bearing interest charges below commercial rates. See INTERNATIONAL DEBT.

**economic exposure** see EXCHANGE RATE EXPOSURE.

**economic growth** an increase in the total real output of goods and services in an economy over time. Economic growth is usually measured in terms of an increase in GROSS DOMESTIC PRODUCT (GDP) over time, or an increase in GDP per head of population to reflect its impact on living standards over time (see NATIONAL INCOME ACCOUNTS). Because of the contribution of economic growth to wealth creation, and the fact that it provides the government with extra resources to provide social amenities (without having to raise taxation), most governments accord a high priority to the promotion of economic growth in formulating their ECONOMIC POLICIES.

The ability of an economy to produce more goods and services on a sustained basis depends on many factors including an increase in the quantity and quality of the labour force, capital stock and natural resources (the basic factor inputs available to it); the efficient use of these resources so as to attain a high level of PRODUCTIVITY; the introduction of new innovative techniques and methods of production and new products. The latter two factors are especially important in the context of a world economy where a country's economic growth rate is materially affected by INTERNATIONAL TRADE influences. Finally, a country's own level of demand needs to be sufficiently buoyant both to ensure the full utilization of its existing resources and to encourage producers to invest in new plant and research and development to enlarge the supply capabilities of the economy over the longer term.

Governments can stimulate the growth process by increasing current spending in the economy through taxation cuts (see FISCAL POLICY) and by increasing the money supply and reducing interest rates (see MONETARY POLICY). Additionally, it can operate on the supply-side of the economy by promoting enterprise initiatives and providing resources for improving productivity and research (see INDUSTRIAL POLICIES).

**economic order quantity model** see STOCKHOLDING MODEL.

**economic planning** a method of controlling the economy that involves the setting of long-term objectives and the formulation of action programmes designed to achieve these objectives. In its most complete form, that of a centrally planned economy, economic planning involves the establishment of a national plan which lays down what goods and services are to be produced, and the quantities of each. Available resources are then allocated between producing units by a system of physical quotas. An alternative form of economic planning is that of 'indicative planning'. This approach does not replace the MARKET SYSTEM but operates by means of it, and involves both sides of industry (management and trade unions) and the government working together to improve the efficiency and productivity of the country's resources. See NATIONAL ECONOMIC DEVELOPMENT COUNCIL, ECONOMY.

**economic policy** the strategies and measures adopted by the government to manage the economy as a means of achieving its economic objectives. In general terms governments are concerned with (at the macro-level) securing full employment (see UNEMPLOYMENT), price stability (see INFLATION), ECONOMIC GROWTH and BALANCE OF PAYMENTS equilibrium, and (at the micro-level) an efficient use of resources. In practice, given the complexities of the economy and its exposure to international influences, the simultaneous achievement of all these objectives is virtually impossible, so that a degree of prioritizing is required. Inevitably, political as well as economic considerations will influence this process.

Various general measures can be employed by governments to achieve their objectives, including FISCAL POLICY (the manipulation of tax rates and government expenditure), MONETARY POLICY (the control of the money supply and interest rates), PRICES AND INCOMES POLICIES (controls on costs and prices) and the management of the EXCHANGE RATE to influence the country's external trade and payments position. These policies are augmented at a more specific level by measures designed to encourage industrial investment, research and development and enterprise, and to protect consumers' interests; see INDUSTRIAL POLICY, REGIONAL POLICY, COMPETITION POLICY.

Fiscal and monetary policies, the main measures used by successive governments in the UK since 1945, operate on the level and distribution of spending in the economy. They are thus essentially demand–side measures. In recent years greater emphasis has been given to the need to improve the supply-side of the economy, reflected, in particular, by attempts to inject greater flexibility into the workings of the labour market by breaking down the power of trade union monopolies.

See BUSINESS CYCLE, MONETARISM.

**economics** the study of the way in which countries endowed with only a *limited* availability of economic resources (natural resources, labour and capital) can best use these resources so as to gain the maximum fulfilment of society's *unlimited* demands for goods and services. Economics has a macroeconomic and a microeconomic dimension. Macroeconomics is concerned with the *overall* efficiency of resource use in the economy, in particular the achievement of full employment, and with the growth of resources over time (see ECONOMIC POLICY). Microeconomics is concerned with the efficient supply of *particular* goods and services (see MARKET SYSTEM).

**economies of scale** the reduction in the unit (average) costs of producing and distributing a product as the size of the firm's operations is increased. The ability to supply a product at a low cost (and hence a low price) represents an important source of COMPETITIVE ADVANTAGE over rival suppliers in markets where price competition is the main form of interfirm rivalry.

Economies of scale are to be found at the level both of the individual plant and of the firm (operating a number of plants). Important plant level economies include the possibility of using superior techniques or organization of production as scale is increased, for example switching from labour intensive BATCH PRODUCTION to continuous capital-intensive MASS PRODUCTION methods of manufacture; and the economies of increased dimensions, where for many types of capital equipment (boilers, tankers, etc.) both set-up and operating costs rise less than proportionately to increases in capacity. Firm-level economies include the ability of large firms to bulk buy raw materials and components on advantageous terms and, likewise, borrow money at preferential rates.

Unit costs, however, do not fall continuously as the scale of the firm's operations is increased; they tend to level off at some point (the *minimum efficient scale* of operation) and remain relatively constant thereafter, or they may rise because of the growing complexities of managing a larger organization (*diseconomies of scale*). Moreover, the potential for exploiting available economies of scale may be limited by the fact that the overall size of the market is too small or that firms' individual market shares are too low. In the latter case, increasing firm size by HORIZONTAL INTEGRATION, particularly through mergers or takeovers, may be one important means of making firms more cost-effective. Where economies of scale are significant, a high level of MARKET CONCENTRATION may also be required to ensure that industry output is produced as efficiently as possible.

See SPECIALIZATION.

**economies of scope** the cost savings which arise by carrying out a number of different activities within the same firm through sharing common inputs or jointly promoting or distributing products. For example, a building society could use its existing branches and staff not only to sell mortgages but also to offer customers other financial services such as insurance, pensions etc.

**economy** a country defined in terms of the total composition of its economic activities and the ultimate location of economic decision making.

The total value of goods and services produced in any one

year is called the *gross domestic product* (see NATIONAL INCOME ACCOUNTS). The contribution made to total output by the various subdivisions of the economy can be split down in various ways: for example, by broad sectors such as the *primary* sector (agriculture), the *industrial* sector (including manufacturing) and the *tertiary* sector (services); or by individual activities (brewing, coal-mining, etc.).

Economic decision making in the economy may be either highly centralized or decentralized. In a *centrally planned economy*, the State owns the means of production (except labour) and decides what goods and services are to be produced in accordance with a national plan. Resources are allocated between producing units, and final outputs between consumers by the use of physical quotas. At the other extreme, in a *private enterprise economy (free market* or *capitalist economy*) the means of production are held by individuals and firms. Economic decision making is highly decentralized with resources being allocated through a large number of individual goods and services markets. It is the MARKET which synchronizes the decisions of buyers and sellers by establishing market prices which determine how much of a product will be produced and sold. In practice, a large number of countries, including the UK, are *mixed economies* with some goods and services being provided by private enterprise and others, typically public-utility type products such as postal services and railways, being supplied by the State. The precise mix of private enterprise and State activities to be found in particular countries, however, does vary substantially between the two extremes and is very much influenced by prevailing political ideologies.

See INDUSTRY, STRUCTURE OF INDUSTRY, NATIONALIZATION VERSUS PRIVATIZATION.

**ECSC** see EUROPEAN COAL AND STEEL COMMUNITY.

**ECU (European Currency Unit),** the unit of account used to value the exchange rates of member countries of the European Union/Community and to settle payments imbalances between members. See EUROPEAN MONETARY SYSTEM.

**EEA** see EUROPEAN ECONOMIC AREA.

**EEF** see ENGINEERING EMPLOYERS FEDERATION.

**EETPU** see ELECTRICAL, ELECTRONIC, TELECOMMUNICATION AND PLUMBING UNION.

**effective exchange rate** see EXCHANGE RATE.

**efficiency** the relationship between the quantities of factor inputs (labour, materials, etc.) used by a firm and the quantity of output which it is able to produce using these inputs. Where a firm is able to produce the same output using fewer inputs or produce more output using the same quantity of inputs then it has improved its efficiency.

See PRODUCTIVITY.

**efficient-market hypothesis** the proposition that all available information which may influence the price of a FINANCIAL SECURITY is reflected in its *current* market price because financial markets are 'efficient' in adjusting prices to information. If markets are indeed efficient it is impossible for an investor to consistently predict how the price of any particular financial security is likely to change and thus outguess the market.

**effort bargain** a term in the SOCIOLOGY OF WORK referring to the implicit trade-offs made by workers between the effort expended on work and the payment received from it.

**EFTA** see EUROPEAN FREE TRADE ASSOCIATION.

**EIS** see ENTERPRISE INVESTMENT SCHEME.

**elasticity of demand** a measure of the degree of responsiveness of DEMAND for a product to a given change in some economic variable, particularly its own price, the prices of competing products and consumers' income. In general terms, if there is a more than proportionate change in quantity demanded as a result of a change in a variable, then demand is said to be *elastic*, while if there is a less than proportionate change, then demand is *inelastic*. Price elasticity of demand is calculated using the formula:

$$\frac{\%\ \text{change in quantity demanded}}{\%\ \text{change in product's own price}}$$

which measures the effect on demand of an increase or decrease in the product's own price. Since the price-quantity demanded relationship determines the firm's total revenue from selling the product, the price elasticity of demand figure thus provides an indication of the way in which a change in price will affect the firm's revenues. For example, if, as in the case of cigarettes as a generic group in the UK, demand is highly inelastic (econometric studies put it at 0.32), then an increase in cigarette prices will increase total industry revenues more than proportionately. However, it is important to note that the demand for each of the many individual brands making up the market is likely to be much more elastic because they face competitive substitutes within the market (i.e. putting up the price of a particular brand is likely to result in buyers switching to other brands, and hence reduce the firm's revenues). The extent to which the demand for a brand is affected by a change in the price of a close substitute brand can be measured by the cross-elasticity of demand formula:

$$\frac{\% \text{ change in quantity demanded of brand A}}{\% \text{ change in price of brand B}}$$

There are various practical difficulties, however, in the way of measuring elasticity values. For example, there is usually insufficient data available to construct a comprehensive 'demand curve' covering a wide range of price-quantity demanded combinations, and to isolate individual brand cross-elasticity effects in a multi-brand setting.

Income elasticity of demand measures the degree of responsiveness of demand for a product to changes in consumers' income over time, namely:

$$\frac{\% \text{ change in quantity demanded}}{\% \text{ change in income}}$$

The concept of income elasticity of demand is useful to corporate planners in indicating which industries are likely to decline or expand over time as income levels rise, and hence can make an important contribution to the formulation of a firm's DIVERSIFICATION and DIVESTMENT strategies.

See PRICE DISCRIMINATION.

**Electrical, Electronic, Telecommunication and Plumbing Union (EETPU)** the UK TRADE UNION notable for espousing a philosophy of 'business unionism' and for seeking SINGLE UNION DEALS, often encroaching on other unions' sphere of influence in the process. The EEPTU was expelled from the TRADES UNION CONGRESS in 1988 for its violation of the BRIDLINGTON RULES governing competition for membership. It merged with the engineering union to form the AMALGAMATED ENGINEERING AND ELECTRICAL UNION in 1992.

**electronic data interchange (EDI)** an interactive COMMUNICATION system which enables two firms to exchange business documents using standard electronic forms and COMPUTERS linked through a service provider. EDI is often a faster, cheaper and more reliable means of exchanging information than traditional paper-based exchanges.

See INFORMATION MANAGEMENT.

**electronic mail (e-mail)** a form of COMMUNICATION which involves sending COMPUTER-originated messages and information across a telecommunications network. E-mail usage is expanding rapidly, partly reflected in the introduction of new facilities which provide an integrated approach to sending messages to any combination of fax, telex and electronic mail addresses.

See INFORMATION MANAGEMENT, NETWORKING.

**electronic point of sale** see EPOS.

**electronic shopping** a form of DIRECT MARKETING in which consumers make purchases from products displayed on their domestic television by means of a telephone or keyboard link to the seller.

**e-mail** see ELECTRONIC MAIL.

**embargo** a complete ban on all INTERNATIONAL TRADE with a particular country or group of countries, or on trade in particular products such as narcotics and defence equipment. See COORDINATING COMMITTEE ON MULTINATIONAL EXPORT CONTROLS.

**emerging country** see DEVELOPING COUNTRY.

**emigration** see POPULATION.

**emoluments** wages, salaries, bonuses and payments in kind paid to employees or self-employed workers and managers. See PAY.

**employee** a person who is employed by an EMPLOYER (firm, government, etc.) on a paid basis to perform a JOB or work task specified in his or her CONTRACT OF EMPLOYMENT. See PAY, WORKER.

**employee attitude survey** see SURVEY.

**employee buy-out** see EMPLOYEE SHARE OWNERSHIP PLAN.

## EMPLOYEE COMMUNICATIONS

MANAGEMENT BUY-OUT, WORKERS' COOPERATIVE.

**employee communications** see COMMUNICATION, CONSULTATION.

**employee involvement** the attempt to increase employees' interest and commitment to their work and to the organization without, however, giving them any role in decision making. SUGGESTION SCHEMES, which encourage employees to think about ways in which work methods could be improved but which generally give them no role in the assessment of their recommendations, are a good example. The term is often used interchangeably with EMPLOYEE PARTICIPATION, but there is a difference in nuance in that the latter usually provides for some, albeit limited, participation in decision making. See TEAM BRIEFING.

**employee participation** the participation of employees in the affairs of the organization through (limited) participation in decision making or acquisition of a stake in the company through EMPLOYEE SHARE OWNERSHIP schemes (financial participation). Participation in decision making is usually at the immediate job level, i.e. employees may be given the opportunity to consider, recommend and implement changes to the way tasks are performed (see JOB DESIGN AND REDESIGN, JAPANIZATION). The philosophy behind participation is that employees have talents and knowledge about their jobs which can be utilized to improve performance, and that involvement in decision-making encourages commitment. It can be contrasted with INDUSTRIAL DEMOCRACY in which employees or their representatives have the *right* to be involved in determining company *policy*. See CONSULTATION, COMMUNITY CHARTER OF FUNDAMENTAL SOCIAL RIGHTS, FIFTH DIRECTIVE, VREDELING DIRECTIVE, EMPLOYEE SHARE OWNERSHIP PLAN.

**employee ratios** accounting ratios which attempt to assess the productivity and efficiency of a firm's labour force; for example, net profit per employee or sales per employee. See ACCOUNTING RATIO.

**employee relations** see INDUSTRIAL RELATIONS.

**employee share ownership** a scheme whereby employees acquire shares in the company in which they are employed. Although employees can of course purchase shares in their company on the open market, or companies can simply choose to donate shares to them, employee share ownership in the UK usually refers to three schemes, established by various Finance Acts, which confer tax advantages if formally approved by the Inland Revenue:

(a) *Approved Deferred Share Trusts* (ADSTs) or approved all-employee profit sharing. In this instance the company allocates a proportion of profits to a trust to buy shares in the company. These are then allocated to eligible employees (full-time employees of five years' standing or more). The company is exempt from corporation tax on profits donated in this way, whilst employees are exempt from income tax on the value of the shares as an addition to their income (as long as they are not sold for five years). Instead they are liable to capital gains tax, but in most cases this will be offset by the employee's capital gains tax allowance, hence no tax is paid.

(b) *Approved All-employee Savings Related Share Option Scheme*. The employee is given the option to buy shares in the company in five or seven years' time at a price fixed at the time of acquiring the option. The finance to purchase the shares is built up by a Save As You Earn (SAYE) savings scheme. If the value of the shares has fallen at the end of this period, the employee can decide not to use the accumulated savings for the share purchase. The employee is exempt from income tax on the benefits gained from the savings scheme and on the growth in value of the shares but is liable to capital gains tax on any profits gained at the sale of the shares. As with ADST schemes, in most cases this liability is more than offset by the capital gains tax allowance. Unlike ADST schemes, however, the company does not gain any tax benefits.

(c) *Approved Discretionary Share Options Scheme* (Executive Option Scheme). In these schemes selected employees, usually top managers, acquire an option to buy shares in the company in three to ten years' time at a price fixed at the time of acquiring the option. Although employees are expected to finance the purchase themselves they often benefit from favourable loan terms offered by the company. In this scheme too the beneficiary is liable to capital gains rather than income tax when the shares are sold. This type of scheme has been the fastest-growing form of employee share ownership in recent years, in part because firms have sought to develop links between individual performance and rewards, in part because top managers have come to expect to receive such benefits as part of the reward package.

Employee share ownership schemes of these types are generally seen by companies as a tax-efficient way of rewarding employees rather than as an extension of INDUSTRIAL DEMOCRACY. They are essentially a FRINGE BENEFIT. Employees may of course gain voting rights at the ANNUAL GENERAL MEETING as a result of acquiring shares but the volume and dispersal of shares is usually such that these shareholders cannot by themselves make a significant impact on company policy. Companies often justify these schemes on the basis that they will promote an identity of interest between employees and their employer, which in turn will lead to improvements in job performance. There is some evidence that some share ownership schemes are associated with attitudes of this sort but it is questionable whether this leads to better individual performance. The link between share benefits (dependent to some extent on growing profitability) and individual effort is at best weak and indirect, and it is therefore doubtful whether they provide a strong incentive effect.

Some observers (for example right-wing politicians) see employee share ownership schemes as a way of weakening employee commitment to TRADE UNIONS and strengthening INDIVIDUALISM and entrepreneurial enthusiasm. But given that employees seem to judge these schemes primarily on their capacity to increase incomes, it is questionable whether any major reorientation of employees' attitudes can be achieved in this way.

See EMPLOYEE SHARE OWNERSHIP PLAN, PROFIT-RELATED-PAY, PROFIT SHARING.

**employee share ownership plan (ESOP)** a method of passing ownership of a company to its employees by gradually transferring SHARES to them. There are several different types of ESOP in the UK. The most common is the 'case-law' ESOP. In this type, a trust has to be established (*Trust A*) to buy shares in the company on behalf of the employees. A separate trust (*Trust B*) is then established to receive a portion of company profits which are then used to purchase shares from Trust A. Trust A uses these receipts to pay off the initial loan whilst Trust B distributes the shares purchased to employees. If employees keep their shares for five years they receive tax concessions relating to their growth in value. If, however, they should chose to sell them they are required to sell them back to Trust B, not on the open market. Similarly, shares must be sold back to the Trust when an individual leaves the company's employment. Over a period of time (say 10 years) the purchase and distribution of shares will pass ownership to the employees. The statutory ESOP, introduced in 1989, has a single trust, normally called an *Employee Share Ownership Trust* (ESOT) or Qualified Employee Share Trust (QUEST). Currently a majority of the trustees must be elected by a majority of employees, and equity must be passed to employees over a twenty year period for the statutory tax benefits to be realised.

Although ESOPs are now common in the USA, there are relatively few in the UK. The advantages claimed for them are similar to other methods of EMPLOYEE SHARE OWNERSHIP. They may stimulate employee interest in company affairs and increase commitment. In acquiring a stake in the company there is an incentive for workers to seek to improve performance. As yet in the UK there is no firm evidence that these benefits are achieved. Other possible advantages include tax breaks and protection from predatory share purchasers. ESOPs may also facilitate INDUSTRIAL DEMOCRACY. As shareholders they may elect a number of representatives to the BOARD OF DIRECTORS (see WORKER DIRECTORS) as well as to the ESOP trusts.

See MANAGEMENT BUY-OUT, EMPLOYEE SHARE OWNERSHIP, PROFIT SHARING.

**employer** an organization (firm, government, etc.) which engages EMPLOYEES to perform JOB tasks related to the types of goods and services produced by the organization. See CONTRACT OF EMPLOYMENT.

**employers' association** an organization of employers in an industry with the function of representing their mutual interests in the promotion of trade (for example, representation at trade fairs) and/or dealing with labour and INDUSTRIAL RELATIONS issues. Regarding the latter, four functions are usually identified:

(a) negotiation of MULTI-EMPLOYER AGREEMENTS regulating rates of pay and conditions of employment in member companies;

(b) operation of a DISPUTES PROCEDURE. Where an INDUSTRIAL DISPUTE arises in a member company the association can step in (if requested) to apply a procedure for resolving the dispute;

(c) provision of advice to member companies on industrial relations and employment questions;

(d) representation of member companies' views to third parties, for example government.

With the growth of COLLECTIVE BARGAINING within companies, employers' associations are not as important in many industries as they once were. Nevertheless, they continue to provide important services for those small companies which do not have the resources to develop these functions in-house.

**employers' liability insurance** INSURANCE which employers are required by law to take out in order to cover their employees against injury or death at work.

**employment** the use of LABOUR and CAPITAL to produce goods and services. See LABOUR FORCE, CAPITAL STOCK.

**Employment Act 1980** a UK statute regulating TRADE UNIONS and INDUSTRIAL RELATIONS. The Act established state payments to finance secret ballots for union elections, for authorizing changes in union rules and for deciding whether STRIKE action should be taken. Individuals were given the right not to be excluded from union membership where a CLOSED SHOP exists. Certain forms of SECONDARY ACTION were made actionable in the civil courts. See EMPLOYMENT ACT 1982, EMPLOYMENT ACT 1988, EMPLOYMENT ACT 1990, TRADE UNION ACT 1984, TRADE UNION REFORM AND EMPLOYMENT RIGHTS ACT 1993.

**Employment Act 1982** a UK statute regulating the CLOSED SHOP and TRADE UNIONS. It required that a closed shop be approved by a substantial majority of the workforce, and that where such a ballot had not been held recently, anyone dismissed for refusing to join a trade union could pursue a claim for UNFAIR DISMISSAL. The Act also nullifies any clauses in commercial CONTRACTS which stipulate that work should be performed by union members or that the parties should recognize unions. The Act removes TRADE UNION IMMUNITIES for union actions which if done by individuals would be actionable in civil law, thereby allowing unions to be sued for damages. See EMPLOYMENT ACT 1980, EMPLOYMENT ACT 1988, EMPLOYMENT ACT 1990, TRADE UNION ACT 1984, TRADE UNION REFORM AND EMPLOYMENT RIGHTS ACT 1993.

**Employment Act 1988** a UK statute establishing legal rights of TRADE UNION members in relation to their unions. Under the Act, union members have the right to prevent their union from authorizing a STRIKE when a secret ballot has not been held, and not to be disciplined by their union for not participating in such action. A Commissioner for the Rights of Trade Union Members was established to support legal action by union members who believe these rights have been infringed. See EMPLOYMENT ACT 1980, EMPLOYMENT ACT 1982, EMPLOYMENT ACT 1990, TRADE UNION ACT 1984, TRADE UNION REFORM AND EMPLOYMENT RIGHTS ACT 1993.

**Employment Act 1989** UK statute aimed at deregulating employment and the LABOUR MARKET. It repealed those laws which controlled the working hours of young workers aged between 16 and 18, and repealed many of the laws which controlled the employment of women e.g. those which prevented women from working in coal mines. Small firms (those employing under 20 workers) were exempted from some requirements imposed by earlier legislation e.g. the requirement to provide a written statement of DISCIPLINARY PROCEDURES to new employees. The Act also abolished the tripartite (see TRIPARTISM) Training Commission, and oversight of training policy and provision passed to the EMPLOYMENT DEPARTMENT. See TRADE UNION REFORM AND EMPLOYMENT RIGHTS ACT 1993.

**Employment Act 1990** a UK statute aimed at reducing unofficial STRIKES. Trade unions were required to actively repudiate unofficial strike action. Employers were permitted to selectively dismiss unofficial strikers (i.e. without fear of UNFAIR DISMISSAL proceedings) and the TRADE UNION IMMUNITY was removed from any strikes called to support those selectively dismissed. The Act also made it unlawful to refuse employment to anybody on the grounds of membership or non-membership of a trade union (see CLOSED SHOP). The immunity for SECONDARY ACTION was removed. See TRADE UNION REFORM AND EMPLOYMENT RIGHTS ACT 1993.

**employment agency** a business which acts as an AGENT on behalf of firms seeking employees and of persons seeking work. Employment agencies maintain lists of job vacancies notified by prospective employers and details of persons seeking work, and match up the two. In addition, they may advertise jobs on behalf of employers and, where instructed, act as recruitment agents by interviewing and shortlisting job applicants.

**Employment Appeals Tribunal** a body which hears appeals against the decisions of INDUSTRIAL TRIBUNALS and the CERTIFICATION OFFICER.

**employment legislation** see LABOUR LAW.

**Employment Training** see TRAINING, TRAINING AND EDUCATION COUNCIL.

**EMS** see EUROPEAN MONETARY SYSTEM.

**enabling authority** a local authority or some other public service organization which coordinates service provision by other, possibly private sector, organizations. In this model of public service provision the public authority no longer provides services itself. Instead it contracts with other organizations to deliver them. The philosophy underlying this model is that private sector organizations can provide public services more effectively and efficiently than public sector organizations. COMPETITIVE TENDERING embodies the 'enabling authority' approach. See NEW PUBLIC MANAGEMENT.

**endgame strategy** or **declining industry strategy** a framework for analysing the nature and causes of decline in an industry and for identifying strategies most appropriate to the firm operating in such an environment. Although an industry which has moved into the decline phase of the PRODUCT LIFE CYCLE is characterized overall by falling demand and problems of excess capacity, it nonetheless may still offer attractive returns to firms possessing COMPETITIVE ADVANTAGES over rival suppliers. For others, immediate exit from the industry rather than hanging on may be appropriate to the situation. Each industry differs in its make-up, so that an appraisal needs to be made of:

(a) the *particular* reasons for decline, the rate at which demand is declining and whether there are growth segments in the market;

(b) the structure of the market (see MARKET STRUCTURE) in terms of levels of MARKET CONCENTRATION, buyer characteristics and factors influencing the volatility of competition;

(c) the firm's own perceived strengths and weaknesses vis-à-vis other competitors in the industry (see SWOT ANALYSIS).

A number of strategic possibilities will emerge from this evaluation including:

(a) to hold or increase the firm's investment in the market by, for example, MERGER/TAKEOVER to expand its market share and, simultaneously, remove excess capacity from the market. This is a high risk strategy but acceptable if the firm possesses competitive advantages (for example, low costs or superior products) and the industry itself exhibits certain favourable endgame characteristics, for example a slow rate of decline in overall demand coupled with the existence of profitable market segments;

(b) to shrink selectively – this strategy involves refocusing the firm by exiting from unprofitable sectors and remaining in profitable ones;

(c) to milk the investment – the firm would continue its operations with a minimum of expenditure and make no effort to maintain its market position;

(d) to divest now – sell the business to competitors wholly or in part, or liquidate. See DIVESTMENT.

See BUSINESS STRATEGY, BARRIERS TO EXIT.

**Engineering Employers Federation (EEF)** the UK federation of EMPLOYERS' ASSOCIATIONS representing employers in the engineering industry. Over 4,000 engineering firms are members of their regional Engineering Employers' Association which in turn are affiliated to the EEF. Member firms are known as federated; nonmembers are nonfederated. Until recently, the EEF negotiated WAGE RATES and HOURS OF WORK nationally with the industry's TRADE UNIONS. Now, wages and conditions are determined at individual companies or workplaces. See MULTI-EMPLOYER AGREEMENT.

**enterprise allowance scheme** financial assistance currently offered by the UK government to assist unemployed people to set up their own businesses.

**Enterprise Investment Scheme (EIS)** a facility introduced in 1994 which offers income tax relief on equity investments in unquoted companies. The EIS (which replaced the *Business Expansion Scheme (BES))* is aimed at assisting smaller businesses in the manufacturing and services industries to raise new capital without having to obtain a STOCK MARKET listing. The scheme specifically excludes investments in private rented housing which had been widely used under the previous BES as a means of avoiding tax.

Under the EIS individuals can invest up to £100,000 in a

company writing off the price paid for their shares against their income tax assessment, and can also become paid directors of the companies they invest in without losing entitlement to tax relief.

See INVESTMENT INCENTIVE.

**enterprise union** see JAPANIZATION, TRADE UNION.

**enterprise zone** a small area of relatively high unemployment where the government is prepared to offer various financial inducements to firms undertaking new investment. See REGIONAL POLICY (UK).

**entrepôt trade** a form of INTERNATIONAL TRADE, mainly confined to COMMODITIES such as tin and tea, where goods are temporarily imported into a country and then subsequently re-exported to other countries as part of a complex chain of physical distribution and financing deals. See FREEPORT.

**entrepreneur** a person who undertakes the risks of establishing and running a new business. Entrepreneurs are characterized by their initiative and enterprise in seeking out new business opportunities; inventing and commercializing new goods and services and methods of production. See VENTURE CAPITAL, INDUSTRIAL POLICY, INTRAPRENEURIAL GROUP, MANAGEMENT BUY-OUT.

**environment** see CONTINGENCY THEORY.

**Environmental Protection Act 1990** see POLLUTION.

**environment monitoring** the practice of keeping a watchful eye on what is happening in the external environment in which a business or organization operates. The objective is to identify threats and opportunities in that environment posed by changing technology, competition, etc. and to help the business or organization be flexible and respond quickly to change.

See SWOT ANALYSIS.

**EPOS (electronic point of sale)** a system for recording sales using sophisticated cash tills which record the total amount to be paid by a customer, provide them with itemized bills and simultaneously adjust the firm's STOCK records to assist the firm to plan its reordering of goods. EPOS is increasingly being used in supermarket checkouts, often linked to BAR-CODE scanners and providing for the direct debiting of customers' bank accounts for the total amount owing.

**Equal Opportunities Commission** see DISCRIMINATION.

**equal opportunities employer** see DISCRIMINATION.

**equal pay** the right for men and women to be paid the same rate of PAY for performing the same job, established in the UK by the Equal Pay Act 1970. Until 1984 it was widely believed that employers could circumvent the spirit of this legislation by segregating men's and women's jobs. Since then employees have been entitled to equal pay for work of equal *value*. Aggrieved employees may pursue their claim to an INDUSTRIAL TRIBUNAL. To determine whether different jobs are of equal value the techniques of JOB EVALUATION are used. See DISCRIMINATION.

**Equal Pay Act 1970** see DISCRIMINATION.

**equal pay for equal value** SEE EQUAL PAY, DISCRIMINATION.

**equation** a means of portraying arithmetically the relationship between VARIABLES. For example, the equation in the form C = £1,000 + 0.9Q suggests a particular relationship between product cost (C) and output (Q). Equations are generally written with a two-bar equals sign (=), the value on the left of the sign being equal to the value on the right of the sign.

**equilibrium market price** the market-clearing price at which the demand for a product is just equal to the supply of it. The *demand curve* in Fig. 38 is downward sloping, indicating that as price falls buyers will be prepared to purchase more of the product; the *supply curve* is upward sloping, indicating that as the price of the product increases suppliers will be prepared to

Fig. 38. **Equilibrium market price.** Graph showing demand and supply curves.

offer more of it. Price OP is the equilibrium market price and OQ the amount of the product transacted. At prices initially higher than OP there is *excess supply* over demand which in a free market situation will cause the price to fall, while at prices initially lower than OP there is *excess demand* over supply which will cause the price to rise. In many markets, however, price levels are likely to be distorted both by the presence of powerful suppliers (see MONOPOLY, CARTEL, COLLUSION) and by governmental PRICE CONTROLS (see AGRICULTURAL POLICY).

**equipment** small items of capital such as a hand drill or screwdriver which are used to produce goods. See PLANT, MACHINERY, CAPITAL STOCK, FIXED ASSET.

**equity** ordinary shareholders' funds, that is, their ORDINARY SHARE capital subscribed plus any RESERVES or ploughed-back profit. Alternatively, equity can be regarded as what would be left to the ordinary shareholders of a company after all the company's debts and liabilities have been met.

**ergonomics** or **human engineering** the study of the interface between people and technology with the objective of achieving a better 'fit' between the two. The twin objectives of ergonomics are the interrelated ones of improvements in efficiency and the provision of better working conditions. For instance, an ergonomist would be concerned to ensure that a typist's chair is of the right height to avoid back and arm strains. As well as minimizing employee dissatisfaction this would prevent productivity from being impaired by physical injury. In more complex technological environments the ergonomist is also concerned with the distribution of functions between human operators and the technology itself. Ergonomics grew out of SCIENTIFIC MANAGEMENT, one strand of which was concerned with the development of technology that could be matched to the task in hand and to the human physique, and human factor psychology (see OCCUPATIONAL PSYCHOLOGY), which was concerned with the impact of environmental factors on work performance.

**ERG Theory** see MOTIVATION.

**ERM** see EUROPEAN MONETARY SYSTEM.

**ESOP** see EMPLOYEE SHARE OWNERSHIP PLAN.

**ESOT** see EMPLOYEE SHARE OWNERSHIP PLAN.

**estate agent** a business which acts as an AGENT on behalf of personal and industrial clients in the buying and selling of land and buildings. Estate agents provide various services for their clients including the valuation and pricing of land and buildings, advice on the attributes of the land or building itself and the locality in which it is situated, and conveyancing, surveying, inspection and MORTGAGE contacts. The provision of estate agency services in the UK is regulated by the Estate Agency Act 1979 which lays down general rules of good conduct and can ban persons who are deemed unfit for this purpose. See CONVEYANCE, BUILDING SOCIETY.

**estate duty** see INHERITANCE TAX.

**estimating** the process of judging the probable expenditure to be incurred in making a product, as a basis for setting a product price. Estimating is generally less detailed and accurate than COSTING where actual costs of jobs are ascertained, but it may suffice in quoting a price for a job.

**ethnic monitoring** see DISCRIMINATION.

**EU** see EUROPEAN UNION.

**Eurobond market** see EUROCURRENCY MARKET.

**Eurocurrency market** or **Eurobond market** a MARKET based in Europe, comprising a web of international banks and money brokers, which is engaged in the borrowing and lending of FOREIGN CURRENCIES such as US dollars *outside* their countries of origin, as a means of financing trade and investment transactions.

The main instrument used in the Eurocurrency market to finance long-term investment is the Eurobond, a form of fixed interest security which is denominated either in a single currency or is syndicated with a 'lead' bank arranging with other banks a multi-currency loan package. Depositors of funds in the Eurocurrency market include commercial banks, companies and central banks, while borrowers for the most part are industrial and financial companies, particularly MULTI-NATIONAL ENTERPRISES, who use Eurofinance during times of domestic credit restrictions and/or when domestic interest rates are high in comparison with Eurocurrency rates.

See LIBOR.

**European Coal and Steel Community (ECSC)** an organization, operating within the EUROPEAN COMMUNITY, now itself part of the EUROPEAN UNION, which is concerned with promoting free trade in coal and steel products, and which acts as a coordinating body in regulating the industries' investment programmes and commercial practices.

**European Commission** see EUROPEAN COMMUNITY.

**European Community (EC)** a regional bloc established by the Treaty of Rome in 1958 and which is now part of the EUROPEAN UNION (established 1993) which has the general objective of integrating the economies of member countries. There were six founding members of the EC: France, Italy, Germany, The Netherlands, Belgium and Luxembourg. The UK, Denmark and Ireland joined the EC in 1973, Greece in 1981 and Spain and Portugal in 1986. Austria, Sweden and Finland joined the EC in 1995, and it is likely that other countries will join in due course. The EC constitutes the leading economic grouping in the world economy, accounting for around 42% of world production and trade in 1994.

The strategic and main operational policies of the EC are formulated by member countries' governments acting through the Council of Ministers (one appointed member per country, one vote) and the democratically-elected European Parliament. The European Commission is responsible for the day-to-day administration and coordination of Community policy, control of the EC's general budget finance and, together with the various specialist agencies set up to run particular programmes (see below), is involved in the detailed implementation of Community policies. The European Court of Justice acts as the final arbiter in cases of dispute between member countries, and between companies, etc., and the European Commission.

The main economic developments within the EC to date include:

(a) the formation of a *common market* providing for FREE TRADE in goods and services through the removal of TARIFFS, QUOTAS and other obstacles to cross-frontier trade, and for the free movement of labour and capital across national boundaries (see INTERNATIONAL TRADE). The EC operates a common external tariff against nonmember countries but this has been progressively reduced through tariff-cuts negotiated through the GENERAL AGREEMENT ON TARIFFS AND TRADE; while tariff-free entry into the EC is provided under various trade pacts with, for example, certain less-developed countries (the Lomé Agreement) and member countries of the EUROPEAN FREE TRADE ASSOCIATION (see EUROPEAN ECONOMIC AREA). A large number of internal obstacles to trade have arisen out of historical differences between countries in the application of, for example technical standards, descriptions of goods, documentation procedures, road and rail regulations, etc. These are to be removed progressively through the 300 or so *directives* emanating from the SINGLE EUROPEAN ACT 1986 (popularly known as the '1992' initiative), which attempts to harmonize and standardize practices across the whole EC bloc;

(b) the free trade philosophy of the EC which is underpinned by the fair trade provisions of the EC's *competition policy* which prohibit price-fixing, market sharing CARTELS, etc. between rival suppliers, and the abuse of a dominant market position, where this serves to reduce or eliminate intra-EC trade. see COMPETITION POLICY (EC);

(c) a *Common Agricultural Policy* (CAP) which provides for the subsidization and protection of the farm sector (see AGRICULTURAL POLICY). Around 75% of EC farm produce benefits directly from the operation of a price support system which maintains EC farm prices at levels usually well in excess of world market prices. Variable tariff rates on imported farm products are used to keep out unwanted imports. The CAP is the largest single component of the EC's total budget, accounting for around 65% of all EC spending in 1994. The CAP has been heavily criticized for encouraging wasteful overproduction of agricultural produce and perpetuating inefficient farming methods and, of course, acting against the interests of consumers. Reform of the CAP is currently a major source of conflict between member countries; see GREEN MONEY.

(d) a *regional* policy whose objective is to remove regional imbalances in industrial activity and employment opportunities so as to achieve a more even spread of economic prosperity both within and between member countries. See REGIONAL POLICY (EC);

(e) the establishment of a mechanism (the EUROPEAN MONETARY SYSTEM) for coordinating member countries' EXCHANGE RATES to provide a greater degree of stability in external currency values as a means of promoting cross-frontier trade;

(f) the creation of a special monetary unit, the *European Currency Unit* (ECU) to provide a common basis for intercountry settlements under the CAP and the EUROPEAN MONETARY SYSTEM.

Over the longer term the EC, as part of the European Union, is to move towards a greater integration of the economies of member countries by the harmonizing of economic policies and the centralization of fiscal and monetary control, for example the replacement of individual national currencies by a single European currency (see EUROPEAN MONETARY SYSTEM). There are those in the European movement who would like to see the tag 'member country' eventually displaced by the EC itself assuming the role of the nation state. See MAASTRICHT TREATY, SUBSIDIARITY.

**European Currency Unit** see EUROPEAN MONETARY SYSTEM.

**European Economic Area (EEA)** an alliance established in 1991 between the member countries of the EUROPEAN COMMUNITY (EC) – now part of the EUROPEAN UNION – and the EUROPEAN FREE TRADE ASSOCIATION (EFTA). The EEA's aim is to extend the EC's 'single market freedoms' in the flow of goods, services, capital and labour to include EFTA. EFTA countries will adopt the harmonization directives currently being implemented under the SINGLE EUROPEAN ACT 1986.

**European Free Trade Association (EFTA)** a regional FREE TRADE BLOC established in 1959 with the general objective of securing the benefits to be derived from greater INTERNATIONAL TRADE. There were originally seven members of EFTA: the UK, Sweden, Switzerland, Austria, Denmark, Norway and Portugal; these countries opted for a less comprehensive integration of their economies than that required by membership of the EUROPEAN COMMUNITY (EC) formed the year previously. In 1973, however, the UK and Denmark left and joined the EC, and Portugal joined the EC in 1986. Three countries have joined EFTA: Finland in 1961, Iceland in 1970 and Liechtenstein in 1991.

The formation of EFTA has resulted in the removal of all import restrictions such as TARIFFS and QUOTAS on trade between member countries, but there has been no attempt, as in the EC, to harmonize restrictions applied against imports from nonmembers, which has remained an area for national jurisdiction.

Over the years EFTA has entered into various trade pacts with the EC (now part of the EUROPEAN UNION) culminatng in the establishment, in 1991, of the EUROPEAN ECONOMIC AREA. However, the whole future of EFTA has been put in the melting pot as three members (Finland, Austria and Sweden) joined the European Union in 1995 and it is possible that others may follow.

**European Investment Bank** see REGIONAL POLICY.

**European Monetary System (EMS)** an institutional arrangement, established in 1979, for coordinating and stabilizing the EXCHANGE RATES of member countries of the EUROPEAN COMMUNITY (EC), which is now part of the EUROPEAN UNION. The EMS is based on a FIXED EXCHANGE RATE SYSTEM and the European Currency Unit (ECU), which is used to value, on a common basis, exchange rates and which also acts as a reserve asset to be used by members, alongside their other INTERNATIONAL RESERVE holdings, to settle payments imbalances between themselves.

The EMS is managed by the *European Monetary Cooperation Fund* (EMCF). Currently membership of the EMS is voluntary and five countries, Greece, Italy, Finland, Sweden and the UK are (as at October 1995) outside the exchange rate arrangements of the EMS, although they are fully involved in the operation of the reserve pool.

Under the EMS *exchange rate mechanism* (ERM) each country's currency is given a fixed central par value specified in terms of the ECU, and the exchange rate between currencies can move to a limited degree around these par values, being controlled by a *parity grid* and *divergence indicator*. The parity grid originally permitted a currency to move up to a limit of 2.25% either side of its central rate but this was increased to 15% in 1993. As a currency moves towards its outer limit the divergence indicator comes into play, requiring the country's central bank to intervene in the foreign exchange market or to adopt appropriate domestic measures (for example alter interest rates) in order to stabilize the rate. If in the view of the EMCF the central rate itself appears to be overvalued or undervalued against other currencies, a country can devalue (see DEVALUATION) or revalue (see REVALUATION) its currency, refixing it at a new central parity rate.

The European Currency Unit, unlike other reserve assets such as gold, has no tangible life of its own. ECU's are created by the Fund in exchange for the in-payment of gold and other reserve assets, and take the form of book-keeping entries recorded in a special account managed by the Fund.

The value of the ECU is based on a weighted 'basket' of members' currencies. In sterling terms it is (currently) worth around 78 pence.

In the long term it is planned (under the MAASTRICHT TREATY, 1991) that the EUROPEAN UNION will move towards eventual monetary unification through:

(a) initially, greater exchange rate harmonization requiring all member countries to join the exchange rate mechanism;

(b) the establishment of a European Central Bank to provide for coordinated monetary policies, leading ultimately to

(c) the replacement of individual members' currencies by a single currency - the 'Euro'.

**European Regional Development Fund** see REGIONAL POLICY.

**European Union (EU)** the 'new' European regional bloc established following the final ratification by all twelve members of the EUROPEAN COMMUNITY of the MAASTRICHT TREATY in November 1993 which provides for a closer unification of the economic, social and political systems of member countries. Responsibilities of the EU include (a) the European Community (established in 1958) with its long-term commitment to economic, monetary and social integration, and two new areas of common responsibilities: (b) foreign policy and defence and (c) co-operation in law enforcement and immigration - both of which will be the concern of the intergovernmental bodies representing all member countries.

In 1995 there were 15 members of the EU: France, Italy, Germany, Netherlands, Belgium, Luxembourg, UK, Denmark, Ireland, Spain, Portugal, Greece, Austria, Finland and Sweden. It is likely that EU membership will be further extended in due course.

For a fuller discussion of the main economic activities of the EU see the entry on EUROPEAN COMMUNITY.

**European Works Council** a pan-European council of employee representatives within transnational firms established to facilitate CONSULTATION between management and employees. Firms with at least 1000 employees in the member states of the EUROPEAN UNION and at least 150 employees in two or more member states are required to establish a European Works Council. This is the first proposal emanating from the

SOCIAL CHAPTER or *Social Protocol* provisions of the MAASTRICHT TREATY. Although this Directive will not apply in the UK, large UK companies with operations in the rest of Europe will be required to establish a European Works Council for their employees elsewhere in Europe.

**excess capacity** see OVERCAPACITY.

**excess demand** see EQUILIBRIUM MARKET PRICE.

**excess supply** see EQUILIBRIUM MARKET PRICE.

**exchange** see MARKET, BARTER.

**exchange controls** see FOREIGN EXCHANGE CONTROLS.

**exchange rate** the price of one country's currency expressed in terms of another country's currency; for example, one UK pound (£) = two US dollars ($). Because there are a large number of countries participating in the international economy, multi-exchange rate systems are required in order to synchronize and, in some cases, coordinate and harmonize exchange rates.

Under a FIXED EXCHANGE RATE SYSTEM, such as the European Union's EUROPEAN MONETARY SYSTEM, exchange rates, once established, will remain unchanged for longish periods. If a particular country's exchange rate gets too far out of line with underlying market conditions, however, and becomes over-valued for example, resulting in that country being persistently in BALANCE OF PAYMENTS deficit, the exchange rate can be devalued (see DEVALUATION), i.e. refixed at a lower level which makes its imports more expensive and its exports cheaper. Similarly, if the exchange rate becomes undervalued, resulting in a country being persistently in balance of payments surplus, the exchange rate can be revalued, i.e. refixed at a higher value, which makes its imports cheaper and its exports more expensive (see REVALUATION).

Over time, exchange rates, if left unregulated by the authorities, will fluctuate according to changes in underlying market conditions, reflecting such things as differences in INFLATION rates and INTEREST RATES between countries. For example, if the prices of UK goods rise faster than the prices of equivalent German goods, people will tend to buy more German goods, causing the Deutschmark to appreciate and the £ to depreciate. On the other hand, if UK interest rates are higher than German interest rates, this will encourage German investors to deposit money in the UK money markets, causing the £ to appreciate against the Deutschmark.

Under a FLOATING EXCHANGE RATE SYSTEM, the exchange rate is free to fluctuate day by day and will fall (see DEPRECIATION) or rise (see APPRECIATION) in line with changing market conditions, serving (in theory) to keep a country's balance of payments more or less in equilibrium on a continuous basis. In practice, however, the uncertainties and SPECULATION associated with free floats tend to produce erratic and random exchange rate movements which act to inhibit trade as well as producing destabilizing domestic effects. For these reasons countries often prefer to 'manage' their exchange rates, both to moderate the degree of short-run fluctuation and to smooth out the long-run trend line.

The term *effective exchange rate* is used to describe a given currency's value in terms of a weighted average of a 'basket' of other currencies. Fig. 39 depicts the effective exchange rate over time of the Pound against other major countries' currencies, for example the US dollar, Japanese yen, German mark, French franc etc. A fall (depreciation) in the effective exchange rate indicates a general improvement in the price competitiveness of a country's products vis-à-vis trade partners.

In FOREIGN EXCHANGE MARKETS the exchange rate may be quoted either in terms of how many units of a foreign currency may be bought or sold per unit of the domestic currency (an *indirect quotation*), or in terms of how many units of domestic currency may be bought or sold per unit of a particular foreign currency (a *direct quotation*). For example, in the UK an indirect quotation of the exchange rate between the Pound and the US dollar might be £1 = $2, whereas a direct quotation would be $1 = 50 pence.

Exchange rates are usually quoted by dealers as a pair of rates, the offer or sell rate and the bid or buy rate, the difference between the two (the *spread*) representing the dealers' profit margin. Currencies which are traded in large volumes, such as the US dollar and German mark, usually have a narrower spread than currencies which are little used in international dealings. Similarly, the spread on current exchange rates quoted in the SPOT MARKET for currencies is usually narrower than the spread on forward prices quoted in the FORWARD MARKET.

See CROSS RATE, EXCHANGE RATE EXPOSURE.

| | |
|------|-----|
| 1990 | 100 |
| 1991 | 98  |
| 1992 | 97  |
| 1993 | 89  |
| 1994 | 89  |
| 1995 | 83  |
| 1996 | 94  |
| 1997 | 104 |

trade-weighted average 1990 = 100

Fig. 39. **Exchange rate.** Effective exchange rate.

**exchange rate exposure** the extent of a firm's potential losses/gains on its overseas operations (measured in domestic currency terms) as a result of EXCHANGE RATE changes. The firm can be exposed to variations in exchange rates in a number of ways:

(a) *translation* or *accounting exposure* arises when consolidating (see CONSOLIDATED ACCOUNTS) the assets, liabilities, revenues and expenses of overseas subsidiaries (expressed in foreign currencies) into the parent company's group accounts (expressed in the parent's domestic currency);

(b) *transactions exposure* arises when a firm exports and imports products and borrows funds from abroad or invests overseas. For example, when a firm exports a product, invoicing the customer in terms of the customer's own local currency, and granting the customer 60 days' credit, then the firm is exposed to the effects of exchange rate variations during the 60-day credit period, which may decrease or increase the domestic currency value of the money due. Were the exchange rate of the foreign currency to fall dramatically vis-à-vis the domestic currency, then the exchange rate loss may completely eliminate any expected profit on the transaction;

(c) *economic* or *cash flow exposure* is concerned with the impact of exchange rate variations on the future cash flows generated by a company's production and marketing operations. Long-term or dramatic changes in exchange rates may well force a firm to rethink its FOREIGN MARKET SERVICING STRATEGY and raw material SOURCING strategy. For instance, a firm which serviced its overseas markets by direct exporting from domestic plants might decide to establish local production units to supply these markets instead, if an exchange rate appreciation were to render its export prices uncompetitive.

There are a number of mechanisms whereby a firm can reduce its exposure to potential losses resulting from exchange rate changes. First, a firm can seek to prevent an exposed position from arising by using such internal exposure management techniques as *currency matching* (matching foreign currency holdings with equal foreign currency borrowings); *leading and lagging* (accelerating or delaying foreign currency payments and receipts where the exchange rate of the currency is expected to change); and MULTILATERAL NETTING of currency receipts and payments between subsidiaries of a MULTINATIONAL ENTERPRISE. Second, the firm can use external contractual arrangements to reduce or eliminate whatever exposure remains, hedging risks by: entering into forward exchange contracts to buy or sell currencies as appropriate (see FORWARD MARKET); FACTORING (selling the firm's trade debts); buying and selling foreign exchange OPTIONS; foreign currency borrowing; the use of export credit guarantees (see EXPORT CREDIT GUARANTEE DEPARTMENT) and currency SWAPS.

**exchange rate mechanism** see EUROPEAN MONETARY SYSTEM.

**excise duty** an INDIRECT TAX imposed by the government on a product, principally those such as tobacco, petrol and alcoholic drinks, the demand for which is highly price-inelastic (see ELASTICITY OF DEMAND). Governments use excise duties both as a means of raising revenue (see BUDGET) and as an instrument of FISCAL POLICY. See CUSTOMS AND EXCISE.

**exclusive dealing** a business practice whereby a supplier contracts distributors/retailers to sell his products on an exclusive basis (i.e. to refrain from handling the products of rival suppliers). Retailers are rewarded for sole representation in a variety of ways including preferential discounts, back-up services and loans. The practice of exclusive dealing may help the supplier boost his sales and protect market share because distributors have an undivided commitment to the product. However, if undertaken by a DOMINANT FIRM, the practice may serve to limit competition in a market by depriving rival suppliers of distribution outlets. See OFFICE OF FAIR TRADING.

**exclusive distribution** a DISTRIBUTION strategy employed by a supplier of a product in which only one RETAILER or WHOLE-SALER is permitted to sell that supplier's product in a particular area or territory. Designated exclusive sales territories may be defined narrowly (city by city) or more broadly (region by region). Exclusive distribution systems can enable physical distribution costs to be lowered and achieve a greater retailer commitment in boosting sales (especially if this is backed by an EXCLUSIVE DEALING arrangement). On the other hand, if the retailer has an insufficient number of shops then, compared with a multiple-retailer approach, sales potential could be limited.

**ex–dividend** *adv.* in a manner which excludes entitlement to the DIVIDEND which attaches to a share. If shares are purchased on the STOCK MARKET 'ex div', the purchasers would not be entitled to the dividend accruing to that share when the dividend is next paid. Compare CUM-DIVIDEND.

**executive committee** the ruling body of an organization, such as a TRADE UNION, whose function is to decide and implement courses of action consistent with the policy and philosophy established by the organization's membership.

**executive director** see DIRECTOR, BOARD OF DIRECTORS.

**executive options scheme** see EMPLOYEE SHARE OWNERSHIP.

**exempt products** see VALUE ADDED TAX.

**Existence, Relatedness and Growth (ERG)** see MOTIVA-TION.

**expectancy theory** see MOTIVATION.

**expectations** the view taken of likely *future* events and changes by persons and firms which serves to influence their *current* economic behaviour. For example, a holder of a FINANCIAL SECURITY may anticipate that its price is likely to fall in the near future, and this may encourage him to sell the security now rather than incur (an expected) reduction in profits or even losses in the future (see SPECULATION, HEDGING); a TRADE UNION may anticipate that INFLATION is likely to rise, which causes it to put in a demand for a wage increase for its members which in part reflects (an expected) higher rate of future inflation.

**expected money value** see DECISION TREE.

**expected number defective** the average number of defective products which a firm expects to obtain from taking a number of samples. If the actual number of defectives from a sample is higher than expected, the production process involved will be investigated to determine the cause of the problem.

See QUALITY CONTROL.

**expected service–perceived service gap** see GAP ANALYSIS.

**expenditure tax** a form of INDIRECT TAX which is added to the selling price of a good or service and which is borne by consumers of these products. VALUE ADDED TAX, EXCISE DUTIES and CUSTOMS DUTIES are the main types of expenditure tax levied in the UK. Expenditure taxes, along with various taxes on income (see DIRECT TAX), are used by the government to raise revenue (see BUDGET) and as a means of regulating the level of spending in the economy (see FISCAL POLICY).

**expense** any expenditure which is chargeable to the trading activities of an accounting period. This includes cash expenditures on materials and labour, and non–cash items of expenditure such as credit purchases and depreciation.

**experience curve** or **learning curve** the cumulative process whereby, as the managers and labour force of a firm gain greater experience of a new technology by repetitive contact, they become more efficient at operating it, which enables unit costs of production to be reduced. Additionally, familiarity with a technology and the development of associated skills and expertise can provide a platform for further technological advances. Thus, a firm's unique embodied experience can enable it to establish COMPETITIVE ADVANTAGES over rival suppliers. See SPECIALIZATION, PRODUCTIVITY.

**expert system** a COMPUTER programme which simulates the problem–solving and decision–making behaviour of a technical expert in a particular field such as engineering and medicine. Like human technical experts, expert systems are able to learn from experience and restructure their knowledge in order to improve their future problem–solving.

**expired costs** costs, the benefits of which have been consumed and used up within the current accounting period and which do not therefore get carried forward into the next account period in the form of closing stock or a prepayment.

**exponential smoothing** see SALES FORECASTING.

**export 1.** a good which is produced in the home country and which is then physically transported to, and sold in, an over-seas market earning foreign exchange for the home country (*visible export*).

**2.** a service which is provided for foreigners either in the home country (for example visits by tourists) or overseas (for example banking, insurance) which likewise generates foreign exchange for the home country (*invisible export*).

**3.** capital which is placed abroad in the form of portfolio investment, foreign direct investment in physical assets, and banking deposits (*capital export*). See FOREIGN INVESTMENT.

Together these items comprise, along with IMPORTS, a country's BALANCE OF PAYMENTS.

See INTERNATIONAL TRADE, EXPORTING, EXPORT CREDIT GUARAN-TEE DEPARTMENT, EXPORT RESTRAINT AGREEMENT, EXPORT SUBSIDY.

**Export Credit Guarantee Department (ECGD)** a UK government department which UNDERWRITES (insures) UK EXPORTS sold on CREDIT against nonpayment by foreign customers whether this is due to insolvency of the customer or, for example, the imposition of exchange controls by foreign governments, etc.

Until 1991 the ECGD provided both short-term and long-term export credits. Guarantees covering 90–95% of the loss of sales revenue were available for most exports sold on up to 6 months' credit, while extended cover is provided for certain exports (for example production engineering products) sold on up to 5 years' credit terms. In addition, the ECGD provides long-term cover (normally up to 15 years) for certain FOREIGN INVESTMENT projects against political risk.

In 1991 the provision of short-term export credits was taken over by a private sector concern, NCM.

See FACTORING.

**exporting** the sale in an overseas market of a product which is produced in the firm's home market.

Exports may be viewed by the firm as merely an extension of home sales, serving to provide extra business as a means of allowing the firm to operate its productive capacity to the full. More fundamentally, exports may be regarded as an important profit centre in their own right, providing the firm with opportunities for worldwide sales expansion and long-term profit growth.

Exporting may be undertaken indirectly or directly. *Indirect* exporting involves the contracting of independent agents to establish wholesale and retail sales contacts, and importers/distributors to handle the physical distribution of the product. Often, however, independent agents/distributors lack the commitment or resources required to maximize the firm's overseas sales potential. For this reason *direct* exporting may be preferred, requiring the appointment of the company's own overseas sales personnel and the establishment of overseas sales offices, depots and sales subsidiaries to handle local distribution and marketing. Exporting may be conducted on a 'stand-alone' basis or, as in the case of MULTINATIONAL ENTERPRISES as part of a more complex FOREIGN MARKET SERVICING STRATEGY involving also licensing and overseas production.

The physical act of transporting goods to export markets may be done by the suppliers' own distribution division or by using the services of independent hauliers, fleet operators and FREIGHT FORWARDERS. Documentation required in connection with export consignments includes a BILL OF LADING, CERTIFICATE OF ORIGIN, WEIGHT NOTE, INSURANCE and (where appropriate) an export licence. Exporting may be undertaken according to a FREE ON BOARD (f.o.b.) contract, a COST, INSURANCE AND FREIGHT (c.i.f.) contract, or a COST AND FREIGHT (c&f) contract.

Export finance is provided by the commercial banks in the form of short-term credits (often underpinned by LETTERS OF CREDIT) and backed in the UK by the government's EXPORT CREDITS GUARANTEE DEPARTMENT (ECGD), FACTORS and FORFAITING HOUSES.

In addition to the ECGD, the DEPARTMENT OF TRADE AND INDUSTRY (DTI) provides various facilities to support UK exports including:

(a) the *Export Market Information Centre* which provides, amongst other things, access to the British Overseas Trade Information Services worldwide statistical database, market-research reports, directories, etc. and an Export Intelligence Service (for subscribers only) providing detailed, up-to-date market and product databases;

(b) the *Export Marketing Research Scheme* which provides professional advice and research on overseas markets, and financial grants to cover exploratory missions;

(c) *Technical Help to Exporters* which provides information and advice in respect of overseas technical standards, national laws covering safety and environmental protection, etc.;

(d) the *Fairs and Promotions* branch which organizes and financially assists exhibitors at overseas trade fairs, sets up contacts with agents and distributors, etc.;

(e) the *Supplier Trade Procedures Board* which provides advice and assistance in preparation of export documentation and provides a system for sending documents by electronic data interchange instead of using paper documents;

(f) the *Projects and Export Policy Division* which provides contacts with overseas governments and companies, and ongoing support for large overseas projects such as power station, railway networks, pipelines, etc.;

(g) finally, the DTI provides information and advice on tariffs, local duties and exchange controls, and in the case of certain specific exports is responsible for issuing export licences.

See CUSTOMS AND EXCISE, INTERNATIONAL TRADE, INTERNATIONAL MARKETING, CHAMBER OF COMMERCE, SUBSIDY, CONSIGNMENT.

**export market** an overseas country to which a firm based in one particular country EXPORTS its products. INTERNATIONAL TRADE provides an opportunity for a firm to increase its sales potential by marketing its products in a number of foreign markets rather than relying solely on sales in its own domestic market. See MARKET DEVELOPMENT, FOREIGN MARKET SERVICING STRATEGY.

**Export Market Information Centre** see EXPORTING.

**Export Market Research Scheme** see EXPORTING.

**export ratio** a measure of the proportion of a firm's sales that are exported, which expresses export sales revenues as a fraction of total sales revenue. To the extent that overseas debts often take longer to collect than money owed by domestic customers, a high export ratio can influence the DEBTORS RATIO.

**export restraint agreement** an undertaking given in respect of a particular product by one country (the exporting country) to another country (the importing country) which limits the volume of EXPORTS, or value of exports, to an agreed maximum number of units or percentage share of the importing country's total domestic sales. Export restraint agreements are a form of PROTECTIONISM designed to shield domestic producers in the importing country from overseas competition and, on occasions, assist that country's balance of payments. See QUOTA.

**export subsidy** a direct payment, or tax concession, made by the government to firms to encourage them to increase their EXPORTS. This is done in order to generate greater foreign exchange earnings, thereby assisting the balance of payments and helping to create additional domestic jobs.

**exposure** see EXCHANGE RATE EXPOSURE.

**exposure draft** a draft STATEMENT OF STANDARD ACCOUNTING PRACTICE published as a discussion document.

**extended internal labour market** see INTERNAL LABOUR MARKET.

**external appraisal** see SWOT.

**external growth** a mode of business growth which involves a firm in expanding its activities by MERGER, TAKEOVER, or JOINT VENTURES, rather than through ORGANIC GROWTH (i.e. internal expansion). External growth may take the form of horizontal, vertical or diversified expansion (see HORIZONTAL INTEGRATION, VERTICAL INTEGRATION, DIVERSIFICATION).

In general terms, external growth allows a firm to expand more rapidly and in a more cost-effective way than internal expansion, while augmenting and widening the firm's resource base. Additionally, external growth has some specific attractions. For example, in the case of *horizontal* growth, a merger with, or takeover of, a competitor can enable a firm significantly to increase its market share while providing scope for exploiting economies of scale through rationalization of the two firms' operations. The alternative of attempting to improve market share through price and product differentiation competition may be prohibitively expensive by comparison. Likewise, in the case of conglomerate expansion, the firm may simply not have the expertise to develop products in non-related areas, whereas external growth allows a firm to move into new activities by acquiring a customized operation and related resource capabilities.

External growth, however, is not without its complications. For example, the merged or acquired firms have to be integrated into the one controlling organization which may require a major streamlining of operations and the creation of new management structures. If this is not done effectively, efficiency may be impaired and financial resources strained.

See BUSINESS STRATEGY, ORGANIC GROWTH, PRODUCT-MARKET MATRIX, FRANCHISE.

**externalities** factors which may result in a benefit or cost to a firm or society which originate, in part, from outside the firm or as an adjunct to productive activity. A firm which does not itself invest in training its labour force, for example, may nonetheless benefit from being able to attract employees who have been trained by other firms or by the government. Pollution is an example of an external cost imposed on society: a chemical company which pollutes the air or contaminates river water incurs only the immediate costs of producing its products, while society suffers the extra costs of cleaning up the atmosphere and river.

**extraordinary items** non-recurring items of expense or revenue which do not arise in the normal course of trading; for example, losses associated with a major reorganization of a company division which involves significant sales of assets. Such losses would be deducted directly from the company's RESERVES below the line rather than being charges against the profits of the trading period, to avoid affecting the results of routine trading operations with one-off non-trading losses.

**extrapolation** see SALES FORECASTING.

# F

**face value** see PAR VALUE 1.

**factor 1.** a firm that purchases TRADE DEBTS from client firms. See FACTORING.

**2.** a firm that buys in bulk and performs a WHOLESALING function.

**3.** an input (for example raw material, labour, capital) which is used to produce a good or provide a service.

**factoring** the provision of finance (and other related services) by one firm (the factor) to another firm (the client) by discounting its unpaid INVOICES issued to customers, i.e. purchasing the client's TRADE DEBTS.

Factors typically provide immediate cash up to the value of 85% of the client's invoices, thus releasing ready money for the client to use for WORKING CAPITAL purposes. The remaining balance, less the fee for providing the facility, is paid over when the factor has received payment from the customer.

In addition, factors are usually prepared to undertake the administration of their clients' sales ledgers, assess credit risks and insure clients against bad debts, thus saving the client the trouble and expense of maintaining his own sales accounts and credit control departments.

Factoring extends to both domestic and export sales. It can be especially useful in the latter context where credit periods on exports are, on average, two to three times longer than on domestic sales and where there are additional complications arising from dealings with relatively unknown foreign customers and an unfamiliarity with local customs and laws.

See EXPORTING, DEBTORS, CREDIT CONTROL.

**factory** a BUSINESS PREMISE used by a firm in the PRODUCTION of goods. See CAPITAL STOCK, FIXED ASSET.

**Factory Inspectorate** see HEALTH AND SAFETY.

**factory layout** the arrangement of machines and equipment within a factory which includes the layout of departments within the factory site, the layout of machines within the departments and the layout of individual work places. The two principal types of factory layout are PRODUCT-FOCUSED LAYOUTS where a product is routed through the factory on a single path, and PROCESS-FOCUSED LAYOUTS where products may follow a variety of routes through job shops in the factory.

In the two above-mentioned layout systems the product moves past stationary production equipment, but in the case of layout by *fixed position* the reverse applies. In the extreme case, for example civil engineering, neither the partly completed nor the finished product moves. Alternatively, as in shipbuilding, the product remains stationary only until it is completed.

Changes in the level of demand, or the need to produce a new product or a redesigned product, may result in a need to reorganize existing plant or to provide additional plant. Obsolescence or failure of existing equipment may result in the decision to install equipment whose characteristics provoke some rearrangements. The need for cost reductions may promote a reappraisal of layouts, as may factory legislation, accidents, etc.

See PRODUCTION, RELATIONSHIP CHART, ACTIVITY CHART.

**failure costs** the cost to a firm of manufacturing defective products. *Internal* failure costs result from defects which arise during the production process, and include the cost of defective items which have to be scrapped (yield loss); the cost of reworking faulty items which have to be corrected (rework costs); and the loss of revenue from having to downgrade a product which has been identified as second quality and has to be sold as substandard at a lower than normal price.

*External* failure costs result from defects which arise after the product has reached the customer and include the cost of replacing or repairing defective products (GUARANTEE OR WARRANTY costs); and legal costs or damages to customers who have suffered physical or financial injury from defective products. An additional external failure cost is the loss of consumer goodwill and cancelled orders which, although difficult to quantify, can have a significant potential impact on sales and profits.

See QUALITY COSTS, QUALITY CONTROL.

**failure rate curve** or **'bath tub curve'** a curve which reflects

## FAILURE RATE CURVE

the RELIABILITY of a component of a product or machine, measured in terms of the proportion of a sample of that component which fails at different phases of its operational life. Fig. 40 shows a typical failure rate curve for a sample of the component which is divided into three phases:

(a) the 'infant' or *burn-in* period of the component is characterized by an initial high rate of failure. The early failure rate then decreases rapidly as surviving components prove themselves to be reliable;

(b) the *adult* or *normal useful life* period of the component is typified by a low and relatively constant rate of component failure;

(c) the *ageing* or *wear-out* period of the component is characterized by a rise in the failure rate as the component reaches the end of its designed life.

Each of these phases will reflect the adequacy of the design of the component, the quality of the materials used to make it, and the consistency with which it is manufactured.

Fig. 40. Failure rate curve. Graph showing a typical curve.

In designing finished products, firms may seek to reduce the extent of early failure of components by laboratory testing of new product designs, and by using feedback from consumer panels and test marketing to perfect the design of the product. In determining GUARANTEE or WARRANTY periods for products, firms need to be aware of when the components of the product are likely to reach the end of their normal useful life and begin to experience rising failure rates. Failure rate profiles for components of factory machines can likewise be employed to plan the firm's MAINTENANCE and machine replacement programmes.

See QUALITY CONTROL.

**Fairs and Promotions** see EXPORTING.

**Fair Trading Act 1973** an Act which consolidated and extended UK competition law by controlling MONOPOLIES, MERGERS AND TAKEOVERS, RESTRICTIVE TRADE AGREEMENTS and RE-SALE PRICES. The Act established a new regulatory authority, the OFFICE OF FAIR TRADING (headed by the Director-General of Fair Trading) with powers to supervise all aspects of COMPETITION POLICY, including the monitoring of changes in market structure, companies' commercial policies, the registration of restrictive trade agreements, and the referral, where appropriate, of cases for investigation and report by the MONOPOLIES AND MERGERS COMMISSION and RESTRICTIVE PRACTICES COURT. The Act also gave the OFT specific responsibilities to oversee other matters affecting consumers' interests, including weights and measures, trade descriptions and voluntary codes of good practice. See CONSUMER PROTECTION.

**Fair Wages Resolution** a UK resolution, passed by the House of Commons in 1891, which stipulated that organizations performing work under contract to the government should pay the going rate and observe conditions of employment established by COLLECTIVE BARGAINING for the industry. These requirements were set out in a fair wages clause incorporated in the contract. Originally designed to discourage sweated labour, the order was rescinded in 1983 on the grounds that it interfered with the normal workings of the labour market.

**family brand** a group of products marketed by a company using a common BRAND NAME. See BRAND EXTENSION (BRAND TRANSFERENCE).

**FAO** see FOOD AND AGRICULTURE ORGANIZATION.

**fashion** see FASHION PRODUCT, TREND 2.

**fashion product** a product for which demand changes frequently because of changes in consumer tastes or product attributes. Where consumer tastes are fickle and consumers seek to be fashionable, suppliers can take advantage of this by frequent restyling of products. See OBSOLESCENCE.

**FAX (Facsimile) machine** a machine capable of transmitting a copy of a document over a telephone link.

**feasible region** see LINEAR PROGRAMMING.

**'federated-firm'** see ENGINEERING EMPLOYERS' FEDERATION (EEF).

**federation** an association of organizations formed to represent and advance their joint interests. In INDUSTRIAL RELATIONS there are both TRADE UNION federations, for example the Confederation of Shipbuilding and Engineering Unions, and federations of EMPLOYERS' ASSOCIATIONS, for example ENGINEERING EMPLOYERS' FEDERATION.

**fee** a payment to an AGENT or professional person/firm such as an accountant or lawyer for performing particular services for clients. Fees may be paid on a *fixed* or *sliding scale* basis related to the value of the transaction or work undertaken.

**fiat currency** or **fiduciary issue** CURRENCY which is issued by a government but not backed by government holdings of gold or other securities. In the 19th century most currency issues were backed by gold, and people could exchange their bank notes for gold on demand. Most modern currency systems, however, are based on nonconvertible bank note issues.

**fidelity bonus** a business practice whereby a supplier rewards distributors/retailers with preferential supply conditions (prompt delivery times, access to supplies in times of shortage, back-up services) in return for their loyal custom. The operation of fidelity bonuses, by encouraging dealers/retailers to place the whole or a substantial part of their orders with the one supplier, may help the supplier increase his sales and protect market share. However, if undertaken by a DOMINANT FIRM, the practice may serve to limit competition in a market by depriving rival suppliers of distribution outlets. See OFFICE OF FAIR TRADING.

**fiduciary issue** see FIAT CURRENCY.

**field studies** see MARKETING INTELLIGENCE.

**FIFO** see STOCK VALUATION.

**FIMBRA** see PERSONAL INVESTMENT AUTHORITY.

**final accounts** financial accounts prepared at the end of an accounting period. Final accounts consist of the PROFIT AND LOSS ACCOUNT and the BALANCE SHEET, and may also include a SOURCES AND USES OF FUNDS STATEMENT for the accounting period.

**final dividend** see DIVIDEND.

**final good** see GOOD.

**finance house** a financial institution which accepts deposits of money from savers and which specializes in the provision of INSTALMENT CREDIT to borrowers and LEASING facilities. See MONETARY SYSTEM, MONETARY POLICY.

**financial accounting** ACCOUNTING activities directed towards the preparation of annual PROFIT-AND-LOSS ACCOUNTS and BALANCE SHEETS in order to report to shareholders on their company's overall (profit) performance. See MANAGEMENT ACCOUNTING.

**financial analysis** see RATIO ANALYSIS, ACCOUNTING RATIOS.

**financial flexibility** see LABOUR FLEXIBILITY.

**Financial Intermediaries, Managers and Brokers Regulatory Association (FIMBRA)** see PERSONAL INVESTMENT AUTHORITY.

**financial investment** see INVESTMENT, PORTFOLIO.

**financial management** the process of obtaining funds to finance a firm and advising on the use of these funds, which involves analysing the flow of funds through the firm. Financial management seeks to improve the market valuation of a firm by improving its future prospective earnings stream, taking due account of the riskiness of earnings. See CAPITAL GEARING, INVESTMENT APPRAISAL, WORKING CAPITAL.

**financial ratio** see ACCOUNTING RATIO.

**financial security** a financial instrument issued by companies, financial institutions and the government as a means of borrowing money and raising new capital. The most commonly used financial securities are SHARES, STOCKS, DEBENTURES, BILLS OF EXCHANGE, TREASURY BILLS and BONDS. Once issued these securities can be bought and sold either on the MONEY MARKETS or on the STOCK MARKET. See WARRANT, CERTIFICATE OF DEPOSIT, CONSOL.

**Financial Services Act 1986** a UK act which provides a regulatory system for the FINANCIAL SECURITIES and INVESTMENT industry. The Act covers the businesses of securities dealing and investment, commodities and financial futures, unit trusts and some insurance (excluding the Lloyds insurance market). Also excluded from its remit is commercial banking, which is supervised by the Bank of England, and mortgage and other business of the building societies, which is regulated separately by the BUILDING SOCIETY ACT 1986.

The main areas covered by the Act are the authorization of securities and investment businesses, and the establishment and enforcement of rules of good and fair business practice. The DEPARTMENT OF TRADE AND INDUSTRY, together with its appointed agency, the Securities and Investment Board (SIB), is responsible for the overall administration of the Act, in conjunction with various Self-Regulatory Organizations (SROs), Recognized Investment Exchanges (RIEs) and Recognized Professional Bodies (RPBs).

The general objective of the legislation is to ensure a high level of investor protection by ensuring that only persons deemed to be 'fit and proper' are authorized to undertake securities and investment business, and that they conduct their business according to standards laid down by the SIB, SROs, RIEs and RPBs; leading, for example, in the former case, to the clarification of the relationship between the firm and its clients, especially as regards disclosure of fees, charges and the capacities in which the firm may act, and, in the latter case, to open and fair pricing.

There are currently three SROs:

(a) IMRO: Investment Management Regulatory Organization, which regulates firms involved in the management and trusteeship of collective investment schemes such as INVESTMENT TRUSTS and PENSION FUNDS;

(b) PIA: Personal Investment Authority, which regulates retail financial services firms providing personal INSURANCE and PENSIONS and UNIT TRUST MANAGEMENT.

(c) SFA: Securities and Futures Authority, which regulates firms dealing in FINANCIAL SECURITIES on the STOCK MARKET and FORWARD MARKET and in COMMODITIES on the Forward Market.

A Recognized Investment Exchange is a body such as the STOCK MARKET, LONDON DERIVATIVES EXCHANGE which provides an organized framework within which transactions can be effected, including facilities for making a market in a financial asset or commodity (see MARKET MAKER), monitoring and reporting completed transactions and providing for settlement and delivery through an appropriate clearing mechanism.

A Recognized Professional Body is an organization such as the Chartered Accountants in England and Wales, which is responsible for regulating its members in relation to their work in advising clients on their investments.

**financial structure** see CAPITAL STRUCTURE, CAPITAL GEARING.

**financial system** a network of financial institutions (COMMERCIAL BANKS, BUILDING SOCIETIES, etc.) and markets (MONEY MARKET, STOCK MARKET), dealing in a variety of financial instruments (BANK DEPOSITS, STOCKS and SHARES, etc.), which are engaged in money transmission activities and the provision of LOAN and CREDIT facilities.

The financial institutions and markets occupy a key position in the economy as intermediaries in channelling savings and other funds to borrowers and investors. In doing this one of their main roles is to reconcile the different requirements of savers and borrowers, thereby facilitating a higher level of saving and investment in the economy than would otherwise be the case. Depositors with financial institutions are seeking a relatively risk-free repository for their monies, combining ready access to their money with a longer term investment return, which provides for current income and/or capital appreciation. Borrowers, in general, require access to funds of varying amounts to finance short, medium and long-term debt and capital investment, often, as is particularly the case with business investments, under conditions of substantial risk. The financial institutions help to reconcile these different requirements in three main ways:

(a) by combining together the deposits and savings of many individuals, thus making it possible to make single large-scale loans;

(b) by pooling the resources of many depositors and savers to provide both for an individual to withdraw his funds at short notice while maintaining, in the round, a substantially large and stable financial base to underpin long-term lending;

(c) by holding a diversified portfolio of assets and lending for a variety of purposes so as to provide for various risk-return combinations.

In the UK the financial system is regulated by the country's CENTRAL BANK (the Bank of England) in combination with various specialized regulatory bodies such as the SECURITIES AND INVESTMENT BOARD.

See FINANCIAL SERVICES ACT 1986, BANKING SYSTEM, CLEARING HOUSE SYSTEM.

**financial year** the period from 1 April to 31 March of the following year used for CORPORATION TAX purposes. Compare FISCAL YEAR.

**firing** see DISMISSAL.

**firm** see BUSINESS.

**first in, first out (FIFO)** see STOCK VALUATION.

**fiscal policy** the regulation of government expenditure and taxation in order to control the level of spending in the economy (see ECONOMIC POLICY).

The fiscal authorities (principally the TREASURY in the UK), can employ a number of taxation measures to control spending: DIRECT TAXES on individuals (INCOME TAX) and companies (CORPORATION TAX) can be increased if spending needs to be reduced, for example, to control inflation, i.e. an increase in income tax reduces people's disposable income, and similarly an increase in corporation tax leaves companies with less profit available to pay dividends and reinvest. Alternatively, spending can be reduced by increasing indirect taxes: an increase in VALUE ADDED TAXES on products in general, or an increase in EXCISE DUTIES on particular products such as petrol and cigarettes will, by increasing their prices, lead to a reduction in purchasing power.

The government can use changes in its own expenditure to affect spending levels; for example, a cut in current purchases of products or capital investment by the government again serves to reduce total spending in the economy.

Taxation and government expenditure are linked together in terms of the government's overall fiscal or BUDGET position: total spending in the economy is reduced by the twin effects of increased taxation and expenditure cuts with the government running a budget surplus. If the objective is to increase spending then the government operates a budget deficit, reducing taxation and increasing its expenditure.

In practice the application of fiscal policy as a *short-term* stabilization technique encounters a number of problems which reduces its effectiveness. Taxation rate changes, particularly alterations to income tax, are administratively cumbersome to initiate and take time to implement: likewise, a substantial proportion of government expenditure on, for example schools, roads, hospitals and defence, reflect *longer-term* economic and social commitments and cannot easily be reversed without lengthy political lobbying. From a technical point of view, changes in taxes or expenditure produce 'multiplier' effects (i.e. some initial change in spending is magnified and transmitted around the economy) but to an indeterminate extent.

Practical experience has indicated that the short-termism approach to economic management has not in fact been especially successful in stabilizing the economy. As a result, *medium-term* management of the economy favoured by the monetarist school has, in recent years, assumed a greater degree of significance.

See MONETARISM, MONETARY POLICY, BUSINESS CYCLE.

**fiscal year** the government's accounting year which, in the UK, runs from 6 April to 5 April of the following year, and in the USA from 1 July to 30 June. The fiscal year is the basic period used by the government in assessing personal INCOME TAX and any income earned during the fiscal year is assessable to taxation at the income tax rates applicable for that fiscal year. Compare FINANCIAL YEAR.

**fishbone chart** a chart that breaks down the PRODUCTION of a product into its constituent operations as a means of identifying the source of a product defect. Fig. 41 (overleaf) shows a simplified fishbone chart for draught beer. Should a poor QUALITY batch of beer be produced this could be due to a malfunction in any one or more of the operations listed, including faulty or unclean equipment (mash mixers and filters, fermentation vessels), incorrect material mixes or poor strains of malt, hop or yeast, or incorrect boiling and cooling temperatures and periods. Fishbone charts can also be used more proactively to detect and *prevent* quality problems on a continuous basis as part of a commitment to TOTAL QUALITY MANAGEMENT. See QUALITY CONTROL.

**Fisher effect** a situation wherein current INTEREST RATES in a country fully reflect the expected rate of INFLATION and the anticipated *real* interest rate (after allowing for inflation). The Fisher effect suggests that interest rates must include an element to compensate lenders for the reduced PURCHASING POWER of the money loaned when it is returned by the borrower – an 'inflation premium', plus a real reward to lenders for making their money available for use by borrowers.

**fixed assets** ASSETS such as buildings and machinery that are

OPERATION

filtering MASHING — Malt is mixed with boiled water and filtered to produce sweet wort

mixing

boiling
HOPPING — Sweet wort is boiled with sugar and hops to produce hopped wort

mixing →

COOLING — Hopped wort is cooled from boiling and run into a fermenting vessel where yeast is added to produce the required strength of alcohol and fermentation takes place

FERMENTATION

BARRELLING — Draught beer is then filtered into barrels/casks for delivery to customers

Fig. 41. **Fishbone chart.** Simplified fishbone chart for draught beer.

bought for long-term use in a firm rather than for resale. Fixed assets are retained in the business for long periods, and generally each year a proportion of their original cost will be written off against PROFITS for DEPRECIATION to reflect the diminishing value of the asset. In a BALANCE SHEET fixed assets are usually shown at cost less depreciation charged to date. Certain fixed assets such as property tend to appreciate in value (see APPRECIATION, definition 1) and need to be revalued periodically to keep their BALANCE SHEET values in line with market values. Other fixed assets such as patents, trademarks and GOODWILL are termed *intangible assets* to distinguish them from tangible assets such as buildings and machinery. All fixed assets are held for the purpose of earning income. See CURRENT ASSETS, REVALUATION, definition 1.

**fixed charge** see CREDITORS.

**fixed costs** any COSTS that do not vary with the level of output because they are linked to a time base rather than to a level of activity (see Fig. 42). Sometimes called period costs, they include rent and rates and depreciation.

Fig. 42. **Fixed costs.** (a) The graph represents total payments made for the use of buildings, plant and equipment, etc., which must be met irrespective of whether output is high or low. (b) The graph represents the continuous decline in average fixed cost as output rises, because a given amount of fixed cost is spread over a greater number of units.

**fixed exchange rate system** a mechanism for synchronizing and coordinating the EXCHANGE RATES of participating countries which involves each country setting a fixed par value for its currency against other countries' currencies; for example, 1 US dollar = 260 Japanese yen. Once an exchange rate value is fixed, countries are expected to maintain this rate for fairly lengthy periods of time, but may choose to devalue their currency (repeg the exchange rate at a new lower rate – see DEVALUATION) or revalue it (repeg the exchange rate at a new higher value – see REVALUATION, definition 2) if their BALANCE OF PAYMENTS is, respectively, in chronic deficit or surplus. Fixed exchange rates are maintained by the country's CENTRAL BANK intervening in the FOREIGN EXCHANGE MARKETS on a day-to-day basis, using its foreign exchange equalization account to buy and sell currencies as appropriate to stabilize the rate around its central par value.

The INTERNATIONAL MONETARY FUND formerly operated a system of fixed exchange rates, while currently most members of the European Union/Community subscribe to the fixed exchange rate requirements of the EUROPEAN MONETARY SYSTEM.

Generally speaking, the business and financial community prefer a relatively fixed exchange rate to FLOATING EXCHANGE RATES, since it enables them to conclude trade and financial transactions at known foreign exchange prices so that the profit and loss implications of these deals can be calculated in advance. The disadvantage with such a system is that governments often tend to delay altering the exchange rate, either because of political factors or because they may choose to deal with balance of payments difficulties by using other measures, so that the pegged rate gets seriously out of line with underlying market tendencies. In consequence, for example, a firm's exports may become progressively less price-competitive in foreign markets because the country's currency is 'overvalued'.

See ECONOMIC POLICY.

**fixed interest financial security** see DEBENTURE.

**fixed interval reorder system** or **reorder point system,** an arrangement whereby STOCK is reordered at regular intervals in variable quantities. In determining the amount to be reordered, account must be taken of usage rate of stock during the interval between placing the order and delivery of the ordered material. Usage during the reorder period should serve to reduce stock to a minimum safety stock level, before then being restored to the planned maximum stock level. With such a periodic review system the stock position is monitored at predetermined intervals and orders placed to bring the stock position up to a target level. See STOCK CONTROL, STOCKHOLDING COSTS.

**fixed overheads** any indirect COSTS that do not vary with the level of output of a product. They include such items as rents and depreciation of fixed assets, whose total cost remains unchanged regardless of changes in the level of activity. Consequently, fixed overhead cost per unit of product will tend to fall as output increases (as OVERHEADS are spread over a larger output). See VARIABLE OVERHEADS, SEMI-VARIABLE OVERHEADS, STANDARD COST.

**fixed quantity reorder system, reorder level system** or **continuous review system** an arrangement whereby a specified quantity of materials is reordered at variable intervals. In determining the interval between orders, account must be taken of the usage rate of STOCK during the interval between placing the order and delivery of the ordered material. With such a continuous review system the stock position is monitored after every withdrawal and when the stock level drops to a pre-determined reorder point a fixed quantity is ordered. See STOCK CONTROL, STOCK HOLDING COST.

**flat organization** an ORGANIZATION which has only a few managerial layers. This avoids excessive bureaucracy (see TALL ORGANIZATION); decision-making is more closely in touch with customer needs and the organization is able to adapt quickly to changes in its external environment.

Small firms are usually flat organizations, but increasingly larger firms have attempted to improve their competitiveness by cutting down on their management structures and by establishing more focused business divisions.

See STRATEGIC BUSINESS UNIT, RIGHTSIZING, HIERARCHY, DE-LAYERING.

**flat yield** see YIELD.

**flexible budget** a BUDGET that is designed to change in accordance with the level of activity actually attained, so that it allows for the variation in COSTS associated with changes in output volume. The costs associated with running a manufacturing plant, for instance, at 50% of capacity are different from running it at 70% or 100% capacity. The budget must allow for variation in plant utilization by distinguishing between FIXED COSTS, VARIABLE COSTS and SEMI-VARIABLE COSTS and their relationship to output. Flexible budgets facilitate more appropriate comparisons between the actual costs associated with the output attained and the budgeted costs for that output level. See BUDGETING, BUDGETARY CONTROL.

**flexible firm** see LABOUR FLEXIBILITY, FLEXIBLE SPECIALIZATION.

**flexible manufacturing system (FMS)** a means of PRODUCTION which makes extensive use of programmed AUTOMATION and COMPUTERS to achieve rapid production of small batches of components or products, whilst maintaining flexibility in manufacturing a wide range of these items. In FMS systems computer-controlled machines can be quickly switched from the production of one component or product to another by re-programming the machines. Such reprogramming also facilitates the smooth running of the production system by allowing a component or product to be processed on several different machines, thus avoiding production bottlenecks or delays caused by machine breakdowns.

**flexible specialization** a form of industrial organization in which firms specialize in certain products but are able to change at short notice to producing different ones. A notable feature is that such flexibility can make it viable to produce small batches of each product. A prerequisite is the use of advanced flexible technology operated by employees with a broad range of skills who are able to surmount traditional job boundaries. Research by sociologists, however, suggests that, in the UK at least, flexible technology is not being fully exploited and that managers are often reluctant to create multi-skilled workforces. See LABOUR FLEXIBILITY.

**flexitime** a method of organizing hours of work which permits some flexibility in the times of starting and finishing each working day. Usually the employee will be required to commence work within certain times (for example between 7.00 and 9.30 a.m.) and to remain at work until a specified time (for example 3.30 p.m.) Within these limits employees can choose day by day their hours of work. However, they will usually be required to work a specified total number of hours over a period of, say, one month. Any shortfalls at the end of the period may be carried forward or result in pay deductions whilst excess hours could be dealt with by additional pay or time off in lieu. Flexitime enables employees to adapt their working day to other commitments. However, it also confers advantages to employers: in so far as it requires precise timings to be kept it can tighten control of hours of work; and because potential absences from work (for example, visit to a doctor) can be pushed outside the flexi-day it can improve utilization of staff and productivity. See ANNUAL HOURS.

**flip flop arbitration** see ARBITRATION.

**floating charge** see DEBENTURES, CREDITORS.

**floating exchange rate system** a mechanism for co-ordinating EXCHANGE RATES between countries' currencies which involves the value of each country's currency in terms of other currencies being determined by the forces of supply and demand in the FOREIGN EXCHANGE MARKET. Over time the exchange rate of a particular currency may rise (appreciate) or fall (depreciate) depending, respectively, on the strength or weakness of its underlying BALANCE OF PAYMENTS position and exposure to SPECULATIVE activity. See APPRECIATION, definition 2, DEPRECIATION, definition 2.

Generally speaking, the business and financial community

dislikes unregulated floating exchange rates since the market tends to produce erratic and destabilizing exchange rate movements, often prompted by currency speculation, which makes it difficult to conclude meaningful trade and investment transactions, because of the uncertainties surrounding the profit-and-loss implications of such deals when exchange rates are fluctuating widely. Governments too dislike disorderly currency markets and prefer where possible to 'manage' their exchange rates both to moderate the excessive short-term fluctuations and to smooth out the underlying longer-term trend line by buying and selling currencies as appropriate out of their foreign exchange equalization account. While this creates a more settled and controlled environment in which to operate, nonetheless firms are usually forced to cover their currency deals in the forward exchange market.

Government intervention in currency markets sometimes goes beyond merely smoothing its exchange rate and may involve a deliberate attempt to manipulate the exchange rate so as to gain a trading advantage over other countries (a so-called *dirty float*). See FORWARD MARKET, INTERNATIONAL MONETARY FUND, ECONOMIC POLICY, CENTRAL BANK, GROUP OF 7 (G7), PURCHASING POWER PARITY, EXCHANGE RATE EXPOSURE.

**floppy disk** a data storage device in which data is stored on a vinyl disk which is inserted in a COMPUTER'S disk drive to enable the computer to 'read' the information contained on it or to 'write' information onto it. Currently most floppy disks are $3\frac{1}{2}''$ or $5\frac{1}{4}''$ diameter and they can store up to 2 megabytes of numbers or letters.

**flotation** the process by which a new company or an established PRIVATE LIMITED COMPANY becomes a PUBLIC LIMITED COMPANY and issues SHARES to the general public. By going public a company is able to raise large amounts of capital by issuing a PROSPECTUS inviting shareholders to subscribe for shares. See SHARE ISSUE.

**flowchart 1.** a graphic representation of a sequence of COMPUTER operations which is used in presenting computer programs.
**2.** a graphic representation of a sequence of production operations. See ACTIVITY CHART.

**flow of funds statement** see SOURCES AND USES OF FUNDS STATEMENT.

**flow production** see MASS PRODUCTION.

**FMS** see FLEXIBLE MANUFACTURING SYSTEM.

**Food and Agricultural Organization (FAO)** an organization run by the UNITED NATIONS whose principal remit is to help increase agricultural efficiency and raise nutritional standards in the DEVELOPING COUNTRIES. The FAO provides technical services and research back-up to those countries which require its assistance.

**Fordism** a form of MASS PRODUCTION characterized by a high degree of job specialization, so called after the pattern of WORK ORGANIZATION and JOB DESIGN extolled by American car entrepreneur Henry Ford (1863–1947). Large numbers of a product could be produced for a mass market using assembly line technology where each worker performs a single task over and over again. Although high specialization can have efficiency advantages this form of work organization is often associated with low levels of JOB SATISFACTION, high LABOUR TURNOVER and ABSENTEEISM and high levels of CONFLICT and INDUSTRIAL DISPUTES.

**forecasting** see SALES FORECASTING, TECHNOLOGICAL FORECASTING.

**foreclosure** the refusal by a VERTICALLY INTEGRATED firm to supply inputs to non-integrated rivals, or distribute their products, as a means of putting them at a competitive disadvantage. In market situations where there are a substantial number of alternative independent supply sources and outlets, rival suppliers are unlikely to be inconvenienced. However, the control by a DOMINANT FIRM of the majority of input sources and outlets, combined with limitations on the establishment of new ones, could have serious anti-competitive consequences. Under UK COMPETITION POLICY, cases of vertical integration may be referred to the MONOPOLIES AND MERGERS COMMISSION for investigation. See REFUSAL TO SUPPLY.

**foreign currency** or **foreign exchange** the CURRENCY of an overseas country, which is purchased by a particular country in exchange for its own currency, which is then used to finance trade and capital transactions between the two countries. See INTERNATIONAL TRADE, FOREIGN EXCHANGE CONTROLS, FOREIGN EXCHANGE MARKET.

**foreign currency translation** the process of denoting the assets and liabilities of a MULTINATIONAL ENTERPRISE'S foreign subsidiary's BALANCE SHEET and the revenues and expenses of the subsidiary's PROFIT-AND-LOSS ACCOUNT, which are expressed in terms of the subsidiary's local currency by translating them into the parent company's domestic currency. This is done in order to prepare CONSOLIDATED ACCOUNTS for the group.

There are two main currency translation methods:

(a) the *closing rate*, or *net investment* method, or *all-current* method, in which all foreign currency items are translated at the EXCHANGE RATE ruling at the date of the balance sheet. With the closing rate method any gains or losses on exchange arising from translation are taken direct to the group balance sheet and dealt with as changes in RESERVES so as not to affect reported PROFIT.

(b) *temporal* method or *current/non-current* method, in which fixed assets and long term liabilities are translated at the exchange rate ruling at the date of their acquisition, and revenues and expenses at an average exchange rate for the year. With the temporal method any differences arising on translation are taken to the profit-and-loss account where they serve to affect recorded profit.

**foreign exchange** see FOREIGN CURRENCY.

**foreign exchange controls** the application of restrictions on the availability of FOREIGN CURRENCIES by a country's central bank, to assist in the removal of a BALANCE OF PAYMENTS deficit and to control disruptive short-run capital inflows and outflows which tend to destabilize the country's EXCHANGE RATE. Because importers need to purchase foreign currencies from the country's central bank (via their commercial banks) in order to buy products from overseas suppliers, by cutting off the supply of foreign currencies the authorities can reduce the amount of IMPORTS to a level compatible with the foreign currency earned by the country's EXPORTS. Exchange controls may be applied not only to limit the total amount of currency available but can also be used to discriminate against particular types of imports, thus serving as a form of PROTECTIONISM. See FOREIGN EXCHANGE MARKET.

**Foreign Exchange Equalization Account** the section of a country's CENTRAL BANK (for example the Bank of England) which uses the country's foreign currency holdings to operate in the FOREIGN EXCHANGE MARKET in order to stabilize the country's currency EXCHANGE RATE.

**foreign exchange market** a MARKET engaged in the buying

and selling of FOREIGN CURRENCIES. Such a market is required because each country involved in INTERNATIONAL TRADE and investment has its own domestic currency and this needs to be exchanged for other currencies in order to finance trade and capital transactions. This function is undertaken by a network of private foreign exchange dealers and a country's monetary authorities acting through its central banks.

The foreign exchange market by its very nature is multinational in scope. The leading centres for foreign exchange dealings are London, New York and Tokyo. In 1995 London's average daily turnover was $464 billion, New York's $244 billion and Tokyo's $161 billion.

Foreign currencies can be transacted on a 'spot' basis for immediate delivery (see SPOT MARKET), or can be bought and sold for future delivery (see FORWARD MARKET). Some two-thirds of London's foreign exchange dealings in 1997 were spot transactions.

The foreign exchange market may be left unregulated by governments, with EXCHANGE RATES between currencies being determined by the free interplay of the forces of demand and supply (see FLOATING EXCHANGE RATE SYSTEM), or they may be subjected to support buying and selling by countries' central banks in order to fix them at particular rates (see FIXED EXCHANGE RATE SYSTEM).

**foreign investment** the purchase of overseas physical and financial assets. Overseas investment in financial assets, in particular by institutional investors, is undertaken primarily to diversify portfolio risk and to obtain higher returns than would be achievable on comparable domestic investments; while physical investment abroad is one main way for a firm to internationalize its operations. Foreign direct investment (FDI) in new manufacturing plants and sales subsidiaries, or the acquisition of established businesses, provide the firm with a more flexible approach to supplying foreign markets. See CAPITAL INFLOW, CAPITAL OUTFLOW, FOREIGN MARKET SERVICING STRATEGY, MULTINATIONAL ENTERPRISE.

**foreign market servicing strategy** the choice of EXPORTING, LICENSING, STRATEGIC ALLIANCES (including JOINT VENTURES) and foreign direct investment (FDI), or some combination of each, by a MULTINATIONAL ENTERPRISE (MNE) as a means of selling its products in overseas markets. Exporting involves production in one or more locations for sale overseas in target markets; licensing involves the assignment of production and selling rights by a MNE to producers in the target market; strategic alliances involve the combining together on a contractual or equity basis the resources and skills of two firms; foreign direct investment involves the establishment of the firm's own production (and selling) facilities in the target market. In resource terms, exporting from established production plants is a relatively inexpensive way of servicing a foreign market, but the firm could be put at a competitive disadvantage either because of local producers' lower cost structures and control of local distribution channels or because of governmental TARIFFS, QUOTAS, etc. and other restrictions on IMPORTS. Licensing enables a firm to gain a rapid penetration of world markets and can be advantageous to a firm lacking the financial resources to set up overseas operations, or where again local firms control distribution channels, but the royalties obtained may represent a poor return for the technology transferred. Strategic alliances can enable complementary resources and skills to be combined, enabling firms to supply products in a more cost-effective way and to increase market penetration. Foreign direct investment can be expensive and risky (although HOST COUNTRIES often offer subsidies, etc. to attract such inward investment), but in many cases the 'presence' effects of operating locally (familiarity with local market conditions and the cultivation of contacts with local suppliers, distributors and retailers) are important factors in building market share over the long run.

MNEs in practice tend to use various combinations of these modes to service global markets because of the added flexibility it gives to their operations. For example, if governments choose to act on imports by raising tariffs, etc. a MNE may substitute in-market FDI for direct exporting.

See FOREIGN INVESTMENT, INTERNATIONAL MARKETING, EXCHANGE RATE EXPOSURE.

**foreman** an alternative term for SUPERVISOR used mainly in manufacturing organizations.

**forfaiting** the provision of finance by one firm (the forfaiter) to another firm (the client) by purchasing goods the client has pre-sold to a customer but for which he has not yet been paid. The forfaiter (which often is a subsidiary of a commercial bank or a specialist firm) buys the client's goods at a discounted cash price, thus releasing ready money for the client to use to finance his WORKING CAPITAL requirements. The forfaiter then arranges to collect the payment when due from the customer to whom the goods have been sold, thus also saving the client the paperwork involved.

Forfaiting extends to both domestic and export sales. It can be especially useful in the latter context in the case of expensive capital equipment involving long delivery dates, and where there are possible complications arising from dealing with relatively unknown customers, exchange rate fluctuations, etc.

See EXPORTING.

**formal organization** see ORGANIZATION.

**forward exchange contract** a contract to exchange a given amount of one foreign currency for another at a specified future date (usually one or three months ahead). For example, if a UK importer is due to pay $100,000 for materials in three months' time, then in order to guarantee the pound cost of these materials it might cover the transaction by entering into a forward exchange contract to buy $100,000 for delivery in three months' time in return for a given amount of pounds, the amount of pounds being determined by the forward exchange rate. See FORWARD MARKET.

**forward exchange market** see FORWARD MARKET.

**forward integration** see VERTICAL INTEGRATION.

**forward market, futures market** or **forward exchange market** a market which provides for the buying and selling of FINANCIAL SECURITIES (shares, stocks), COMMODITIES (rubber, tin, etc.) and FOREIGN CURRENCIES for delivery at some future point in time, as opposed to a SPOT MARKET which provides for immediate delivery. Forward positions are taken by traders in a particular financial asset or commodity whose price can fluctuate greatly over time, in order to minimize the risk and uncertainty surrounding their business dealings in the immediate future (i.e. hedge against adverse price movements), and by dealers and speculators (see SPECULATION) hoping to earn windfall profits from correctly anticipating price movements.

Traders seek to minimize uncertainty about future prices by buying or selling *futures*, particularly OPTIONS, i.e. contracts that promise to buy or sell a commodity or financial asset at a price agreed upon now for delivery at some later point in time, usually within a three-month period. For example, a producer of chocolate could contract to buy a given amount of cocoa at today's price plus a percentage risk premium for delivery in two months' time. Even if the price of cocoa were to go up markedly, the manufacturer knows that he is still able to buy at the (lower) contract price, and is thus able to plan his raw material outlays accordingly. Similarly, the producers of cocoa can contract to sell the commodity at an agreed price now for delivery in the near future in order to cover themselves against adverse price changes.

In between the original buyers and producers, using futures as a hedge to minimize risk, stand the various dealers and speculators who do not themselves actually *physically* hold commodities and financial assets but buy or sell the paper contracts to such items according to their view of probable price movements.

Forward prices reflect anticipated future demand and supply conditions for a financial security, foreign currency or commodity being traded. Specifically, the forward prices will be based partially on current spot prices but will also take into account interest rate and inflation rate trends. The difference between the current spot rate of a foreign currency and the forward exchange rate constitutes the 'forward margin'. The forward margin can be at either a discount or a premium to the spot rate.

The LONDON INTERNATIONAL FINANCIAL FUTURES MARKET (LIFFE), which includes the London Traded Option Market and the London Commodity Market, constitutes the largest European Union centre for forward dealings in securities and commodities. The forward markets in the UK are regulated by the SECURITIES AND FUTURES AUTHORITY (SFA) in accordance with various standards of good practice laid down under the FINANCIAL SERVICES ACT 1986. Globally, the Chicago Board of Trade is the world's largest forward market, followed by the Chicago Mercantile Exchange and the LIFFE.

See COMMODITY MARKET, FOREIGN EXCHANGE MARKET, STOCK MARKET, CONTANGO, COVERED INTEREST ARBITRAGE, EXCHANGE RATE EXPOSURE.

# FOUR O'S OF PURCHASING

**Four O's of purchasing** the objects and objectives of a purchase, and the organization and operation of buying.

The Four O's help to answer important marketing questions about:

(a) *Objects* – what general uses will the product have?

(b) *Objectives* – what specific functions do buyers expect the product to perform?

(c) *Organization* – who within an organization has power to authorize a purchase?

(d) *Operations* – what procurement procedures do they employ in purchasing it, for example, by inviting tenders?

The answers to these questions will assist a company in formulating its MARKETING MIX.

**Four P's of marketing** product, price, promotion and place, the key variables of the MARKETING MIX.

(a) *Product*: a good or service offered to consumers which satisfies a want or need. Product management involves decisions about PRODUCT LINES, the PRODUCT MIX, BRANDS and PACKAGING;

(b) *Price*: the amount of money which consumers are required to pay for a product or service. Decisions have to be made about the basic price, trade discounts, allowances and special deals, credit terms and carriage terms. Various PRICING METHODS may be employed;

(c) *Promotion*: the means of stimulating demand for the firm's products. Promotion decisions involve consideration of the MEDIA to be used for ADVERTISING the firm's products, SALES PROMOTION and other aspects of the PROMOTIONAL MIX;

(d) *Place*: the physical DISTRIBUTION of the firm's products into the hands of customers. This involves the selection of appropriate DISTRIBUTION CHANNELS which maximize marketing effectiveness.

**four-shift working** see SHIFT WORK.

**franchise** the granting by one company to another company (exclusive franchise) or a number of companies (non-exclusive franchise) of the right/s to supply its products. A franchise is a contractual arrangement which is entered into for a specified period of time, with the franchisee paying a royalty to the franchisor for the rights assigned. Examples of franchises include the McDonald Burger and Kentucky Fried Chicken diner chains, Tie Rack and Dyno-Rod.

Franchises are a form of co-partnership, offering mutual benefits. They allow the franchisor to expand sales rapidly and widely, sometimes on a global basis, without having to raise large amounts of capital, by building on the efforts of a highly motivated team of entrepreneurs. Individual franchisees are usually required to contribute the bulk of the investment in physical assets and hence have a personal interest in the success of the venture. For his part, the franchisee obtains access to an innovative product or novel selling method, with the franchisor providing back-up, technical assistance, specialized equipment and advertising and promotion.

See VERTICAL MARKETING SYSTEM, BUSINESS STRATEGY, EXTERNAL GROWTH.

**franked investment income** interest or dividends received from FINANCIAL SECURITIES net after CORPORATION TAX has been deducted. To avoid taxing such investment income twice, any such income received by a company which has bought financial securities is granted a TAX CREDIT for the tax already paid so that it is not subject to further corporation tax.

**Fraser's five-fold grading system** see RECRUITMENT AND SELECTION.

**fraud** the gaining of financial advantage by a person who deliberately deceives another person or business, by mispresenting himself.

**'free balance'** see ALLOCATION, definition 2.

**free enterprise economy** see ECONOMY.

**freehold property** property which is legally owned outright by a person or business. Contrast LEASEHOLD PROPERTY.

**free issue** raw materials or components which a factory operative can collect from the materials stores without having to obtain a duly authorized MATERIALS REQUISITION.

**free on board (f.o.b.)** a term used to denote the respective contractual obligations of sellers and buyers of a good which is exported. Under a f.o.b. contract the seller pays the cost of transporting the goods to the port of shipment and loading charges, plus all insurance cover up to this point. From then on it is the buyer who bears the cost of transporting, and insuring, the good to its final destination. See COST, INSURANCE AND FREIGHT, COST AND FREIGHT, EXPORTING.

**freeport** or **free trade zone** an area usually forming part of an airport or shipping port into which goods can be imported without incurring import or customs duties, provided the goods are to be subsequently exported either in their original form or as intermediate products within a final good. See ENTREPÔT TRADE.

**free trade** the EXPORT and IMPORT of goods and services between countries totally unhindered by restrictions such as TARIFFS and QUOTAS. In general, free trade leads to a higher level of economic welfare in so far as it favours the location of economic activities in those countries best suited to their production, resulting, through the trade mechanism, in worldwide consumption gains in the form of lower prices and greater product availability.

See INTERNATIONAL TRADE, FREE TRADE BLOC, GENERAL AGREEMENT ON TARIFFS AND TRADE.

**free trade area** see FREE TRADE BLOC.

**free trade bloc** a territorial grouping of countries that have dismantled all restrictions on cross-frontier trade between themselves, including the removal of TARIFFS, QUOTAS and EXCHANGE CONTROLS. The objective of a free trade bloc is to promote the economic welfare of member countries by reducing the prices of internationally traded goods and services and by making them more widely available, and by providing a greater opportunity for industrial specialization and a more efficient use of productive resources (see INTERNATIONAL TRADE).

There are three main types of free trade bloc:

(a) *Free trade area*, where members eliminate trade barriers between themselves but each independently continues to operate its own particular barrier against nonmembers. (See EUROPEAN FREE TRADE AREA, NORTH AMERICAN FREE TRADE AGREEMENT);

(b) *Customs union*, where members eliminate trade barriers between themselves, but establish uniform barriers against nonmembers, in particular common external tariff rates;

(c) *Common market*, that is, a customs union which also provides for the free movement of labour and capital across national boundaries (see EUROPEAN UNION/COMMUNITY).

**free trade zone** see FREEPORT.

**freight** or **cargo** goods that are in the process of being physically transported from a factory or depot to a customer by road, rail, sea or air, involving both domestically and internationally traded goods. The movement of goods may be done by the suppliers' own distribution division or by independent fleet operators and FREIGHT FORWARDERS. See COST AND FREIGHT, COST, INSURANCE AND FREIGHT, BALTIC MERCANTILE AND SHIPPING EXCHANGE.

**freight forwarder** or **forwarding agent** a firm which specializes in the physical movement of goods in transit, arranging the collection of goods from factory, depot, etc., and delivering them direct to the customer in the case of domestic consignments, and to seaports, airports, etc. in the case of exported goods. In the latter case the forwarder also handles the documentation required by the customs authorities and the booking arrangements. See EXPORTING.

**frequency distribution** a means of summarizing large amounts of data by grouping observations into convenient classes, and then showing how these observations are distributed among the different classes. A numerical frequency distribution groups data according to numerical size, for example income bands as in Fig. 43 (a) overleaf.

For certain purposes it is useful to have a numerical frequency distribution which groups observations in terms of cumulative size. This shows how many cases fall above or below certain values. For example, Fig. 43 (b) shows how a distribution, with cases falling into income classes, can be converted into a cumulate 'less than' distribution.

A qualitative frequency distribution sorts data into categories according to some qualitative description such as industry group, as in Fig. 43 (c).

See HISTOGRAM.

**frictional unemployment** see UNEMPLOYMENT.

**friendly society** a business organization which is owned by its members. Friendly societies were the forerunners of many modern INSURANCE COMPANIES and BUILDING SOCIETIES. See REGISTRAR OF FRIENDLY SOCIETIES, BUILDING SOCIETY ACT, 1986.

**fringe benefit** or **perk** any benefit offered to employees in addition to their WAGE or SALARY, for example luncheon vouchers, company car or mileage allowance, EMPLOYEE SHARE OWNERSHIP PLAN and private health insurance and employer contributions to a PENSION scheme. Fringe benefits are generally awarded to all employees in an organization or to all those in a particular category of staff, for example manage-

# FRINGE BENEFIT

| Numerical distribution | | Cumulative numerical distribution | |
|---|---|---|---|
| Weekly income (£) | number | Weekly income (£) | number |
| 0–100 | 400 | 100 or less | 400 |
| 101–200 | 300 | 200 or less | 700 |
| 201–300 | 200 | 300 or less | 900 |
| 301–400 | 100 | 400 or less | 1,000 |
| | 1,000 | | |
| (a) | | (b) | |

Qualitative distribution

| Industry | Numbers employed |
|---|---|
| Agriculture/Mining | 100,000 |
| Manufacturing | 300,000 |
| Construction/Building | 200,000 |
| Services/Retail | 400,000 |

(c)

Fig. 43. **Frequency distribution.** Data grouped according to (a) numerical size, (b) cumulative size, (c) qualitative distribution.

ment staff. In general, clerical and managerial employees receive more favourable benefits than manual employees (but see STAFF STATUS).

Since fringe benefits are distributed in this way they often provide only a weak incentive for individuals to improve their job performance (an exception is where the size of a company car is related to job position in the organization, so that promotion results in a new and bigger car). The primary advantage they offer to employers and employees is that they often attract lower rates of taxation than is found with monetary rewards. In addition they provide a means of improving remuneration when a PRICES AND INCOMES POLICY restricts growth in monetary incomes. An extensive range of fringe benefits may also contribute to good working relationships in the organization (see HUMAN RELATIONS) though perceived inequity of distribution can lead to conflict.

In many cases fringe benefits are introduced in an *ad hoc*

way rather than as part of a coordinated approach to managing remuneration. As a result their cost can escalate out of control. Recent research has shown that for a substantial number of firms in the UK fringe benefits are forming an increasing element of employment costs.

See EMPLOYEE SHARE OWNERSHIP.

**full-cost pricing** see COST-BASED PRICING.

**full employment** see ECONOMIC POLICY.

**full-line forcing** a business practice whereby a supplier encourages distributors/retailers to stock or provide not only his principal products or services but additionally other products or services from his range. For example, an oil company might require a filling station contracted to sell its petrol also to sell its brands of lubricants, anti-freeze and other motoring accessories. The practice of full line forcing may help the supplier increase his total sales and reinforce brand loyalty. However, if undertaken by a DOMINANT FIRM, the practice may serve to limit competition in a market by depriving rival suppliers of distribution outlets. See OFFICE OF FAIR TRADING.

**full-line strategy** a product line strategy which involves offering an extensive number of variations of a product.

See PRODUCT RANGE, contrast LIMITED-LINE STRATEGY.

**full-time official** an official employed by a TRADE UNION to undertake COLLECTIVE BARGAINING with managements, recruitment of new members and administration of union affairs. See SHOP STEWARD.

**functional budget** a BUDGET which relates to a specific function of a business organization e.g., marketing, production, research and development, purchasing etc.

**functional flexibility** see LABOUR FLEXIBILITY.

**functional foremen** see SCIENTIFIC MANAGEMENT.

**functional layout** a means of organizing production which involves grouping together equipment, machinery and personnel according to the function which they perform in the production process, for example drilling, grinding and assembly. See BATCH PRODUCTION.

**functional structure** an ORGANIZATION structure where activities are grouped into DEPARTMENTS by function, and formal COORDINATION occurs at the apex. (See Fig. 44.)

Such structures provide a generally effective means of coordination both within departments and across the organization as a whole, when there is a *single* product or service. They also provide clear career paths for functional specialists, though there is a possibility that loyalty to departments will displace loyalty to the organization. Functional structures become less appropriate when an organization *diversifies* – it can be difficult to adapt functions to possibly varying product or service requirements since the centralization of authority in this model tends to encourage uniformity.

This type of structure is often referred to as 'U-form' since authority within the organization can be traced up the CHAIN OF COMMAND to a unitary source.

See PRODUCT-BASED STRUCTURE. MATRIX STRUCTURE, CRITICAL FUNCTION STRUCTURE.

Fig. 44. **Functional structure.** A typical example.

**funding** the process of replacing maturing short-term LOANS by long-term loans in order to reduce the ratio of short-term borrowing to long-term borrowing. Funding is undertaken by the government in its management of the NATIONAL DEBT, and by companies who use the proceeds of DEBENTURE and LOAN STOCK issues to pay off short-term borrowings and overdrafts.

**funds** the WORKING CAPITAL of a business, consisting of money tied up in stocks and debtors plus cash, less money owed to creditors. Any change in net working capital has an effect in increasing or decreasing funds.

**funds flow analysis** a means of analysing the movement of funds within a company by comparing successive BALANCE SHEETS to note where additional funds have come from and where they have been deployed in the business. See also SOURCES AND USES OF FUNDS STATEMENT.

**funds flow statement** see SOURCES AND USES OF FUNDS STATE-MENT.

**futures market** see FORWARD MARKET.

# G

**gainsharing a** PAY system where a proportion of employees' pay is linked to gains in productivity or reductions in costs. Its benefits are thought to include greater acceptance of changes in technology and work methods, more information sharing, more effective teamwork and greater personal effort. It can be used in organizations where profit-sharing schemes are inappropriate or impossible e.g. not-for-profit and public service organizations.

Two common forms of gainsharing are the Scanlon Plan where a portion of wages is based on movements in the ratio of the total wages bill to the total value of sales, and the Rucker Plan where wages are related to movements in the ratio of the total wages bill to total VALUE ADDED. The former provides an incentive to maximize saleable output whilst the latter encourages cost reduction.

**Gantt chart** a chart used for PRODUCTION SCHEDULING purposes which lists orders on the left of the chart and time along the right of the chart as in Fig. 45, depicting the scheduling of orders on a day-by-day or week-by-week basis using bar lines to show the start and completion dates of each order. A similar chart can be used to show machine availability and utilization rates in producing orders.

**gap analysis** a technique used in the marketing of services to identify to what extent customers' *expectations* match up to the *perceived* level of services received. In some cases customers may get better service than they expected – a positive 'expected service–perceived service' gap – thus encouraging them to purchase the supplier's service again. By contrast, a negative 'expected service–perceived service' gap may apply such that customers will show their dissatisfaction with the

| order no | customer | date | | | | | |
|----------|----------|--------|--------|--------|--------|--------|--------|
| | | week 1 | week 2 | week 3 | week 4 | week 5 | week 6 |
| 001 | Pass | ▬▬▬▬ | | | | | |
| 002 | Lowes | | | ▬▬▬▬▬▬ | | | |
| 003 | Chadwick | | ▬▬▬▬▬▬▬▬▬ | | | | |
| 004 | Pendleton | | | | | ▬▬▬▬▬▬ | |
| 005 | Smith | ▬▬▬▬▬▬ | | | | | |

Fig. 45. **Gantt chart.** A typical example.

supplier's service by ceasing to purchase it. Gap analysis identifies a number of potential problem areas which can emerge, including: (i) *management perception–consumer expectations gap:* the supplier fails to identify or understand consumers' expected service needs; (ii) *management perception–service quality specification gap:* the supplier knows what customers expect but fails to establish satisfactory service quality specifications resulting in the provision of an inferior service; (iii) *service quality specification–service delivery gap:* service quality specifications may be satisfactory but the firm's service delivery is unsatisfactory because, for example, contact persons are inefficient/unhelpful; *service delivery–external communications gap:* the supplier 'misleads' customers by promising (through advertisements etc.) more than the supplier can actually deliver.

Gap analysis thus helps managers identify and remove existing and potential negative service gaps which reflect the firm's *own* failings in meeting customers' demands for a quality service.

**'garbage can' model of decision making** a pattern of decision making in organizations, identified by the American Professor of Management, James March (1928– ), in which organizational members generate a stream of problems and solutions, especially when choices need to be made. These are in effect 'dumped' into a 'garbage can'; only a small minority of solutions will be incorporated in the final decision (if one is made at all). The basis of this model is that organizational members frequently have favoured courses of action: wherever they can they seize the opportunity provided by a problem or the organization's needs to make a choice to advocate the implementation of their solution. In this sense organizations can be said to be a set of 'free floating' solutions waiting for problems to arise. Decisions can be seen as a more or less fortuitous by-product of problems, solutions and choices coming together at a particular junction. See ORGANIZATIONAL ANALYSIS, 'ORGANIZED ANARCHY'.

**gatekeeper** a person who controls important information flows within an organization. The person concerned may have control over the information which goes up or down the organizational structure or in and out of the organization.

**GATT** see GENERAL AGREEMENT ON TARIFFS AND TRADE.

**gazumping** a situation in which a seller of an asset such as a house, having already agreed informally to sell the asset to one buyer at an agreed price, subsequently sells the asset to another buyer at a higher price.

**GDP** see GROSS DOMESTIC PRODUCT.

**gearing** see CAPITAL GEARING.

**General Agreement on Tariffs and Trade (GATT)** an international organization established in 1947 to promote the expansion of INTERNATIONAL TRADE through the removal of TARIFFS and other restrictions on cross-frontier trade. GATT operates in two principal ways:

(a) by arranging for countries to receive foreign tariff reductions in return for tariff cuts of their own (reciprocity);

(b) by requiring that a country should apply its lowest tariff for any particular product to all of its suppliers (the 'most favoured nation' rule).

GATT has supervised eleven major multilateral rounds of tariff negotiations, including the 'Kennedy Round' of 1962–67 which secured an average cut in tariff rates on manufactures of around 35% and the 'Tokyo Round' of 1973–79 which provided further significant reductions in tariffs.

The 'Uruguay Round' of 1988–93 produced further cuts in tariffs on manufactures, lowering the overall tariff rates applied by the developed countries from 6.3% to 3.9%. Importantly, the Uruguay Round also led to sizeable reductions in tariffs and quotas on trade in agricultural produce and went some way towards liberalizing trade in services and in PATENT recognitions.

These GATT initiatives, together with the work of the

INTERNATIONAL MONETARY FUND, the formation of FREE TRADE BLOCS (in particular, the EUROPEAN UNION/COMMUNITY and the EUROPEAN FREE TRADE ASSOCIATION) and high growth rates in the industrial countries, led to a record expansion of world trade up to the 1970s. The OPEC oil price increase of 1973 and the subsequent onset of recessionary conditions in the world economy, however, has reduced the impact of GATT and has led to a renaissance of PROTECTIONISM based on national self-interest. The 'new protectionism', as it is referred to, is based not on tariffs but on various measures which are much less transparent and diffuse and therefore more difficult to control on a uniform basis, including EXPORT RESTRAINT AGREEMENTS, LOCAL CONTENT RULES, import licensing restrictions, subsidies given to domestic industries, etc.

The GATT was replaced by the World Trade Organization (WTO) in 1995, which will provide a more permanent forum for trade negotiations and stronger powers to adjudicate in trade disputes between member countries.

See DUMPING.

**General Municipal Boilermakers – Association of Professional, Clerical and Computer Staff Partnership (GMB-APEX Partnership)** the UK's third largest TRADE UNION formed out of a merger between the GMB (a general union) and APEX (a white-collar union) in 1989. It currently has around 800,000 members.

**general union** see TRADE UNION.

**generic** a term that is used to identify a PRODUCT or product class as a whole (for example, 'cigarettes') rather than an individual supplier's BRAND of the product (for example, 'Marlboro' cigarettes).

**geographical pricing** the PRICING of products to customers based in different locations. In some cases differential PRICES may be charged to reflect the respective costs of physical DISTRIBUTION involved in moving goods from the factory to the buyer.

In other cases firms may simplify their pricing arrangements by means of a 'uniform delivered price system' which involves charging the same price to all customers irrespective of their location (for example post office letters). Alternatively, customers may be grouped into a number of delivery zones and a common price charged to all customers in each zone.

Such 'basing point price systems' involve some cross-subsidization of delivery costs between customers in the interests of maximizing the firm's total sales.

See PRICE DISCRIMINATION.

**geographical segmentation** a form of MARKET SEGMENTATION which divides a market into geographical areas on the basis of common customer characteristics. Geographical segmentation also provides a means of dividing a MARKET into sales regions and then subdividing them into sales territories to assist with the efficient deployment of sales representatives to service customers.

**geographic mobility** see LABOUR MOBILITY.

**Gesellschaft mit beschrankter Haftung (GmbH)** the German equivalent of a private limited company. See JOINT-STOCK COMPANY.

**gilt-edged security** a BOND issued by the government or a company as a means of borrowing money. Such bonds are called gilt-edged because they are a low-risk form of lending in so far as governments and well-established large companies rarely default on their debts.

**glass ceiling** the impenetrable yet invisible barrier which prevents most women from reaching senior management positions, depite attempts to tackle DISCRIMINATION in employment over the last twenty-five years. The glass ceiling exists because male senior managers tend to believe that the values and talents necessary for senior management positions are more likely to be found in men. In other words male managers recruit new managers in their own image.

**global brand** a BRAND which is sold in a large number of national markets on the basis of a single unique BRAND NAME, for example Coca Cola, rather than using different brand names for each separate national market. Such global brands offer considerable economies of scale in marketing and production, though care must be exercised in developing a brand name which is in keeping with the customs and sentiments of all the target nations. See MULTINATIONAL ENTERPRISE.

**globalization** see INTERNATIONALIZATION.

**Globex** an international futures trading system which enables futures contracts to be traded outside the trading hours of their national FORWARD MARKETS. Globex is run by REUTERS and its members include the Chicago Mercantile Exchange, Matif (of France) and DTB (of Germany). However, it has failed to attract the support of the LONDON DERIVATIVES EXCHANGE, the world's third largest futures market, while the world's largest futures exchange, the Chicago Board of Trade, withdrew from Globex in 1994.

**GNP** see GROSS NATIONAL PRODUCT.

**GNVQ** see NATIONAL VOCATIONAL QUALIFICATION.

**goal displacement** the process whereby an organization's primary objectives (for example the provision of services to consumers) come to take second place to other subsidiary objectives (such as monitoring employee performance). Writers on ORGANIZATIONS have shown how there is the ever-present danger that the means adopted to achieve organizational goals will become ends in themselves and displace the original goals. This tension is inevitable because organizations generally need to develop procedures to guide their members' job activities. But time and effort have to be expended to ensure that the procedures are adhered to and that they are effective. In this way operation of the procedures can come to dominate the activities of managers to the exclusion of attaining the goals the procedures were initially intended to achieve. See BUREAUCRACY.

**goals** see BUSINESS OBJECTIVES.

**going concern** see ACCOUNTING PRINCIPLES.

**going-rate pricing** see COMPETITION-BASED PRICING.

**gold** a mineral that is used both as an industrial base metal and for ornamental purposes, and is held by governments as part of their stock of INTERNATIONAL RESERVE assets in order to finance balance of payments deficits. Formerly, in the UK and many other countries, gold coins formed the basis of the domestic MONEY SUPPLY, but gold has now been replaced by bank notes and brass and nickel coins as the cash component of the money supply. See BULLION MARKET. WORLD GOLD COUNCIL.

**goldbricking** a hoarding of output by employees when PIECEWORK is in operation. Employees do not declare their full daily output, preferring to hide it and then declare it at a later date. Payment for it will thus be received in the future. This enables employees to regulate their earnings over time. On some days they can take it easy but by releasing previous output to management they can achieve their usual level of pay. See

QUOTA RESTRICTION.

**golden handcuff** a form of BONUS PAYMENT (cash or share allocation) made to retain key staff. Bonuses are not paid out immediately but at some set future date provided the person is still working for the firm.

**golden handshake** a generous severance payment made to an employee as an inducement to leave an organization. The phrase is also sometimes used to describe payments made to retiring employees as a sign of gratitude for their services. See REDUNDANCY.

**golden hello** a large lump-sum payment made to a new employee of an organization as an inducement to join it.

**golden parachute** see TAKEOVER BID.

**golden share** an arrangement which enables the government to intercede in the affairs of a company which has been privatized (i.e. sold by the government to private investors). A typical 'golden share' stipulation is a limitation on the number of shares which can be owned by any *single* investor, which thus enables the government to block an unwelcome TAKEOVER bid. 'Golden shares' may be waivered or held for a limited period only, but in some cases (British Gas, British Telecom, for example) they are held on a permanent basis (or until such time as the government decides to remove them). See NATIONALIZATION VERSUS PRIVATIZATION.

**good** or **commodity** an economic PRODUCT which is produced to meet some personal or business demand. Goods which are purchased by individuals are called *consumer goods* or *final goods*, while goods purchased by businesses are referred to variously as *producer goods*, *capital goods*, *industrial goods* or *intermediate goods*.

Some consumer goods (nondurables), such as bread and toothpaste, are used up immediately or within days of purchase, while others, referred to as *consumer durables*, such as cars, washing machines and televisions, are 'consumed' over a time scale often running into several years and are often considered to constitute part of an individual's personal assets or wealth.

Producer goods are items which are purchased by manufacturers, etc. to be used as factor inputs in producing other goods or services. They too may be used up in the short term (for example nuts and bolts, engines, etc.) as the production cycle repeats itself, or they may constitute the firm's stock of longer-lasting (durable) fixed capital assets such as plants, equipment and machinery.

The provision of goods (for example, a motor car, a perfume etc.) involve a number of characteristics which set them apart from the provision of a SERVICE (for example, window cleaning), in particular *tangibility* – the ability of a customer to see, touch, taste or smell the good, and *separability* – the fact that goods are typically produced and consumed at different points in time and thus can be stored. See MARKETING.

**goods (inwards) received records** documents used to inform the PURCHASING and production scheduling departments that goods have arrived from suppliers and are now in the materials store or warehouse.

**goods on approval** products which are supplied to a prospective buyer on the understanding that they will only be purchased if they prove to be suitable to the buyer.

**goodwill** the difference at a particular time between the STOCK MARKET valuation of a FIRM and the sum of its NET ASSETS recorded in a BALANCE SHEET. If another firm wishes to acquire this firm, goodwill represents the premium which the buyer must be prepared to pay for the firm over and above its asset value, because of the firm's trade contacts, reputation, established BRAND names, management expertise and general 'know-how'. Where a firm has a poor trading record its market value as a going concern to a potential buyer may be less than the balance sheet value of its assets, in which case goodwill is negative.

Goodwill is an intangible FIXED ASSET and may be shown in a company's balance sheet. However, many companies write off the goodwill premium which they pay to acquire a new subsidiary company immediately against their current year's profits with the result that goodwill does not appear in their balance sheets.

**government securities** see BOND, TREASURY BILL.

**GP Fundholder** a UK doctors' practice which is given funds to purchase healthcare services, e.g. hospital treatment for its patients. A recent innovation in UK healthcare, its novelty is that doctors are able to buy services directly for their patients rather than referring their patients to the local hospital under the general contract in the locality between the health authority 'purchaser' and NHS TRUST 'provider' of health services (see PURCHASER-PROVIDER SPLIT).

**graduated measured day work** see MEASURED DAY WORK.

**graph** a means of portraying data in pictorial form that shows the relationship between an independent VARIABLE and a dependent variable by labelling and scaling the two axes of the graph to represent the two variables; plotting joint values of the two in the space between the axes; and joining these values with a line. Frequently graphs show time as the independent variable, depicting by means of a line how the dependent variable has changed over time.

**graphology** the study of handwriting and its associations with character types. There is some evidence that certain writing styles are associated with certain character traits. For this reason graphology is sometimes used as a quasi-PSYCHOLOGICAL TEST in RECRUITMENT AND SELECTION.

**green audit** an examination of an organization's production, distribution and marketing activities which concentrates upon the environmental impact of these activities. Green audits can assist an organization in identifying sources of environmental pollution or excessive resource usage so that it can then seek to improve its performance.

**'green' consumers** buyers who are influenced by environmental considerations in purchasing products. For example, a typical green consumer of petrol would favour the purchase of a lead-free brand. Pressures from green consumer groups like Friends of the Earth or Greenpeace have on occasions forced companies to adopt production and waste disposal methods which reduce pollution levels. See CONSUMERISM.

**greenfield investment** the establishment of a new manufacturing plant, workshop, office, etc. by a firm. Greenfield investment is undertaken by a 'start-up' (i.e. new) business and by existing firms as a means of expanding their activities (see ORGANIC GROWTH). Establishing a new plant may be preferred to inheriting existing plants through takeovers and mergers (see EXTERNAL GROWTH), because it gives the firm greater flexibility in choosing an appropriate location (see INDUSTRIAL LOCATION). It enables it to build a scale of plant most appropriate to its operations and to instal modern manufacturing processes, techniques and work practices, thus avoiding, for example, various problems associated with the rationalization and reorganization of existing plants and the removal of restrictive labour practices. See MARKET ENTRY, BARRIERS TO ENTRY.

**greenmail** see TAKEOVER BID.

**green money** or **monetary compensatory amounts** the system used by the Common Agricultural Policy of the EUROPEAN UNION/COMMUNITY to convert the common prices agreed for farm products into the national currency of member countries and to realign prices when the exchange rates of those currencies change.

**grievance** a complaint by an employee arising out of his or her employment. For instance, a typical grievance is that a mistake has been made in the calculation of wages and that a worker has been underpaid. If not sorted out satisfactorily grievances can lead to resentment or even INDUSTRIAL DISPUTES. See GRIEVANCE PROCEDURE, DISCRIMINATION.

**grievance procedure** a set of rules stipulating the procedures to be followed when an employee has a complaint arising out of his or her employment. Usually they require that the complaint be formally submitted in writing, that the employee and the immediate manager attempt to resolve the problem and that, failing that, the issue be dealt with by higher levels of management. Where TRADE UNIONS are recognized by management there may well be a facility for a union representative to become involved in grievance resolution. In some cases the grievance procedure forms part of the PROCEDURAL AGREEMENT governing COLLECTIVE BARGAINING. Most, but not all, UK organizations operate a formal grievance procedure; it is a statutory requirement, however, that all employees other than those in small firms be notified, in the documentation setting out their CONTRACT OF EMPLOYMENT, as to what steps they can take if they have a grievance. See DISPUTES PROCEDURE.

**gross domestic product (GDP)** the total money value of all final goods and services produced in an economy over a one-year period. See NATIONAL INCOME ACCOUNTS.

**grossing up** the process in the UK of converting *net* of tax payments of DIVIDENDS, INTEREST, etc., into *gross* figures by adding back the tax credits attached to those dividends or interest payments. This is done in order to allow an individual investor's INCOME TAX assessment to be based on his gross income. See CORPORATION TAX.

**gross margin** see PROFIT MARGIN, MARK UP.

**gross national product (GNP)** the total money value of all final goods and services produced in an economy over a one-year period (gross domestic product) plus net property income from abroad (net profits, dividends, rent and interest). See NATIONAL INCOME ACCOUNTS.

**gross profit** the difference between SALES REVENUE and the COST OF SALES before the deduction of selling, distribution, administration and other costs in the PROFIT-AND-LOSS ACCOUNT.

**group 1.** a collection of people who interact with each other, are aware of each other and see themselves as a group. Very small groups, where each member knows the others well and can interact in a face-to-face manner, are often termed *primary groups*. Those with a larger membership where individuals are unable to interact directly with all the members are called *secondary groups*. Much of the work conducted in ORGANIZATIONS is done by groups. Work groups may take the form of either a number of people undertaking a particular task, directed by a manager (see MANAGEMENT) or SUPERVISOR, or a team in which coordination of a range of activities takes place and where status is more equal. The distinction is not a hard and fast one, but groups of production workers are generally referred to as 'work groups' whilst groups of managers tend to be referred to as teams. Both are *formal groups* in that they are consciously established to achieve certain work goals. By contrast, *informal groups* are those which emerge naturally, are based primarily on friendship, shared attributes or status, and whose membership does not necessarily coincide with that of formal groups. An early indication of the importance of social groups in organizations was provided by the HAWTHORNE STUDIES and exemplified in HUMAN RELATIONS philosophy. The Hawthorne researchers found that informal groups could emerge alongside formal groups, with work norms which contradicted those of management. An earlier investigation in the research programme, however, seemed to find that a style of management (see MANAGEMENT STYLE, LEADERSHIP) which displayed an interest in workers could help collections of workers to cohere into effective groups, committed to managerial goals.

Subsequently managers have adopted a variety of means to influence the activities of groups so as to harness them in support of managerial goals. One such measure is basing pay or bonuses on group output, so as to provide a stimulus to group members to work effectively together and to pressurize recalcitrant members into following group policy. Similarly, the creation of 'semiautonomous work groups' (see JOB DESIGN AND REDESIGN) with the power to allocate group members' tasks is designed to heighten both group cohesion and commitment to effective task performance. However, a question that still nevertheless vexes managers is why some groups are effective whilst others are not. For this reason substantial research has been conducted into group development and dynamics (i.e. the stages of growth that they go through and the patterns of interaction within them). One approach has suggested that groups go through four stages of development:

(a) *forming* (i.e. getting to know each other);

(b) *storming* (initial conflict as individuals compete for leadership positions and to influence the direction taken by the group);

(c) *norming* (the establishment of shared values);

(d) *performing* (where the group utilizes its strengths to perform desired activities). Many groups find difficulty in moving beyond the second and third stages. Team–building exercises, to encourage group cohesion, are an attempt to solve such problems. Research has shown that individual contributions to groups differ, and that in some cases they are effective whilst in others they are not. Management writer Meredith Belbin (1926– ) has argued that each individual has a preferred team role and a secondary role which he or she adopts if unable to occupy his or her preferred role. These roles are *chairman* (setting the agenda), *shaper* (defining the task), *plant* (generating ideas), *monitor/evaluator* (evaluating ideas), *company worker* (organizing the group), *resource investigator* (seeking out resources), *team worker* (maintaining group cohesion) and *finisher* (ensuring deadlines are kept). On the basis of research of this type managers have attempted to influence group performance by selecting appropriate team members.

Whilst team working is generally thought to be a useful approach to achieving organizational goals, it can have negative effects. The most damaging of these is *groupthink*, where pressures towards group conformity stifle creativity.

See TEAM BRIEFING.

**2.** a collection of interrelated JOINT-STOCK COMPANIES which usually consists of a HOLDING COMPANY and a number of SUBSIDIARY COMPANIES and ASSOCIATED COMPANIES which tends to operate as a single business unit.

**group accounts** see CONSOLIDATED ACCOUNTS.

**group discussion** see MOTIVATIONAL RESEARCH.

**group incentive bonus scheme** a form of PAYMENT BY RESULTS in which WAGES may be supplemented by additional payments based on the performance of the work group, the establishment or the enterprise as a whole rather than the performance of the individual worker (INCENTIVE BONUS SCHEME). For example, in addition to being paid a GUARANTEED BASIC WAGE, workers in a work group could be paid a 'bonus' for exceeding pre-determined production targets. See PRIESTMAN PLAN, PERFORMANCE-RELATED PAY.

**Group of 7 (G7)** a group of seven major countries which in the late 1980s committed themselves to promote stable EXCHANGE RATES between their currencies in order to strengthen the world economy at a time when FLOATING EXCHANGE RATE SYSTEMS were threatening to undermine world economic recovery. The finance ministers and central bank governors of the US, Japan, Germany, France, UK, Italy and Canada meet regularly and establish informal limits to exchange rate fluctuations between their currencies. See INTERNATIONAL MONETARY FUND.

**group replacement** a PREVENTIVE MAINTENANCE system which replaces groups of items such as lightbulbs at predetermined intervals, even though they may not all have come to the end of their life. This is done because group replacement can be more cost-effective than the replacement of individual items as they fail, if the cost of replacement units is low and the labour and other costs of replacing them are high.

**group survey** see MARKETING INTELLIGENCE.

**group technology (GT)** a method of PRODUCTION which involves grouping together several products or components which are sufficiently similar in terms of their processing requirements for them to be produced using the same machines, with a minimal amount of machine resetting from product to product. GT requires the establishment of a separate area (or 'cell') in the factory and the laying down of a PRODUCTION LINE to handle flows of the products included in the group.

GT systems are used to produce low-volume products or components. By providing for the *continuous* production of a series of low-volume products it is possible to obtain benefits similar to those of high-volume MASS PRODUCTION using a production-line or assembly-line operation (i.e. less SET-UP time, reduced CYCLE TIMES, etc.).

**'groupthink'** see GROUP.

**growth phase** see PRODUCT LIFE CYCLE.

**GT** see GROUP TECHNOLOGY.

**guarantee** or **warranty** a legally binding promise by the seller of a product to the purchaser that in the event of the product failing to work properly the seller will either replace or repair it free of charge, or refund the purchase price. Guarantees and warranties usually operate for a limited time-period from the date of purchase, though some products like cars may relate guarantee conditions to both time and mileage. Guarantees and warranties are an important means of promoting a product, in so far as they assure the buyer about the product's expected quality and reliability. See CUSTOMER SERVICE, MARKETING MIX.

**guaranteed basic wage** the amount which a worker will receive in remuneration irrespective of the level of company output. For example, in an INCENTIVE SCHEME, should a worker's output fall short of the target set, the guaranteed basic WAGE will still be paid.

# H

**'halo effect'** the regarding of an individual by others, especially his or her superiors, as especially good at his or her job. The reality may be different but, because the belief is strongly held, any shortcomings may not be perceived. Those employees who have the halo effect often achieve rapid promotion, with the result that their occupancy of particular job roles may be brief. Any aspects of their performance which are not satisfactory may not come to light for some time, hence the halo effect remains undiminished. However, those with this attribute often attract resentment from their more discerning colleagues. The opposite of the halo effect is the *horns effect*, where an employee is viewed badly whatever his or her actual performance. See PETER PRINCIPLE.

**Halsey Plan** see ROWAN PLAN.

**handling** see MATERIALS HANDLING.

**hard currency** a FOREIGN CURRENCY that is in strong demand, but in short supply on the FOREIGN EXCHANGE MARKET. This usually arises when a country is in persistent balance of payments surplus. Compare SOFT CURRENCY.

**hard disk** a data storage device in which data is stored on a magnetic disk embodied in a COMPUTER. Most hard disks can store large amounts of data, such as 20 megabytes of numbers or letters.

**'hard sell'** a forceful and robust approach to marketing a BRAND or product. This style of ADVERTISING or PERSONAL SELLING can sometimes be successful in convincing undecided buyers. See 'SOFT SELL'.

**hardware** the electrical circuits and electromechanical devices that make up a COMPUTER system, including the CPU (central processing unit), DISK DRIVES, keyboard, and VDU (visual display unit).

**harmonization** see STAFF STATUS.

**harmonization of accounts** the process of reducing differences in accounting practices between countries. Differences arise because of countries' different legal and commercial systems, differences in types of business organization and their ownership, varying taxation rules and variations in the strength of the accounting profession between countries. Harmonization of accounting on an international basis has been fostered by the International Accounting Standards Committee which prepares international accounting standards as a basis for national STATEMENTS OF RECOMMENDED PRACTICE. On a regional basis, the European Union/Community (EU) has issued a number of Company Law Directives which have prescribed the form and content of ANNUAL REPORTS AND ACCOUNTS for all EU countries, set out common rules on ASSET valuation and offered common rules on CONSOLIDATED ACCOUNTS.

# HAWTHORNE STUDIES

**Hawthorne Studies** a series of investigations into workers' attitudes and behaviour conducted in the late 1920s and early 1930s at Western Electric Company's plant at Hawthorne, Chicago, which provided the empirical underpinning for the management approach known as HUMAN RELATIONS. The research programme had four main stages. In the *first* (inconclusive) experiments the researchers tested the effect of environmental factors, such as the quality of lighting, on worker productivity. The suspicion that social factors may have been an important intervening variable led to the *second* stage. Here six women were placed in the Relay Assembly Test Room and a set of changes were made to their working conditions, such as alterations to the duration of work-breaks. Somewhat oddly, output rose throughout the experiments even when conditions were restored to their pre-experimental state. The only consistent variable seemed to be the presence of the researcher in the test room. From this was derived the so-called Hawthorne Effect – that people behave differently when they know they are under observation. Human relations writing further suggested that the observer had acted as a quasi-supervisor and had stimulated a growth in output by (a) showing interest in the workforce and thereby increasing JOB SATISFACTION and (b) helping the women to cohere as an effective team.

The *third* stage was a large scale programme of interviews (about 10,000) with workers, which found that employees were more complex social beings than had been assumed in management theory to date. Following on from this the *fourth* stage involved the observation of a work GROUP in the Bank Wiring Observation Room. Here it was found that an informal policy of restricting output was in operation. For the researchers this showed the importance of group influences on individual behaviour and how this could frustrate managerial objectives.

Overall human relations theory claimed that the Hawthorne studies showed that people were social beings, who both developed and were influenced by social networks out of a need to belong to a community. The task for management was to understand these processes and to intervene to mould them in the organization's favour. Whether this is the correct interpretation of the studies is open to question. The

Hawthorne studies suffered from methodological weaknesses and, contrary to their conclusions, their data provides some evidence that financial incentives rather than social pressures are the main influence on worker behaviour.

See SOCIOLOGY OF WORK.

**Hay-MSL evaluation** see JOB EVALUATION.

**health and safety** the regulation of organizations' working methods so as to discourage dangerous practices. It is usually understood to focus on the avoidance of accidents rather than the active promotion of good health, although the latter can form part of a health and safety policy.

Concern for safety can be worthwhile for employers, as well as for employees. Absence from work due to accidents at work is costly. Nevertheless in many firms health and safety is not given the attention it deserves, in part because the benefits of safe working conditions may only become apparent once accidents have occurred, in part because the encouragement of safe working methods can slow down production speeds.

In the UK, legislation has regulated working conditions since the mid-nineteenth century. The main legislation today is the Health and Safety at Work Act 1974. This requires employers to formulate a written safety policy, places an obligation on employees to observe safety rules, and allows for the appointment of TRADE UNION safety representatives with time off from normal duties to attend to safety matters. The Act established the Health and Safety Commission to formulate safety regulations and codes of practice, and the Health and Safety Executive to enforce the provisions of the Act. The Factory Inspectorate is responsible for ensuring that employers obey safety regulations. They have the right to enter places of work to carry out investigations and to serve notice on employers to change potentially unsafe working methods. However, critics argue that the Inspectorate is too understaffed to provide an effective deterrent to those employers who choose to follow dangerous practices.

**hedge fund** a pool of capital which fund managers (for example, international banks) used to speculate on the foreign exchange, stock and commodity markets. Fund managers aim to make windfall profits by 'correctly' guessing future price movements. Their activities, which have become increasingly global and largely unsupervised by national regulatory frameworks, have, on occasion, served to destabilize the financial markets. See HEDGING, OPTIONS, FORWARD MARKET, DERIVATIVE.

**hedging** the act of reducing uncertainty about future (unknown) price movements in a COMMODITY (rubber, tea, etc.), FINANCIAL SECURITY (share, stock etc.) and FOREIGN CURRENCY. This can be done by undertaking forward sales or purchases of the commodity, security or currency in the FORWARD MARKET; or by taking out an OPTION which limits the option holder's exposure to price fluctuations. See EXCHANGE RATE EXPOSURE, HEDGE FUND.

**heterarchy** an ORGANIZATION without a HIERARCHY or leader. All members of the organization have equal authority and involvement in decision-making. Such an organizational form is difficult to sustain beyond the smallest organizations because of the need to coordinate the organization's activities. See WORKERS' COOPERATIVE.

**H-form** a form of company structure in which constituent companies are completely or partially owned by a HOLDING COMPANY. Generally such structures arise out of merger or acquisition activity. The product range, production facilities and management structures are often left largely unchanged, and constituent companies can thus be said to be *undigested*. Little direct control is exercised by the holding company other than receipt of profits. The absence of central direction is often contrasted with that in the *M-form company* but in so far as the holding company confines itself to acquisitions, divestment and simple financial control it could be said to be a 'pure' form of the latter. H-form companies were at one time a common feature of UK industry but in the last thirty years the structure and activities of many have been rationalized (*digested*) to form multi-divisional companies. See PRODUCT-BASED STRUCTURE.

**hidden** or **disguised price rise** a decrease in the quantity or quality of a good or service sold at an unchanged price. Suppliers may reduce the quantity or quality of a good in order to improve unit profit margins or contain cost increases, but need to be mindful of consumers' reactions to these moves once they have become aware of the situation.

**hidden reserve** the undervaluation of the ASSETS, or overvaluation of the LIABILITIES, of a firm in its BALANCE SHEET. For example, the value of a firm's land and buildings may be shown in the balance sheet at HISTORIC COST or original cost, whereas the current market price of those assets may be considerably higher. Thus, if the assets were to be revalued to reflect current market values the difference would be formally recorded in the balance sheet as an addition to capital RESERVES. See INFLATION ACCOUNTING.

**hierarchy 1.** any pattern of social relationships where some individuals have AUTHORITY over others.

**2.** the vertical structure of an ORGANIZATION. Generally there will be a number of management levels in the hierarchy with each having authority over the one beneath it. In a very small organization there might be only two levels in the hierarchy – the manager and the managed. In larger organizations the number will be greater, though it is rarely above eight. Organizations with a high number of levels are said to be *tall* whilst those with only two or three are said to be *flat*. There is an inverse relationship with the SPAN OF CONTROL. Where the latter is high, i.e. each manager supervises a large number of subordinates, there will be a tendency towards a flat structure. For the same number of total staff, a low span of control will be associated with a tall structure.

See ORGANIZATION CHART, DE-LAYERING.

**hierarchy of needs** see MOTIVATION.

**high geared** see CAPITAL GEARING.

**hire purchase** see INSTALMENT CREDIT.

**hiring** see RECRUITMENT AND SELECTION.

**histogram** see BAR CHART.

**historic cost** the original cost of purchasing an ASSET (such as an item of machinery). For accountancy purposes, the asset is entered in a firm's BALANCE SHEET at historic cost. However, allowance has to be made for the REPLACEMENT COST of the asset which, because of INFLATION, may well be considerably greater than the original price paid. Thus, DEPRECIATION provisions which are generally based on the historic cost of assets may be inadequate in a period of rapidly rising prices. See INFLATION ACCOUNTING, MARKET VALUE.

**historical costing** COSTING systems where costs and revenues are calculated after the end of the accounting period in which they are incurred. Historical costing permits the accurate calculation of costs afterwards but is of little use for forward planning purposes. Contrast PREDETERMINED COSTING.

**hoarding** the nonproductive retention of resources, products or money. Rather than release particular workers when demand for its products falls, a firm may retain them so as to be in a position to expand production again quickly when demand picks up. Hoarding of money may be practised by people who are reluctant to use the banking system, etc. as a repository for their savings.

**holding company** a JOINT-STOCK COMPANY that controls another company or companies. Ownership may be *complete* (100%) or *partial* (ownership of 50%+ of the voting shares in the company). Such ownership confers powers to control the policies of SUBSIDIARY COMPANIES. The holding company will report the accounting results of these subsidiary companies as part of the accounting results for the group of companies.

In addition, the holding company may own between 20% and 50% of the voting shares of an ASSOCIATED COMPANY, which will continue to produce its own annual accounts and retain a degree of independence, though subject to the influence of the holding company.

Holding companies are most frequently used as a means of achieving diversified or conglomerate growth, with the firm operating separate companies in different lines of production activity, but with each company subject to varying degrees of centralized control by the *parent company*. See CONSOLIDATED ACCOUNTS, H-FORM, DIVERSIFICATION.

**holding cost** see STOCKHOLDING COST.

**homeworking** work performed at home for an organization or individual. Such work is usually performed by those confined to the home for some reason (for example child-care commitments) and usually involves simple assembly or packaging and dispatch, though there are more sophisticated variants (see NETWORKING). It is commonly found in the clothing industry, either for simple manufacture at the bottom-end of the market, or for creation of one-off fashion design at the top end. Payment is usually based on output, and rates of pay are often very low. Since homeworkers are usually freelance, not employees, they receive little employment or earnings protection and do not contribute directly to the social INSURANCE system. For this reason homeworking can be advantageous to those business people who place a premium on minimizing labour costs as part of a policy of competing on prices.

Labour costs may be kept at a level which makes it not financially worthwhile to automate the production process on the employer's premises. A recurrent problem, however, is a high drop-out rate amongst homeworkers (see LABOUR TURN-OVER). Once they are no longer confined to the home conventional employment may be more financially and socially rewarding.

**horizontal integration 1.** the specialization of a firm at a particular level in the production or distribution of a product.
**2.** the increase in MARKET CONCENTRATION arising from the ORGANIC GROWTH of firms, or, more specifically, EXTERNAL GROWTH through MERGERS and TAKEOVERS, and the subsequent integration of firms supplying the same product.

Horizontal integration may be advantageous to firms if it permits them to lower unit costs by exploiting ECONOMIES OF SCALE, and to increase their market share, enabling them to exercise greater control over market conditions. There are, however, limits to horizontal integration as a growth strategy for the firm. Overall market demand may be static or declining (see PRODUCT LIFE CYCLE), making it necessary for firms to seek new growth opportunities through DIVERSIFICATION. In addition, firms' ability to increase market share by merger and takeover may be restricted by COMPETITION POLICY. In the UK, for example, mergers and takeovers which take a firm's market share of a product above 25% may be challenged by the OFFICE OF FAIR TRADING.

See BUSINESS STRATEGY, COMPETITIVE ADVANTAGE, PRODUCT MARKET MATRIX.

**horizontal segregation** the division of a workforce by sex or some other criteria. It is common for certain jobs in an organization to be performed solely by women, whilst other jobs at the same level are performed by men. Most female employees in the UK work only with other women. This practice has a long history due to gender stereotyping but has been reinforced by legislation aimed at tackling DISCRIMINA-TION. To avoid claims by women for equal pay many employers removed all males from certain occupations so that there is no directly comparable male wage. The emergence of 'equal pay for work of equal value' undermines the rationale for this practice.

**'horns effect'** see 'HALO EFFECT'.

**host country** a country which is a recipient of FOREIGN INVEST-
MENT by a MULTINATIONAL ENTERPRISE (MNE), including the
establishment of new plants, joint ventures, takeovers and
mergers and the extension of the MNE's existing operations in
the country. Inward investment may arise due to the 'natural'
attractions of the host country to the MNE both in terms of
the SOURCING of inputs (for example, large deposits of raw
materials, or a low-wage labour force) and as a market
providing growth prospects for the firm's products. Additionally, the host country itself may seek to attract
internationally-mobile capital by offering various fiscal and
financial inducements (for example, tax exemptions and investment subsidies) in order to strengthen its economy. The
potential gains to a country from inward investment include
various general macroeconomic effects, for example, higher
levels of domestic investment (important when domestic savings are too low to finance this); and increased employment
and exports, which serve to benefit the economy as a whole
by raising the level of national income and promoting industrialization (important in the case of the less developed
countries). At the microeconomic level, inward investment
may serve to make firms and industries more competitive in
international markets through technology transfer (acquiring
innovative processes and products) and the acquisition of
marketing and managerial skills. On the debit side, inward investment may lead to key industries being controlled by
foreign corporate interests and heightened dangers of loss of
sovereignty over their economies by host country governments. For these reasons, governmental regulation or agreed
codes of conduct may be required to sustain a mutually beneficial commitment to inward investment. See CAPITAL INFLOW,
FOREIGN MARKET SERVICING STRATEGY.

**hot money** short-term CAPITAL INFLOWS and CAPITAL OUTFLOWS
between countries which occur in anticipation of likely
EXCHANGE RATE changes (devaluations and revaluations), or in
response to INTEREST RATE differentials between financial
centres. See SPECULATION, ARBITRAGE.

**hours of work** the number of hours an employee is contracted to work each week for his or her employer. See CON-
TRACT OF EMPLOYMENT.

**human asset accounting** see PERSONNEL MANAGEMENT.

**human engineering** see ERGONOMICS.

**human factor psychology** see OCCUPATIONAL PSYCHOLOGY.

**human relations** a concept of the MANAGEMENT of human resources based on the belief that the character of social relationships at work has a profound effect on employee performance. The task of management is to understand and influence these so as to gain employee commitment to organizational goals and to improve individual and collective performance. The main way of doing this, according to human relations theory, is for management to be seen to be taking an active interest in employee aspirations and welfare, which in turn will stimulate the development of work GROUPS which cohere well and are committed to the formal objectives of the organization.

The main architect of human relations was Professor Elton Mayo (1880–1949) of Harvard University. He based his work on the investigations known as the HAWTHORNE STUDIES, though it is debatable how far Mayo was actually involved in these. The key findings of these studies were that informal work groups which operate against the organization's objectives could emerge and that friendly supervision was correlated with steady improvements in employee performance. Mayo placed these findings in a broader philosophy of modern industrial society. He claimed that people had a fundamental 'need to belong' (more powerful than economic needs) which had not been actualized in industrial society (see ANOMIE), and they therefore suffered a sense of loss which could be overcome by the creation of a *community* at work. The Hawthorne studies, according to Mayo, showed how managerial action could achieve this: the friendly supervisor had helped workers to cohere in an effective social group.

The upshot of this is that MANAGEMENT STYLE is a key consideration in the management of people. Managers should display concern for people as well as simply getting the job done. It can be argued that human relations put a welcome emphasis on the human dimension at work. However, the concept can be criticized for its manipulative character in that it advocates that managers should mould social relationships in a way that is conducive to organizational goals. It also requires that managers stifle the expression of interests which are contrary to those of the organization. Hence human relations practice can be hostile to trade unions. Human relations has also been criticized on the grounds that it understates the influence of other factors, such as financial incentives and job design (see JOB DESIGN AND REDESIGN), on worker behaviour and JOB SATISFACTION. Despite these criticisms human relations was an important stage in the development of the SOCIOLOGY OF WORK, in that it focused attention on the role of work groups and social factors in influencing individual attitudes and behaviour. Human relations was fashionable amongst managers in the UK in the 1940s and 1950s but lost favour subsequently. It has had something of a revival recently in the guise of such management methods as TEAM BRIEFING.

See SOCIOLOGY OF WORK.

**human resource management (HRM)** see PERSONNEL MANAGEMENT.

**hygiene factor** see MOTIVATION.

**hyperinflation** a very high level of INFLATION.

**hypermarket** see SUPERMARKET.


# I


**ICAEW** see INSTITUTE OF CHARTERED ACCOUNTANTS IN ENGLAND AND WALES.

**ICAS** see INSTITUE OF CHARTERED ACCOUNTANTS IN SCOTLAND.

**idea generation** a systematic search for new product ideas. Idea generation may involve BRAINSTORMING, visits to other countries to seek out new product opportunities, or simply monitoring the external environment in which the firm operates. See NEW PRODUCT DEVELOPMENT.

**ideal type** see BUREAUCRACY.

**idle time** the time during which a machine or PRODUCTION operative is not producing components or products. Idle time can be caused by machine breakdowns, delays in obtaining raw materials or components, production delays at earlier phases of the production process, worker illness or injury, or industrial disputes. Idle time leads to lost output and reduces

MACHINE UTILIZATION rates.

**ILO** see INTERNATIONAL LABOUR OFFICE.

**IM** see INSTITUTE OF MANAGMENT.

**image building** an aspect of SALES PROMOTION which seeks to influence buyers' perceptions of a BRAND in a favourable way, thus reinforcing BRAND LOYALTY.

See also COMPANY IMAGE, PRODUCT IMAGE.

**IMF** see INTERNATIONAL MONETARY FUND.

**immigration** see POPULATION.

**immunities** see TRADE UNION IMMUNITIES.

**imperfect competition** a MARKET STRUCTURE characterized by non-standardized products and BARRIERS TO ENTRY. Whether the number of suppliers are many (MONOPOLISTIC COMPETITION) or few (OLIGOPOLY), key features of imperfect competition are the efforts by each supplier to offer a distinctive branded product (see PRODUCT DIFFERENTIATION) as a means of establishing COMPETITIVE ADVANTAGE over rival suppliers; while barriers to entry serve to limit attempts by newcomers to enter the market. In basic economic analysis imperfect competition as compared with PERFECT COMPETITION is depicted as resulting in an inferior market performance, specifically lower industry output levels and higher costs and prices. However, this model ignores certain benefits arising from product differentiation competition, including greater consumer choice and lower overall supply costs resulting from mass marketing.

**implicit cost** or **imputed cost** the OPPORTUNITY COST to a FIRM of using resources owned by the firm itself to produce its output. For example, if a firm occupies a building that it owns, it forgoes the opportunity of renting it out for some other use. Thus, implicit costs represent the sacrifice of income that could have been earned by renting out (or selling) the firm's resources to others.

To achieve an accurate measure of the total cost of producing goods or services, the firm must *impute* a rent to itself using a SHADOW PRICE based upon the current market rates for renting the property.

See PROFIT, EXPLICIT COST.

**implied terms** those conditions of employment which are implicit rather than explicitly stated in the CONTRACT OF EMPLOYMENT between employer and employee. These normally derive from common law (e.g. that employees should normally obey reasonable instructions from the employer).

**import 1.** a good which is produced in a foreign country and which is then physically transported to and sold in the home market, leading to an outflow of foreign exchange from the home country (visible import).

**2.** a service which is provided for the home country by foreign interests, either in the home country (banking, insurance) or overseas (for example, travel abroad), again leading to an outflow of foreign exchange from the home country (*invisible* import).

**3.** capital which is invested in the home country in the form of portfolio investment, foreign direct investment in physical assets and banking deposits (*capital* imports).

Together these items comprise, along with EXPORTS, a country's BALANCE OF PAYMENTS. See INTERNATIONAL TRADE, IMPORT DUTY, IMPORTING, IMPORT PENETRATION.

**import deposit** a sum of money paid to the government by importers of a specified good on arrival of the good in the country prior to its eventual sale. Import deposits are used primarily to discourage imports as a means of protecting a country's BALANCE OF PAYMENTS.

**import duty** a TAX levied by the government on imported products (see TARIFFS) as a means of protecting domestic industries from foreign competition, in order to assist the country's BALANCE OF PAYMENTS and to raise revenue for the government. See PROTECTIONISM.

**importing** the sale in the home market of a product which is produced in a foreign country. Domestic producers may IMPORT particular materials, components and final products either because they are unobtainable from domestic sources or because foreign producers can supply an input more cheaply or supply an alternative version of the final product. Similarly, importing may be undertaken (indirectly or directly) by foreign-based firms as an adjunct to their EXPORTING operations. In some cases locally based agents may be contracted by overseas producers to develop sales outlets and importers/distributors may be appointed to handle physical distribution. In other cases, in order to build up a stronger position in the market, foreign producers may prefer instead to establish their own sales offices and subsidiary companies to handle local distribution and marketing. See INTERNATIONAL TRADE, MULTI-

NATIONAL ENTERPRISE, PARALLEL IMPORTING, CUSTOMS AND EXCISE.

**import penetration** the proportion of domestic consumption accounted for by IMPORTS. In the case of particular products the displacement of domestic supply by imports may be beneficial, allowing consumers access to products at lower prices than can be obtained from local producers (see INTERNATIONAL TRADE). Widespread import penetration across the economy, however, when unmatched by an equivalent volume of exports, can result in BALANCE OF PAYMENT difficulties, falling domestic output and job losses (see UNEMPLOYMENT). In the case of the UK, import penetration in the competitive manufacturing sector has increased substantially, imports rising from 7% of domestic consumption of manufactures in 1955 to 38% in 1997. See also STRUCTURE OF INDUSTRY.

**import surcharge** an extra duty placed on an imported good by the government, over and above existing rates of import duty, customs duty or tariff. Import duties are used primarily to discourage imports as a means of protecting the country's BALANCE OF PAYMENTS.

**imprest** a system used to control the expenditure of petty cash. An opening balance of petty cash (called the imprest) is made available to cover the petty cash expenses for the next accounting period. At the end of the period, whatever cash has been spent is replenished to restore the petty cash balance. This system tends to limit any losses, for example, via fraud, because the maximum that can be misappropriated in any one period is the imprest or opening balance.

**impulse buy** see PRE-PURCHASE BEHAVIOUR.

**imputation system** see CORPORATION TAX.

**IMRO** see INVESTMENT MANAGEMENT REGULATORY ORGANIZATION.

**incentive bonus scheme** a form of PAYMENT BY RESULTS whereby an individual's WAGES may be supplemented by additional payments based on achievement of output or sales targets. See GROUP INCENTIVE SCHEME, PIECEWORK, PRIESTMAN PLAN, ROWAN or HALSEY PLAN, PERFORMANCE-RELATED PAY.

**income** money received by individuals, firms and other organizations in the form of WAGES, SALARIES, RENT, INTEREST, COMMISSIONS, FEES and PROFIT, together with grants, unemployment benefit, old age pensions, etc. See EARNED INCOME.

**income-and-expenditure account** see PROFIT-AND-LOSS ACCOUNT.

## INCOME DISTRIBUTION

**income distribution** see DISTRIBUTION OF INCOME.

**income-elasticity of demand** see ELASTICITY OF DEMAND.

**income measurement** the calculation of the PROFIT or LOSS of a firm. See PROFIT AND LOSS ACCOUNT, ACCOUNTING.

**income per head** see PER CAPITA INCOME.

**income segmentation** a form of MARKET SEGMENTATION which divides consumers into groups according to their income levels. See SOCIOECONOMIC GROUP.

**incomes policy** see PRICES AND INCOMES POLICY.

**income statement** see PROFIT-AND-LOSS ACCOUNT.

**income support** see TRANSFER PAYMENT, SOCIAL SECURITY BENEFIT, AGRICULTURAL POLICY.

**income tax** a DIRECT TAX imposed by the government on the INCOME (wages, rent, dividends) received by persons. The government uses income tax in order to raise revenue (see BUDGET), as a means of redistributing income (see DISTRIBUTION OF INCOME) and as an instrument of FISCAL POLICY. Income tax is usually paid on a progressive scale so that the greater the individual's earnings, the greater the rate of tax which is levied, up to some predetermined upper limit (currently 40% in the UK); low levels of income are usually tax exempt (by granting individuals an INCOME TAX ALLOWANCE), while the remainder is taxed according to various *bands* of income at rising tax rates up to the upper limit. In the UK, for example, there are currently *three* taxable income bands with taxable income up to £4,100 being taxed at 20%, £4,101 to £26,100 of income being taxed at 23% and any income above this being taxed at 40% (as at 1997/8).

In the UK, the INLAND REVENUE assesses and collects taxes on behalf of the government for a fiscal year from 6 April to 5 April the following year.

Ideally, a progressive income tax structure should promote social equity by redistributing income but also encourage enterprise and initiative by avoiding penal rates of taxation at the upper end of the scale and, together with the SOCIAL SECURITY provisions, provide suitable incentives to work at the lower end of the scale.

See NEGATIVE INCOME TAX.

**income-tax allowance** or **personal allowance** the amount of income that a person is allowed to earn before beginning to pay INCOME TAX. In the UK, for example, the personal allowance is currently (1997/8) £4,045 for a single person. In addition, older persons, widows, single-parent families, married couples and blind persons receive an extra personal allowance so that they are able to earn more before paying tax.

**income-tax schedules** the classification by the INLAND REVENUE in the UK of various sources of INCOME to facilitate the assessment of TAXATION liability upon an individual. There are 6 schedules lettered A to F. Briefly, the income source of each schedule is as follows:

Schedule A: land and property

Schedule B: woodlands run as a business (not now used)

Schedule C: INTEREST and DIVIDENDS from public bodies (including government)

Schedule D: trades, businesses, professions and vocations, interest received gross

Schedule E: WAGES from employment (collected under the PAY-AS-YOU-EARN system – PAYE)

Schedule F: company distributions.

There are considerable rules and regulations concerning INCOME TAX and the expenses allowable against income.

**incorporation** see COMPANY FORMATION.

**incremental pay scale** a graduated PAY scale upon which an employee's position is determined usually by a combination of age, experience and length of service. After each year of service the employee will generally be given an increment, i.e. moved one position up the scale. However, organizations are increasingly determining movement on such pay scales according to job performance.

**indemnity** an arrangement whereby a financial institution such as an INSURANCE COMPANY agrees to compensate a client for any financial losses suffered as a result of damage, theft or loss of the client's property.

**in-depth interviews** see MOTIVATIONAL RESEARCH.

**index-linked** (of an income payment such as a wage, or the value of an asset such as a house), connected to a PRICE INDEX in some predetermined proportion, so that, for example, if the retail price index increases, a wage payment will be automatically adjusted by the same proportion. Indexation is a means of protecting the PURCHASING POWER of an income payment or the value of an asset against erosion by INFLATION.

**index number** a single numerical value that reflects the relative size of a variable in one time period compared with its size in some predetermined base period. For example, a retail PRICE INDEX takes a SAMPLE of goods and services in each period and measures the average price of this typical basket of goods and services, showing this average price in the form of a single index number.

There are two broad types of index number:

(a) a *base-weighted* index number that uses *base-year* weights. For example, in calculating a price index the respective quantities of various products bought in the base year would be noted and the prices of these products combined to form a single price index number. At some later time, the new prices of these products would be combined to form a new price index number making *no allowance* for changes in the relative quantities of the products bought over time as their prices change;

(b) a *current-weighted* index number that uses *current-year* weights, for example, in calculating a price index the respective quantities of various products bought in the base year would be noted and the prices of these products combined to form a single price index number. At some later time the new prices of these products would be combined to form a new price index number, making *allowance* for changes in the relative quantities of the products bought over time as their prices change. See SHARE PRICE INDEX.

**indicative planning** see ECONOMIC PLANNING, NATIONAL ECONOMIC DEVELOPMENT COUNCIL.

**indirect cost** see OVERHEADS, COST.

**indirect exporting** see EXPORTING.

**indirect investment** any expenditure on FINANCIAL SECURITIES such as STOCKS and SHARES. This is sometimes referred to as *financial* or *portfolio investment*. See INVESTMENT.

**indirect labour** that part of the labour force in a firm which is not directly concerned with the manufacture of a good or the provision of a service. Indirect-labour cost depends on the amount of remuneration paid to all those factory employees who are not directly engaged in making products but who provide support services, for example supervision and clerical work. The wages of such indirect labour are usually counted as part of production OVERHEADS. See DIRECT LABOUR, FIXED COST, STANDARD COST.

**indirect materials** any raw materials which, while they are not incorporated in a product, are nonetheless consumed in the production process, for example lubricants and moulds for metal castings. The cost of such indirect materials is usually counted as part of production OVERHEADS. See DIRECT MATERIALS, FIXED COST, STANDARD COST.

**indirect quotation** see EXCHANGE RATE.

**indirect tax** a TAX imposed by the government on goods and services (which is incorporated into the product's final price) in order to raise revenues and as an instrument of FISCAL POLICY in managing the economy. The main forms of indirect tax in the UK are VALUE ADDED TAX, EXCISE DUTY and CUSTOMS DUTY. See BUDGET (GOVERNMENT), EXPENDITURE TAX.

**individualism** the philosophy that individuals have their own unique set of wants and interests, and that they should be given free rein to pursue them. Those promoting this philosophy therefore advocate the removal of laws and regulations governing how people should behave. In the economic and business spheres, they argue, regulation stifles entrepreneurial creativity and inhibits responsiveness to market forces; if people can be freed from regulation they will become more highly motivated to succeed, whilst markets will be able to function more effectively, leading to benefits to society at large. They tend to be critical of TRADE UNIONS since they believe that unions elevate group over individual interests, and place restrictions on both their members' and managers' freedom to behave as they wish. Critics of this philosophy argue, however, that interests are in fact often shared (for example between groups of employees), that power resources are unequal and hence that collective action is therefore often necessary, and that unbridled pursuit of individual goals can damage the interests of others. See COLLECTIVISM, DEREGULATION.

**individual labour law** see LABOUR LAW.

**indivisibilities** the physical inability, or economic inappropriateness, of running a machine or some other piece of equipment at below its optimal operational capacity. For example, because of design and technical specifications a machine may optimally carry out 4,000 operations per day, it being physically impossible to build two 'half-machines' in its stead, each performing only 2,000 operations. Given this situation, a firm requiring, say, a machine which carried out 3,000 operations per day would be forced to invest in the minimum-sized machine of 4,000 operations per day capacity. As a result the machine would be under-utilized and the unit of AVERAGE COST would be greater than if the machine were optimally employed.

Indivisibilities may pose particular problems in the context of a PRODUCTION-LINE operation where a number of processes and machines, each having different optimal capacities, may be required. Suppose a firm needs to combine process A machines capable of carrying out 5,000 operations per day and process B machines capable of carrying out 2,000 operations per day. Only by producing 10,000 units a day, employing two process A machines and five process B machines, would the firm be able to use both types of machine in a cost-effective way. Any output level below this would result in either one or other machine, or both, being under-utilized. See MACHINE UTILIZATION, PRODUCTION-LINE BALANCING.

**induction** the initial TRAINING an employee may receive at the commencement of employment to familiarize him or her with the workings of the organization.

**induction crisis** a trauma suffered by new employees where the reality of their new employment differs sharply from their expectations. A widespread phenomenon, it generally results from a failure by management to portray accurately the job and organization at the RECRUITMENT AND SELECTION stage, and from neglect of the process of initial TRAINING and familiarization. Induction crises frequently result in decisions to quit. See LABOUR TURNOVER.

**indulgency pattern** a term coined by an American sociologist, Alvin Gouldner (1920–80), to refer to a relaxed approach to organizational rules by both management and workers, leading to generally harmonious relationships between them. See BUREAUCRACY, ORGANIZATION.

**industrial action** measures taken by one or more workers either to bring pressure to bear on employers during the course of an INDUSTRIAL DISPUTE or as a response to their conditions of work and employment. Industrial action can therefore be an element of a strategy to win concessions from employers, or an expression of discontent and CONFLICT (or both). Generally the most dramatic form of industrial action is where employees withdraw their labour by going on STRIKE. There are other methods, however, many of which are less costly to employees since they do not usually result in complete loss of wages for the duration of the action. These include:

(a) the *overtime ban*, where employees refuse to work any time in excess of the hours stipulated in their CONTRACT OF EMPLOYMENT;

(b) the *go-slow*, where employees work at a slower rate than usual;

(c) the *work-to-rule*, where employees observe strictly the terms of their job description and their contract of employment, thereby requiring a greater level of direct supervision by management than is usual and restricting FLEXIBILITY.

The success of these forms of action is based on the fact that the work process usually requires a degree of cooperation and flexibility from the workforce in excess of that which can be formally embodied in the contract. Withdrawal of this co-operation can thus be an effective sanction. These forms of action are especially useful to those occupational groups who are prohibited from withdrawing their labour or who find STRIKE action morally repugnant.

A rarer form of industrial action is the *work-in* or *occupation* ('sit-in') where workers take over the running of the workplace, usually in response to a threat of closure.

Workers may also take *individual* action either as an expression of discontent or as an element of a personal strategy to improve their working life. ABSENTEEISM, where workers stay away from work, and *quitting* altogether (see LABOUR TURNOVER) are good examples of this. *Sabotage* (i.e. deliberate interference with equipment and the work process) is often seen as an individual outburst of dissatisfaction but it can also be a collective action carefully designed to regulate the pace of work.

Although attention generally focuses on action taken by workers, *employers* also take industrial action on occasions. For instance they may *lock-out* the workforce (i.e. prevent their employees from entering the workplace) in an attempt to secure concessions or to counter employee action during a dispute. A more indirect form of action is where they deliberately foster a STRIKE or other form of employee action, possibly as a way of reducing labour costs when the order book is low.

See ALIENATION, JOB SATISFACTION, SECONDARY ACTION.

**industrial buyer** a BUYER whose function it is to acquire raw materials, bought-out finished components, services and equipment on behalf of his or her company. See INDUSTRIAL MARKETING, BUYER BEHAVIOUR.

**industrial conflict** see CONFLICT, INDUSTRIAL ACTION, INDUSTRIAL DISPUTE, STRIKE.

**industrial democracy** the participation of the workforce in the government of organizations. Various approaches to industrial democracy provide employees or their representatives with varying degrees of power to influence decision-making processes in their organization. All, however, involve the creation of institutions and mechanisms to permit transmission of employee interests and objectives into these processes.

Industrial democracy can take a number of forms:

(a) *workers' control*, where the workforce is the sole source of authority within the organization, even though the organization might be actually owned by another (i.e. the state), and managers are required to operate to policy determined by the collectivity. This can be said to be direct form of democracy in that potentially all workers are deeply involved in the formulation of policy;

(b) *workers' cooperative*, where the organization is actually owned by the employees, and where the management (selected by and possibly from the workforce) acts in accordance with policies formulated by or sanctioned by the workforce. See WORKERS' COOPERATIVE;

(c) *worker directors*, who are representatives of the workforce who sit on the BOARD OF DIRECTORS and are involved in determining broad company policy. In contrast to other forms of industrial democracy it is not anticipated that worker representatives will have a close involvement in operational decisions. However, in the CO-DETERMINATION system in West Germany, worker directors operate in tandem with works councils, which have a more substantial involvement in these areas of management. See WORKER DIRECTOR;

(d) *collective bargaining* which is a form of industrial democracy in that it involves management formally relinquishing the right to take all decisions in the organization. See

COLLECTIVE BARGAINING.

These various forms of industrial democracy can be contrasted with EMPLOYEE PARTICIPATION and EMPLOYEE INVOLVEMENT, where employee involvement is often confined to immediate job issues and where employees or their representatives have few formal rights in decision making. In recent years in the UK interest has shifted from industrial democracy to these other forms of participation which, from a managerial perspective, provide the benefits of involvement without the costs of relinquishing managerial rights in decision making. However, pressures from the EUROPEAN COMMUNITY for an expansion of industrial democracy may act as a powerful countervailing force in the coming years.

See BULLOCK REPORT, SOCIAL CHAPTER.

**industrial dispute** a dispute between an employer (or group of employers) and one or more workers usually arising over pay and conditions of employment, allocation of work, work discipline etc. The current official definition in the UK states that it is a dispute between workers and *their* employer (i.e. not another employer) and that it relates mainly or wholly to their conditions of employment (see CONTRACT OF EMPLOYMENT). The definition excludes disputes *between* workers (thereby excluding inter-TRADE UNION conflicts). Disputes that fall outside the official definition (for example INDUSTRIAL ACTION taken by workers or trade unions in furtherance of political objectives) are not covered by TRADE UNION IMMUNITIES and hence those involved are liable to legal action by employers in the civil courts.

A large number of UK employers are party (either directly or indirectly through EMPLOYERS' ASSOCIATIONS) to a DISPUTES PROCEDURE or GRIEVANCE PROCEDURE which governs how disputes of this kind should be dealt with and resolved. Where such procedures are absent or where it is not possible to resolve the dispute in this way, some form of INDUSTRIAL ACTION such as a STRIKE may occur. Industrial disputes may be settled in a number of ways, including voluntary agreement between the parties concerned or through some form of third party intervention.

See ARBITRATION, COLLECTIVE BARGAINING, CONCILIATION, CONFLICT, MEDIATION.

**industrial estate** a purpose-built site designated for industrial and commercial use which is separate from residential accommodation, often located on the outskirts of major urban conurbations close to motorways and other transportation systems. In the main, industrial estates offer low-cost work space for light manufacturing industries and warehouse distribution facilities. A large proportion of the investment in infrastructure and buildings is provided by local authorities. See INDUSTRIAL LOCATION.

**industrial goods** raw materials, components, machinery, equipment, etc., which are used by firms as 'factor inputs' in the production of other goods. See GOOD, INDUSTRIAL MARKETING.

**industrial location** the geographical site or sites selected by a firm to perform its economic functions. The choice of an appropriate location is influenced by a range of considerations but two are particularly important:

(a) the nature and characteristics of the industrial activity that the firm performs (for example raw material extraction or crop cultivation, the manufacture of intermediate or final products, the provision of a service) and

(b) the relative costs of production at different locations balanced against the cost of physical distribution to target markets, and the importance of closeness to customers as a basis for establishing COMPETITIVE ADVANTAGES over rival suppliers.

Some activities are highly location-specific. For example, the extraction of iron ore can only occur where there are deposits of the metal. Likewise many service activities, for example retailing, have to be located in and around customer catchment areas, while some suppliers of components may find it advantageous to operate alongside their key customers in order to synchronize better the latter's input-production requirements. The manufacture of final products tends to be more 'footloose'. Certain locations may be preferred for their production advantages, because of, for example, lower labour costs, or the availability of investment subsidies (see REGIONAL POLICY) or the supply of skilled workers and access to related facilities. On the other hand, high distribution costs, especially in the case of bulky, low value added products, or, in the international context, the imposition of tariffs and quotas on imports, tend to favour a market-orientated location.

See GREENFIELD INVESTMENT, INDUSTRIAL ESTATE, MULTINATIONAL ENTERPRISE.

**industrial marketing** the MARKETING of goods and services to INDUSTRIAL BUYERS. The major characteristics of industrial marketing are that:

(a) industrial buyers tend to be fewer and possess greater bargaining power than final consumers;

(b) DISTRIBUTION CHANNELS tend to be more complex, with more intermediate steps in production, wholesaling and retailing than for consumer goods;

(c) the sales force in most cases needs to have a detailed technical knowledge of the products/services in which they are dealing because of the generally greater complexity of industrial products;

(d) PERSONAL SELLING plays a greater role in marketing industrial products and sales representatives have to make more pricing decisions on discounts and spend more time demonstrating products and dealing with technical queries;

(e) the PROMOTIONAL MIX for industrial goods tends to be different from that for consumer goods, with little use of MASS ADVERTISING MEDIA and greater emphasis on targeted advertising through trade/professional journals, industrial directories, direct mail, and samples and brochures.

See BUYER BEHAVIOUR.

**industrial policy** a policy concerned with promoting industrial efficiency and competitiveness, industrial regeneration and expansion and the creation of employment opportunities. Industrial policy can be broadly based, encompassing, for example, measures to increase competition (see COMPETITION POLICY) and promote regional development (see REGIONAL POLICY), as well as specific across-the-board measures to stimulate efficiency and the adoption of new technology; or it can be more narrowly focused involving selective intervention in particular industries or support for particular projects and firms. Industrial policy in most countries is both *reactive* (responding, for example, to cases of market failure by acting to restructure and rationalize declining industries or support failing, 'lame duck' firms) and *proactive* (acting as a catalyst for change by encouraging, for example, the establishment of new businesses and the development of new technologies).

Between 1962 and 1992 the NATIONAL ECONOMIC DEVELOPMENT

COUNCIL (NEDC) and its satellites, the Economic Development ment Committees were responsible for the formulation of strategic programmes for improving efficiency and international competitiveness.

Currently in the UK, the thrust of industrial policy is directed towards strengthening the industrial base of the economy in a number of ways, including:

(a) the promotion of greater domestic competition by attacking in particular, CARTELS, anti-competitive practices and MERGERS and TAKEOVERS, together with the privatization and DEREGULATION of state-owned industries (see NATIONALIZATION VERSUS PRIVATIZATION);

(b) the stimulation of overseas trade by the provision of back-up export support services by the DEPARTMENT OF TRADE AND INDUSTRY (DTI) and its arms, the Export Market Information Centre, EXPORT CREDIT GUARANTEE DEPARTMENT, etc. (see EXPORTING);

(c) the regeneration of regions in industrial decline by the provision of financial support programmes for firms prepared to locate in *assisted areas, enterprise zones* and *inner city* development areas. (see REGIONAL POLICY);

(d) the encouragement of innovation and the adoption of new technologies through DTI-sponsored 'collaborative research' between industry and government/university research departments and TECHNOLOGY TRANSFER programmes, the SMART scheme, Regional Technology Centres and the activities of the BRITISH TECHNOLOGY GROUP;

(e) the promotion of vocational training, again partly funded by the DTI, together with more general initiatives to create employment opportunities. See TRAINING.

Finally, in recent years particular emphasis has been placed on the small-firm sector of the economy. To encourage business start-ups and assist with initial development problems, the DTI offers a LOAN GUARANTEE SCHEME, which together with the ENTERPRISE INVESTMENT SCHEME, provides financial backing to small firms. Additionally, the DTI will pay half the costs of 5–15 days consultancy services for firms (with fewer than 500 employees) requiring help with key management functions, and assist innovative efforts through the SMART scheme. Regional enterprise grants are available for small firms undertaking new invest-

ment in areas designated as 'assisted areas' under UK RE-
GIONAL POLICY.

See MARKET STRUCTURE, MARKET PERFORMANCE, SCIENCE PARK,
SUBSIDY, INVESTMENT INCENTIVE.

**industrial product** see SELLER.

**industrial relations** 1. the general state of relationships
between management, TRADE UNIONS and workforce.
2. the process of determining rates of pay and conditions of
employment by COLLECTIVE BARGAINING, the institutions and
procedures in which this is done, and the relationships
between the key people (for example SHOP STEWARDS and industrial relations managers) involved.

Industrial relations can therefore refer to both the day-to-day
relationship between workers and their supervisor and the
more specialized activity of formal NEGOTIATIONS and CON-
SULTATION. The main subjects of industrial relations include
PAY and conditions and, from the employers' perspective,
achieving desired levels of productivity, in part through the
enforcement of work discipline. Industrial relations problems
can arise where employees believe that too much effort is required from them for a given set of rewards or that work discipline is harsh or inequitable.

Industrial relations is often also referred to as 'labour relations' or (more commonly today) 'employee relations'. Many
managers prefer the latter term since it is thought to avoid the
connotations of conflict and trade unionism associated with
both 'industrial relations' and 'labour relations'.

Within organizations, industrial relations management is
often one of the duties of PERSONNEL MANAGEMENT, although in
many cases negotiation over pay is done by managers whose
primary responsibilities lie outside the field. Much of the day-
to-day conduct of industrial relations is undertaken by LINE
MANAGERS.

In the UK, industrial relations has been widely viewed as a
major national problem since the 1960s. Comparatively low
labour PRODUCTIVITY, spiralling wage claims, over-mighty and
irresponsible TRADE UNIONS, and an apparently high incidence
of STRIKES were thought by some to be significant factors in
the UK's deteriorating economic performance. Others argued
that low productivity was due more to a failure by employers
to invest, and that union militancy was the inevitable result of

badly-trained managers treating their workforces as little more than factors of production.

The Royal Commission on Trades Unions and Employers' Associations (DONOVAN COMMISSION), which reported in 1968, found that many of the UK's industrial relations problems could be attributed to the breakdown in the private sector of a system of COLLECTIVE BARGAINING based at industry level, and its partial replacement by uncontrolled bargaining within individual companies. The Commission recommended that the latter be brought under control, that SHOP STEWARD organization be encouraged by management, and that managers operate more formal procedures to deal with GRIEVANCES. During the 1970s these prescriptions were adopted by many companies, though perhaps more because of the expansion of LABOUR LAW than Donovan's exhortations. Many firms shifted collective bargaining over pay and conditions to the plant or company and established GRIEVANCE PROCEDURES and DISCIPLINARY PROCEDURES. Despite these reforms, however, pay settlements often exceeded the rate of inflation, and governments used PRICES AND INCOMES POLICY for much of the decade.

In the 1980s the focus of concern about industrial relations shifted to the public sector. The government believed that many organizations in this sector could achieve significant efficiency improvements were it not for union RESTRICTIVE LABOUR PRACTICES. Their efforts to reform these, coupled with restraints on public sector pay, led to a series of major national strikes in this sector during the decade. At the same time the government attempted to reform industrial relations in all sectors through a series of statutes regulating trade union activities.

See EMPLOYMENT ACT 1980, EMPLOYMENT ACT 1982, EMPLOYMENT ACT 1988, EMPLOYMENT ACT 1990, TRADE UNION ACT 1984, TRADE UNION REFORM AND EMPLOYMENT RIGHTS ACT 1993.

**industrial relations audit** a systematic examination and assessment of the quality and effectiveness of existing INDUSTRIAL RELATIONS procedures in an organization. The aim is not so much to quantify precisely their costs and benefits but to determine whether they are the most appropriate for the organization's needs. Issues that usually need to be considered are the incidence and resolution of grievances and conflicts, and the structure of and approach to COLLECTIVE BARGAINING over PAY and conditions of employment.

**Industrial Society** a UK organization which aims to promote public awareness of industry and to encourage good practice amongst managers, especially in relation to EMPLOYEE INVOLVEMENT. In recent years the INDUSTRIAL SOCIETY has strongly recommended the practice of TEAM BRIEFING.

**industrial sociology** see SOCIOLOGY OF WORK.

**Industrial Training Board** see TRAINING.

**Industrial Tribunal** a 'labour court' which adjudicates on claims that individuals have been unlawfully treated by their employers. In the UK, UNFAIR DISMISSAL claims are by far the largest part of the Tribunals' caseload. When established in 1964 it was hoped that the Tribunal system would provide an informal and inexpensive means of protecting employment rights. This has not been borne out, as it is now common for the parties, especially managements, to be represented by solicitors and barristers. See ADVISORY, CONCILIATION AND ARBITRATION SERVICE, CONCILIATION, DISCRIMINATION.

**industrial union** see TRADE UNION.

**industry** a branch of commercial enterprise concerned with the output of related goods or services. For example, the beer/brewing industry might be defined as all those firms that produce bitter and mild ales, lagers, stouts and ciders. However, beer production might be seen also as constituting part of a wider and bigger industry, the 'alcoholic beverages industry' which includes the production of spirits and wines as well as beer. Thus, there are specification problems with respect to how widely or narrowly a particular industry is defined. Moreover, STANDARD INDUSTRIAL CLASSIFICATIONS typically group together products on the basis of their *supply* characteristics, such as the use of common raw materials and manufacturing processes. This may or may not coincide with how goods and services are grouped together to define MARKETS, which requires account to be taken also of how products are seen from the point of view of buyers (that is, their *demand* characteristics). Thus although mens' and womens' shoes are produced using the same materials and manufacturing processes, and often by the same firms, they are not considered by buyers as close *substitutes*, and hence, from a MARKETING point of view, they must be treated as constituting separate markets. See STRUCTURE OF INDUSTRY.

**industry-wide bargaining** see COLLECTIVE BARGAINING, MULTI-EMPLOYER AGREEMENT.

**inertia selling** the practice of attempting to sell goods by sending them to people who have not requested them in the hope that the recipients will keep and pay for these goods. See UNSOLICITED GOODS AND SERVICES ACT.

**inflation** an increase in the general level of PRICES in an economy that is sustained over time. The rate of inflation can be measured using, for example, a retail PRICE INDEX which shows the annual percentage change in consumer prices. Because of the distorting effects of inflation on the functioning of the economy and the harm it does to certain sections of the community (particularly those people on fixed incomes), most governments accord a high priority to the control of inflation when formulating their ECONOMIC POLICIES.

There are two main causes of inflation:

(a) the presence of excess demand beyond the output capacity of the economy to supply goods and services, which 'pulls up' prices (*demand-pull* inflation);

(b) an increase in input costs – wages, raw materials and components – which 'push up' final prices (*cost-push* inflation).

According to the monetarist school (see MONETARISM), demand-pull inflation is caused by the excessive creation of money and they prescribe strict controls on the MONEY SUPPLY as a means of reducing excess spending (see MONETARY POLICY). Likewise the Keynesian school advocates cuts in spending as the way of tackling excess demand, but in their case mainly by increasing taxes and reducing government expenditure (see FISCAL POLICY). Cost-push inflation tends to be associated particularly with excessive increases in money wage rates (i.e. wage rates greater than can be paid for by increases in the underlying rate of productivity growth) and with occasional explosions in commodity prices (the OPEC oil price increases of 1973 and 1979 being a case in point). Cost-push inflation caused by excessive wage demands can be modified or eliminated either directly by the use of controls on prices and incomes (see PRICES AND INCOMES POLICY) or more indirectly by 'moral suasion' and measures to reduce the monopoly power of trade unions.

In general the business community dislikes inflation. It is administratively inconvenient and expensive constantly to change price lists and allow for the effects of inflation on firms' cash-flow positions and the valuation of assets (see INFLATION ACCOUNTING). A more important consideration is the effect of inflation on firms' competitive positions in the domestic and overseas markets against foreign rivals. Specifically, high rates of inflation, unless offset by compensatory EXCHANGE RATE movements, have the effect of making imports relatively cheaper and exporting more expensive, thus putting firms at a growing price disadvantage or squeezing their profit margins.

See PURCHASING POWER, INDEX-LINKED.

**inflation accounting** adjustments to a firm's accounts to allow for the effects of INFLATION and arrive at a view of the real profitability of the firm. In a period of rising prices when the purchasing power of the money unit is declining, profit calculations based upon the HISTORIC COST of STOCKS and FIXED ASSETS are likely to overstate the real profit position. Various methods of allowing for the effects of inflation on the PROFIT-AND-LOSS ACCOUNT and the BALANCE SHEET have been tried.

One relatively simple method of inflation-adjusting a firm's accounting results is the *current purchasing-power method*. This uses a PRICE INDEX number to adjust the calculated profit figure from the profit-and-loss account, and to express it in real terms. A more detailed method is the *current cost-accounting method*. This produces a supplementary current-cost profit-and-loss account and balance sheet. In these current-cost accounts the deduction from revenue for COST OF SALES is based upon the REPLACEMENT COST of the goods sold (cost of sales adjustment); while DEPRECIATION is calculated on the replacement cost of fixed assets used and not on their historic cost (depreciation adjustment).

See REVALUATION PROVISION, APPRECIATION, definition 1.

**influencers** individuals whose views, advice and recommendations are respected and acted upon during the making of a buying decision. Such individuals may often be OPINION LEADERS and they can provide useful market research data to a company in drawing up product specifications. See MARKETING RESEARCH.

**informal organization** see ORGANIZATION.

**information agreement** an agreement between rival suppliers which involves them in furnishing each other with details of their prices, discount terms, output and sales figures, profit margins etc. Although some of the information exchanged may be innocuous and could be obtained from normal trade sources (for example, rivals' prices), some data is of a highly confidential nature, and prompts one to ask why firms are prepared to disclose such information to competitors. In the UK, concern that information exchanges between competitors might well be used as a cloak for COLLUSION between firms has led to the requirement that certain information agreements (specifically those covering the price and terms and conditions of goods) must be registered with the OFFICE OF FAIR TRADING. See COMPETITION POLICY.

**information highway** a national or international ('super' highway) network which links up businesses and homes with information service providers (cable television, video tele phones, interactive shopping etc.). Each user has a 'connection box' which links them via a cable to all kinds of services. In the case of cable television, for example, a customer connected to the highway could select a film from a large 'menu' and then receive it down the wire a few minutes later. See INTER-NET.

**information management** the process of gathering, processing and interpreting data both from the firm's external environment and from inside the firm, generally using the information technology provided by COMPUTERS.

All business functions such as production, marketing and distribution involve both physical tasks and parallel information-processing activities. Computers, communications devices and other information technology hardware can be deployed to perform routine accounting, record keeping and order processing functions cheaply and efficiently. In addition to these basic data-processing tasks, information technology has enabled firms to collect more data than previously could be handled by the firm and subject it to more detailed analysis. This has the advantage of dovetailing production, marketing and distribution activities within the firm. In addition, greater communication with customers and suppliers through their computers facilitates closer relationships with these customers and suppliers, leading to, for example, just-in-time production and supply (see JUST-IN-TIME (JIT) SYSTEM). Such information technologies as COMPUTER-AIDED DESIGN and

COMPUTER-AIDED MANUFACTURE facilitate the rapid development of new products or modification of existing products and the prompt production of such products through FLEXIBLE MANUFACTURING SYSTEMS, thereby allowing the firm to gain a COMPETITIVE ADVANTAGE by responding rapidly to changing customer requirements. See COMMUNICATION, BUSINESS PROCESS RE-ENGINEERING.

**information technology** see INFORMATION MANAGEMENT.

**informative advertising** see ADVERTISING.

**infrastructure** the investment by central government and local authorities in railways, roads, airports, shipping ports, schools, universities, hospitals, etc.

Infrastructure can play an important facilitating role in improving a country's industrial performance by providing, for example, a good communications network, and a stock of well educated and trained workers, scientists and technologists.

**inheritance tax** a form of WEALTH TAX imposed by the UK government on a proportion of a person's private assets when these assets are transferred to the person's beneficiaries. Currently (as at April 1997) 'chargeable assets' such as houses, stocks and shares, etc. up to a maximum of £215,000 are tax-exempt. Above £215,000 inheritance tax is levied at a flat rate of 40%. Assets transferred more than seven years before the donor's death are exempt from inheritance tax, while assets transferred between three and seven years before death are taxed at lower rates.

Inheritance tax superseded earlier UK arrangements for taxing wealth, including estate duty or death duty and capital transfer tax.

**initial allowances** see CAPITAL ALLOWANCES.

**injunction** a court order issued to a person or company requiring them to desist from behaving in ways which are harmful to other people. See CONTRACT, TORT.

**Inland Revenue** the UK government department that is responsible for assessing individual and corporate TAXATION liabilities (HM Inspector of Taxes), and for the collection of taxation monies due (HM Collector of Taxes). In the US the Internal Revenue Service performs similar functions.

**innovation** see RESEARCH AND DEVELOPMENT.

**input** resources such as raw material, labour and capital which are used by a firm to produce goods and services (OUTPUT).

**input-output control** a means of managing the relationship between the amount of work or jobs arriving at a work station (input) and the rate at which work is completed by that work station (output). The output rate will depend upon the capacity of the work station and the load or volume of work still to be processed by that work station.

See PRODUCTION-LINE BALANCING.

**input tax** see VALUE ADDED TAX.

**inseparability** a characteristic of most SERVICES (for example, window cleaning, legal advice etc.) that reflects the fact that they are produced and consumed at the same time and thus cannot be stored.

Contrast GOODS.

**insider dealing** transactions in FINANCIAL SECURITIES by persons having access to privileged (secret and confidential) information not yet available to the general investing public, and who in consequence stand to profit from exploiting this knowledge. For example, an employee of a merchant bank engaged in working out the financial details of a prospective TAKEOVER BID by a client firm for another company, might himself or through intermediaries buy shares in the target company prior to the public announcement of the bid.

In the UK, a case of suspected insider dealing can be investigated by the 'City Panel on Takeovers and Mergers' under the provisions of the Company Securities (Insider Dealing) Act 1985. This Act interprets insider dealers to include not only company officials and their advisers, but also government officials and members of securities regulatory bodies who might come into possession of unpublished information.

See CITY CODE ON TAKEOVERS AND MERGERS, FINANCIAL SERVICES ACT 1986, STOCK MARKET.

**insolvency** or **bankruptcy** a condition under which an individual or firm's LIABILITIES to CREDITORS exceed ASSETS. The individual or firm is therefore unable to discharge all accumulated liabilities from realizable assets. Insolvency occurs after a period in which an individual's expenditure has exceeded his income, or a firm's costs have exceeded its sales revenues (when LOSSES are made). In the UK the treatment of insolvent companies is governed by the terms of the Insolvency Act 1986. A number of possible steps are involved.

The first stage is often a *voluntary arrangement* under which the company and its creditors agree to a scheme of reduced or delayed debt payments. If it proves impossible to TURNROUND the company within a reasonable time the firm may ask the bankruptcy court to arrange for the company to be put into administration where an Administrator is appointed to try to reorganize the company and run it, and who will liquidate the company only if he is unable to rehabilitate it.

If the Administrator is successful in rehabilitating the company then it may be returned to its management. Otherwise the next stage is *receivership* where the Administrator may continue to run the company while selling assets to pay off secured creditors such as DEBENTURE holders whose loans are secured by a fixed charge on a particular asset.

Should the firm's fortunes continue to deteriorate the Administrator may have no alternative but to *wind up* the firm, i.e. LIQUIDATE its available assets, the proceeds being distributed amongst creditors. In this event the Administrator adopts the role of liquidator, whose function is to sell off the company's assets and pay back creditors.

When a joint-stock company's assets are liquidated then the proceeds of liquidation will be paid fully to firstly, 'preferential creditors' (the INLAND REVENUE for tax due, employees for wages owed etc.); secondly, other creditors (banks for loans and TRADE CREDITORS); thirdly, PREFERENCE SHAREHOLDERS; and finally, ORDINARY SHAREHOLDERS, if any funds still remain.

In the UK, under the terms of the Company Directors Disqualification Act 1986, if directors of a joint-stock company continue trading after they should have known that it was insolvent, then they can be charged with wrongful trading, lose the protection of limited liability and become personally responsible for the firm's debts. They may also be declared unfit to be directors and disqualified from acting as directors or managers of any company for up to 15 years.

**Insolvency Act 1986** see INSOLVENCY.

**inspection 1.** the examination of raw materials, work in progress and finished goods to check that these items comply with predetermined QUALITY standards. The principal purpose of inspection is the identification of rejects, thereby ensuring that the standards set are maintained by weeding out unacceptable items (DEFECTIVE WORK). Inspection can involve examination of all items, or just a sample of items where the cost of examination is high.

**2.** the inspection of buildings, plant, machinery and equipment which is also necessary to identify MAINTENANCE problems which might cause machine failure and disruption to production, or inconsistent machine performance which would affect product quality.

See QUALITY CONTROL, QUALITY COSTS.

**instalment credit** or **hire purchase** a contractual means of purchasing a product over an extended period of time using a CREDIT facility provided either by a financial institution such as a FINANCE HOUSE, or by the firm selling the product concerned. An initial down payment is usually required followed by monthly fixed payments (including interest charges) for a specified period. See MONETARY POLICY, CONSUMER CREDIT ACT 1974.

**Institute of Chartered Accountants in England and Wales (ICAEW)** the largest of the UK bodies of professional accountants, whose members primarily undertake auditing and provide taxation advice.

**Institute of Chartered Accountants in Scotland (ICAS)** a body of professional accountants who practise primarily in Scotland.

**Institute of Directors** the UK organization representing the interests and views of company directors. Its membership is drawn especially from smaller businesses and hence its policies tend to reflect the interests of small employers. In particular it advocates reduction of those regulations governing how businesses operate, including those relating to employment protection, which are believed to stifle entrepreneurial initiative.

**Institute of Management (IM)** the main UK organization representing managers in general whose main aim is to improve standards of MANAGEMENT. The IM was formed in 1992 through the merger of the British Institute of Management and the Institution of Industrial Managers, and it currently has over 350,000 members. To be admitted to membership, managers must possess appropriate managerial experience and pass various examinations.

See MANAGEMENT CHARTER, PROFESSIONAL.

**Institute of Personnel Management (IPM)** the main UK body representing personnel managers and publicizing the benefits of effective PERSONNEL MANAGEMENT. It operates a system of training and examination of personnel managers so as to promote professional standards of personnel work. Currently it has over 30,000 members. See PROFESSIONAL.

**institutional investors** the financial institutions that collect savings and other deposits and invest *long*-term in corporate STOCKS and SHARES, government fixed interest securities (BONDS), property and overseas securities. In the UK, PENSION FUNDS, INSURANCE COMPANIES, UNIT TRUSTS and INVESTMENT TRUST COMPANIES, together with the SAVINGS BANKS, INVESTMENT BANKS and specialized VENTURE CAPITAL agencies such as the 3i's (formerly Investors in Industry), constitute the main investing institutions. In many other countries the COMMERCIAL BANKS are major long-term investors. (In most ŏf these countries the lack of any established STOCK MARKET and the availability of private capital from individuals was the main historical reason for their closer tie-in with industrial companies.)

Institutional investors have grown rapidly in the UK since the 1950s, encouraged in particular by tax concessions on contractual pension and life insurance schemes, and they now constitute the primary means of channelling personal savings into corporate investment. In 1995, pension funds, insurance companies, unit trusts and investment trust companies collectively owned around 58% of UK ordinary shares, compared with around 20% held by private individuals.

In the UK, the pensions funds, insurance companies, unit trusts and investment trust companies are represented collectively by the Institutional Investors Committee, which acts on their behalf in dealings with other institutional bodies such as the Securities and Investment Board, etc. (see FINANCIAL SERVICES ACT 1986) and the government.

See FINANCIAL SYSTEM.

**Institutional Investors Committee** the body which represents the collective interests of the PENSION FUNDS, INSURANCE COMPANIES, UNIT TRUSTS and INVESTMENT TRUST COMPANIES in the UK.

**institutionalization of conflict** see CONFLICT.

**instrumentalism** see ORIENTATION TO WORK.

**insurance** a method of protecting a person or firm against financial loss resulting from damage to, or theft of, personal and business assets (general insurance), and death and injury (life and accident insurance). Insurance may be obtained directly from an INSURANCE COMPANY or through an intermediary such as an INSURANCE BROKER/AGENT. In return for an insurance premium the person or firm obtains insurance cover against financial risks. See ASSURANCE; COST, INSURANCE AND FREIGHT.

**insurance broker** or **insurance agent** a person or firm which acts as an intermediary in bringing together clients seeking INSURANCE cover and INSURANCE COMPANIES offering suitable policies. In some cases the agent may simply introduce the two parties to each other and receive a commission from the insurance company; or the agent may be employed by a particular insurance company to sell insurance policies on its behalf, partly on salary and partly on commission. Insurance brokers are usually independent intermediaries who are able to negotiate with a number of insurance companies on behalf of clients in order to secure for them the most advantageous cover and terms, as well as handling claims and offering general insurance advice. Most of the larger insurance brokers are members of LLOYDS, a corporation of brokers and insurance companies. Insurance brokers are regulated by the PERSONAL INVESTMENT AUTHORITY in accordance with various standards of good practice laid down under the FINANCIAL SERVICES ACT 1986.

**insurance company** a financial institution which UNDERWRITES the risk of loss of, or damage to, personal and business assets (general INSURANCE) and life and limb (life and accident insurance). Some companies specialize in one or other of these areas, but others (referred to as 'composites') operate in both sectors. Insurance companies issue insurance policies to cover a variety of contingencies (fire, flooding, breakage, theft, death, etc.), involving potential financial loss to policy holders or their dependants in return for regular payments of a premium. An insurance company operates by pooling risk among a large number of policyholders; premiums are based on the probability of a particular event occurring and the average financial loss associated with each. This is done by the company's actuarial staff using statistical techniques to analyse past claims. For very large insurance risks an insurance company may resort to *reinsurance* sharing the insurance premium with other insurers in proportion to the share of potential claim which they are prepared to accept. In addition, many insurance companies offer contractual savings schemes (see ASSURANCE).

Insurance companies use the premiums they receive not only to settle day-to-day claims but also to generate additional income and profit by investing their funds in FINANCIAL SECURITIES, particularly UK and overseas government fixed-interest bonds and corporate stocks and shares (see INSTITUTIONAL INVESTORS). Their portfolios attempt to maintain a careful balance between immediate liquidity needs and longer-term investment returns. Life insurance business, in particular, because of its long-term contractual nature, is especially conducive to offering long-term investment returns to policy holders as well as the insurance company. *With profit* life insurance policies are now commonplace, as are *unit-linked* policies which are directly related to fund performance (see UNIT TRUST). Life insurance policies linked to the provision of MORTGAGE finance for house purchase are another innovation.

Most insurance companies are members of LLOYDS, a corporation of insurers and INSURANCE BROKERS. Insurance companies in the UK are represented by the Association of British Insurers which provides a forum for the discussion of matters of general concern to members and acts on behalf of members in dealings with other institutional bodies such as the Institutional Investors Committee and the government. The investment and management of funds by insurance companies is regulated by the PERSONAL INVESTMENT AUTHORITY in accordance with various standards of good practice laid down under the FINANCIAL SERVICES ACT 1986.

**intangibility** a characteristic of most SERVICES (for example, window cleaning, legal advice etc.) that reflects the inability of a customer to see, touch, taste or smell the service.

Contrast GOOD.

**intangible fixed assets** nonphysical FIXED ASSETS such as GOODWILL, PATENTS AND TRADEMARKS, which have a money value.

**integrated marketing** a business approach which stresses the need to coordinate all functions, departments and personnel in a firm and to harness their endeavours towards a common goal of attracting and retaining customers (see MARKETING CONCEPT).

Integrated marketing stresses how the activities of all functions and personnel in a firm have marketing implications. For example, the manner in which the firm operates its credit control procedures could win or lose customers, or customers could be put off by a poor delivery service.

Whether integrated marketing is effective depends to a large extent upon the position held by marketing in a business's ORGANIZATION STRUCTURE:

(a) if marketing is regarded as just one of a number of business functions alongside production, finance and personnel, insufficient integration will occur;

(b) if marketing includes all subfunctions from other departments which affect customers – credit control, customer service and distribution, then a fuller degree of integration will be attained;

(c) if a company fully accepts the marketing concept then marketing will be classed as the principal function, with all other functions (production, finance, personnel) being subordinate to it.

**integrative bargaining** SEE COLLECTIVE BARGAINING.

**intellectual property right** the legal ownership by a person or business of a COPYRIGHT, DESIGN, PATENT or TRADE MARK attached to a particular product or process which protects the owner against unauthorized imitation.

**intensive distribution** a physical DISTRIBUTION approach which seeks to maximize a firm's sales potential by attempting to ensure that its products are stocked by as many sales outlets as possible.

**interaction** SEE OCCUPATIONAL PSYCHOLOGY.

**interbank clearing rate** SEE INTEREST RATE.

**interest** the charge made for borrowing money in the form of a LOAN. Interest is payable on a number of short-term and long-term borrowing forms including LOANS, OVERDRAFTS, MORTGAGES, INSTALMENT CREDIT, LEASING, LOAN STOCK, DEBENTURES, BONDS, TREASURY BILLS and BILLS OF EXCHANGE.

Interest charges may be fixed or variable and payable weekly, monthly or annually depending on the size of the loan and the length of the loan period. When a loan is extended on a fixed-interest basis the rate remains unchanged throughout the life of the loan. However, in times of inflation the real or effective interest rate as opposed to the loan's agreed or nominal interest rate will fall as inflation reduces the PURCHASING POWER of money. In this case, where the lender is able to vary the interest charge, then the interest rate can be raised to offset the effects of inflation. For this reason, whereas most short-term loans are extended on fixed-interest terms, variable terms are usually applied to long-term loans.

Interest may be computed on a *simple* or *compound* basis. Simple interest is based only on the original amount of the loan, whereas compound interest is based on the original amount of the loan *plus* previous accumulated interest. For example, a £100 loan paying simple interest at 10% would accumulate to £110 at the end of the first year and £120 (i.e. £100 + £10 + £10) at the end of the second, whereas with compound interest the loan would accumulate to £121 at the end of the second year (i.e. £100 + £10 + £11 [10% of £110]).

See INTEREST RATE, APR.

**interest cover** or **times interest earned** a measure of the extent to which a firm's earnings (profit before tax) cover INTEREST payments due on LOANS. It expresses profit as a ratio of interest due.

**interest rate** the particular amount of INTEREST which a borrower is required to pay to a lender for borrowing a particular sum of money to finance spending on consumption and the purchase of capital assets.

The rate of interest charged for any particular transaction will depend on such considerations as the purpose and duration of the loan, the amount of money borrowed, the COLLATERAL SECURITY offered (if any) and the creditworthiness of the borrower, all factors influencing the degree of perceived risk involved in making the loan as seen by the lender.

A number of key short-term interest rates may be identified in the UK including:

(a) *interbank clearing rate*: the rate of interest at which the COMMERCIAL BANKS lend short-term sterling funds to one another;

(b) *bill-discounting rate*: the rate of interest at which the CENTRAL BANK (Bank of England) is prepared to lend money to the DISCOUNT HOUSES in its capacity as 'lender of last resort' (i.e. if the discount houses are forced to borrow from the Bank because of their inability to obtain sufficient loans from the commercial banks to cover their TREASURY BILL positions);

(c) *base rate*: the 'floor' rate of interest which is used by the commercial banks as the basis for charging interest on loans and overdrafts to their customers. Typically, banks would charge an interest rate only slightly above base rate to large established business customers whose risks of default are small, and administrative charges low; whereas they would charge a rate much higher than base rate to, for example, a small new business.

These rates of interest (and others) are highly interrelated. The level of interest rates is determined by the forces of supply and demand for short-term finance in the MONEY MARKET, subject to manipulation by the Bank of England as part of its application of MONETARY POLICY. Formerly, base rates etc. were linked directly to *bank rate*, but nowadays the authorities seek to control the level of interest rates more indirectly by *open market operations*, buying or selling monetary instruments such as treasury bills to reduce or increase the availability of loanable funds.

The rate of interest or COST OF CAPITAL is an important factor in relation to companies' investment decisions. See INVESTMENT APPRAISAL.

In a situation of INFLATION where prices are rising rapidly, it is important to distinguish between the 'nominal' interest rate stipulated in a LOAN contract and the 'real' rate of interest which allows for the effects of inflation in reducing the REAL VALUE or PURCHASING POWER of the interest received.

See APR, LIBOR, DISCOUNT RATE, SWAP.

**interest-rate swap** see SWAP.

**interest yield** the INTEREST paid on a BOND or LOAN STOCK etc., expressed as a percentage of the current market price of the bond or stock. For example, a bond offering an interest payment of £10 per year and having a current market price of £50 would have a yield of 20%.

**interference allowance** see ALLOWANCES.

**interfirm comparison** the comparison of one firm's accounting results with those of other firms in the same or similar industries. Such comparisons require the summarization of PROFIT-AND-LOSS ACCOUNT and BALANCE SHEET data in the form of ACCOUNTING RATIOS so that comparisons can be made between firms. Some industry trade associations and commercial organizations, such as the Centre for Interfirm Comparisons, operate industry-wide interfirm comparison schemes, whereby firms submit their accounting results on a confidential basis and receive in return information about their major competitors, these competitors being anonymously labelled company A, company B, etc. Alternatively a firm may use the published ANNUAL REPORT AND ACCOUNTS of competitors for comparison.

Interfirm comparisons allow a company's managers to gauge their *comparative* performance and are a useful adjunct to historical comparisons which merely look at the company's own performance over time.

**interim dividend** see DIVIDEND.

**interim report** an abbreviated form of the ANNUAL REPORT AND ACCOUNTS issued by the directors of a JOINT-STOCK COMPANY to SHAREHOLDERS during the accounting year. Interim reports are often prepared half-yearly to keep shareholders informed of a company's performance between the receipt of full end-year accounts. Such interim reports are not necessarily AUDITED.

**intermediaries** see DISTRIBUTION CHANNEL, MARKET INTERMEDIARY.

**intermediate area** a region of economic decline designated under UK REGIONAL POLICY as in need of industrial regeneration. Financial assistance in the form of REGIONAL SELECTIVE ASSISTANCE is also available to manufacturing and service businesses prepared to undertake new investments in the area.

**intermediate good** see GOOD.

**intermediation** the role of financial institutions such as COMMERCIAL BANKS and BUILDING SOCIETIES as intermediaries in channelling funds from lenders to borrowers.

**intermittent production** see BATCH PRODUCTION.

**internal audit** see AUDIT.

**internal appraisal** see SWOT ANALYSIS.

**internal customer** a division or department of a vertically integrated firm (see VERTICAL INTEGRATION) which acts as a BUYER for raw materials, components or services supplied by other divisions or departments of the firm. The TRANSFER PRICE at which materials, components or services are 'bought' from *internal suppliers* by internal customers needs to be considered by managers; and the QUALITY standards of these items needs to be agreed.

See TOTAL QUALITY MANAGEMENT.

**internal financing** the ability to finance a firm's growth from retained earnings. A company's NET PROFIT can be paid out in DIVIDENDS or retained for internal financing, or some mixture of these two. Generally, shareholders look for some immediate income in the form of dividends and some growth in the capital value of their shares (which depends on growth of the company). By paying out more dividends, growth is slowed. Achieving the optimum solution between two conflicting objectives is an important area of study in FINANCIAL MANAGEMENT. See COST OF CAPITAL, RETENTION RATIO, RESERVES.

**internal growth** see ORGANIC GROWTH.

**internalization** the combining in one firm of two or more related activities, as opposed to those activities being undertaken separately by different firms. VERTICAL INTEGRATION where a series of vertically-related operations are combined together is the most frequent example of internalization. Internalization results from firms' desire to reduce their costs by achieving production economies in sequential operations, stock-holding economies and the avoidance of transaction costs in arranging contracts with outside suppliers or distributors. Security of input supplies and access to outlets may be additional considerations.

Diversified or conglomerate firms which operate in many different markets can internalize the funding of their capital investment programmes by recycling funds from some operating divisions to headquarters, which are then reallocated to other operating divisions. This avoids the need for these divisions to have to raise funds externally through a STOCK MARKET.

Internalization can also be a feature of the FOREIGN MARKET SERVICING STRATEGIES of MULTINATIONAL ENTERPRISES (MNEs); for example, MNEs may opt to replace the licensing of foreign producers and instead set up overseas manufacturing plants, the better to protect and exploit innovatory products.

See DIVERSIFICATION, TRANSFER PRICE.

**internal labour market** a MARKET for LABOUR which operates within the organization. In other words, recruits for JOB positions in the organization are sought from within the stock of existing employees. In the 'pure' form, recruits from the labour market outside are sought for the lowest level jobs only ('points of entry'). These individuals then pass up through the organizational hierarchy, filling higher level posts as these become vacant. Economists and sociologists have discerned a long-term trend towards internalization of labour markets during which, as industrial societies and technology have developed, technology has become increasingly firm-specific.

It has thus become increasingly difficult to find applicants already possessing suitable skills on the open market. The pay of employees in internal labour markets is set according to the firm's criteria and objectives. Some argue, therefore, that they are not really markets at all; the price of labour is not determined primarily by supply and demand.

The benefits of internalization stem from the individual becoming wedded to the organization by virtue of the fact that his or her skills and knowledge are not saleable elsewhere. The organization can invest heavily in training without fear of 'poaching' by other employers. A stock of skills and knowledge can therefore be built-up. A potential disadvantage of internal labour markets is that the supply of 'new blood' is restricted and the organization may become insulated from new ideas.

Few organizations in the UK adopt the 'pure' form, though some have come close to it. In the past, many top managers on the railways have started their careers in jobs at the bottom of the railway hierarchy. Most modern large organizations use a mixture of external and internal labour markets. They have a number of points of entry (for example separate ones for production and managerial jobs) whilst jobs may be advertised both internally and externally, with the former often occurring first. One common form of internal labour market is the 'extended internal labour market', where external recruits are sought from those related to, or otherwise closely associated with, existing employees.

See JAPANIZATION, LABOUR MARKET.

**internal market** the creation of a network of divisions within an organization such as a public authority (the National Health Service for example) or a vertically integrated firm (see VERTICAL INTEGRATION), each division standing in a supplying or buying relationship with other divisions. To promote efficiency and cost effectiveness each division may be required to operate as a PROFIT CENTRE thus imposing the same commercial 'discipline' on an organization as if it was dealing with external suppliers and buyers. See PURCHASER-PROVIDER SPLIT.

**internal rate of return** see DISCOUNTED CASH FLOW.

**Internal Revenue Service (IRS)** the United States equivalent of the British INLAND REVENUE which is responsible for assessing and collecting taxes.

**internal supplier** see INTERNAL CUSTOMER.

**International Bank for Reconstruction and Development** see WORLD BANK.

**international commodity agreement** a form of CARTEL arrangement between producers in a number of countries (often organized by their governments) which operate to regulate the supply and prices of a particular COMMODITY such as tin, copper etc. on world markets. Commodity agreements seek to increase both the foreign currency available to governments and the income of producers by establishing relatively stable prices for commodities whose prices tend to fluctuate erratically when left to market forces. See BUFFER STOCK.

**international debt** the outstanding LOANS owed by borrowing countries to the WORLD BANK, INTERNATIONAL MONETARY FUND, CENTRAL BANKS and private sector COMMERCIAL BANKS, and other lending institutions. In the main, debtor countries are the less developed countries who, because they have been unable to earn sufficient foreign exchange from exports to pay for the capital imports, etc. required to finance their development programmes, have been forced to fill the gap by borrowing. Since the 1970s the debt problems of the less-developed countries have escalated, and despite the introduction of various debt rescheduling packages, many countries have been unable to service their interest charges and have reneged on capital repayments. See ECONOMIC AID.

**international Fisher effect** a situation where current INTEREST RATE differentials between countries fully reflect expected changes in the EXCHANGE RATES of their currencies. For example, if UK investors anticipate that the German D-mark will appreciate by 10% against the pound over the coming year, then they would be prepared to accept an interest rate approximately 10% less per annum on a D-mark denominated financial security than that which could be expected from an equivalent investment denominated in pounds. For borrowers the cost of equivalent loans in alternative currencies like the D-mark and pound will be the same regardless of the rate of interest.

**internationalization** or **globalization** the expansion of a firm into foreign economies by EXPORTING, but more specifically by FOREIGN INVESTMENT in the establishment of components factories, manufacturing plants and sales subsidiaries. See MULTINATIONAL ENTERPRISE, FOREIGN MARKET SERVICING STRATEGY.

International growth provides additional sales opportunities for firms constrained by the small size of their national markets and serves to reduce their dependency on a single national market to generate profits. See STRATEGIC DIRECTION.

**International Labour Office (ILO)** an organization run by the UNITED NATIONS whose basic remit is to assist in the improvement of social and working conditions throughout the world. The ILO provides technical assistance to countries with manpower training, advises governments on labour standards and work practices, and publishes regular series of international labour statistics.

**international liquidity** see INTERNATIONAL RESERVES.

**international marketing** the MARKETING of a firm's products in a number of overseas markets as opposed to selling only in the firm's domestic market. In a limited number of cases a firm may be able to promote its product as a GLOBAL BRAND using the same broad MARKETING MIX format across all its export markets (for example Coca Cola). More generally, however, differences in language, culture, laws and buyer characteristics (for example right-hand drive cars in the UK, left-hand drive cars in Europe) will require a firm to adopt a more customized approach to EXPORTING (see DIFFERENTIATED MARKETING STRATEGY). Products may have to be substantially adapted to meet foreign requirements or even new products developed to cater for those markets. The firm's marketing approach too may require significant modification to allow for differences in promotion (see PROMOTIONAL MIX) and DISTRIBUTION CHANNELS. In many cases lack of local knowledge and contacts may make it imperative for a firm to use overseas SALES AGENTS to market their products. See MARKET SEGMENTATION, ROLL-OUT MARKETING, MULTINATIONAL ENTERPRISE, FOREIGN MARKET SERVICING STRATEGY.

**International Monetary Fund (IMF),** an international organization established in 1947 to promote, alongside the GENERAL AGREEMENT ON TARIFFS AND TRADE, the expansion of INTERNATIONAL TRADE in a way consistent with the maintenance of BALANCE OF PAYMENTS equilibrium by individual member countries. This has involved the Fund in negotiating the removal of restrictions (such as FOREIGN EXCHANGE CONTROLS) on the convertibility of currencies, the establishment of 'orderly' EXCHANGE RATES between members' currencies and the provision of borrowing facilities and INTERNATIONAL RESERVES to members in balance of payments difficulties.

Up to the 1970s the IMF supervised a FIXED EXCHANGE RATE SYSTEM and established 'fixed' pivotal values for members' currencies for concluding trade and capital transactions. Countries could devalue or revalue their currency to a new fixed rate when their balance of payments situation warranted it, subject to Fund negotiation and approval. This procedure ensured that currency realignments were decided by multilateral agreement rather than initiated as a unilateral act. In the early 1970s, however, with a continued weakening of the US dollar, the pivotal currency in the Fund's operations, and the onset of a world recession, a large number of currencies were 'floated' to provide a greater degree of exchange rate flexibility (see FLOATING EXCHANGE RATE SYSTEM). Most major currencies have continued to float although fixed exchange rate arrangements have been reintroduced on a limited basis (see EUROPEAN MONETARY SYSTEM). As a result of these developments the Fund has lost formal control over exchange rate movements, but member countries are still obliged, in theory, to maintain orderly exchange rates, avoiding in particular the manipulation of their exchange rates to disadvantage trade partners.

The Fund's resources consist of a pool of foreign currencies (see FOREIGN EXCHANGE) and international reserve assets (excluding gold, however) subscribed by its members. Each country is allocated a 'subscription quota', weighted according to its economic status, and is required to pay 75% of its quota in its own currency and the remainder in international reserve assets. Included in the Fund's stock of reserve assets is the SPECIAL DRAWING RIGHT (SDR) unit, an asset which the Fund itself creates and holds in the form of a book-keeping entry (i.e. unlike currencies, SDRs have no tangible life of their own), and which is valued in terms of a weighted average of five major currencies. Countries needing extra resources over and above their own nationally-held reserves to finance a balance of payments deficit may borrow (i.e. exercise their 'drawing rights' on) the currencies they require from the Fund. A substantial proportion of these borrowings, however, are subject to the

Fund's 'conditionality' rules, whereby the Fund stipulates the measures a member must implement to remove its payments deficit. Borrowings are normally required to be repaid within three to five years, but the INTERNATIONAL DEBT problem has not only forced the Fund to 'roll-over' credits but has led to the establishment of various new facilities to accommodate its poorer members.

See GROUP OF 7.

**international reserves** or **international liquidity** monetary assets that are used to settle BALANCE OF PAYMENTS deficits between countries; specifically, GOLD, certain FOREIGN CURRENCIES (particularly the US dollar, German Deutschmark, Swiss franc and Japanese yen), INTERNATIONAL MONETARY FUND 'Drawing Rights' and 'Special Drawing Rights'. Additionally, members of the EUROPEAN MONETARY SYSTEM use the 'European Currency Unit' for settlement purposes.

**International Standard** see ISO 9000.

**International Standardization Organization (ISO)** a body which produces international standards for products and processes. The ISO seeks to produce standards which harmonize national standards established by individual countries. In designing products and processes firms must generally meet the QUALITY, performance and safety standards laid down by the ISO if their products and processes are to be acceptable to consumers.

See BRITISH STANDARDS INSTITUTION, ISO 9000.

**international trade** cross-frontier trade between countries in goods and services, with differences between countries in their COMPETITIVE ADVANTAGES (or 'comparative advantages') to supply particular products providing the basis of an international division of labour (location of production) and an associated flow of EXPORTS and IMPORTS between countries. International trade can bring both consumption and production gains to a country, serving to raise its living standards and improve its productive efficiency. International trade enables countries to consume some goods and services more cheaply by importing them, and also to obtain some resources and products from other countries which would otherwise be totally unavailable because domestic producers are unable to supply them (for example a scarce raw material or high-technology product). International trade promotes productive efficiency by encouraging a reallocation of resources away from areas of the economy best served by imports into industries where the country itself has a comparative advantage over trade partners.

Inter-country variations in comparative advantage are reflected both in terms of their differential cost structures (i.e. price competitiveness) and different skill levels (i.e. product differentiation competitiveness). These, in turn, are determined in large measure by the country's basic factor endowments (natural resources, labour and capital) and degree of economic maturity (level of per capita income, general cost and price levels, scientific and technical skills, etc.). Resource availability and skills indicate the product range which a country is technically capable of supplying, while *relative* cost, price and product differentiation factors dictate which of these products it is economically appropriate for the country to produce, i.e. those products in which it has a comparative advantage over other countries.

In its more simplified form, a two country – two product world economy, the theory of comparative advantage generates the following international production and trade relationship: assuming country A is well endowed with cheap labour and country B is well endowed with capital (capital is cheap relative to labour), and that product X is labour-intensive and product Y is capital-intensive, then country A will have a comparative advantage over B in the production of X, while country B will have a comparative advantage over A in the production of Y. It follows that both countries stand to gain from SPECIALIZATION and trade: country A produces X and exports some of it in exchange for imports of Y, while country B produces Y and trades some of it for imports of X.

A basic assumption of this presentation is that factor endowments, and hence comparative advantages, are 'fixed'. Dynamically, however, comparative advantage may well change. It may do so in response to a number of influences including:

(a) the initiation by a country's government of structural programmes leading to resource redeployment. For example, a country which seemingly has a comparative advantage in the supply of primary products such as cotton and wheat may nevertheless abandon or de-emphasize it in favour of a drive towards industrialization and the establishment of comparative advantage in higher value-added manufactured goods;

(b) international capital movements and technology transfer, and relocation of production by MULTINATIONAL ENTERPRISES. For example, Malaysia developed a comparative advantage in the production of natural rubber only after UK entrepreneurs established and invested in rubber tree plantations there.

Consideration of the benefits of international trade suggests that the optimization of such benefits is best achieved by conditions of FREE TRADE (i.e. the absence of restrictions on trade such as TARIFFS and QUOTAS), a view given operational validity by the international community by the establishment of the GENERAL AGREEMENT ON TARIFFS AND TRADE and the formation of various regional FREE TRADE BLOCS. In practice, however, the benefits of international trade are often unequally divided between countries, and this inevitably tends to produce situations where national self interest is put before international obligations.

See PROTECTIONISM, FOREIGN CURRENCY, FOREIGN EXCHANGE MARKET, BALANCE OF PAYMENTS, DUMPING, IMPORTING, PARALLEL IMPORTING, COUNTERTRADE, EMBARGO.

**Internet** an electronic network linking COMPUTERS in businesses, government departments etc. around the world via phone lines and fibre-optic cables. See ELECTRONIC MAIL, BULLETIN BOARD, MODEM, INFORMATION HIGHWAY.

**interstage store** a work in progress STORE located between two production departments which serves to minimize production delays (IDLE TIME) by providing adequate levels of interprocess STOCKS.

**intrapreneurial group** a group of employees within an organization who are encouraged to act as ENTREPRENEURS by 'selling' their goods and services in competition with other groups, to other groups or departments within the organization. No real money necessarily changes hands. Instead notional payments may be made and received. However, they may seek contracts with other organizations. The allocation of work within the group can be determined by members of the group. The potential benefits of this form of organization are that by providing profit incentives and facilitating identification of individual and group output, employee motivation is increased, while inter-group competition can keep costs down.

On the negative side, the encouragement of sectional interests could harm those of the organization as a whole.

Variants of this idea have been popular in the UK in recent years. Many organizations have pushed responsibility for profits down to as low a level as possible in the organization (see STRATEGIC BUSINESS UNIT), whilst many have developed the use of notional transfer payments between departments so as to identify and control the costs of activities. This can be particularly relevant to the work of those service departments (such as personnel) whose contribution to the 'bottom-line' is otherwise difficult to quantify.

**introduction** a method of raising new SHARE CAPITAL by issuing company shares at an agreed price to STOCKBROKERS and MARKET MAKERS rather than to the general public. Introductions are usually employed by established companies as a means of raising new capital with less administrative expense than other forms of SHARE ISSUE.

**introduction phase** see PRODUCT LIFE CYCLE.

**invention** see RESEARCH AND DEVELOPMENT.

**inventory** the STOCKS of finished goods, WORK IN PROGRESS and raw materials held by businesses. See INVENTORY INVESTMENT, STOCKHOLDING COSTS.

**inventory control** see STOCK CONTROL.

**inventory investment** the INVESTMENT in raw materials, WORK IN PROGRESS and finished STOCK. In contrast to FIXED INVESTMENT, inventories are constantly being 'turned over' as the production cycle repeats itself, with raw materials being purchased, converted first into work in progress, then into finished goods, then finally being sold.

The level of inventory investment made by a firm will depend upon its forecasts about future demand and its resulting output plans, and the amount of stock it needs to allow for delivery delays on raw materials and production delays in serving customers with appropriate buffer stocks to cover unforeseen contingencies. Frequently firms find that actual levels of demand differ from their forecasts, so that demand is less than expected and firms find that stocks of unsold goods build up (unintended inventory investment); or that demand exceeds expectations so that stocks run down (unintended inventory disinvestment). The cost of inventory investment includes order and delivery costs, deterioration and obsolescence of stock and interest charges on funds invested in stock. Firms seek to minimize these costs by establishing economic order quantities and optimum stockholding levels.

See STOCKHOLDING COSTS.

**investment 1.** *physical* or real investment: capital expenditure on the purchase of assets such as plant, machinery and equipment (FIXED CAPITAL assets) and STOCKS or INVENTORY (WORKING CAPITAL assets). Fixed capital investment is undertaken by firms, both to replace worn-out and obsolete capital items (see DEPRECIATION) and to increase the firm's total assets (see CAPITAL EMPLOYED), so as to enable it to produce a greater volume of products, and, by investing in the latest technology, to remain competitive. In aggregate terms, net additions to the country's CAPITAL STOCK increase the economy's productive capacity, thus making an important contribution to the achievement of higher rates of ECONOMIC GROWTH and improved living standards.

**2.** *financial* investment: expenditure on the purchase of financial securities such as SHARES and BONDS. PORTFOLIO investment is undertaken by individuals, companies and financial institutions as a means of earning income in the form of dividend, interest and rent payments and through capital appreciation.

See STOCK MARKET, FINANCIAL SYSTEM, FOREIGN INVESTMENT, SAVINGS, INVESTMENT INCENTIVE, INVESTMENT APPRAISAL, ACCOUNTING RETURN, PAYBACK METHOD, DISCOUNTED CASH FLOW.

**investment appraisal** the process of evaluating the desirability of INVESTMENT proposals covering such things as the replacement of worn-out plant and machinery, the establishment of a new factory, the takeover of another company, new product development or a sales promotion campaign.

Generally the desirability of an investment will be considered in terms of the PROFIT it will yield and managers will prefer those investments which promise the largest profit. Alternatively, they could measure the CASH FLOW associated with a project, and award priority to projects which promise the best contribution towards future cash flows. In making investment decisions managers will undertake investments which promise a rate of return greater than the cost of capital needed to finance it.

There are several techniques which can be used to assess investment opportunities, some based upon accounting profit measures, others upon cash flows. These methods include the ACCOUNTING RETURN, PAYBACK PERIOD and DISCOUNTED CASH FLOW.

**investment bank** a BANK which accepts deposits of money from savers and which specializes in investments in SHARE CAPITAL and the provision of LOAN finance for corporate borrowers. See BANKING SYSTEM.

**investment centre** an organizational subunit of a firm which is fully independent with full control over its costs and revenues (that is, a PROFIT CENTRE) but which also has responsibility for raising capital and for long-term investment.

**investment grant** see INVESTMENT INCENTIVE.

**investment incentive** a financial inducement given by the government to a firm as a means of encouraging new INVESTMENT. Such inducements can include cash grants to defray part of the costs of building a new factory and/or installing new machines and equipment; low interest rates; interest-free LOANS; or tax relief on the firm's profits. Investment incentives can be used to stimulate investment in general, or they can be targeted to encourage certain types of investment and to influence the geographical location of new investment. See INDUSTRIAL POLICY, REGIONAL POLICY, SUBSIDY, ENTERPRISE INVESTMENT SCHEME.

**investment income** income which a company derives from TRADE INVESTMENTS rather than normal trading activities.

**Investment Management Regulatory Organization (IMRO)** a body responsible for regulating firms involved in the management and trusteeship of collective investment schemes (such as unit trusts) and pension funds. See FINANCIAL SERVICES ACT 1986.

**investment ratios** ratios which are used to assess the performance of a company's shares, for example, PRICE EARNINGS RATIO, EARNINGS PER SHARE and EARNINGS YIELD. In addition to being of great interest to the ordinary shareholders, investment ratios are also of interest to potential investors, analysts and competitors.

**investment trust company** a financial institution which issues its own shares to the investing public and which specializes in investment in FINANCIAL SECURITIES, mainly UK and overseas corporate stocks and shares and government fixed-interest securities. They tend to be attractive to smaller investors who wish to secure a wider spread of risk than they could achieve for themselves by direct investment in a limited number of securities, or who require professional management of their investments.

Investment trust company shares are bought and sold on the STOCK MARKET so that, like other securities, their prices can go up or down reflecting general stock market price trends, but more particularly the company's own performance. Investment trust companies vary in the portfolios they put together and the expertise with which they are managed, so that the portfolio performance of different companies has varied from mediocre to excellent over the years.

In recent years most investment trust company shares have traded at a substantial DISCOUNT on their asset values (i.e. asset backing per share), partly reflecting small investors' preference for UNIT TRUSTS as an alternative investment medium.

Investment trust companies in the UK are represented by the Association of Investment Trust Companies (AITC), which provides a forum for the discussion of matters of general concern to members, and acts on behalf of members in dealings with other institutional bodies such as the Institutional Investors Committee and the government. The investment and management of funds by investment trust companies is regulated by the INVESTMENT MANAGEMENT REGULATORY ORGANIZATION in accordance with various standards of good practice laid down under the FINANCIAL SERVICES ACT 1986.

See INSTITUTIONAL INVESTORS, FINANCIAL SYSTEM.

**investor** a person, company or institution which uses either its own SAVINGS or LOAN finance to acquire financial and physical assets such as SHARES and BONDS, factories and offices, etc. See INVESTMENT, FINANCIAL SYSTEM.

**Investors in People** a recent UK government initiative to encourage ORGANIZATIONS to train their workforces. Those registering with the initiative are assisted to undertake a systematic analysis of BUSINESS STRATEGY and the training needs that result from this (see TRAINING). The organization is required to design and implement training programmes to meet these needs, and to agree personal training and development programmes with each emloyee, linked to the achievement of NATIONAL VOCATIONAL QUALIFICATIONS where possible. The extent to which the organization meets the training targets set is assessed by external assessors, and those found to have met them are given an Investors in People award.

**invisible assets** see INTANGIBLE FIXED ASSETS.

**invisible export** see EXPORT, BALANCE OF PAYMENTS.

**invisible import** see IMPORT, BALANCE OF PAYMENTS.

**invoice** a document sent by a supplier to a customer that itemizes the products supplied to the customer, their prices, and the total amount of money owed by the customer for these products. An invoice is usually sent after the products have been shipped with their associated DELIVERY NOTE, and serves to inform the customer that payment is required. See STATEMENT OF ACCOUNT.

**invoice factoring** see FACTORING.

**inward investment** see CAPITAL INFLOW, HOST COUNTRY.

**IPM** see INSTITUTE OF PERSONAL MANAGEMENT.

**irregular variations** see SALES FORECASTING.

**IRS** see INTERNAL REVENUE SERVICE.

**ISO** see INTERNATIONAL STANDARDIZATION ORGANIZATION.

**ISO 9000** a QUALITY standard drawn up by the INTERNATIONAL STANDARDIZATION ORGANIZATION. ISO 9000 is identical to the BRITISH STANDARDS INSTITUTION's quality standard BS 5750. To obtain certification a supplier is required to establish, document and maintain an effective and economical quality system.

**issued share capital** the amount of its AUTHORIZED SHARE CAPITAL that a JOINT-STOCK COMPANY has issued to SHARE-HOLDERS in order to raise CAPITAL. This amount is disclosed in the company's BALANCE SHEET.

Issued share capital shows the initial investments made by shareholders in the company, though this investment is often increased to the extent that profits are retained in the firm and added to RESERVES rather than all being distributed as dividends. The market value of the issued share capital can differ considerably from its PAR VALUE, since market values depend upon the price at which issued shares are currently being sold on the STOCK MARKET.

**issue price** the price at which a SHARE or DEBENTURE is issued, which is not necessarily equal to its PAR VALUE (see SHARE PRE-MIUM).

**issuing house** a division of a MERCHANT BANK or similar organization that arranges and UNDERWRITES the issue of new STOCKS and SHARES on behalf of corporate clients, for an agreed fee. See SHARE ISSUE.

# J

**Japanization** the adoption by organizations elsewhere of work organization and employment practices usually found in large Japanese companies. The notion of Japanization usually suggests that such practices are implemented in a fairly systematic way as part of a strategy to improve individual and organizational performance. The model is large private-sector companies in Japan, which generally have the following policies (known as the 'sacred treasures') in the employment and industrial relations sphere: enterprise unions (see TRADE UNIONS), pay systems based on seniority and length of service (see INCREMENTAL PAY SCALE) and lifetime security of employment. Companies elsewhere have rarely adopted these policies in full but some have adapted them in the context of their own national industrial relations systems. For instance, the fashion for SINGLE UNION DEALS in the UK represents a partial Japanization, inspired by the practice in Japanese companies of establishing production facilities in the UK (see below). Guaranteed lifetime employment is a rarity in the UK but firms who are said to be following the Japanese example often provide more favourable conditions of employment than is found in other organizations (see STAFF STATUS).

Firms embarking on Japanization usually adopt one or more of the following policies and practices in the sphere of work organization:

(a) *quality circles* (QCs). These consist of a work group and its supervisor who meet formally at regular intervals to assess the effectiveness and efficiency of its part of the production or service process, and to discuss and suggest possible improvements. In this way the knowledge and experience of operatives can be tapped and put to good use, whilst the attempt to involve them may increase their commitment. For QCs to work it is essential that top management be committed to them, and that they take their recommendations seriously.

(b) *just-in-time (Kanban) production.* In this system the quantity of stocks is kept to the minimum level necessary for immediate production. For this to succeed the production system has to be designed to facilitate regular flows of semi-finished goods between each stage of production, and all stages have to be very closely monitored. It therefore requires a highly systematic approach to organizing production. It also necessitates close relationships with suppliers so that delivery of new stock can be assured. Firms that adopt this system also find that the quantity and quality of training of all those involved in production has to be increased. See JUST IN TIME (JIT) SYSTEM.

A number of Japanese companies, for example Nissan and Toshiba, have established factories in the UK recently. Whilst they tend to use Japanese methods of work organization, they tend to use variants of Japanese employment practices adapted to local conditions. For instance, a number of companies have attempted to combine elements of Japanese and UK industrial relations by signing NO STRIKE AGREEMENTS with pendulum ARBITRATION as a component of SINGLE UNION DEALS. A notable feature of these companies is their systematic and strategic approach to employment and industrial relations issues.

The notion of Japanization is somewhat ironic since many so-called Japanese practices were in fact earlier imported by the Japanese (from the USA) to combat industrial unrest. It is not universally accepted that progressive employment policies are the key to Japan's recent economic success: many economists would argue that high tariff barriers have been equally important.

**JIT** see JUST-IN-TIME (JIT) SYSTEM.

**job 1.** a work task or series of work tasks to be performed. For factory operatives the work tasks are often clearly defined as a specific set of machining or assembly operations. By contrast, at senior management level, work tasks are less clearly defined and managers have more discretion as to the range of tasks to be performed and how they are performed.

**2.** a unit of good or service for which costs can be ascertained. The job or cost unit could consist of a single order. Alternatively, the job or cost unit could be a batch or group of identical products passing together through production.

**job analysis** a process of research to identify the tasks comprising a particular JOB and to determine whether they could be organized in a more productive or satisfying way. It is preferable not to analyse individual jobs in isolation but to examine the workflow in its entirety, since tasks could potentially be usefully shifted from one person or job to another. Job analysis can be carried out by simple observation of the workflow or by more scientific scrutiny (see WORK STUDY), and can make use of interviews with job holders. It can form the first step in compiling a list of job characteristics (job specification) for the RECRUITMENT AND SELECTION process or for investigating whether a different JOB DESIGN is feasible.

**jobbing** the function of buying and selling FINANCIAL SECURITIES such as STOCKS, SHARES and BONDS on the STOCK MARKET by a dealer who acts as a principal in 'making a market' in these securities. See MARKET MAKER.

**jobbing production** see PRODUCTION.

**job card** a document which records the materials and direct labour cost of a job. These ledger records collect data from MATERIALS REQUISITIONS and TIME SHEETS to ascertain the cost of a job.

**job costing** see PRODUCT COSTING.

**job description** a statement of the work tasks which constitute a JOB and the responsibilities of the employee in performing that job. Job descriptions usually form part of an employee's CONTRACT OF EMPLOYMENT.

**job design and redesign** the process or outcome of grouping together work tasks to form individual JOBS. Jobs may comprise a single or small number of tasks (for example repetitive production work on an assembly line) or a considerable range (for example the job of a manager). Some jobs involve substantial decision-making whilst others require very little.

Job design is often said to have two main dimensions – SPECIALIZATION and discretion. The key questions facing the job designer are: how specialized a set of tasks should the individual perform? and how far should the individual decide which tasks are to be undertaken at a given moment and in what way? As regards the latter, it has been suggested that

jobs could be categorized according to a TIME SPAN OF DISCRE-
TION: the length of time that passes before a worker's task
performance is checked and assessed by a superior.

Job design has an important effect on JOB SATISFACTION.
Those jobs which are highly specialized and which involve
little discretion often give rise to dissatisfaction, which may
find expression in CONFLICT, INDUSTRIAL DISPUTES, ABSENTEEISM
and LABOUR TURNOVER. Although specialization can be viewed
as an efficient approach to job design these side-effects can
lead to low levels of PRODUCTIVITY. To enhance job satisfaction
and productivity some analysts have advocated job redesign.
Most notable is the Quality of Working Life (QWL) movement, a loose knit body of academics, managers and trade
unionists, which from the 1970s onwards advocated sweeping
changes to prevailing patterns of job design.

The changes recommended include:

(a) *job enlargement*, where additional tasks are given to the
worker so as to provide more variety. In other words it is the
horizontal expansion of the tasks;

(b) *job enrichment*, where workers are given greater scope in
deciding how the tasks should be performed. Here the range
of tasks is extended vertically, to enrich the quality of the job
for the worker;

(c) *job rotation*, where workers rotate around the jobs in
their department on a regular basis, on the grounds that greater variety will lead to greater job satisfaction.

As can be seen, these changes involve modification to the
key dimensions of specialization and discretion. A more radical
approach still is the creation of semiautonomous work groups.
Here workers are allowed to decide amongst themselves how
to distribute and execute work tasks. This could involve replacing assembly-line working, where each individual performs
an allotted task in a pre-planned series of tasks, by group
working where who does what could be decided on a day-to-
day basis.

See FORDISM, SCIENTIFIC MANAGEMENT, WORK ORGANIZATION.

**job enlargement** see JOB DESIGN AND REDESIGN.

**job enrichment** see JOB DESIGN AND REDESIGN.

**job evaluation** a set of procedures to assess the relative worth
of groups of jobs in an organization so as to place them in a
rank order. This can then provide the basis of a grading and

pay structure. Job evaluation is more widely used for assessing managerial and white-collar rather than blue-collar jobs but its use amongst the latter has been growing steadily in recent years. The primary advantage of job evaluation is that it puts differences in rates of pay between jobs on a systematic footing. By so doing the rationale for pay differences can be clearly shown. It is generally recommended that only broadly similar jobs (job family) be evaluated in a particular exercise, i.e. manual and managerial jobs are too different to be meaningfully evaluated together. It is also recommended that trade union representatives be fully involved (where TRADE UNIONS are present) in the evaluation to ensure that the eventual ranking is accepted as fair.

There are a number of different ways of conducting job evaluation:

(a) *non-analytic*: these approaches do not break jobs into constituent factors but compare 'whole' jobs.

    (i)    *job ranking*. Here jobs are simply placed in an order on the basis of the content of job description that is felt to be fair by the evaluators.

    (ii)   *paired comparisons*. Here each job is compared with each other job and points are awarded for the comparative importance in each case. The total number of points for each job provides the basis for the rank order.

    (iii)  *job classification*. In this case the number and definition of grades are produced first, and then jobs are allocated to these grades according to the degree of 'fit' between job description and grade definition.

(b) *Analytic*: in approaches of this sort jobs are broken down into their core factors, such as degree of skill, responsibility, etc. and are then compared on the basis of these.

    (i)    *factor comparison*. Various facets of jobs, such as skill and responsibility, are considered and each is given a ranking. Jobs are then compared, factor by factor, to provide a grading structure.

    (ii)   *points rating*. The factors in each job are given a points score based on the importance of the factor relative to the others. The points for each factor are totalled for each job to produce a final rank order.

    (iii)  *Hay-MSL Evaluation*. This is a variant of the points rating system used for evaluating managerial jobs. The amount of knowledge, problem-solving and responsibility involved in each job is assessed, and each factor compared against the other to produce a final ranking.

The analytic approaches are plainly more rigorous than the non-analytic. Even these, however, cannot eliminate subjectivity. Job evaluators have to make decisions on the scores for each factor that can never be fully objective. Any score will inevitably involve an element of judgment. However, analytic job evaluation does enable jobs to be compared in a systematic and consistent way. Now that equal pay for men and women should be based on work of equal value, job evaluation free of sex bias is especially important. Those operating job evaluation schemes have to ensure that sexual discrimination does not enter into the ranking of jobs. The courts have decided that only analytic schemes may be used as a defence in an equal pay for equal value claim (see DISCRIMINATION). Where such a claim is made, the techniques of job evaluation are used to assess whether it is justified.

**job grading** see JOB EVALUATION.

**job redesign** see JOB DESIGN AND REDESIGN.

**job rights** the rights which employees may claim as theirs by virtue of performing a certain JOB. These may be an amalgam of their work conditions as laid down in a CONTRACT OF EMPLOYMENT: statutory rights, customary duties and benefits associated with a particular job. A good example of job rights is that of the (now abolished) Dock Labour Scheme: registered dockers were paid a wage even when there was no work available. Assertion of job rights is often a method of defence when managers seek to reorganize some aspect of work and employment.

**job rotation** see JOB DESIGN.

**job satisfaction** the satisfaction that an individual gains (or does not gain) from his or her job. It is generally believed that satisfied employees will be more highly motivated and will work more productively than dissatisfied employees. Job dissatisfaction may lead to ABSENTEEISM, LABOUR TURNOVER, INDUSTRIAL ACTION, etc.

The study of job satisfaction and its determinants has traditionally formed an important component of the SOCIOLOGY OF WORK. HUMAN RELATIONS writers argued that job satisfaction could be encouraged by managerial policies and practices that encouraged a sense of belonging. The rationale for this is that (in their view) people want to belong to a community: by experiencing a community at work workers will feel satisfaction in their work (see ANOMIE). More commonly, technology has been viewed as an important casual factor in job dissatisfaction. American sociologist Robert Blauner (1929– ) argued that, in general, job satisfaction declined in the shift from craft through machine to assembly-line technology but then increased with the adoption of continuous process production, i.e. that found in modern petrochemical plants. In his view, the experience of dissatisfaction could have four dimensions: a sense of powerlessness, of meaninglessness, of isolation and of self-estrangement (see ALIENATION). Today most writers and practitioners take the view that, whilst technology can have certain effects on job satisfaction, there is no necessary form of WORK ORGANIZATION associated with any particular type of technology (see SOCIO-TECHNICAL SYSTEM). It is, therefore, possible to modify work organization to make work more satisfying (see JOB DESIGN AND REDESIGN).

Other writers, however, have followed Karl Marx (1818–83) in asserting that job dissatisfaction is an endemic feature arising from ALIENATION in capitalist society and hence can never be eliminated whilst capitalism remains in existence.

In recent years many analysts of job satisfaction have argued that in looking for the causes of dissatisfaction the focus of study should be widened from analysis of the job itself. Psychologists have argued that workers' experience of job satisfaction is influenced by their expectations of the job. If they have expected that a job would be tedious their dissatisfaction tends not to be as great as if they had expected it to be exciting. In a not dissimilar vein, sociologists have suggested that workers' experience of dissatisfaction is determined to some extent by their ORIENTATIONS TO WORK. If their primary reason for undertaking a certain job is to achieve a high income they do not experience strong dissatisfaction even if the job is tedious and repetitive (as long as it pays well). As one sociologist put it, 'they see the wound but feel no pain'.

**job security** the degree of certainty of continued employment with a particular organization. Job security is generally a function of statutory employment rights (i.e. protection against

UNFAIR DISMISSAL), other elements of the CONTRACT OF EMPLOYMENT and the financial wellbeing of the organization. It can be said to be low where a company is suffering sustained losses or where the employment contract places a limit on the duration of employment (which may also debar the employee from certain statutory rights). Even where these conditions are not present, job security may be threatened by rationalizations which remove the need for certain jobs and hence lead to REDUNDANCY. See TEMPORARY WORK.

**job sharing** the carrying out by two or more individuals between them of the duties of a particular JOB, each being paid pro rata according to the number of hours worked. For instance, two people might share a 40 hours per week job with each working 20 hours and each paid half the wage or salary attached to the post. The advantage to job sharers is that both may work part-time in jobs that are more highly paid than is usual for most PART-TIME jobs. It is more common for potential sharers to approach employers with a job-share package than for employers to initiate this form of working themselves. Employers are generally wary of job sharing because it can increase employment costs (for example INSURANCE payments), because the division of duties and responsibilities may be difficult to specify, and because the competences of job sharers may be perceived as unbalanced.

**job specialization** see SPECIALIZATION, JOB DESIGN AND REDESIGN.

**job specification** see RECRUITMENT AND SELECTION.

**joint account** a BANK or BUILDING SOCIETY account opened in the name of two or more people.

**joint consultation** see CONSULTATION.

**joint costs** the COSTS involved in producing several products from the same process, for example petrol, diesel, tar, etc. which derive from a common oil-refining process. Joint costs such as oil-refinery running costs are difficult to allocate precisely between the different products in determining the exact cost of each. See COSTING, BY-PRODUCT.

**Joint Industrial Council** see MULTI-EMPLOYER AGREEMENT.

**joint products** products which emerge from the same production process; for example, petrol, diesel and tar from a common oil refining process.
See JOINT COSTS, BY-PRODUCT.

**joint-stock company** a form of company in which a number

of people contribute funds to finance a FIRM in return for SHARES in the company. Joint-stock companies are able to raise funds by issuing shares to large numbers of SHAREHOLDERS and thus are able to raise more capital to finance their operations than could a SOLE PROPRIETOR or even a PARTNERSHIP. Once a joint-stock company is formed then it becomes a separate legal entity apart from its shareholders, able to enter into contracts with suppliers and customers. Joint-stock companies are managed by the BOARD OF DIRECTORS appointed by share-holders. The directors must report on the progress of the company to the shareholders at an ANNUAL GENERAL MEETING where shareholders can in principle vote to remove existing directors if they are dissatisfied with their performance.

The development of joint-stock companies was given a con-siderable boost by the introduction of the principle of LIMITED LIABILITY which limited the maximum loss which a shareholder was liable for in the event of company failure. This protection for shareholders encouraged many more of them to invest in companies.

There are two main forms of joint-stock company:

(a) *private limited company*. Under UK Company Law the maximum number of shareholders in a private company is limited to 50 and the shares issued by the company cannot be bought and sold on the STOCK EXCHANGE. Such companies carry the term limited (Ltd) after their name;

(b) *public limited company*. Under UK Company Law there must be a minimum of seven shareholders in a public company, but otherwise a company can have an unlimited number of shareholders. Shares in a public company can be bought and sold on the stock exchange and so can be bought by the general public. Such companies carry the term public limited company (plc) after their name.

Most big firms are public companies since this is the only practical way of obtaining access to large amounts of capital. Although the shareholders are the owners of a public company, very often it is the company's management which in fact controls its affairs. See FLOTATION, SHARE ISSUE.

**joint venture** a business owned jointly by two (or more, in come cases) independent firms who continue to function separately in all other respects but pool together their resources in a particular line of activity. Firms set up joint ventures for a variety of reasons. The combining together of the resources of the two firms may facilitate the establishment of a larger-scale operation giving the joint venture access to economics of scale and increasing its penetration of the market. A joint venture is often a particularly effective way of exploiting complementary resources and skills, with one firm, for example, contributing new technology and products and the other providing marketing expertise and distribution channels. In the international context, joint ventures with local partners are often used by MULTINATIONAL ENTERPRISES as a means of entering unfamiliar foreign markets (see FOREIGN MARKET SERVICING STRATEGY).

Joint ventures are usually a less expensive way of expanding a firm's business interests than undertaking full mergers and takeovers (see EXTERNAL GROWTH); and they also allow firms to withdraw from a particular activity more easily (see DIVESTMENT). The main problem with joint ventures centres on the need to secure agreement between the two partners (especially if it is a 50–50 arrangement) as to how the business should be managed and developed. See BUSINESS STRATEGY, STRATEGIC ALLIANCE.

**journal** or **day book** a book of original entry in which information from documents and vouchers such as invoices and cheque stubs is entered, prior to entering or 'posting' this information to DOUBLE-ENTRY ACCOUNTS in the LEDGER. For example, the sales day book records invoices issued to customers in order of date and invoice number; these are then entered in the personal account of each customer in the sales ledger. Likewise the purchases day book records invoices received from suppliers in order of date; and these details are then posted or entered in the personal account of each supplier in the purchases ledger.

**junk bond** or **mezzanine debt** colloquial terms used to describe high-interest, high-risk LOAN STOCK which is issued by a company as a means of borrowing money to finance a TAKEOVER BID, MANAGEMENT BUY-OUT, or MANAGEMENT BUY-IN. A so-called 'leveraged' takeover bid or buy-out involves the company in increasing the proportion of its debt capital to equity capital, that is, increasing its CAPITAL GEARING.

Junk bond/mezzanine debt has come to the fore in recent years to plug the gap between the use of conventional loan finance such as DEBENTURES and the issue of SHARE CAPITAL, and the prices required to be paid for some takeover victims and DIVESTMENTS. Holders of mezzanine debt rank below conventional debt holders in terms of the repayment of loans, for which they receive a higher interest return or some shares in the company, or both. Mezzanine debt is often provided on a *bridging loan* basis; that is, it is used by a company to finance a takeover which, if successful, is then repaid out of the proceeds of disposing of some of the victim firm's businesses.

**juridification** The process whereby the law has come to exert an increasing influence on the employment relationship and the conduct of industrial relations. In the UK, for instance, a range of statutory employment rights have been created since the 1960s, such as protection against UNFAIR DISMISSAL. In the 1970s some statutory support for COLLECTIVE BARGAINING was provided though some elements of this were subsequently repealed. In the 1980s the expansion of legislation governing the conduct of INDUSTRIAL DISPUTES has increasingly drawn the courts into the regulation of industrial relations.

**just-in-time (JIT) system** a PRODUCTION MANAGEMENT system in which materials, components and products are produced for, or delivered to, the next stage of production (or customers) at the exact time they are needed. JIT seeks to minimize the amount of work-in-progress STOCKS held by a firm by synchronizing the flow of materials between production processes; and to economize on finished product stocks by matching the final assembly of products with the rate of customers' orders.

JIT is especially suited to high-volume production where uniform PRODUCTION-LINE OR ASSEMBLY-LINE schedules are operated on a continuous basis. Key elements in the successful application of JIT systems are:

(a) a high degree of cooperation and coordination with the (usually) single outside supplier of each particular material or component, who undertakes to supply on demand small consignments at frequent intervals and who carries sufficient stocks to permit immediate delivery;

(b) an internal control procedure which assists the smooth movement of materials and components from process to process at the required time. An illustration of this is provided by the Japanese car company Toyota's *Kanban* (card) system which uses cards attached to component containers to monitor the flow of production through its factories.

The advantages of JIT include the reduction of stockholding costs; reduced space requirements; and faster manufacturing rates. On the other hand, JIT systems leave the firm more vulnerable to production losses occasioned by delivery hold-ups or component defects.

See PRODUCTION SCHEDULING, MATERIALS REQUIREMENTS PLAN-NING, MATERIALS PLANNING, JAPANIZATION.

# K

**Kabushiki Kaisha** The Japanese equivalent of a public limited company. See JOINT-STOCK COMPANY.

**kanban** see JUST-IN-TIME (JIT) SYSTEM, JAPANIZATION.

**keyboard** a typewriter–style COMPUTER data input device.

**key factor** SEE LIMITING FACTOR.

**know-how** skill, expertise and trade contacts developed by a business over time, which serve to enhance its COMPETITIVE ADVANTAGE over rival suppliers.

**knowledge worker** a person who works in a professional or managerial capacity and whose tasks involve creating, process-ing and interpreting information.

# L

**label** a paper or plastic attachment to a product, or part of the product's PACKAGING, which provides information about the product.

**labour** the human input to work activity. See JOB, CAPITAL.

**labour cost variance** the difference between the standard DIR-ECT LABOUR cost of a product (standard labour time × standard wage rate) and its actual direct labour cost (actual labour time × actual wage rate). This difference can be broken down into two parts:

(a) *labour efficiency variance*, which involves calculating the difference between the standard labour time specified and the actual labour time, converted into money terms by multiplying by the standard wage rate;

(b) *labour rate variance*, which involves calculating the difference between the predetermined standard wage rate and the actual wage rate, multiplied by the actual labour time.

With this distinction it is possible to trace whether an adverse direct labour cost variance is due to lower labour efficiency or higher wage rates. See STANDARD COST.

**labour flexibility** the ability of a firm to modify the employment and utilization of its labour force in the face of changing labour and product market conditions.

Several forms of labour flexibility can be identified:

(a) *numerical flexibility*, where the level and type of employment can be varied. For instance, PART-TIME WORK and TEMPORARY WORK can enable the employer to adjust the size of the labour force;

(b) *functional flexibility*, where the utilization of employees can be varied. Here the employer seeks to remove DEMARCATION LINES and RESTRICTIVE LABOUR PRACTICES so that, in theory at least, workers can perform a greater range of tasks. Further TRAINING may be necessary to achieve this;

(c) *temporal flexibility*, where the hours of work can be varied so as to match them to production or operations requirements. Use of part-time work, COMPRESSED HOURS and ANNUAL HOURS systems may assist this;

(d) *financial flexibility*, where levels of payment to employees can be varied in line with changes in profitability or individual performance. See PROFIT-RELATED PAY, MERIT PAY.

Firms require some degree of flexibility because of the inherent uncertainty of markets. However, it has arguably become more necessary in recent years because of intensifying competition in product markets. A firm which achieves flexibility in most or all of the dimensions above may be described as a 'flexible firm'. Such a firm would be composed of a *core workforce* of functionally flexible, well-paid employees and a *peripheral workforce* of numerically flexible PART-TIME

WORKERS and temporal workers. Labour flexibility is usually viewed as a benefit to management; however, it can also benefit employees when it enables them to fit in paid employment with other (for example, domestic) commitments.

See FLEXIBLE SPECIALIZATION, FLEXITIME, TEMPORARY WORK.

**labour force** or **workforce 1.** the total number of people employed by a firm or some other organization to produce goods and services.
**2.** the total number of people in an ECONOMY available to produce goods and services. The total working population is usually defined to consist of all those persons currently in employment, either as employees or self-employed, together with those persons who are officially registered with the government as being currently unemployed but available for work. The figure excludes people working in the BLACK ECONOMY. See STRUCTURE OF INDUSTRY.

**labour hour rate** a COST RATE which is used in ABSORPTION COSTING to charge the OVERHEADS of a department or COST CENTRE in the cost of a product or job. It is usually used for those departments or cost centres which are less mechanized, and is computed by dividing the budgeted overheads which have been assigned to the department or cost centre by the estimated total number of labour hours for the period, to arrive at a rate per labour hour. The overhead charge for any product or job will depend upon the number of labour hours required for its production.

See also ABSORPTION.

**labour intensiveness** the extent to which labour is used in the PRODUCTION of goods and services. Where labour is relatively cheap and capital is comparatively expensive then firms will be inclined to use large amounts of labour in their production processes.

See CAPITAL LABOUR RATIO. Compare CAPITAL INTENSIVENESS.

**labour law** the body of legislation and judicial decisions concerned with INDUSTRIAL RELATIONS, TRADE UNIONS and employment. Labour law has two main forms:

(a) *individual labour law,* relating to the rights and obligations of individual employees. From the 1960s onwards the volume of law in this area has grown considerably, partly as a response to European Union/Community legislation. The Employment Act 1975 was particularly important as it established the right not to be unfairly dismissed (see UNFAIR DIS-MISSAL). Other important legislation in this era proscribed DIS-CRIMINATION on grounds of race or sex. In the 1980s individual rights were weakened somewhat. For example, the qualifying period for the right not to be unfairly dismissed was extended. However, legislation by the European Union counterbalanced this trend to some extent;

(b) *collective labour laws*, relating to the activities of TRADE UNIONS and the conduct of INDUSTRIAL RELATIONS and COLLEC-TIVE BARGAINING. Traditionally, the law has not played an important role in industrial relations, and agreements made between unions and employers are not legally binding (see VOLUNTARISM). However, industrial relations has become in-creasingly subject to legal intervention in recent years (see JUR-IDIFICATION). In the 1970s a statutory union recognition procedure was established (now repealed) by the Employment Act 1975. This law also required that employers consult over REDUNDANCIES and pass to unions information relevant to collective bargaining (see DISCLOSURE OF INFORMATION). In the 1980s the conduct of STRIKES, TRADE UNION IMMUNITIES, SECOND-ARY ACTION, and the CLOSED SHOP were all the subjects of legislation, much of it aimed at eradicating what the govern-ment saw as trade union abuses. Since much of this legislation put the onus on aggrieved employers to pursue action in the civil courts, judicial involvement in industrial relations in-creased during the 1980s.

See EMPLOYMENT ACT 1980, EMPLOYMENT ACT 1982, EMPLOYMENT ACT 1988, EMPLOYMENT ACT 1989, TRADE UNION ACT 1984, TRADE UNION REFORM AND EMPLOYMENT RIGHTS ACT 1993.

**labour management** the activity or part of MANAGEMENT con-cerned with all aspects of managing the work of others. It in-volves both the managing of production itself and activities such as selection of labour, discipline etc. With the growing specialization of management in recent decades these activities have often been separated, with some becoming the respons-ibility of PERSONNEL MANAGEMENT. For this reason the term 'labour management' is not in widespread use today.

**labour market** a MARKET which brings together those persons seeking work (the supply of labour) and firms, government and other organizations seeking to fill JOB vacancies (the demand for labour). The labour market in practice is highly fragmented reflecting the diversity of work tasks, which range from unskilled or low-skill work (labourers, drivers, machine operators etc.) to tasks calling for specialist skills and expertise (research scientists, surgeons, managers, etc.). See INTERNAL LABOUR MARKET, PAY, COLLECTIVE BARGAINING, PAY DIFFERENTIAL, LABOUR MOBILITY.

**labour mobility** the movement of workers between firms, industries and regions in response to PAY DIFFERENTIALS and employment opportunities. Occupational mobility (the movement of workers between different types of JOB) depends upon, for example, the facilities for TRAINING and retraining workers provided by firms and the government, and upon the transferability of workers' occupational PENSIONS. Geographical mobility (the movement of workers between areas) depends upon, for example, the availability and cost of housing, relocation costs and social amenities (schools etc.).

**labour process** see SOCIOLOGY OF WORK.

**labour relations** see INDUSTRIAL RELATIONS.

**labour turnover** the proportion of an organization's labour force which leaves its employment over a given period. It can be composed of retirements, deaths, dismissals, redundancy or voluntary resignation. In general labour turnover is strongly influenced by the business cycle. In a period of growth when employment opportunities are expanding, turnover will increase. A certain amount of turnover is believed to be a good thing (as well as inevitable), since it enables the labour force to be revitalized. However, a high level of turnover in an organization can indicate that pay and conditions of employment are perceived as inadequate or that the organization is badly managed.

Two basic measures of leaving rate can be used:

(a) *wastage index*

$$\frac{\text{number of employees leaving in a period}}{\text{average number of employees in a period}} \times 100$$

(b) *stability index*

$$\frac{\text{number of employees with one year of service or more}}{\text{number employed one year ago}} \times 100$$

The wastage index is a fairly crude measure because it provides little indication of which employees are leaving. By contrast, the stability index can be used to pinpoint whether those quitting are new recruits or more established employees, and how long the duration of employment tends to be. This is important because turnover is often concentrated amongst new recruits (see INDUCTION CRISIS).

Turnover rates differ between industries. In general, those organizations with well-developed career structures have lower annual rates of turnover than those which rely heavily on the labour market to fill vacancies.

See INTERNAL LABOUR MARKET, JOB SATISFACTION.

**LAFTA** see LATIN AMERICAN FREE TRADE ASSOCIATION.

**laissez-faire** an economic doctrine which emphasizes the superiority of a 'free' MARKET SYSTEM over state regulation of individual markets and of the ECONOMY in general.

**lame duck** a firm which is experiencing trading difficulties and making persistent losses which threaten its survival. If such firms are seen as strategically important, governments may be prepared to provide them with financial support. See INDUSTRIAL POLICY.

**LAN** see LOCAL AREA NETWORK.

**laptop** a small battery-powered portable COMPUTER.

**last-in, first-out** see REDUNDANCY.

**last-in, first-out (LIFO)** see STOCK VALUATION.

**last offer arbitration** see ARBITRATION.

**Latin American Free Trade Association (LAFTA)** the former regional alliance established in 1960 to promote FREE TRADE between its ten members: Argentina, Brazil, Paraguay, Mexico, Venezuela, Chile, Colombia, Equador, Peru and Bolivia. In 1995, a new trade bloc, *Mercosur*, was established, creating a customs union between Brazil, Uruguay, Argentina and Paraguay. Mexico is now a member of the NORTH AMERICAN FREE TRADE AGREEMENT.

**launch** the introduction of a NEW PRODUCT onto the market. See PRODUCT LIFE CYCLE, TEST MARKETING, PROMOTIONAL MIX, ADVERTISING EFFECTIVENESS TESTS.

**LAUTRO** see PERSONAL INVESTMENT AUTHORITY.

**lay-off** the termination of an employee's employment with an organization due to reduced demand for the goods or services produced by the organization. Lay-offs may be temporary, in which case employees will be re-employed when demand increases again, or permanent.

See REDUNDANCY.

**lay official** a TRADE UNION representative who is not actually employed by a union, and who performs union duties in his or her spare time or in time made available by their employer. See SHOP STEWARD.

**lead body** see NATIONAL VOCATIONAL QUALIFICATION.

**leadership** the process of influencing others to achieve certain goals. Effective leadership is often seen as the outcome of leadership qualities (traits) which some people have and some do not. In this conception, leadership is often seen as an autocratic activity, and leadership qualities are thought to include strength of personality, charisma, etc. Unfortunately, research into associated traits has been unable to prove conclusively a positive relationship between aspects of personality and effective management.

Academic work on leadership then shifted its attention away from what leaders are to what managers actually do in leadership roles. Two basic approaches to leadership were identified and have formed the core of theories of leadership and MANAGEMENT STYLE ever since. These are *concern for production*, as exemplified by SCIENTIFIC MANAGEMENT, and *concern for people*, as found in HUMAN RELATIONS philosophy. In the former, managers concentrate on getting the job done and their leadership style is essentially directive. In the latter, managers devote their efforts to ensuring that their subordinates are satisfied in their jobs, on the basis that a contented worker is an effective one. These twin dimensions are combined together in the Managerial Grid, devised by Americans Robert Blake (1918– ) and Jane Mouton (1930– ), as shown in Fig. 46. In their view the most effective form of management is Team Management, where leaders show a marked concern for people and for getting the job done.

However, research findings do not fully support this contention, leading some analysts to suggest that the *situation* in which leadership occurs needs to be considered too. American writer Fred Fiedler (1922– ) has suggested that the extent to which tasks are structured and the nature of the leader–subordinate relationship (including the power resources

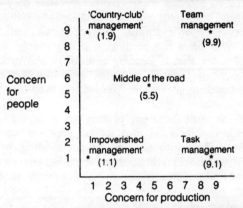

Fig. 46. **Leadership**. Blake and Mouton's managerial grid.

of the leader) influence the effectiveness of leadership styles. A task–oriented approach is most effective where tasks are either highly structured or fairly unstructured and where the leader–subordinate relationship is very good or very poor. It is in the middling positions that a people–oriented style is most effective. Fiedler believed that managers find it difficult to change their styles and therefore advocated that managers should attempt to modify the situation to enhance effectiveness. Other writers, however, have argued, in what has come to be known as 'situational management', that leaders should adapt their style to the demands of the situation. It has been suggested that a critical factor is the job 'maturity' of subordinates, i.e. their capacity to direct their own job performance. At low levels of maturity a task-orientation is most appropriate to provide direction. As maturity increases leaders should adopt a people–orientation to provide support whilst reducing the amount of task direction. As individuals reach full maturity the manager can reduce both task- and people-orientation and allow individuals to perform the job as they see fit. In a sense, at this point successful leadership is the absence of overt leadership.

**leading and lagging** see EXCHANGE RATE EXPOSURE.

**leading indicators** the statistical time series that past experience has shown tends to reflect later changes, and which thus can be used to forecast these changes because they precede the changes in a consistent manner and by a relatively constant time interval. For example, current birth statistics would provide a firm basis for predicting primary school admissions five or six years ahead. Leading indicators like orders for new machine tools, overtime/short-time working in manufacturing and housebuilding starts are frequently used for SALES FORE-CASTING.

**lead time** the time between placing an order or reorder and the goods being received into stores. STOCK CONTROL systems take the lead time into account when deciding upon reorder levels, placing orders whilst there is sufficient safety stock or BUFFER STOCK to meet production requirements during the lead time.

**learning curve** see EXPERIENCE CURVE.

**learning for work** see TRAINING.

**lease** a legal contract under which the owner (the lessor) of an ASSET such as a building or piece of machinery grants to a person or company (the lessee) the right to use that asset for a specified period of time in return for the payment of an agreed rental. See LEASING, LEASEBACK.

**leaseback** an arrangement which involves the selling of an ASSET by the owner to another person or company on condition that the asset is then LEASED (rented back) to the original owner for a specified period of time at an agreed rental. Leaseback is used primarily as a means of raising finance from the sale of surplus properties while allowing the firm to continue its existing business operations. See LEASING.

**leasehold property** property which is LEASED to a person or firm (the lessee) from its legal owners (the lessor) for an agreed period of time. Contrast FREEHOLD PROPERTY.

**leasing** the hiring out by one firm (the lessor) of an ASSET such as a factory building, piece of machinery or vehicle to another firm (the lessee) in return for the payment of an agreed rental. The lessor retains the ownership of the asset concerned and will repossess the asset on the expiry of the contract, or beforehand should the client require a replacement. A leasing arrangement can be useful to a client company in so far as it enables it to employ assets without having to tie up large amounts of capital for long periods of time. See LEASE, LEASE-BACK, OFF-BALANCE SHEET FINANCING, FINANCE HOUSE.

**LEC** see LOCAL ENTERPRISE COMPANY.

**ledger** the ACCOUNTING records that keep a note of a firm's day-to-day financial transactions with outside parties. For example, the purchases or CREDITORS ledger would show the value of raw materials or services purchased from each supplier, payments made to suppliers for these, and any amounts still owing to suppliers. Similarly, the sales or DEBTORS ledger would show the value of goods or services sold to each customer, amounts they have paid for these, and any amounts still owed by customers. In former times such ledger accounts took the form of bound ledgers in which entries were recorded by hand; nowadays they are generally kept as computer records. Fig. 47 shows the main ledger accounts. See DOUBLE-ENTRY ACCOUNTS.

SALES LEDGER (Debtors' Ledger)
Account for each *customer*

PURCHASES LEDGER (Creditors' Ledger)
Account for each *supplier*

ASSET LEDGER (Plant Register)
Account for each *asset*

CASH ACCOUNT (Cash Book)
Record of all cash *incomings* and *outgoings*

*NOMINAL LEDGER*
Account for each *income* or *expense*

PAYROLL ACCOUNT
Record for each *employee*

Fig. 47. **Ledger**. The main ledger accounts.

**legal tender** that part of a country's MONEY SUPPLY which, in the eyes of the law, is *totally* acceptable in discharge of a payment or debt. Coins and bank notes (CURRENCY) issued by the government fulfil this requirement. By contrast, a dealer or creditor is within his legal rights to refuse to accept as payment for a purchase or repayment of a debt a cheque drawn against a bank account.

**lender** a person, company or institution that provides a BORROWER with MONEY or some other asset (for example machinery, property) in the form of a LOAN, MORTGAGE or LEASING arrangement in order to finance consumption and investment. See DEBT, FINANCIAL SYSTEM, COLLATERAL SECURITY.

**'lender of last resort'** the role of the Bank of England in making funds available to the DISCOUNT HOUSES when they are unable to cover their short-term liabilities from their own resources or from loans from the commercial banks. See DISCOUNT MARKET, INTEREST RATE, CENTRAL BANK.

**letter of credit** a document used to effect payment for internationally traded goods, usually as part of a contract for the sale of goods which ensures that the supplier receives prompt and guaranteed payment while the purchaser obtains a short-term CREDIT line. In brief, under this facility, a purchaser in country A of goods supplied by a firm in country B can arrange a letter of credit from his bank (the credit issuing bank) authorizing it to make payment to the supplier either through a branch of the bank in country B or, more usually, through a bank (the negotiating bank) holding the supplier's account. Under a contract of sale of goods this will be done on the presentation to the negotiating bank of documents stipulated in the letter of credit, such as the bill of lading, insurance policy, certificate of origin, etc. In the case of certain letters of credit relating to particular transactions and customers located in heavily indebted countries, a secondary market has developed to offset political as well as commercial risk. See EXPORTING.

**levels of hierarchy** see HIERARCHY.

**leverage** see CAPITAL GEARING.

**leveraged bid** see TAKEOVER BID.

**LGS** see LOAN GUARANTEE SCHEME.

**liability** a claim on the resources of an individual or business in respect of monies borrowed. A liability is thus a form of DEBT, for example a bank overdraft or LOAN, a building society MORTGAGE. See ASSET, BALANCE SHEET.

**LIBOR (London Interbank Offered Rate)** the INTEREST RATE on dollar and other foreign currency deposits at which larger banks are prepared to borrow and lend these currencies in the EUROCURRENCY MARKET. The LIBOR rates reflect market conditions for international funds, and are widely used by the banks as a basis for determining the interest rates charged on dollar and foreign currency loans to business customers.

**licence 1.** the assignment by one firm to another (exclusive licence) or a number of firms (non-exclusive licence) of the right to use its technology or distribution network or to produce its product. Similarly, the grant by the government to an authority (for example an airport) or firm of the rights to supply a particular product. Licences are contractual arrangements which are entered into usually for a specified period of time, with the licensee paying a lump sum payment and/or a royalty or fee for the rights assigned. For an innovating firm with limited financial resources of its own, licensing offers a means of obtaining extensive national and international sales potential (see FOREIGN MARKET SERVICING STRATEGY) and a quick return on its risk capital. The danger is that the firm, by providing actual and potential (long run) competitors with its know-how etc., will lose control of core technology and products to rival producers. To safeguard this and also to provide greater technological collaboration between firms working both in complementary and diverse areas, a *cross-licensing* arrangement may be established involving the reciprocal licensing of each other's products or technology.

**2.** a document issued by a licensing authority as a means of ensuring that persons or premises are 'fit and proper' for the activities in which they are engaged, for example, an investment adviser or premises for the consumption of alcoholic drink.

**3.** a document which shows proof of legal ownership (or entitlement) or compliance with a statutory or private requirement in which a fee is payable, for example a television licence issued by the government, or a private fishing licence.

See EXPORT LICENCE.

**Life Assurance and Unit Trust Regulatory Organization (LAUTRO)** see PERSONAL INVESTMENT AUTHORITY.

**life cycle** see PRODUCT LIFE CYCLE.

**life style** an individual's living pattern as expressed by his or her interests, values, activities and opinions. Life styles influence people's buying behaviour and thus the types of products they are likely to purchase. See SOCIOECONOMIC GROUP, BUYER BEHAVIOUR.

**LIFFE (London International Financial Futures Exchange)** see LONDON DERIVATIVES EXCHANGE.

**limited company (Ltd)** see JOINT-STOCK COMPANY.

**limited liability** an arrangement that limits the maximum LOSS which a SHAREHOLDER is liable for in the event of company failure to the SHARE CAPITAL which he originally subscribed.

The principle of limited liability limits a shareholder's maximum loss in the event of his company failing to the original share capital which he invested, no further claims by creditors against the shareholder's other assets being permitted. Once shareholders were protected in this way many more people were encouraged to invest in companies and JOINT-STOCK COMPANIES grew rapidly. To warn potential creditors that any claims by creditors will be limited in total to the amount of the company's share capital, such companies carry the term: 'Limited' (Ltd) or 'Public Limited Company' (Plc) after their names.

When a business is subject to *unlimited liability*, as is the case with SOLE PROPRIETORS and unlimited PARTNERSHIPS, the owners of the business are liable in full for the debts of the business if it fails. This may involve their losing not only the capital that they have put into the business, but also most of their personal assets.

When the directors of a joint-stock company continue trading after they should have known the company was insolvent (see INSOLVENCY), they can lose the protection of limited liability and become personally responsible for the firm's debts.

**limited-line strategy** a product line strategy which involves offering only a small number of variations of a product.
See PRODUCT RANGE. Contrast FULL-LINE STRATEGY.

**limiting factor** or **key factor** the critical constraint upon a firm's budgeted activity level. In most circumstances the limiting factor will be the amounts that the company can sell, but in certain cases the limiting factor might be shortage of production capacity, shortages of particular raw materials or the like. Here planning will be aimed at devising a sales programme which generates maximum profit from these limited resources. For example, Fig. 48 shows how a firm with limited production capacity might seek to maximize its CONTRIBUTION by concentrating upon production of the product which requires fewer direct labour hours to make. See BUDGET, BUDGETING, LINEAR PROGRAMMING.

**line and staff** an approach to structuring ORGANIZATIONS which distinguishes between those who are in the line or CHAIN OF COMMAND and are directly involved in the achievement of the

| | Chairs £ | Sofas £ |
|---|---|---|
| Selling price | 120 | 160 |
| Unit Variable Cost | 100 | 130 |
| | 20 | 30 |
| Direct labour hours per unit | 4 hours | 8 hours |
| Contribution per direct labour hour | £5 | £7.25 |

What 10,000 direct labour hours capacity can make:

| | | | |
|---|---|---|---|
| | 10,000 ÷ 4 | or | 10,000 ÷ 8 |
| | 2,500 units | or | 1,250 units |
| Contributions: | 2,500 units × £20 | or | 1,250 units × £30 |
| | £50,000 | or | £37,500 |

Fig. 48. **Limiting factor**. Contributions and constraints.

organization's primary goals (line), and those who provide advice or a supporting service to them (staff). Typically, staff functions include those such as management services and personnel. However, the distinction is often less clear cut in practice because staff functions may exercise authority on behalf of line managers or acquire informal power and authority of their own. In addition, there is usually a line of command within staff departments. See MANAGEMENT.

**linear programming** a technique for utilizing limited resources to meet a desired objective, such as minimizing cost or maximizing profit, where the resource limits are expressed as constraints.

For example, consider a firm making only two products, bookcases and chairs, and trying to decide how many of each to make. The company's output will be limited by the productive resources which it has available, and these are depicted graphically in Fig. 49 where output of bookcases is represented on the horizontal axis and output of chairs on the vertical axis. If the company has only 40 hours of machine time available each week, while a bookcase needs 2 hours of machine time to make and a chair 2 hours of machine time, then the maximum output with the available machine would be represented by line XY. If there were only 42 hours of labour available, and each bookcase needs 3 hours' work while each chair needs 1.5 hours' work, then the maximum output with the available labour force would be represented by line RT.

Fig. 49. **Linear programming.** Limitations on productive resources.

The area OXZT represents all feasible combinations of bookcases and chairs which can be produced with the limited machine-hours and man-hours available (the *feasible region*).

If each bookcase (b) sold makes a profit of £5, and each chair (c) £4, then in order to maximize profit the firm would seek to maximize output:

$$5b + 4c.$$

For example, in order to earn a profit of £60 the company could produce 12 bookcases or 15 chairs or some combination of the two, as represented by the broken line MP in Fig. 49. Combinations of bookcases and chairs corresponding to larger total profits can be represented by other lines such as LN, which are parallel to MP but further out from the origin O. The line LN represents the largest profit which the firm can earn with its available man-hours and machine-hours, since it is the highest broken line which just touches the resource constraints represented by the feasible region OXZT. The firm will therefore settle at point Z producing OV chairs per week and OW bookcases each week in order to maximize its profits from available resources.

Linear programming also provides information about the value of additional resources to a company. For example, it shows how much extra profit could be earned by increasing the number of machine-hours or man-hours available, and thus indicates the maximum amount which the company should pay for additional units of these resources. These maximum amounts which the company could afford to pay for additional resources without prejudicing profitability are called SHADOW PRICES of the machine-hour and man-hour resources.

Where a company produces more than two outputs, two-dimensional graphical analysis is impossible. However, an optimum combination of outputs can still be calculated using a similar reasoning process called the *simplex method*.

**line balancing** see PRODUCTION-LINE BALANCING.

**line manager** a manager who has direct AUTHORITY over other employees in the ORGANIZATION. They exercise authority down the CHAIN OF COMMAND shown in the ORGANIZATION CHART. Often the term is used to denote those managers who have direct authority over production or clerical employees at the base of the organization. See LINE AND STAFF, MANAGEMENT.

**line of balance (LOB) chart** a chart which combines information on agreed product DELIVERY DATES with data on the availability of components required to make the products. LOB charts are used in PRODUCTION SCHEDULING to ensure that the correct number of components are available at the appropriate times, so that final assembly of the product can be completed by its scheduled date in time to meet promised delivery dates.

**liquid assets** those CURRENT ASSETS which are held in the form of cash, or assets which can be quickly converted into cash, notably DEBTORS but not STOCK. A company's liquid current assets show how much it could quickly raise in cash to meet the immediate demands of its CREDITORS if they were all to press for prompt payment.

**liquidation** the process by which a JOINT-STOCK COMPANY'S existence as a legal entity ceases by the *winding-up* of the company. Such a process can be initiated at the behest of the CREDITORS where the company is insolvent (a compulsory winding-up), or by the company directors or SHAREHOLDERS, in which case it is known as a voluntary winding-up.

The person appointed as liquidator, either by the company

directors/shareholders or by the creditors, sells off the company's ASSETS for as much as they will realize. The proceeds of the sale are used to discharge any outstanding liabilities to the creditors of the company. If there are insufficient funds to pay all creditors (INSOLVENCY), preferential creditors are paid first (for example the INLAND REVENUE for tax due), then ordinary creditors pro rata. If there is a surplus after payment of all creditors this is distributed pro rata amongst the ordinary shareholders of the company.

See also LIMITED LIABILITY, SHAREHOLDERS, CAPITAL.

**liquidator** see LIQUIDATION, INSOLVENCY.

**liquidity** the possession by a person or business of a stock of monetary assets which can be used directly to finance the purchase of goods and services and capital assets. See MONEY, MONEY SUPPLY.

**liquidity ratio** see CURRENT RATIO.

**listed company** a public limited JOINT-STOCK COMPANY (Plc) whose shares are traded on the main STOCK MARKET. In the UK, to obtain a full listing on the main stock exchange a company is required to provide comprehensive information about its activities. Smaller companies unable or unwilling to provide the comprehensive information required for a full listing may seek to satisfy the less exacting information requirements of the UNLISTED SECURITIES MARKET and have their shares traded there. See QUOTED COMPANY.

**list price** the published PRICE of a good or service. The actual price paid by the buyer is often lower than this because suppliers are prepared to offer trade discounts for BULKBUYING.

**Lloyds (of London)** a corporation whose membership comprises a group of some 31,000 INSURANCE BROKERS and INSURANCE COMPANIES engaged in the UNDERWRITING of INSURANCE risks. Lloyds itself does not perform any underwriting business; its member brokers and insurers either act individually in arranging insurance cover for clients, or, in the case of particular types of insurance risk, operate together on a consortium or syndicated basis. What Lloyds does is to provide a forum for organizing syndicated insurance groupings and to validate the integrity of its members in the eyes of the public (i.e. members of Lloyds are expected to conduct their business in a fair and honest way and to deposit funds with it as a surety).

**load** the work which is assigned to a work station (machine or operative) during a specified period of time. See PRODUCTION-LINE BALANCING.

**loading** the balancing out of work loads over the available CAPACITY of a machine or item of equipment. Effective machine loading seeks to identify and avoid over- or under-loaded machines or equipment. See PRODUCTION-LINE BALANCING.

**loan** the advance of a specified sum of MONEY to a person or business (the BORROWER) by other persons or businesses, or more particularly by a specialist financial institution (the LENDER) which makes its profits from the INTEREST charged on loans. The provision of loans by COMMERCIAL BANKS, FINANCE HOUSES, BUILDING SOCIETIES etc. is an important source of CREDIT in the economy, serving to underpin a substantial amount of spending on current consumption and the acquisition of personal and business assets.

Loans may be advanced on an *unsecured* or *secured* basis; in the latter case the lender requires the borrower to offer some form of COLLATERAL SECURITY (for example property deeds) which the lender may retain in the event of the borrower defaulting on the repayment of the loan.

See BANK LOAN, INSTALMENT CREDIT, MORTGAGE, LOAN STOCK, DEBENTURE, LOAN GUARANTEE SCHEME, INTEREST RATE, SOFT LOAN.

**loan capital** or **debt capital** the money employed in a company that has been borrowed from external sources for fixed periods of time by the issue of fixed–interest financial securities such as DEBENTURES. The providers of loan capital do not normally share in the profits of the company but are rewarded by means of regular INTEREST payments which must be paid under the terms of the loan contract. Interest payments are a business expense which must be charged against revenues in calculating profits. See SHARE CAPITAL, BALANCE SHEET, CAPITAL GEARING.

**Loan Guarantee Scheme (LGS)** a facility for encouraging the COMMERCIAL BANKS to provide LOAN finance to small firms who, because of the high risk involved or lack of collateral, are unable to obtain conventional loans. Under the scheme, the DEPARTMENT OF TRADE AND INDUSTRY guarantees repayment to the bank of (currently) 70% of the loan on default in return for an annual premium of 2.5% on the guaranteed portion of the loan.

**LOB** see LINE OF BALANCE.

**local area network (LAN)** a network of PERSONAL COMPUTERS used to undertake routine data processing functions in a business. Over the years these networks have become more complex and to this extent a 'system crash' or failure can be highly disruptive and expensive. Old-style PC networks were device-sharing facilities giving people access to a departmental printer or fax. If they went down, people could still carry on working. In modern networks, however, people use PCs to log on to the network for all their software, including word processing and databases, and to access information held on software in other departments.

See INFORMATION MANAGEMENT.

**local content rule** or **rule of origin** the stipulation by a country that for a product to qualify as an authentic domestically manufactured product (that is, originating in that country) the product must be manufactured predominantly from locally supplied as opposed to imported components. Local content rules are used by governments mainly to prevent the operation of so called 'screwdriver' plants (plants producing final products from mainly imported components) established to circumvent TARIFFS, QUOTAS and ANTI-DUMPING DUTIES imposed on imported final products.

The application of local content rules poses two particular measurement issues:

(a) the proportion of the final product that is to be sourced domestically (see SOURCING) for the product to qualify as a locally produced one. The chosen cut-off point is inevitably arbitrary and often subject to political manipulation, i.e. governments may use local content rules to discriminate against imports as a form of PROTECTIONISM;

(b) the extent of the local content that is to be measured; for example, either the *number* of components or their *value* might form the basis of measurement. Using the number alone as a basis is unsatisfactory because a large number of minor components might be supplied locally (superficially indicating a high proportion of local content) whereas only a few but major components are imported. For this reason many countries, including the UK, prefer a VALUE-ADDED criterion, measuring the proportion of the product's ex-factory price which is accounted for by locally produced and imported components, respectively.

See DUMPING, CERTIFICATE OF ORIGIN.

**Local Enterprise Company (LEC)** the Scottish equivalent of the TRAINING AND ENTERPRISE COUNCILS found in England and Wales. See also TRAINING.

**local tax** a TAX on property or persons by local authorities/councils which, together with central government grants, is used to finance the provision of various local services. Before 1990, in the UK, *rates* were levied on eligible properties; between April 1990 (April 1989 in Scotland) and April 1993 a *community charge* (*poll tax*) was levied on eligible persons; since April 1993 a *council tax* has been levied on eligible properties. The current means of raising local taxes, the council tax, is based on the rateable value of local properties, the amount payable in the case of residential dwellings being adjusted to take into account such things as the number of people living in the property, their incomes, and any disabilities they suffer.

See UNIFORM BUSINESS RATE.

**lock-out** see INDUSTRIAL ACTION.

**logistics** the functions involved in moving raw materials and components into the firm, the movement of work-in-progress and stocks within the firm and the movement of finished products out of the firm.

See MATERIALS MANAGEMENT, MATERIALS REQUIREMENT PLANNING, STOCK CONTROL, DISTRIBUTION, MARKETING LOGISTICS.

**logo** a company name or BRAND NAME written or illustrated in a distinctive way to heighten customers' recognition of the company or product concerned. See BRAND MARK.

**log on** the procedure for gaining access to a COMPUTER.

**London Interbank Offered Rate** see LIBOR.

**London International Financial Futures Exchange (LIFFE)** a FORWARD MARKET which is engaged in the buying and selling of FINANCIAL SECURITIES and COMMODITIES. LIFFE's operations have been expanded by the absorption of two other exchanges, the London Traded Option Market in 1990 and the London Commodity Market in 1995. See FINANCIAL SERVICES ACT 1986.

**London International Stock Exchange** see STOCK MARKET.

**London Metal Exchange** see COMMODITY MARKET.

**London Traded Option Market (LTOM)** see LONDON DER-IVATIVES EXCHANGE.

**long position** a situation in which a dealer or MARKET MAKER in a particular COMMODITY, FINANCIAL SECURITY or FOREIGN CURRENCY is selling less than he is buying, so that his working stock of the item increases (i.e. becomes 'long').

**Longs** BONDS, DEBENTURES and PREFERENCE SHARES which have a redemption date of 15 years or more.

**long-term capital employed** or **net worth** any long-term funds employed in a firm. For companies this takes the form of SHAREHOLDERS' CAPITAL EMPLOYED plus long-term loans such as DEBENTURES.

**long term debt** see LOAN CAPITAL.

**loss** the shortfall between a firm's sales revenues received from the sale of its products and the total costs incurred in producing the firm's output (see BREAK-EVEN ANALYSIS). Losses may be of a temporary nature occasioned by, for example, a downturn in demand (see BUSINESS CYCLE) or due to an exceptional level of expenditures (such as the launch of a series of new products). Short-term losses are usually financed by a firm running down its RESERVES or by an increase in borrowings. Losses which are sustained over time typically arise from a firm's poor competitive position in a market (see COMPETITIVE ADVANTAGE), and unless competitiveness can be restored market exit or DIVESTMENT may be the only practical way of remedying the situation. See MARKET SYSTEM.

**loss leading** the practice whereby a RETAILER sells a manufacturer's branded product at a PRICE below bought-in cost. Loss leading is used by retailers to attract customers into their stores in the hope that buyers will then purchase a selection of full-price products in addition to cut-price items, thus making a profit on the purchases taken as a whole. In the short run, manufacturers of products subjected to loss leading may well benefit from increased sales and profits (i.e. it is the retailer, not the manufacturer, who incurs the loss), but over the longer term the practice may undermine the product's price-quality reputation with consumers. In the UK, under the RESALE PRICE ACTS, manufacturers can take court action to stop retailers using their products as loss leaders.

**lot size** see BATCH SIZE.

**low geared** see CAPITAL GEARING.

**low pay** wages or salaries that are considered to be low relative to the average level of PAY or relative to needs. Official definitions tend to adopt the latter approach. Low pay is viewed as income that is insufficient to meet officially defined needs and hence can be supplemented by various state benefits (for example social security). Many argue, however, that poverty or impoverished lifestyle extends beyond the group able to claim such benefits, and therefore they prefer a relative definition. In the past the *lowest decile* of male earnings has been used as a yardstick, but increasingly in the UK the Council of Europe's 'decency threshold' of *two-thirds of median pay* has been adopted as a definition by those concerned to combat low pay.

Low pay, however defined, tends to be concentrated amongst certain social groups and industries. It is concentrated amongst the female workforce, and is especially prevalent in certain service industries, such as hotel and catering and hairdressing, and in such primary industries as agriculture. Some recent reports have indicated that nearly half the UK's employed adult workforce is receiving pay that falls below the decency threshold.

Opinions differ on how to tackle low pay. Some argue that attention should be focused on supply-side factors such as education and training. Others maintain that a statutory minimum wage is the answer. Although this is found in most European Union/Community countries it has not found favour with UK policy-makers. It has been argued that it would drive firms' costs up, causing bankruptcies and unemployment. Trade unions too have been wary of a minimum wage in the past because of their dislike of governmental interference in pay determination, but this attitude seems to be changing. Until recently a selective statutory minimum wage system was in operation in the UK. The rates of pay stipulated by WAGES COUNCILS for certain occupations were legally binding. Wages Councils, however, were abolished in 1993.

See DISCRIMINATION.

**Ltd (limited company)** see JOINT-STOCK COMPANY.
**LTOM** see LONDON DERIVATIVES EXCHANGE.

# M

**Maastricht Treaty 1991** an agreement between member countries of the EUROPEAN UNION which aims to provide for a closer unification of the economic and political systems of member countries. The Treaty contains a number of elements, in particular, economic and monetary harmonization (building on the existing frameworks of the EUROPEAN COMMUNITY), political unification in such areas as foreign policy and defence and greater co-operation in areas such as law enforcement and immigration.

In the case of economic and monetary union the Treaty proposes a three-stage plan for the irrevocable change to a single currency, the 'Euro'. The plan (arising from the 'Delors proposals') makes participation in the exchange rate mechanism of the EUROPEAN MONETARY SYSTEM a pre-requisite for all countries participating in the first stage (1991-94). In the second transitional stage, which started in 1994, a *European Monetary Institute* was created, as the forerunner to a European CENTRAL BANK. In 1996, the Institute and the European Commission will report on the fitness of each country for inclusion in the ECU zone, based on stiff criteria of 'economic convergence', which includes low inflation rates and under 3% for government debt ratios.

The third stage, locking all currencies together and placing monetary policy under the control of an independent central bank, will begin if, by 1996, a majority of seven members have met the convergence criteria and vote to decide on a starting date. Otherwise, the central bank will begin work in 1998 and the third stage will start on 1 January 1999.

See SUBSIDIARITY, SOCIAL CHAPTER.

**machine bureaucracy** an ORGANIZATION characterised by a high reliance on rules to govern how its members perform their jobs and interact with each other. Organizations of this type are usually found in stable environments. See MECHANIS-

TIC AND ORGANISMIC.

**machine code** COMPUTER instructions written as a form of zero/one combinations which the computer can execute by activating off/on electrical pulses. All 'higher level' computer program languages like BASIC or COBOL have to be translated into machine code for use in a computer.

**machine hour rate** a COST RATE which is used in ABSORPTION COSTING to charge the OVERHEADS of a department or COST CENTRE in the cost of a product or job. It is usually used for those departments or cost centres which are highly mechanized, and is computed by dividing the budgeted overheads which have been assigned to the department or cost centre by the estimated total number of machine hours for the period, to arrive at the rate per machine hour. The overhead charge for any product or job will depend upon the number of machine hours required for its production.

See also ABSORPTION.

**machine register** see PLANT REGISTER.

**machinery 1.** items of capital such as a lathe or ROBOT welder which are used in production. See PLANT, EQUIPMENT, CAPITAL STOCK, FIXED ASSET.

**2.** procedures for the conduct of negotiations between trade unions and management and the settlement of disputes. See PROCEDURAL AGREEMENT, GRIEVANCE PROCEDURE, DISPUTES PROCEDURE.

**machine utilization** the extent to which the productive capacity of a machine is used during a specified period of time. Machine utilization can be expressed as a percentage, for example:

$$\frac{\text{machine hours used}}{\text{total machine hours available}} \times 100$$

In order to maximize machine utilization, firms must examine IDLE TIME records to find out why machine time is being lost and take steps to remedy the situation.

**mail order** a DIRECT MARKETING means of retailing products to consumers through the post. Mail order firms supply catalogues to prospective customers who either themselves or through agents make purchases for delivery to their homes.

Mail order concerns typically combine wholesaling (stocking large quantities of products and breaking bulk) and retailing functions, supplying customers from a central warehouse. Such firms compete mainly by offering customers convenience (i.e. home shopping) and by the provision of INSTALMENT CREDIT facilities on purchases. Mail order methods may also be used to sell industrial products. See RETAILER, WHOLESALER, DISTRIBUTION CHANNEL.

**mainframe** a large-scale COMPUTER with big data-storage facilities which is often accessible simultaneously from many terminals. Mainframe computers are used by large data-processing departments in businesses for sales and purchase ledger record-keeping, etc.

As MICROCOMPUTERS and MINICOMPUTERS become more powerful in terms of data-processing, speed and data-storage capacity, the distinction between the three types of computer has become blurred.

**mainstream corporation tax** see CORPORATION TAX.

**maintainability** the ability of a product or component to be kept in a state in which it can perform its required function when maintained.

See MAINTENANCE.

**maintenance** the management process of repairing and maintaining buildings, plant, machinery and equipment to avoid breakdowns and disruption to production.

Effective maintenance requires the firm to draw up appropriate plans and timetables, taking into account the frequency of maintenance required, available personnel, ordering and stocking of spare parts etc.

The maintenance function provides an important service to production, marketing and administration departments. Routine maintenance within a firm is often undertaken by the firm's own maintenance department, while major refurbishment of machines may be contracted to specialist outside firms.

See PREVENTIVE MAINTENANCE, INSPECTION, WORK-BASED MAINTENANCE, TIME-BASED MAINTENANCE, PRODUCTION MANAGEMENT.

**make for stock** see PRODUCTION SCHEDULING.

**make-or-buy decision** the strategic choice confronting the firm as to whether it purchases its raw materials and components requirements from outside suppliers or produces them for itself as part of a vertically-integrated operation (see VERTICAL INTEGRATION). The main factors influencing this decision are the relative costs and risks involved. The main advantage of outside suppliers who specialize in the production of an input and produce for a large number of customers (not just one as in the case of self supply), is that they are able to benefit from the lower costs associated with economies of large-scale operations (see ECONOMIES OF SCALE). Thus, it may be cheaper to a user to buy in the input rather than to produce it internally; the more so if the firm has access to a number of supply sources (both domestic and international) and can take full advantage of price competition between them. Set against this are the risks in certain cases of over-dependency on particular suppliers, leading to possible problems of overcharging and disruptions to the firm's production schedules arising from supply shortages, failure to meet delivery times, and inputs lacking the desired degree of quality or precision. See SOURCING, PURCHASING.

**make to order** see PRODUCTION SCHEDULING.

**management** the process of organizing and directing human and physical resources within an ORGANIZATION so as to meet defined objectives. The key management roles are:

(a) *planning* how to carry out the various activities which are required to achieve the objective. This involves establishing an action programme (see BUSINESS PLAN) and an appropriate organization structure within which tasks can be subdivided (for example into production, personnel, marketing and finance); RESPONSIBILITY for them delegated; and PAY and reward systems instituted (see JOB DESIGN AND REDESIGN, WORK ORGANIZATION);

(b) CONTROL, by comparing current performance with that planned in order to monitor progress of the work. Such comparisons reveal where additional resources may be needed to achieve desired performance or when plans may need to be modified in the light of experience;

(c) COORDINATION of the tasks being undertaken, which involves synchronizing and balancing work loads and ensuring effective collaboration between the various DEPARTMENTS and GROUPS within the organization;

(d) MOTIVATION of the members of the organization, encouraging them to work effectively in performing their assigned task.

CLASSICAL MANAGEMENT THEORY portrayed management as a rational activity largely concerned with establishing routines and procedures for administering the work. More recently this emphasis has been questioned in a number of respects. Research has shown that much of the manager's working day is spent on tasks other than those suggested in this approach, for example attending retirement presentations, responding to telephone enquiries etc. Much of the manager's job involves ad hoc reactions to events. Other research has shown that managers 'muddle through', aiming at achieving satisfactory rather than optimum outcomes (see SATISFICING).

Recent writing on management has emphasized the LEADERSHIP aspect of the managerial function. The key issue here concerns the means by which managers can achieve effective performance from their subordinates. Two basic approaches are identified in the literature (on MANAGEMENT STYLE):

(a) *task orientation*, where managers' relationship with their subordinates is essentially directive, being primarily focused on getting the job done;

(b) *people orientation*, where managers show a greater concern for their subordinates' well-being, on the grounds that a contented workforce performs effectively.

Some believe that good leaders are born with certain personal qualities whilst others believe that these can be instilled through MANAGEMENT DEVELOPMENT. Whatever perspective is taken it should be remembered that leadership involves more than a leader: it also involves subordinates and a context. Good leadership is that which produces appropriate behaviour from others in particular situations.

See ORGANIZATIONAL ANALYSIS, BOARD OF DIRECTORS.

**management accounting** any accounting activities geared to the preparation of information for managers to help them plan and control a company's operations. Management accounts generally provide more detailed information than financial accounts; for example, breaking down revenues and costs between different products, factories or departments to provide comparative data and to help reveal profitable and unprofitable activities. Management accounts also tend to provide information about performance more frequently than financial accounts, with monthly or even weekly management accounts rather than annual financial accounts, to give managers prompt feedback and to enable them to act quickly to check inefficiencies. Management accounts are geared to estimates of future costs and revenues rather than simply reporting past revenues and costs as financial accounts do, thereby providing valuable management information for preparing accurate estimates and tenders and for use in negotiating price changes.

Fig. 50 shows how more detailed analysis of revenues and costs can provide more useful information than total information as reported in the PROFIT-AND-LOSS ACCOUNT.

Compare FINANCIAL ACCOUNTING. See also BUDGETING.

| | Profit-&-Loss Account Total £ | Beds £ | Divans £ | Suites £ |
|---|---|---|---|---|
| Sales | 300,000 | 190,000 | 70,000 | 40,000 |
| less costs | 274,000 | 178,000 | 52,000 | 44,000 |
| Profit (loss) | 26,000 | 12,000 | 18,000 | (4,000) |
| Profit as % of sales | 8.6% | 6.3% | 25.7% | Zero |

Fig. 50. **Management accounting.** Trading results: Y Company Plc for year ending 19xx.

**management buy-in** the TAKEOVER of a company, or of a division of a company, by a small group of shareholders (often ex-managers of the company) who then form the nucleus of a new management team to run the company or division. As with a MANAGEMENT BUY-OUT (the takeover of a company by its *existing* management) management buy-ins are often financed by the issue of loan capital subscribed by financial institutions such as merchant banks and venture capital specialists. See JUNK BOND/MEZZANINE DEBT.

**management buy-out** the TAKEOVER of a firm, or of a division of a firm, by its existing management team from, in the former case, the shareholders of the firm, or in the latter case, the firm's main board of directors subject to shareholder approval. The purchase of a division of a diversified firm (see DIVERSIFICATION) by its management is a form of DIVESTMENT which can be beneficial to both parties. The disposer's motive is usually to get out of a particular activity which is no longer considered to fit in with its strategic plans for developing the business, and to use the monies released to strengthen its activities or acquire new businesses. From the buyer's point of view, there is the challenge of running one's own business and the potential for making a greater success of an activity which perhaps, because of insufficient support from above in its divisional form, had previously been underperforming. The rekindling of entrepreneurship in the hands of owner-managers is seen to be a key advantage of a management buy-out.

A critical factor in the success of a management buy-out, apart from the obvious need for managerial competence (and a little luck!) is the price paid for the business and the related financial package for acquiring it. The members of the management team will provide a percentage of the purchase price from their own personal funds and own a large amount of the SHARE CAPITAL, with the balance of funds often being provided by LOANS from merchant banks and venture capital specialists. Alternatively, the balance can be obtained by selling shares to the workforce either directly, or indirectly to a trust, as part of an EMPLOYEE SHARE OWNERSHIP PLAN. One advantage of this solution is that it enables the management team to avoid an overdependency on outside interests and unrealistic CAPITAL GEARING levels.

See JUNK BOND, MANAGEMENT BUY-IN, DEMERGER, BUSINESS STRATEGY, VENTURE CAPITAL.

**management by exception** a system whereby only the important variations from plan are brought to management attention. This avoids managers becoming too bogged down with paperwork containing unimportant detail. See VARIANCE ANALYSIS.

**management by objectives (MBO)** an approach to MANAGEMENT, popularized by American management writer Peter Drucker (1909–  ), which emphasizes the need for clear organizational objectives which can be incorporated in the actions of individual managers. In Drucker's view organizations have a multiplicity of objectives; these should be clarified and prioritized so that all managers understand what the most important goals of the organization are. Then individual managers should set objectives for themselves, in conjunction with their superiors, which will assist in meeting organizational goals. This approach was popular in the 1960s and 1970s but subsequently fell from favour because all too often objectives were *imposed* on managers rather than generated by them, and because the extent to which objectives were met was often used simply to evaluate managers rather than as a basis to improve performance. Genuine commitment was difficult to engender in these circumstances. This approach to management has made a comeback recently with the emphasis attached to objective-setting in the PERFORMANCE APPRAISAL process.

**management by walking around (MBWA)** an approach to MANAGEMENT which emphasizes the value of observing what goes on in the ORGANIZATION and of displaying a high profile to subordinates. In this model, good managers are those who spend much of their time discussing work issues with colleagues and subordinates, rather than those who rely on issuing formal instructions from the seclusion of their offices. By wandering around in this way the manager will come to recognize and understand the informal relationships and activities that can both facilitate and obstruct the achievement of organizational goals. A manager who adopts this approach will thus be well placed to achieve organizational change. MBWA can be seen as a derivative of HUMAN RELATIONS philosophy in that it stresses the importance of informal relationships, and assumes that managerial visibility on the shop floor will be favourably interpreted and received by subordinates as an expression of managerial interest in them, thereby leading to good job performance. Compare MANAGEMENT BY OBJECTIVES.

**Management Charter** an initiative in the UK by the Council for Management Education and Development to create a national qualification of Chartered Manager. Managers thus qualified would become PROFESSIONALS like accountants or lawyers. Professionalization would require identification of the core skills or 'competencies' of management, and a system of training and examination in these areas. Critics of this proposal have argued that management is so diverse that it is difficult to identify a core of competencies that are relevant to all managers. Furthermore certain management skills, such as those relating to managing people, are not easily translatable into a simple set of skills that can be assessed by formal examination. See MANAGEMENT DEVELOPMENT.

**management consultant** a person or firm which specializes in advising companies and other organizations on matters relating to their business strategy, organizational structure and the management of operations in functional areas such as marketing and production. Management consultants are employed to examine a company's current business practices and management, with a view to making recommendations for change aimed at improving efficiency and profitability. Unlike 'insiders', often with a vested interest in maintaining the status quo, the use of an independent team of consultants can provide an objective and detached assessment of what a firm needs to do in order to strengthen its organization.

**management development** the preparation of managers for future work roles. It can have two components:

(a) The passing of *specific* skills to managers using programmes of TRAINING; and

(b) the *general* development of abilities thought to be useful to managers such as awareness, problem solving, etc.

Whilst the former can be straightforward, the latter is usually more difficult because development of this kind is not very tangible, therefore it is difficult to evaluate the worth of development programmes.

The core of most management development programmes is short courses, run either in-house or by consultants, on such topics as managing difficult employees and interpreting customer needs. Usually selection of participants will be done by managers' superiors, possibly as a result of development needs identified during PERFORMANCE APPRAISAL. In some cases, however, courses are offered on a cafeteria basis, i.e. individuals choose what they think they need most. A more sustained programme of individual development can be had by enrolling for a Master in Business Administration course at a university or polytechnic.

One type of course, less popular now than in the 1970s, is that involving 'T groups' or 'sensitivity training'. Over a period of days participants meet in a group and explore the patterns of interaction between group members. Its rationale is that it can heighten awareness of others and understanding of oneself, thereby promoting a more perceptive approach to management. Many individuals, however, find this experience unpleasant as it can raise awkward truths which many would prefer left unstated.

Partly because of doubts about the effectiveness of the class-room approach to development, *action learning* has become popular in recent years. Here managers are presented with real problems, possibly arising in an organization other than their own. The theory is that concentration on dealing with these will enhance problem-solving abilities.

Another approach currently popular is that of mentoring. Here a junior manager is paired with an experienced and successful manager (mentor) who acts as a role model. The trainee is to learn good management by example, reviewing his or her progress in regular meetings with the mentor. The benefit claimed of mentoring is that it facilitates development of personal qualities and managerial skills which cannot easily be taught by formal training. For mentoring to be successful it is essential that a good personal relationship is established and that those responsible for management development fully appreciate which qualities are desirable and can discover which managers possess them.

Many UK organizations do not devote enough resources to development. The reasons for this include the difficulties of evaluating its benefits and the reluctance of organizations to release individuals from their normal duties to participate in development programmes. Those involved in the MANAGEMENT CHARTER initiative have proposed that this be rectified by developing a CODE OF PRACTICE establishing minimum standards of management development. All organizations subscribing to the Charter would abide by the proposed code.

**management–employee buy-out** a MANAGEMENT BUY-OUT where non-managerial employees also participate in the buy-out either directly by buying equity or loaning capital or indirectly via an EMPLOYEE SHARE OWNERSHIP PLAN.

**management information system** a procedure which is concerned with getting appropriate information to managers as and when they need it.

See INFORMATION MANAGEMENT.

**management style 1.** the general character of management's approach to INDUSTRIAL RELATIONS. The starting point for considering management style is usually the contrast between two frames of reference (i.e. perspectives) concerning industrial relations:

(a) *unitary frame of reference*, where employee and managerial interests are believed to be the same, and hence TRADE UNIONS are viewed as illegitimate. They are seen as trouble-makers who provoke CONFLICT where no real conflict exists. Those subscribing to this philosophy often portray the organization as a team where each member is dependent on the others in the team. There is also usually a strong emphasis on management's prerogative of taking decisions, justified on the basis that they are working for the good of all in the organization;

(b) *pluralist frame of reference*, where it is accepted that employees' interests may differ from those of management or the organization on occasion, and that trade unions are a legitimate expression of this. It is necessary to create procedures for resolving these differences so that conflict, which is damaging to all, can be avoided. Research has shown that in the UK most managers adopt a pluralist approach as a recognition of the reality of industrial relations, rather than as a philosophy to which they positively subscribe. See PLURALISM.

These frames of reference are embodied in contrasting management styles. Early analysis suggested that there were two distinct styles corresponding to these frames of reference. Now industrial relations research indicates that a greater number of styles can be discerned:

(a) *traditionalist*, where the unitary frame of reference is displayed in open and aggressive hostility to trade unions. This style is often found in small companies;

(b) *sophisticated paternalist*, where union avoidance is achieved through use of sophisticated PERSONNEL MANAGEMENT and HUMAN RELATIONS policies rather than simple aggression against unions;

(c) *sophisticated moderns*, i.e.

(i) *constitutionalists*, where unions are recognized, and the rights and obligations of management and unions are clearly defined in a PROCEDURAL AGREEMENT; and

(ii) *consultors*, where unions are recognized but management prefer not to codify everything in a formal agreement. Great emphasis is placed on CONSULTATION.

(d) *standard modern*, where management's approach is essentially reactive rather than in accordance with any clear strategy or philosophy. This is perhaps the most common approach in UK manufacturing industry.

Although the notion of industrial relations style can be criticized for a lack of clarity – it is an amalgam of philosophies, statements, policies and actions – it is useful as a shorthand term to designate clusters of attributes which can be found in reality.

**2.** (in ORGANIZATIONAL ANALYSIS) the character of LEADERSHIP and MANAGEMENT. In the literature, management style refers to two different, though closely related phenomena: the leadership styles of individual managers and the prevailing style or CULTURE of the organization. In the former a basic distinction is made between *concern for production* and *concern for people*, exemplified on the one hand by the autocratic, task-centred approach of SCIENTIFIC MANAGEMENT and on the other by the concern for employee welfare found in HUMAN RELATIONS. In recent writing on leadership these concepts have been considered in relation to the situation in which leadership is exercised, the characteristics of those to be led, and the relationship to managerial effectiveness. The underlying distinction is also found in analysis of collective management style. The best known example is Douglas McGregor's (1906–64) THEORY X AND Y. In Theory X approaches, emphasis is placed on coercion to get the task done, whilst in Theory Y organizations, employees are allowed greater freedom on the grounds that this will lead to better job performance. A more sophisticated variant was developed by Rensis Likert (1903–81). He discerned four styles or systems of management:

(a) *exploitative autocratic*, where decision-making is autocratic and where employee compliance is achieved through coercion;

(b) *benevolent authoritative*, where decision-making is still largely centralized but managers appear to take some note of employee views and interests;

(c) *consultative*, where managers seek EMPLOYEE INVOLVEMENT but nevertheless still take the lead in policy formulation and decision-making;

(d) *democratic*, where there is some genuine devolution of decision-making to subordinates, especially in relation to job performance (see JOB DESIGN AND REDESIGN).

Likert believed that in the long run the democratic style would be most effective because it would reduce job dissatisfaction and build up employee commitment. As in industrial relations analysis, notions of style such as Likert's seem to correspond with distinct organizational types. Similarly, there is the problem that they can be somewhat imprecise in analytical terms. See NEO-HUMAN RELATIONS.

**managerial grid** see LEADERSHIP.

**manpower planning** the process of determining the demand and supply of labour to ensure that the organization (or national economy) has the right people with the right skills at the right time. The starting point for manpower planning is consideration of the demand for labour required by the organization. Then a stocks and flows analysis should be undertaken:

(a) *stocks*, the number of existing staff and their profits in terms of age, skills etc.;

(b) *flows*, the movement of people through the organization, especially those out of the organization and those within the organization, for example promotions, transfers, etc.

By using wastage analysis (see LABOUR TURNOVER) it should be possible to forecast what the employment numbers and the profile of the workforce will be in the future. Any gap between this and the labour requirements of the business strategy will need to be filled by RECRUITMENT AND SELECTION of new staff, TRAINING etc.

Manpower planning fell into some degree of disrepute during the early 1980s because the future was viewed as so uncertain that reliable forecasts were difficult to make. However, some planning is better than none and generally speaking those organizations which undertake some measure of planning are better situated to respond to future developments than those which do not. The shortage of school leavers in the UK in the early 1990s and the need to find ways of covering potential shortfalls in employee numbers has given a renewed respectability to manpower planning. Sophisticated manpower planning does not concentrate exclusively on the future, however. It aims to identify weaknesses in and upgrade the quality of the current workforce.

**Manpower Services Commission** see TRAINING.

**manual worker** see WORKER.

**manufacturer** see PRODUCER.

**manufacturing account** an accounting statement which summarizes the main items of manufacturing cost with a view to determining the cost of finished goods manufactured. The cost of finished goods manufactured can then be entered in the PROFIT-AND-LOSS ACCOUNT as the equivalent of purchases for a purely trading company, in order to determine the cost of goods sold and gross profit. Fig. 51 shows a typical manufacturing account.

| | | £ | £ |
|---|---|---|---|
| Raw Materials used: | opening stock | 100,000 | |
| | add purchases | 330,000 | |
| | less closing stock | 130,000 | 300,000 |
| direct labour | | | 200,000 |
| direct cost | | | 500,000 |
| factory overheads | | | 100,000 |
| total manufacturing cost: | | | 600,000 |
| add opening work in progress | | 60,000 | |
| less closing work in progress | | 110,000 | (50,000) |
| cost of finished goods manufactured | | | 550,000 |

Fig. 51. **Manufacturing account**. Manufacturing account of Y Company for year ending 19xx.

**manufacturing cycle** see CYCLE TIME.

**manufacturing resource planning (MRP II)** a computer-based PRODUCTION planning system which integrates *all* the resource requirements of a firm, including not only the control of raw materials and components (the central concern of MATERIALS REQUIREMENTS PLANNING – MRP) but also labour, machines and other resource needs. See PRODUCTION MANAGEMENT.

**Manufacturing, Science and Finance Union (MSF)** a UK TRADE UNION representing technical and professional employees across a range of industries, including the health service. It was formed out of a merger of the Association of Scientific, Technical and Managerial Staffs (ASTMS) and the Technical and Supervisory Section (TASS) of the Amalgamated Union of Engineering Workers (AUEW) in 1988. It has about 480,000 members and is currently the UK's fifth largest union.

**margin** the difference between selling price and cost price of a PRODUCT or FINANCIAL SECURITY. See PROFIT MARGIN, SPREAD.

**marginal cost** the extra cost that is incurred by a firm in increasing OUTPUT by one unit. Given that FIXED COSTS do not vary with output, marginal costs are entirely marginal VARIABLE COSTS. Marginal cost generally includes the DIRECT MATER-

IALS and DIRECT LABOUR COST of a product along with VARIABLE OVERHEADS. See MARGINAL REVENUE.

**marginal costing** a system of product COSTING which assigns variable materials and labour costs to units of product manufactured but which does not assign fixed OVERHEAD costs to products. Fig. 52 shows an illustration of marginal costing.

|  | TOTAL £ | Tables £ | Chairs £ | Stools £ |
|---|---|---|---|---|
| Sales | 500 | 200 | 200 | 100 |
| Material cost | 250 | 100 | 75 | 75 |
| Wages | 100 | 35 | 50 | 15 |
| VARIABLE COST | 350 | 135 | 125 | 90 |
| CONTRIBUTION | 150 | 65 | 75 | 100 |
| FIXED COSTS | 100 | | | |
| PROFIT (LOSS) | 50 | | | |
| | | | | |
| Contribution: Sales % | 30% | 32% | 37% | 10% |
| Contribution per £ wages | £1.50 | £1.90 | £1.50 | £0.70 |
| Contribution per £ mat | £0.60 | £0.70 | £1.00 | £0.10 |

Fig. 52. **Marginal costing.** A typical example.

With marginal costing, work in progress and finished goods stocks are valued at direct materials and direct labour costs only, and fixed overhead costs are charged as a single block against revenues in the period when they are incurred. By contrast, with ABSORPTION COSTING fixed overhead costs are included in the value of work in progress and finished goods stock.

See CONTRIBUTION, BREAK-EVEN.

**marginal-cost pricing** see COST-BASED PRICING.

**marginal revenue** the extra revenue that is obtained by a firm from the sale of additional units of product. If firms are profit maximizers they will seek to equate marginal revenue with MARGINAL COST to establish that price output/sales combination which yields an optimal return.

See BUSINESS OBJECTIVE.

**market** an exchange mechanism which brings together the sellers and buyers of a product. Markets, in practice, embrace a number of product, spatial and physical dimensions. In terms of product, a market can be defined as consisting of a group of goods or services which are viewed as *substitute* products by buyers. Thus, from a MARKETING point of view, womens' shoes and mens' shoes would be represented as constituting separate markets, that is, markets catering for the needs of different buyers (see MARKET SEGMENTATION).

Spatially, a market may be local, regional, national or international in scope, depending on such considerations as transport costs, product characteristics and the homogeneity of buyer tastes. For example, because of a high ratio of transport costs to value added, cement and plasterboard markets tend to be localized. Likewise, Bavarian beer caters for a specialized regional taste, while Coca Cola, by contrast, is sold worldwide as a global brand.

Physically, seller and buyer exchanges may be transacted in a well-defined market place (for example a local fish market or wool exchange), or in a much more amorphous way (for example the buying and selling of stocks and shares by telephone through a nexus of international dealing offices). Finally, in some markets sellers deal directly with final buyers, while in others transactions are conducted through a chain of intermediaries such as wholesalers and retailers, brokers and banks.

Markets constitute the battlegrounds of business. Corporate success depends fundamentally on identifying and exploiting positions of COMPETITIVE ADVANTAGE which requires the effective application of appropriate strategies of PRODUCTION, MARKETING, etc.

See COMMODITY MARKET, MONEY MARKET, STOCK MARKET, SPOT MARKET, FORWARD MARKET, INDUSTRY, MARKET STRUCTURE, MARKET SYSTEM, EQUILIBRIUM MARKET PRICE.

**market capitalization** the total value of a company's ISSUED SHARE CAPITAL as determined by its current share price on the STOCK MARKET.

**market challengers** the sellers of a product who rank second, third etc. in terms of MARKET SHARE and are in a close position to challenge the current MARKET LEADER. However, they may choose not to attack the market leader to increase their own market share, but may merely seek to maintain their existing market position by passively following the market leader's product, pricing and promotional strategies.

**market channel** see DISTRIBUTION CHANNEL.

# MARKET CONCENTRATION

**market concentration** the extent to which the production of a particular good or service is controlled by the leading suppliers (*seller concentration*), and the extent to which the purchase of a product is controlled by the leading buyers (*buyer concentration*). The degree of seller concentration in a MARKET is often measured by a CONCENTRATION RATIO which shows the proportion of market sales accounted for by the largest five, or ten, suppliers.

The significance of market concentration for BUSINESS STRATEGY and MARKETING lies in its effect on the nature and intensity of competition. Structurally, as the level of seller concentration in a market progressively increases, 'competition between the many' becomes 'competition between the few' until, at the extreme, the market is totally monopolized by a single supplier (see MARKET STRUCTURE). In terms of MARKET CONDUCT, as supply becomes concentrated in fewer and fewer hands (OLIGOPOLY), suppliers may seek to avoid mutually, ruinous price competition and channel their main marketing efforts into sales promotion and product innovation, activities which offer a more profitable and effective way of establishing COMPETITIVE ADVANTAGE over rivals.

Buyer concentration can also affect the competitive situation. In many markets (particularly end-consumer markets) buyers are too small to influence supply conditions, but in others (particularly in intermediary goods markets and in retailing), buying power is concentrated and purchasers are able to obtain bulk-buying discounts from suppliers.

See ECONOMIES OF SCALE, HORIZONTAL INTEGRATION, COMPETITION POLICY, MONOPOLY.

**market conduct** the behavioural characteristics of suppliers and buyers operating in a MARKET/INDUSTRY. Key elements of market conduct include:

(a) the BUSINESS OBJECTIVES of suppliers (for example profit and sales growth targets), and the product requirements of buyers (for example low prices, product performance and sophistication);

(b) the MARKETING instruments and strategies available to firms which can be used to establish COMPETITIVE ADVANTAGE over rival suppliers. These include various pricing tactics (MARKET PENETRATION PRICING, MARKET SKIMMING, PRICING, etc.) and MARKETING-MIX combinations such as advertising and sales promotion, quality variations, packaging and design etc. The choice of appropriate marketing strategies will, of course, vary from market to market depending on product characteristics and, critically, on an understanding of those product attributes which command buyer satisfaction (see MARKET RESEARCH);

(c) the mutual interdependency of suppliers which serves to constrain individual freedom of action and often leads, particularly in markets characterized by high seller concentration, to coordinated behaviour patterns, for example PRICE LEADERSHIP and COLLUSION;

(d) the relationships between suppliers and buyers, in particular the impact of bulkbuying policies (see MARKET CONCENTRATION, MARKET STRUCTURE).

In sum, most markets exhibit both competitive and cooperative tendencies, and firms must be mindful of these forces in formulating appropriate business strategies. COMPETITION POLICY interest in market conduct is centred on the potentially adverse effect of market power on MARKET PERFORMANCE, either exercised by a DOMINANT FIRM or deriving from collusion between firms.

See MARKET STRUCTURE-CONDUCT-PERFORMANCE SCHEMA.

**market development** a BUSINESS STRATEGY pursued by a firm aimed at increasing sales of the firm's *existing* products by finding *new* markets for those products. This strategy could involve the firm in building up a network of export markets, or in finding new applications or uses for its product. See PRODUCT – MARKET MATRIX.

**market entry** the entry into a MARKET of a new supplier in the form of either a GREENFIELD operation (i.e. an additional supply source) or the MERGER with, or TAKEOVER of, an existing supplier. Market entry constitutes a major BUSINESS STRATEGY decision, reflecting a strategic initiative on the part of a firm to develop, or reshape, its product/market positioning. Such entry occurs largely in response to the perceived long–run profit potential of the target market, which in turn is importantly influenced by the size of the market and its perceived growth potential, both with respect to the expansion of total primary demand and particular market segments. Successful new entry requires the firm not only to overcome any initial BARRIERS TO ENTRY, but also to develop a long–term strategy for establishing and sustaining COMPETITIVE ADVANTAGE over rival suppliers. See MARKET SYSTEM.

**market exit** the exit from a MARKET of an established supplier. Market exit constitutes a major BUSINESS STRATEGY decision, reflecting a strategic initiative on the part of a firm to reshape its product/market positioning. Such exit occurs largely in response to a sustained LOSS-making situation or poor PROFIT rate or low perceived growth potential. Successful exit requires the firm to overcome any BARRIERS TO EXIT. See DIVESTMENT.

**market follower** see MARKET CHALLENGER.

**marketing** the managerial process of identifying customer requirements and satisfying them by providing customers with appropriate products in order to achieve the organization's objectives. Marketing goes beyond merely selling what the firm produces, but starts by identifying underlying consumer needs through MARKETING RESEARCH; generating products which satisfy these needs through NEW PRODUCT DEVELOPMENT; promoting these products to consumers through various MARKETING MIX policies (pricing, advertising, sales promotion etc.); and physically distributing products to customers through DISTRIBUTION CHANNELS. See MARKETING CONCEPT, INTEGRATED MARKETING, CONSUMER ORIENTATION, PRODUCTION ORIENTATION, MARKETING STRATEGY, GAP ANALYSIS.

**marketing allocation** the division of a company's SALES BUDGET between its PRODUCTS, MARKET SEGMENTS and SALES TERRITORIES.

**marketing audit** see SWOT ANALYSIS.

**marketing concept** a business philosophy which aims at the generation of profits by the recognition and satisfaction of customer needs.

The marketing concept emphasizes the need for a business to adopt a CONSUMER ORIENTATION, that is to start by identifying the needs of consumers and then develop products with the attributes and characteristics to meet these needs.

The marketing concept stresses the superiority of a customer-based marketing approach over a PRODUCTION ORIENTATION which is largely concerned with persuading customers to buy what the firm has chosen to produce.

See INTEGRATED MARKETING, MARKETING MIX.

**marketing effort** the total amount of resources which a firm puts into the MARKETING MIX in order to stimulate demand for its goods and services (see SALES BUDGET). However, the firm's overall marketing success will depend not only on its marketing effort but also on the *effectiveness* of that expenditure in securing customers, and a firm would aim to generate greater sales than its competitors from an equivalent level of expenditure.

**marketing intelligence** information about developments in a firm's market environment that can assist executives in formulating marketing plans. Such intelligence could include details of new products being introduced by competitors, and price changes, or more general economic and social statistics published by government and other bodies.

Various techniques may be employed to gather market intelligence. *Field studies* may be undertaken among samples of the population employing personally conducted or postal QUESTIONNAIRES, telephone and personal interviews, and group surveys; *focus groups*, which involve detailed discussions among small groups of invited respondents called together on one or two occasions; *desk research* can be employed using secondary published information and reports from government or other sources; finally, information about existing products or prototypes can be gained by recruiting *panels* of consumers who report regularly on their experience of using products, by setting up controlled experiments to test consumers' reactions to products and advertising messages, and by direct observation of customers who are buying or using a product or service.

Intelligence gathering is undertaken to seek out new market opportunities and identify possible threats to the sales of existing products.

See MARKETING RESEARCH.

**marketing logistics** the analysis, planning, organization and control of all movement and storage operations connected with the PRODUCTION and DISTRIBUTION of goods.

Whereas distribution is concerned with simply moving products to customers, marketing logistics incorporates a broader responsibility for product distribution management which includes moving raw materials to factories, moving work in progress through the factory and moving finished goods from the factory to consumers. Such an integrated system involves siting of factories and warehouses and DISTRIBUTION CHANNELS used, in order to maximize the effectiveness of the system.

See JUST-IN-TIME.

**marketing management** the process of setting objectives, formulating policy, analysis, planning, implementation and control of activities aimed at the effective selling of the firm's goods or services. See MARKETING, MANAGEMENT.

**marketing mix** the range of measures used by firms to market their products to buyers. Important facets of the marketing mix are:

(a) the product offering, in particular the QUALITY, styling and variety of the firm's established products (see PRODUCT RANGE), and its ability to provide buyers with new products over time (see NEW PRODUCT DEVELOPMENT);

(b) the prices charged for the firm's products (see PRICING, PRICING METHODS);

(c) the means used by the firm to promote its products, including ADVERTISING, SALES PROMOTION, MERCHANDIZING, PERSONAL SELLING, PACKAGING and PUBLIC RELATIONS;

(d) the provision of various on-going CUSTOMER SERVICES, particularly AFTER SALES SERVICE facilities and GUARANTEES;

(e) the means used to distribute the product into the hands of buyers (see DISTRIBUTION CHANNEL).

The relative importance of these elements will vary according to the *particular* buyer characteristics of the MARKET or MARKET SEGMENTS being served by a product. Thus, to take a broad example, in marketing *consumer* goods such factors as advertising, sales promotion and packaging might be emphasized, while in marketing *industrial* goods technical features of the product, price and personal selling might be stressed.

See CONSUMER ORIENTATION.

**marketing myopia** the tendency for firms to take a narrow view of the MARKETS they currently serve based upon their present product offerings and thus to ignore broader market opportunities. For example, a producer who viewed his market solely as that for 'potato crisps' would be ignoring the potential for selling related products into the much broader 'snack products' market. See PRODUCT-MARKET MATRIX.

**marketing objectives** the general and specific aims which a firm sets for itself in selling its products. Marketing objectives together with similar objectives for the other functional areas of the firm (production, finance etc.) are closely related to the firm's overall BUSINESS OBJECTIVES. Operationally, marketing objectives may either be stated in general terms such as simply the increase of sales year by year, or set as quantitative targets: a minimum 10% increase in sales per annum, or an increase in the market share of a particular product from its current level of say 20% of the market to 30% over a five-year period. Such explicit objectives provide a focus for the deployment of the firm's resources and the application of appropriate MARKET-ING STRATEGIES to achieve them.

**marketing research** the systematic and objective classification, collection, analysis and reporting of information about a particular marketing problem. Marketing research can be ad hoc and specific or continuous and general.

Ad hoc (or one-off) marketing research sets out to obtain specific information which is needed for a particular purpose, for example a study of consumer attitudes and perceptions about an existing product. This information could then be used to modify the product or change the MARKETING MIX used to promote it.

Continuous (or on-going) marketing research involves monitoring of the firm's market environment on a regular basis. Such research provides intelligence about competitors and their pricing and marketing policies, effects of proposed legislation on company brands, the potential impact of economic changes such as total consumer spending and social trends such as environmental awareness.

Marketing research uses a variety of techniques such as indepth interviews and group surveys which can be used primarily for MOTIVATIONAL RESEARCH; in addition, field studies can be undertaken using QUESTIONNAIRES and interviews, and desk research of records and data, these being used primarily for MARKETING INTELLIGENCE. Finally, techniques such as consumer panels, market experiments and observation may be used to gain information about existing products.

Businesses carry out marketing research to enable them to identify market trends; to find out about market characteristics; to forecast market potential; to analyse MARKET SHARE; to find a MARKET SEGMENT; and to test consumer acceptance of new or existing products.

See CONSUMER ORIENTATION, NEW-PRODUCT DEVELOPMENT.

**marketing strategy** a STRATEGY employed by a firm to attain its MARKETING OBJECTIVES, which in turn is closely related to the achievement of the firm's overall BUSINESS OBJECTIVES. Three basic marketing strategies may be distinguished:

(a) an UNDIFFERENTIATED MARKETING STRATEGY which uses the same MARKETING MIX format with respect to price, advertising etc. right across a market;

(b) a DIFFERENTIATED MARKETING STRATEGY which uses a variety of marketing mix formats each tailored to meet the requirements of particular MARKET SEGMENTS;

(c) a CONCENTRATED MARKETING STRATEGY which focuses the firm's marketing efforts on a single market segment.

Where a firm operates in a number of product markets (see DIVERSIFICATION) it may use a combination of these strategies, depending upon the nature of the products being supplied and the buyer characteristics of the market (see BUYER BEHAVIOUR).

See BUSINESS STRATEGY.

**market intermediary** a business such as a WHOLESALER which acts as a 'middleman' in moving goods through a DISTRIBUTION CHANNEL, or an AGENT (for example, an INSURANCE BROKER) which brings together buyers and sellers of insurance.

See TRADER/DEALER.

**market leader** the seller of a product who holds the largest MARKET SHARE. Generally firms become market leaders by establishing positions of COMPETITIVE ADVANTAGE over rival suppliers. See MARKET CHALLENGERS.

**market maker** a firm attached to the STOCK MARKET which is engaged in the buying and selling of FINANCIAL SECURITIES such as STOCKS, SHARES and BONDS and thereby acts to establish a market PRICE for these securities. Market making firms in the UK have (since the 1986 stock market reforms) combined the roles of jobber (acting as a *principal* in the buying and selling of securities) and stockbroker (acting as an *agent* on behalf of clients wishing to sell or buy securities); although the stockbroking function is still performed by firms specialized in that activity alone.

A market making firm usually specializes in a small group of securities, for example the shares of companies in a particular industry. The firm makes its profit out of the difference between the price at which it buys a security and the (higher) price at which it sells. The firm marks its buying and selling prices upwards or downwards according to whether its holding of a security is falling or increasing. For example, if there is a strong demand for a particular share, then as the firm sells some of its holdings it will mark the share price up to reflect its growing scarcity value. See BID PRICE, SHARE PURCHASE/SALE, DUAL CAPACITY.

**market niche** see MARKET SEGMENT.

**market penetration** a BUSINESS STRATEGY pursued by a firm which is aimed at increasing the sales of the firm's *existing* products in its *present* markets thereby increasing its MARKET SHARE in those markets. This strategy involves the deployment of various MARKETING MIX elements (pricing, advertising etc.), together with appropriate MARKET SEGMENTATION policies aimed at competing more aggressively against rival suppliers. See PRODUCT MARKET MATRIX, MARKET PENETRATION PRICING, CONCENTRATED MARKETING STRATEGY.

**market penetration pricing** a pricing policy that involves charging a comparatively low PRICE for a product in order to secure growing sales and a high market share. This policy can be adopted by a firm where consumers are price sensitive. More specifically such a tactic may be used as a means of securing entry to a market, or where its product has moved into the growth phase of its PRODUCT LIFE CYCLE. Contrast MARKET SKIMMING PRICE. See PRICING OBJECTIVES, PRICING METHODS, DUMPING, MARKET ENTRY, ELASTICITY OF DEMAND, MARKET PENETRATION.

**market performance** the effectiveness of suppliers in a MARKET/INDUSTRY in utilizing economic resource to their maximum efficiency and to the ultimate benefit of consumers. Key elements of market performance include:

(a) productive efficiency – the cost effectiveness of firms in producing their outputs. Ideally, outputs should be produced in plants of optimal scale, that is, plant sizes which fully exploit available ECONOMIES OF SCALE so that minimum cost levels are attained;

(b) distributive efficiency – the utilization of cost-effective channels of distribution and marketing techniques so as to minimize distribution costs;

(c) the setting of 'fair' prices to consumers, that is, prices which are consistent with the real economic costs of supplying the product, including a reasonable (i.e. non-monopolistic) profit return to suppliers;

(d) product performance – the satisfaction of consumer demands for product variety and sophistication, that is, the maximization of consumer choice and value-for-money attributes;

(e) technological progressiveness – the introduction of process and product innovations which enable supply costs and prices to be reduced in real terms and which provide consumers with technically superior products (see RESEARCH AND DEVELOPMENT).

Market performance is determined primarily by MARKET STRUCTURE and MARKET CONDUCT. For example, in markets where economies of scale are significant, a high level of MARKET CONCENTRATION may be required in order to minimize supply costs. In conduct terms, price COMPETITION between firms is likely to benefit consumers whereas COLLUSION is likely to have an adverse effect on consumer welfare. These and other elements of market structure and conduct are a major concern of a government's COMPETITION POLICY and INDUSTRIAL POLICY.

See MARKET STRUCTURE-CONDUCT-PERFORMANCE SCHEMA.

**market positioning** the comparative position which a company's BRAND of a product holds vis-à-vis competitors' brands in the opinion of consumers in a particular MARKET or MARKET SEGMENT. For example, a brand may be perceived as a sophisticated, high quality, 'up market' brand or a basic, low quality, 'down market' brand. See MARKET SEGMENTATION.

The technique of 'perceptual mapping' is often used to chart consumers' perceptions of brands currently on offer and to identify opportunities for launching new brands or to reposition an existing brand. This technique involves identifying perceived product characteristics which may be used to classify consumer opinions about brands of a product. Thus, in Fig. 53 the two axes of the 'map' show the perceived product attributes, 'strong'/'mild' and 'ordinary'/'classy' for cigarettes while B1 to B9 on the map indicate consumers' perceptions of existing brands of cigarettes on offer in terms of these characteristics. Brands show market segments which are currently being serviced by existing brands and 'clusters' of brands suggest larger volume segments.

A positioning strategy seeks to differentiate the firm's brand from competitors' brands in terms of product characteristics

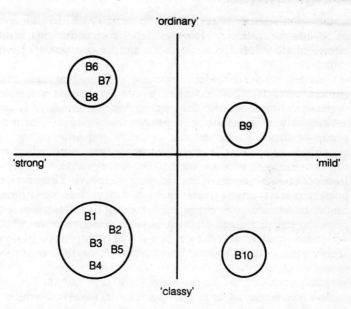

Fig. 53. **Market positioning.** Perceptual map.

and 'image' so as to maximize sales potential. In positioning brands a firm may choose to offer a 'copy-cat' or 'me-too' brand in a well-served market segment which is very similar to competing brands, with minimal PRODUCT DIFFERENTIATION (Brands B1 to B5 in the figure). This stratagem may be viable where this segment represents a high proportion of total market sales so that even a small brand share would result in large sales. Alternatively, a firm's MARKETING RESEARCH may reveal untapped demand potential in different market segments, so that it may choose to distance its brand from competing brands with a high degree of product differentiation, introducing a new brand (B10).

See PRICE QUALITY TRADE-OFF, PRICING POLICY, PRODUCT SEGMENTATION, PRODUCT IMAGE, PRODUCT VARIETY, BRAND EXTENSION.

**market potential** the total size of the MARKET for a product at a given time, measured in either volume or value terms. A single seller's share of the market potential will depend upon its MARKETING effort. However, the cumulative marketing efforts of all sellers can serve to expand market potential over time.

Changes in the broader economic environment can affect market potential. For example, a rise in interest rates will decrease the total DEMAND for certain electrical goods.

**market power** or **monopoly power** the ability of a firm (or group of firms) to dictate market prices and other terms and conditions of supply. Market power derives essentially from the possession of a dominant market share (see MONOPOLY) or from COLLUSION between the leading suppliers. Where firms possess market power there exists a danger that such power might be abused; for example, the charging of monopolistic prices to the detriment of consumers or selective price cuts to drive out smaller competitors. See COMPETITION POLICY, MARKET STRUCTURE, MARKET CONDUCT, MARKET PERFORMANCE, DOMINANT FIRM.

**market-product matrix** see PRODUCT-MARKET MATRIX.

**market research** an aspect of MARKETING RESEARCH which is concerned with the collection and analysis of information about a particular market.

**market research agency** a firm which carries out MARKETING RESEARCH on behalf of clients.

**market risk** or **non-diversifiable risk** that part of total risk (within the CAPITAL-ASSET PRICING MODEL) attributable to the holding of a security, or portfolio of securities, which depends upon variations in general security prices on the STOCK MARKET. Market risk is associated with general market variations as measured by a market index, such as the Financial Times All-Share Index or the Dow-Jones Index. Unlike SPECIFIC RISK, it is not possible to diversify market risk away, because however large the portfolio of shares held, they are all influenced by the market generally to a greater or lesser extent. See BETA COEFFICIENT.

**market segment** a part of a MARKET which has its own distinct customer profile and buyer characteristics such that, for MARKETING purposes, it can be targeted separately from other segments of the market. See MARKET SEGMENTATION, DIFFERENTIATED MARKETING STRATEGY, CONCENTRATED MARKETING STRATEGY.

**market segmentation** the division of a MARKET into identifiable submarkets or segments each having its own particular customer profile and BUYER characteristics. A market can often be divided up broadly into major customer segments as well as more narrowly into various submarkets within each of these segments. In MARKETING terms, markets can be segmented in a number of ways as Fig. 54 (overleaf) indicates, pyramiding down from the identification of major subgroups of customers, and their particular product-type requirements and preferences with reference to such things as range of quality gradations, colouring and packaging. Further elements in market segmentation include the distribution outlets used by buyers to make purchases and the geographical boundaries of the market.

Depending upon the complexity of a market as revealed by market segment analysis, a firm may choose to operate 'across the board' or decide to focus on a limited number of segments. Since most markets in practice possess segmentation characteristics to a greater or lesser degree, an UNDIFFERENTIATED MARKETING STRATEGY involving a uniform MARKETING MIX approach across all segments is likely to be of only limited effectiveness. A more attractive approach in these circumstances is a DIFFERENTIATED MARKETING STRATEGY involving various 'customized' marketing mix formulations, each tailored to match the buyer characteristics of the segments targeted. A third approach, a CONCENTRATED MARKETING STRATEGY, may be applied where the firm decides to target the whole of its marketing effort on one particular segment.

See SOCIOECONOMIC GROUP, CONSUMER SEGMENTATION, DISTRIBUTION CHANNEL, PRODUCT RANGE, PRODUCT ATTRIBUTES, PACKAGING, INTERNATIONAL MARKETING, BRAND EXTENSION, MARKET POSITIONING, CUSTOMIZATION.

**market share** the proportion of total sales of a product accounted for by an individual BRAND of the product or all brands of the product offered by a firm in a particular MARKET.

A firm's market share relative to competitors' market share provides an indicator of its success in marketing its brand(s) over time. Some minimum market share may be necessary to achieve sufficient sales volume to enable the firm to produce efficiently (see ECONOMIES OF SCALE). Beyond this the firm may aspire to market leadership of the whole market or may seek

Fig. 54. Market segmentation. A matrix for paint.

to achieve high market share in one or more MARKET SEG-
MENTS.

Market shares can be only meaningfully related to a precise
definition of the market serviced by the firm both in geographic terms (for example UK snack product sales or
European snack product sales), and in product scope (for
example, potato crisps and other snack products).

See MARKET LEADER, MARKET CHALLENGERS, MARKET CONCEN-
TRATION, COMPETITION POLICY.

**market-skimming pricing** a pricing policy that involves
charging a comparatively high price for a product to secure
large profit margins. This policy can be adopted by a firm
where consumers are not price sensitive. More specifically,
such a tactic may be used where a new product is still in the
introductory phase of its PRODUCT LIFECYCLE and embodies
novel features which enable it to command a premium price.
Contrast with MARKET PENETRATION PRICING. See PRICING OBJEC-
TIVES, PRICING METHODS, ELASTICITY OF DEMAND.

**market structure** the organizational characteristics of a
MARKET/INDUSTRY. Key elements of market structure include:

(a) the number of suppliers and their relative size distribution, indicating the extent of seller concentration in the market
(see MARKET CONCENTRATION, CONCENTRATION RATIO);

(b) the number of buyers and their relative size distribution,
indicating the extent of buyer concentration in the market;

(c) the nature of the product, whether it is a standardized
good or service, or differentiated in a variety of ways (see
PRODUCT DIFFERENTIATION);

(d) the condition of entry to the market, that is, the extent
and severity of BARRIERS TO ENTRY confronting potential newcomers;

(e) the degree of VERTICAL INTEGRATION, that is, the extent to
which suppliers produce their own input requirements, or
possess their own distribution outlets for their products.

These aspects of market structure, together with underlying
cost and demand conditions, are significant in so far as they
have a *strategic* influence on the nature and intensity of
competitive behaviour in a market (see MARKET CONDUCT) and
hence on MARKET PERFORMANCE. To illustrate: the greater the
level of seller concentration, the more heightened is the degree
of mutual interdependency such that the actions of one firm

will have a discernible effect on the market position of other firms, causing them to respond with actions of their own. In this situation, for example, recognition that aggressive price competition is likely to prove mutually ruinous may well encourage suppliers to focus their competitive efforts on sales promotion and product innovation as these provide a more effective means of establishing COMPETITIVE ADVANTAGE. In turn, the greater the scope for the deployment of product differentiation strategies, the more prominent this area of competition is likely to become. Barriers to entry may arise naturally from the supply characteristics of the market (for example cost advantages to established firms arising from ECONOMIES OF SCALE), or they can be created predatorily by established firms to keep newcomers out (for example the use of EXCLUSIVE DEALING practices). In either case established firms are protected from new competition. Likewise, vertical integration by a DOMINANT FIRM may limit competition in a market by depriving rivals and potential entrants of inputs or distribution outlets. Additionally, a firm which is diversified into a number of markets (see DIVERSIFICATION) may be able to cross-subsidize its activities in a particular market in order to advance its position in that market.

In sum, market structure provides the backdrop to a firm's strategic actions as it seeks to establish competitive advantage over rivals, but, importantly, can itself be altered and controlled by firms' actions; for example, firms may seek to increase their market shares by TAKEOVERS and MERGERS, thereby raising the level of seller concentration.

COMPETITION POLICY interest in market structure centres on the association of market structure and conduct, and their impact on market performance. Mergers and takeovers, for example, which would reduce competition, may be prohibited on the grounds that they would unduly increase a firm's power to control market prices and profit levels.

See MARKET STRUCTURE-CONDUCT-PERFORMANCE SCHEMA, MONOPOLISTIC COMPETITION, MONOPOLY, OLIGOPOLY, PERFECT COMPETITION.

**market structure-conduct-performance schema** a conceptual framework which identifies key characteristics of MARKET STRUCTURE, MARKET CONDUCT and MARKET PERFORMANCE (see Fig. 55), and facilitates analysis of the interrelationships

# MARKET STRUCTURE-CONDUCT-PERFORMANCE SCHEMA

**MARKET CONDUCT**
1. BUSINESS OBJECTIVES
2. MARKETING POLICIES: PRICES, PRODUCT RANGE, ADVERTISING, ETC.
3. INTERFIRM CO-ORDINATION (COMPETITION/COLLUSION)

**MARKET STRUCTURE**
1. EXTENT OF SELLER/ BUYER CONCENTRATION
2. PRODUCT CHARACTER (HOMOGENEOUS/ DIFFERENTIATED)
3. CONDITION OF ENTRY
4. VERTICAL INTEGRATION

**MARKET PERFORMANCE**
1. EFFICIENT SUPPLY (LOW PRODUCTION & MARKETING COSTS)
2. 'FAIR' PRICES
3. PROCESS INNOVATION
4. PRODUCT INNOVATION

**PUBLIC POLICY**
1. COMPETITION POLICY
2. INDUSTRIAL POLICY

Fig. 55. **Market structure-conduct-performance schema.**

between these variables. The structure–conduct–performance schema is useful for the achievement of COMPETITIVE ADVANTAGE over rivals. Structure and conduct patterns enable an analysis to be made of the 'forces driving competition' in a market, which, together with observation of market performance results, enables an assessment to be made of the actual and potential strengths and weaknesses of established suppliers. Established firms may be relatively cost-inefficient because of their failure to exploit ECONOMIES OF SCALE, or, because of inertia or limited marketing vision, neglect potentially lucrative market niches. Consideration of such factors may provide for successful MARKET ENTRY based on the establishment of optimal scale plant and MARKET SEGMENTATION strategies. The schema is particularly relevant to COMPETITION POLICY and INDUSTRIAL POLICY bodies in applying appropriate remedial measures to redress poor performance. For example, structural initiatives involving mergers and rationalization schemes may be the preferred means of reorganizing markets to eliminate excess capacity, or, alternatively, mergers between the leading firms in a market may be vetoed because they would lead to an undesirable degree of monopolization. Likewise, conduct measures may be used to improve cost efficiency and lower 'excessive' market prices and profit levels by, for example, the prohibition of price-fixing CARTELS, or the imposition of PRICE CONTROLS on dominant suppliers.

**market system** or **price system** an ECONOMY in which basic decisions about the allocation of resources, which goods and services are produced and in what quantities, are determined by the interaction of buyers and sellers in factor and product MARKETS, as shown in Fig. 56.

The firm is a key element in the market system operating in product markets where it sells products, and factor markets where it buys or hires resources. The market system embraces both types of market and operates so as to ensure that resources are allocated broadly in line with consumer demand.

A simplified illustration of this process is given below. Suppose initially that tea and coffee prices were such as to equate demand and supply for these products in their respective markets (see EQUILIBRIUM MARKET PRICE), but then there was a change in consumer demand away from tea and towards coffee, as shown in Fig. 57. The increased demand for coffee, coupled with an unchanged coffee supply in the short run, would result in an excess demand for coffee at the prevailing price and would thus cause its price to rise. By the same token, the fall in demand for tea, coupled with an unchanged tea supply in the short run, would initially result in an excess supply of tea at the prevailing price and the price of tea would fall as suppliers sought to clear unsold stocks.

The relative profitability of supplying tea and coffee will also change as their relative prices change. The increase in demand and prices in the coffee market will increase coffee producers' profits, while tea suppliers faced with falling demand and prices will find their profits declining. In the longer run, coffee producers will invest in new plant and hire more labour to expand supply, and new firms will be induced by the higher profits to enter the market. As supply expands prices will fall and a new, lower-level, equilibrium market price will be reached. By contrast, as demand and prices fall

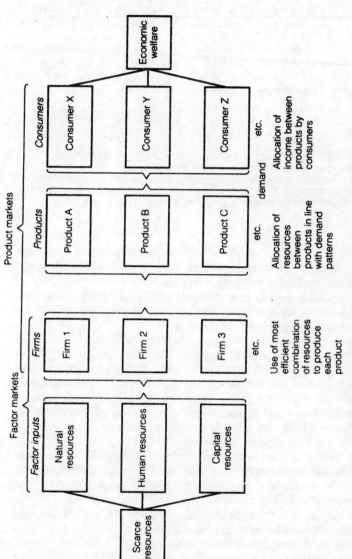

Fig. 56. **Market system.** Diagram showing the interaction of buyers and sellers in factor and product markets.

## MARKET TARGETING

|  | Product markets | | Factor markets | |
|---|---|---|---|---|
|  | coffee market | tea market | coffee inputs | tea inputs |
| Short-run | D = S | D = S | DF = SF | DF = SF |
|  | D ↑ | D ↓ |  |  |
|  | D > S | D < S |  |  |
|  | P ↑ | P ↓ |  |  |
|  | Pr ↑ | Pr ↓ |  |  |
| Long run | market entry | market exit | DF ↑ | DF ↓ |
|  | S ↑ | S ↓ | DF > SF | DF < SF |
|  | P ↓ | P ↑ | Pf ↑ | Pf ↓ |
|  | Pr ↓ | Pr ↑ |  |  |
|  | D = S | D = S |  |  |

Key:  D = product demand;  S = product supply;  P = price of products;
Pr = profits of suppliers;  Pf = price of factor input;
SF = factor supply;  DF = factor demand

Fig. 57. **Market system**. A simplified illustration of the effect of a change in demand.

in the tea market, suppliers will see their profits falling and less efficient loss-making firms will be forced out of the market, while the remaining suppliers will cut their output. The resulting decline in the supply will cause prices to harden and a new higher-level, equilibrium market price will be reached.

These changes in product markets will have knock-on effects in factor markets, as Fig. 57 shows. The higher profitability of coffee production will enable coffee producers to pay higher returns to the factor inputs they use, thus attracting additional resources into the industry; by contrast, falling demand, prices and profitability in the tea industry will release resources which can now be redeployed in the coffee industry and in other expanding industries.

In practice, the market mechanism described above may well work imperfectly. For example, it may not be possible for new producers to enter the coffee market because of significant BARRIERS TO ENTRY; in this case established firms may decide not to expand coffee supply but exploit the increased demand by raising prices further.

**market targeting** see MARKET SEGMENT.

**market testing** the process of putting a good or service on to the market to gauge its viability. The term has been used in the UK in the context of the privatization and deregulation of public sector products.

**market value** the amount that a firm's FIXED ASSETS and CURRENT ASSETS such as STOCKS could be sold for on the open market. In a company's BALANCE SHEET such assets are usually recorded at their HISTORIC COST though market value may be substantially higher, reflecting current prices.

**mark-up** the PROFIT MARGIN on a good or service which can be expressed as a percentage of the cost of the product or a percentage of its selling price. See PRICING METHODS, COST-BASED PRICING.

**mark-up pricing** see COST-BASED PRICING.

**mass marketing** the process of promoting the sales of large numbers of a product in order to facilitate MASS PRODUCTION of the product. See PROMOTIONAL MIX.

**mass media** see MEDIA.

**mass production** a method of organizing PRODUCTION whereby a component or product such as a motor car passes through a sequence of predetermined operations or processes which constitute a PRODUCTION LINE OR ASSEMBLY LINE. Mass production systems are used to make components or products in comparatively large quantities using specialized machines on a continuous basis. See PRODUCT-FOCUSED LAYOUT, PRODUCTION SCHEDULING.

**master budget** a summary budgeted PROFIT-AND-LOSS ACCOUNT and budgeted BALANCE SHEET, incorporating the component functional budgets (sales, production, distribution etc.) as approved and employed by a firm's managers. See BUDGET, BUDGETING.

**matching** the process of matching revenues and profits with the associated expenses incurred in earning these revenues. See ACCRUALS PRINCIPLE OF ACCOUNTING.

**materials** inputs into the PRODUCTION process most of which are embodied in the finished goods being manufactured. Materials include raw materials such as metal ores and cotton, and manufactured components. The materials which are embodied in the finished product are known as DIRECT MATERIALS whereas other materials such as lubricants and other consumables which are used up during the production process are known as INDIRECT MATERIALS.

See VALUE ADDED.

## MATERIALITY

**materiality** see ACCOUNTING PRINCIPLES.

**materials cost variance** the difference between the standard DIRECT MATERIALS cost of a product (standard materials usage × standard materials price) and its actual direct materials cost (actual materials usage × actual materials price). This difference can be broken down into two parts:

(a) *materials quantity variance*, which involves calculating the difference between the standard quantity of materials specified and the actual quantity used, converted into money terms by multiplying by the standard materials price;

(b) *materials price variance*, which involves calculating the difference between the standard price of materials specified and the actual price paid, multiplied by the actual quantity of materials used.

With this distinction it is possible to trace whether an adverse direct materials cost variance is due to excess usage of materials or to higher materials prices. See STANDARD COST.

**materials flow management** the organization of the flow of materials within a factory based upon the breaking down of manufacturing processes into detailed elements. The aim of materials flow management is to reduce manufacturing throughput time by seeking to reduce waste in the process.

Materials flow analysis generally involves three main types of documentation: *assembly drawings* which specify how the components in a manufactured product should be put together; *assembly charts* which are derived from the assembly drawings and which show each sequential step in the assembly process; *operations process sheets* or *routing sheets* which are derived from the assembly chart and which show in detail the operations and routing required for each individual component along with any tools and equipment needed.

In addition, where firms seek to analyse and improve materials flows they may employ ACTIVITY CHARTS which represent assembly activities in terms of standardized symbols.

**materials handling** see MATERIALS MANAGEMENT.

**materials management** the administration and control of the materials used by a firm in the PRODUCTION process. This has two main aspects:

(a) the ordering and maintaining of STOCKS of materials so as to ensure that adequate amounts of materials are available at all times, thus enabling production to go ahead without interruption while at the same time attempting to minimize stockholding costs (see PURCHASING, MATERIALS REQUIREMENTS PLANNING, STOCK CONTROL, STOCKHOLDING MODEL);

(b) materials handling, the physical movement of materials from place to place, their packaging (in pallets and containers) and their storage (see INTERSTAGE STORE) as they proceed through various production processes. Materials handling seeks to minimize internal transport costs and damage to, and wastage of, materials. See MATERIALS FLOW ANALYSIS.

**materials price variance** See MATERIALS COST VARIANCE.

**materials quantity variance** see MATERIALS COST VARIANCE.

**materials requirement planning (MRP)** a planning system for scheduling STOCK replenishment so as to ensure that adequate amounts of materials are available at all times thus enabling PRODUCTION to go ahead without interruption. Key features of MRP are the calculation of raw material and component requirements from the PRODUCTION SCHEDULES of the products in which the materials are to be embodied, and the time phasing of replenishment orders for materials so that they arrive in good time to avoid a *stockout* situation which would halt production. Thus, if production schedules indicate that stock of a particular material will need to be replenished in week 7 to avoid a stockout and the time it takes for the new stock to be delivered after the placement of the order is 2 weeks, then the order will need to be issued in week 5. See STOCK CONTROL, JUST-IN-TIME, MANUFACTURING RESOURCE PLANNING, MATERIALS MANAGEMENT.

**materials requisition** a document which is used to authorize and record the issue of materials or components to production from stores. Information from the requisition is used to update the STORES RECORD CARD (bin card) and the STORES LEDGER, and to ascertain the DIRECT MATERIALS used on jobs or products as well as the INDIRECT MATERIALS used by various COST CENTRES.

**materials usage variance** see MATERIALS COST VARIANCE.

**maternity rights** the rights pregnant women and the mothers of very young children have in relation to their employment. Pregnant women in the UK have a right to a minimum of 14 weeks' maternity leave, and any dismissal of a female employee on the grounds of pregnancy constitutes UNFAIR DISMISSAL. Pregnant women also have the right to their usual employment benefits during these 14 weeks such as continuing use of their company car. These rights, based on a directive of the European Union, extend previous law on maternity rights which required minimum periods of employment.

See SICK PAY.

**matrix 1.** an ORGANIZATION structure in which individuals report to managers in more than one DEPARTMENT or function. The simple CHAIN OF COMMAND found in the classic BUREAUCRACY is replaced by (potentially) a multiplicity of reporting relationships. This type of structure may characterize part of the organization – for project team management for instance, where a project manager assumes authority over team members drawn from a number of departments – or it may extend to the entire organization. See Fig. 58.

Fig. 58. **Matrix.** The matrix structure.

There is no standard form of matrix. Managers may have *equal* formal authority over subordinates or alternatively one of these may have *primary* authority with the others, assuming authority on particular issues, as in the dotted-line relationship (see ORGANIZATION CHART). The benefits of matrix organization are said to be that it facilitates interdepartmental coordination during innovation, and, by weakening departmental boundaries, encourages greater flexibility and creativity. However, many organizations that have assumed this form have found that the absence of clarity in lines of authority and responsibility can lead to inertia and conflict.

See FUNCTIONAL STRUCTURE, PRODUCT-BASED STRUCTURE, CRITICAL FUNCTION STRUCTURE.

**2.** a rectangular array of numerical or alphabetical data displayed as rows and columns. Matrices may be of any dimension, for example three rows and two columns. Multiplying rows by columns gives the number of elements in a matrix, which in our example is six. Matrices are employed in SPREAD-SHEETS to present and manipulate data.

**maturity date** see REDEMPTION DATE.

**maturity phase** see PRODUCT LIFE CYCLE.

**maximum stock level** the highest planned level of STOCK for a particular item in a STOCK CONTROL system.

**MBO** see MANAGEMENT BY OBJECTIVES.

**MBWA** see MANAGEMENT BY WALKING AROUND.

**mean** see AVERAGE.

**means test** the scrutiny of an individual's personal and financial circumstances to determine whether or not he or she qualifies to receive SOCIAL SECURITY BENEFITS.

**measured day work** a system of PAY in which WAGES are output-based but do not fluctuate in response to short-term fluctuations in output. Typically, possible daily output will be established through WORK MEASUREMENT. Individuals' pay will then be based on the understanding that they will usually achieve this level of output. Pay relativities are established by JOB EVALUATION. The notable feature of measured day work is that daily output and WAGE RATES are usually set at higher levels than industry norms, and thus represent an attempt to achieve high output without the attendant INDUSTRIAL RELATIONS problems often associated with PIECEWORK. A variant is 'graduated measured day work' where an individual can choose from a range of output/wage options.

**mechanistic and organismic organizations** terms used by the British writers Tom Burns and G M Stalker to contrast two very different types of ORGANIZATION. *Mechanistic* organizations are characterized by high and rigid job specialization and centralized decision-making with vertical channels of communication. *Organismic* organizations, by contrast, display loose job definitions, greater horizontal communication and some devolution of decision-making to lower levels of the HIERARCHY. The nature of the environment is a critical determinant: stable conditions tend to encourage mechanistic organizations whilst fast-changing product markets tend to encourage the organismic form. See BUREAUCRACY, CONTINGENCY THEORY, CULTURE.

**media** the channels of communication available to a firm (or some other organization) through which the firm's products can be advertised to prospective buyers. The main media channels available in the UK and other major economies include commercial television and radio, newspapers and magazines, technical journals, poster sites, cinemas and theatres, display cards (on buses, in restaurants etc.) and direct mailing. A firm's selection of appropriate media for its ADVERTISEMENTS will depend critically on whether the whole MARKET or particular MARKET SEGMENTS are being targeted (for example, in the former case national newspapers may be used, in the latter case, appropriate specialist journals and magazines); the desired degree of ADVERTISING FREQUENCY required (daily, weekly, etc.); and the relative costs of placing advertisements in the various media combined with the firm's advertising budget limits. See ADVERTISING.

**median** a method of representing the middle of a set of numbers by a single number, i.e. the value of the middle item when the items are arranged in increasing order of magnitude. For example, if five people had weekly incomes of £100, £130, £150, £250 and £400 then the median income of the group would be £150 (the middle figure). See also AVERAGE, MODE.

**mediation** a method of resolving INDUSTRIAL DISPUTES in which a neutral third party acts as a go-between to the parties in dispute. Typically, the mediator introduces proposals of his or her own as an aid to continued NEGOTIATIONS. It is a useful form of intervention where disputes have become especially acrimonious and the disputants are entrenched in their bargaining positions. Conceptually it is midway between CONCILIATION and ARBITRATION. See ADVISORY, CONCILIATION AND ARBITRATION SERVICES (ACAS), COLLECTIVE BARGAINING.

**medium of exchange** see MONEY.

**Mediums** BONDS, DEBENTURES and PREFERENCE SHARES which have a redemption date of between 5 and 15 years.

**memorandum of association** a legal document which must be filed with the REGISTRAR OF COMPANIES before a JOINT-STOCK COMPANY can be incorporated, and which governs the external relationship between the company and third parties. The memorandum must contain certain compulsory clauses stating:

    (a) the name of the company;

    (b) the objects of the company;

(c) the country in which the company is situated;

(d) whether it is limited by shares or other means;

(e) the amount and division of share capital;

(f) the signature of the subscribers forming the company, each of whom must take at least one share. See ARTICLES OF ASSOCIATION.

**memory** the part of a COMPUTER that stores information. The two main types of computer memory are RAM (Random Access Memory) and ROM (Read Only Memory). HARD DISKS and FLOPPY DISKS provide additional memory capacity for storing computer programs and data.

**mentoring** see MANAGEMENT DEVELOPMENT.

**merchandise** an alternative term for a GOOD or COMMODITY.

**merchandising** in-store promotional activity by manufacturers or retailers at the point of sale, designed to stimulate SALES. Such merchandising makes considerable use of POINT-OF-SALE DISPLAY materials and special buying incentives such as free trial samples, money–off packs and gifts. See SALES PROMOTION, PROMOTIONAL MIX.

**merchant** a business such as a RETAILER or WHOLESALER which acts as an intermediary in a DISTRIBUTION CHANNEL. Merchants 'take title' to goods (that is, purchase goods) which they then on–sell to customers.

**merchantable quality** a legal term used to describe products whch are satisfactory insofar as they are fit for the purpose intended. See SALE OF GOODS ACT, 1979.

**merchant bank** a BANK which offers a range of financial facilities and services to clients. The merchant banks are still involved in what was their original business, namely the provision of merchandise finance, in the form of 'acceptance' notes on BILLS OF EXCHANGE to importers and exporters to cover products in transit. They have extended their interests variously into investment management, stockbroking, MARKET MAKING and corporate finance (see VENTURE CAPITAL). In the latter capacity, merchant banks arrange new stock and share issues on behalf of corporate clients (see SHARE ISSUES) and UNDERWRITE such issues. Merchant banks nowadays play a particularly prominent role in advising corporate clients on MERGERS and TAKEOVER BID tactics and in putting together the financial terms and details of such deals. See BANKING SYSTEM.

**Mercosur** see LATIN AMERICAN FREE TRADE ASSOCIATION.

**merger** or **amalgamation** the combining together of two or more firms into a single business on a basis that is mutually agreed by the firms' managements and approved by their shareholders. Mergers are one form of EXTERNAL GROWTH involving firms in expanding in a horizontal, vertical or conglomerate direction:

(a) *Horizontal* mergers (mergers between firms in the same market) may enable the firms to lower their costs, by taking advantage of the economies of large-scale production and marketing and by increasing the market share of the combined group, thereby putting it on a stronger competitive footing (see HORIZONTAL INTEGRATION);

(b) *Vertical* mergers (mergers between firms operating at different levels in the same market) may enable the firms to lower their costs by combining together in one operation a number of sequentially linked processes and by cutting stockholding costs, while control of inputs and market outlets gives the firm greater security of supplies and access to distribution channels, often at a competitive advantage over non-integrated rivals (see VERTICAL INTEGRATION);

(c) *Conglomerate* mergers (mergers between firms engaged in unrelated markets) enable risk to be spread, and provide an opportunity to develop better the resources of each by cross-transference of management, production and marketing expertise and by the targeting of finance to areas of growth potential (see DIVERSIFICATION).

In terms of their wider impact on the functioning of market processes, mergers may, on the one hand, promote greater efficiency in resource use and lower market costs and prices, or, on the other hand, reduce competition and heighten the dangers of monopolistic control over markets. Thus they may simultaneously involve both benefits and detriments. For this reason, in the UK, mergers and TAKEOVERS which create or extend a firm's market share of a particular product in excess of 25%, or where the value of assets combined is over £70 million, can be referred by the OFFICE OF FAIR TRADING to the MONOPOLIES AND MERGERS COMMISSION to determine whether or not they are in the public interest.

See MARKET ENTRY, BARRIERS TO ENTRY, CITY CODE ON TAKEOVERS AND MERGERS, DEMERGER, BUSINESS STRATEGY, MERCHANT BANK.

**merit pay** see PERFORMANCE-RATED PAY.

**merit rating** see PERFORMANCE-RELATED PAY.

**method study** an aspect of WORK STUDY which involves the systematic recording and analysis of the way in which a JOB is performed, with a view to developing and applying easier and more efficient methods of performing the task. More effective work methods can help increase PRODUCTIVITY and reduce labour costs.

Method study involves a number of steps:

(a) the selection of the work to be studied, giving priority to permanent jobs with a high labour content where potential cost savings are substantial;

(b) the recording of the existing work method. For DIRECT LABOUR involved in repetitive tasks this can be done by using an ACTIVITY CHART to record all the work tasks performed by a person and/or machine using standard symbols for the activities: operation, transportation, inspection etc. Alternatively, video tape records of the work being performed by direct operatives can be used. For managers, staff and INDIRECT LABOUR involved in a wide range of tasks ACTIVITY SAMPLING can provide information about the relative time spent on each main activity undertaken;

(c) the critical examination of these records to establish the purpose, place and sequence of activities, and the means by which they are performed, in order to facilitate

(d) the development of an improved work method by eliminating unnecessary activities, combining activities, changing their sequence or simplifying them;

(e) the installation of the new method and provision of appropriate training for

(f) the maintenance of the new work practice.

Method study is generally undertaken prior to WORK MEASUREMENT.

**'me-too' product** see MARKET POSITIONING.

**mezzanine debt** see JUNK BOND.

**MFA** see MULTI-FIBRE AGREEMENT.

**M-form** see PRODUCT-BASED STRUCTURE.

**microcomputer** a small-scale COMPUTER with modest data storage facilities, usually comprising a CPU (central processing unit), DISK DRIVES, KEYBOARD and monitor or VDU (visual display unit). Stand-alone computers can be designed as desktop machines or as portable LAPTOP units.

As microcomputers have become more powerful in terms of data processing speed and data storage capacity the distinction between them and MINICOMPUTERS has become blurred.

**middleman** a person or firm which acts as an intermediary between a seller of a good or service and the buyer of that good or service. See WHOLESALER, AGENT, MARKET INTERMEDIARY.

**middle manager** any manager who occupies a middle position in the HIERARCHY of an ORGANIZATION, located between those senior managers who formulate business strategy and those with direct responsibility for overseeing the work of production or of clerical employees. In practice the term is used imprecisely; it can also refer to those managers who do not contribute directly to the organization's primary output and to those who do not have direct responsibility for budgets or overseeing the work of others (see LINE AND STAFF). In recent years many organizations have sought to reduce the number of their middle managers; information technology has rendered some of their information-processing role unnecessary, whilst many have claimed that the absence of responsibility has led to poor job performance. See MANAGEMENT.

**middle price** the price of a FINANCIAL SECURITY, FOREIGN CURRENCY or COMMODITY which lies half way between the bid (buy) and offer (sell) price quoted by market makers or dealers. Share prices, commodity prices and exchange rates published in newspapers are generally middle prices. See BID PRICE.

**minicomputer** a medium-scale COMPUTER with sizeable data storage facilities which is often accessible simultaneously from several terminals.

As MICROCOMPUTERS and minicomputers have become more powerful in terms of data-processing speed and data-storage capacity, the distinction between them and MAINFRAME computers has become blurred.

**minimum agreement** see MULTIEMPLOYER AGREEMENT.

**minimum efficient scale** see ECONOMIES OF SCALE.

**minimum stock level** the lowest planned level of STOCK for a particular item prior to replenishment in a STOCK CONTROL system.

**minimum wage rate** the stipulation by the government or

by agreement between trade unions and employers of a minimum rate of PAY for a specified JOB. Minimum wage rates are often decreed by government for particular kinds of work to ensure that employees are able to enjoy a basic standard of living. Until recently minimum wages rates were stipulated for some occupations by WAGES COUNCILS. The abolition of the Wages Councils is believed to have added to the problem of LOW PAY in the UK and some are now calling for a statutory minimum wage to apply to virtually all types of employment. See LOW PAY.

**minority interest** that part of a subsidiary company's listed SHARE CAPITAL which is not owned by the HOLDING COMPANY. Where the holding company owns more than 50% of the shares of a subsidiary company then it is able to control that company, but where it owns less than 100% of the shares then the minority interest of other shareholders in the subsidiary company must be recognized. In compiling CONSOLIDATED ACCOUNTS the claims of minority interests in certain group assets located in subsidiary companies must be recognized, and their entitlement to a share in the profits of subsidiary companies must be allowed for. See PREACQUISITION PROFITS.

**minutes** a summarized transcript or record of items discussed at a meeting and any proposals or resolutions made at the meeting.

**MIRAS (Mortgage Interest Relief at Source)** an arrangement whereby interest payments on a MORTGAGE used to purchase or improve a person's home are allowed against that person's INCOME TAX.

**mission statement** an explicit written statement of an ORGANIZATION's long-term aims and objectives. Mission statements are designed to give substance to the perceived purposes of the organization and provide all employees with an indication of what they are attempting to achieve through their collective endeavours. See BUSINESS OBJECTIVES.

**mixed economy** see ECONOMY.

**MMC** see MONOPOLIES AND MERGERS COMMISSION.

**MNE** see MULTINATIONAL ENTERPRISE.

**mobility barrier** an obstacle which protects firms in one STRATEGIC GROUP in a market from entry by firms currently in some other strategic group. See BARRIERS TO ENTRY. Thus, for example, a producer of general chemicals may be unable to enter the 'speciality' chemical segment because it lacks the technical expertise to do so or because of patent protection.

**'mock bureaucracy'** see BUREAUCRACY.

**mode** a method of representing a set of numbers by a single number which is the value which occurs most often, that is, the one with the highest frequency. For example, if five people had weekly incomes of £100, £100, £150, £250 and £400 then the modal income would be £100 (the most common income). See also AVERAGE, MEDIAN.

**modem** a device used to connect a COMPUTER to the public telephone network to enable the computer to transmit or receive information from other computers sited some distance away.

**modern apprenticeship** see TRAINING.

**modular design** a product DESIGN which facilitates the production of a wide variety of styles of a product using a limited range of common interchangeable components.

**Mondragon** see WORKERS' COOPERATIVE.

**monetarism** a body of economic ideas concerning the role of MONEY, in particular the MONEY SUPPLY, in the functioning of the economy. The historical roots of modern monetarism lie in the *quantity theory of money*: $MV = PT$, where $M$ = money supply, $V$ = velocity of circulation of money, $P$ = general price level, $T$ = the number of goods and services produced by the economy. In simple terms, assuming $V$ to be constant and $T$ to be fixed in the short run, then an increase in $M$ results in an increase in $P$, i.e. the quantity theory provides an explanation of INFLATION in the economy. The theory thus emphasizes the importance of the need for a *long-term* balanced relationship between the amount of money available to finance purchases of goods and services, on the one hand, and the ability of the economy to produce such goods and services, on the other. Thus, in order to avoid inflation the growth of the money supply must not exceed the supply capacity (i.e. growth rate) of the economy over time. See MONETARY POLICY, ECONOMIC POLICY.

**Monetary Compensation Amount** see GREEN MONEY.

**monetary policy** the regulation of the MONEY SUPPLY, CREDIT and INTEREST RATES in order to control the level of spending in the economy (see ECONOMIC POLICY).

The monetary authorities (principally the Bank of England in the UK) can employ a number of measures to regulate the money supply, in particular that part of it which is used to underpin the provision of credit, including open market operations in government BONDS and TREASURY BILLS, special deposits and directives (see CENTRAL BANK).

*Open market operations* are targeted at the liquidity base of the banking system and involve the sale or purchase of bonds and Treasury bills which alters the amount of bank deposits held by the COMMERCIAL BANKS and thus their capacity to advance LOANS and OVERDRAFTS to customers. For example, if the authorities wish to reduce the money supply they can sell long-dated bonds to the general public. Buyers pay for these bonds by running down their bank deposits – an important constituent of the money supply – which forces the banks in turn to reduce the volume of their lending.

A *special deposit* call by the authorities requires the banks to place a specified proportion of their liquid assets on deposit with the Bank of England which are then 'frozen', i.e. they cannot be used by the banks as the basis for advancing loans and overdrafts to customers, again reducing the money supply. A *directive* is a request by the Bank of England to the banks to keep their total lending below a specified global ceiling or to reduce their lending for particular purposes (for example car purchase).

The authorities can also operate INSTALMENT CREDIT controls on lending by FINANCE HOUSES to limit spending. They can, for example, discourage potential borrowers from using instalment facilities by increasing the down payment required and by reducing the time period of the loan; the former stipulation requires the borrower to find more ready cash, while the latter increases the effective interest charge payable.

The authorities may seek to influence interest rates more widely rather than just on particular categories of borrowing. In May 1997, responsibility for setting interest rates was handed over by the government to the Bank of England, thereby making the determination of monetary policy 'independent' of political control.

In practice, the application of monetary policy is fraught with difficulties. The main problem is that there is no single reliable definition of the money supply (see MONEY SUPPLY for details), so that any attempt to target a particular specification of the money supply tends to be undermined by asset-switching from other categories. To illustrate briefly: if the authorities target M3 (mainly currency plus bank deposits) for control purposes and use the various instruments noted above to reduce the level of bank deposits, this may not be sufficient in itself to reduce spending. Spenders may simply switch to 'M4' type money, running down their building society deposits to finance current purchases.

For most of the period since 1945, monetary policy has been used as a short-term stabilization technique but has largely taken second place to FISCAL POLICY. However, with the recent upsurge in monetarist ideas, control of the money supply on a longer-term basis has taken centre stage in the application of economic policy.

See MONETARISM, BUSINESS CYCLE.

**monetary system** the assets which make up a country's MONEY SUPPLY and the institutions involved in deposit-taking, money transmission and the provision of credit facilities, together constitute the monetary side of the ECONOMY.

The money supply consists of a number of assets (bank notes, coins etc.), denominated in terms of MONETARY UNITS (pounds and pence in the case of the UK). The institutions involved in handling money include various BANKS, FINANCE HOUSES, BUILDING SOCIETIES etc. The monetary system of a country is controlled by its CENTRAL BANK which uses a number of techniques to regulate the supply of money and interest rates (see MONETARY POLICY).

The monetary system also has an external dimension in that participation by countries in INTERNATIONAL TRADE and FOREIGN INVESTMENT requires the establishment of interactive mechanisms such as EXCHANGE RATES and INTERNATIONAL RESERVES.

See INTERNATIONAL MONETARY FUND.

**monetary unit** one of the units of CURRENCY used in a country as the basis of payments and lending and borrowing transactions. The units of currency used in the UK, for example, are pounds and pence, while in France they are the franc and centime. The monetary units of different countries are related to each other for INTERNATIONAL TRADE and INVESTMENT purposes through their EXCHANGE RATE values.

**money** an asset which is generally acceptable as a means of payment in the sale and purchase of products and other assets and for concluding borrowing and lending transactions. The use of money enables products and assets to be priced in terms of the monetary units of the country (pence and pounds in the UK, for example), and to be exchanged using money as a common *medium of exchange* rather than the bartering of one product against another. Money also acts as a *store of value* (money can be held over a period of time and used to finance future payments) and as a *unit of account* (money is used to measure and record the value of products and assets, as for example in compiling the country's NATIONAL INCOME accounts). See MONEY SUPPLY, MONETARY POLICY.

**money market** a MARKET engaged in the short-term lending and borrowing of MONEY, linking together the financial institutions (COMMERCIAL BANKS, DISCOUNT HOUSES etc.), companies and the government. To take one example: a company with surplus short-term funds might deposit these funds with its commercial bank, which in turn places them on 'call' (deposit) with a discount house. The discount house in turn uses the money to purchase TREASURY BILLS issued by the government. See DISCOUNT MARKET.

**money supply** the stock of MONEY in an economy. The money supply can be specified in a variety of ways (see Fig. 59): narrow definitions of the money supply include only a limited number of assets, while broader definitions extend the range of assets included; for example, the 'M0' (narrow) money supply comprises currency (notes and coins), COMMERCIAL BANKS' till money and their operational balances at the Bank of England; 'M3' (broad) money supply is made up of M0 plus sight and time deposits with the commercial banks and UK public sector sterling deposits.

The size of the money supply is an important determinant of the level of spending in the economy and its control is a particular concern of MONETARY POLICY. However, the monetary authorities have a problem because given the number of possible definitions of the money supply, it is difficult for them to decide which is the most appropriate money supply category to target for control purposes. Moreover, having targeted a particular definition they face the added difficulty of actually controlling it because of the potential for asset-switching from one category of money to another.

For most of the 1980s the authorities targeted M3 for con-

## MONEY VALUES

| Initials | Definition | Amount £ billion (December 1996) |
|----------|------------|----------------------------------|
| *'Narrow' money (Money held predominantly for spending)* | | |
| MO | Bank notes and coin in circulation plus banks' till money and operational balances at Bank of England | 25 |
| M1 | M0 plus UK private sector sight bank deposits | |
| *Broad Money (Money for spending and/or as a store of value)* | | |
| M3 | M1 plus UK private sector time bank deposits and UK public sector sterling deposits | |
| M4 | M3 plus net building society deposits | 712 |

Fig. 59. **Money Supply**. Money supply definitions
(Source: Bank of England *Quarterly Bulletin*, December 1997.)

trol purposes, but in recent years have switched to M0 and
M4 as 'indicators' of monetary conditions.

See LEGAL TENDER.

**money values** see REAL VALUES.

**Monopolies and Mergers Commission (MMC)** a regulatory body responsible, in part, for the implementation of
UK COMPETITION POLICY. The basic remit of the MMC is to
investigate and report on cases of MONOPOLY, MERGER and
TAKEOVER and ANTI-COMPETITIVE PRACTICES referred to it by the
OFFICE OF FAIR TRADING (OFT) to determine whether or not they
operate against the public interest.

The term *public interest* is not specifically defined in competition law so it has been left to the MMC itself to determine what constitutes offence to the public interest in the particular situations before it. In monopoly cases, the MMC examines the actions of DOMINANT FIRMS for evidence of the abuse of market power; for example, the charging of excessive prices resulting in monopoly profits being earned, or the use of PRICE DISCRIMINATION in ways harmful to the consuming public, together with the use of various predatory practices such as selective price cutting and restrictions on distribution which put smaller rivals at a competitive disadvantage and create BARRIERS TO ENTRY. Practices such as EXCLUSIVE DEALING, REFUSAL TO SUPPLY, AGGREGATED REBATES, etc., which produce few economic benefits and whose main effect is to restrict competition, are invariably condemned by the MMC.

In merger and takeover cases, the MMC examines the potential benefits likely to arise from the merger (for example, the scope for reducing costs and better research and development opportunities); alongside possible detriments (for example, increased market power bringing with it the danger of higher prices and restrictions on competition). Under present law, however, mergers are not required to exhibit *net* benefit and can only be opposed if they are judged to seriously reduce competition or impair efficiency.

The MMC only has powers of recommendation when it finds offence to the public interest; for example, it can recommend price cuts and price controls to eliminate monopoly prices; the prohibition of offending anti-competitive practices; and the prohibition of undesirable mergers and takeovers. It is then, however, up to the OFT to implement these recommendations, or otherwise, as it sees fit.

**monopolistic competition** a MARKET STRUCTURE characterized by many small suppliers and non-standardized products. Competition between suppliers is focused on offering distinctive branded products (see PRODUCT DIFFERENTIATION) rather than price competition. Although each supplier has a degree of monopoly control over his *own* product (via his brand name), the presence of a large number of similar competing products ensures that no individual supplier can control the market as a whole. See IMPERFECT COMPETITION.

**monopoly** a MARKET STRUCTURE characterized by a single

supplier and high barriers to entry. In practice, the term 'monopoly' is usually given a wider interpretation, particularly within the context of COMPETITION POLICY, to cover DOMINANT FIRM situations and COLLUSION between rival suppliers. Monopoly is often depicted as an inefficient form of market organization since the lack of effective competition tends to remove the monopolist's incentive to reduce industry supply costs. Worse still, monopolists may abuse their market power both with respect to consumers (for example, by charging excessive prices), and actual and potential competitors (for example, by depriving them of market access through EXCLUSIVE DEALING practices). On the other hand, MARKET CONCENTRATION may lower industry supply costs by enabling firms to take advantage of ECONOMIES OF SCALE, and it is to be noted that governments go out of their way to encourage patent monopolies (see PATENT) as a means of encouraging innovation. See CONCENTRATION RATIO, MONOPOLY OF SCALE.

**monopoly of scale** the dominance of a market by an individual firm which often derives from the firm's ability to take advantage of economies of large-scale production and distribution (see ECONOMIES OF SCALE). UK COMPETITION POLICY gives the term a more specific connotation, defining a monopoly of scale situation as one in which a firm supplies more than 25% or more of a particular product. The inference is that while such a firm may generate benefits in the way of cost efficiencies, it is also in a position to exercise MARKET POWER to the potential detriment of both consumers and smaller competitors. See DOMINANT FIRM, MONOPOLY.

**monopoly policy** a policy concerned with the regulation of MONOPOLIES, MERGERS and TAKEOVERS, RESTRICTIVE TRADE AGREEMENTS, RESALE PRICES and ANTI-COMPETITIVE PRACTICES. See COMPETITION POLICY for further discussion of these areas.

**monopoly power** see MARKET POWER.

**moonlighter** a person who is officially registered as being unemployed and receives unemployment benefit, but who in reality undertakes paid work in the unofficial so-called BLACK ECONOMY. Alternatively, moonlighting is where an employee undertakes a *second* job 'on the side' during the normal working hours of his or her main employment.

**moratorium** the suspension of repayment of DEBT, or INTEREST, for a specified period of time; for example, the freezing of debt repayment obligations extended by governments and private banks of advanced countries to a developing country which is experiencing acute balance of payments difficulties, or the suspension of debt payments owing to dealers in a commodity market which has suffered a dramatic price collapse.

**mortgage** the advance of a LOAN to a person or business (the borrower/mortgagor) by other persons or businesses, in particular financial institutions such as BUILDING SOCIETIES and COMMERCIAL BANKS (the lender/mortgagee) which is used to acquire some asset, most notably a property such as a house, office or factory. A mortgage is a form of CREDIT which is extended for a specified period of time either on fixed INTEREST terms, or more usually, given the long duration of most mortgages, on variable interest terms. Under an ordinary mortgage, interest and the repayment of the principal loaned is paid on a regular instalment basis over the life of the mortgage. In the case of endowment mortgages (which are linked to a life INSURANCE policy) interest is paid on a regular instalment basis to the building society and the life insurance premium likewise to an INSURANCE COMPANY, with the principal being repaid in full out of the proceeds of the life insurance policy (either on the death of the mortgagor or on completion of the mortgage contract period). The deeds giving entitlement to ownership of the property remain with the building society as collateral security (against default on the loan), until it is repaid in full, when they are transferred to the mortgagor who then becomes the legal owner of the property. See SECOND MORTGAGE, MIRAS.

**Mortgage Interest Relief at Source** see MIRAS.

**most favoured nation rule** see GENERAL AGREEMENT ON TARIFFS AND TRADE.

**mothballing** see CAPACITY.

**motion study** see WORK STUDY.

**motivation** the force or process which impels people to behave in the way that they do. In a work setting, motivation can be viewed as that which determines whether workers expend the degree of effort necessary to achieve required task objectives. In OCCUPATIONAL PSYCHOLOGY two basic conceptions of motivation can be discerned: 'needs' theory and 'expectancy' theory. Possibly the best known of the former is

# MOTIVATION

the 'hierarchy of needs' identified by Abraham Maslow (1908–70). He argued that individuals have intrinsic needs which they are impelled to seek to satisfy. These needs, which are ordered in a hierarchy are *physical needs* (food, warmth, shelter), *security needs* (safety, home), *ego needs* (esteem, status) and *self-actualization needs* (the realization of individual potential). Initially, the lower order needs such as safety determine behaviour but once these are satisfied higher order needs come to dominate. Maslow's theory has been widely criticized, however, for assuming that such needs are universal and that they are always ordered in this particular hierarchy.

Other needs theories include Herzberg's 'Two Factor Theory of Motivation'. He argued that people are motivated by two kinds of need: *hygiene factors* (those basic needs such as shelter which, if not satisfied, lead to unhappiness but whose satisfaction does not in itself lead to happiness); and *motivators* (those higher order needs which when satisfied lead to contentment). The importance of this theory in a work setting is its insistence that managers have to ensure that both hygiene factors (i.e. pay, working conditions) and motivation (i.e. the need for personal fulfilment) are satisfied for a workforce to be content and highly motivated.

A further 'needs' theory is the ERG (Existence, Relatedness and Growth) theory of Clayton Alderfer (1940– ). Like Maslow he suggests that there is a hierarchy of needs but that the less a high level need is satisfied the more important a lower level need becomes. Hence demands for more pay in fact really reflect a desire for work to be made more satisfying.

The main alternative approach to 'needs' theories is the 'expectancy' approach associated with Victor Vroom (1932– ). This suggests that individuals are motivated to act in certain ways not by some basic inner need but by the strength of the expectation that the action will achieve a result seen by them as desirable. The desire for a particular outcome is known as the 'valence'. This theory is essentially a 'process' theory: it emphasizes the process of motivation rather than the nature or content of particular motivators. The strength of people's motivation will be determined by weighing up how much they want something and how far they believe a certain action will contribute to achieving it.

**motivational research** the measurement of attitudes and preferences likely to affect BUYER BEHAVIOUR. Motivational research is concerned with exploring the underlying reasons why consumers buy products, which can range from functional requirements to psychological needs like status and esteem. There are various techniques which may be employed to explore consumers' psychological needs, including in-depth interviews, psychoanalytical tests and group discussions. The results of motivational research can be used to generate ideas for new products, reposition existing products, and design ADVERTISING COPY to appeal specifically to the motives identified. See MARKETING RESEARCH.

**mouse** a device used to move a pointer around a COMPUTER screen.

**moving average** see SALES FORECASTING.

**MRP** see MATERIALS REQUIREMENT PLANNING.

**MRPII** see MANUFACTURING RESOURCE PLANNING.

**MSDOS** see DOS (DISK OPERATING SYSTEM).

**MSF** see MANUFACTURING, SCIENCE AND FINANCE UNION.

**multi-channel marketing system** see DISTRIBUTION CHANNEL.

**multi-divisional company** see PRODUCT-BASED STRUCTURE.

**multi-employer agreement** (in INDUSTRIAL RELATIONS) an agreement between a group of employers and TRADE UNIONS governing rates of pay and conditions of employment in all of these companies. In multi-employer COLLECTIVE BARGAINING in the UK the employers' interests are usually represented by an EMPLOYERS' ASSOCIATION, which aspires to represent all employers in that particular industry. Such agreements are thus often also called 'industry-wide agreements'. On the union side, the negotiations are usually conducted by paid regional or national officials rather than lay SHOP STEWARDS. The forum in which the agreement is made is known in some industries as a joint industrial council.

Multi-employer collective bargaining agreements developed in the UK from the 1920s onwards, partly in response to the recommendations of the Whitley Committee. In the post-World War II period multi-employer agreements came to be supplemented by bargaining within individual plants (see DONOVAN COMMISSION), and since the 1960s there has been a shift away from reliance on multi-employer agreements. Nevertheless multi-employer agreements still provide the core framework for regulating pay and conditions in some industries, especially those composed of a large number of small companies. In this context three types of multi-employer agreement can be identified:

(a) *minimum agreements*: where the agreement sets a minimum rate of pay which can be supplemented by individual employers. Revision upwards of the minimum rate of pay does not automatically push up the actual rate of pay for most employed; instead it increases the rate of pay only of those employed at the minimum rate. Agreements of this kind can therefore be said to provide a safety-net for the lowest paid. The determination of actual rates of pay for other employees is achieved through collective bargaining *within* firms. Multi-employer bargaining of this type therefore coexists with single employer bargaining. This type of agreement was found in the UK engineering industry until recently;

(b) *partial agreements*: where some but not all aspects of pay and conditions are regulated by the agreement. For instance, the regulation of pay rates is more detailed than in the minimum agreement but they are still minima which may be supplemented by individual employers;

(c) *comprehensive agreements*: where most or all aspects of pay and conditions are tightly regulated in accordance with the agreement and there is little scope for individual employers to modify these. Electrical contracting is a good example of this in the UK.

**multi-employer bargaining** see COLLECTIVE BARGAINING, MULTI-EMPLOYER AGREEMENT.

**Multi-Fibre Agreement (MFA)** a trading arrangement between some 80 developed and developing countries which regulates international trade in textile and clothing products. The MFA attempts to preserve 'orderly' market conditions in the developed economies by using QUOTAS to limit imports from the developing countries. See PROTECTIONISM.

**multilateral netting** an arrangement whereby two or more associated companies offset their receipts and payments with each other, leaving a single net intra-company receipt or payment balance. Multilateral netting is used particularly by MULTINATIONAL ENTERPRISES which operate many overseas subsidiaries trading in different national currencies, in order to simplify the settlement of intra-group indebtedness. Multilateral netting also serves to reduce a company's EXCHANGE RATE EXPOSURE by minimizing the amount of external purchases and sales of foreign currencies.

**multi-level marketing** a system of selling a firm's product which involves a 'pyramid' of sales persons. Persons sell the product to friends, acquaintances etc. but are also offered a financial inducement to recruit other people as sales persons who, in turn, recruit yet more sales persons. In this way, person A recruits person B who recruits person C and so on thus creating an expanding chain of sales persons, each receiving a commission on their own sales and additionally further commissions based on the sales of people they have recruited directly or indirectly.

**multinational company** see MULTINATIONAL ENTERPRISE.

**multinational enterprise (MNE), multinational company (MNC)** or **transnational company** a firm that *owns* production, sales and other revenue-generating assets in a number of countries. Foreign direct investment by MNEs in the establishment or acquisition of overseas raw material and components operations, production plants and sales subsidiaries occurs because of the potentially greater cost-effectiveness and profitability in SOURCING inputs and servicing markets (see FOREIGN MARKET SERVICING STRATEGY) through a direct presence in a number of locations, rather than sole reliance on a single home base and IMPORTS and EXPORTS as the basis of the firms' international operations.

A firm may possess various COMPETITIVE ADVANTAGES over rival suppliers ('firm-specific advantages') in the form of patented process technology or a unique branded product which it can better exploit and protect by establishing overseas supply facilities. Direct investment may enable a firm to reduce its distribution costs and keep in touch more closely with local market conditions – changes in consumer tastes, competitors' actions etc. Moreover, direct investment enables a firm both to avoid governmental restrictions on market access such as TARIFFS and QUOTAS, and be able to benefit from other 'country-specific advantages' such as the availability of government cash grants and subsidies on inward investment. In the case of sourcing, direct investment allows the MNE to take advantage of some countries' lower labour costs or provides access to superior technological know-how.

## MULTIPLE ACTIVITY CHART

See BUSINESS STRATEGY, CAPITAL INFLOW, HOST COUNTRY, FOREIGN INVESTMENT, INDUSTRIAL LOCATION, INTERNALIZATION, TRANSFER PRICE, OFFSHORE PRODUCTION, INTERNATIONAL MARKETING, FOREIGN CURRENCY TRANSLATION, DOUBLE TAXATION, UNITARY TAXATION, WITHHOLDING TAX, EXCHANGE RATE EXPOSURE.

**multiple activity chart** see ACTIVITY CHART.

**multi-unionism** the presence of a number of potentially competing TRADE UNIONS in a workplace or organization, accompanied in some organizations by separate COLLECTIVE BARGAINING arrangements. It is believed to have a detrimental effect on INDUSTRIAL RELATIONS because it encourages disputes over DEMARCATION LINES, PAY DIFFERENTIALS etc. Once an integral element of UK industrial relations, the rationalization of bargaining procedures and the decline in the number of unions have reduced its extent and significance.

**multi-unit pricing** the sale of more than one unit of a product at a price lower than the total of individual units' prices. This technique is used as a form of SALES PROMOTION (for example, 'two-for-the price-of-one' offers).

**mutuality** the principle that managers should not change any aspect of WORK ORGANIZATION without first securing the agreement of SHOP STEWARDS or TRADE UNION officials. See COLLECTIVE BARGAINING.

# N

**Naamloze Vennootschap (N.V.)** the Dutch equivalent of a British public limited company. See JOINT-STOCK COMPANY.

**NAFTA** see NORTH AMERICAN FREE TRADE AGREEMENT.

**National Association of Pension Funds (NAPF)** the TRADE ASSOCIATION which represents the collective interests of PENSION FUNDS in the UK.

**National Association of Schoolmasters and Union of Women Teachers (NAS/UWT)** the second largest teaching TRADE UNION in the UK. Unlike the NATIONAL UNION OF TEACHERS, its membership is concentrated in secondary education. Currently its membership is around 210,000, and it is the UK's tenth largest union.

**national debt** the money owed by the government to domestic and overseas lenders. Governments frequently spend more than their current receipts from taxation and are required to cover the ensuing budget deficit by issuing financial securities such as TREASURY BILLS and BONDS. See BUDGET (GOVERNMENT).

**National Council for Vocational Qualifications** the body overseeing the system of NATIONAL VOCATIONAL QUALIFICATIONS in England and Wales. See also TRAINING, TRAINING AND ENTERPRISE COUNCIL.

**National Economic Development Council (NEDC)** an organization which, together with its satellite agencies, the Economic Development Committees (EDCs) and the National Economic Development Organization (NEDO) operated between 1962 and 1992 to help improve Britain's economic performance. See INDUSTRIAL POLICY.

**National Economic Development Organization** see NATIONAL ECONOMIC DEVELOPMENT COUNCIL.

**National Education and Training Target** see TRAINING.

**National Farmers' Union (NFU)** the EMPLOYER'S ASSOCIATION representing employers in agriculture.

**national income** the total money value of the income accruing from a country's economic activity over a one-year period. See NATIONAL INCOME ACCOUNTS.

**national income accounts** a financial statement of the total income (or output) generated in an economy over a particular period of time, usually one year. The national income accounts provide a useful money measure of economic activity in the economy and are used by governments in the formulation of their economic policies. By calculating national income per head of population an indication is given of the country's general prosperity (i.e. living standards); this can then be used to compare living standards over time or to make international comparisons of living standards.

National income can be measured in three ways:

(a) the *value added* or *output* method sums together the value added by each economic activity (beer production, banking services etc.) in producing the year's output. This total figure is known as the gross domestic product (GDP); *net property income from abroad* (net profits, rent, dividends, interest) is added

NATIONAL INSURANCE

on to GDP to arrive at the *gross national product* (GNP). Because some of the nation's capital stock is used up in producing current output, allowance must be made for DEPRECIATION (capital consumption). Net national product (GNP minus depreciation of the capital stock) is called national income;

(a) the *income* method sums together all the factor incomes (wages and salaries, rent and profits) received from producing the year's output. These factor incomes are equal in total to the total of value added = GDP. Again, net property income from abroad must be added to GDP to arrive at GNP and depreciation deducted to give the national income figure;

(c) The *expenditure* method sums together all of the expenditures on the year's output to give a figure for total domestic expenditure. Since some domestic expenditure will be on imported goods and some domestic output is exported (reflecting expenditure by foreigners), it is necessary to deduct the value of imports and add the value of exports to the total domestic expenditure figure to arrive at GNP. Again depreciation must be deducted from GNP to arrive at the figure for national income.

**national insurance** SEE SOCIAL SECURITY BENEFITS.

**national insurance contributions** the payments made by employers and their employees to the UK government up to a specified maximum limit. National insurance contributions, together with other government budgetary receipts, are used to finance state pensions, sick pay, unemployment benefits, etc.

There are currently (1997/8) four classes of national insurance contributions. Under the most common class, Class 1, employees and employers pay no contributions on weekly earnings of below £62; on earnings between £62 and £465 employees pay contributions at the rate of 2% on the first £62 of weekly earnings and at the rate of 10% on weekly earnings between £62 and £465 (the upper limit). Employers' contributions are on a sliding-scale, ranging upwards from 3% (weekly earnings £62–£110) to 10% (weekly earnings greater than £210–no limit). Self-employed persons pay Class 2 contributions at the fixed rate of £6.15 per week on annual earnings above £3,480 and additionally at a rate of 6.0% (under Class 4) on earnings between £7,010 and £24,180.

See BUDGET (GOVERNMENT).

**nationalization versus privatization** the taking into public ownership, in the case of nationalization, of an entire industry or an individual firm, and, in the case of privatization (denationalization), the removal of an industry or firm from the public sector and its sale back to the private sector.

In a fully centrally planned ECONOMY, most if not all of industry is owned by the State, while in a free enterprise economy, industry is in private hands. In a mixed economy such as the UK, some industries are State-owned, but most are in the private sector. In the 1980s in the UK the political tide placed a greater emphasis on free enterprise and this led the government to embark on a widespread privatization programme which (to date) has included the sale of the gas, telecommunications, water, electricity and steel industries, together with various individual businesses including BP, BAA, TSB and Amersham.

The extent of State involvement in industrial activity is motivated by a number of political and economic considerations. The main rationale underlying State ownership of all industry is the view that the collective ownership of the means of production 'by the people for the people' is preferable to a situation in which the ownership of the means of production is in the hands of the 'capitalist class' who are able to exploit their élite position to the detriment of the populace at large. State control of industry enables the economy as a whole to be organized in accordance with some central plan, which by interlocking and synchronizing the input–output requirements of industry, is able to secure an efficient allocation of productive resources. Critics of State-owned economic systems argue, however, that in practice they tend to be 'captured and corrupted' by powerful State officials, and that their top-heavy bureaucratic structures result in a highly inefficient organization of production and insensitivity to what customers actually want. Free enterprise advocates argue that a decentralized, MARKET-based system leads to a more efficient allocation of productive resources in line with the demands of buyers, and that in pursuit of individual self-interest (the profit motive) it will produce economic results (lower costs and prices, innovative new products) which are beneficial to society as a whole.

The main economic justification for an individual industry

to be nationalized (as opposed to all industry) is that production can be more efficiently organized on a single-supplier basis with cost reductions accruing through economies of scale and the elimination of wasteful duplication. Critics argue, however, that while this may be a theoretical possibility, the reality is that operating economies are usually dissipated by the higher administrative costs of running large bureaucracies, especially where, due to lack of competition, there is no imperative to seek cost savings. Advocates of privatization, in particular, place emphasis on competition and capital market sanctions as a means of promoting greater efficiency, i.e. firms which are inefficient vis-à-vis competitors will suffer losses and will either go bankrupt or be taken over.

The main problem with privatization is the extent to which competition can in fact be introduced into sectors hitherto confined to State monopolies, either by breaking up an existing State corporation into a number of separate private companies (as for electricity) or by encouraging new entry (as in gas and telecommunications). Because of this it has been necessary in some cases to establish a regulatory authority (Ofgas and Oftel, respectively, for gas and telecommunications), backed up by the possibility of a reference to the MONOPOLIES AND MERGERS COMMISSION, to control the industry.

**national plan** see ECONOMIC PLANNING.

**National Research and Development Corporation** see BRITISH TECHNOLOGY GROUP.

**national savings certificate** a FINANCIAL SECURITY issued by the UK government as a means of raising money for the government and encouraging private SAVING. National Savings Certificates are issued in small denominations through post offices and banks; holders receive interest on them which is free of income tax, but the number held by any one person is limited to (currently) 10,000.

**National Union of Mineworkers (NUM)** an industrial TRADE UNION representing clerical and manual employees in the UK coal industry. As an industrial union its fortunes have been closely dependent on those of the coal industry. The closure of a large number of coal mines in recent years has led to substantial membership losses for the union. Its preeminence in the industry has been challenged by the emergence of the Union of Democratic Mineworkers in the

1984–85 strike. The NUM now has under 10,000 members, compared with over 150,000 in 1984.

**National Union of Teachers (NUT)** the largest teaching TRADE UNION in the UK with members in both primary and secondary education. Currently it has over 200,000 members, and is the UK's ninth largest trade union.

**National Vocational Qualification** a qualification in England and Wales recognizing competence in a vocational or technical subject, usually awarded after a period of vocational TRAINING and formal assessment. Competence is primarily defined as the ability to perform a task successfully. The NVQ system has been developed to encourage firms to train more systematically and to encourage training in transferable SKILLS (i.e. skills of use to more than one organization). The UK government's intention is that there will be national standards of competence for all occupations, established by *lead bodies* for each occupation/industry. Many NVQ subjects are highly specific and are primarily concerned with task performance rather than more diffuse conceptual understanding (the ability to understand as well as perform a task is sometimes referred to as competency). Some NVQs, however, are broader and less immediately technical in scope, and are perceived as more practically focused alternatives to traditional academic qualifications such as A-Levels: these tend to be known as General NVQs or more usually GNVQs. NVQs are arranged in a set of 5 levels, ranging from basic to professional level.

The NVQ system is a major attempt to improve on the UK's poor record in vocational training. Critics of NVQs allege, however, that many NVQ courses pay insufficient attention to the development of the conceptual skills necessary to understand technical processes fully. It is also difficult to identify discrete competences required for many tasks and occupations, particularly those that are highly complex in character.

**NCVQ** see NATIONAL COUNCIL FOR VOCATIONAL QUALIFICATION.

**NEDC** see NATIONAL ECONOMIC DEVELOPMENT COUNCIL.

**needs** or **wants** the physical, psychological and social requirements of human beings. The identification of consumer needs and the development and MARKETING of appropriate products to satisfy these needs lies at the heart of all business activity. See BUYER BEHAVIOUR, NEW PRODUCT DEVELOPMENT, OCCUPA-

# NEGATIVE INCOME TAX

**negative income tax** a form of TAXATION which involves establishing a socially and economically acceptable minimum or 'threshold' level of income for individuals, taxing those above it on a progressive basis (see INCOME TAX) and giving tax credits or rebates to those people below it.

Advocates of such a tax structure for the UK argue that in combining the tax and SOCIAL SECURITY systems, not only would this be easier and more cost-effective to administer but, importantly, it would remove many of the anomalies of the present dual systems; in particular, cases where people receive more income (benefits) from not working than from taking paid employment.

**negotiation** the process by which two or more parties attempt to achieve agreement on matters of mutual interest. It can occur at the interpersonal level, for example, to resolve who does the washing-up on a particular evening; or at the organizational and societal level, for example, negotiations between TRADE UNIONS and employers over the size of an annual pay award (see COLLECTIVE BARGAINING). It can be viewed as a way of resolving CONFLICTS of interest in a way that is at least acceptable, if not ideal, to all concerned. Negotiation between two parties can be relatively straightforward but becomes much more complex when more are involved.

Research into negotiation has established that the process works most smoothly when each party listens fully to the other so that the points of difference can be delineated precisely. In many cases this does not happen, with the result that each party's view of the other's position is in fact erroneous. Listening is also essential during hard bargaining to pick up any signals that the other party is prepared to change its bargaining position.

Inexperienced negotiators often believe that negotiation is a zero-sum activity: that one party's gain must be the other's loss. However, such an outcome is rarely effective in the long term. The defeated party may well harbour such resentment that when it is in a more favourable position it will strike back. More experienced negotiators tend to view bargaining as a positive-sum activity: all parties can gain something from the process. Negotiation is the activity through which the possibilities are explored. However in some cases, during IN-DUSTRIAL DISPUTES for example, negotiators find it impossible to reach agreement. At this point it can be useful to enlist the services of a neutral third party to conduct ARBITRATION, CON-CILIATION or MEDIATION.

**neo-human relations** a body of theories, mainly developed in the 1950s and 1960s within the realm of OCCUPATIONAL PSYCHOLOGY, which suggested that prevailing patterns of WORK ORGANIZATION, leaving individuals with 'narrow' jobs and little responsibility, frustrate workers' needs for 'self-actualization' (i.e. development of their full potential) and hence lead to low levels of JOB SATISFACTION. The solution was seen to be the re-design of jobs (see JOB DESIGN and JOB REDESIGN), and especially job enrichment to make work more satisfying. As part of this process managers had to learn to trust their subordinates to act correctly without close or punitive supervision. In turn satisfied workers would become committed to organizational goals and their performance would improve. The emphasis of neo-human relations differs from that of human relations in that it assumes that worker-behaviour is determined by mater-ial factors, such as work technology, as well as social relation-ships. Actual change in jobs is seen to be necessary as well as changes in MANAGEMENT STYLE. See ALIENATION, HUMAN RELA-TIONS, THEORY X AND Y.

**net assets** the combined amount of a company's FIXED ASSETS and WORKING CAPITAL (net current assets) as recorded in the company's BALANCE SHEET. The book value of a company's net assets provides a rough guide to the value of the company's resources being used to generate profit. Compare TOTAL ASSETS.

**net asset value** the asset value of a company to its ordinary shareholders. This consists of the BALANCE SHEET value of total assets (FIXED ASSETS plus CURRENT ASSETS) less CURRENT LIABILITIES, DEBENTURES, LOAN STOCKS and PREFERENCE SHARES. These net assets can be divided by the number of ordinary shares to indicate the net asset value per share.

**net book value** or **written down value** the accounting value of a FIXED ASSET in a firm's BALANCE SHEET that represents its original cost less cumulative DEPRECIATION charged to date.

**net current assets** see WORKING CAPITAL.

**net income** see NET PROFIT.

**net investment method** see FOREIGN CURRENCY TRANSLATION.

**net margin** see NET PROFIT.

**net present value** see INVESTMENT APPRAISAL, DISCOUNTED CASH FLOW.

**net profit** the difference between a firm's SALES REVENUE and all COSTS. In accounting terms net profit is the difference between GROSS PROFIT and the costs involved in running a firm (including DEPRECIATION costs and INTEREST charges). In the UK, net profit may be expressed before or after deduction of CORPORATION TAX. See PROFIT, PROFIT-AND-LOSS ACCOUNT.

**net realizable value** the amount for which a FIXED ASSET or CURRENT ASSET can be sold, less any selling expenses involved. Net realizable value of an asset may be below its NET BOOK VALUE in which case the ACCOUNTING PRINCIPLE of prudence would suggest that the value of the asset in the company's LEDGER accounts should be adjusted downward to avoid over-stating asset values in the BALANCE SHEET.

**NETT** see TRAINING.

**netting** see MULTILATERAL NETTING.

**network analysis** or **programme evaluation and review technique (PERT)** a method of planning, scheduling and controlling projects involving interrelated but distinct elements of work, or *activities*. Activities and their interrelationships are depicted in a *network* of arrowed links representing activities. For example, Fig. 60 shows a simple schematic network for the construction of a kitchen extension, with planned activities and their estimated duration in weeks. Certain activities (like preparing the ground) have to be performed before the next stage of production can be embarked upon (like constructing the shell of the building). The sequential path which takes the least time to complete the project is called the 'critical path' (here the route a-b-c-d-e-f, taking 20 weeks) and any delay to these critical activities will delay the project completion. Other activities (like preparing the ground) are non-critical and can be delayed (in this case by up to one week) without delaying the overall project. Such non-critical activities embody an amount of *slack* time (one week in the example). The total amount of slack time for all non-critical activities shows the extent to which these activities can be delayed before affecting the project completion date.

Network analysis is often applied to large-scale projects in

Fig. 60. **Network analysis.** Network for constructing kitchen extension. (w=weeks).

civil engineering and shipbuilding or to major repair or maintenance projects or new product launches. It is used to identify problem areas where bottlenecks may occur and where additional resources may be needed.

**networking 1.** a form of WORK ORGANIZATION in which tasks are subcontracted to people who work away from the office (at home for instance) but who are connected to office information systems via COMPUTER-based ELECTRONIC MAIL and similar communications links. Usually networked staff are former employees who have become SELF-EMPLOYED and are now paid on a fee basis. Networking can be advantageous to all parties: employers benefit from lower employment costs whilst networked staff gain more control over their working time.

**2.** the establishment by a manager of contacts with other people whose knowledge and expertise might prove useful to the manager.

**3.** the linking of a number of firms or business units within a firm in order to develop a supply chain for a product. This could involve, for example, business unit (A) supplying components to business unit (B) which assembles these components into a final product which is then marketed by business unit (C). See MULTINATIONAL ENTERPRISE, JUST IN TIME.

**4.** the process of linking together a number of PERSONAL COMPUTERS in order to facilitate communication between them. See LOCAL AREA NETWORK.

**net worth** see LONG-TERM CAPITAL EMPLOYED.

**newly industrializing country (NIC)** see DEVELOPING COUNTRY.

**new product** a good or service which is sufficiently different from existing products to be regarded as new by consumers. The degree of newness of a product depends upon the extent of its novelty and whether it embodies product attributes not previously available, and can range from relatively minor adaptations of existing products to entirely different product offerings like microwave ovens. Products which are radically different can rapidly establish COMPETITIVE ADVANTAGE as they open up an entirely new market and dominate the early stages of the PRODUCT LIFE CYCLE. See NEW-PRODUCT DEVELOPMENT, DIFFUSION PROCESS.

**new product development** the process of creating NEW PRODUCTS by a firm as part of its ongoing PRODUCT STRATEGY. New product development involves a number of steps as indicated in Fig. 61. New product ideas can arise from two broad sources:

(a) product concepts based on ideas for new products generated by the firm's own marketing or production staff, or ideas from customers or suppliers;

(b) product technology generated by the firm's RESEARCH AND DEVELOPMENT department or licensed from outside the firm.

Any product ideas arising from either of these sources are then subjected to an initial product screening which explores their viability in terms of possible consumer acceptance, technological feasibility and likely cost. Product ideas which seem viable in terms of this initial screening justify further development expenditures and proceed to the next phase. This phase involves:

(a) further testing of the product concept to gauge its consumer acceptability, perhaps using consumer discussion groups and questionnaire field research;

(b) product design to make product prototypes and test them in a laboratory situation.

The results of these two processes will then be subjected to further screening on marketing, technology and cost grounds, and a product design will be agreed upon for product ideas which survive the second screening. In order to test further both consumer acceptability and the operating efficiency of the product design, prototypes may be distributed to a consumer test panel for their use and results collected from them. Feed-

Fig. 61. **New product development.** Steps in the process of developing a new product.

back from this pre-test can then be used to make final modifications to the product design if the basic design proves to be broadly acceptable.

Finally the firm may undertake extensive MARKETING RE-SEARCH into the potential market for the designed product, establish pilot production facilities for it and test market it in a limited geographical area in order to gauge consumer reaction. If TEST MARKETING proves successful then full-scale production facilities will be created and a full product launch undertaken, backed up by appropriate advertising and sales promotion.

A very high proportion of new product ideas are eliminated by the firm through its screening processes. Despite this only a small proportion of those surviving new products which are launched succeed in establishing themselves in the market. See CONCURRENT ENGINEERING.

**new public management** a new approach to the administration and delivery of public services which has found favour in the UK and elsewhere in the last fifteen years, and can be contrasted with 'old' public administration. Its hallmark is greater emphasis on private sector styles of management and efficiency. Large public bureaucracies with centralized decision-making have been broken up into smaller units with each unit operating at 'arms-length' from each other on the basis of explicit contracts, as in UK central government (see AGENCY STATUS) and the health service (see PURCHASER-PROVIDER SPLIT). These contracts typically include a range of output targets, and the organizations' achievement of these is measured by a set of PERFORMANCE INDICATORS. Competitive pressures have been increased in these organizations by the use of COMPETITIVE TENDERING which in some cases has resulted in private sector firms taking over the delivery of public services. The rationale for these changes is that the costs of public service provision will be easier to identify and hence to reduce. Furthermore, the fragmentation of public organizations will facilitate flexibility, and hence make service delivery more effective and efficient. An important component of the new public management has been a new approach to industrial relations: PERFORMANCE-RELATED PAY has been increasingly adopted in place of standardized pay systems. Critics of new public management argue, however, that the emphasis on entrepreneurial styles of management could weaken the commitment of public sector employees to disinterested public service, and at the extreme encourage corruption. See also CITIZENS' CHARTER.

**Next Steps** see AGENCY STATUS.

**NFU** see NATIONAL FARMERS' UNION.

**NHS Trust** an organization running health-care provision in the UK's National Health Service (NHS) at 'arms-length' from the other parts of the health service. NHS Trusts manage publicly-owned facilities such as hospitals and are accountable to central government in respect of their financial management but have operational autonomy in certain respects e.g. setting the pay and conditions of some employees. It is argued that hospital managers have greater freedom to manage than under the previous system of health service administration, and that this will lead to more effective and efficient use of resources. Controversy has surrounded the creation of NHS Trusts because local political influence on health-care delivery has been reduced, with critics arguing that the self-governing nature of some Trust functions is a form of privatization. Supporters argue that, besides the advantages listed above, consumer influences on health care policy are more appropriately filtered through the health authorities and GP FUNDHOLDERS which purchase health services on their behalf from the Trusts (see PURCHASER-PROVIDER SPLIT). See NEW PUBLIC MANAGEMENT.

**niche** see MARKET SEGMENT.

**Nikkei Index** see SHARE PRICE INDEX.

**'nineteen ninety-two'** the deadline set by the EUROPEAN COMMUNITY for the implementation of the various measures for creating a truly unified internal common market arising from the SINGLE EUROPEAN ACT 1986.

**nominal accounts** records of items of income received by a business, such as rents from properties, or of expenses incurred, such as rates paid. This LEDGER information is summarized periodically in the PROFIT-AND-LOSS ACCOUNT. Contrast with REAL ACCOUNTS.

**nominal capital** see AUTHORIZED or REGISTERED SHARE CAPITAL.

**nominal ledger** the LEDGER which is used to record a firm's income and expenses.

**nominal share capital** see AUTHORIZED CAPITAL.

**nominal share value** see PAR VALUE.

**nominal values** the face value of an asset, wage, profit etc. expressed in current money prices without any adjustment for changes in the level of prices over time. Compare REAL VALUE.

**nominee** a company or trust which holds FINANCIAL SECURITIES on behalf of a person or other company. Nominees may be professional investment managers who hold portfolios of financial securities on behalf of investors (see UNIT TRUST). Alternatively, nominees may be used to buy and hold shares in a particular company on behalf of investors who wish to remain anonymous (often prior to making a TAKEOVER BID for the company). However, UK company law provisions on the DISCLOSURE OF SHAREHOLDINGS make it difficult for a BENEFICIAL OWNER to accumulate large blocks of shares in a company without being forced to reveal his identity. See SHARE REGISTER.

**non-core business** see CORE BUSINESS.

**non-executive director** see DIRECTOR, BOARD OF DIRECTORS.

**non-diversifiable risk** see CAPITAL-ASSET PRICING MODEL.

**non-personal communication channels** see COMMUNICATION CHANNELS.

**non-productive time** see IDLE TIME.

**non-voting shares** or **'A' shares** ORDINARY SHARES which do not have any voting rights at a company's ANNUAL GENERAL MEETING. Non-voting shares often arose because company founders or directors sought to raise new share capital without diluting their control, by issuing large numbers of non-voting shares but retaining control of the original voting shares. Holders of voting shares have an advantage in company takeovers or disputes about company policy and so may have a higher market value than non-voting shares. Most STOCK MARKETS discourage companies from issuing new non-voting shares.

**no par value share** a company SHARE which has no face value. Such shares are used in North America. Contrast PAR VALUE SHARE.

**normal curve** a FREQUENCY DISTRIBUTION which has a bell-shaped symmetrical pattern like Fig. 62. The normal curve can be defined in terms of its AVERAGE and STANDARD DEVIATION and once these are known it is possible to calculate the height of the curve (the frequency) corresponding to any given numerical value.

By changing the scale of a normal distribution it is possible to produce a normal curve with a zero average and unit standard deviation like Fig. 62. This normal curve has a total area equal to 1.0 and the PROBABILITY of getting a particular numerical value which is a given number of standard deviations to the left or right of the average can be estimated directly from the area under the curve as in Fig. 62. Where frequency distributions can be approximated by a normal curve, then about 68% of cases fall within one standard deviation of the mean. 95% of cases fall within two standard deviations of the mean and 99% of cases fall within three standard deviations from the mean.

Normal curves are used in statistical QUALITY CONTROL to establish the limits of variation in the size or other characteristic of a product which is to be regarded as acceptable in SAMPLES of a product being tested. For example, if a

Fig. 62. **Normal curve.** A normal curve with a zero average and unit standard deviation.

component is intended to measure an average of 100 mm across and the standard deviation is 2 mm, then the testers would expect 95% of a sample of components to measure between 96 mm and 104 mm across, and 99% of the sample to measure between 94 mm and 106 mm across. If the latter range of sizes was felt be acceptable in terms of the technical performance of the product, then this CONFIDENCE INTERVAL would lead to the whole batch of components being rejected if more than 1% of sample components were larger or smaller than these broad limits. By contrast, if a tougher criterion was imposed and only components measuring 96 mm to 104 mm across were to be regarded as technically acceptable, then 95% of sample components would be acceptable, and if more than 5% of the sample were larger or smaller than these size limits then the whole batch of components would be rejected.

**normal useful life** see FAILURE RATE CURVE.

**North America Free Trade Agreement (NAFTA)** a regional FREE TRADE area established in 1989 by the USA and Canada, which was extended to include Mexico in 1994. NAFTA aims to remove trade barriers for most manufactured goods, raw materials and agricultural produce over a 10 year period, as well as restrictions on cross border investment, banking and financial services.

See FREE TRADE BLOC.

**no-strike agreement** an agreement between an employer and a TRADE UNION in which the latter undertakes not to initiate or support STRIKE action by employees of the company. A number of Japanese companies which have recently established production facilities in the UK have reached agreements of this type. However, since collective agreements have no legal force in the UK there can be no absolute prohibition of strike action. Such agreements therefore can be viewed primarily as declarations of intent.

In fact most PROCEDURAL AGREEMENTS in INDUSTRIAL RELATIONS in the UK contain provisions which preclude strikes while issues are still under consideration within the COLLECTIVE BARGAINING procedures. Perhaps the main novelty of the new agreements is that most contain a provision for third party intervention, often in the form of pendulum ARBITRATION, should management and union be unable to resolve their differences.

See JAPANIZATION, SINGLE UNION AGREEMENT.

**NUM** see NATIONAL UNION OF MINEWORKERS.

**numeraire** a monetary unit which is used for valuing, on a common basis, international transactions in goods and services, and inter-governmental and central banks' financial settlements. The EUROPEAN MONETARY UNIT (ECU) is used to denominate financial transactions between members of the EUROPEAN MONETARY SYSTEM, while the US dollar is used as the numeraire of the international oil trade.

**numerical control** a system of controlling an automatic machine by means of a programme of instructions (often COMPUTER based) which relate to the particular operations being performed on a component. Machines which are operated by numerical control usually work with greater speed and accuracy than machines operated by hand and are particularly suited to MASS PRODUCTION OR PRODUCTION LINE manufacture.

**numerical flexibility** see LABOUR FLEXIBILITY.
**NUPE** see UNISON.
**NUT** see NATIONAL UNION OF TEACHERS.
**N.V.** see NAAMLOZE VENNOOTSCHAP.
**NVQ** see NATIONAL VOCATIONAL QUALIFICATION.

# O

**objective and task method** a means of managing activities which involves the formulation of specific objectives and the tasks which have to be performed in order to achieve them.
**objectives** see BUSINESS OBJECTIVES.
**objectivity** see ACCOUNTING PRINCIPLES.
**observed time** the time it takes an operator to perform a task when being observed for time study purposes. Observed times do not take into account contingencies like machine breakdowns or the operator's ability, and are simply the time taken by the particular operator being observed to complete the task. Thus, when setting a STANDARD TIME for a particular task several different operatives of differing levels of ability will be observed, and a contingency ALLOWANCE added. See WORK MEASUREMENT.
**obsolescence 1.** the tendency for products to become outmoded and to reach the end of their effective PRODUCT LIFE CYCLE. Obsolescence may be due to changes in style, fashion, materials used and the functions performed. With rapidly advancing technology and more fickle public tastes, product life cycles are tending to shorten as new, more sophisticated products supersede established products. Firms may respond by frequently updating their existing products in order to lengthen their life cycle. Alternatively, firms may deliberately follow a strategy of 'planned obsolescence' by bringing out a continuous stream of new products both to establish COMPETITIVE ADVANTAGE over rival suppliers, and to increase their total sales by inducing customers to replace products more frequently. See NEW-PRODUCT DEVELOPMENT, FASHION PRODUCT,

PRODUCT STRATEGY.

**2.** the reduction in the value of a FIXED ASSET because of a significant change in demand or technology which renders the asset out of date, or comparatively inefficient.

Renting or LEASING plant, machinery and equipment avoids the risk of obsolescence, since at the end of the rental or lease period a firm may rent or lease a more modern fixed asset.

**occupational mobility** see LABOUR MOBILITY.

**occupational pension** see PENSION.

**occupational psychology** the branch of psychology concerned with the study of individual and group attributes and behaviour in work settings. Its potential benefit to managers is that understanding these can facilitate prediction and modification of future behaviour. Occupational psychology is therefore highly relevant to all aspects of organizational activities where individual performance and interaction are relevant to overall organizational performance, i.e. RECRUITMENT AND SELECTION, PERFORMANCE APPRAISAL.

Occupational psychology developed out of what came to be known as *human factor psychology*. This area of psychology is concerned with the relationship between the worker and the working environment. Specifically, it is concerned with the impact of environmental factors, such as the level of illumination on work performance, and how the environment can be changed to improve both job performance and JOB SATISFACTION. It is thus closely related to ERGONOMICS AND HUMAN ENGINEERING. Human factor psychology developed out of a concern to identify the causes of fatigue at work. Initially fatigue was considered solely as a physiological phenomenon, i.e. adverse physical effects would be experienced as work pace reached a certain level. As time went on, however, it was realized that fatigue was at least in part a psychological occurrence and might arise from boredom which in turn could be traced to the character of JOB DESIGN AND REDESIGN.

Although human factor psychology continues to be an important element of occupational psychology, it is fair to say that the central concerns of the discipline relate to the central issues in psychology generally: *motivation*, *learning* and *personality*. Two basic approaches can be discerned in the study of MOTIVATION. One rests on the belief that people have certain basic needs which govern their behaviour (*content* or *needs theory*); the other, known as *expectancy theory*, suggests that individuals are motivated not by some inner need but the strength of their expectation that their actions will achieve a desired result, whatever that is.

The second main concern of occupational psychology is organizational learning. How do individuals learn (or how can they be taught) desirable modes of work behaviour? Once again there are two main approaches:

(a) *Behavioural psychology* suggests that there is a direct relationship between stimulus and response. A certain stimulus will cause a certain behavioural response. Psychologist B F Skinner (1904–90) is especially associated with this approach, which is notable for excluding mental processes themselves from analysis. He argued that behaviour could be conditioned or reinforced by using stimuli. In Skinner's view two forms of condition can be discerned:

(i) *respondent conditioning*, where there is a simple direct and temporal relationship between a certain stimulus and a certain response;

(ii) *operant conditioning*, where a range of environmental factors serves to shape behaviour over time, without there being a simple relationship between one stimulus and one response.

For example, a positive approach to performance appraisal by a boss can over time lead to good work performance by a subordinate. Recurrent praise by the boss will lead to better performance at some point in the future;

(b) The alternative approach to behavioural psychology is *cognitive psychology*. This emphasizes individual interpretation and understanding, and the active role of individuals in establishing their own objectives. A managerial strategy based on this approach would therefore attempt to influence individual goals and thought processes so as to make them complementary to the objectives of the organization.

The third main area of study and analysis is that of personality. Psychologists attempt to pinpoint the dimensions of personality (for example aggression, confidence etc.) and to determine which aspects are shaped by which experiences and whether some in fact are inherited ('nature–nurture debate'). The concern of occupational psychologists is to determine which aspects of personality are especially relevant to work performance, and whether certain traits are associated with effectiveness. It is widely believed, by managers if not by psychologists themselves, that certain traits, for example assertiveness, are LEADERSHIP qualities; hence an attempt to determine whether individuals possess these is often an important part of the recruitment and selection process. (See PSYCHOLOGICAL TESTS, BEHAVIOURALLY ANCHORED RATING SCALE, BEHAVIOURAL OBSERVATION SCALE, PERSONALITY INVENTORY.)

Besides these three core areas of occupational psychology, practitioners also deal with individual problems at work, such as stress. The method normally employed here is counselling. In face-to-face interviews the psychologist will encourage the individual to explore and understand the nature of the problem and to devise appropriate ways of dealing with it. The counsellor has a dual function: he or she listens (which can be highly important to the client) and also attempts to direct the way the client thinks about the problem.

**OECD** see ORGANIZATION FOR ECONOMIC COOPERATION AND DEVELOPMENT.

**off-balance sheet financing** the payment for use of an ASSET by hiring (LEASING) it rather than buying it. If a company wishes to install a new £50,000 photocopier it may enter into a lease agreement and agree to pay £12,000 per year over five years rather than buy the copier. Each year £12,000 is charged against profits in the company's PROFIT AND LOSS ACCOUNT. The copier does not appear in the BALANCE SHEET as a FIXED ASSET because the firm does not own it, but shows up as an annual operating cost which may be offset against PROFIT for TAXATION purposes. Off-balance sheet financing enables a company to make use of expensive assets without having to invest large sums of money in buying them. It also enables a company to keep its LONG-TERM CAPITAL EMPLOYED as small as possible, improving its measured RETURN ON CAPITAL EMPLOYED. See LEASEBACK.

**offer** see CONTRACT.

**offer for sale** a method of raising new SHARE CAPITAL by issuing company shares to the general public at a prearranged fixed price or by tender.

A company usually makes an offer for sale by placing its PROSPECTUS and application form for shares in a newspaper to invite the public to subscribe for shares. The application details will specify the deadline by which all application forms and accompanying cheques from prospective buyers must be received. At the deadline date, lists will be closed and shares allocated among successful subscribers (see ALLOTMENT); monies will be returned to unsuccessful applicants. See SHARE ISSUE, OVERSUBSCRIPTION.

**offer price** see BID PRICE.

**office** BUSINESS PREMISES used by a firm in the provision of services. See CAPITAL STOCK, FIXED ASSET.

**Office of Fair Trading** an authority established by the FAIR TRADING ACT 1973, to administer all aspects of UK COMPETITION POLICY, specifically the control of MONOPOLIES, MERGERS and TAKEOVERS, RESTRICTIVE TRADE AGREEMENTS, RESALE PRICES and ANTI-COMPETITIVE PRACTICES. The OFT, headed by the Director General of Fair Trading, collects data on industrial structure, monitors changes in market concentration and merger and takeover activity, and investigates and acts on information received from interested parties concerning allegedly 'abusive' behaviour in respect of trade practices, prices, discounts and other terms and conditions of sale. Where appropriate, the OFT may decide to refer particular cases for further investigation and report to the MONOPOLIES AND MERGERS COMMISSION and the RESTRICTIVE PRACTICES COURT. The OFT also has other main responsibilities with regard to the protection of consumers' interests generally, including taking action against unscrupulous trade practices such as false description of goods and inaccurate weights and measures, and the regulation of consumer credit. See CONSUMER PROTECTION, TRADE DESCRIPTIONS ACTS 1968 and 1972, WEIGHTS AND MEASURES ACT 1963, CONSUMER CREDIT ACT 1974, ESTATE AGENCY ACT 1979, CONTROL OF MISLEADING ADVERTISEMENTS REGULATIONS 1988.

**Official List** the prices of STOCKS and SHARES published daily by the UK STOCK MARKET. The prices quoted are the prices ruling at the close of the day's trading and are based on the average of the bid and offer prices. See BID PRICE.

**off-line** *adj.* (of COMPUTER equipment) currently not under the control of the central processing unit (CPU).

**offshore fund** money and FINANCIAL SECURITIES held by a FINANCIAL INSTITUTION which has its registered office in an overseas country (usually a TAX HAVEN such as Bermuda, the Cayman Islands or Jersey).

**offshore production** the devolvement, by a MULTINATIONAL ENTERPRISE engaged in the manufacture of a final product in a particular country, of part of its production operations to one or more of its overseas plants. In its strictest sense the term 'offshore production' refers specifically to the production overseas of *components* which are then exported and incorporated into the final product at the firm's main plant. With the increasing globalization of multinational firms' activities, the term is sometimes used also to describe the overseas production of some of the firm's *final products* which are then exported and sold alongside the firm's locally produced items as part of a comprehensive product range offering. Offshore production is undertaken primarily to enable a firm to maintain its international competitiveness by taking advantage of the lower labour costs of, and the financial subsidies offered by, HOST COUNTRIES wishing to attract FOREIGN INVESTMENT. See SOURCING.

**oligopoly** a MARKET STRUCTURE characterized by concentrated supply conditions (i.e. a few large firms supply the bulk of industry output) and high barriers to entry. A key feature of oligopoly is the mutual interdependency of the leading suppliers, which has a major impact on the nature and intensity of their competitive relationships. For example, a price cut by one firm may seem advantageous as a unilateral act, but if rival suppliers are forced to follow suit rather than risk losing market share, such a move may escalate into a 'price war' leading to all firms suffering reduced profitability. For this reason, oligopolists tend to prefer to coordinate their price behaviour (see PRICE LEADERSHIP, CARTEL) and to seek instead to establish COMPETITIVE ADVANTAGE over rival suppliers through PRODUCT DIFFERENTIATION initiatives.

In basic economic analysis oligopoly is often depicted as an inefficient form of market organization since the emphasis on product differentiation strategies tends to push up industry cost levels, while the avoidance of price competition tends to result in consumers paying excessive prices. On the other hand, large oligopolistic firms are often in a position to take full advantage of economies of large scale production and marketing (see ECONOMIES OF SCALE), thereby lowering industry supply costs; while product differentiation competition may well further benefit consumers through the availability of wider choice and new, innovative products.

See IMPERFECT COMPETITION.

**ombudsman** a UK body which is responsible for settling disputes between suppliers of goods and services and their customers, and public agencies and their clients. For example, the *Insurance Ombudsman* handles disputes between insurance companies and policyholders. The scheme is voluntary and not all insurers are members. By contrast, the *Building Societies Ombudsman* is a statutory scheme and all building societies are members. The *Revenue Adjudicator* considers complaints about delays, errors or discourtesy by INLAND REVENUE staff.

In most cases Ombudsmen have powers to award compensation to injured parties.

**one worker–multiple machines production (OWMM)** a method of PRODUCTION which involves one worker operating a number of *different* machines on a PRODUCTION LINE.

OWMM is usually employed in situations where production volumes are not high enough to justify a big production line involving a large number of operatives. OWMM economizes on the use of labour while enabling advantage to be taken of benefits of a production-line operation (for example less SET-UP time).

**on-line** *adj.* (of COMPUTER equipment) currently under the control of the central processing unit (CPU).

**OPEC** see ORGANIZATION OF PETROLEUM EXPORTING COUNTRIES.

**open market operation** the sale or purchase by the monetary authorities of Government BONDS and TREASURY BILLS as a means of controlling the MONEY SUPPLY. See MONETARY POLICY for further discussion.

**open union** see TRADE UNION.

**operant conditioning** see OCCUPATIONAL PSYCHOLOGY.

**operating characteristic curve** a line which shows the relationship between the QUALITY of batches of raw materials or components and the probability of accepting any given batch. Fig 63 shows an operating characteristic curve in which the vertical axis represents the probability of accepting a batch of raw materials or components (or the percentage of batches accepted from multiple batches) while the horizontal axis shows the percentage of defective units in a batch or batches of materials or components.

The operating characteristic curve is used as part of an

ACCEPTANCE SAMPLING scheme and shows the performance of the sampling plan for any batch quality characteristic.

Fig. 63. Operating characteristic curve.

**operating profit/loss** the profit (or loss) arising from the manufacturing and trading operations of a business. Operating profit is not usually the same as NET PROFIT in the PROFIT-AND-LOSS ACCOUNT since it excludes non-operating income or expenditure such as dividends received on investments or loan interest paid.

**operational research** the application of mathematical and statistical techniques to industrial processes as a means of establishing optimal operating procedures and systems. Such techniques as LINEAR PROGRAMMING, NETWORK ANALYSIS, computer-based SIMULATION techniques, COMPUTER-AIDED DESIGN and STOCKHOLDING MODELS can be used in various areas of a firm's operations to establish cost-effective and efficient working practices.

**operations management** see PRODUCTION MANAGEMENT.

**operations planning** the planning of a firm's production operations including:
(a) the operations or work tasks to be performed;
(b) the order in which they will be carried out;
(c) the time which each operation should take;
(d) the layout of plant and machinery in the factory. Effec-

456

tive operations planning enables production to flow easily throughout the factory, secures an efficient utilization of machines and labour, and facilities good PRODUCTION SCHEDULING. See PRODUCTION-LINE BALANCING.

**operating process sheets** see MATERIALS FLOW MANAGEMENT.

**opinion leaders** individuals whose knowledge, skill or personality gives them an ability to influence other members of their REFERENCE GROUPS. In marketing goods and services, businesses try to identify opinion leaders and get them to try, use and endorse their product. See INFLUENCERS.

**opportunities and threats** see SWOT ANALYSIS.

**opportunity-based maintenance** the performance of routine MAINTENANCE tasks outside normal production periods so as to avoid disruption to production operations.

**opportunity cost** a comparator against which to measure the return on the use of resources in some *particular* activity, as compared to the return which the *same* resources could earn in some other *alternative* activity. For example, a firm may employ its limited factory capacity in the production of dining tables or alternatively coffee tables, and would measure the opportunity cost of manufacturing dining tables in terms of the profits it might have earned from making coffee tables. See LINEAR PROGRAMMING.

**Opportunity 2000** an initiative by a group of employers (including the government) in the early 1990s to improve the position of female employees. Those subscribing to the initiative have introduced measures to overcome VERTICAL SEGREGATION and the GLASS CEILING, such as CAREER BREAKS. See DISCRIMINATION.

**option** a contractual right to buy (a 'call' option) or sell (a 'put' option) or buy/sell (a 'double' option) a FINANCIAL SECURITY such as a SHARE, FOREIGN CURRENCY, or a COMMODITY such as tea or tin, at an agreed (predetermined) price at any time within three months of the contract date. Option rights are purchased for a percentage of the share price etc. which varies according to the observed volatility of the share etc. (i.e. the magnitude of fluctuation in its price over the recent past).

Options are of two types: non-tradeable and tradeable. In the latter case the option itself can be bought and sold, which gives the option holder a greater degree of flexibility; for example, if, in the case of a 'put' option, the share price should start to go down instead of up as anticipated, the option holder can cut his losses by selling his option. Options are frequently used to speculate (see SPECULATION) or hedge (see HEDGING) against future market prices.

The LONDON TRADED OPTION MARKET and the LONDON INTERNATIONAL FINANCIAL FUTURES EXCHANGE (which were merged in 1990) constitute the largest European Union centre for dealings in options and other forward contracts. See FORWARD MARKET.

**optional extra** a product which can be added to a basic product to enhance its performance or style, for example a sun roof or a radio cassette which may be added to a basic model of car. Optional extras are used by a seller to increase the market appeal of the basic product. See OPTIONAL EXTRAS PRICING, PRODUCT RANGE.

**optional extras pricing** the PRICING of OPTIONAL EXTRAS. Here, sellers must consider the cumulative price of the extras alongside the price of the basic model, vis-à-vis the price of the next most sophisticated model in the product line which incorporates these extras as standard features. See PRODUCT RANGE.

**ordering cost** the cost of placing an order for raw materials or components or machines, which includes management and clerical time, stationery, postage and other PURCHASING department costs. See STOCKHOLDING MODEL.

**order interval** the time interval between placings of orders for new STOCK. See STOCK CONTROL.

**order level** see STOCK CONTROL.

**order quantity** the quantity of an item to be ordered when STOCKS of the item fall to a predetermined minimum stock level. The reorder quantity should serve to replenish stock to the planned maximum stock level. The optimum order quantity may be ascertained by means of a STOCKHOLDING MODEL. See STOCK CONTROL.

**order processing** the procedure followed by a firm from receipt of a customer order to despatch or delivery and invoicing of the goods or services concerned. This procedure usually involves vetting the customer's credit limit and authorization of the customer's order; recording orders and sending copy orders to appropriate personnel, for example stores, despatch and accounts; and finally advising customers and sales personnel of delivery dates. See DELIVERY NOTE, INVOICE.

**ordinary shares** or **equity** a FINANCIAL SECURITY issued to those individuals and institutions who provide long-term finance for JOINT-STOCK COMPANIES. Ordinary SHAREHOLDERS are entitled to any net profits made by their company after all expenses (including interest charges and tax) have been paid and they generally receive some or all of these profits in the form of DIVIDENDS. In the event of the company being wound up they are entitled to any remaining ASSETS of the business after all debts and the claims of PREFERENCE SHAREHOLDERS have been discharged. Ordinary shareholders generally have voting rights at company ANNUAL GENERAL MEETINGS which depend upon the number of shares which they hold. However, some UK and overseas companies have both voting and NON-VOTING SHARES, where the company founders or directors have sought to raise new share capital without diluting their control by issuing non-voting shares. See also SHARE CAPITAL.

**organic growth** or **internal growth** a mode of business growth which is self generated (that is, expansion from within) rather then being achieved externally through MERGERS and TAKEOVERS. Organic growth typically involves a firm in improving its market share by developing new products and generally outperforming competitors (see HORIZONTAL INTEGRATION), and through market development (that is, finding new markets for existing products). Organic growth may also involve firms in expanding vertically into supply sources and market outlets (see VERTICAL INTEGRATION), as well as DIVERSIFICATION into new product areas.

The advantages of organic growth include the ability to capitalize on the firm's existing core skills and knowledge, to use up spare production capacity and to match available resources to the firm's expansion rate over time. Internal growth may be the only alternative where no suitable acquisition exists or where the product is in the early phase of the PRODUCT LIFE CYCLE. The disadvantages of organic growth are that in relying too extensively on internally generated resources, the firm may fail to develop acceptable products to sustain its position in existing markets, while existing skills and know-how may be too limited to support a more broadly based expansion programme.

For this reason, firms often rely on a combination of internal and external growth modes to internationalize their operations and undertake product/market diversifications.

See EXTERNAL GROWTH, BUSINESS STRATEGY, PRODUCT – MARKET MATRIX, NEW-PRODUCT DEVELOPMENT.

**organismic organizations** see MECHANISTIC AND ORGANISMIC ORGANIZATIONS.

**organization** a social grouping designed to achieve certain goals. In the modern world much of the provision of goods and services is undertaken by organizations, and they are the main providers of paid employment. The core features of the modern organization were outlined by Max Weber (1864–1920) in his analysis of BUREAUCRACY. In his view the bureaucratic organization was the dominant mode of organization in modern industrial societies. Organizations of this sort are often also called *formal organizations* since they exist independently of the individuals who belong to them at any given time, and the roles and activities of organization members are formally prescribed at least to some extent. *Informal organization*, by contrast, is where the differentiation of roles (for example leader, follower) is not formally specified and where roles emerge naturally. Small GROUPS are often referred to as informal organizations. They can be a source of difficulty within formal organizations because their respective roles and goals may conflict.

All formal organizations have a structure of roles and a set of arrangements to achieve the organization's objectives. This is known as the organization's *design*. It embraces the distribution of tasks that organization members perform and the mechanisms of coordination and control. Design is thus more than the simple lines of AUTHORITY and ACCOUNTABILITY shown in the ORGANIZATION CHART. In ORGANIZATIONAL ANALYSIS three dimensions of structure are usually seen as fundamental:

(a) *centralization*: the number of levels in the HIERARCHY and the extent to which decisions are taken at the top of the organization;

(b) *specialization*: the extent to which the total activities of the organization are broken down into specialized jobs for individuals. See JOB DESIGN AND REDESIGN;

(c) *standardization*: the extent to which the conduct of activities necessary to achieve the organization's goals are controlled and coordinated by standard, written rules.

Organizations differ along these dimensions. Small dynamic organizations in high growth sectors are often characterized by low centralization, specialization and standardization; by contrast, public administration often exhibits the opposite (see MECHANISTIC AND ORGANISMIC ORGANIZATIONS).

See WORK ORGANIZATION, ORGANIZATIONAL STRUCTURE, PRODUCT-BASED STRUCTURE, FUNCTIONAL STRUCTURE, MATRIX STRUCTURE, H-FORM, TALL ORGANIZATION, FLAT ORGANIZATION.

**organizational analysis** the analysis and comparison of ORGANIZATIONS, especially their structure and the processes of decision-making within them. It is thus concerned with JOB DESIGN and the way work is organized (see WORK ORGANIZATION) in an organization. The body of knowledge on this subject is known as organization theory. Initially, theories in this area were concerned with developing universal principles of MANAGEMENT and organization structure, such as the optimum number of subordinates a manager should oversee (see CLASSICAL MANAGEMENT THEORY, SCIENTIFIC MANAGEMENT). Later analysts became aware of the differences between organizations. CONTINGENCY THEORY explores these differences, the reasons for them and the impact on performance (see also MECHANISTIC AND ORGANISMIC ORGANIZATIONS).

In recent years organizational analysis has been much concerned with decision-making processes in organizations. Researchers have investigated the types of decision that are taken by top managers and how the decisions are taken (for example by individuals or committee). There is considerable evidence that decisions are often not the outcome of a rational process of investigation and consideration but instead are substantially influenced by political processes within the organization. A further limit on rationality is the difficulty of obtaining sufficient information to make optimal decisions (see SATISFICE). As a result decision making rarely occurs in the preplanned, rational way suggested in some of the literature on BUSINESS STRATEGY. Instead the parameters of the decision may change during the decision-making process. Much decision making may be characterized as 'muddling through'.

**organizational behaviour** an umbrella term for theories and disciplines concerned with human behaviour in ORGANIZATIONS and the influences upon it. Approaches with this focus include INDUSTRIAL RELATIONS, OCCUPATIONAL PSYCHOLOGY, ORGANIZA-

TIONAL ANALYSIS and the SOCIOLOGY OF WORK. Though the boundaries between these are not distinct, they differ according to the emphasis they accord to individual or collective behaviour, and the relative importance they attach to structural (societal or organizational) or inter-personal determinants.

**organizational commitment** the extent to which an employee is committed to an ORGANIZATION. It has both attitudinal components (i.e. the degree to which individuals identify with the goals of the firm) and behavioural aspects (i.e. the likelihood of an employee leaving the firm), and as such has been criticized for being a muddled concept. There are a number of standard scales for measuring commitment, and they are commonly applied using SURVEY methods.

**organizational culture** see CULTURE.

**organizational slack** the tendency for bureaucratic ORGANIZATIONS to use more resources than are strictly necessary to perform the functions of the organization, with the result that resources are used inefficiently and costs rise. See NATIONALIZATION VERSUS PRIVATIZATION.

**organizational structure** the particular way in which a firm or public authority is structured in order to perform its economic, social etc. activities.

A firm may be structured in two main ways: in a PRODUCT-BASED STRUCTURE activities are grouped together according to product, with each product being supported by its *own* functional teams of marketing, production, finance etc.; in a FUNCTIONAL STRUCTURE activities are grouped into departments by function – marketing, production, finance etc – which support *all* the firm's products.

Organizational structure can also be looked at in terms of the number of management layers involved, TALL ORGANIZATIONS having many management levels and FLAT ORGANIZATIONS only a few management levels.

The way in which a firm is organized around products and functions and the number of management layers can have a significant effect on the efficiency of the firm and its ability to respond quickly to changes in its market environment.

See CORPORATE RESTRUCTURING, BUSINESS PROCESS RE-ENGINEERING.

**organization chart** a diagrammatic representation of the job titles and the formal patterns of AUTHORITY and RESPONSIBILITY

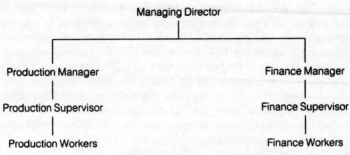

Fig. 64. **Organization chart.** A simple **example.**

in an ORGANIZATION. See Fig. 64.

Generally, such charts display the managerial HIERARCHY though they can be used to show all job positions within the organization. Though such charts are useful for presenting the overall structure, undue reliance should not be placed on such charts for the understanding of how organizations actually function. They rarely show the actual nature of job responsibilities.

They do not indicate what levels of cooperation may be necessary between departments, they do not show the actual communication flows nor the informal patterns of authority which may coexist with the formal channels. Organizations are usually much more complex and fluid than the organization chart suggests. In so far as the chart highlights the formal CHAIN OF COMMAND they can be said to embody a mechanistic conception of organization.

More sophisticated organization charts may show 'dotted-line' relationships as well as the formal line of command. This is a representation of a relationship between two employees where one has no direct-line authority over the other but is empowered to give instruction on particular issues.

Fig. 65. **Organization chart.** A 'dotted line' relationship.

## ORGANIZATION DESIGN

In Fig. 65 the Personnel Manager has a 'dotted line' relationship with the Area Manager, enabling him or her to give instructions on personnel issues. In theory the Personnel Manager's authority to do this flows from the powers of the General Manager. In practice those giving instructions through the 'dotted-line' may build up their own power base.

See BUREAUCRACY, HIERARCHY, MECHANISTIC AND ORGANISMIC, SPAN OF CONTROL, LINE AND STAFF, PRODUCT-BASED STRUCTURE, FUNCTIONAL STRUCTURE, MATRIX STRUCTURE, DE-LAYERING, BUSINESS PROCESS RE-ENGINEERING.

**organization design** see ORGANIZATION.

**organization development (OD)** the process of improving organization performance by improving the pattern of interaction between members of the ORGANIZATION. The philosophy behind OD is that the core features of organization, such as task specialization, tend to obstruct the full use of individual talents and hence inhibit effectiveness. MECHANISTIC organizations can benefit from being loosened-up to enable faster response to environmental change. To do this individuals need to understand what others do and what motivates them, as well as themselves, and to identify the barriers to personal and group effectiveness. OD facilitates this through use of behavioural techniques such as T-Groups (see MANAGEMENT DEVELOPMENT). Many are wary of OD, partly because it seems to delve into the private domain and partly because its benefits are difficult to quantify. Also, if power relationships in the organization are left unchanged individuals may become resentful: they have been encouraged to modify their behaviour but their bosses, it seems, have not. See CULTURE, GROUP.

**Organization for Economic Cooperation and Development (OECD)** an international organization whose membership comprises mainly the economically advanced countries of the world. The OECD provides a regular forum for discussions among government finance and trade ministers on economic matters affecting their mutual interests, particularly the promotion of economic growth and international trade, and it coordinates the provision of ECONOMIC AID to the less developed countries. The OECD is a main source of international economic data and regularly compiles and publishes standardized inter-country statistics.

**Organization of Petroleum Exporting Countries**

**(OPEC)** an organization established in 1960 to look after the oil interests of its 13 member countries: Saudi Arabia, Kuwait, Iran, Iraq, Venezuela, Qatar, Indonesia, Libya, Abu Dhabi, Algeria, Nigeria, Ecuador and Gabon.

OPEC has exerted a major influence over the world economy since 1973 when it quadrupled the price of oil, with further price increases taking oil prices to around US$28 a barrel in 1979. In the 1980s oil prices fell back sharply (being as low as $10 a barrel in 1986) due to a combination of factors, including weak demand, the development of alternative oil fields (the North Sea in particular) and squabbling between OPEC members leading to overproduction. In response, OPEC has established formal production quotas limiting output and this has led to higher prices. See CARTEL.

**organization structure** see ORGANIZATION.

**organization theory** see ORGANIZATIONAL ANALYSIS.

**organized anarchy** a behavioural model of how ORGANIZATIONS function which emphasizes the limits of rational action (compare with the rational model of BUREAUCRACY). As developed by the American management writers Richard Cyert (1921– ) and James March (1928– ), this model suggests that organizations tend to formulate objectives *in response* to their activities rather than *in advance*, that organizational members do not fully comprehend the workings of the organization, and that their involvement in organizational activities is fluid and unpredictable. As a result, much of what organizations do can be said to be ad hoc and somewhat anarchic in character. However, the structure and procedures of the organization prevent unrestrained anarchy. See GARBAGE-CAN MODEL OF DECISION MAKING, DISJOINTED INCREMENTALISM, ORGANIZATIONAL ANALYSIS.

**orientation to work** the objectives and expectations that employees have of their work, and which influences their interpretation of their work experience, thereby determining to some extent their JOB SATISFACTION. The notion of orientations to work first gained currency in the SOCIOLOGY OF WORK in the late 1960s after the publication of a major study of workers' attitudes (the Affluent Worker study) in a car assembly factory. The researchers found that these workers assessed the satisfaction obtained from their jobs not in absolute terms but in relation to what they wanted from their employment. Thus the technology, for instance, did not directly determine the level of job satisfaction; the orientations developed out of people's social experiences outside work. Three types of orientation were identified.

(a) *solidaristic*, where the value of work lies in its capacity to provide intrinsic satisfaction and social contact with other workers. Work is a central life interest and work friendships extend outside the factory gate.

(b) *bureaucratic*, where the worker sees work in terms of a lifelong career, and work satisfaction depends on the extent to which work meets career and status aspirations.

(c) *instrumental*, where no intrinsic satisfaction from work is sought and work has primarily an economic value to the worker. Those with this orientation attach little importance to friendship with workmates and tend to lead a 'privatized' existence separate from the rest of the community.

It was argued that the 'affluent workers' had the latter orientation. Although the work was undeniably tedious these employees did not express dissatisfaction with their jobs as long as high incomes could be gained. The Affluent Worker study was a landmark in the sociology of work because it emphasized the importance of the meanings people attach to their work.

**OTC** see OVER THE COUNTER MARKET.

**output** goods and services produced by a firm using resource INPUTS.

**output tax** see VALUE-ADDED TAX.

**outsourcing** the buying-in of components, finished products and services from outside suppliers rather than self supply from within the firm. In some cases this is done because it is more cost-effective to use outside suppliers (see MAKE OR BUY) or because outside suppliers are more technically competent or can supply a greater range of items. See SOURCING, VERTICAL INTEGRATION.

**outward investment** see CAPITAL OUTFLOW.

**overcapacity** a situation in which a firm or industry has too much production CAPACITY on hand relative to current demand levels. This may be only temporary because of a downturn in the BUSINESS CYCLE. Alternatively, the decline in demand may be permanent (see PRODUCT LIFE CYCLE) or due to the industry having overinvested in new plant relative to long-run demand potential. In this case, overcapacity, leading to greater competition for limited sales is often removed by the disappearance of inefficient firms from the industry, or by RATIONALIZATION schemes involving the MERGER of firms and closure of redundant plant.

**overdraft** a financial facility for advancing MONEY to an individual or business (the borrower) by a COMMERCIAL BANK, SAVINGS BANK etc. (the lender). An overdraft is a form of CREDIT which allows the borrower to withdraw as much money as required up to a prearranged total limit, whereupon interest is charged at a rate related to the base rate of interest on outstanding balances (see INTEREST RATE). In the case of businesses, overdraft facilities are often provided on an indefinite basis, thus providing the borrower with a continuous line of credit used mainly to finance WORKING CAPITAL requirements. See BANK LOAN.

**overhead** or **indirect cost** any COST that is not directly associated with a product, that is, all costs other than DIRECT MATERIALS cost and DIRECT LABOUR cost. Production overheads (factory overheads) include the cost of INDIRECT MATERIALS and INDIRECT LABOUR along with other production expenses like factory heat, light and power, and depreciation of plant and machinery. The cost of factory departments such as maintenance, materials stores and the canteen which render services to producing departments are similarly part of production overheads. Most SELLING COSTS and DISTRIBUTION COSTS and all ADMINISTRATION COSTS are also counted as overheads since they cannot usually be directly related to units of product. See also FIXED COST, STANDARD COST.

**overhead–cost variance** the difference between the standard overhead cost of a product and its actual overhead cost. Use of COST RATES for charging OVERHEADS to products will recover the overheads actually incurred only if actual overhead costs correspond with BUDGET and if actual output is the same as budgeted output. If actual expenditure is larger than the budgeted amount, then the standard overhead cost per unit of product will be smaller than actual unit overheads incurred and overheads will be under-recovered in the price set (*expenditure variance*). Again, if actual output turns out to be smaller than planned output, then fixed overheads will remain as under-recovered overheads (*volume variance*). By contrast, over-recovery of overheads occurs when actual overhead costs are less than budget and/or more is produced than planned. See ABSORPTION, STANDARD COST.

**overmanning** the employment of more workers than is strictly required to perform efficiently a particular set of work tasks. This can occur because of an inefficient organization of work by management or through the operation of RESTRICTIVE LABOUR PRACTICES.

**overriding discount** see AGGREGATED REBATE.

**Overseas Technical Information Centre** see TECHNOLOGY TRANSFER.

**oversubscription** a situation in which the number of SHARES applied for in a new SHARE ISSUE exceeds the numbers to be issued. This requires the ISSUING HOUSE responsible for handling the share issue to devise some formula for allocating the shares. By contrast, *undersubscription* occurs when the number of shares applied for falls short of the number on offer, requiring the issuing house which has underwritten the shares to buy the surplus shares itself. See CALLED-UP CAPITAL, PAID-UP CAPITAL.

**over-the-counter market (OTC)** a MARKET for corporate SHARES which have not obtained a full listing on the main STOCK MARKET. The UK's OTC market was abolished in 1992.

**overtime** extra hours of work undertaken by an employee that are additional to the number of hours specified as constituting the 'basic' working week, and for which employees are paid a WAGE RATE higher than the 'basic' wage. Firms often resort to overtime working to meet sudden increases in orders, viewing overtime by the existing workforce as a more flexible and cheaper alternative to taking on extra workers. An *overtime ban* by employees can thus be a highly effective form of INDUSTRIAL ACTION.

**overtime ban** see INDUSTRIAL ACTION.

**overtrading** a situation in which a firm expands its production and sales without making sufficient provision for additional funds to finance the extra WORKING CAPITAL needed. Where this happens the firm will run into LIQUIDITY problems and can find itself unable to find the cash to pay suppliers or wages. See also WORKING-CAPITAL RATIO, CURRENT RATIO, CASH FLOW.

**OWMM** see ONE WORKER-MULTIPLE MACHINES PRODUCTION.

**own-label brand** a product which is sold by a RETAILER bearing the retailer's own BRAND NAME. In some cases own-label brands are manufactured by the retailer as part of a vertically integrated manufacturing–retailing operation (Boots the Chemist, for instance, both produces and retails a large number of its own pharmaceutical and cosmetic products). More usually, however, retailers' 'own labels' are produced by independent manufacturers on a contract basis. In many cases, these are the very same manufacturers who produce their own (manufacturers') branded products which sell in competition alongside the retailers' own-label version! The attraction to the manufacturer in producing 'own labels' is that they bring in a substantial volume of extra business on a regular basis. On the other hand, however, there is a danger that the own-label versions of the product will reduce the sales of the manufacturers' main branded products, especially as retailers tend to sell their own-label brands at lower prices than they sell the manufacturer's brand. For the retailer, own-label brands may increase unit profit margins and provide extra sales potential by building up store loyalty (for example, Heinz' baked beans can be bought in Tesco, Sainsbury's etc. but Tesco's baked beans can be bought only in Tesco).

# P

**P** see CONTROL CHART.

**packaging** the means of physically protecting and selling a product. Functionally, packaging protects products whilst they are in transit and being stored, enables products to be sold in convenient retail packs in standard WEIGHTS AND MEASURES, and identifies the contents of the package by means of labelling.

In addition, packaging may play an important part in marketing a product, particularly when products are being sold on a SELF SERVICE basis. The attractiveness of the colour and design of the package is important in attracting the attention of the buyer. In addition, the use of BRAND NAMES on packaging reinforces the perceptions of the brand at the point of sale.

Packaging can take a variety of forms including metal and plastic containers, and paper and cardboard cartons, and a firm's choice of packaging material will depend upon the characteristics of the product (for example, liquid or solid), the comparative cost of the material and its appearance and customer appeal.

See PROMOTIONAL MIX.

**pac-man defence** see TAKEOVER BID.

**paid-up capital** the amount of CALLED-UP CAPITAL which shareholders have paid to date, where a JOINT-STOCK COMPANY issues shares with phased payment terms. For example, a company may issue £1 shares with 50p payable immediately upon *application* by intending shareholders, a further 25p upon *allotment* of shares to shareholders and the final 25p three months later. Here the paid-up capital three months after allotment would be £1 per share times the number of shares allotted, equal to called-up capital, unless there is a shortfall from shareholders who have failed to pay their final 25p instalments (*calls in arrears*). See SHARE ISSUE.

**pallet** a portable platform or container used for transporting raw materials, work in progress and finished goods.

**parallel importing** the practice whereby independent importers buy a particular manufacturer's product from a low-priced market source and sell it in direct competition with the manufacturer's appointed distributors in the local market, usually at a lower price. Parallel importing has been prominent in the European Community where differences between member countries' price levels, along with manufacturers' practices of granting lucrative EXCLUSIVE DEALING rights to selected local distributors, have created profitable segments for independents to exploit.

Parallel importing is seen as beneficial by advocates of FREE TRADE and COMPETITION POLICY as it breaks down barriers to INTERNATIONAL TRADE and PRICE DISCRIMINATION between markets, leading to a greater harmonization of international price levels. See IMPORTING.

**parallel loan** see BACK-TO-BACK LOAN.

**parallel system** a means of improving the RELIABILITY of a product or machine by incorporating two or more components in the product or machine to operate in parallel, so that if one of the components fails, the product or machine will still continue to operate. Parallel systems are incorporated within products such as aircraft, where the importance of safety considerations warrants the extra cost of additional components.

**parent company** see HOLDING COMPANY.

**parenting** the manner in which the senior managers of a company manage their subordinate companies or business units. Good parenting in the form of clear goals for business unit managers, monitoring of their performance, appropriate rewards and tight financial controls can improve the performance of these business units.

See DIVERSIFICATION.

**Pareto analysis** see ABC ANALYSIS.

**Pareto distribution** the tendency for a small proportion of the number of objects or items being considered to account for a large proportion of the feature under examination. More crudely, the Pareto 'law' suggests that 20% of items account for 80% of the total amount of stock or sales or whatever. In the case of stock, the Pareto law implies that a small proportion of the total number of items stocked accounts for a large proportion of the total value of stock held.

The business significance of the Pareto distribution is that if management devotes the greater part of its time to controlling the most important 20% of the stock items held, it is, in effect, controlling a large proportion of the total value of the firm's stocks. See ABC ANALYSIS.

**Parkinson's law** an observation by English management writer C Northcote Parkinson (1909–93) that 'work expands to fill the time available for its completion'. As a result employees generally feel overworked whatever their actual workload. A solution favoured by managers and officials alike is the appointment of more subordinates to relieve them of some of their workload. However, the greater the number of staff the more difficult the task of COORDINATION. Hence there is a tendency for certain coordinative mechanisms, such as committees, to proliferate. This in turn generates additional work which is reflected in pressure to increase employee numbers even further. Hence organizations have a tendency to grow in staff numbers even though the base workload may be unchanging. Parkinson's writings are generally viewed as humorous and perceptive asides on organizational life rather than propositions to be empirically tested.

**partial agreement** see MULTI-EMPLOYER AGREEMENT.

**participating preference share** see PREFERENCE SHARE.

**participation** see EMPLOYEE PARTICIPATION.

**partly paid capital** the difference between CALLED UP CAPITAL and PAID UP CAPITAL where shares are issued with phased payment terms.

**partnership** a BUSINESS owned and controlled by two or more persons who subscribe capital and share decision-taking as specified by a partnership agreement. Generally partners have *unlimited liability* for any debts incurred by the partnership and any of them may enter into contracts on behalf of the partnership. Partnerships are particularly prevalent in professional services, for example accounting, surveying and insurance. See SLEEPING PARTNER, SOLE PROPRIETORSHIP, JOINT-STOCK COMPANY, LIMITED LIABILITY.

**part-time work** employment where the hours of work are substantially fewer than the usual working week. In the UK, part-time work is officially defined as that which is under 30 hours each week. Below this number national insurance contributions do not have to be made. Part-time workers are therefore excluded from certain national insurance benefits (see MATERNITY RIGHTS).

The advantage of part-time working to employers is that it can be relatively cheap as insurance contributions may not have to be made. It also enables them to adapt production or the provision of services to variations in demand, for example, a shop may stay open into the evening by employing part-time workers to cover the evening work. Part-time work can also be advantageous to employees themselves in so far as it allows them to fit work in with other commitments.

In the UK in recent years, growth in part-time work has formed a large part of the growth in employment. Approximately 25% of the employed labour force are now in part-time jobs. Most of these are women. It is often said that paid work is not as central a life interest to part-time workers as it is to full-timers and as a result pressure for high rates of pay is somewhat less. For these reasons also, TRADE UNIONS find it difficult to recruit and mobilize part-time workers. Thus, part-time work is generally not well paid, with the result that some employers find it attractive to replace full-time work-forces with part-time ones.

See LABOUR FLEXIBILITY, LOW PAY, TEMPORARY WORK.

**party plan** see DIRECT SELLING.

**par value 1.** the face or nominal value of a SHARE in the UK. Par values may be of any amount, though 25p or £1 are the most common par values. The par value of a share bears little relationship to its market value, which is determined by demand and supply for the shares. A company can change the par value of its shares by a reorganization or SHARE SPLIT, for example issuing four 25p par value shares for every £1 share held.

**2.** the fixed price of a FOREIGN CURRENCY under a FIXED RATE EXCHANGE SYSTEM.

**patent** a grant of ownership rights by the government to a person or business in respect of the invention of an entirely new product or manufacturing process or a significant development of an existing product or process. In the UK, under the COPYRIGHT, DESIGNS AND PATENTS ACT 1988, the PATENT OFFICE can grant a patentee a monopoly to make, use or sell the invention for a maximum of twenty years from the date on which the patent was first filed. In order to obtain a patent approval, inventors are required to supply full details of the invention to the Patents Office and satisfy that body that the invention contains original features and that it has a demonstrable industrial application.

The monopoly protection given by a patent is not enforced by the Patent Office itself. It is the responsibility of patentees to look after their rights by detecting whether someone else is infringing them and then seeking redress for infringement through the courts.

Patents registered in one country may be valid in other countries if filed in a country which is party to a reciprocal treaty. The UK, for example, is a member of the 13-country European Patent Convention which allows inventors to obtain patent rights in the EPC countries by filing a single European patent application. Globally, patent applications are administered by the World Intellectual Property Organization (WIPO) under the Patent Co-operation Treaty which enables investors to apply for registration in member countries with a single registration. WIPO has no powers of enforcement.

However, under a GATT accord (negotiated at the 'Uruguay Round') it was agreed to give investors a minimum patent term of 20 years in all member countries with members being obliged to enforce patent protection on patents recognised by each others national authorities.

The patent system has the twin objectives of both encouraging inventors to undertake the risks and expenses of breaking new ground by offering them temporary monopoly rights to profit from their work, and providing for the eventual dissemination of advances in technology to the benefit of society as a whole.

See RESEARCH AND DEVELOPMENT, BRAND.

**Patent Office** a UK body which is responsible for the administration of various aspects of 'intellectual property rights' legislation, in particular the COPYRIGHT, DESIGNS AND PATENTS ACTS 1988, the Registered Designs Act 1949 and the Trade Marks Act 1938. The Patent Office is the sole authority for the granting of PATENT rights on product and process inventions and for the registration of industrial designs (see DESIGN RIGHTS) and TRADEMARKS.

**paternalism** an approach to the management of employees or subordinates in which considerable importance is attached to looking after their interests as viewed and defined by the employer or superior. Paternalism is often associated with hostility to TRADE UNIONS since unions attempt to give independent expression to employee interests. See MANAGEMENT STYLE, WELFARE.

**paternity leave** time allowed off work to male employees on the birth of their children. Men have no statutory rights in this respect (compare MATERNITY RIGHTS); paternity leave is therefore a benefit offered voluntarily by employers, or in agreement with trade unions. It is usually no more than a few days in duration.

**pay** the money paid to an employee for performing specified work tasks or JOBS. Payment to employees for the labour they provide takes two main forms:

(a) PAYMENT BY TIME, principally weekly WAGES and OVERTIME, together with monthly SALARIES;

(b) PAYMENT BY RESULTS, principally PIECEWORK, INCENTIVE BONUSES, GROUP INCENTIVE BONUSES.

The main distinction between the two is that 'payment by

time' systems remunerate workers for the amount of labour supplied (i.e. the *input* of labour) per time period (hourly, weekly etc.) irrespective of the amount of output produced; whereas 'payment by results' systems remunerate workers specifically for the amount or value of the *output* produced in a given time period. 'Payment by results' is favoured by many firms because it is thought to provide a strong financial incentive for workers to strive to maximize their output rather than work at a more leisurely pace, but the firm may be required to install appropriate INSPECTION systems to ensure that extra output has not been achieved at the expense of product quality and reliability.

Pay rates are determined by a number of factors including the forces of supply and demand for particular types of job in the LABOUR MARKET, the bargaining power of TRADE UNIONS (see COLLECTIVE BARGAINING) and the general economic climate (see, for example, PRICES AND INCOMES POLICY).

In addition to receipt of money employees may receive various other work-related benefits such as free or subsidized meals, travel allowances, a company car, etc. (see FRINGE BENEFITS).

See ATTENDANCE BONUS, MERIT PAY, COMMISSION, FEE, PERFORMANCE-RELATED PAY, CAFETERIA BENEFITS, COMPARABILITY, INCREMENTAL PAY SCALE, WORK MEASUREMENT, PROFIT-RELATED PAY, EMPLOYEE SHARE OWNERSHIP, PAY DIFFERENTIALS, LOW PAY, GAIN-SHARING.

**pay-as-you-earn (PAYE),** a scheme for collecting INCOME TAX due from the earnings of an individual by deducting the tax owing before an employer pays WAGES or SALARIES. PAYE is *not* a tax, merely a *scheme* for the collection of tax. See INCOME TAX SCHEDULES.

**payback method** see PAYBACK PERIOD.

**payback period** a criterion used in INVESTMENT APPRAISAL to evaluate the desirability of an INVESTMENT project. Payback calculations involve measuring the CASH FLOWS associated with a project and indicate how long it takes for an investment to generate sufficient cash to recover in full its original capital outlay. For example, if a machine costs £5,000 to purchase at the start of year 1, then generates net cash inflows from the sale of products made by the machine of £5,000 in year 1 and £3,000 in year 2 then it would recoup the initial cash outlay in the first year. If a firm's target payback period for new investment projects was, say, two years or less, then this particular project would be undertaken.

Whether or not the machine pays back its initial outlay in one year depends upon how accurate the future estimates of sales volumes, selling prices, materials costs etc. turn out to be. Since all investments involve assessments of future revenues and costs they are all subject to a degree of uncertainty. This problem, in part, can be handled by undertaking sensitivity analysis, by making not one but three estimates for each item of project cost or revenue ('optimistic', 'most likely', 'pessimistic') to indicate the range of possible outcomes.

**pay bargaining** see COLLECTIVE BARGAINING.

**pay differential** the difference between the WAGE RATES of different groups of workers. Pay differentials arise for a number of reasons:

(a) differences in skills, training and responsibilities between occupations (for example, doctors are paid more than nurses, managers more than factory operatives);

(b) differences in growth rates and PRODUCTIVITY levels between firms and industries, with high-growth, high-productivity firms and industries paying more;

(c) differences in regional employment levels reflecting differences in the supply and demand for labour in particular localities, with pay in prosperous areas generally being higher than pay in depressed areas.

Pay differentials serve to encourage LABOUR MOBILITY between occupations, industries and regions, facilitating the movement of workers into sectors of the economy where they can be more efficiently employed.

Maintenance of differentials is believed to foster poor INDUSTRIAL RELATIONS and encourage inflationary wage spirals; as one group wins a pay increase so another seeks a similar one to maintain the differential.

See COLLECTIVE BARGAINING, COMPARABILITY, INFLATION.

**PAYE** see PAY-AS-YOU-EARN.

**pay freeze** see PRICES AND INCOMES POLICY.

**payment by results** a PAY system in which a worker's WAGES and other payments received are related to the amount (or value) of output produced. See PIECEWORK, INCENTIVE BONUS

SCHEME, GROUP INCENTIVE SCHEME, MERIT PAY, WORK STUDY.

**payment by time** a PAY system in which a worker's WAGES are typically a function of the hourly 'basic' WAGE RATE for the job and the number of hours constituting the 'basic' working week, plus any OVERTIME payments. See SALARY, WORK STUDY.

**payment in advance** see PREPAYMENT.

**payment system** see PAY.

**pay restraint** see PRICES AND INCOMES POLICY.

**pay review body** a committee whose function is to recommend levels of PAY for 'top people' (for example judges) and other groups of public sector PROFESSIONALS (for example hospital doctors and nurses) where it is believed by government that COLLECTIVE BARGAINING is an inappropriate method of pay determination. The acceptance of the pay review system by these occupational groups is premised on the assumption that the awards of these bodies will be honoured and financed by government (as the ultimate paymaster).

**payroll accounts** LEDGER accounts which show for each of a firm's employees the amount of gross salary or wage payment due, deductions of income tax and national insurance and the net amount of income to be paid out each week or month. Gross wages may be based on hours worked, for time-paid workers; or on units of output completed, for piece-rate paid workers.

**pay round** the series of negotiations between employers and TRADE UNIONS (COLLECTIVE BARGAINING) that takes place throughout UK industry each year to determine WAGE RATES, SALARIES and other forms of PAY. The inflationary pressures that are said to result from an annual pay round have led some to advocate pay deals of two or three years' duration. So far only a small minority of pay deals have taken this form, and the annual pay round remains firmly entrenched.

**PC** see PERSONAL COMPUTER.

**pendulum arbitration** see ARBITRATION.

**penetration pricing** see MARKET PENETRATION PRICING.

**pension** a payment received by individuals who have retired from paid employment or have reached the government's pensionable age, in the form of a regular weekly or monthly income, or as a lump sum. There are three main types of pension scheme:

    (a) *state retirement pensions* operated by the Government,

whereby the employee pays NATIONAL INSURANCE CONTRIBU-
TIONS over his working life, giving entitlement to an old age
pension on retirement of an amount considered to provide
some minimum standard of living. Pension payments are
INDEX-LINKED to protect recipients against erosion by inflation;

(b) *occupational pensions* operated by private sector employers
whereby the employee and the employer each make regular
contributions to a PENSION FUND or INSURANCE COMPANY
scheme, the pensioner then receiving a pension which is related to the amount of his contributions (annual contributions
× number of years worked);

(c) *personal pension plans* (*PPP*) operated by insurance
companies, pension funds and other financial institutions
which provide 'customized' pension arrangements for individuals depending on their personal circumstances. Since a
PPP scheme is not tied to a particular employer the problem
of transferring pension rights should the person move jobs is
much reduced. See CONTRACTING OUT.

**pension fund** a financial institution which specializes in the
management and administration of personal and corporate PEN-
SION schemes. Pension funds collect regular contributions from
individuals, employees and employers in the case of occupational pension schemes, and make payments to retired beneficiaries.

Pension funds use the monies they receive not only to make
day-to-day disbursements to pensioners but also to generate
additional income and profit by investing their funds in
FINANCIAL SECURITIES, mainly UK and overseas government
fixed-interest bonds, corporate stocks and shares and property
bonds (see INSTITUTIONAL INVESTORS). Their portfolios attempt
to maintain a careful balance between immediate liquidity
needs and longer term investment returns.

The pension fund movement in the UK is represented by
the National Association of Pension Funds (NAPF), which
provides a forum for the discussion of matters of general concern to members and acts on behalf of members in dealings
with other institutional bodies such as the Institutional Investors Committee and the Government. The investment and
management of monies by pension funds are regulated by the
INVESTMENT MANAGEMENT REGULATORY ORGANIZATION (for in-
company pension funds) and by the PERSONAL INVESTMENT

AUTHORITY (for retail pension funds) in accordance with various standards of good practice laid down under the FINANCIAL SERVICES ACTS 1986.

**PEP** see PERSONAL EQUITY PLAN.

**per capita income** or **income per head** the GROSS NATIONAL PRODUCT (national income) of a country divided by the size of its population. This gives the *average* income per head of population if it were all shared out equally. In 1995, the UK had a per capita level of $18,700, Japan $39,640, and the USA $26,980. Most developing countries, by contrast, had a per capita income level of under $1,000 in 1994. See DISTRIBUTION OF INCOME.

**percent defective control chart (P)** see CONTROL CHART.

**percentage-of-sales method** a rule of thumb used for determining a firm's SALES PROMOTION budget. The budgeted amount is calculated as a percentage of the product's past or projected sales revenue. See BUDGETING.

**percentiles** the numerical values that divide a group of numerical observations into 100 parts, each containing an equal number of observations. Compare QUARTILES, DECILES.

**percentual mapping** see MARKET POSITIONING.

**perfect competition** a MARKET STRUCTURE characterized by a multitude of small suppliers and buyers, standardized products and no barriers to entry or exit. Perfect competition is depicted in basic economic analysis as an 'ideal' form of market organization, resulting in the largest possible industry output and the lowest possible industry prices *given* the underlying cost structures of firms. However, a major criticism of perfect competition as a resource-allocation model centres on its small firm cost structure assumption. By ignoring the existence of ECONOMIES OF SCALE the model seriously underestimates the scope for lowering industry supply costs and prices, and hence increasing industry output, by concentrating production in the largest firms. Additionally, of course, outside certain commodity markets, very few actual markets approximate the other structural features of perfect competition, since most markets are characterized to a greater or lesser degree by non-standardized (branded) products and barriers to entry. See IMPERFECT COMPETITION.

**performance appraisal** the process of considering and evaluating the performance of an employee with the objective of improving JOB performance. The information generated during appraisal can be used as a basis for measures to improve JOB SATISFACTION, career planning, MANPOWER PLANNING, TRAINING and as a basis for deciding levels of PAY.

Appraisal usually involves an employee and his immediate superior, although in some organizations employees appraise themselves (self-appraisal) or, much more rarely, are appraised by their immediate colleagues or subordinates. Whoever the appraiser, the focus of appraisal can take a number of forms:

(a) attitudes displayed at work. Experts believe this to be an undesirable form of appraisal since attitudes are not necessarily relevant to job performance whilst appraiser prejudice can bias the outcome;

(b) behaviour in work tasks, for example the proportion of incoming telephone calls answered in a period;

(c) meeting of objectives. These can be decided by the superior but in appraisal of managers it is usual for objectives to be agreed in advance (see MANAGEMENT BY OBJECTIVES).

For the last especially, interviews are the main vehicle for appraisal. Although the information generated can itself be of great use, there is a tendency for appraisal to involve an assessment of individual performance and competence. Often performance is condensed into an overall rating, ranging from 'excellent' to 'very poor'. Apart from the difficulties of producing such a rating – it often involves a judgmental leap from the data provided – this can introduce tension into the process. In so far as individuals feel they are on trial an element of distrust may enter the process and the validity of the information may become questionable.

These dangers become greater when pay is linked to the appraisal process (performance-related pay). Usually, the overall rating achieved will determine whether an employee receives a bonus (MERIT PAY) or is moved up the pay scale. This provides an incentive for individuals to exaggerate their achievement or to establish easily-met objectives, whilst the poor performer denied an increase is as likely to feel resentment as to be motivated to improve his or her performance.

See CRITICAL INCIDENT TECHNIQUE, BEHAVIOURALLY-ANCHORED RATING SCALE, BEHAVIOURAL OBSERVATION SCALE.

**performance indicator** a proxy measure of organizational performance often used where profit or 'bottom-line' indicators are either inadequate or irrelevant guides to performance. Non-profit-making organizations or those with a multiplicity of objectives can find such indicators especially beneficial. Their use has been encouraged in the UK public sector in recent years, though private sector companies can also find them useful to measure and develop their quality of services. In the public sector their primary use has generally been to measure the relationship of inputs to outputs, thereby providing an indication of both efficiency and of the quality of output (effectiveness). Use of these indicators is thought to improve managerial decision making and resource allocation. However, selection of appropriate indicators can be problematic whilst measurement and recording of output can be difficult. See MANAGEMENT BY OBJECTIVES.

**performance-related pay** a PAY system where part of an employee's pay is based on his or her performance. It is based on the principle, common to all PAYMENT BY RESULTS, that the opportunity to increase pay will act as an incentive to employees to work harder or more productively. At its simplest, performance-related pay may take the form of an annual cash bonus based on a simple subjective assessment of employee performance over the previous year. Most large organizations take a more systematic approach and attempt to base performance pay on more objective criteria. One approach, often used with clerical staff, is to observe employee behaviour, e.g. the number of telephone calls answered within a specified time period. A more common approach is based on systematic PERFORMANCE APPRAISAL. Typically a set of objectives will be agreed between the employee and the manager: the employee's achievement of these will be reviewed a year later, and an assessment made of his or her performance. Often this is expressed on a scale ranging from 'very good' to 'very unsatisfactory' (or similar) known as a merit rating. The performance pay is attached to the merit rating. The resulting payment may be an annual bonus, a percentage addition to monthly salary, or an extra increment. This payment may be made in addition to an annual cost of living pay increase or in place of it. Those deemed to be performing badly may be denied not just the performance supplement but also a cost of living increase.

The use of performance pay has been increasing in recent

years, especially in the public sector (see CITIZENS' CHARTER) and particularly amongst white collar and managerial employees. In most cases, however, it forms a relatively small portion of total pay. It has been associated with moves towards limiting the involvement of trade unions in pay determination, and is often introduced hand in hand with PERSONAL CONTRACTS. It is often criticized on the ground that good performers do not need financial incentives whilst financial penalties demotivate rather than incentivize poor performers. In any case poor performance may be due to factors other than lack of commitment or ability in individual employees. A further problem with performance pay systems is their tendency to encourage DISCRIMINATION against female employees and those from ethnic minorities.

**performers' rights** the legal protection given to persons and businesses from the making of unauthorized films, broadcasts, recordings or cable transmission of their performances.

In the UK, the Performers' Protection Acts 1958–72, as updated by the COPYRIGHT, DESIGNS AND PATENTS ACT 1988, give protection to original performances for 50 years. In cases of infringement, performers may seek an injunction through the courts preventing further abuses, with offenders liable to pay unlimited damages/fines and to prison sentences in extreme cases.

**period costs** FIXED COSTS that are completely written off in the calculation of profit in the accounting period to which they relate and are not carried forward to subsequent accounting periods by being included in the valuation of unsold stock.

See MARGINAL COSTING, CONTRIBUTION and BREAK EVEN ANALYSIS.

**periodic review system of stock control** see FIXED INTERVAL REORDER SYSTEM.

**peripheral workforce** see LABOUR FLEXIBILITY.

**perk** see FRINGE BENEFIT.

**perpetual stock system** see STOCK CONTROL, BIN CARD.

**personal accounts** the accounts which are recorded in the sales ledger and purchases ledger of debtors and creditors respectively. A business has to keep a record within its recording system of how much is owing from each individual customer and to each individual supplier. See LEDGER.

**personal allowance** see INCOME TAX ALLOWANCE.

**personal computer (PC)** a small COMPUTER used as a desktop data processing facility in business and for personal use. In the office, PCs and desk-top workstations are often linked together in LOCAL AREA NETWORKS enabling them to share data and peripherals such as printers, fax machines, scanners etc. For many tasks the PC has replaced the large mainframe computer (see DOWNSIZING).

See INFORMATION MANAGEMENT.

**personal contract** a CONTRACT OF EMPLOYMENT which is determined solely by the employer and employee, and covers only that one employee. Many of the collective agreements underlying the terms of employment contracts, such as standardized conditions of employment reached by agreement by employer and trade unions, are explicitly excluded. The main purpose of most personal contracts is to take employees' pay out of the ambit of COLLECTIVE BARGAINING and to remove or limit employees' rights to representation by a trade union, thereby weakening trade unions. Instead an employee's pay is determined on a personal basis between employer and employee. For this reason personal contracts are often introduced alongside PERFORMANCE-RELATED PAY. Personal contracts often appear attractive to employees because it is common for substantial cash inducements to be given to encourage employees to sign them (see TRADE UNION REFORM AND EMPLOYMENT RIGHTS ACT 1993) and because they appear to be more personalized than previous contracts. In practice most personal contracts are standardized with employees given little opportunity to negotiate over the contract's terms. Furthermore, most give greater discretion to employers than those they are replacing.

**personal equity plan (PEP)** a scheme introduced by the Government in 1987 to encourage small savers to invest in UK ORDINARY SHARES. An individual can invest up to (currently) £9,000 per year in shares listed on the main STOCK MARKET or AIM (see UNLISTED SECURITIES MARKET) and, provided the sums involved remain invested for a calendar year, any income or capital gain received is exempt from tax. Up to £6,000 can be invested in a general (multi-share) PEP and £3,000 in a single-share PEP.

**personal goals** the individual goals or objectives of people working within a business or organization. In some cases these goals may run counter to and conflict with the goals/objectives of the business or organization. Possible goal conflict makes it important that the business or organization communicates its own goals clearly to all appropriate personnel and encourages them to adopt these goals as their own.

**Personal Investment Authority (PIA)** a UK body which is responsible for regulating retail financial services firms providing personal INSURANCE and PENSIONS and UNIT TRUST management. The PIA was established in 1994, taking over the activities of two previous regulatory bodies – the Financial Intermediaries, Managers and Brokers Regulatory Association (FIMBRA) and the Life Assurance and Unit Trust Regulatory Organization (LAUTRO).

See FINANCIAL SERVICES ACT 1986.

**personality inventory** a profile of an individual's personality traits. Such profiles are usually constructed by asking subjects a series of questions about their behaviour in various situations and about their character. From these responses a profile or inventory of characteristics in key personality areas can be constructed. For example, a profile of an individual's degree of confidence, thoughtfulness, consideration for others etc. can be built up. In theory, there are no right or wrong answers to the questions asked but this is not always the case in practice. Inventories of this sort have been popular of late in RECRUITMENT AND SELECTION, especially of managerial employees. This reflects an emphasis on the importance of leadership qualities and an implicit belief that they are in part innate and not acquired. However, inventories of this sort can be flawed in a number of ways, hence their use as predictors of future performance is questionable:

(a) subjects can often discern the answers desired by the selectors;

(b) the presence of certain personality characteristics implied by certain answers may be dubious; for instance, 'lack of confidence' cannot be straightforwardly derived from a response such as 'I have not felt able to say anything at recent seminars'; it may have reflected an awareness that one's knowledge of the seminar topic was decidedly limited;

(c) the qualities seen as desirable by selectors (for example confidence) may not in fact be beneficial in actual work situations.

Despite these flaws the apparent insight the profile gives into the personality and characteristics of job applicants will ensure its continued popularity.

See PSYCHOLOGICAL TEST.

**personal pension plan** see PENSION.

**personal selling** a means of increasing the sales of a firm's product which involves direct contact between the firm's SALES REPRESENTATIVES and prospective customers. Unlike passive means of communicating with buyers such as ADVERTISING, face-to-face meetings with customers facilitate a more pro-active approach, with sales representatives being able to explain fully the details of a product, advise and answer customer queries about it, and, where appropriate, demonstrate the workings of the product. See PROMOTIONAL MIX.

**personnel function** see PERSONNEL MANAGEMENT.

**personnel information system** the collection of information on its employees stored by an organization. At its most basic such information will usually comprise employees' names and addresses, length of service and attendance, and will be maintained by the PERSONNEL MANAGEMENT department. It is common for this information to be kept separate from pay records (which are usually maintained by the finance department). Until the widespread adoption of computerized data bases, many organizations found it difficult to analyse this information for MANPOWER PLANNING purposes; it was instead used mainly to deal with problems relating to individual employees. In addition such information was not readily available to other management departments. Nor did it generally include information on, for instance, skills and training which production departments, for instance, would find useful. A sophisticated personnel information system will comprise an extensive data base capable of retrieval and analysis by all management functions.

**personnel management** the branch of management concerned with administering the employment relationship and with achieving effective use of the human resources available to the organization. The rationale for employing personnel managers is that specialized knowledge of aspects of 'people management' – RECRUITMENT AND SELECTION, TRAINING, PERFORMANCE APPRAISAL, WELFARE, PAYMENT SYSTEMS, LABOUR LAW, INDUSTRIAL RELATIONS – will lead to better managerial and organizational performance. High standards of management in these areas will reduce certain potential costs such as those arising from ABSENTEEISM, LABOUR TURNOVER and INDUSTRIAL DISPUTES. Personnel management typically involves routine administration of employment matters, for example maintenance of personnel records (see PERSONNEL INFORMATION SYSTEM), provision of specialized advice on personnel issues to other managers, creation of procedures (for example DISCIPLINARY PROCEDURES) to guide and control the activities of these managers and, in some cases, conduct of COLLECTIVE BARGAINING with TRADE UNIONS. Often people management is largely undertaken by others, such as LINE MANAGERS; the objective of personnel managers is usually to ensure that these managers act consistently and equitably. The full range of personnel activities, be they undertaken by personnel managers or others, is known as the *personnel function*. In the UK personnel management developed out of the industrial welfare movement earlier in the twentieth century. These origins, coupled with the emphasis in personnel management on fairness (in part for good business reasons), lead some managers to view personnel managers with suspicion. They are sometimes seen as 'soft' on the workers and as not 'proper' managers. In part this may also be due to resentment at the interference of personnel managers in what they view as their area of decision making. These attitudes are reflected in status insecurity amongst some personnel managers; they feel that they stand midway between workers and management, and are not properly part of either.

One development that has raised the status of personnel management in the UK in recent years is the emergence of *human resource management* (HRM). Some argue that HRM is nothing new; it is simply personnel management with a new title, adopted by personnel managers to advance their interests. Others argue that HRM does possess distinctive characteristics. These include greater sophistication in the use of personnel techniques (for example wider adoption of PSYCHOLOGICAL TESTS in employee selection); a concern with resource maximization (exemplified in an emphasis on training and MANAGEMENT DEVELOPMENT) rather than the traditional one of cost minimization; and a closer integration of personnel management activity with BUSINESS STRATEGY. In addition, many of the more routine aspects of personnel work are passed to line managers, leaving human resources managers with the task of devising strategies to guide and train them in these activities.

An advanced form of HRM, rarely practised, is *human asset accounting*. This approach attempts to assign an accounting value to the organization's human resources, and to determine whether these assets appreciate or depreciate in the same way as do capital resources. In this way HRM can be brought into the calculation of the 'bottom line'. The rationale of this approach is that the value of an organization's human resources has an important bearing on its long-term health. By generating data of this sort it provides managers with a higher quality of information upon which to base human resource decisions, and encourages them to adopt a more long-term perspective in the utilization of their workforces.

See INSTITUTE OF PERSONNEL MANAGEMENT, MANPOWER PLANNING.

**person-oriented culture** see CULTURE.

**person specification** see RECRUITMENT AND SELECTION.

**persuasive advertising** see ADVERTISING.

**PERT (programme evaluation and review technique)** see NETWORK ANALYSIS.

**Peter Principle** the principle, formulated by the American management writer Laurence Peter (1919–   ), that in organizations people are promoted to the level of their incompetence. Individuals rise through ORGANIZATION hierarchies because job vacancies continually arise and need to be filled. The criteria for promotion is successful performance in current and previous posts. But at some point individuals are promoted to posts which are beyond the range of their abilities. From then on their job performance is characterized by incompetence, and promotion will cease. Individuals thus come to stay in jobs which they cannot adequately perform. Hence the principle that 'every employee tends to move to their level of incompetence'.

Every organization will contain a number of people in this situation. Indeed, in time 'every post tends to be occupied by an employee who is incompetent'. Thus organizational performance will virtually always be at suboptimum levels. The Peter Principle is generally viewed as a perceptive and humorous insight into organizational processes rather than as a proposition worthy of empirical investigation.

**petty cash** small sums of money held by a person or business to pay for small items of expenditure.

**Phillips curve** an empirical observation of the relationship between the level of UNEMPLOYMENT and the rate of change of WAGE RATES, and, by inference, the rate of change of final prices (INFLATION), indicating that as unemployment falls the rate of inflation rises, and vice versa. See ECONOMIC POLICY.

**physical distribution** see DISTRIBUTION.

**picket** a person involved in a STRIKE who seeks to prevent other persons from gaining access to a place of work during an INDUSTRIAL DISPUTE. In the UK, picketing one's own place of work is lawful; picketing other people's places of work (*secondary picketing*) is unlawful. See SECONDARY ACTION.

**piecework** a system of PAY in which an individual's WAGE is related to his or her output. In some cases payments are based entirely on the volume of output (for example fruit picking), in others employees receive a 'floor' wage supplemented by additional payments proportional to the value of the time saved where output is achieved in less than the time allotted. The latter relies on the calculation of standard times to perform given tasks and hence usually makes extensive use of WORK MEASUREMENT. In the past, piecework has often given rise to INDUSTRIAL RELATIONS difficulties, especially when workers are unable to achieve normal expected bonuses because of factors outside their control, for example non-availability of stock.

**pie chart** a chart that portrays data in pictorial form, showing the relative share of each category in a total by means of the relative size of its 'slice' of a circular 'pie'.

**pioneering customer** see DIFFUSION PROCESS, PRODUCT LIFE CYCLE.

**PIMS (Profit Impact of Market Strategy)** a database covering over 3000 businesses in Europe and North America which contains information on firms' sales, market shares, investment etc. and market characteristics (growth rates, concentration, customer power, etc.) and which seeks to establish associations between these variables and firms' profit performance. See BUSINESS STRATEGY, COMPETITIVE STRATEGY.

**place** an aspect of DISTRIBUTION concerned with ensuring that a firm's products are available for consumers to purchase at appropriate locations.

See DISTRIBUTION CHANNEL, MARKETING LOGISTICS, FOUR P'S OF MARKETING.

**placing** a means of raising new SHARE CAPITAL by issuing company shares to a selected group of investors rather than to the investing public at large. See SHARE ISSUE.

**planned obsolescence** see OBSOLESCENCE.

**planning** see BUSINESS STRATEGY, ECONOMIC PLANNING.

**plant** large items of capital such as a PRODUCTION LINE or furnace used in production. See MACHINERY, EQUIPMENT, CAPITAL STOCK, FIXED ASSET.

**plant-and-machinery per employee** an accounting measure of a firm's degree of mechanization, which expresses the firm's plant and machinery as a ratio of its number of employees.

See CAPITAL LABOUR RATIO, PRODUCTIVITY.

**plant bargaining** see COLLECTIVE BARGAINING.

**plant hire** see LEASING.

**plant layout** see FACTORY LAYOUT.

**plant register** a record of information about each item of plant, machinery and equipment employed by a firm. Typically a plant register will include details of: description of the particular item and its expected life; its cost and DEPRECIATION details; its location; its MAINTENANCE requirements; any special operating considerations, such as safety features and breakdown implications; details of GUARANTEES and service contracts.

**Plc (public limited company)** see JOINT-STOCK COMPANY.

**ploughed-back profit** see RETAINED PROFIT or UNDISTRIBUTED PROFIT.

**pluralism** a diffusion of power and interests in a society or ORGANIZATION, such that there is a plurality of interest groups. Those who subscribe to pluralism argue that there will inevitably be differences between individuals or groups in any complex social institution over, for instance, the distribution of rewards.

Pluralists claim that it is better to accept these differences than to suppress them, because once they are brought into the open it is possible to find mechanisms for resolving potential conflict to the benefit of all. In INDUSTRIAL RELATIONS the pluralist frame of reference is held by those who believe that the interests of management and workers will inevitably differ on occasions, for example over the size of an annual pay increase. They argue that it is better to accept that TRADE UNIONS are the legitimate expressions of *employee* interests rather than to refuse recognition on the grounds that employer–employee interests are identical. If the latter policy is adopted CONFLICT may break out without warning and with no acceptable means of resolving it. If, on the other hand, unions are recognized then management and unions can work together to devise procedures (for example GRIEVANCE PROCEDURES) that will prevent differences of interest from developing into open conflict and provide a means of resolving conflict if it should occur.

See MANAGEMENT STYLE.

**pluralist frame of reference** see MANAGEMENT STYLE.

**point of sale** see RETAIL OUTLET.

**point of sale display** promotional material, such as banners and posters or demonstrations of a product inside a SHOP or store, which is used as a means of stimulating SALES. Such in-store displays and demonstrations are often used alongside an ADVERTISING campaign, and serve to reinforce and capitalize upon that advertising by attracting customers' attention whilst in the store. See SALES PROMOTION, MERCHANDISING.

**poison pill** see TAKEOVER BID.

**political fund** a fund maintained by a TRADE UNION or other body for the purpose of supporting a political party. In the UK such funds must be clearly distinct from other union budgets and union members have the right to be exempt from making payments into it. The TRADE UNION ACT 1984 requires that unions maintaining a political fund must ballot their members on its continuation at least every ten years.

**poll tax** a tax that is levied at a fixed rate per head of population. See LOCAL TAX.

**polluter pays principle** see POLLUTION.

**pollution** the contamination of the environment by the discharge of industrial substances, smoke emissions and the dumping of waste materials and products. In the past, little attention was paid to the social costs of polluting the atmosphere, rivers, the countryside etc., but increasingly governments have passed more onerous regulations covering the use and disposal of industrial materials and production methods. As a consequence industry itself is being forced to invest in appropriate pollution control and limitation systems, and take a more proactive approach to the production and marketing of products which are environment-friendly.

In the UK the basic approach of government policy on the environment is that pollution should be prevented at source and that the polluter should pay for the necessary controls (the *polluter pays principle*). The main measure for achieving this is the Environmental Protection Act 1990. Under the Act the Inspectorate of Pollution is charged with the task of getting businesses to use the best available technology and techniques to prevent or minimize pollution in industrial processes.

Firms which do not comply with the new controls face fines of up to £20,000 in the magistrates' court, and unlimited fines in the Crown Court. Clean-up costs incurred by the enforcing authorities can also be recovered from the polluter. See GREEN CONSUMER, RECYCLING, EXTERNALITIES.

**polyvalence** the acquisition and application of a range of SKILLS. A polyvalent worker is one with a variety of job competencies and hence is able to perform a range of tasks which transcend traditional job boundaries. See LABOUR FLEXIBILITY.

**population 1.** the total number of people resident in a country at a particular point in time. The UK, for example, had a population of 59 million people in 1997. The size of the population is determined by past and present birth and death rates, together with net migration trends – the number of people leaving the country to live abroad (emigration) compared with the number entering the country to take up residence (immigration). The UK birth rate is currently 13 births per 1000 of the population per annum and the death rate 12 per 1000 of the population per annum. In most advanced countries, both birth and death rates have declined over the long run because of rising living standards and improved medical care; this has produced slow-growing, ageing populations.

The total size of the population and its composition in terms of proportion of males to females and age-group distributions, combined with various SOCIOECONOMIC factors influencing buying characteristics, are important to businesses in assessing the market potential for their products.

**2.** all possible observations of a certain phenomenon in statistical analysis, for example incomes of all people resident in a country. Where it is too time-consuming and expensive to record all possible observations it is necessary to take a SAMPLE, for example the incomes of 1000 citizens, and generalize about the incomes of all citizens from this sample. See STATISTICAL INFERENCE.

**porcupine** see TAKEOVER BID.

**portable computer** see COMPUTER.

**portfolio 1.** a collection of FINANCIAL SECURITIES held by an investor. Typically an investor would want to hold a number of different financial securities to spread his risk, and would seek a mixture of them, some offering high short-term DIVIDEND payments with others offering long-term capital appreciation as their market prices rise. See PORTFOLIO THEORY, INVESTMENT.
**2.** a collection of products marketed by a firm. See PRODUCT RANGE, PRODUCT-MARKET MATRIX, BOSTON MATRIX.

**portfolio theory** the study of the way in which an individual investor may achieve the maximum expected return from a varied PORTFOLIO of FINANCIAL SECURITIES which has attached to it a given level of risk. Alternatively the portfolio may achieve for the investor a minimum amount of risk for a given level of expected return. Return on a security consists of INTEREST or DIVIDEND, plus or minus any CAPITAL GAIN or loss from holding the security over a given time period. The *expected* return on the collection of securities within the portfolio is the weighted average of the expected returns on the individual INVESTMENTS that comprise the portfolio. However, the important thing is that the risk attaching to a portfolio (its variability) is smaller than the variability of each individual investment. See CAPITAL ASSET PRICING MODEL, EFFICIENT MARKET HYPOTHESIS, UNCERTAINTY.

**positioning** see MARKET POSITIONING.

**post** *v.* an accounting term, meaning to enter the details of a transaction in a firm's LEDGER accounts from the details provided in the firm's JOURNAL.

**post-acquisition profits** the profits made by a company after the date of its acquisition or TAKEOVER by the HOLDING COMPANY. Such post-acquisition profits belong to the new shareholders of the company. See PRE-ACQUISITION PROFITS.

**post-balance sheet events** events occurring after the date of the annual BALANCE SHEET, that is, in the next ACCOUNTING PERIOD. Where events such as the outcome of a major legal trial or an important technological or market change have a significant effect upon the value of company ASSETS the BOARD OF DIRECTORS are required to spell out the financial implications of such events to shareholders in the Directors' Report in the ANNUAL REPORT AND ACCOUNTS.

**post-entry closed shop** see CLOSED SHOP.

**post-purchase behaviour** the stage in buyer decision-making where buyers take further action after making the purchase. Specifically sellers are interested as part of their MARKETING RESEARCH in whether buyers are satisfied or dissatisfied with their purchase since this will have a critical effect on BRAND LOYALTY and the likelihood of repeat purchases. Firms use buyer studies to elicit information about post-purchase behaviour. See BUYER BEHAVIOUR, PRE-PURCHASE BEHAVIOUR.

**post-testing** see ADVERTISING EFFECTIVENESS TEST.

**pound (£)** the standard monetary unit of the UK. See CURRENCY, STERLING.

**power culture** see CULTURE.

**PR** see PUBLIC RELATIONS.

**pre-acquisition profits** the profits made by a company up to the date of its acquisition or TAKEOVER by the HOLDING COMPANY. Such pre-acquisition profits belong to the original shareholders of that company and where the holding company acquires less than 100% of the subsidiary company's shares then a proportion of the pre-acquisition profits belong to the MINORITY INTERESTS. See POST-ACQUISITION PROFITS.

**precedence diagram** a chart which depicts the sequence of operations involved in an assembly operation by specifying which operations need to be completed prior to subsequent operations commencing. Precedence diagrams are a means of planning and controlling PRODUCTION operations.

**predatory pricing** a PRICING strategy which is aimed at the removal of troublesome competitors. It can take a number of specific forms including selective price cutting on particular brands or selective price cuts in particular sales territories, and the application of a PRICE SQUEEZE by a vertically-integrated supplier on non-integrated rivals.

See PRICE WAR, LOSS LEADER, DUMPING, COMPETITION POLICY.

**pre-determined costing** COSTING systems such as BUDGETARY CONTROL and STANDARD COSTING, where costs and revenues are estimated in advance of the start of the accounting period in which they are to be incurred. Contrast HISTORICAL COSTING.

**predetermined motion time system** see WORK MEASUREMENT.

**pre–entry closed shop** see CLOSED SHOP.

**preference share** or **preferred stock** a FINANCIAL SECURITY issued to those individuals and institutions who provide long-term finance for JOINT-STOCK COMPANIES. Preference shares pay a fixed rate of DIVIDEND and are generally given priority over ORDINARY SHARES in receiving dividend. In the event of the company being wound up they also have first claim on any remaining ASSETS of the business after all debts have been discharged. Cumulative preference shares are entitled to be paid any arrears of their dividend before ordinary shares receive any dividends.

Certain preference shares, called Participating Preference Shares, entitle holders not only to a fixed dividend rate but also to an additional distribution of profit in good trading years. Generally, preference SHAREHOLDERS have no voting rights at company ANNUAL GENERAL MEETINGS, though under the terms of a firm's ARTICLES OF ASSOCIATION they may be granted voting rights where their dividends are in arrears.

See SHARE CAPITAL.

**preferential creditor** see INSOLVENCY.

**preferred stock** see PREFERENCE SHARE.

**preliminary expenses** the initial costs incurred in forming a JOINT-STOCK COMPANY, such as preparing a PROSPECTUS and issuing SHARES, prior to the company commencing trading.

**premium 1.** an addition to the published LIST PRICE of a product charged by a supplier to a customer. The premium could be charged for guaranteeing rapid delivery of the product, or could reflect the temporary scarcity of the product. A 'premium price' over similar products might be charged by a supplier who is able to convince buyers that his product is superior in some respect to competitors' offerings.
**2.** the purchase of a BOND for more than its nominal value. The price which people are prepared to pay for a bond can be more than its nominal value if the nominal rate of interest on that bond exceeds current market interest rates.
**3.** the sale of new STOCKS and SHARES at an enhanced price. In the UK this involves the issue of a new share at a price above its nominal value. Where shares have no nominal value it in-

volves the sale of new shares above their current market price.
**4.** the rating of a particular company's shares at a price above the average market price of the shares of other companies operating in the same sector, the 'premium' reflecting investors' general optimism that this company is likely to perform much better than the others.

**5.** the amount by which a foreign currency's spot exchange rate stands above its 'official' par value under a FIXED EXCHANGE RATE system which allows some degree of short-term fluctuation either side of the par value.

**6.** the annual payment made to an INSURANCE COMPANY by persons or firms taking out an insurance policy.

**premium bond** a FINANCIAL SECURITY issued by the UK government as a means of raising money for the government and encouraging private SAVING. Premium bonds are issued in small denominations, but do not pay interest, nor can a capital gain be obtained on redemption, since they are issued and redeemed at their face value. Their appeal lies in the prospect of a 'gambler's chance' of winning a substantial lump sum of money in a monthly prize lottery (numbers being drawn electronically by 'ERNIE').

**prepayment** or **payment in advance** an expense which is paid in one trading period but which is properly chargeable against the revenues or profits of future trading periods. For example, if a company preparing accounts for the year to 31 December pays its annual rent on 1 April, then only three quarters of that rent relates to the current trading period, the remaining quarter being a prepayment for use of the building from 1 January to 31 March in the next trading period. Prepayments are counted as part of the company's assets at the end of the trading period and are usually included as part of DEBTORS in the firm's BALANCE SHEET. See ACCRUAL.

**pre-purchase behaviour** the stage in buyer decision-making where potential buyers get information about a product through advertisements, sales brochures and personal contacts. The degree of search behaviour undertaken by prospective buyers will vary according to the cost and technical complexity of the product and buyers' previous experience of the product. Purchasing decisions may be carefully pre-planned or may be a spontaneous, impulse buy. As part of their MARKETING RESEARCH firms use MOTIVATIONAL RESEARCH to identify buyer needs in order to influence pre-purchase behaviour through ADVERTISING and SALES PROMOTION. See BUYER BEHAVIOUR, POST-PURCHASE BEHAVIOUR.

**present value** see DISCOUNTED CASH FLOW.

**present value tables** tables which are used in INVESTMENT APPRAISAL undertaken by means of DISCOUNTED CASH FLOW. The tables show how much we need to invest now, at a certain rate of interest and for a particular period of time, to produce £1. For example, the tables show that if we want to produce £1 in 5 years' time at 10%, we will need to invest £0.621 now. Alternatively, the tables show that £1 receivable in 5 years' time, taking into account a rate of interest 10%, will be worth only 62p (that is, £0.621).

**president** a North American term for the chief executive or MANAGING DIRECTOR of a corporation or JOINT-STOCK COMPANY.

**pretest 1.** a trial launch of a product to a sample group of consumers to test the product's operational efficiency and consumer acceptability. See NEW-PRODUCT DEVELOPMENT.

**2.** see ADVERTISING EFFECTIVENESS TEST.

**3.** see QUALITY CONTROL.

**prevention costs** see QUALITY COSTS.

**preventive maintenance** a planned MAINTENANCE programme aimed at minimizing or eliminating breakdowns to buildings, plant, machinery and equipment with their consequent disruption to production, or inconsistent machine operation which might affect product quality. A preventive maintenance programme would involve keeping an up-to-date PLANT REGISTER which notes the maintenance requirements of each machine; scheduling the frequency of inspections, lubrication and overhauls for each machine; GROUP REPLACEMENT of parts, where appropriate, or replacement of parts as they fail (see CONDITION-BASED MAINTENANCE); making modifications and improvements which increase reliability and at the same time bring the plant, machinery or equipment up to date.

**price** the money value of a unit of a GOOD, SERVICE, FINANCIAL SECURITY or ASSET which a buyer is required to pay a seller to purchase the item. Usually the price of a product is fixed by the seller in advance on the basis of the costs of producing and selling the product and the seller's desired profit margin. In other cases, however, prices are variable, being determined by prevailing demand and supply conditions as with the sale, for example, of a STOCK or SHARE, a house or items sold at an auction.

Because a purchase involves a money outlay on the part of buyers who operate within a budget constraint, the price of a product is an important factor in the buying decision. It may well be the paramount consideration in many cases, but for some purchases other elements in the MARKETING MIX (product quality and performance etc.) may be equally if not more important. Thus, although many products (especially COMMODITY-TYPE PRODUCTS) tend to be sold at low, competitive prices, many others can be sold at higher prices, providing customers with a variety of price–quality trade-offs and other product attributes.

See MARKET STRUCTURE, MONOPOLY, BUYER'S MARKET, SELLER'S MARKET, PRICING, PRICING OBJECTIVES, PRICING METHODS, FOUR P'S OF MARKETING.

**price competition** see COMPETITION.

**price controls** the regulation by a government agency of the PRICES permitted to be charged for a product. Price controls can be targeted specifically to benefit particular groups of buyers or suppliers, or can be applied more generally in the context of, for example, controlling INFLATION (see PRICES AND INCOMES POLICY). In the former case, price controls may be used to benefit consumers of a product by, for example, preventing suppliers from charging MONOPOLY prices (see COMPETITION POLICY), or by keeping the price of some 'essential' product at a low level (see SUBSIDY). Alternatively, the government may wish to encourage the greater supply of a product, to the benefit of suppliers, by setting minimum prices for the product which are higher than the free market price. The EUROPEAN UNION'S support system for agricultural produce prices is a case in point (see AGRICULTURAL POLICY). See RATE OF RETURN REGULATION.

**price discrimination** the ability of a supplier to sell the *same* good or service in a number of *separate* MARKETS at *different* PRICES. Markets can be separated in various ways such as by different consumer requirements (for example bulk and low volume gas supplies to industrial and household consumers, respectively); by the nature of the product itself (for example original and replacement components for washing machines) and by geographical locations (for example domestic and foreign markets). In order for price discrimination to be viable, markets must differ in their demand profiles (that is, exhibit different demand elasticities, so that higher prices can be charged where demand is inelastic and lower prices charged when demand is elastic), and the supplier must be able to 'seal off' each market so that customers in lower-priced markets cannot resell to those in higher-priced markets.

Price discrimination can help a supplier to increase his sales and profits, improve market share and contribute to the full capacity utilization of manufacturing plant. However, price discrimination may be exercised by a DOMINANT FIRM in a predatory manner aimed at removing troublesome competition or as a means of exploiting buyers. See OFFICE OF FAIR TRADING, ELASTICITY OF DEMAND, PRICE-SQUEEZE, DEMAND-BASED PRICING.

**price–earnings ratio** a ratio used to appraise a quoted public company's profit performance, which expresses the market PRICE of the company's SHARES as a multiple of its PROFIT. For example, if a company's profit amounted to £1 per share and the price of its shares was £10 each on the STOCK MARKET, then its price–earnings ratio would be 10:1. Where a company's prospects are considered by the stock market to be good, then it is likely that the company's share price will rise, producing a higher price–earnings ratio. Price–earnings ratio is the mirror image of EARNINGS YIELD. See EARNINGS PER SHARE.

**price elasticity of demand** see ELASTICITY OF DEMAND.

**price index 1.** a weighted average of the prices of a general 'basket' of goods and services produced in an economy over time, which is used in particular to indicate the rate of INFLATION. The Retail Price Index (RPI) is one commonly-used index, measuring the average level of the prices of final goods and services purchased by consumers. Each product in the index is weighted according to its relative importance in total consumer expenditure. A suitable base year is selected to commence the series (for example, index value 1980=100) and subsequent price changes are then reflected in changes in the index value over time (for example, 1989=200, indicating an annual rate of inflation of 10%). See INDEX-LINKED, PURCHASING POWER.

**2.** a weighted average of the prices of particular classes of financial securities or commodities, for example the Financial Times 100 share index or all-share index. See SHARE PRICE IN-

DEX.

**price leadership** a situation where a particular supplier is generally accepted by other suppliers as the 'lead' firm in changing market PRICES. Price leadership takes two main forms:

(a) DOMINANT FIRM price leadership: where the largest firm in terms of market share (and/or the lowest cost producer) leads off price changes (usually price increases) which other firms are prepared to follow because the price established yields them adequate profits or, occasionally, because of the power of the dominant firm to punish non-compliance (by, for example, subjecting non-following firms to selective price cutting);

(b) barometric price leadership: where a particular firm, often a smaller firm, is 'adopted' as the price leader because it has proved adept at reading changing market conditions.

Price leadership systems are often seen by suppliers as a useful way of coordinating their price policies so as to limit price competition and avoid ruinous price wars (see OLIGOPOLY). They may, however, act as a cloak for COLLUSION, and as such operate in a way detrimental to the interests of consumers. See MARKET CONDUCT, COMPETITION POLICY.

**Price Marking (Bargain Offers) Order 1979** a UK directive (made under the PRICES ACT 1974) which prohibits traders from making vague or misleading PRICE claims such as 'worth £10 our price £5' and 'reductions of up to 50%', and comparisons with prices of other unspecified traders. Genuine bargain offer price claims must be related to the seller's previous prices (specifically a price the trader has charged for at least 28 consecutive days during the previous six months) or to the manufacturer's RECOMMENDED RETAIL PRICE. See TRADE DESCRIPTIONS ACT 1968, CONSUMER PROTECTION, DEPARTMENT OF TRADE AND INDUSTRY.

**price promotion** a form of SALES PROMOTION employed by manufacturers and retailers which involves 'introductory-price' offers, 'money-off' packs, 'two-for-the-price-of-one' packs and 'special-price' offers. In addition to increasing the sales potential of the products whose prices have been temporarily cut, price promotions also serve to attract customers into shops. See SALE, LOSS LEADING.

**price–quality trade-offs** a firm's MARKETING policy on what QUALITY of product or BRAND to sell and the PRICE at which it is sold. Such decisions can be made only in the context of the quality of rivals' brands and the prices they are charging. In this context, quality refers to both durability and performance and to technical sophistication.

A firm may choose to offer a high-quality brand and sell it at a high price to appeal to a particular quality-conscious MARKET SEGMENT; or to produce a lower-quality brand to sell at a lower price to a more price-conscious segment. In terms of MARKET POSITIONING a firm, for example, may choose to upgrade slightly the quality of its brand and offer it at an unchanged price to make it more competitive; alternatively, the firm may modify a low-quality, low-price brand by significantly upgrading its quality and offering it at the same price to appeal to a new medium-quality price-conscious segment. Businesses often offer several different qualities or specifications of a product as a product line in order to appeal simultaneously to several market segments.

See PRODUCT RANGE, PSYCHOLOGICAL PRICING.

**Prices Act 1974** a UK Act which empowers the Secretary of State for Trade and Industry to issue 'orders', as appropriate, to protect consumers from vague, inaccurate and confusing PRICE claims made by traders. See PRICE MARKING (BARGAIN OFFERS) ORDER 1979, DEPARTMENT OF TRADE AND INDUSTRY, CONSUMER PROTECTION.

**prices and incomes policy** the application of controls on PRICES and INCOMES (particularly wages) in order to stop or slow down INFLATION in an economy.

Prices and incomes policies can be applied on a voluntary or statutory (mandatory) basis. In the former case, the government lays down guidelines for price and wage increases, appealing to industrialists and trade unions to moderate their actions, but experience has shown this approach to be largely ineffectual. A statutory prices and incomes policy can work for limited periods provided it is backed by strong penalties for non-compliance. This approach typically involves an initial standstill phase of up to one year in which price and wage increases are prohibited, followed by a further period of one to three years, providing for some degree of relaxation but nonetheless limiting increases either to levels below some specified 'ceiling', say 5% per annum, or more particularly the use of various formulas for linking price rises to non-absorbable cost increases and wage increases to increases in PRODUCTIVITY. Prices and incomes policies require the establishment of one or more regulatory bodies to administer them (such as the Pay Board and the Price Commission which formerly operated in the UK).

Critics of prices and incomes policies, while viewing them as a useful way of applying a 'short, sharp shock' to the economy to reduce inflationary expectations, see their long-term use as perverse: such controls are incompatible with the normal functioning of a market economy, resulting in an in-efficient allocation of resources and the stifling of enterprise and initiative. See ECONOMIC POLICY.

**price squeeze** the charging of discriminatory prices by a vertically integrated firm (see VERTICAL INTEGRATION) for the supply of inputs to non-integrated rivals, as a means of putting them at a competitive disadvantage. This occurs when the integrated firm produces both the input and the finished product, while the unintegrated firms produce only the finished product but have to rely on the integrated firm for their input supply. A 'squeeze' is applied if the integrated firm charges the non-integrated firms a *high* price for the input but sells its own finished product at a *low* price, thus allowing non-integrated firms only minimal profits or forcing losses on them. In market situations where there is a substantial number of alternative, independent supply sources, rival producers are unlikely to be harmed. However, the control by a DOMINANT FIRM of the input, combined with limitations on the establish-ment of new sources of supply, could have serious anti-competitive consequences. Under UK COMPETITION POLICY cases of vertical integration may be referred to the MONOPOLIES AND MERGERS COMMISSION for investigation. See PRICE DIS-CRIMINATION, TRANSFER PRICE.

**price support** see AGRICULTURAL POLICY.

**price system** see MARKET SYSTEM.

**price war** a situation of aggressive price cutting by a group of rival suppliers as a means of gaining sales at each other's expense. Since price wars, however, tend to be mutually ruinous by destroying the profitability of the market, they are normally avoided, with suppliers preferring to compete instead through various PRODUCT DIFFERENTIATION strategies. See OLIGOPOLY, CARTEL, COLLUSION, PRICE LEADERSHIP.

## PRICING

**pricing** the decision-making process involved in setting a PRICE for a good or service. For most products, pricing decisions cannot be made in isolation but must consider all aspects of the MARKETING MIX, prices of the firm's related products, competitors' prices, product COSTS, DEMAND and the firm's PRICING OBJECTIVES. See PRICING POLICY, PRICING METHODS, PRICE–QUALITY TRADE-OFF, BY-PRODUCT PRICING, PRODUCT LINE PRICING, CAPTIVE PRODUCT PRICING, OPTIONAL EXTRAS PRICING, GEOGRAPHICAL PRICING, PSYCHOLOGICAL PRICING.

**pricing methods** the approaches used by firms to PRICE goods or services. Three basic pricing methods may be distinguished:

(a) a COST-BASED PRICING method which relates the price of a product to the costs involved in producing and distributing it;

(b) a DEMAND-BASED PRICING method which relates the price of a product to the intensity of total demand for it and acknowledges differences in demand intensities between subgroups of buyers;

(c) a COMPETITION-BASED PRICING method which relates the price of a product to the prices charged by rivals. In practice, firms use a combination of these methods in setting their prices. See PRICING OBJECTIVES, PRICING POLICY.

**pricing objectives** the general and specific aims which a firm sets for itself in establishing the PRICE of its products. Pricing objectives are closely tied in with a firm's MARKETING OBJECTIVES which in turn are closely related to the achievement of the firm's overall BUSINESS OBJECTIVES.

Unit price × quantity sold is a key determinant of the firm's revenues which together with its underlying cost structures will determine the amount of PROFIT earned by the firm. Pricing objectives may be expressed generally in terms of achieving higher profit returns or related, for example, to some specified targeted RATE OF RETURN ON CAPITAL EMPLOYED. More specifically, in the case of particular products the pricing objective may be to increase MARKET SHARE in existing markets, or to enter a new market. In addition, a firm may seek to achieve price stability so as to avoid excessive fluctuations in its PROFIT MARGINS and the administrative costs associated with changing prices (for example, reprinting price lists).

See PRICING, PRICING METHODS, PRICING POLICY, MARKET PENETRATION PRICING.

**pricing policy** the overall policy pursued by a multiproduct firm in PRICING its products. At the specific level pricing policy will include PRODUCT LINE PRICING, establishing price differentials between the brands making up a line, for example prices of the basic and de luxe versions of the Ford Escort car. At a general level, pricing policy would also embrace price relativities *between* product lines, for example prices of the Ford Escort, Sierra and Fiesta cars.

Other areas involving a multidimensional pricing approach include BY-PRODUCT PRICING, CAPTIVE PRODUCT PRICING, OPTIONAL EXTRAS PRICING, PRICE–QUALITY TRADE-OFF, SELECTIVE PRICE CUTTING.

**Priestman plan** a GROUP INCENTIVE SCHEME in which employees are paid a guaranteed basic wage plus a percentage based on the percentage by which output exceeded the target output. The principal problem for a business which wants to use this system is the setting of the target output figure: setting it too low will lead to large bonus payments, setting it too high will reduce the incentive for workers.

**prime cost** see DIRECT COST, COST.

**printer** a COMPUTER output device for producing hard copy of text or diagrammatic material on paper.

**prior charges** INTEREST payments on DEBENTURES and LOAN STOCK which must be paid by a company before any dividend payments can be made to shareholders. See ORDINARY SHARE, PREFERENCE SHARE.

**priority–based budgeting** a management accounting technique that seeks to improve profitability by requiring managers to reassess their activities and determine priorities. Priority-based BUDGETING aims to reduce costs and channel company resources into high–priority areas of the business.

**prior year adjustments** adjustments applicable to prior years arising from changes in ACCOUNTING PRINCIPLES, for example the use of a different DEPRECIATION rule for fixed assets. Prior year adjustments are made to ensure that previous years' accounting results (recalculated on the basis of the new accounting policy) are *consistent* with those of the current year (measured on the same new basis).

**private enterprise economy** see ECONOMY.

**private label brand** see OWN-LABEL BRAND.

**private ledger** a ledger that is used to keep the accounts relating to the directors and possibly other highly confidential accounts. Generally access to the private ledger is restricted to certain authorized personnel.

**private limited company (Ltd)** see JOINT-STOCK COMPANY.

**privatization** or **denationalization** the transference of ownership of an industry or firm from the State to private interests. For further discussion, see the entry NATIONALIZATION VERSUS PRIVATIZATION.

**probability** the likelihood of a particular uncertain event occurring, measured on a scale from 0.0 (the event is impossible) to 1.0 (the event is certain to occur). People usually estimate probabilities on the basis of the relative frequency with which an event has occurred in the past, and generalize from this past experience. In some circumstances it is easy to estimate the proportion of occasions on which an event occurs, for example, the probability of getting 'heads' when flipping a coin is 0.5 because with such a coin in the long run we would get 50% 'heads' and 50% 'tails'. In estimating probabilities in business situations though, there may be no or only a few previous experiences which can be used to gauge the relative frequency of an event occurring. See UNCERTAINTY AND RISK.

**procedural agreement 1.** any agreement between two parties which establishes procedures for future discussion and negotiations over issues of mutual interest.

**2.** (in INDUSTRIAL RELATIONS) an agreement between employers and trade union officials or representatives governing the conduct of negotiations and joint consultation over pay, conditions of employment etc. See COLLECTIVE BARGAINING.

**process chart** see ACTIVITY CHART.

**process costing** a system for determining the cost of products made in a PROCESS PRODUCTION plant like an oil refinery. The continuous nature of such a process and the uniformity of the products emerging from it make it difficult to identify specific units of output. The cost of any particular unit must, therefore, be taken as the average cost of manufacture over a period. Process costing is further complicated by the tendency to experience process wastage from chemical reaction or evaporation and the production of waste products which have to be allowed for in costing products emerging from the process. Furthermore, in making the main product, BY-PRODUCTS may arise from the production process, making it difficult to determine the respective cost of main and by-products since they result from common expenditures on raw materials and processing of these materials. See BY-PRODUCT PRICING.

**process-focused layout** a FACTORY LAYOUT in which all PRODUCTION operations of a similar nature are grouped together in the same department or part of the factory. For example, separate areas may exist for drilling operations, milling, grinding, assembly and so on (see Fig. 66). Process layout is appropriate where small quantities of a large range of products are to be manufactured, as for example in BATCH PRODUCTION or jobbing production. The nature of the layout permits flexibility in production, i.e. complex products, requiring processing in most of the functional departments, may be made alongside simple products requiring processing in only a few departments. This same flexibility, however, brings disadvantages, since batch production in process layouts necessitates frequent machine resetting; it normally operates with a comparatively high level of work in progress; and through-put time is high. Specialist supervision is possible, and the grouping of operatives of a similar type and skill within the same department promotes cohesiveness and enables individual incentive payment schemes to be used. The provision of services (for example water, power, removal of scrap) is simpler than in other forms of layout, but the cost of materials handling is high. See PRODUCT-FOCUSED LAYOUT, SET-UP COST, SET-UP TIME.

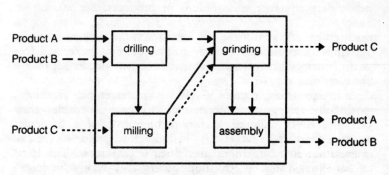

Fig. 66. **Process-focused layout.** A simple example.

**processor** an electronic device within a COMPUTER which is capable of interpreting and executing instructions.

**process production** a system of PRODUCTION in which a product passes through several processes or stages of production which are operated on a continuous basis; for example in oil refining and petrochemicals plants where the processes involve liquid or semisolid materials. In manufacturing a main product, say petrol, from such a production process, BY-PRODUCTS like tar or creosote may unavoidably arise. See PROCESS COSTING.

**procurement lead time** see STOCK CONTROL.

**producer** or **manufacturer** a business which is engaged in making consumer goods and capital goods using factor inputs such as raw materials, labour and capital. See VALUE ADDED.

**producer good** see GOOD.

**producers' cooperative** see WORKERS' COOPERATIVE.

**product** a generic term which covers both GOODS and SERVICES. *Final products* are goods and services which are purchased by consumers, while *intermediate products* are goods and services which are used by producers as factor inputs in producing other goods and services. See FOUR P'S OF MARKETING.

**product attributes** the various characteristics of a product which satisfy some particular consumer need. Product attributes such as quality, size, weight, price and reliability will affect the buyer decision-making process. Buyers will tend to rank attributes according to their perceptions and needs. Companies generally focus on particular attributes when they advertise their brands or products. See MARKETING MIX.

**product-based structure** an ORGANIZATION structure where activities are grouped according to product or service, and formal COORDINATION of management functions occurs separately for each. See Fig. 67.

Although this structure duplicates management functions, potentially losing some economies of scale, it enables their activities to be tailored to the requirements of a particular product and its market. It is, therefore, said to be an appropriate structure for a diversified organization. The locus of AUTHORITY and coordination occurs at a relatively decentralized level (compared with FUNCTIONAL STRUCTURES), thereby facilitating swift adjustment to changing market conditions. The geographically based structure takes a similar form: each

Fig. 67. **Product-based structure**. A typical example.

unit is based on a particular geographical area. Mixed geographical–product-based structures are quite common.

An extension of this form is the multidivisional or M-form company. Here the units are organized as separate divisions or profit centres, with considerable autonomy in operational decision-making. Questions of strategy, i.e. which markets to be in and hence what divisions to have, are reserved to a head office. This also acts as a banker, setting profit targets for the divisions, receiving surpluses from them and providing capital. In practice this separation of responsibilities is not so clear cut: head offices often interfere in operational decisions which they perceive to be of great importance. This multi-divisional form is the predominant structure amongst large companies in the UK.

See STRATEGIC BUSINESS UNIT, PROFIT CENTRE, FUNCTIONAL STRUCTURE, CRITICAL FUNCTION STRUCTURE, MATRIX STRUCTURE.

**product champion** a marketing executive within a company who has specific responsibility for a *particular* product. Product champions may be needed in large multiproduct companies to provide a focus for integrating marketing, production and distribution of the product.

**product class** see PRODUCT RANGE.

**product concept** an idea for a product which is capable of fulfilling consumer needs. See NEW-PRODUCT DEVELOPMENT.

**product cost** the total cost of making a product which comprises its DIRECT MATERIALS cost and its DIRECT LABOUR cost plus its OVERHEAD cost. Product costs may be based upon the actual costs incurred in making products or the anticipated costs of making products in some future period. See STANDARD COST.

**product costing** or **job costing** a cost accounting method which applies to separate contracts, jobs or batches of products. Product costing seeks to determine PRODUCT COST which will include materials, labour and overheads.

**product depth** the number of variants of a product offered by a firm in each of its product lines. See PRODUCT RANGE.

**product design** see DESIGN.

**product development** a BUSINESS STRATEGY pursued by a firm aimed at increasing sales by developing *new* products which can be sold in its *existing* markets (see PRODUCT-MARKET MATRIX) or new products which take the firm into *new* markets. (See DIVERSIFICATION). In the former case, product development is especially important given both the life-cycle tendencies of products (see PRODUCT LIFE CYCLE) and in maintaining the firm's competitiveness. Most individual BRANDS follow a typical cycle of introduction, growth, maturity and eventual decline so that it is vital for the firm to develop and launch a constant stream of new brands to replace those in decline. Moreover, the ability of a firm to introduce innovatory new brands is often a key means of establishing a COMPETITIVE ADVANTAGE over rival suppliers. Developing new products involves the firm in undertaking MARKETING RESEARCH and committing resources to product RESEARCH AND DEVELOPMENT. See NEW-PRODUCT DEVELOPMENT, BOSTON MATRIX.

**product differentiation** the means by which suppliers attempt to distinguish their own products from those offered by competitors. There are two basic ways in which products can be differentiated:

(a) by variations in the physical appearance and attributes of the product based on differences in design, styling, colouring and packaging, and differences in quality, composition, innovatory features and performance results;

(b) broadly similar products may be differentiated in the minds of buyers by the use of ADVERTISING and sales promotion techniques which emphasize imputed or subjective aspects of the product: for example 'better than', 'cleaner and whiter than'.

The purpose of product differentiation is to create and

sustain a demand for the firm's products by nurturing consumer BRAND LOYALTY. Product differentiation is an important means of establishing COMPETITIVE ADVANTAGE over rival suppliers, and in some market structures, most notably OLIGOPOLY, it is regarded as constituting a more effective competitive strategy than price competition. The attraction of product-differentiation competition over price competition lies in the fact that whereas price cuts, for example, can be quickly and completely matched by competitors, a successful advertising campaign or the introduction of an innovatory product is less easily imitated. Moreover, whereas price competition lowers firms' profitability, product differentiation tends to preserve and even enhance profit returns. In particular, the establishment of product uniqueness may allow firms to command premium prices over competitors' offerings. Finally, product differentiation may serve to act as a BARRIER TO ENTRY, thereby protecting existing market shares against new competition.

See BRAND PROLIFERATION, IMPERFECT COMPETITION, MARKET CONDUCT, RESEARCH AND DEVELOPMENT, PRODUCT MIX, MARKETING MIX, DIFFERENTIATED MARKETING STRATEGY, MARKET POSITIONING.

**product diversification** a BUSINESS STRATEGY pursued by a firm aimed at increasing sales by developing (or acquiring) new products for new markets.

See PRODUCT-MARKET MATRIX, DIVERSIFICATION.

**product family** see PRODUCT RANGE.

**product-focused layout** a FACTORY LAYOUT in which the equipment is arranged according to the needs of the product and in the same sequence as the operations (for example drilling, milling, grinding, assembly) necessary for production (see Fig. 68). Each production-line or assembly-line layout requires sufficient and stable demand to ensure a high utilization of equipment and a regular supply of raw materials and components. Failure in the supply of a piece of equipment results in the entire production line stopping, and quite remote failures can often result in disproportionately high losses.

The provision of machine services (power, maintenance, etc.) is difficult in product-type layouts, since where particularly elaborate machinery is used quite different pieces of equipment with different characteristics and requirements may be located adjacent to one another. A mixture of skills and operations frequently occurs, resulting in difficulties of payment and supervision; usually, however, little specialized supervision is required since the work performed is often highly rationalized. Minimum floor space is required, work in progress is minimized and through-put time is low. The requirements for handling materials are small and machine utilization is high.

A product layout is appropriate for the production of a small range of products in very large quantities and is a comparatively rigid production system. See PRODUCTION-LINE, PROCESS-FOCUSED LAYOUT.

Fig. 68. **Product-focused layout.** A simple example.

**product group** see PRODUCT RANGE.

**product image** the perceptions and attitudes of consumers towards an existing or proposed new product. Product image is affected both by the physical attributes of the product itself and by the psychological or imputed values of the buyer which can be cultivated and manipulated by ADVERTISING and other promotional forms. See BUYER BEHAVIOUR, MARKET POSITIONING, PSYCHOLOGICAL PRICING.

**product imitation** a MARKET POSITIONING strategy involving the introduction of a product which emulates or copies a product already on the market (in so far as it is legally possible under PATENT and TRADEMARK laws). Product imitation may be used to exploit high-volume market segments or to compete with new innovative products in a rapidly growing market (see PRODUCT LIFE CYCLE).

**product innovation** the improvement of existing products or the development of new products. Product innovation involves considerable expense in financing the generation of ideas, product design, development and testing, and since a high proportion of new products fail to secure customer acceptance it involves a high degree of risk. See RESEARCH AND DEVELOPMENT, NEW-PRODUCT DEVELOPMENT.

**production** the conversion process for transforming inputs such as materials, labour and capital into goods and services.

In the case of goods, production processes may be divided into three broad categories:

(a) *process* production involves the continuous production of a good in bulk often by chemical means, for example petrochemicals. Process production is used whenever raw materials in liquid or gaseous form need to be blended, heated or distilled, and the flow of these materials is facilitated by using pipelines which connect the various production stages;

(b) *mass* production involves the PRODUCTION-LINE OR ASSEMBLY-LINE production in very large numbers of goods such as motor cars or domestic appliances using PRODUCT-FOCUSED LAYOUTS. Mass production is used wherever demand for a product is sufficiently large and the product sufficiently standardized to justify laying out a specialized production line or assembly line for it in order to achieve the cost savings associated with ECONOMIES OF SCALE;

(c) *batch* production involves the manufacturing of similar goods together in batches and is used where demand is insufficient or the product cannot be standardized to enable mass production to be used. In batch production, batches of a product are subjected to a series of processes such as machining, drilling and grinding in work stations specializing in these processes, with machines generally being reset after each batch, ready to process the next batch (see PROCESS-FOCUSED LAYOUT).

In addition, a number of hybrid production systems such as GROUP TECHNOLOGY and FLEXIBLE MANUFACTURING SYSTEMS combine various features of mass production and batch production methods, using AUTOMATION to facilitate the low-cost production of a variety of low-volume components or products.

Mass production and batch production are generally undertaken for STOCK and customer orders are met by drawing on this stock. Alternatively, the firm may manufacture to individual customer orders rather than for stock, that is, engage in jobbing production. See VALUE ADDED.

**production budget** see BUDGET.

**production capacity** see CAPACITY.

**production control** the coordination and monitoring of production programmes and targets. Production control involves a number of activities, in particular:

(a) minimizing operational variations from production schedules, PROGRESS CHASING and dealing with problems so as to avoid losing output;

(b) controlling manufacturing costs by monitoring the use of materials and labour inputs and taking action to avoid wastage where necessary (see COST CONTROL);

(c) controlling product quality by inspection to detect defective products and taking action to remedy deficiencies (see QUALITY CONTROL);

(d) controlling MACHINE UTILIZATION by monitoring machine usage and avoiding idle time or machine down-time.

See also PRODUCTION MANAGEMENT, PRODUCTION SCHEDULING.

**production line** or **assembly line** a means of organizing PRODUCTION whereby a product is manufactured by passing it through a series of operations, further materials or components being added as appropriate. This method of production is used in, for example, the production of motor cars and electrical products such as television sets.

In planning an assembly line careful attention must be paid to PRODUCTION-LINE BALANCING to ensure that all operations are synchronized so as to produce a preplanned volume of output.

Assembly-line methods usually involve breaking down production operations into many small tasks. This has the benefit of reducing the complexity of each task, reducing the skill demanded of production operatives and reducing training costs. Such lines also create opportunities to use specialized purpose-built machines to undertake particular production or assembly processes (see AUTOMATION, ROBOT). Assembly line methods also facilitate the use of special materials-handling devices like conveyor belts which reduce materials-handling costs. Finally, use of assembly lines serves to reduce stock holdings of raw materials and components between production processes by making it easier to estimate daily production and usage.

On the other hand, assembly lines are vulnerable to breakdowns and disruptions since a breakdown at any point on the assembly line stops the whole production process. In addition, the speed at which the line is operated can cause stress problems for operatives. Finally, the limited and repetitive nature of each operation can lead to worker demotivation. To counter such motivational problems some companies use job enrichment programmes whereby operatives undertake a wider range of activities, or interchange between activities (see JOB DESIGN AND REDESIGN).

See PRODUCT-FOCUSED LAYOUT, JUST-IN-TIME (JIT) SYSTEM.

**production-line balancing** or **assembly-line balancing** the assignment of *equal* amounts of work to sequential work stations on the production line. This is necessary to avoid idle time or 'balancing loss' since the work stations at each production stage (for example drilling, milling, etc. in Fig. 69), although having different types of work to perform, are all required to work on the same number of items in any one time period (12 per hour in Fig. 69).

The task of production-line planning requires the total work to be divided among work stations where a worker or group of workers performs the same operation continuously on successive items. Alternatively, certain work stations may employ automatic machines (numerically-controlled machine tools or robots) to perform operations. The output of production lines is determined by the 'cycle time' at the work stations, i.e. the time it takes for the workers or machine to complete the work task required. The number of work stations at each production stage must be balanced so that each production stage can deal with the same number of items (i.e. 12 in Fig. 69). If the average cycle time is, say, five minutes, then the output from the last work station, and consequently from the production line as a whole, is one item every five minutes or twelve items per hour.

A planned work pace of twelve items per hour could leave some machines underutilized; for example, the milling work station could be capable of producing 15 items per hour or one every four minutes but will be constrained to operate at less than capacity to maintain the same output rate as prior and succeeding work stations. By contrast, if only one grinding work station rather than two were available this would create a 'bottleneck' constraining the output of the whole production line to just six units per hour.

Whereas machine-based work stations have constant cycle times, work stations using human operatives are likely to experience a degree of variability in cycle time from the STANDARD TIMES established by work measurement techniques. To deal with this variability some flexibility can be built into the production line by introducing buffer stocks of materials or components between work stations. Buffer stocks also serve to prevent disruption to later 'down stream' production operations if machine breakdowns or labour problems have occurred at earlier production phases.

See INDIVISIBILITIES, INPUT-OUTPUT CONTROL.

Fig. 69. **Production-line balancing.** A simple example.

**production management** or **operations management** the administration of the conversion process which transforms labour, materials and capital inputs into final products.

Production management involves:

(a) planning the design and construction of the production system. System design decisions include such things as the determination of manufacturing methods – batch production, mass production (see PRODUCTION), acquisition and arrangement of plant (see FACTORY LAYOUT), and the establishment of schedules for the production of each item (see PRODUCTION SCHEDULING);

(b) controlling the operation, performance and running of the physical facilities and predetermined production plans which constitute the production system. Decisions relating to the operation of the production system involve PRODUCTION CONTROL, PURCHASING, QUALITY CONTROL, STOCK CONTROL, WORK STUDY, and MAINTENANCE of equipment.

See also MATERIALS MANAGEMENT, MATERIALS REQUIREMENTS PLANNING, JUST-IN-TIME (JIT) SYSTEM, MANUFACTURING RESOURCE PLANNING, DISTRIBUTION RESOURCE PLANNING, NETWORK ANALYSIS, WORLD CLASS MANUFACTURING.

**production orientation** the business philosophy of a company which emphasizes the *selling* of goods and services that it produces, through intensive use of advertising and sales promotion, but which pays only limited attention to the underlying needs of consumers. Such a philosophy is often found in companies dominated by production and engineering managers and stresses the pursuit of technical excellence of products. Since such products have not been designed with the needs of consumers sufficiently in mind they risk being rejected by them. Contrast with CONSUMER ORIENTATION.

**production scheduling** the detailed planning of PRODUCTION so as to achieve production targets within specified timetables and avoid production bottlenecks, while making effective use of labour resources and ensuring a high rate of machine utilization. Production scheduling is generally undertaken by the production planning department and will be based upon orders received for products or forecasts of product demand. Where a firm schedules its production on the basis of *making to order* then it will plan its production in response to customers' specific orders and promised delivery dates. On the other hand, where a firm schedules its production on the basis of *making for stock* it will plan its production to maintain adequate STOCK levels of finished products from which it can, in turn, satisfy customer orders.

Production scheduling in BATCH PRODUCTION is concerned with fitting new orders into the spaces available in the manufacturing programmes. This requires knowledge of:

(a) the production operations required for the manufacture of each product, the order in which these operations must be undertaken and the machine or work stations at which operations will be performed;

(b) the available capacity of machines or work stations;

(c) the relative priorities of existing jobs;

(d) available labour and materials;

(e) the required delivery or completion date for the job.

Almost all production scheduling in batch production involves the successive subtraction of operation times from the required completion date. This is known as *due date* or *reverse scheduling*. The principal problem in due date scheduling is to decide what allowances shall be made for idle or waiting time. Operation times are known sufficiently accurately, but waiting times between operations are variable. Production schedules of this type are usually depicted upon bar charts (see GANTT CHART). The advantage of this type of presentation is that the load on any machine or on any department is clear at a glance, and available or spare capacity is easily identified. It will also indicate which resources are overloaded so that activities can be rescheduled or some of the work subcontracted.

Production scheduling in MASS PRODUCTION is more straightforward since usually a much more limited number of products is involved, sequences of production operations are predetermined and production is generally for stock rather than in response to direct customer orders.

Once production schedules have been established then PRODUCTION CONTROL will be concerned to ensure that products are manufactured according to the previously-determined production plan.

See LINE OF BALANCE CHART, BACKLOG, ACTIVITY CHART, JUST-IN-TIME (JIT) SYSTEM, MATERIALS FLOW MANAGEMENT, DISPATCH.

**productivity** the relationship between the physical output of a product and the factor inputs which have gone into producing that output. Productivity is usually measured in terms of *output per man hour*, an improvement in productivity showing up as an increase in output per man hour.

Productivity is important to a firm because it enables the firm to establish a COMPETITIVE ADVANTAGE over rival suppliers: a *given output* can be produced at a lower resource cost, enabling a firm to supply this output at a lower price; or alternatively the firm can now produce more output from the *same amount* of inputs, enabling the firm to increase its total profit return. A high rate of growth of output per man hour also puts the firm in a better position to absorb inflationary cost pressures arising from wage increases and increases in raw material prices, should it be difficult (see PRICES AND INCOMES controls) or competitively inopportune to increase prices on a pro rata basis.

A firm can improve its productivity in a variety of ways, including the adoption of better working practices (particularly the removal of RESTRICTIVE LABOUR PRACTICES) and pay-incentive schemes (for example PROFIT-RELATED PAY and PROFIT-SHARING schemes); the adoption of methods for economizing on the STOCKHOLDING of raw materials (for example the JUST-IN-TIME stock ordering system). An especially important source of productivity improvement is the use of superior production methods (for example switching from labour–intensive BATCH PRODUCTION to continuous capital-intensive MASS-PRODUCTION processes), and investment in the latest 'state-of-the-art' technologies (for example COMPUTER-AIDED MANUFACTURING systems (CAM)).

See ECONOMIC GROWTH, EXPERIENCE CURVE, SPECIALIZATION.

**productivity bargaining** see COLLECTIVE BARGAINING, PRODUCTIVITY.

**product life cycle** the typical sales pattern of a PRODUCT over time from its introduction on to the market and its eventual decline as it is displaced by new, more innovative products or until demand for it falls, due to a change in consumer tastes.

The product life cycle for product A, as illustrated in Fig. 70, has four main phases: introduction/launch, growth, maturity/saturation and decline. Each phase can be characterized by the adoption of various MARKETING MIX formats (price, advertising, sales promotions etc.) to encourage both potential buyers to purchase the product and distributors to stock it):

(a) *introduction/launch*. This occurs following the successful technical development of a NEW PRODUCT and indications, from MARKETING RESEARCH and TEST MARKETING trials, that the product is likely to be a commercial success. In the introductory phase, sales volume is relatively low and limited in the main to *pioneering customers*. Firms may adopt a high MARKET SKIMMING PRICING policy aimed at high-income, price-insensitive buyers, or, alternatively, they may wish to accelerate the move into the growth phase by a low MARKET PENETRATION PRICING policy backed by heavy advertising and other promotional spending to obtain the maximum physical distribution and consumer interest in the product;

(b) *growth* phase. In this stage, sales volume expands rapidly as the product increasingly commands acceptance by the mass market of consumers. The introduction of imitation brands by competitors tends to heighten competitive pressures, but at this stage the collective and cumulative marketing effort of

Fig. 70. **Product life cycle.** Product B is launched before product A declines. A1 shows that product life may be extended by product modification.

suppliers expands the overall size of the market, resulting in sales gains for most producers;

(c) *maturity/saturation* phase. In this stage sales are largely repeat purchases to existing customers, since the majority of potential buyers have already made their first purchases. As the market becomes progressively saturated, firms are unable to benefit from further expansion of the market as a whole and must instead compete to increase or maintain their market share. It is at this point that BRAND LOYALTY becomes critical, leading to a heavy emphasis on advertising and sales promotion and back-up AFTER SALES SERVICE etc. Fierce price competition is likely to be resisted, especially if the market is oligopolistic in structure (see OLIGOPOLY), in order to preserve the profitability of the market; firms may, however, have no choice but to compete on price if consumers see the product as increasingly a standardized item despite efforts by suppliers to differentiate their own particular brand of it;

(d) *decline*. This phase is characterized by falling sales. If left to follow this downward path, the product will eventually die as sales fall to very low levels, although long before this the firm may withdraw it from the market. However, the rate of decline may be slow and protracted in the absence of rapid technological change and bolstered by entrenched customer tastes, so that suppliers may continue to earn good profits from the product. (See ENDGAME STRATEGY).

In view of the product life cycle, firms must not only pay particular attention to how best to exploit their established products at various stages of their life cycle, but, importantly, must formulate appropriate PRODUCT RANGE strategies so as to provide for a balanced portfolio of new products, growth products and mature products. Thus, for example, as demand for product A begins to decline the firm must have *already* launched new products such as B as part of a regular programme of new product launches (see Fig. 70). In addition, it may be possible to modify an existing product such as A in order to extend its life cycle as depicted by A1 in the figure (see PRODUCT MODIFICATION).

See NEW-PRODUCT DEVELOPMENT, OBSOLESCENCE, BOSTON MATRIX.

**product line** a number of closely-related versions of a product, for example variants of the Ford Escort car. See PRODUCT RANGE, PRODUCT LINE PRICING.

**product line pricing** the PRICING of all the different variants or models of a product which together constitute a product line, for example prices of the 'basic', 'de luxe' and 'super de luxe' versions of the Ford Escort car. Product line pricing seeks to establish appropriate price differentials between the brands making up a line, in relation to the relative quality, sophistication and cost of each brand, vis-à-vis equivalent competitors' offerings and the prices they are charging. In pricing a product line, price relativities *between* lines may also have to be considered, for example prices of the Ford Sierra, Escort and Fiesta cars, since there can be overlaps between product lines, like that between the super de luxe model of the Ford Escort and the basic model of the Ford Sierra. See PRODUCT RANGE, PRICING POLICY.

**product manager** or **brand manager** a manager who is responsible for planning and implementing the MARKETING of a particular product or brand.

**product–market matrix** a framework for highlighting and analysing the various growth opportunities open to a firm which are used by corporate planners in formulating the firm's BUSINESS STRATEGY.

**MARKET**

|  |  | Present | New |
|---|---|---|---|
| PRODUCT | Present | (a) market penetration | (b) market development |
|  | New | (c) product development | (d) diversification |

Fig. 71. **Product — market matrix**. A matrix showing four major strategies for growth.

Fig. 71 shows the matrix which depicts products on one axis and markets on the other. By way of example let us consider a firm currently specializing in the production of rayon in the UK, a man-made fibre which is currently sold to UK textile fabricators to be made up into clothing. The matrix indicates that the firm has four main strategic possibilities open to it to develop its business (a fifth option, that of VERTICAL INTEGRATION, is closely linked with strategy (a):

(a) it can seek to achieve a greater penetration of its *existing* MARKET, increasing its share of the textile fabrication market by various competitive means – low costs and prices, product differentiation (see COMPETITIVE ADVANTAGE). However, if the firm is already a dominant supplier, or if the market itself is in the mature phase of the PRODUCT LIFE CYCLE, growth opportunities are strictly limited (see HORIZONTAL INTEGRATION);

(b) the firm can aim to develop *new markets* for its existing products, capitalizing on the firm's production expertise. In our example, the firm could adapt rayon for use as a packaging material for products such as crisps and cigarettes, or the firm could globalize its operations by selling rayon into international markets (see MULTINATIONAL ENTERPRISE);

(c) the firm can seek to develop *new products* for its existing markets, exploiting the firm's marketing strengths. Our rayon firm could, for example, add other synthetic fibres to its product range, or blend together rayon with natural wool to create 'hybrid' fabrics of various strengths and textures for use by clothiers. This strategy, however, suffers from the same general limitations as strategy (a) above;

(d) the firm could aim to diversify (see DIVERSIFICATION) away from its existing activity by developing *new products* for *new markets*. The rayon firm might decide that the clothing industry overall had too little long-term growth potential, or that it had become too competitive to make decent profit returns. In this case, DIVESTMENT of its original business interests or a gradual move away from rayon production into, say, the electronics industry may be considered. This is generally the highest-risk strategy since it takes the firm furthest away from its core expertise in production and marketing. For this reason, merger and takeover (EXTERNAL GROWTH) rather than ORGANIC GROWTH is often the most viable way of developing entirely new business interests for the firm.

See BOSTON MATRIX.

**product–market strategies** see PRODUCT–MARKET MATRIX.

**product mix** see PRODUCT RANGE.

**product modification** the alteration by a firm of an existing product to update it and improve its competitiveness in serving existing MARKET SEGMENTS or to modify it to serve new market segments. Where technological change is rapid or where consumer tastes are changing rapidly, appropriate product modifications may be necessary to extend its life (see PRODUCT LIFE CYCLE). See PRODUCT STRATEGY.

**product obsolescence** see OBSOLESCENCE.

**product portfolio** see PRODUCT RANGE.

**product positioning** see MARKET POSITIONING.

**product range** the number of PRODUCTS and BRANDS sold by a firm. Depending upon the firm's degree of SPECIALIZATION or DIVERSIFICATION its product range may be classified as follows:

## PRODUCT RATIONALIZATION

(a) *product line* or *product class*: a number of closely-related products. The products in a line may serve a particular consumer segment or price range, or may be used together by the consumer, or may employ common distribution outlets. For example, a motorcar supplier such as Ford offers a number of different versions of a particular model, say the Fiesta (differentiated by engine size, trim, accessories etc.), within a limited price band designated in Fig. 72 as 'basic', 'de luxe' and 'super de luxe'. Alternatively, a kitchenware supplier may market together as a product line such items as food mixers, toasters and kettles;

(b) *product group* or *product family*: a combination of individual PRODUCT LINES which together constitute a firm's product offering to a particular MARKET. A motorcar supplier like Ford, for instance, offers a number of different car models (Granada, Mondeo, Escort and Fiesta) to serve different segments of the motorcar market (see Fig. 72);

(c) *product mix*: all the PRODUCT GROUPS and PRODUCT LINES which together constitute a firm's *total* product offering. The firm's product range might be closely related or very diverse depending upon the spread of the firm's business interests. Ford's product mix, for instance, consists primarily of motorcars, trucks and tractors, while a more diversified company such as Hanson markets bricks, food products, dry batteries and many other different products.

See MARKET SEGMENTATION, PRODUCT LIFE CYCLE, PRODUCT–MARKET MATRIX, MARKETING MIX, PRODUCT LINE PRICING, PRODUCT VARIETY.

**product rationalization** the withdrawal by a firm of a product or products from the market. A firm may withdraw a product because demand for it has fallen to the extent that it is no longer profitable to sell (see PRODUCT LIFE CYCLE), or the firm may decide to withdraw a number of products from its PRODUCT RANGE in order to cut costs or focus its marketing efforts more narrowly. See PRODUCT STRATEGY, RATIONALIZATION, DIVESTMENT.

**product sampling** a form of SALES PROMOTION in which consumers are given a free trial sample of a brand so as to induce them to then purchase it.

**product segmentation** an approach to marketing which involves defining a firm's PRODUCT ATTRIBUTES and then compar-

b = basic model
dl = de luxe
sdl = super de luxe

Fig. 72. **Product range.** An example from the car-manufacturing industry.

ing them with consumers' buying characteristics. This enables a firm to identify how the firm's *own* brand or brands are perceived by potential consumers compared to competitors' brands, and can be used to position the firm's brands relative to competitors' brands. See MARKET POSITIONING.

**product specification** a detailed inventory of all the raw materials and components which comprise a product and their exact sizes and qualities (a 'bill of materials'). The product specification will also list all the manufacturing and assembly processes involved in making the product. Once a product specification is drawn up it can be used for PRODUCT COSTING purposes and as a basis for PRODUCTION SCHEDULING.

Product specifications for consumer products are strongly influenced by MARKETING considerations relating to the features and performance of the product considered to be appealing to buyers. For example, the product specification for a car could include comfort, speed, reliability, safety features etc.

## PRODUCT STRATEGY

**product strategy** a firm's policy on the range of PRODUCTS which it supplies. Product strategy involves the periodic updating and modification of the firm's existing products or brands (see PRODUCT RANGE); the introduction of NEW PRODUCTS; and the phasing out of old products whose sales are declining, in order to release production and marketing resources which can be devoted to newer, more active products.

Technological innovation results in new products, new cost-reducing production technologies and new materials. Some innovations can serve to improve existing products or reduce their production costs and so prolong their lives. However, many such technological changes serve to limit the lives of products, shortening the PRODUCT LIFE CYCLE and speeding the onset of decline as new products supersede existing products. Furthermore, rapid changes in consumer tastes may render a particular product obsolete after only a short time, as with, for example, fashion products. Consequently, a company's product development policy needs to maintain a constant stream of new products over time if it is to succeed in meeting its growth and profitability goals. Product range strategy should provide for launching new products and deleting old ones so as to avoid having a disproportionate number of products at any one stage of their lives. Indeed firms may deliberately follow a strategy of planned obsolescence, bringing out a continuous stream of new products as a means of increasing their total sales by inducing customers to replace products more frequently.

See PRODUCT MODIFICATION, PRODUCT RATIONALIZATION, NEW-PRODUCT DEVELOPMENT.

**product variety** the number and range of BRANDS or PRODUCTS offered by a supplier. How many variants of a product a supplier markets will depend on the degree to which the market is segmented and the number of product variants offered by competitors. In making product variety decisions the firm must consider how to *position* its brands so as to serve its target market segments without excessive duplication of brands in any segment, and the additional costs of producing small volumes of many varieties with consequent loss of standardization economies. See MARKET SEGMENTATION, PRODUCT POSITIONING, BRAND PROLIFERATION, PRODUCT RANGE.

**product warranty** see GUARANTEE.

PROFESSIONAL

**product width** the number of different product lines offered by a firm. See PRODUCT RANGE.

**professional** a person with a recognized set of skills and knowledge which qualifies them to practise a certain occupation. Usually this knowledge is gained from lengthy TRAINING and is certified by examination, often by a professional association. This pattern of entry to an occupation is similar to that of apprenticeships; however, the professions are usually understood to be those occupations which are located at the top of the occupational structure in terms of status, for example doctors, architects, lawyers etc. In so far as professional associations (for example the Law Society) stipulate the form and content of training and examination, they define the nature of the job tasks and the work standards that should be achieved and they control entry into the profession. Once individuals have been admitted to the profession it is customary in most instances for them to join the association. Professional associations are similar to craft unions (see TRADE UNION) in that they seek to maintain high incomes for their members by restricting entry to these occupations. Some associations (especially those governing public-sector professionals) are registered as trade unions and have become more similar to other unions in recent years, in that they have felt forced to mount industrial action or publicity campaigns to influence government and management policy decisions.

The notion of professionalism, i.e. that professional workers are special by virtue of their knowledge, has been much criticized in recent years. Critics have claimed that it is used to advance sectional interests, for example high income levels, and to prevent regulation by government or employers of the way tasks are carried out. Attempts have been made to weaken the power of certain professions; for instance, the recent trend in the UK Health Service for the allocation of resources to be determined on grounds of efficiency and effectiveness by management teams rather than on medical grounds as defined by doctors and consultants.

MANAGEMENT *per se* has generally not been viewed as a profession in the UK because there has been little agreement on the skills and knowledge which are integral to management, and no professional body has been able to enforce minimum standards. However, numerous associations concerned with particular aspects of management, for example the INSTITUTE OF PERSONNEL MANAGEMENT, have identified training requirements and hold examinations in an attempt to achieve professional status. Recently the MANAGEMENT CHARTER initiative has attempted to identify core 'competences' of management as a first step to creating a profession of management.

**professional association** see PROFESSIONAL.

**professional bureaucracy** an ORGANIZATION where much of the work is done by PROFESSIONALS. The organization depends on the extensive knowledge of these employees. This tends to encourage a certain degree of DECENTRALIZATION since it is difficult for superiors who do not possess the specialized knowledge to CONTROL what their subordinates do. There may well be conflict as managers attempt to enforce control.

**profit** the difference that arises when a firm's SALES REVENUE is greater than its TOTAL COSTS. GROSS PROFIT is the difference between SALES REVENUE and the COST OF SALES, while NET PROFIT is equal to gross profit less selling distribution, administration and financing costs. PROFIT AFTER TAX is the net profit attributable to shareholders after taxes have been paid.

Profit depends on two main factors:

(a) *average profit margins* or profit per £1 of sales. If costs increase the profit margins will be squeezed; if competition forces selling prices downward margins will be similarly squeezed, and vice versa;

(b) *sales turnover*. Any increase in sales value will tend to increase profits.

See PROFIT AND LOSS ACCOUNT.

**profitability** the PROFIT earned by a firm in relation to the size of the firm, measured in terms of total ASSETS employed, long term capital or number of employees. See RETURN ON CAPITAL EMPLOYED.

**profit after tax** the NET PROFIT attributable to SHAREHOLDERS of a company after all costs and taxes have been deducted. This is the amount left to be paid out as DIVIDENDS to shareholders as a return on their investment or to be ploughed back into the business as undistributed profits to add to the company's RESERVES.

**profit–and–loss account** or **income statement** an accounting statement that shows a firm's SALES REVENUE generated over a trading period and all the relevant costs experienced in earning that revenue. In the account, the COST OF SALES is deducted from sales revenue to calculate GROSS PROFIT; then the other costs involved are deducted from the gross profit to show any NET PROFIT earned.

In effect, the profit-and-loss account provides a summarized financial video-recording of the firm's trading activities. Fig. 73 shows the typical layout of a profit and loss account.

|  |  | £ | £ |
|---|---|---|---|
| Sales revenue |  |  | 980,000 |
| less cost of sales: | opening stock of finished good | 80,000 |  |
|  | add purchases of finished good | 550,000 |  |
|  | deduct closing stock of finished good | 100,000 | 530,000 |
| Gross profit |  |  | 450,000 |
| Overhead costs: | manufacturing | 60,000 |  |
|  | selling and distribution | 90,000 |  |
|  | administration | 40,000 |  |
|  | financing | 10,000 | 200,000 |
| Net profit |  |  | 250,000 |

Fig. 73. **Profit-and-loss account.** Profit-and-loss account of Y Co for year ending 31 December 19xx.

**profit-and-loss appropriation account** an account that shows how any NET PROFIT recorded in the PROFIT AND LOSS ACCOUNT is divided between TAX payments, DIVIDEND payments and RESERVES.

**profit centre** an organizational subunit of a firm given responsibility for minimizing COSTS and maximizing REVENUE within its limited sphere of operations. Profit centres facilitate management control by helping to ascertain a unit's performance and profitability. Profit centres are, in effect, independent business units controlled by a local manager and financed by the parent company. See also COST CENTRE, INVESTMENT CENTRE.

**Profit Impact of Market Strategy** see PIMS.

**profit margin** the difference between the SELLING PRICE of a product and its PRODUCTION COST and SELLING COST. The size of the profit margin will depend upon the percentage profit mark-up which a firm adds to costs in determining its selling price. The size of the profit margin is measured by the PROFIT-MARGINS RATIO.

**profit-margins ratio** or **profit-to-sales ratio** a measure of a firm's PROFIT MARGINS, which expresses the firm's PROFITS as a percentage of its SALES REVENUE. Competitive pressure on selling prices or cost increases serve to squeeze profit margins and affect profits. The profit-margins ratio has a significant impact upon a firm's RETURN ON CAPITAL EMPLOYED.

**profit per employee** an accounting ratio which expresses a firm's PROFIT as a proportion of its size, measured in terms of numbers of employees. Where a company employs a high proportion of part-time workers, employee numbers may need to be adjusted to full-time equivalent numbers to assist comparability. Alternatively profit may be expressed as a proportion of total employee remuneration.

**profit-related pay (PRP)** a system of PAY where all or some of an employee's WAGE or SALARY is directly based on or related to company profitability (see PROFIT). The total level of pay will therefore vary in relation to movements in profitability. Since 1987 the UK government has tried to encourage this form of payment by exempting a portion of it from income tax. The objective has been to encourage moderation in wage demands during COLLECTIVE BARGAINING, and to combat the unemployment effect of 'wage stickiness' – i.e. that wages tend to remain unchanged when profitability declines causing firms to adjust by reducing employment levels. Initially the take-up of PRP was limited. The reason is thought to be that companies feared that it would lead TRADE UNIONS to seek greater DISCLOSURE OF INFORMATION on sensitive financial matters, and that unions would take existing levels of pay as the base for any PRP scheme in such a way that the addition of a supplementary profit-based element would increase unit labour costs. Some companies also believed PRP to be complex to administer. However, the tax breaks on PRP were substantially increased in the early 1990s and since then the number of PRP schemes has multiplied. It is believed that many of these PRP schemes are not new but are conversions of existing PROFIT SHARING schemes. It is questionable also how far pay actually falls in response to falls in profit. It is widely anticipated that restrictions may be imposed on PRP schemes by the government to rectify the tax revenue losses to the

Treasury since the tax breaks were increased.

**profit sharing** the distribution of some portion of PROFITS to the employees of a company. It can take the form of an annual cash bonus based on the previous year's profits or it can form an element of weekly or monthly pay (see PROFIT-RELATED PAY). Less direct forms of profit sharing include allocation to employees of shares in the company, paid for out of company profits, and providing employees with the option to buy shares at some point in the future at current prices, thereby enabling them to benefit from both the share dividend and any growth in share value resulting from increases in profitability (see EMPLOYEE SHARE OWNERSHIP). Profit sharing is often advocated to improve employee commitment and thereby improve PRODUCTIVITY. The evidence is as yet uncertain about the efficiency benefits but most research to date has indicated that profit sharing in isolation fails to secure significant and enduring changes in employee attitudes.

**profit–volume ratio** a ratio used in MARGINAL COSTING and BREAKEVEN analysis which shows the CONTRIBUTION as a percentage of sales. For example, if the profit–volume ratio is 42%, then for every £100 of sales a contribution towards fixed costs and profit of £42 will be generated, provided that selling prices and unit variable costs do not change.

**pro forma** *adj.* prescribing a set form or procedure. For instance, a *pro forma* invoice may be sent to a customer in advance of a transaction to facilitate paperwork, or a *pro forma* projected SOURCES AND USES OF FUNDS STATEMENT may be constructed to show the bank manager the anticipated future financial situation as a basis for negotiating a short-term LOAN.

**program** see COMPUTER PROGRAM.

**programme evaluation and review technique (PERT)** see NETWORK ANALYSIS.

**progress chasing** the task of monitoring the progress of PRODUCTION orders through all stages of production from the time when the order is placed to the time when the work is completed, so as to detect variations of the order or production batch from schedule. This involves identifying jobs which have been started late or which are running behind schedule and the causes of deviations from schedule, for example because materials or components were not ordered in time. It also involves corrective action to overcome bottlenecks and ensure that jobs are completed by the scheduled date to help the business to keep to its delivery promises. See PRODUCTION MANAGEMENT, PRODUCTION CONTROL.

**Projects and Exports Policy Division** see EXPORTING.

**promotion 1.** the means of bringing products to the attention of consumers and persuading them to buy those products. See PROMOTIONAL MIX, ADVERTISING, SALES PROMOTION, MERCHANDIZING, PERSONAL SELLING, PACKAGING, PUBLIC RELATIONS.
**2.** the elevation of a person to a position of greater authority and responsibility. See ORGANIZATION CHART.

**promotional allowance** a financial inducement which is offered by sellers of a product to wholesalers or retailers as a means of encouraging them to take part in a SALES PROMOTION campaign.

**promotional mix** the means which a firm can use to inform prospective customers of the nature and attributes of its products and to persuade them to buy and repeat-purchase those products. The promotional mix is made up of ADVERTISING, SALES PROMOTION, MERCHANDISING, PACKAGING, PERSONAL SELLING and PUBLIC RELATIONS.

*Advertising* involves the placement of ADVERTISEMENTS in the MEDIA (commercial television, newspapers etc); *sales promotion* embraces such things as money-off-packs and free trial samples; *merchandising* is concerned with in-store promotions and displays; *packaging* assists in emphasizing the attractiveness of products; *personal selling* involves visits by a firm's SALES REPRESENTATIVES to prospective customers. Finally, *public relations* is aimed at promoting the COMPANY'S IMAGE in general to establish a favourable public attitude towards the firm and its products.

In practice, most firms will use a combination of these methods to sell their products, varying the mix according to the product and buyer characteristics of a particular MARKET or MARKET SEGMENT. For example, low-price, frequently-bought consumer goods like tea are mostly promoted by mass media advertising and sales promotions, while high-price industrial or consumer goods such as cars are promoted largely by personal selling. See FOUR P'S OF MARKETING.

**promotional price** see PRICE PROMOTION.

**promotional sample** a free pack of a product given to prospective consumers to encourage them to try and subsequently to purchase the product. See SALES PROMOTION.

**promotion-line union** see TRADE UNION.

**proof of purchase** a receipt which is given by the seller of a product to a buyer at the time of purchase, which the buyer can then use to claim a refund, product exchange or repair under GUARANTEE conditions (see SALE OF GOODS ACT 1979). In the case of special offers and promotions, detachable vouchers or labels incorporated in the product packaging may be used as proof of purchase and entitlement to the offer or promotion (see SALES PROMOTION).

**proprietor** the owner of a business. See SOLE PROPRIETORSHIP, PARTNERSHIP, JOINT-STOCK COMPANY.

**prospectus** a document prepared by a JOINT-STOCK COMPANY as an invitation to the public to subscribe for shares in the company. The prospectus gives details of the company's past trading record, current capital structure and borrowings. Prospectuses are published as the first stage of an *offer for sale* of shares. See SHARE ISSUE.

**protectionism** the measures taken by a country to protect certain of its domestic industries from foreign competition and, on occasion, to assist the country's balance of payments. In some cases this is done because the government considers that an industry faces unfair competition from dumped products (see DUMPING), or because an industry needs protecting to give it time to undertake a structural reorganization to make it more efficient. Developing countries often protect newly established industries (so-called 'infant industries') in order to foster the industrialization of their economies. Less justifiable are those cases where governments protect mature and inefficient industries (like the textile industry in Europe and North America) or pander to sectional interests (for example agriculture in the European Union) for political reasons rather than the strict economic logic of the situation.

Operationally, protectionism comes in a number of guises. The most transparent forms of it are the imposition of taxes on imports (TARIFFS) and the use of physical controls to limit imports to a specified number of units (QUOTAS). Less obvious, or indirect, forms of protectionism include EXPORT RESTRAINT AGREEMENTS, LOCAL CONTENT RULES, government SUBSIDIES to domestic industries, and government procurement policies favouring domestic suppliers.

Protectionism, because it is motivated by and promotes national self-interest, is invariably harmful to the interests of other trading countries and brings with it the danger of retaliatory action on their part and the escalation of trade restrictions, ultimately leading to a reduction in the growth of, or even a fall in, INTERNATIONAL TRADE.

See also FREE TRADE, GENERAL AGREEMENT ON TARIFFS AND TRADE.

**prototype** an early, pre-market, model of a product which is being developed. Small numbers of prototypes of new products are often constructed to aid the process of testing the performance and consumer acceptability of the product prior to deciding whether or not to engage in full-scale commercial production and marketing of the product.

See NEW PRODUCT DEVELOPMENT.

**provision** the sums charged in DOUBLE ENTRY ACCOUNTS against a firm's PROFITS in anticipation of costs which are likely to arise in the future. The most common general provision made by firms is the provision for DOUBTFUL DEBTS which is established in anticipation of some customers not paying what they owe. In addition, a firm may make a specific provision against, say, a damages claim which is presently not yet settled. Provisions are aimed at trying to ensure that profits are not overstated by making sure that all a firm's costs are charged, even those whose precise amount is not yet certain.

See REVALUATION PROVISION, DEFERRED TAX.

**proxy** an authorization to a person or firm to act in place of another. During a JOINT-STOCK COMPANY'S ANNUAL GENERAL MEETING, for example, a SHAREHOLDER may be unable to attend and vote on items contained in the agenda. The shareholder may therefore give written authorization for someone else to attend and vote at the meeting in his stead. A shareholder's proxy is frequently given to the incumbent board of directors to vote with as they think fit, hence the term 'proxy vote'.

**PRP** see PROFIT-RELATED PAY.

**prudence** see ACCOUNTING PRINCIPLES.

**PSBR** see PUBLIC SECTOR BORROWING REQUIREMENT.

**psychological pricing** an approach to PRICING which pays particular attention to the effect which a product's PRICE has upon consumers' perceptions of the product. This has a number of dimensions, including:

(a) the charging of very high prices for certain (generally high-quality) consumer products to convey an impression of product exclusiveness. High prices may appeal to particular high-income customers who wish to possess the product as a status symbol ('conspicuous consumption');

(b) the charging of high prices for technologically sophisticated consumer products in order to convey an impression of superior product quality and performance. This may play an important part in the buying decision when consumers are ignorant about the comparative properties of the brands of the product facing them, and thus use price as an indicator of quality;

(c) the charging of a price for a product which is just below a 'round figure' threshold price (for example 99 pence rather than £1) so as to create an impression that the product's price is *considerably* below the threshold;

(d) the charging of relatively low prices for frequently purchased and familiar products so as to create or reinforce an impression of value for money.

**psychological test** a test of an individual's level of achievement or aptitude. There are two main types of test:

(a) *achievement test:* this tests an individual's acquired knowledge and skills, for example a driving test;

(b) *aptitude test*: this tests fundamental abilities or aptitudes, such as mental ability (for example, an intelligence test) or perceptual abilities.

Whereas (a) is used to determine what skills an individual already possesses, the purpose of (b) is to discover his or her capacity to acquire new skills in future. Tests of both types are often utilized in RECRUITMENT AND SELECTION. Achievement tests can be used to verify information that a candidate has submitted in his application, and aptitude tests can be used to gauge how individuals will respond to new challenges and hence to provide a degree of prediction of future work performance. See PERSONALITY INVENTORY.

**psychometric testing** see PERSONALITY INVENTORY, PSYCHOLOGICAL TEST.

**public interest** a yardstick used in the application of COMPETITION POLICY in the UK to judge whether or not a particular action or practice pursued by a supplier of a product, or a change in the structure of a market by, for example, MERGER or TAKEOVER, is 'good' or 'bad' in terms of its effects on efficiency and the interests of consumers. As interpreted under UK law, the term 'public interest' is a flexible concept requiring the facts in each specific case to be presented and adjudicated on. For example, high rates of profit are not necessarily condemned if firms can show they have been innovative and are highly efficient; a merger which reduces competition may not be declared against the public interest if there are seen to be offsetting benefits, for example economies of scale. CARTELS, by contrast, are usually condemned as operating against the public interest.

**public limited company (Plc)** see JOINT-STOCK COMPANY.

**public opinion** see COMPANY IMAGE, PUBLIC RELATIONS.

**public relations (PR)** a general means of promoting a business's COMPANY IMAGE with a view to encouraging customers to buy its products and investors to buy its shares, as well, for example, as influencing government policies on issues relevant to the company. Companies often appoint a PR officer to liaise with the MEDIA in providing them with information and news about the company's activities and its record on such matters as CONSUMER PROTECTION and environmental pollution. Sponsorship of sport and the arts, etc. represent an indirect way of building up customer goodwill towards the company's products. See PROMOTIONAL MIX.

**public sector borrowing requirement (PSBR)** the amount of money the government requires to borrow in order to finance a budget deficit (see BUDGET (GOVERNMENT)). The government can finance the PSBR in two basic ways:

(a) by the issue of short-dated TREASURY BILLS which are purchased in the main by DISCOUNT HOUSES and COMMERCIAL BANKS;

(b) by the issue of long-dated government BONDS which are purchased by INSTITUTIONAL INVESTORS (pension funds etc.) and by the general public.

How the government varies the borrowing between these two categories has an important effect on the level (and distribution) of spending in the economy. The issue of Treasury Bills increases the 'liquidity base' of the banking system, enabling it to make more credit available (i.e. it increases the MONEY SUPPLY and thus raises spending in the economy); by contrast, the issue of bonds reduces the liquidity base of the banking system as buyers of bonds run down their bank deposits to purchase them (i.e. it reduces the money supply and availability of credit, serving to decrease spending in the economy). See ECONOMIC POLICY, FISCAL POLICY, MONETARY POLICY.

**public utility** an undertaking which provides a certain basic good or service such as gas, electricity or telecommunications. In some countries public utilities are mainly owned by the State, while in others they are privately owned but subject to regulation by the government. See RATE OF RETURN REGULATION, NATIONALIZATION VERSUS PRIVATIZATION.

**published accounts** see ANNUAL REPORT AND ACCOUNTS.

**'pull' strategy** a selling approach which emphasizes 'pulling' products through the DISTRIBUTION CHANNELS by spending on ADVERTISING and consumer promotions (free samples etc.) to increase the final demand for the products, so that consumers' demand encourages wholesalers and retailers to stock it.

In practice, SALES PROMOTIONS campaigns usually use trade promotions as well to encourage wholesalers and retailers to 'push' the product. See 'PUSH' STRATEGY.

**punishment–centred bureaucracy** see BUREAUCRACY.

**purchaser–provider split** the new system of health service provision in the UK in which the hitherto unified management system of the National Health Service has been split into purchasers (health authorities and GP FUNDHOLDERS) who buy health services on behalf of the population from health care providers such as hospitals (most of which are now run by NHS TRUSTS). This new system is also referred to as the *internal market*. Its architects argue that the true costs of health–care delivery are now easier to identify and that the new structure provides incentives to reduce costs. The NHS internal market is based on a similar philosophy to that behind the notion of the ENABLING AUTHORITY and COMPETITIVE TENDERING in local government. See NEW PUBLIC MANAGEMENT.

**purchases day book** see JOURNAL OR DAY BOOK, ACCOUNTING.

**purchases journal** see JOURNAL OR DAY BOOK, ACCOUNTING.

**purchases ledger** see LEDGER, ACCOUNTING.

**purchasing** the business function which is involved in procuring raw materials, components, finished goods and capital equipment, ordering and acquiring supplies of these items at competitive prices. Purchasing is charged with the task of maintaining adequate STOCKS of raw materials, components or finished goods, and placing orders to top up stocks as necessary. This involves seeking out and evaluating suppliers in terms of the quality of their offerings, reliability, delivery times and after-sales service, as well as prices. For standard commodities, industrial buyers will generally buy largely on price, seeking quotations or tenders from suppliers. The buyer can choose to place large orders with just one or two suppliers to secure BULK-BUYING price discounts or he or she may choose to spread orders among several suppliers to diversify supplies and avoid the risk of disruption to production if a single supplier defaults. Finally, industrial buyers need to keep up to date with materials and product prices and new materials becoming available in order to provide intelligence to production and marketing colleagues. See MATERIALS MANAGEMENT, JUST IN TIME (JIT) SYSTEM.

**purchasing power** the amount of goods and services which can be purchased by a specified sum of money, *given* the prices of those goods and services. The greater the quantity of products which can be bought with, say, £20, the greater is the purchasing power of that sum of money. If prices go up (INFLATION), however, then purchasing power will fall. What is important for people and business is the long-run relationship of prices and the amount of money they have available to spend. If prices double, for example, but because people's wages are INDEX-LINKED, (i.e. related to a PRICE INDEX), wages also double, then purchasing power remains unchanged.

**purchasing power parity** the tendency for the EXCHANGE RATE between the currencies of two countries to reflect long-term differences in the INFLATION rates of these countries under a FLOATING EXCHANGE RATE SYSTEM. Thus, for example, if the inflation rate in country A were 10% per annum and that of country B 6% per annum, then in order to maintain parity between the PURCHASING POWER of the two currencies, country A's currency would have to depreciate by 4% against country B's currency.

**'push' strategy** a selling approach which emphasizes 'pushing' products into wholesale and retail outlets using its salesforce and trade promotions (PROMOTIONAL ALLOWANCES etc.) to persuade WHOLESALERS and RETAILERS to stock and promote the product.

In practice, SALES PROMOTION campaigns usually use consumer promotions and ADVERTISING as well, in order to encourage consumers to demand the product and to 'pull' it through the distribution system.

See 'PULL' STRATEGY.

**put option** see OPTION.

**pyramid selling** a form of MULTI-LEVEL MARKETING which involves a 'pyramid' of sales persons who recruit other people thus creating an expanding chain of sales persons.

# Q

**qualified report** see AUDIT.

**quality** the totality of the attributes of a good or service which meet the requirements of BUYERS or customers. The materials which make up the product, the design and engineering of the product, product performance, reliability and durability are all important characteristics of the 'quality package', which ultimately influence customers to buy a product and repeat-purchase it.

Product quality is an important source of PRODUCT DIFFER-ENTIATION, enabling firms to establish BRAND LOYALTY and COMPETITIVE ADVANTAGE over rival suppliers.

See PRODUCT ATTRIBUTES, TOTAL QUALITY MANAGEMENT, QUALITY CONTROL, BRITISH STANDARDS INSTITUTION, BS5750, INTER-NATIONAL STANDARDIZATION ORGANIZATION, ISO 9000.

**quality assurance** an overall organizational commitment to the detection and prevention of QUALITY problems in order to maintain specified levels of product quality. Quality assurance involves managers and employees from all functional areas (production, marketing, purchasing etc.) in collaborating to design and produce more reliable goods or services ('quality assurance groups'). In addition, small groups of supervisors and employees within each functional area may be formed to identify and solve quality problems (QUALITY CIRCLES). See TOTAL QUALITY MANAGEMENT, QUALITY CONTROL.

## QUALITY AUDIT

**quality audit** a systematic and independent examination to determine whether QUALITY activities comply with planned arrangements and whether these arrangements are implemented effectively.

**quality circle** a body of employees who meet periodically, usually under the guidance of a supervisor, to discuss ways in which the QUALITY of the organization's products or service can be improved. See JAPANIZATION, EMPLOYEE PARTICIPATION.

**quality control** the task of ensuring that the QUALITY of a product or service meets specified performance criteria. Quality control involves a number of activities, in particular:

(a) interpretation of PRODUCT SPECIFICATIONS;

(b) INSPECTION of products at each stage of production, including SAMPLING procedures to select items for testing and the use of testing equipment to check the performance of components or products and detect those that are defective. The results of such tests enable production operations to be modified quickly, for example by changing machine settings, to prevent further defectives being made and thereby saving on rectification costs or the later processing costs of items which would eventually have to be scrapped;

(c) cooperation with design, marketing, production and research and development over improvements in product quality;

(d) undertaking periodic quality audits to review the effectiveness of quality control procedures.

See TOTAL QUALITY MANAGEMENT, PRODUCTION CONTROL, QUALITY ASSURANCE, FISHBONE CHART, QUALITY CIRCLE, SCRAP, CONTROL CHART, FAILURE COSTS, NORMAL CURVE, ACCEPTANCE SAMPLING, CONTROL COSTS.

**quality control chart** see CONTROL CHART.

**quality costs** the costs which are incurred by a firm in ensuring that its products meet customers' QUALITY requirements. Quality costs fall into three main categories.

First, *prevention costs* which are the costs of pre-production activities aimed at preventing defects (these include the determination of quality requirements and specifications, the creation of quality planning procedures and quality assurance systems aimed at achieving the quality objective, the training of operatives, etc).

Second, *appraisal costs* which are the costs associated with the evaluation of materials, processes, products and services to ensure that they conform to pre-determined specifications.

Third, *failure costs* which are the costs incurred when defective products are made. Failure costs themselves include both internal failure costs (costs of scrap, re-working and machine downtime) and external failure costs (warranty charges, returned goods and allowances).

Figure 74 depicts the relationship between the costs of prevention, appraisal and failure, and the ability of the firm to meet customers' quality requirements. When the ability to provide a quality acceptable to customers is low, quality costs are typically high, largely because of failure costs. As ability is improved by a greater investment in prevention and appraisal, failure costs can be reduced significantly leading to a marked fall in total quality costs.

Fig. 74. Quality costs.

**quality council** a body of senior managers representing the main functional areas and departments within a firm and QUALITY specialists who meet periodically to identify quality problems and devise appropriate solutions to these problems. This may include setting-up a QUALITY IMPROVEMENT TEAM to deal with a particular quality problem.

**quality improvement team** a body of managers drawn from the main functional areas and departments within a firm whose purpose is to implement a particular QUALITY programme throughout the business. Quality improvement teams typically report to a QUALITY COUNCIL.

**quality management** see TOTAL QUALITY MANAGEMENT.

**quality of a product** the ability of a product to perform its function and fulfill its expectations in terms of reliability, durability, ease of operation/servicing and repair or other valued PRODUCT ATTRIBUTES. See PRICE–QUALITY TRADE-OFF, QUALITY CONTROL, TOTAL QUALITY MANAGEMENT.

**quality of working life movement** a loose-knit body of academics, managers and trade unions who from the 1970s onwards advocated changes to prevailing patterns of JOB DESIGN so as to improve employee JOB SATISFACTION.

**quality policy** the overall intentions of an organization with regard to QUALITY as formally expressed by senior management.

See TOTAL QUALITY MANAGEMENT.

**quality standard** see BS 5750, ISO 9000.

**quality system** the organizational structure, responsibilities, procedures and processes for implementing QUALITY management.

See TOTAL QUALITY MANAGEMENT.

**quango (quasi-autonomous non-governmental organization)** an executive body which is responsible for overseeing a designated area of public sector activities and spending. Two examples of quangos are the *Funding Agency for Schools* and the *School Curriculum and Assessment Authority*.

**quantity discount** a price reduction from a supplier's LIST PRICE given to buyers of products according to the quantities that they purchase. Such BULK-BUYING discounts are often termed 'trade discounts', and they could be based on the size of a single order or could take the form of an AGGREGATED REBATE on the volume of cumulative purchases over a period of time. Quantity discounts are used both to secure orders against competitors and by encouraging larger, less frequent orders, to reduce the supplier's order and delivery cost.

**quartiles** the numerical values that divide a group of numerical observations into four parts, each containing an equal number of observations. Quartiles are frequently applied to data arranged in decreasing numerical order. Thus, in Fig.75, for example, one-quarter of the eight observations exceed the first quartile (9); while one-half exceed the second quartile (6); and three-quarters exceed the third quartile (3).

Compare DECILES, PERCENTILES.

Fig. 75. **Quartiles.** An example containing eight observations.

**QUEST** see EMPLOYEE SHARE OWNERSHIP PLAN.

**questionnaire** a structured list of questions which is used to obtain information. It is frequently used in MARKETING RESEARCH to help identify consumers' needs and motivations and to gauge their reactions to present product offerings. Considerable care and skill needs to be exercised in the preparation, development and testing of questionnaires before they are used, and in interpreting the results obtained.

Questionnaires may be designed to take a highly structured form, involving detailed questions requiring simply yes/no answers or multiple choices, or ratings on a scale. Such questionnaires are generally used to elicit simple information and are often administered to large samples of potential respondents through the post. Alternatively, semi-structured questionnaires may be used, which are generally administered personally to smaller samples of potential respondents and give interviewees more flexibility in answering set questions and elaborating on their answers when responding to supplementary questions. For some purposes unstructured questionnaires may be used with small samples of respondents to provide brief guidelines to personal interviewers as to the main areas to be investigated in their discussions with respondents. Such questionnaires are often used as part of a pilot survey as a basis for compiling a more structured questionnaire.

The confidence with which the results of a questionnaire can be used depends on the response rate, that is, the actual proportion of contacted consumers who complete and return a postal questionnaire or answer fully the personally conducted questionnaires.

See MARKETING INTELLIGENCE.

**queue** the build-up of customers who are delayed while waiting for service. Queueing can occur in a retail outlet where shoppers queue at supermarket checkouts or cars queue on petrol station forecourts. Similar queueing problems occur in factories where components queue to be processed on machines.

Variability in the demand for service and the variable time to complete service makes it difficult to judge the level of service to provide for customers. Where numerous service channels are provided, customers will experience few delays even when many customers arrive simultaneously for service. On the other hand, providing numerous service channels involves large labour costs, as in the case of supermarket checkout staff or bank clerks, or large investment in physical facilities, such as tanker berths or airport runways.

Queueing models employing statistical techniques can be used to analyse queues and to balance the cost of resources used to provide service against the cost of the time lost by customers while waiting for service. These models consider the number of potential customers; the likely rate at which they arrive; whether they arrive singly or in batches; the number of parallel queues; maximum queue length; order of service (first come, first served or prioritized); number of servers; likely service time; and whether customers are served singly or in batches. For complex queues, SIMULATION techniques may be employed to decide the level of service to provide and how to organize the service facilities.

**quick assets** quickly realizable CURRENT ASSETS (DEBTORS and cash) which are available to pay off CURRENT LIABILITIES. See CURRENT RATIO.

**quick ratio** see CURRENT RATIO.

**quota** an administrative limitation on the production of, or trade in, a particular product imposed by suppliers or by the government.

(a) Producers' CARTELS typically place a limitation on the total output of a product so as deliberately to restrict its supply to a predetermined level and then use a quota system to allocate output between member firms;

(b) Trade quotas are imposed by governments as a means of restricting IMPORTS of a product to a specified level in order to protect domestic producers (see PROTECTIONISM) and assist the country's BALANCE OF PAYMENTS, or, alternatively, they can be used by exporting countries as a means of restricting exports (see EXPORT RESTRAINT AGREEMENT). Unlike TARIFFS where suppliers may be prepared to absorb the duties imposed in order to maintain their sales, quotas reduce the volume of foreign sales in the home market and in some cases may completely deprive a firm of access to the market. For this reason MULTINATIONAL ENTERPRISES may set up a local manufacturing plant to replace exports to the market.

See FOREIGN MARKET SERVICING STRATEGY, LOCAL CONTENT RULE.

**quota restriction** a restriction of output by workers where PIECEWORK is in operation. The rationale behind it is that management or the RATE FIXER would be tempted to reduce the payment or the time allowed per unit of output if output were to exceed initial expectations. By keeping output below the possible maximum, workers deter management from *decreasing* payment rates, or time allowed, and may even prompt them to *increase* them so as to stimulate greater effort on the workers' part. See GOLDBRICKING.

**quotation 1.** the price and terms on which a firm is prepared to supply a good or service. Quotations often include detailed technical specifications of the product to be supplied, delivery dates and credit terms. Several suppliers may quote for a contract put out to TENDER by the purchaser.

**2.** the price at which a MARKET MAKER is prepared to buy or sell a FINANCIAL SECURITY (STOCKS, SHARES etc.) or FOREIGN CURRENCY. Market makers often quote two prices, the price at which they are prepared to *buy* a financial security or currency and the price at which they are prepared to *sell* the security or currency.

**3.** permission from a STOCK MARKET's regulatory authority for a company's shares to be traded in that market. See LISTED COMPANY.

**quoted company** a public limited JOINT-STOCK COMPANY (Plc) whose shares are traded either on the main STOCK MARKET or related secondary markets such as the UNLISTED SECURITIES

MARKET. See LISTED COMPANY.

**quoted investments** investments in FINANCIAL SECURITIES such as SHARES and DEBENTURES which are 'quoted' on a STOCK MARKET. Where a company holds such quoted investments they will be shown in its BALANCE SHEET at their purchase price with a supplementary note showing their current market value. See TRADE INVESTMENT.

# R

**Race Relations Act 1976** see DISCRIMINATION.

**RAM (Random Access Memory)** a COMPUTER memory device from which data can be read and on to which data can be written. The contents of such memory can be added to, or erased, by an operator. RAM is incorporated in microchips which allow the operative access to any part of the memory without having to move sequentially through the contents of the memory from start to finish.

**R & D** see RESEARCH AND DEVELOPMENT.

**Random Access Memory** see RAM.

**range** the differences between the largest observation and the smallest observation within a group of numerical observations. For example, if five products had prices of £5, £4, £3, £2 and £1, then the range of prices should be £5 − £1=£4. The range provides a quick indication of the variability of a set of data, although it is not a very accurate indication because it considers only the two extreme values in the group and so ignores the dispersion of the remaining observations which lie between the extremes. See also AVERAGE DEVIATION, STANDARD DEVIATION.

**rate fixer** the person responsible for establishing the WAGE RATE per unit of output or the payment per time saved in PIECE-WORK systems of wage payment.

**rate of exchange** see EXCHANGE RATE.

**rate of interest** see INTEREST RATE.

**rate of pay** see WAGE RATE.

**rate of return** the PROFITS earned by a business, measured as a percentage of the ASSETS employed in the business. See RETURN ON CAPITAL EMPLOYED.

**rate of return regulation** the control of a firm's or industry's level of profitability by the stipulation of maximum-permitted RATES OF RETURN ON CAPITAL EMPLOYED or investment. Such regulation is undertaken by government agencies to prevent the charging of 'excessive' prices by private sector monopolies and public utilities.

Simple rate of return stipulations are objectionable on the grounds that they do nothing to promote greater efficiency; if a firm reduces its costs and achieves a higher profit than stipulated, a price cut is ordered to remove them – so why bother to cut costs in the first place? Likewise, if costs go up prices can be put up by an equivalent amount to preserve the same permitted level of profitability. For this reason, more sophisticated cost-based and/or price-based formulas are often used to encourage cost savings; for example, only some cost increases may be allowed to be passed on in higher prices, the rest having to be absorbed by productivity increases if profits are to be maintained. The formula used in the UK to regulate British Telecom's prices (currently, increases in the Retail Price Index minus 3%) is a variant of this approach. See PRICE CONTROLS, COMPETITION POLICY.

**rates** see UNIFORM BUSINESS RATE, COMMUNITY CHARGE.

**ratio analysis** the calculation and use of ACCOUNTING RATIOS to analyse the trading performance, liquidity and financial security of a company over time and by comparison with other firms. See INTERFIRM COMPARISON.

**rationalization** the restructuring of a firm or industry to enable it to become more efficient or to reduce OVERCAPACITY. In some cases this may involve the firm in closing high-cost plant and concentrating production in larger, more modern plants; or it may involve the streamlining of a firm's organizational structure and reducing overhead costs. In the context of an industry, rationalization may require firms to merge, or inefficient firms to leave the industry, leading to higher levels of MARKET CONCENTRATION. See PRODUCT RATIONALIZATION, DIVESTMENT.

**rational–legal authority** see AUTHORITY.

**raw materials** basic materials such as iron ore, bauxite, wheat and coffee, which are converted into finished goods or components in the PRODUCTION process. See DIRECT MATERIALS, VALUE ADDED.

**Read Only Memory** see ROM.

**real accounts** ACCOUNTS or LEDGER records that deal with assets and liabilities, for example the asset ledger. Assets and liabilities appearing in the real accounts are summarized periodically in the BALANCE SHEET. Contrast with NOMINAL ACCOUNT.

**real values** the value of an asset, wage, profit, etc. adjusted for changes in the level of prices (particularly INFLATION) over time; that is, expressing the value in terms of *constant* prices not current money prices. Thus, while workers' money wages may have increased due to inflation, giving the appearance that they are now better off, their real wage may well have remained the same; i.e. if wages go up at exactly the same rate as inflation, the PURCHASING POWER of that wage (the real wage) remains unchanged; if money wages go up by less than the rate of inflation then real wages will fall. See INFLATION ACCOUNTING. Compare with NOMINAL VALUES.

**recall test** see ADVERTISING EFFECTIVENESS TEST.

**receipts and payments account** a simplified form of PROFIT AND LOSS ACCOUNT which focuses upon cash received and cash paid over an accounting period, ignoring credit transactions, prepayments, accruals and depreciation.

**receiver** see INSOLVENCY, LIQUIDATION.

**recession** see BUSINESS CYCLE.

**recognition test** see ADVERTISING EFFECTIVENESS TESTS.

**Recognized Investment Exchange (RIE)** a body validated by the FINANCIAL SERVICES ACT 1986 as meeting the regulatory requirements of the Act in respect of dealings in financial securities and commodities.

**Recognized Professional Body** a professional body such as the Chartered Accountants of England and Wales, which is recognized as a self-regulating organization for maintaining standards of good business practice under the terms of the UK FINANCIAL SERVICES ACT 1986.

**recommended resale price** the stipulation by a manufacturer of a 'suggested' retail selling PRICE for his product. Suppliers have no powers legally to enforce such prices and the actual prices paid by consumers are usually much lower than those recommended, depending on the intensity of price competition between retailers. Retailers find the 'recommended price' tag a useful benchmark on which to base special offers and clearance sale prices. See RESALE PRICE MAINTENANCE, PRICE MARKING (BARGAIN OFFERS) ORDER 1979.

**recovery** see BUSINESS CYCLE.

**recovery rate** see COST RATE.

**recruitment agency** see RECRUITMENT AND SELECTION, EMPLOYMENT AGENCY.

**recruitment and selection** the process of filling JOB vacancies in an organization by hiring new employees. It is a recurring process for most organizations because new entrants will be needed to replace those leaving (see LABOUR TURNOVER). The challenge is to find and employ people with skills, knowledge and experience which match those required by the organization, and whose future performance will be conducive to the good of the organization. This latter is especially problematic since it is difficult to predict future performance on the basis of the past, and when much of the information flow during the recruitment and selection process is controlled by the job applicant. Many organizations now use quite sophisticated methods to deal with these issues, especially in the selection of managerial employees. Equally, in many cases recruitment and selection is handled in a haphazard way.

There are a number of stages to recruitment and selection, each of which should ideally be carefully managed by organizations.

(a) Creation of a *job specification*, i.e. the main characteristics of a job. Ideally this should be the result of careful JOB ANALYSIS;

(b) Creation of a *person specification*, i.e. the personal characteristics that match the requirements of the job specification. Two checklists are often used to guide recruiters here:

*Fraser's Five-Fold Grading System*
 (i)   impact upon others (appearance etc.)
 (ii)  qualifications
 (iii) innate abilities
 (iv)  motivation
 (v)   adjustment (i.e. ability to respond positively
       in new situations).
*Rodger's Seven-Point Plan*

    (i)   physical make–up
    (ii)  attainments
    (iii) general intelligence
    (iv) special aptitudes
    (v)  interests
    (vi) disposition
    (vii) circumstances

(c) *recruitment*, i.e. the search for suitable applicants, using advertising, executive search agencies, etc. (see EMPLOYMENT AGENCY);

(d) *screening*, i.e. scrutiny of applications to determine which candidates appear to be capable of filling the post;

(e) *selection*, i.e. choosing the person to be employed. This can be the most difficult stage of the process for the reasons outlined above. The selection interview is the most favoured method but it is not without its problems, chiefly interviewer bias and (often) incompetence. PSYCHOLOGICAL TESTS and PERSONALITY INVENTORIES to determine abilities and to construct character profiles are being increasingly employed as a supplement to the interview, with the aim of uncovering the 'real' nature of the applicant in an apparently objective way. Some organizations also make use of the 'assessment centre' – a range of tests to determine suitability, including observation of candidates in complex decision-making and leadership situations.

The character of all stages of the selection and recruitment process can be influenced by the opinions of those operating it in such a way that DISCRIMINATION can occur. Legislation now prohibits explicit race or sex discrimination. However, members of disadvantaged groups may still be reluctant to apply for many types of job. To tackle this, many organizations now style themselves as 'equal opportunities employers' in their recruitment material. See GLASS CEILING.

**rectification costs** the cost of additional work which has to be performed in order to bring defective or damaged components or products up to standard. See QUALITY CONTROL.

**recycling** the reprocessing of materials, containers and goods which would otherwise have been thrown away, to be used in the manufacture of some other product; for example the pulping of old newspapers to produce egg boxes and writing paper, and the melting down of used metal drinks cans to make new containers.

Recycling can help businesses keep their production costs down since materials which are recycled are generally less expensive than primary raw materials, and it helps the economy by conserving scarce natural resources and saving on energy costs: recycling paper preserves forests and is estimated to result in a 70% saving of energy compared to processing new timber. Recycling also helps control environmental pollution by reducing the need for waste dumps.

**redeemable financial security** a financial security such as a DEBENTURE, PREFERENCE SHARE or BOND issued for a fixed period of time and repayable on maturity.

Sometimes the borrowing company arranges debentures or loans which are repayable at the option of the company within certain time limits, the earliest and latest repayment dates being set out in the debenture or loan contract.

**redemption date** or **maturity date** the repayment date of a REDEEMABLE FINANCIAL SECURITY.

**redemption yield** see YIELD.

**rediscounting** the secondary purchase and sale of BILLS OF EXCHANGE, TREASURY BILLS and BONDS between their original issue and final redemption. When a bill of exchange is first issued it is usually purchased (i.e. 'discounted') by a DISCOUNT HOUSE. The discount house may hold on to the bill until maturity, or it may choose to on-sell it to another discount house, in which case the bill is then 'rediscounted'.

For example, if a bill with a face value of £1,000 redeemable in one year's time is sold initially for £900 (giving a £100 discount on its formal redemption value), then it might be resold or rediscounted for £950 after six months.

See DISCOUNT, DISCOUNT MARKET.

**red tape** rules which stipulate in great detail how the members of an organization should carry out their duties, and which are seen to inhibit flexibility and detract from effectiveness. See BUREAUCRACY, GOAL DISPLACEMENT.

**reducing balance depreciation** see DEPRECIATION.

**redundancy** the termination of an individual's employment when the employer ceases trading or the job ceases to be required because of rationalization, change of product etc. When an employer decides to make part or all of a workforce redundant, notice must be given to the trade unions involved

# REDUNDANCY

(30 days where from 10 to 100 workers are involved, 90 days when 100+ workers are to be made redundant), setting out the number and type of employees to be made redundant. The employer must then consult with these unions. These requirements were thought to implement the European Community's Collective Redundancy Directive of 1975. However, a recent European Court of Justice ruling indicates that UK legislation is insufficient since no statutory rights to representation apply to non-union firms. UK legislation will need to be amended to give all employees a statutory right to elect representatives for the purposes of consultation over redundancy.

Employees with more than two years' service are statutorily entitled to a redundancy or severance payment. For adult employees under 40 this is one week's pay for each year of service, for those of 40 plus it is one and a half week's pay for each year up to a maximum of twenty years. Until 1986 employers could claim part of this back from a Redundancy Fund (now abolished) to which all employers contributed. Many employers choose to make payments substantially above the statutory level (in some public sector organizations there are special schemes to support this) to sweeten the pill of redundancy.

Selection of employees for redundancy can be a traumatic process and, if the organization is to continue trading, needs to be conducted fairly if the morale of those remaining is not to be irretrievably dented. A favoured option is to seek voluntary recruits for redundancy among older employees, backed up by generous redundancy payments and possibly early access to pension benefits. An alternative method is 'last-in-first-out', i.e. those with shorter service are selected for redundancy. Whilst superficially fair the problem with this is that it potentially removes those young workers who have most to offer the organization in the long term.

Whatever the method chosen, redundancy is undoubtedly a distressing process for all those involved. Some more progressive organizations offer counselling services to aid adjustment and to rebuild confidence. Others, especially where very large numbers have been made redundant, have set up employment agencies in an attempt to find alternative work. Although trade unions sometimes declare their intention to fight redundancies, they and their members are generally unwilling to take any form of industrial action since this could imperil redundancy payments. Unions, therefore, usually come to devote their efforts to ensuring that individuals are treated fairly by those handling the redundancy process.

**redundancy fund** see REDUNDANCY.

**reference group** a social group with which an individual identifies or to membership of which he or she aspires. The activities and values of the reference group provide a basis for the individual's beliefs and lifestyles. For example, young people often identify with rock stars.

The need to imitate the lifestyle of such idols can be exploited in MARKETING. Promotional material such as advertisements may feature these heroes, thereby suggesting that if consumers purchase a particular product they will be like their chosen reference group, and be viewed as such by others.

**refusal to supply** a business practice whereby a supplier acts to cut off supplies of his product to a distributor, either because the distributor has been found to be unsatisfactory in handling the product (i.e. failing to meet the terms of his CONTRACT), or as a means of coercing the distributor to accept such practices as EXCLUSIVE DEALING AND TIE-IN SALES. In the UK, a refusal to supply which is suspected of having detrimental effects on competition can be investigated by the OFFICE OF FAIR TRADING and THE MONOPOLIES AND MERGERS COMMISSION.

**regional enterprise grants** cash grants given to small manufacturing and service businesses (with under 25 employees) which are prepared to undertake new investment in areas designated as 'development areas' under UK REGIONAL POLICY.

**regional policy** a policy concerned with promoting a balanced distribution of industrial activity, employment and wealth as between the various geographical areas of a country. The main thrust of regional policy in most countries is to ensure a fairly even spread of industry around the regions, so as to rectify or prevent economic decline and UNEMPLOYMENT in some regions while avoiding congestion problems in more prosperous ones. A particular emphasis of regional policy is the regeneration of impoverished regions by encouraging new firms and industries to locate and invest in these areas (the so-called 'inward investment' approach to the regional problem). The rationale behind this approach is that the problems of the depressed areas stem largely from overspecialization in industries which have gone into decline (for example coal mining in South Wales, ship building in North-East England) rather than from any fundamental economic disadvantage. Accordingly, what is required is a diversification of the industrial base of such areas so as to provide new employment opportunities which, in turn, by increasing spending in the region, will help to create further jobs in, for example, local component suppliers, retailing and financial services.

The 'inward investment' approach to regional policy is implemented in three main ways: the provision of financial inducements (investment grants, tax and rent relief etc.) to firms prepared to locate in designated *assisted areas* to offset investment costs, together with other payments to cover, for example, retraining expenses; the use of physical controls on factory and office buildings to prevent firms from expanding in non-designated areas; investment by the government in improved road and rail communications and local amenities to increase the general attractiveness of these regions to potential investors. Critics of this approach to regional policy argue that directing firms to locate in areas which they might not otherwise have chosen to go to and subsidizing these activities might impair their efficiency. However, there is little evidence to suggest that this has been the case.

A possible alternative approach, that of encouraging labour migration out of depressed regions, has not found favour; not only does it tend to accentuate the problems of the depressed areas themselves (loss of skilled workers, reduced local spending etc.), but also it creates added difficulties for 'receiving areas', particularly if they are already overburdened with respect to housing, schools etc.

UK regional policy has as its main aim the reduction of disparities in unemployment between the regions and also the regeneration of smaller localities suffering particularly acute unemployment problems. To this end the government, through the DEPARTMENT OF TRADE AND INDUSTRY (DTI), offers financial aid and other services to firms located in, or who are prepared to establish new plants and offices in, the areas designated as 'assisted areas' – development areas and intermediate areas (see Fig. 76) – and also to firms located in 'enterprise zones' and various inner city areas. *Development areas* were originally those areas suffering from very high levels of unemployment, *intermediate areas* less so and the two qualified for different levels of assistance. However, currently, apart from the treatment of small firms, the distinction is largely superfluous. Financial aid in the assisted areas is of four main types, applicable both to manufacturing and to service activities:

(a) REGIONAL SELECTIVE ASSISTANCE in the form of cash grants. This is potential available to *all* firms undertaking investments in the development and intermediate areas. Such aid, however, is discretionary – 'selectivity' requires that the investment project should have a good chance of paying its way, that assistance is vital for the project to go ahead (for example, without the grant the project could not go ahead at all, or only on a smaller scale), and that the project should contribute to both the regional and the national economy. A project grant is based on the fixed capital costs of a project and the number of jobs it is expected to create or safeguard. The amount of grant is negotiated for the minimum necessary for the project to go ahead on the basis proposed. This is obviously open to manipulation, but has been useful in enabling the development areas to attract foreign firms into the UK. It was the availability of a regional assistance grant that ensured the location of the Nissan car assembly plant in Washington, Tyne and Wear;

(b) *Regional enterprise grants*. These are available *only* to small firms (with under 25 employees) located in the development areas, and cover investment – 15% of the cost of plant and equipment and other fixed assets up to a maximum grant of £5,000; and innovation – 50% of the cost of new and improved products and processes up to a maximum grant of £25,000;

(c) *Training grants*. These are available to cover up to 40% (up to 80% including a matching grant from the European Community's Social Fund) of the cost of providing trainees (under 25 years of age and employed on a project qualifying for regional selective assistance) with new technological skills;

(d) *Consultancy grants*. These are available to firms (with under 500 employees) to cover two-thirds of the cost of from 5 to 15 days' consultancy services in key functional areas – marketing, production etc.

Regional assistance is also available through the following:

(a) *Enterprise zones*: There are 25 enterprise zones in the UK, the first 11 being set up by the government in 1981 to provide a 'magnet' for business expansion in localities of high unemployment. Firms in these areas are exempt from the payment of rates for 10 years and qualify for 100% investment allowances;

(b) *Development Corporations/Agencies*: The Government has promoted the establishment of 11 urban development corporations, starting in 1982 with the London and Liverpool dockland development schemes, as well as contributing financially to 'self-help' regional organizations, such as the Humberside Business Development Unit. In Scotland and Wales, Scottish Enterprise and the Welsh Development Agency, respectively, have played an important role in industrial regeneration by attracting, in particular, overseas information technology and consumer electronics businesses;

(c) The European Union's *Regional Development Fund*, Investment Bank and the European Coal and Steel Community.

In the European Union, the overriding aim of policy is to reduce economic disparities between member states. This involves both supporting areas of industrial decline in the older industrialized countries of the Union and assisting the underdeveloped regions. A number of EU institutions are involved in this process, including the European Social Fund, the European Investment Bank, the European Coal and Steel Community, and, in particular, the European Regional Development Fund (ERDF). The ERDF has provided cash grants for a broad spectrum of projects in areas of industrial decline, ranging from tourism infrastructure in Wales to a regional airport in Lorraine. Support for such projects remains important, but increasingly the emphasis has shifted towards assisting the least developed areas of the Union, i.e. those regions needing to catch up in terms of *per capita* income levels – Greece, Portugal and parts of Ireland, Spain and Italy. In these areas the ERDF supports infrastructure projects such as roads, railways, electricity and gas distribution, and provides funds to modernize traditional industries and establish new ones.

The European Investment Bank provides loans for schemes and investment projects of regional significance as well as projects considered to be beneficial in promoting the economic

Fig. 76. Regional policy.

integration of the Union; while the European Coal and Steel Community provides loans to projects in areas specifically suffering job losses from the rundown of the coal and steel industries. Loans available from these two institutions are for up to half the fixed asset costs of the project.

**regional selective assistance** a cash grant which is given on a discretionary basis to manufacturing and service businesses which are prepared to undertake new investment in areas designated as 'development areas' and 'intermediate areas' under UK REGIONAL POLICY.

**Regional Technology Centres** see TECHNOLOGY TRANSFER.

**registered office** the official address of a JOINT-STOCK COMPANY to which all official correspondence must be sent.

**registered share capital** see AUTHORIZED SHARE CAPITAL.

**register of charges** a record of the claims on a JOINT-STOCK COMPANY'S assets (MORTGAGES, DEBENTURES etc.), which is kept at the company's head office with the COMPANY REGISTRAR for inspection by shareholders and creditors.

**Registrar** see COMPANY REGISTRAR, REGISTRAR OF COMPANIES.

**Registrar of Companies** the official (responsible to the DEPARTMENT OF TRADE AND INDUSTRY) who maintains a record of all JOINT-STOCK COMPANIES operating in the UK. All joint-stock companies must lodge a copy of their MEMORANDUM OF ASSOCIATION and ARTICLES OF ASSOCIATION with the Registrar at Companies House when they are first formed, and larger companies must continue to file their ANNUAL RETURN, ANNUAL REPORT AND ACCOUNTS and a REGISTER OF CHARGES on their assets with the Registrar each year. Any potential lender or investor can inspect the company records lodged with the Registrar in order to gain background information about a particular company.

**Registrar of Friendly Societies** the official (responsible to the DEPARTMENT OF TRADE AND INDUSTRY) who maintains a record of all FRIENDLY SOCIETIES in the UK and supervises their activities.

**registration fee** a charge made by a JOINT-STOCK COMPANY for recording the transfer of ownership of STOCKS and SHARES.

**regression analysis** a statistical technique for estimating the EQUATION which best fits sets of observations of dependent VARIABLES and independent variables, so generating the best estimate of the true underlying relationship between these variables. From this estimated equation it is then possible to forecast what the (unknown) dependent variable will be for a given value of the (known) independent variable.

In the case of a linear equation with just one independent variable and a dependent variable (for example disposable income and sales), the problem is to fit a straight line to a set of data consisting of pairs of SAMPLE observations of income (Y) and sales (s). Fig. 77 shows such a set of paired observations plotted in GRAPH form, and it is necessary to find the equation of the line which provides the best possible fit to this data, for this line will yield the best predictions of the dependent variable. The line of best fit to the data should be chosen so that the sum of the squares of the vertical distances between the points and the line should be a minimum. This method of *ordinary least squares* is applied in most regressions. The *goodness of fit* of the regression line to the sample observations is measured by the CORRELATION COEFFICIENT.

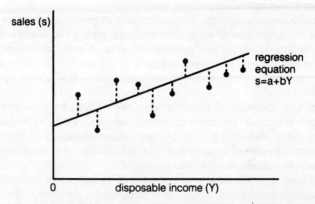

Fig. 77. **Regression analysis.** Paired observations and the line of best fit.

In arithmetic terms the line depicted in Fig. 77 is a linear equation of the form:

$$s = a + bY$$

where the coefficients of the equation, $a$ and $b$, are estimates (based on sample observations) of the true population parameters. These constants, $a$ and $b$, obtained with the method of ordinary least squares, are called the estimated regression coefficients, and once their numerical values have been determined then they can be used to predict values of the dependent variable (s) from values of the independent variable (Y). For example, if the estimated regression coefficients of $a$ and $b$ were 1000 and 0.9 respectively, then the regression equation would be $s = 1000 + 0.9$ Y and we could predict that for a disposable income of £10,000 sales would be:

$$
\begin{aligned}
s &= 1000 + 0.9Y \\
&= 1000 + 0.9 \times 10\,000 \\
&= 10\,000
\end{aligned}
$$

The regression equation will not provide an exact prediction of the dependent variable for any given value of the independent variable, because the regression coefficients estimated from sample observations are merely the best estimate of the true population parameters, and are subject to chance variations.

To acknowledge the imperfections in any estimated regression equation based on a sample in depicting the true underlying relationship in the population as a whole, the regression equation is generally written as:

$$s = a + bY + e$$

with the addition of a *residual* or *error term*, *e*, to reflect the residual effect of chance variations and the effects of other independent variables (such as, say, interest rates on consumer credit) which influence sales but which are not explicitly included in the regression equation.

Where it is felt that more than one independent variable has a significant effect upon the dependent variable, then the technique of *multiple linear regression* will be employed. The technique involves formulating a multiple linear regression equation involving two or more independent variables, such as:

$$s + a + bY + dI + e$$

where I is the interest rate on consumer credit and *d* is an additional regression coefficient attached to this extra independent variable. Estimation of this multiple linear regression equation by the method of ordinary least squares involves fitting a three-dimensional plane or surface to a set of sample observations of sales, disposable income and interest rates in such a way as to minimize the squared deviations of the observation from the plane. In arithmetic terms the sample observations can be used to generate numerical estimates of the three regression coefficients (*a*, *b* and *d*) in the above equation.

Regression analysis is used in SALES FORECASTING to estimate trend lines in time series analysis and causal links with variables which affect sales; and in ECONOMETRICS to measure relationships between economic variables.

**reinforcement advertising** or **reminder advertising** ADVERTISEMENTS which seek to remind and 'reassure' established buyers of a product of the product's merits and values to them, thereby helping to reinforce BRAND LOYALTY.

**reinsurance** see INSURANCE COMPANY.

**related company** see ASSOCIATED COMPANY.

**relationship chart (REL chart)** a means of depicting the pattern and extent of inter-departmental movement of items within a factory. REL or cross charts are used to collect information about relationships between factory departments, identifying the numbers of items per day moved from each department and which department receives them. This information can be used to establish the best relative location for each department, thus assisting in planning FACTORY LAYOUT.

**relaxation allowance** see ALLOWANCES.

**REL chart** see RELATIONSHIP CHART.

**reliability** the extent to which a product fulfils its function over a period of time.

The reliability of a product depends upon its design characteristics, the quality of materials and components embodied within it and the care with which it is made and assembled.

A product's reliability is an important part of its performance in use and thus affects the appeal of the product to customers and the likelihood of their buying it. See BRAND LOYALTY.

See QUALITY CONTROL, FAILURE RATE CURVE, PARALLEL SYSTEM.

**reminder advertising** see REINFORCEMENT ADVERTISING.

**remuneration** the PAY or reward to workers and managers for their labour services, in the form of WAGES, SALARIES and bonuses.

**remuneration per employee** an accounting ratio which is used to assess the average remuneration of the labour force. It is computed by dividing the total wages and salaries paid to employees for the accounting period by the average number of employees on the payroll during the period.

**renunciation form** a form attached to the ALLOTMENT letter in respect of a new SHARE ISSUE or a RIGHTS ISSUE to existing shareholders, enabling a shareholder to sell his or her shares, or giving the right to additional shares in the period before receiving the SHARE CERTIFICATE.

**reorder level** a predetermined level for a particular item to which STOCKS must fall before an order for more of the item is placed. In fixing the reorder level, account has to be taken of the anticipated usage of the item during the reorder period. See STOCK CONTROL.

**reorder point** the time at which an order is placed for new STOCK. See STOCK CONTROL.

**reorder point system** see FIXED INTERVAL REORDER SYSTEM, STOCK CONTROL.

**repeat purchases** further purchases of a product by a BUYER who, after having tried the product, is sufficiently satisfied with it to make additional purchases. See BRAND LOYALTY.

**replacement cost** the cost of replacing a FIXED ASSET (such as an item of machinery) or STOCK. Unlike HISTORIC COST – the original cost of acquiring an asset – replacement cost makes due allowance for the effects of INFLATION in increasing asset prices over time. Prudence requires that stocks are valued in a company's accounts at historic or replacement cost, whichever is the lower. See also REVALUATION PROVISION, INFLATION ACCOUNTING, APPRECIATION, DEFINITION 1.

**replacement investment** the INVESTMENT that is undertaken to replace a firm's plant and equipment which has become worn out or obsolete.

**replacement parts** product components which are stocked by suppliers of capital goods and consumer durables in anticipation of component failures. The comprehensiveness of a supplier's component stocks is an important part of his AFTER SALES SERVICE.

**repositioning** changing a BRAND'S design, physical properties or the image it projects to alter the 'position' of the brand in a market.

See MARKET POSITIONING.

**representative bureaucracy** see BUREAUCRACY.

**resale price maintenance (rpm)** a business practice whereby a supplier stipulates the PRICE at which his product is to be sold by retailers. By establishing a *uniform* retail price (that is, by preventing price cutting) the supplier may aim to ensure that his product is available through most retail outlets, as well as preserving the price–quality image of the product. On the other hand, in the absence of rpm, price competition between retailers may well increase the sales of the product. However the problem for many suppliers is that the growth of large multiple retailers has led to the demand for bulk buying concessions (bigger discounts) to support price–cutting tactics; this has served to squeeze suppliers' profit margins. In the event, rpm is virtually prohibited by UK COMPETITION POLICY on the grounds that it deprives consumers of the benefit of lower prices and gives too much protection to inefficient retailers. See OFFICE OF FAIR TRADING, RECOMMENDED RESALE PRICE, RESALE PRICES ACTS (1964, 1976).

**Resale Prices Acts (1964, 1976)** a body of UK legislation providing for the control of RESALE PRICE MAINTENANCE by suppliers of a product. The Acts make the practice of rpm illegal unless it is specifically exempted by the OFFICE OF FAIR TRADING, usually after investigation by the RESTRICTIVE PRACTICES COURT. Under the Acts, suppliers must satisfy the Court that not only does rpm benefit buyers in one or more specified ways (for example through greater convenience, or the provision of after-sales services) but that, *on balance*, these benefits are greater than any detriments (for example higher prices resulting from the elimination of retail price competition). The Acts make one concession to manufacturers, allowing them legally to prevent a retailer from pricing products as a LOSS LEADER (i.e. selling the product at below bought-in cost). See COMPETITION POLICY (UK), RECOMMENDED RESALE PRICE.

**research and development (R&D)** the commitment of resources by a firm to scientific research (both 'pure' and 'applied') and the refinement and modification of research ideas and prototypes aimed at the ultimate development of commercially viable processes and products. Thus, R&D is concerned both with *invention* (the act of discovering new methods and techniques of manufacture and new products) and *innovation* (the task of bringing these inventions to the marketplace).

Invention is often an inspirational act, and studies have shown that the large firm with its well-equipped laboratories and research teams has been no more successful than the individual inventor working alone with minimal facilities. Innovation, however, is usually very resource-intensive and the substantial capital outlays required to pursue development work, coupled with a high risk of failing to come up with a marketable product, tend to favour the larger business which is able to cross-subsidize R&D out of profits from existing products and also pool risks. Nonetheless, in many industries small innovative firms continue to coexist alongside large firms as in, for example, computer software and electronics.

From an organizational point of view, R&D activities may be performed within a separate department but with links with the main operating divisions of the firm. Alternatively, a more customized approach may be preferred, involving the decentralization of R&D and a close integration of R&D work with the firm's ongoing production and marketing operations.

In technologically dynamic industries the ability to develop new processes which lower supply costs and introduce innovative NEW PRODUCTS is often a critical factor in establishing COMPETITIVE ADVANTAGE over rival suppliers. Although it may be possible to buy in the latest technology and products from other firms through LICENSING deals, this may represent a poor substitute in competitive terms for the establishment of the firm's own internal pool of skills and experience; i.e. it is the difference between the firm being able to assume the position of technological leader in the industry and it becoming a 'me too' follower.

See PATENT, DIVERSIFICATION, PRODUCT DIFFERENTIATION, SCIENCE PARK, SMART SCHEME, INDUSTRIAL POLICY, DEPARTMENT OF TRADE AND INDUSTRY, NEW-PRODUCT DEVELOPMENT, TECHNOLOGICAL FORECASTING.

**reserves 1.** any additional claims of company shareholders which reflect increases in the value of company ASSETS in the BALANCE SHEET. Revenue reserves arise when some after-tax profit is retained in the business to finance the acquisition of extra assets, rather than being paid out as DIVIDENDS (see Fig. 78). Capital reserves arise when company assets such as buildings are revalued to reflect their increased market value due to inflation. Reserves serve to increase SHAREHOLDERS' CAPITAL EMPLOYED in a company.

See also RETAINED PROFITS, CAPITALIZATION ISSUE, RETENTIONS RATIO, APPRECIATION, SENSE 1, REVALUATION PROVISION, INFLATION ACCOUNTING.

**2.** the proportion of a bank's total assets which it keeps in the form of liquid assets.

**3.** monetary assets held by countries to finance balance of payments deficits.

See INTERNATIONAL RESERVES.

**residual value** or **scrap value** the amount for which a FIXED ASSET can be sold at the end of its useful working life. The anticipated residual value is taken into account in calculating the amount of DEPRECIATION to be charged against PROFITS each year for the use of the asset during its life. In many cases re-

| Balance Sheet at Dec XX | £ | Balance Sheet at Dec XY | £ | Balance Sheet at Dec XZ | £ |
|---|---|---|---|---|---|
| Fixed Assets | 10,000 | Fixed Assets | 13,000 | Fixed Assets | 13,000 |
| Net Current | | Net Current | | Net Current | |
| Assets | 3,000 | Assets | 4,000 | Assets | 2,000 |
| Net Assets | 13,000 | Net Assets | 17,000 | Net Assets | 15,000 |
| Share Capital | 10,000 | Share Capital | 10,000 | Share Capital | 10,000 |
| Reserves | 3,000 | Reserves | 7,000 | Reserves | 5,000 |
| | 13,000 | | 17,000 | | 15,000 |

| | Profit and Loss A/c yr end XY | | Profit and Loss A/c yr end XZ | |
|---|---|---|---|---|
| | | £ | | £ |
| Sales | | 20,000 | Sales | 15,000 |
| Costs | | 16,000 | Costs | 17,000 |
| Profit | | 4,000 | | (2,000) |

Fig. 78. **Reserves.** Reserves and profit.

sidual values are assumed to be nil, given the small residual values of many fixed assets and the difficulties of forecasting what such values may be many years ahead.

**resource allocation** see MARKET SYSTEM, ALLOCATION.

**respondent conditioning** see OCCUPATIONAL PSYCHOLOGY.

**responsibility** the obligation to carry out specified duties and tasks. For instance, someone who has responsibility for cash transactions in an ORGANIZATION is obliged either to carry them out himself or herself or to ensure that others do so. Failure to do so can result in action being taken against the person with responsibility for them. A common problem in organizations is that responsibilities are weakly defined: it is not fully clear who is responsible for what, with the result that certain functions are not carried out effectively. Similarly, some office holders are unwilling to take full responsibility for their actions and decisions. See ACCOUNTABILITY, AUTHORITY.

**responsibility centre** see COST CENTRE, REVENUE CENTRE, PROFIT CENTRE.

**restrictive labour practice** a practice, usually operated by a TRADE UNION or group of employees, which inhibits

PRODUCTIVITY. A union may insist that certain work tasks are undertaken by several employees when arguably a smaller number of workers would be sufficient to perform the tasks (*overmanning*); efficiency may be impaired by DEMARCATION LINES, laid down by different unions operating in the same plant, which serve to limit job interchangeability. See COLLEC TIVE BARGAINING.

**Restrictive Practices Acts (1956, 1968, 1976)** a body of UK legislation providing for the control of RESTRICTIVE TRADE AGREEMENTS between rival suppliers. The Acts make the operation of a restrictive trade agreement illegal unless it is specifically exempted by the OFFICE OF FAIR TRADING, usually after investigation by the RESTRICTIVE PRACTICES COURT. Under the Acts, parties to such an agreement must satisfy the Court that not only do the restrictions contained in the agreement confer benefits in one or more specified ways (for example by reducing costs and prices through greater specialization, or by helping exports and reducing unemployment), but that, *on balance*, these benefits are greater than any detriments (for example higher prices resulting from the elimination of price competition or the protection of inefficient producers). See COMPETITION POLICY (UK).

**Restrictive Practices Court (RPC)** a regulatory body responsible, in part, for the implementation of UK COMPETITION POLICY. The basic remit of the RPC is to investigate and report on cases of RESTRICTIVE TRADE AGREEMENTS, INFORMATION AGREEMENTS and RESALE PRICE MAINTENANCE referred to it by the OFFICE OF FAIR TRADING (OFT) to determine whether or not they operate against the public interest.

Restrictive trade agreements and information agreements between rival suppliers involving restrictions on competition, in particular price fixing and market sharing, are generally presumed (under RESTRICTIVE PRACTICES legislation) to operate *against* the public interest and the onus is on the parties to them to prove otherwise to the satisfaction of the RPC. In order to be permitted to continue, agreements must not only confer benefits in one or more of eight ways specified by the legislation (that the agreement is beneficial, for example, because it lowers supply costs, creates employment, increases exports, etc.), but also, crucially, that such benefits, *on balance*, must outweigh any detriments (for example, higher prices, protection of inefficient suppliers, etc.). Agreements found by the RPC to operate against the public interest are automatically illegal.

Only a small handful of those agreements defended before the Court have been upheld, while the vast majority of agreements originally registered with the OFT have been abandoned voluntarily without a formal Court trial. Thus, outwardly the attack on CARTELS in the UK, as in the European Union, has been highly successful, but recently there has been an increase in the number of 'secret' (illegal) agreements unearthed by the OFT.

The RPC is also charged under the RESALE PRICES legislation with investigating cases of RESALE PRICE MAINTENANCE where, again, the presumption is that the practice operates against the public interest, with firms wishing to apply rpm to their products being required to show, on balance, that the practice yields net benefits. Rpm has been upheld by the Court in only two cases.

See COLLUSION.

**restrictive trade agreement** an agreement entered into by two or more suppliers of a product which contains restrictions relating to such matters as prices, terms and conditions of supply, restrictions on the type of persons or businesses supplied etc. Such agreements, while conferring advantages to those firms party to them (for example enabling them to charge higher prices), may serve to limit or suppress competition in a market to the detriment of other suppliers and to the buying public. For this reason COMPETITION POLICY in many countries, most notably the US and the European Union, prohibits the more offensive forms of restrictive agreements (CARTELS), in particular those relating to price fixing, market sharing and restrictions on production and capacity. In the UK, restrictive trade agreements are required to be registered with the OFFICE OF FAIR TRADING and can only continue if they are cleared by the RESTRICTIVE PRACTICES COURT. UK law requires that not only must such agreements confer benefit in one or more of a number of ways (for example lower costs, help for exports etc), but, *on balance*, such benefits must outweigh any detriments (for example higher prices, restrictions on supply etc). In practice only a very small number of agreements have managed to satisfy this 'balancing' requirement.

The term restrictive trade agreement can be used also for an agreement entered into between a supplier and his distributors if it contains restrictions (for example EXCLUSIVE DEALING provisions) which deprive other suppliers of access to distribution outlets. See COLLUSION, CARTEL, RESTRICTIVE PRACTICES ACTS (1956, 1968, 1976).

**restructuring** see CORPORATE RE-ENGINEERING.

**retail cooperative** an organization that is owned by its consumers. This form of organization provides an alternative mechanism for a firm to identify consumer wants: meetings with consumers replace market forces. In many cases not all consumers hold share capital. Nevertheless, they will receive a small annual dividend based on profits on sales. In this instance ownership is notional rather than real. See WORKERS' CO-OPERATIVE.

**retailer** a business which stocks a particular type of product (such as a shoe shop) or an extensive range of products (such as a DEPARTMENT STORE) for sale to consumers. Retailers operate at the final end of a DISTRIBUTION CHANNEL for a product or products, which also involves MANUFACTURERS and WHOLE-SALERS.

Although some retailers (for example, butchers) are involved in the preparation and packaging of products before their final sale and provide personal service, most retailers are engaged in selling prepacked, complete items on a self-service basis. Formerly, in the UK and elsewhere, retailers played a relatively passive role in the distribution channel, merely providing a convenient point of sale for manufacturers' products (in many trades at prices controlled by the manufacturers through RE-SALE PRICE MAINTENANCE). However, with the emergence of large CHAIN STORE retailers (SUPERMARKETS, DO-IT-YOURSELF groups) the 'balance of power' in the channel has switched towards retailers. Retailers have been able to use their BULK-BUYING power to obtain substantial price discounts from manufacturers and this, together with the demise of rpm, has given retailers greater discretion in the use of price as a competitive weapon (see DISCOUNT STORE). Moreover, the larger retailer groups have established an extensive OWN-LABEL BRAND business in direct competition to manufacturers' brands, which has also increased their MARKETING MIX opportunities to compete against other retailers.

See SPECIALIST SHOP, CATEGORY DISCOUNTER, WAREHOUSE CLUB, MAIL ORDER.

**retailing** the function of selling products to the ultimate buyers of those products. See RETAILER, DISTRIBUTION CHANNEL.

**retail outlet** business premises or facilities for selling products to CONSUMERS. A retail outlet may take the form of a SHOP or STORE which buyers visit to make purchases, or it could be an AUTOMATIC VENDING MACHINE or kiosk located in a hotel or restaurant. Apart from 'points of sale' geographically located within easy reach of prospective customers, retail sales can be made by direct delivery or through the post to a buyer's home as, for example, in MAIL ORDER selling. See RETAILER, DISTRIBUTION CHANNEL, EPOS.

**retail price index** see PRICE INDEX.

**retail services mix** the range of services offered by a RETAILER to its customers to encourage loyalty to the store. Some of the main elements of the retail services mix include special displays, convenient opening hours, easy exchanges and returns, restaurants and parking facilities.

**retained profit** or **undistributed profit** any after-tax PROFIT that is reinvested (*ploughed back*) in the firm rather than being paid out to the owners of the company in DIVIDENDS. Such retained earnings form a valuable source of capital to be invested in additional FIXED ASSETS and CURRENT ASSETS. They serve to swell the value of the company to the shareholders and increase SHAREHOLDERS' CAPITAL EMPLOYED by adding to revenue RESERVES. See also RETENTIONS RATIO.

**retentions ratio** a measure of the proportion of NET PROFIT which a company ploughs back into the business rather than distributing it to shareholders. Specifically the retentions ratio expresses net profit after tax and interest less DIVIDENDS declared/paid as a percentage of net profit. Thus, for example, if a company retains three-quarters of its profits and pays out only one-quarter as dividends, then its retentions ratio is 75%. The retentions ratio is the opposite of the DISTRIBUTION RATIO. See also RESERVES, RETAINED PROFITS.

**retirement** the termination of an individual's working career at a certain age with the expectation that he or she will no longer undertake paid employment. In the UK the normal retirement age for men has been 65 and for women 60. European law has a big effect on retirement benefits in the

UK. For some time it has been required that men and women have the same pension rights in occupational schemes despite differing retirement ages, thereby meaning that women's benefits are more favourable than men's. The European Court of Justice has now ruled that benefits should be the same. This could mean that the retirement age for women will become 65. Another recent innovation, stemming from the Court, is that part-time workers can no longer be excluded from occupational pension schemes. Until recently many occupational pension schemes excluded part-time workers but the Court has ruled that since many part-time employees are female, exclusion could be a form of DISCRIMINATION.

**retrenchment** see DIVESTMENT.

**return on assets** see RETURN ON CAPITAL EMPLOYED.

**return on capital employed (ROCE)** an accounting measure of a firm's PROFITABILITY, which expresses the firm's PROFITS for an accounting period as a percentage of its period-end capital employed. Generally, profit is taken before deduction of tax and is related to LONG-TERM CAPITAL EMPLOYED, though broader comparisons are possible, which relate profit before tax and interest payments to all ASSETS employed, and narrower comparisons which relate after-tax profit to shareholders' capital. A firm's return on capital depends upon its PROFIT MARGINS RATIO and its ASSET TURNOVER RATIO, the first being a multiple of the last two, thus

$$\frac{\text{profit}}{\text{long term capital}} = \frac{\text{profit}}{\text{sales}} \times \frac{\text{sales}}{\text{long term capital}}$$

Return on capital employed provides a key measure of management performance in earning profits from the assets which they control. To improve return on capital employed managers need to:

(a) improve profit margins either by reducing unit production and selling costs, or by increasing selling prices of products;

(b) improve asset turnover either by increasing sales volumes using present assets, or by reducing the FIXED ASSETS and CURRENT ASSETS employed to achieve present sales volumes.

**return on equity** see RETURN ON SHAREHOLDERS' FUNDS.

**return on investment** see RETURN ON CAPITAL EMPLOYED, RE-TURN ON SHAREHOLDERS' FUNDS.

**return on shareholders' funds** an accounting measure of the rate of return that shareholders have obtained on the capital which they have invested in the business. It is calculated by dividing PROFIT after interest and tax by SHAREHOLDERS' CAPITAL EMPLOYED (issued share capital plus RESERVES).

**Reuters** a company which collects and disseminates world-wide general news items for press publication and which provides support facilities for the financial markets.

See GLOBEX.

**revaluation 1.** the increase in the valuation of a FIXED ASSET to its current market value. Revaluation of fixed assets such as land and buildings may be necessary to reflect their APPRECIATION as property prices rise. Where revaluation takes place, the increase in the value of the fixed asset over its NET BOOK VALUE is added to the company's RESERVES.

**2.** an administered increase in the EXCHANGE RATE of a currency against other currencies under a FIXED EXCHANGE RATE SYSTEM; for example, an increase in the value of the UK pound (£) against the US dollar ($) from one fixed or 'pegged' level to a higher level, say, from £1 = $2 to £1 = $3. Governments resort to revaluations as a means of eliminating a BALANCE OF PAYMENTS surplus. The effect of a revaluation is to make imports (in the local currency) cheaper, thereby inducing an increase in import demand, and exports (in the local currency) more expensive, thereby reducing export demand.

Whether or not a revaluation 'works' in restoring balance of payments equilibrium depends on a number of factors, includ-ing the reaction of domestic firms and the effect of the government's other policies over the longer term (for example the control of inflation). For business, a revaluation makes imports more price-competitive, putting pressure on domestic producers either to cut their prices or, alternatively, to depend more on advertising and sales promotion. Likewise, in export markets a firm may choose to hold its prices, accepting lower profit margins, rather than increase them, in order to maintain market share. Thus, in the short run revaluations threaten firms' current profitability and market position, putting firms under pressure to cut costs by improving productivity and generally placing a greater emphasis on PRODUCT DIFFERENTIATION as a means of remaining competitive against overseas suppliers. Contrast with DEVALUATION.

**revaluation provision** an accounting PROVISION made for the increased cost of replacing a FIXED ASSET, over and above its HISTORIC COST. DEPRECIATION charges spread the original cost of a fixed asset over its estimated life, preventing the cost of the asset from being ignored in calculating net profit and so preventing the firm's LONG-TERM CAPITAL EMPLOYED from being distributed as DIVIDENDS. However, where the REPLACEMENT COST of a fixed asset is expected to exceed its original cost, a prudent firm may withhold additional profits instead of distributing them, in anticipation of having to pay this additional sum. See INFLATION ACCOUNTING.

**revenue 1.** the money received by a firm from the sale of its output of GOODS or SERVICES (SALES REVENUE).

**2.** money received by the government from TAXATION.

**revenue account** see PROFIT-AND-LOSS ACCOUNT.

**revenue centre** an organizational subunit of a firm under the control of a manager, who is able to affect output levels and revenues but has no direct control over costs. See COST CENTRE, PROFIT CENTRE.

**revenue expenditure** expenditure that is written off completely in the PROFIT-AND-LOSS ACCOUNT in the ACCOUNTING PERIOD to which it relates. Contrast CAPITAL EXPENDITURE.

**reverse takeover** the TAKEOVER of one company by another company which has a lower stock market valuation (i.e. the value of the bidder's ISSUED SHARE CAPITAL traded on the stock market is less than that of the victim firm). A reverse takeover bid usually involves the bidding firm issuing shares or raising LOAN CAPITAL to finance the deal.

**reverse yield gap** see YIELD GAP.

**rework costs** see FAILURE COSTS.

**RIE** see RECOGNIZED INVESTMENT EXCHANGE.

**right first time** see ZERO DEFECTS.

**rights issue** the issue by a JOINT-STOCK COMPANY of additional SHARES to existing SHAREHOLDERS at a price which is generally a little below the current market price. Rights are issued to existing shareholders in proportion to their existing shareholdings, and shareholders can sell their rights if they do not wish to subscribe for extra shares. Compare CAPITALIZATION ISSUE.

**rightsizing** a colloquial term for an ORGANIZATION'S re-structuring efforts to improve its efficiency and cost-effectiveness which involve reducing the size of its work force.

**risk** see UNCERTAINTY AND RISK.

**risk analysis** the systematic analysis of the degree of risk attaching to capital projects. Risk reflects the variability of expected future return from a capital INVESTMENT, and as such the statistical technique of probability may be applied to assist a decision. See also CAPITAL BUDGETING, UNCERTAINTY AND RISK, DECISION TREE.

**risk capital** any business capital subscribed by an individual ENTREPRENEUR or group of ORDINARY SHAREHOLDERS which entails some risk of loss in the event of the enterprise failing.

**risk premium** the additional return on an INVESTMENT which an investor requires to compensate for the possibility of losing all or part of that investment if future events prove adverse. The size of the risk premium will depend to an extent upon the personality of the investor. Some cautious investors are 'risk averse' and require a substantial risk premium to induce them to undertake risky investments. Other less cautious investors are 'gamblers' and demand little risk premium. Attitudes to risk also depend upon the size of the potential gains or losses involved. Where a project risks making a loss which is so large as to endanger the future solvency of the investor then investors would tend to adopt a cautious view about the downside risk involved, even when such losses are highly unlikely, and would demand a substantial risk premium. See DECISION TREE, UNCERTAINTY AND RISK, CAPITAL ASSET PRICING MODEL.

**Road Haulage Association Limited** the EMPLOYERS' ASSOCIATION representing employers in the road haulage industry. As well as representing their interests in the political sphere, this association negotiates WAGE RATES with the industry's TRADE UNIONS. See MULTI-EMPLOYER AGREEMENT.

**robot** a form of programmable automatic machine that performs repetitive PRODUCTION tasks in place of human operatives on a PRODUCTION LINE. Robots can be used for tasks such as welding or spray painting, which can be unhealthy for human operatives to perform, and assembly tasks, which can be performed more rapidly and consistently than by human workers. The use of robots can therefore improve the PRODUCTIVITY of production operations and the QUALITY of products.

**ROCE** see RETURN ON CAPITAL EMPLOYED.

**Rodger's seven-point plan** see RECRUITMENT AND SELECTION.

**role culture** see CULTURE.

**rolling settlement** see ACCOUNT PERIOD, TALISMAN.

**rollout marketing** the planned introduction of a firm's products to its target markets one area at a time. The firm will seek to rank sales areas according to their market potential and competition so as to determine the order in which each area will be targeted. See MARKETING SEGMENTATION, INTERNATIONAL MARKETING.

**ROM (Read Only Memory)** a COMPUTER memory device from which data can be read but which cannot be written on to. The contents of such memory are fixed when the computer is manufactured, being incorporated in ROM microchips.

**routing sheets** see MATERIALS FLOW MANAGEMENT.

**Rowan** or **Halsey Plan** a form of PAYMENT BY RESULTS where a component of WAGES is based on the achievement by a factory worker of output in excess of a predetermined output target.

**Royal College of Nursing** the main professional body for nursing staff in the UK. Faced with far-reaching changes in the health service recently, the RCN has increasingly acted as a TRADE UNION, taking some limited forms of INDUSTRIAL ACTION. Nevertheless, it has maintained its policy against STRIKE action despite challenges to it from some sections of the membership. With over 300,000 members it is the UK's sixth largest union.

**Royal Mint** see CENTRAL BANK.

**royalties** payments made for the use of an INTELLECTUAL PROPERTY RIGHT (copyrights, patents etc.) or physical property rights (mineral extraction rights etc.).

**RPC** see RESTRICTIVE PRACTICES COURT.

**RPI** see PRICE INDEX.

**rpm** see RESALE PRICE MAINTENANCE.

**Rucker Plan** see GAINSHARING.

**rule of origin** see LOCAL CONTENT RULE.

**rule of thumb** an aid to decision-making involving the use of conventions or mechanistic formulas to determine prices, production schedules, advertising budgets etc. Rules of thumb are used as rough guides or approximations when, because of uncertainty, it is impossible to determine optimal solutions. Many firms, for example, use cost-based formulas to set prices, adding a conventional unit profit mark-up to costs, in the absence of totally reliable information about demand. Similarly, firms often set the value of their advertising budget as a fixed percentage of their sales revenue. See COST-BASED PRICING, UNCERTAINTY AND RISK.

**run** to start executing a specific PROGRAM on a COMPUTER.

# S

**SA** see SOCIÉTÉ ANONYME.

**sabotage** see INDUSTRIAL ACTION.

**safety** see HEALTH AND SAFETY.

**safety stock** see STOCK CONTROL.

**salary** a payment made to employees for the use of their labour. Unlike WAGES, salaries are not strictly related to the actual number of hours worked (though the CONTRACT OF EMPLOYMENT will usually stipulate the required working hours each week). Instead salaries are expressed in an annual sum, a portion of which is paid to the employee each month. An employee's salary is generally a function of the individual's age and experience, and the level of the job in the organization. Increasingly, an element of the employee's salary is based on some measure of individual performance. See INCREMENTAL PAY SCALE, PERFORMANCE APPRAISAL, MERIT PAY.

**sale 1.** the purchase of a good or service by a buyer from a seller at a stated PRICE or, in some instances, through a BARTER or COUNTERTRADE arrangement.

**2.** price reductions applied to individual items or across the board for a limited period of time by a seller, to increase sales of existing products (a sales period), to clear old stocks prior to selling new lines (an end of season sale), or to sell off the stock of a bankrupt business (a closing down sale).

**3.** a specially convened gathering of sellers and buyers organized as a one-off event such as a jumble sale or on a regular basis such as a monthly AUCTION of second-hand cars.

**sale and leaseback** see LEASEBACK.

**Sale of Goods Act 1979** a UK Act which provides protection to the purchaser of a GOOD by laying down certain legal obligations which a supplier must fulfil as part of the CONTRACT OF SALE. These obligations include that the goods supplied correspond with the description of the goods and that goods are of merchantable quality, that is, 'fit for the purpose' for which they are intended.

See CONSUMER PROTECTION.

**Sale of Goods and Services Act 1982** a UK Act which provides protection to the purchaser of a SERVICE (which may also involve the provision of a GOOD, for example, the supply of new parts in servicing a car) by laying down certain legal obligations which a supplier must fulfil as part of the CONTRACT OF SALE. These obligations include compliance with description and 'fitness for purpose' (see SALE OF GOODS ACT 1979) and that the supplier will use 'reasonable' care and skill in providing the service.

See CONSUMER PROTECTION.

**sales agency** a business which specializes in promoting the SALES of a client firm. Typically agents do not take title to goods but are employed on a commission basis by, for example, a producer to obtain new wholesale customers or new retail accounts. A company may employ a sales agency to handle its entire selling activities or to augment its own sales force. Agents are often used by smaller companies and are particularly useful in the context of INTERNATIONAL MARKETING where foreign agents familiar with overseas markets and distribution networks can be used to establish an EXPORT market for a firm's products. See SALES COMMISSION.

**sales analysis** the recording, analysis and evaluation of a firm's SALES data. Sales analysis is usually designed to give a breakdown of sales by product, by sales person, by sales area, and by customer (age group, sex etc.). See SALES FORECASTING.

**sales commission** incentive payments made to the firm's own SALES REPRESENTATIVES for reaching/exceeding specified SALES targets. Where a firm employs AGENTS to sell its products, commissions are used as the primary form of remuneration.

See SALES AGENCY.

**sales concept** a business philosophy which aims at the generation of profits through the selling and promotion of products. The sales concept is an extension of a firm's PRODUCTION ORIENTATION where emphasis is placed on the effective selling of what the firm has chosen to produce. Contrast MARKETING CONCEPT.

**sales conviction test** see ADVERTISING EFFECTIVENESS TESTS.

**sales force** the salespeople employed by a firm to sell its goods or services. Their functions range from relatively passive tasks such as taking repeat orders from established customers and making deliveries, to more active PERSONAL SELLING aimed at securing additional business from established and new customers.

The sales force can consist of:

(a) SALES REPRESENTATIVES who visit wholesalers, retailers or final customers, making face-to-face contact with those prospective buyers as a means of selling;

(b) telephone sales staff who contact prospective customers by telephone to establish an initial contact which can then be followed up by a visit from a sales representative;

(c) product demonstrators who operate in wholesale or retail stores or visit customers to provide an opportunity for prospective buyers to see a product in action or to sample it;

(d) sales managers who are responsible for organizing and controlling the activities of the field sales force, and the recruitment, selection and training of sales-force personnel.

In organizing the field sales force, sales persons may be required to represent *all* the firm's products in small SALES TERRITORIES, or may specialize in selling limited product lines in larger territories.

**sales forecasting** the process of predicting future product demand to help in making decisions about marketing expenditure, investment in production capacity and the scheduling of factory output. Various sales forecasting methods can be used to make predictions about both future levels of industry demand and the company's own particular sales (which depend on its market share). These methods vary greatly in terms of their subjectivity, sophistication, data requirements and cost, and a manager's choice of method will depend on the level of accuracy he requires, on the distance into the future to be forecast, and on expense. The main forecasting methods are:

(a) *survey* methods, the most subjective of the demand-estimating techniques available. Surveys generally involve the use of interviews or mailed QUESTIONNAIRES asking individual consumers about their future buying intentions, alternatively, opinions of the sales force may be obtained. Such data can often be useful for making short-term projections about future spending, and, in the case of new products, surveys may provide one of the few methods available in the absence of historical data. However, their subjectivity can detract from their accuracy. Buyers may be unwilling to give correct answers for reasons of commercial secrecy, or be uncertain about their future buying intentions; or interviewer bias may occur in the way in which questions are asked. Sales-force opinions represent 'second-hand' data and can be distorted by optimism or pessimism of sales representatives. For these reasons surveys are frequently used to supplement rather than replace other forecasting methods.

(b) *Extrapolation* methods employ time-series data, using past sales to predict future sales. These techniques assume that the historical relationship between past and future sales will continue to hold. Time-series data usually comprise:

(i)   *secular trend*, which shows the relatively smooth, regular movement of the time series over the long term.

(ii)  *cyclical variation*, which consists of medium-term, regular repeating patterns, generally associated with BUSINESS CYCLES. The recurring upswings and downswings in economic activity are superimposed upon the secular trend.

(iii) *seasonal variation*, which consists of short-term regular repeating patterns, generally associated with different seasons of the year. These seasonal variations are superimposed upon the secular trend and cyclical variations.

(iv)  *irregular variations*, which are erratic fluctuations in the time series caused by unpredictable, chance events. These irregular variations are superimposed upon the secular trend, cyclical variation and seasonal variation (see Fig. 79).

Time-series analysis is concerned with isolating the effect of

Fig. 79. **Sales forecasting.** Time-series analysis.

each of these influences upon a time series with a view to using them to project this past experience into the future. In order to identify the underlying secular trend in a time series, the forecaster may 'fit' a line by eye to time-series observations depicted on a graph. Alternatively, the forecaster may use a moving average to smooth the time series and help identify the underlying trend. For example, he could use a five-period *moving average*, replacing each consecutive observation by the average of that observation and the two preceding and two succeeding observations. *Exponential smoothing* provides yet another technique which can be used to smooth time-series data. It is similar to the moving-average method but gives greater weight to more recent observations in calculating the average. In order to identify the effect of seasonal variations, the forecaster can construct a measure of seasonal variation (called the *seasonal index*) and use this to 'deseasonalize' the time-series data and show how the time series would look if there were no seasonal fluctuations. Once the trend has been identified it is possible to extrapolate that trend, and estimate trend values for time periods beyond the present time period. In Fig. 79, for example, the trend for time periods up to and including time *t* can be extrapolated to time *t*+1. Such trend-projection techniques are generally more useful for longer-term forecasting than short-term estimation. Their big drawback is that they make no attempt to represent the factors which causally affect demand, simply assuming that historical relationships involved in the time series will continue into the future. This renders them unable to predict sharp upturns or downturns in sales associated with dramatic changes in demand-influencing variables.

(c) *Barometric* methods seek to predict the future value of sales from the present values of particular statistical indicators which have a consistent relationship with sales. Such leading indicators as business capital investment plans and new house-building starts can be used as a barometer for forecasting product demand, and they can be useful for predicting sharp changes in demand.

(d) *Econometric* methods predict future sales by examining other variables which are causally related to it. Econometric models link variables in the form of equations which can be estimated statistically and then used as a basis for forecasting. Judgment has to be exercised in identifying the independent variables which causally affect demand. For example, in order to predict future quantity of a product demanded ($Qd$) we would formulate an equation linking it to product price ($P$) and disposable income ($Y$):

$$Qd = a + bP = cY$$

then use past data to estimate the numerical value of the coefficients $a$, $b$ and $c$. This method can be expensive in terms of data collection and processing costs, but it can produce reasonably accurate forecasts and offers the opportunity to learn from past forecasting mistakes by amending the forecasting equations, adding new independent variables etc., to improve future forecasts.

Ultimately no forecasting method will generate consistently accurate forecasts. This means that managers need to exercise judgement in choosing which forecasting methods to use and in combining information compiled from several different forecasting methods in arriving at a judgment about future demand conditions. Moreover, in making any forecast the forecaster must allow for a margin of error in the forecast, anticipating that future demand may be higher or lower than the forecast value.

**sales journal** see JOURNAL, ACCOUNTING.

**sales ledger** see LEDGER, ACCOUNTING.

**salesmanship** the art of SELLING.

**sales-per-employee ratio** a measure of a firm's sales/size relation, that expresses the firm's SALES REVENUE as a ratio of its size measured in terms of number of employees.

Where a company employs a high proportion of part-time workers, employee numbers may need to be adjusted to full-time equivalent numbers to assist comparability. Alternatively sales may be expressed as a proportion of total employee remuneration.

It is useful to compare sales per employee in a firm with the company's average employee remuneration.

**sales per square foot** a common measure of efficiency in RETAILING which relates sales revenue generated to the OVERHEAD costs (rent, rates, heating, lighting, etc.) of providing selling space.

**sales potential** a particular seller's share of MARKET POTENTIAL.

**sales promotion** the measures used by firms alongside other elements of the PROMOTIONAL MIX (advertising, personal selling etc.) to increase the SALES of their products.

In the case of CONSUMER GOODS, while ADVERTISING seeks to develop and sustain sales by creating BRAND LOYALTY over the long run, sales promotions are largely used in short, sharp bursts to support, for example, the introduction of a new brand, to renew interest in a product whose sales have fallen and, periodically, to stimulate extra demand for a well-established brand. A variety of techniques are used for these purposes, including: free-trial samples, money-off packs, 'two-for-the-price-of-one' offers, extra quantities for the same price, product competitions offering prizes, coupons offering gifts, trading stamps, in-store demonstrations, point-of-sale displays, etc.

These methods can succeed only if the product being promoted is widely available for consumers to buy, so that it is important also to encourage retailers to stock it. This is done using various trade promotions including special cash offers on purchases, free extra quantities, gifts and prizes.

In the case of industrial products, trade fairs, exhibitions and demonstrations are used to back up the most commonly used mode, PERSONAL SELLING.

See MERCHANDISING, PACKAGING.

**sales representative (rep)** or **sales executive** a salesperson employed to represent his or her company's products to prospective buyers and to engage in DIRECT SELLING of these products. Sales representatives usually visit potential buyers at the buyers' premises and are generally responsible for visiting numbers of customers within their designated sales territory.

Sales representatives are responsible for securing repeat orders from established customers, gaining orders from new customers, informing customers about their firm's new products and collecting market intelligence from customers. In many cases the selling task also involves representatives in demonstrating products, offering technical advice and arranging credit terms. Sales representatives are often remunerated partly by means of SALES COMMISSION in order to provide them with incentives to secure sales.

See PERSONAL SELLING, CALLS.

**sales response** the rate at which SALES of a product or brand change as a result of changes in marketing expenditure or price. In order to make rational decisions about marketing expenditures on products or brands, firms need to estimate the likely sales response of each product or brand. See ELASTICITY OF DEMAND.

**sales revenue** the income generated from the sale of GOODS and SERVICES. Sales revenue depends upon the volume of a product sold and the price of the product.

In a company's PROFIT-AND-LOSS ACCOUNT, sales revenue is generally recorded net of VAT and any trade discounts given, for subsequent comparison with costs.

**sales–revenue variance** the difference between the budgeted value of SALES and the actual value of sales achieved. This variance can be broken down into two parts:

(a) *sales–price variance*, which shows the difference between the predetermined price of a product and the actual price;

(b) *sales–volume variance*, which indicates the extent to which sales revenue has been lost because smaller volumes of products were sold than were budgeted for.

Both of these are affected by sales mix, and the *sales–mix variance* shows the effect on revenue of achieving an actual mix of sales different from the product mix anticipated in the sales budget.

**sales territory** a geographical area containing potential customers who can be approached through DIRECT SELLING and to which salespersons can be assigned. The number and sizes of territories scheduled by a firm will depend upon such considerations as numbers and size of potential customers to be covered, how densely they are grouped (since this affects travelling time between customers) and the complexity of the selling operation (which will determine the number and length of sales calls required). Where a sales territory contains insufficient potential customers to warrant the cost of deploying its own sales personnel (see SALES REPRESENTATIVE) a firm may instead choose to sell its products through a SALES AGENCY.

**sales to fixed assets ratio** an efficiency ratio which looks at the sales generated by a firm in relation to its fixed assets. It is computed by dividing sales by fixed assets and provides a measure of fixed asset utilization. See ACCOUNTING RATIO.

**sales volume** the quantity of a firm's product or brand sold within a given time period. Sales volumes are important because of their implications for sales revenues (volumes multiplied by prices) and for PRODUCTION SCHEDULING and production costs, especially where a high rate of capacity utilization is necessary to BREAK EVEN.

**salvage value** see SCRAP.

**sample 1.** part of a total population that can be analysed to make inferences about the whole population (see SAMPLING).

**2.** a small amount of raw material or finished product whose quality or performance can be tested as a guide to the quality or performance of a whole batch of material or product (see QUALITY CONTROL, ACCEPTANCE SAMPLING).

**3.** a small trial pack of a product or brand which is used to encourage buyers to try it out (see SALES PROMOTION).

**sampling** the selection of part of a total population of consumers or products whose behaviour or performance can be analysed, in order to make inferences about the behaviour or performance of the total population, without the difficulty and expense of undertaking a complete census of the whole population.

Samples may be chosen *randomly*, with every consumer or product in the population having an equal chance of being included. Random samples are most commonly used by firms in QUALITY CONTROL where they are used as a basis for selecting products, components or materials for quality testing.

Alternatively, samples may be chosen by dividing up the total population into a number of distinct *sub-groups* or strata, then selecting a *proportionate number* of consumers or products from each sub-group since this is quicker and cheaper than random sampling. In MARKETING RESEARCH and opinion polling, *quota* sampling is usually employed where interviewers select the particular consumers to be interviewed, choosing the numbers of these consumers in proportion to their occurrence in the total population.

Samples may be:

(a) *cross-sectional*, where sample observations are collected at a particular point in time, for example data on company sales and the incomes of consumers in the current year, embracing a wide range of different income groups, as a basis for investigating the relationship between sales and income;

(b) *longitudinal*, where sample observations are collected over a number of time periods, for example data on changes in company sales over a number of years and changes in consumer incomes over the same time periods, as a basis for investigating the relationship between sales and income.

See STATISTICAL INFERENCES, QUESTIONNAIRE.

**SARL** see SOCIÉTÉ À RESPONSABILITÉ LIMITÉE.

**satisfice** an approach to decision-making which aspires to achieve satisfactory but not optimum results. It can be a rational approach because it accepts that the perfect knowledge necessary to make the best decision is usually unattainable. Instead decision-makers will act in accordance with RULES OF THUMB which they know will at least achieve acceptable results. See ORGANIZATIONAL ANALYSIS, BUSINESS OBJECTIVES.

**saturation phase** see PRODUCT LIFE CYCLE.

**saver** a person, company or institution who sets aside a proportion of current income by forgoing immediate spending on consumption. See SAVINGS.

**savings** the proportion of income of a person (personal saving), company or institution (retained profits) that is not spent on current consumption. Savings are typically placed on deposit with a BANK, BUILDING SOCIETY, etc., or used to acquire financial and physical assets such as SHARES or plant. By forgoing immediate spending on consumption, savers seek to augment their future income through dividends, interest and rent receipts and through capital appreciation.

In real terms, savings are important in that they finance physical INVESTMENT in the economy, enabling a country to increase its CAPITAL STOCK and hence its overall capacity to produce a greater volume of products.

See FINANCIAL SYSTEM, NATIONAL SAVINGS CERTIFICATE.

**savings bank** a BANK which offers clients a variety of savings accounts to attract deposits, mainly from the general public, and which specializes in investments in financial securities such as STOCKS and SHARES and government BONDS. In recent times, however, some savings banks, such as the Trustee Savings Bank, have become JOINT-STOCK COMPANIES and operate more like the COMMERCIAL BANKS, offering their clients money transmission services (cheque books and credit cards), bank loans and mortgages, and other financial services.

**SBU** see STRATEGIC BUSINESS UNIT.

**'scab'** see BLACKLEG.

**scalar concept** a principle of ORGANIZATION design whereby job posts are arranged hierarchically with clear lines of AUTHORITY passing down the HIERARCHY. This view is a central component of CLASSICAL MANAGEMENT THEORY.

**Scanlon Plan** see GAINSHARING.

**scatter diagram** a graphical representation of the pairs of values of the independent VARIABLE and dependent variable. In order to make sense of such data, we need to examine the pattern of the graphed observations with a view to fitting a line to the graph which adequately represents the relationship between the independent and dependent variable.

**scenario writing** see TECHNOLOGICAL FORECASTING.

**scheduling** see PRODUCTION SCHEDULING.

**'science of muddling through'** see DISJOINTED INCREMENTALISM.

**science park** or **business park** a cluster of firms, mainly high-technology businesses, which are located together on a purpose-built site adjacent to a university, polytechnic or some other centre of research, which facilitates the transfer of basic technology and know-how from research laboratories to commercial applications. The term is also applied more generally to embrace *technology parks* or *technopoles* (commonly found in Continental Europe), where emphasis is on attracting established research-based companies and *innovation centres* which cater for smaller high-technology companies.

In most countries a large proportion of the investment in science-park infrastructure and buildings is provided by the public sector as part of a wider programme to stimulate regional enterprise and promote technological advance.

See RESEARCH AND DEVELOPMENT, REGIONAL POLICY, INDUSTRIAL POLICY.

**scientific management** an approach to JOB DESIGN advocated by F. W. Taylor (1856–1915), an American WORK STUDY engineer. Taylor sought to increase output by improving management competence and by careful attention to job design. Specifically, he advocated close analysis of job tasks through the methods of work study as a basis for achieving an extreme degree of job specialization. All decision-making about task performance was to pass to management, who were to create 'thinking departments' to analyse and plan work tasks. Supervision of performance was to be undertaken by 'functional foremen', responsible for particular aspects of the production process (for example maintenance). Workers would be motivated by pay incentives to work to the full extent of their abilities, and the best workers should be selected for each particular job. Taylor believed that adoption of his system would lead to high levels of efficiency. In reality his theory ignored the importance of JOB SATISFACTION. Adoption of his methods led to STRIKES and CONFLICT. See FORDISM, METHOD STUDY.

**Scottish Enterprise (SE)** an organization whose general remit is to foster the industrial regeneration of Scotland as a means of creating employment and improving living standards. Scottish Enterprise provides financial assistance and other support to manufacturing and service businesses prepared to undertake new investment in the region, as well as supporting infrastructure projects and training. See REGIONAL POLICY.

**Scotvec** the Scottish Council for Vocational Training. The Scottish equivalent of the NATIONAL COUNCIL FOR VOCATIONAL QUALIFICATIONS in England and Wales, it oversees vocational training in Scotland and the SVQ, the Scottish version of the NATIONAL VOCATIONAL QUALIFICATION. See TRAINING, TRAINING AND ENTERPRISE COUNCIL, LOCAL ENTERPRISE COMPANY.

**scrap** seriously defective or damaged components or products that are rejected by a firm's QUALITY CONTROL system as incapable of being rectified and which have to be disposed of for the salvage value of their materials.

**scrap value** see RESIDUAL VALUE.

**screening** the process of evaluating product ideas in terms of

# SECURITIES AND EXCHANGE COMMISSION

consumer acceptance, technical feasibility and cost. See NEW PRODUCT DEVELOPMENT.

**scrip issue** see CAPITALIZATION ISSUE.

**SDR** see INTERNATIONAL MONETARY FUND.

**SE** see SCOTTISH ENTERPRISE.

**sealed-bid pricing** see COMPETITION-BASED PRICING.

**sealed minimum stock** a STOCK CONTROL system for STOCK items where re-orders are placed when the sealed minimum stock level is reached. Sealed stock systems tend to be used for inexpensive items such a rivets, which are available to operatives on free issue. The reorder stock level is sealed in a bag and this bag is opened only when all the other stock has been used up. A tag or card attached to the bag is used to initiate a replenishment order.

**SEAQ** see STOCK MARKET.

**seasonal index** see SALES FORECASTING.

**seasonal unemployment** see UNEMPLOYMENT.

**seasonal variation** see SALES FORECASTING.

**secondary action** a form of INDUSTRIAL ACTION in which a group of employees STRIKE or take some other action against their employer, as a means of putting pressure on another employer currently engaged in an industrial dispute with his or her workforce. By taking industrial action, the provision of goods and services from the one employer to the employer in dispute can be disrupted. In legal terms, secondary action can be said to involve a breach of the CONTRACT OF EMPLOYMENT that leads to a breach of commercial contract. Until the EMPLOYMENT ACT 1980, lawful secondary action included action taken by employees in support of employees of organizations who had no direct commercial relationship with their own, for example sympathy strikes. The 1980 Act made secondary action lawful only when the firms involved had contracts with each other. The EMPLOYMENT ACT 1990 made all secondary action unlawful.

**second mortgage** a second LOAN raised by a property owner against the COLLATERAL SECURITY of his or her property. See MORTGAGE.

**secular trend** see SALES FORECASTING.

**secured creditor** see CREDITORS.

**Securities and Exchange Commission** the US government body that regulates the operations of the New York STOCK

## SECURITIES AND FUTURES AUTHORITY

MARKET.

**Securities and Futures Authority (SFA)** a UK body which is responsible for regulating firms dealing in FINANCIAL SECURITIES on the STOCK MARKET and FORWARD MARKET and in COMMODITIES on the Forward Market.

The SFA was established in 1991 through the merger of two previous regulatory bodies – The Securities Association (TSA) and the Association of Futures Brokers and Dealers (AFBD). See FINANCIAL SERVICES ACT 1986.

**Securities and Investment Board (SIB)** an authority established under the FINANCIAL SERVICES ACT 1986 which is responsible for regulating, in part, the UK financial investment industry. It oversees the functioning of the STOCK MARKET and FORWARD MARKET and the rulebooks of the markets' three Self-Regulating Organisations – the PERSONAL INVESTMENT AUTHORITY, the INVESTMENT MANAGEMENT REGULATORY ORGANIZATION and the SECURITIES AND FUTURES AUTHORITY.

The SIB's main objective is to achieve a high level of investor protection by ensuring that persons and firms who provide any form of investment service are properly authorized to undertake this task by meeting appropriate standards of honesty, competence and solvency.

**securitization** an arrangement which involves putting together a claim on particular assets of a business which is then sold as a negotiable security in the financial markets. Securitization is mainly undertaken by financial institutions; assets involved typically include commercial paper, mortgages, car loans, export credits and credit card receivables.

Securitization enables the issuing institution to raise ready cash, thus improving its liquidity. Purchasers of such securities seek to profit by obtaining claims on assets at less than their redemption value, but they may choose to on-sell their claims in the market.

**Security 1.** a FINANCIAL SECURITY such as a STOCK, SHARE or BOND.

**2.** the provision of a 'collateral' to obtain a LOAN. See COLLATERAL SECURITY.

**segmental reporting** the practice of reporting separately on the SALES REVENUES, COSTS and PROFITS of different segments of a company's business. Company law in the UK requires the DIRECTOR'S REPORT to offer information to shareholders about the performance of different market segments or sectors of the company. Segmental reporting is often necessary in large groups which are highly diversified, operating in many different markets at home and abroad.

**selection** see RECRUITMENT AND SELECTION.

**selective distribution** A DISTRIBUTION strategy used by manufacturers which makes a product available only to certain RETAILERS rather than to retailers in general. 'Approved' retailers are required to meet standards set by the manufacturer with regard, for example, to presentation of the product, and to employ trained staff who can advise customers about the product.

**selective price cutting** a PRICING strategy which involves price cuts on particular brands or in particular sales territories in order to boost demand. More predatorily, price cuts may be deployed in order to remove competitors.

**self-appraisal** see PERFORMANCE APPRAISAL.

**self-management** see WORKERS' COOPERATIVE.

**Self-Regulatory Organization (SRO)** a UK body established under the FINANCIAL SERVICES ACT 1986 which is responsible for regulating specified investment services. There are currently (1995) three SROs: the PERSONAL INVESTMENT AUTHORITY, the INVESTMENT MANAGEMENT REGULATORY ORGANIZATION and the SECURITIES AND FUTURES AUTHORITY.

**self service** a form of retailing whereby customers of RETAIL OUTLETS (shop, filling station etc.) select for themselves the goods they wish to purchase and pay for them at a checkout. Self service can be applied to both large- and small-scale retailing operations and by cutting down on operating costs (i.e. eliminating the wages of sales assistants) it can assist a retailer or some other business (restaurant, cafeteria, etc.) to become more price competitive. See RETAILER.

**seller** a supplier of a GOOD, SERVICE or FINANCIAL SECURITY. In the first two cases, a broad distinction can be made between suppliers of goods and services such as raw materials, components, plant and equipment which are used to produce other products (that is, suppliers of *industrial products*) and sellers of products for personal consumption (that is, suppliers of *consumer products*).

The distinction between these two groups is important in terms of the application of appropriate MARKETING STRATEGIES.

## SELLER CONCENTRATION

**seller concentration** see MARKET CONCENTRATION.

**seller's market** a MARKET situation in which the demand for a product or financial security is greater than the supply of it at existing PRICES, which leads to the bidding-up of prices to the advantage of sellers. Compare BUYER'S MARKET.

**selling** the process of persuading potential BUYERS to purchase products. This process is undertaken by a firm's SALES REPRESENTATIVES who visit buyers, or by sales assistants in retail shops or by wholesalers. See PERSONAL SELLING, SALES FORCE.

**selling costs** the expenditures incurred by suppliers in creating and sustaining a demand for their products. Selling costs include ADVERTISING expenditures; packaging and styling; salaries, commissions and travelling expenses of sales personnel; and the cost of shops and showrooms. See also PROMOTIONAL MIX, PRODUCT DIFFERENTIATION, OVERHEADS.

**semiautonomous work groups** see JOB DESIGN AND REDESIGN.

**semivariable overheads** any OVERHEADS that are partly FIXED OVERHEADS and partly VARIABLE OVERHEADS with respect to output, so that they vary roughly with output but not in exact proportion to it. They include such items as electricity and telephone costs which combine a fixed quarterly payment with a charge per unit consumed. In arithmetic terms, semi-variable costs (S) can be represented as:

$$S = F + V.Q$$

where $F$ is the fixed cost element, $V$ is variable cost per unit and $Q$ is output.

To facilitate cost analysis, semi-variable overhead costs are often broken down into their fixed and variable parts, leaving only two categories of cost:

*Variable Costs* = direct materials + direct labour
+ variable overheads + variable component
of semivariable overheads.

*Fixed Costs* = fixed overhead + fixed element of
semivariable overheads.

This allows accountants to represent the behaviour of costs graphically by straight lines using BREAK-EVEN ANALYSIS.

**senior manager** a manager who has a substantial role in formulating the objectives and policy of the ORGANIZATION. Usually managers at the top of the HIERARCHY are described in this way but where there is substantial DECENTRALIZATION of decision-making, managers at lower reaches of the organization may have this status. See MANAGEMENT.

**sensitivity analysis** a means of testing the extent to which the results of an analysis of an INVESTMENT project or company budget would change if one or more of the assumptions on which the analysis is based were to change. For example, in estimating the rate of return on an investment, such as a new machine, a firm will need to input various assumptions about the cost of the machine, the anticipated life of the machine, its running costs, annual output, residual value etc. Sensitivity analysis shows how much the expected rate of return on the machine would change if any one of these factors were to be higher or lower than originally expected. Sensitivity analysis thus allows managers to anticipate a range of possible outcomes where uncertainty about the factors involved make it impossible to predict the exact outcome. See UNCERTAINTY AND RISK, DISCOUNTED CASH FLOW.

**sensitivity training** see MANAGEMENT DEVELOPMENT.

**SEPON (Stock Exchange Pool Nominees)** the official UK STOCK MARKET company which receives details of all STOCKS and SHARES transfers, and facilitates prompt settlement of accounts and transfer of SHARE CERTIFICATES, making use of the TALISMAN computerized transfer system.

**sequestration** the confiscation of an organization's assets by a court following contempt of court by the organization. Its assets come under the control of a sequestrator, usually an accountant, until the organization can show that it has purged its contempt. Sequestration can be used to ensure that funds are available to pay any fines resulting from the contempt of court. In the late 1980s a number of TRADE UNIONS were subject to sequestration orders, in most cases as a result of violating the law on SECONDARY ACTION and strike ballots.

**service** an economic activity which is performed to meet a personal or business demand. Some services are either specifically personal (for example hairdressing, dentistry), or business (for example factory maintenance, freight forwarding), but a large number are multifaceted, catering for both sectors, for example, household and industrial painting, telephone services.

The provision of most services (for example, window cleaning) involves a number of characteristics which set them apart from the provision of a GOOD (for example, a motorcar), in particular *intangibility* – the inability of a customer to see, touch, taste or smell the service, and *inseparability* – the fact that services are produced and consumed at the same time and thus cannot be stored. See MARKETING, GAP ANALYSIS.

See PRODUCT.

**service contract** a CONTRACT OF EMPLOYMENT covering the terms and conditions applied to directors and senior managers of a joint-stock company.

**service level** see STOCK CONTROL.

**settlement day** see ACCOUNT PERIOD.

**set-up cost** the cost involved in preparing and setting up a machine for the next work task, including cleaning, replacement of cutting tools or jigs etc. Set-up costs include the labour costs of preparing machines, the cost of new tools and frequently higher scrap rates immediately after machine resetting.

**set-up time** the time involved in setting up a machine ready for the next work task. Set-up times represent IDLE TIME when machines are not producing output, and production managers will seek to set up machines as quickly as possible and return them to production mode. In BATCH PRODUCTION, in particular, set-up times are an important constraint upon factory output, and firms may prefer long production runs making particular components in order to minimize the number of machine resettings needed. See MACHINE UTILIZATION, ALLOWANCES.

**severance pay** see REDUNDANCY.

**sex discrimination** see DISCRIMINATION.

**Sex Discrimination Act 1975** see DISCRIMINATION.

**SFA** see SECURITIES AND FUTURES AUTHORITY.

**shadow price** the imputed PRICE or value of a good or service where such a price or value cannot be determined accurately owing to the absence of a market for the good or service, or to gross distortions in any markets which exist. To impute a price or value is to make the best estimate possible of what that price or value would be if a normal market existed.

One use of shadow pricing is when intra-firm trading occurs. The inputs of company division B may be the outputs of company division A. The products in which the two company divisions trade may not have an equivalent market price because no open market for them exists (for example intermediate components or managerial services). The transactions are given shadow prices, usually based on estimated costs plus a return on the capital involved.

A particular application of shadow pricing can be found in LINEAR PROGRAMMING where the solution to a problem yields hypothetical prices for scarce factor inputs, showing how much additional profit would result from an extra unit of each fully used resource.

See TRANSFER PRICE.

**share** a FINANCIAL SECURITY issued by a JOINT-STOCK COMPANY as a means of raising long-term capital. Purchasers of shares pay money into the company's bank account and in return receive a SHARE CERTIFICATE signifying their ownership of the shares and have their ownership recorded in the company's SHARE REGISTER. The SHAREHOLDERS of a company are its legal owners and are entitled to a share in its profits. Shares are traded on the STOCK MARKET. There are two broad kinds of shares: PREFERENCE SHARES and ORDINARY SHARES. See also SHARE CAPITAL, SHARE ISSUE, CAPITAL GEARING.

**share capital** the money employed in a JOINT-STOCK COMPANY that has been subscribed by the SHAREHOLDERS of the company in the form of ORDINARY SHARES (equity) and PREFERENCE SHARES, and which will remain as a permanent source of finance as long as the company remains in existence. See also LOAN CAPITAL, CAPITAL GEARING, STOCK.

**share certificate** a document which is issued to a SHAREHOLDER in a company, which serves as proof of ownership of SHARES in the company. See TRANSFER DEED.

**shareholders** the individuals and institutions who contribute funds to finance a JOINT-STOCK COMPANY in return for SHARES in that company. There are two main types of shareholder:

(a) holders of PREFERENCE SHARES who are entitled to a fixed DIVIDEND from a company's PROFITS (before ordinary shareholders receive anything), and who have first claim on any remaining assets of the business after all debts have been discharged;

(b) holders of ORDINARY SHARES who are entitled to a dividend from a company's profits after all other outlays have been met and who are entitled to any remaining ASSETS of the business in the event of the company being wound up (LIQUIDATED).

## SHAREHOLDERS' CAPITAL EMPLOYED

Generally only ordinary shareholders are entitled to vote at ANNUAL GENERAL MEETINGS and elect DIRECTORS, since they bear most of the risk.

**shareholders' capital employed** SHARE CAPITAL originally invested by SHAREHOLDERS plus any RESERVES which arise, for example, as retained profits are ploughed back into the company.

**share issue** the process of issuing shares in a JOINT-STOCK COMPANY.

New share capital is most frequently raised through issuing houses or merchant banks which arrange for the sale of shares on behalf of client companies. Shares can be issued in a variety of ways, such as direct to the general public by way of an 'offer for sale' (or an 'introduction') at a prearranged fixed price; an 'offer for sale by TENDER' where the issue price is determined by averaging out the bid prices offered by prospective purchasers of the share subject to a minimum price bid; a RIGHTS ISSUE of shares to existing shareholders at a fixed price; or a *placing* of the shares at an arranged price with selected investors, often INSTITUTIONAL INVESTORS.

Where shares are issued by means of an offer for sale the company issues a PROSPECTUS inviting members of the public to subscribe for shares, such *applications* for shares being accompanied either by a proportion of the purchase price of the shares or by the full purchase price. Then the company arranges for the ALLOTMENT of shares to intending shareholders. If the share issue is oversubscribed with more applications for shares than the number of shares being issued, then the firm must use some formula to allocate shares among applicants. To cover for the possibility that the share issue will be undersubscribed companies usually contract with a merchant bank to have the issue underwritten, the bank purchasing any unsold shares. Successful applicants then pay any balance of the share price or a second instalment towards the final price in response to a 'call' by the company. At this stage the names of successful applicants are entered on the company's SHARE REGISTER and they become entitled to full shareholders' rights, including the right to receive ANNUAL REPORTS AND ACCOUNTS and to vote at the company's ANNUAL GENERAL MEETING.

See STOCK MARKET, CALLED-UP CAPITAL, PAID-UP CAPITAL, ALLOT-

MENT, SHARE CERTIFICATE.

**share option** a contractual right to buy a SHARE in a company at a predetermined price within a predetermined period. A company seeking to raise new capital can grant existing shareholders options to buy new shares in proportion to their existing shareholdings. Shareholders can either exercise their options and buy the shares or can sell their option rights on the STOCK MARKET. Share options can also be granted by a company to its employees as a means of improving their motivation and loyalty to the company.

See RIGHTS ISSUE, EMPLOYEE SHARE OWNERSHIP.

**share ownership plan** see EMPLOYEE SHARE OWNERSHIP PLAN.

**share portfolio** see PORTFOLIO.

**share premium** the proceeds from issuing SHARES at a price higher than their PAR VALUE or present market value. Such proceeds are added to a JOINT-STOCK COMPANY'S revenue RESERVES.

**share price index** a means of measuring changes in the aggregate value of a particular 'basket' of company shares, usually ORDINARY SHARES. The Financial Times 30 share index, 100 share index and all-share index are used in the UK to measure the value of ordinary shares quoted on the London STOCK MARKET. A similar role is performed in the US by the *Dow-Jones index*, and in Japan by the *Nikkei index*.

In technical terms, a share price index is compiled by noting the prices of the shares included in the index at some 'base' point in time (for example, 2 January 1993) and assigning an index number (say 1000) to begin the series. If share prices generally start to increase then this is translated into an upward movement in the value of the index (for example, the value of the index at 2 January 1994 may be, say, 1500, indicating that share prices on average have increased by 50% over a one-year period). Likewise, general falls in share prices are recorded as a decline in the value of the index.

Share price indices reflect the corporate sector's underlying profit and growth record and also act like a barometer of investor confidence or lack of it, about the state of industry and the economy generally.

See PRICE INDEX.

**share purchase/sale** the process of buying and selling STOCKS and SHARES on the STOCK MARKET. This involves a number of procedures where small purchases or sales are involved:

(a) the buyer/seller can approach a STOCKBROKER or COMMERCIAL BANK and instruct them to buy or sell a specific number of shares in a particular company. The stockbroker or bank will then undertake this task for a commission (a minimum fixed amount or a percentage of the value of the transaction);

(b) the stockbroker or bank approaches a MARKET MAKER (formerly called a 'jobber') to buy or sell the shares as instructed. The market maker holds a stock of shares and other financial securities in a limited range of companies determined by the market maker's speciality. The market maker will quote two prices to the stockbroker or bank, a lower 'bid' price at which the market maker is prepared to buy shares, and a higher 'offer' price at which he is prepared to sell the shares. The difference or 'spread' between these prices provides the market maker's profit margin. In quoting two prices the market maker does not know whether the stockbroker intends to buy or sell shares and the stockbroker will only disclose whether he wishes to buy or sell and conclude the transaction if he finds the market maker's prices competitive with those being quoted by other market makers. At this stage a 'bargain' is struck and legal title to the shares passes to the buyer; contrast 'order-driven' exchanges – see TRADEPOINT.

(c) Trading in the stock market takes place within a 'rolling settlement' system (see ACCOUNT PERIOD) in which settlement for purchases and sales takes place five working days after a deal has been struck.

(d) In order to record the transfer of ownership of the shares to the buyer, the market maker will notify the COMPANY REGISTRAR of the company whose shares have been bought, who will amend his share register and issue a new share certificate to the buyer and cancel share certificates held by the seller. See TALISMAN, CREST.

INSTITUTIONAL INVESTORS such as pension funds follow a broadly similar procedure in transacting shares, though they often bypass stockbrokers and sometimes market makers, buying and selling large volumes of securities direct between themselves.

See SPECULATION.

**share register** a record of a company's SHAREHOLDERS which lists the names and addresses of shareholders and the number of shares and other company securities held by them. The COMPANY SECRETARY is legally obliged to maintain an up-to-date record of all share owners, which necessitates noting all transfers of ownership of shares shortly after they are bought and sold on the STOCK MARKET. TRANSFER DEEDS are used to record share purchases and these in turn are used to update the share register and issue new SHARE CERTIFICATES.

Where shares are held by NOMINEES it is impossible to identify the ultimate beneficial holders of these shares. However in the UK, where an individual shareholder acquires more than 3% of a company's issued shares through one or more nominees, the company's directors are legally entitled to insist on knowing the identity of the shareholder.

**share split** or **stock split** an increase in the number of SHARES in a JOINT-STOCK COMPANY matched by an offsetting reduction in the PAR VALUE of each share so that it does not affect the capitalization of the company. For example, Company X has 10,000 authorized, issued and fully paid up shares each with a par value of £1; and total SHAREHOLDERS' CAPITAL is shown in the BALANCE SHEET at £10,000. The STOCK MARKET values the company at around £100,000, making each share worth £10. The company wishes to attract a wider shareholder base by reducing the market PRICE of each share, and so undertakes a two-for-one stock split, giving existing shareholders two new 50p shares for each £1 share held. The company now has 20,000 authorized, issued and fully paid up shares of 50p nominal value, and capitalization of the company remains unchanged at £10,000. However, now the stock-market price of the shares will be around £5, which hopefully will improve the marketability of the shares. See also SHARE CAPITAL.

**shark repellents** see TAKEOVER BID.

**shelf space** the amount of space allocated to a particular product or brand by a wholesaler or retailer. Shelf space is particularly important in the case of consumer goods sold through self-service retail outlets such as SUPERMARKETS, where the amount and location of shelf space devoted to a brand can have a significant impact upon sales volume.

**shell company** a company whose shares are currently listed on the STOCK MARKET but which is not actively trading. The share prices of such companies are generally very low and they may offer an attractive means for a business without a stock-market listing to acquire one by TAKEOVER.

**shift pay** see SHIFT WORK.

**shift work** a method of organizing work which enables production or services to be operated beyond normal working hours. Employees' working days are known as shifts and may be timed to commence at varying times of the day or night. Where shifts are of equal lengths it is common for employees to rotate around them, working, say 'earlies' one week, 'lates' the next.

There are several forms of shift-work:

(a) *double-day shifts*, where there are two shifts of equal length each working day, usually 6 a.m. to 2 p.m. and 2 p.m. to 10 p.m.;

(b) *three-shift working*, where there are three shifts of equal length so that operations can be maintained round the clock either throughout the week including weekends (*continuous*) or from Monday to Friday (*discontinuous*). Where there are peaks of activity, a four-shift system can be used to provide some overlap at certain times of the day;

(c) *continental shift*, where there is a three-shift system but workers change from shift to shift every two or three days rather than each week;

(d) *split-shift working*, where an employee's working day is cut in two, with a middle period off duty. This may be found in industries such as public transport, where demand peaks in the early morning and late afternoon;

(e) *permanent night shifts*, where a separate group of employees work solely at night, thereby achieving the benefit of an extended working day but without disturbing the working patterns of day employees;

(f) *'twilight' shift working*, where a separate group of part-time workers (see PART-TIME WORK) take over from the day shift in the late afternoon and work through until mid or late evening. By this method the productive day is extended but some of the costs of shift work are avoided, such as the need to pay a shift *premium* (see below).

Most shift systems involve a regular pattern of signing-on times but in some cases, for example the railway industry, signing-on times vary from day to day (though they usually broadly correspond to a three-shift working system).

The benefits of shift work to employers include more intensive use of production facilities and, especially in service industries, the capacity to adapt operations to the pattern of demand. Also, some forms of technology, for example in the chemical industry, need to be operated continuously and require some form of shift working. Maintaining productivity in shift work can be problematic, however. People are generally less productive in the small hours of the night, whilst control of performance may be ineffective (witness the occasional media horror stories about night-shift workers getting a good night's sleep alongside their machines). It is recognized that shift work imposes costs on employees, chiefly in the disruption to their social and domestic life. For this reason it is common for some form of shift premium to be paid on top of the hourly pay rate, especially when night work is involved. There is also some evidence that frequent changes to waking hours damage body rhythms and can be harmful to health in the long term.

**shop** a business premise which is engaged in the retailing of products to customers who visit the shop or store to make purchases. The range of merchandise they stock and sell varies considerably from, at one extreme, total specialization on the one product (as in a shoe shop, for example) to retail operations involving thousands of different lines (as in a large DEPARTMENT STORE). Shop sizes too vary considerably, ranging upwards from small 'corner shop' premises to massive 'hypermarket' complexes (see SUPERMARKET). See RETAIL OUTLET, RETAILER, DISTRIBUTION CHANNEL.

**Shop Act 1950** an Act applying to England and Wales which contains provisions relating to SHOP opening times and shop workers' hours. The Act requires every shop to be closed on Sundays except for the sale of a restricted list of products but this has now been amended by the Sunday Trading Act. Daily opening hours are also governed in so far as all shops (with a limited number of exceptions such as shops having an off-licence to sell liquor) must be closed by 8 p.m. except for one 'late day' per week which is until 9 p.m. There are no statutory provisions covering the time shops may open in the morning.

Local courts have the power to fine a trader up to a maximum of £1,000 per offence for infringements of the Act.

## SHOP FLOOR

In 1994 the Sunday Trading Act made it legal for retailers to open their stores on Sundays. Small shops are permitted to open as normal but larger shops (for example, supermarkets) are restricted to a maximum of six hours.

**shop floor** the basic level within an organization at which goods (or services) are produced. In a typical manufacturing business the shop floor would consist of operatives working in a factory to produce components or finished goods under the supervision of first line managers.

See SUPERVISOR, SHOP STEWARD.

**shopping goods** products such as motorcars which represent a major purchasing decision and thus justify the buyer in 'shopping around' to compare suitability, price, quality and style. Contrast with CONVENIENCE GOODS.

**shop steward** a shop-floor employee who represents his/her colleagues' interests in workplace negotiations with management. Their functions include rectifying with management GRIEVANCES arising at work and the maintenance or creation of patterns of WORK ORGANIZATION desired by their constituents. Although shop stewards are usually TRADE UNION members and are viewed as union, representatives, they often function independently of the rest of the union. However, until CHECK-OFF AGREEMENTS became widespread, it was common for shop stewards to collect union membership subscriptions.

From the 1950s, shop stewards in UK manufacturing industry became increasingly involved in informal workplace negotiations over pay and work organization, which supplemented the formal, industry-wide system of COLLECTIVE BARGAINING. Since then bargaining has been rationalized, involving a shift to plant- and company-level bargaining, thereby giving some shop stewards a much greater formal role in pay bargaining. In organizations where shop stewards have this function there will generally be a hierarchy with only the more senior shop stewards taking a direct part in negotiations with management. Where more than one union is present (see MULTI-UNIONISM) there may well be a joint shop stewards committee to pursue the unions' interests collectively.

**short position** a situation where a dealer or MARKET MAKER in a particular COMMODITY, FINANCIAL SECURITY or FOREIGN CURRENCY is selling more than he is buying so that his working stock of the item becomes depleted (i.e. runs short).

**Shorts** BONDS and DEBENTURES which have a redemption date of less than five years.

**SIB** see SECURITIES AND INVESTMENTS BOARD.

**SIC** see STANDARD INDUSTRIAL CLASSIFICATION.

**sick pay** the payments made to an employee who is unable to work normally due to illness. In principle these payments could be made in place of a wage, from a national insurance fund, or by the employers themselves. The current system of 'statutory sick pay' in the UK (in operation since 1986) combines elements of both. The employer makes payments to the sick employee at a level determined by social security regulations, which are financed out of the National Insurance contributions held by the employer. No payments can be made until the fourth day of absence (unless there has been a previous period of absence due to illness shortly before). After seven days of absence a doctor's certificate is necessary; prior to that the employee provides self-certification. After a prolonged period of sickness absence (currently 28 weeks) responsibility for payment transfers to the Department of Social Security.

Many UK employers choose to operate their own sick-pay scheme alongside statutory sick pay, and provide more favourable benefits than the state scheme. Although, traditionally, occupational sick-pay schemes have been applied to managerial and white-collar rather than to blue-collar workers, most UK employees are now covered by such a scheme. Often they will provide for the employee to receive full pay for up to 28 weeks. Provision of favourable sick pay is often thought to encourage ABSENTEEISM but the evidence suggests that this a short-run phenomenon largely confined to the period immediately after the scheme is introduced.

**sight deposit** see COMMERCIAL BANK.

**SIMO chart** see SIMULTANEOUS MOTION CHART.

**simple interest** see INTEREST.

**simple structure** an ORGANIZATION where the formal structure is in a rudimentary state, with few rules and regulations to govern how work is done or AUTHORITY exercised. Small organizations in their early stages of development often take this form.

**simplex method** see LINEAR PROGRAMMING.

**simulation** a technique for dealing with complex resource-allocation problems which cannot be solved exactly by LINEAR PROGRAMMING or similar analytical methods. The technique involves creating a typical life history of a system to represent the actual problem and its rules of operation. Repeated runs of the simulation, slightly altering the operating rules each time, provides experimentation aimed at discovering methods of improving the performance of the system. Such simulation techniques are frequently employed in examining STOCKHOLDING and QUEUE problems. For example, in simulating a queue problem, such as cars queueing at a petrol-station forecourt, it is possible to note how well existing service facilities are coping with customers and the extent to which existing service capacity is utilized. It is also possible to investigate the effects of such changes as increasing the number of service channels or changing the arrangement of channels to discover ways of improving the performance of the garage.

**simultaneous motion chart (SIMO chart)** a chart used in METHOD STUDY to record a worker's rapid hand movements in performing work tasks. The work elements involved are often identified using slowed down video-recordings or films and presented in chart form using THERBLIG symbols. SIMO charts can be used to identify non-productive pauses or awkward hand motions caused by poor workplace layout or badly designed tools. See WORK MEASUREMENT.

**single-bin system** see STOCK CONTROL.

**single capacity** the restriction on firms in the STOCK MARKET which requires them to operate *either* as a MARKET MAKER, buying and selling shares on their own account, *or* as a STOCKBROKER, acting on behalf of clients. See DUAL CAPACITY.

**single employer bargaining** see COLLECTIVE BARGAINING.

**Single European Act 1986** (referred to popularly as the '1992' initiative) an Act which extended the principles enshrined in the founding legislation of the EUROPEAN COMMUNITY (now part of the EUROPEAN UNION) with the objective of creating a 'single market' (by 1992) by the removal of various internal obstacles to the free movement of goods, services, capital and persons between the member states of the Union. Under the Act, the European Commission has submitted some 400 Directives for eliminating disparities between members in respect of physical, technical and fiscal rules and regulations, so as to create a unified Union-wide set of practices: for example, individuals and freight transport will be able to move across national frontiers without undergoing passport and customs checks; common technical specifications are to be introduced relating to product descriptions and design, health and safety standards, etc.; while VAT and other sales taxes are to be applied on a uniform basis. See EUROPEAN ECONOMIC AREA.

**single table bargaining** a form of COLLECTIVE BARGAINING where all the trade unions in an organization sit together in negotiations over pay and conditions of employment. The alternative is separate negotiations between each union and management. The benefit of single table bargaining is that it inhibits leapfrog bargaining where each bargaining group tries to outdo the others. The trend in the UK is towards greater use of single table bargaining in those organizations that negotiate with trade unions.

**single union deal** an agreement between an employer and a TRADE UNION in which the former agrees to recognize the one union in respect of employee representation and COLLECTIVE BARGAINING. In return the union may agree to prohibit strike action by its members (see NO-STRIKE AGREEMENT). Such agreements are not new but they have been the subject of contention recently (especially in relation to Japanese and other foreign companies establishing factories in the UK), because signing such agreements has sometimes resulted in certain trade unions moving outside their traditional sphere of influence to represent occupational groups normally represented by another union. See JAPANIZATION.

**sinking fund** a fund into which periodic payments are made which, with compound INTEREST, will ultimately be sufficient to meet a known future capital commitment or discharge a LIABILITY. Such a fund may be used to finance the replacement of FIXED ASSETS at the end of their useful life or to purchase back company loan stock or DEBENTURES upon maturity. See also DEPRECIATION, sense 1.

**sit-in** see INDUSTRIAL ACTION.

**'sitting next to Nelly'** see TRAINING.

**situational leadership** see LEADERSHIP.

**skill** any competence possessed by someone; in an employment context it often refers to a combination of knowledge and manual dexterity amongst manual workers. JOBS are often categorized as *skilled, semiskilled* or *unskilled* according to the level of skills apparently required to perform them. However, many argue that there is a mismatch between skills that are actually necessary to perform certain jobs and the nomenclature of the job. Jobs classed as skilled may in reality require little skill (perhaps because of the introduction of new technology) whilst unskilled jobs may require more knowledge than is often recognized (tacit skills). It is therefore argued by some that skills are socially constructed. By defining certain jobs as skilled, entry to them can be restricted to those who possess certain recognized competencies or characteristics. If acquisition of these can be controlled then entry to the job can be restricted. In this way the rewards stemming from the job can be maintained at a high level. This has traditionally been the strategy of craft TRADE UNIONS and of PROFESSIONALS. See SOCIOLOGY OF WORK, TRAINING.

**skills gap** see TRAINING.

**skimming pricing** see MARKET SKIMMING PRICING.

**slack** see NETWORK ANALYSIS, ORGANIZATIONAL SLACK.

**sleeping partner** a partner in a PARTNERSHIP who contributes capital to finance the business but takes no active part in managing the company. Sleeping partners still retain unlimited liability for the debts of the partnership alongside active partners.

**slump** see BUSINESS CYCLE.

**SMART scheme (Small Firms Merit Award for Research and Technology)** a programme sponsored by the DEPARTMENT OF TRADE AND INDUSTRY, designed to stimulate innovation effort by individuals and small firms (with under 50 employees), by providing initial finance for projects in the hope that they will eventually attract conventional loan finance or investment. Assistance is provided in two stages: the first year the DTI will finance 75% of the cost of approved projects (up to a maximum of £45,000); if the first year's results are promising, the DTI will provide a further 50% grant (up to a maximum of £60,000) over the following year. See INDUSTRIAL POLICY, RESEARCH AND DEVELOPMENT.

**social audit** an examination of an organization's employment and equal opportunities performance, its responsiveness to customers; its environmental impact (pollution); and its impact upon the community. Social audits can assist an organization

in identifying deficiencies in its performance in the above respects, so that the organization can develop policies to
improve its performance.

See AUDIT, GREEN AUDIT.

**Social Chapter** the EUROPEAN UNION (EU) protocol which establishes (under the MAASTRICHT TREATY) a set of basic rights at
work throughout the EU. These include the right to join a
TRADE UNION, the right to take INDUSTRIAL ACTION, the right to
equal treatment for men and women (including equal pay),
and various provisions relating to collective REDUNDANCIES. It
also seeks to encourage CONSULTATION and PARTICIPATION.

These provisions have been accepted by all EU members
except the UK whose (current) view is that these are matters
of SUBSIDIARITY (to be determined by the individual member
state rather than on an EU-wide level). See EUROPEAN WORKS
COUNCIL.

**social class stratification** the division, into groups, of people
who tend to possess similar characteristics in terms of values,
interests, aspirations and behaviour. See SOCIO-ECONOMIC
GROUP.

**social group** see GROUP.

**social responsibility** a business philosophy which stresses the
need for firms to behave as good corporate citizens, not
merely obeying the law but conducting their production and
marketing activities in a manner which avoids causing
environmental pollution or exhausting finite world resources.
Some businesses have begun to behave in a more socially responsible manner, partly because their managers want to do
so, and partly because of fear of environmentalist and consumer pressure groups and the media, and concern for their
public image. It is argued that socially responsible behaviour
can pay off in the long run, even where it involves some
short-term sacrifice of profit. See CONSUMERISM, COMPANY
IMAGE.

**social security benefits** benefits provided by the government
as a means of assisting low-income members of society such
as the unemployed (unemployment benefits), the retired (basic
old age pensions), the sick (sick pay and free medical treatment), the disabled, single-parent families etc.

In the UK such social security benefits are provided as part
of the governments' 'national insurance' scheme administered

by the Department of Social Security and financed mainly by NATIONAL INSURANCE CONTRIBUTIONS paid by employees and employers. See BUDGET (GOVERNMENT), NEGATIVE INCOME TAX.

**societal marketing** the satisfaction of the needs and wants of consumers in an effective and efficient manner which avoids environmental pollution or waste of the Earth's resources. See SOCIAL RESPONSIBILITY.

**Société Anonyme (SA)** the French equivalent of a public limited company (Plc). See JOINT STOCK COMPANY.

**Société À Responsabilité Limitée (SARL)** the French equivalent of a private limited company (Ltd). See JOINT STOCK COMPANY.

**socioeconomic group** the potential BUYERS of a product grouped together in terms of certain common personal and economic characteristics. Such groups are likely to differ in the level and pattern of their spending and thus can be used as the basis for identifying strategic MARKET SEGMENTS which can then be exploited by targeting 'customized' products to meet the particular customer requirements of those segments.

A commonly used *general* method of classifying potential customers is the 'A to E' social-class grading system:

GRADE A – 'upper middle class': higher managerial, administrative or professional occupations;

GRADE B – 'middle class': middle to senior managers and administrators;

GRADE C1 – 'lower middle class': junior managers, supervisory and clerical grades;

GRADE C2 – 'skilled working class': qualified tradespersons;

GRADE D – 'working class': semiskilled and unskilled workers such as labourers;

GRADE E – pensioners.

For most consumer product marketing, a much finer, more detailed customer profile is required based on such data as sex (male, female), age (1–4, 5–10, 11–18, 19–34, 35–49, etc.), income level (£50,000+, under £5,000), housing status (owner-occupier, council-house tenant), etc.

Using such information it is possible, for example, to establish the approximate number of professional, high-income earning women, in the age bracket 35–49, who might provide a potential market for a new premium price exotic perfume.

See MARKET SEGMENTATION.

**sociology of work** a branch of sociology concerned with the attitudes, behaviour and relationships of those engaged in productive activity. As such, it has a number of levels of concern: the individual WORKER, the work GROUP, the ORGANIZATION and society. Traditionally the subject was known as industrial sociology and tended to focus on the attitudes and behaviour of production workers in industry. In recent years its subject matter has widened to take account of the shifts in occupational structure and the importance of work activities conducted outside formal employment (for example DOMESTIC LABOUR).

Industrial sociology emerged in the 1930s with the HAWTHORNE STUDIES. These studies were concerned with the social determinants of job behaviour, especially worker productivity. A notable feature of the Hawthorne studies was the (at the time) novel finding that JOB SATISFACTION was strongly influenced by the social experience of work and that satisfaction was itself an important determinant of worker output. These studies also highlighted the importance of GROUP influences on individual behaviour. Subsequent research in the new discipline was concerned with deepening the analysis of group dynamics and development, and with pinpointing more precisely the determinants of job satisfaction. For a while technological determinism – the notion that technology is the dominant influence on attitudes and behaviour – held sway (see ALIENATION). However, in the 1950s and 1960s, a growing body of thought suggested that there was no necessary relationship between technology and the social organization of work (see SOCIOTECHNICAL SYSTEM, JOB DESIGN AND REDESIGN) and hence a given type of technology could be used in various ways with varying effects on worker satisfaction. In addition sociologists came to appreciate the importance of individuals' expectations and requirements from work in determining their assessment of the quality of work experience (see ORIENTATIONS TO WORK).

In recent years the subject matter of the sociology of work has changed somewhat. Radical commentators have shifted the discipline to some extent to focus more explicitly on the structure of the relationship between employees and employers, and the inequities that flow from this. Arguing that the relationship is essentially one of exploitation, 'labour process' writers have argued that we need to examine the whole process by which employers achieve the 'subordination' of labour. In other words, how do employers control their workforces? It has been argued that there is a long-run tendency for employers to use the principle of SCIENTIFIC MANAGEMENT to reduce their reliance on workers' skills and independent thought. Control of labour is to be achieved by reducing workers to simple 'cogs in the machine'. Critics have argued that many managements lack this degree of planning, and that workers resist such objectives anyway. Both radical sociologists and their critics share, however, a concern with CONFLICT at work and its sources.

In response to the growing participation of women in paid employment in recent years, sociologists have come to examine the characteristics of gender relationships at work, focusing especially on the inequalities of work and its rewards between the sexes, as well as the interrelationship between work and broader societal experiences. In addition, changes in the labour market – the decline of manufacturing employment, for instance – have generally caused sociologists to widen their focus from (male) production workers in paid employment to all kinds of work activity.

See also ANOMIE, LABOUR FLEXIBILITY, FLEXIBLE SPECIALIZATION, HOMEWORKING, PART-TIME WORK.

**socio-technical system** an approach within ORGANIZATION THEORY, associated with the Tavistock Institute in London, which stresses that WORK ORGANIZATION has both a technical and a social dimension. In a study of coal mining, researchers found that the replacement of group working by MASS PRODUCTION methods had disrupted the prevailing social systems with adverse effects on JOB SATISFACTION. With the specialization of work tasks, miners had fewer opportunities for job rotation, and the cohesive work groups were fragmented. The researchers concluded that, to be effective, work organization should not be determined by technology alone but should take account of the prevailing social system. They found that several forms of work organization, each with its own social and psychological effects, were compatible with a given level of technology. It was thus possible to choose a method of work organization that was efficient and also provided benefits to the participants. See JOB DESIGN AND REDESIGN.

**soft currency** a FOREIGN CURRENCY that is in weak demand, but in abundant supply on the FOREIGN EXCHANGE MARKET. This situation usually arises when a country is in persistent balance-of-payments deficit. Compare HARD CURRENCY.

**soft loan** a LOAN that bears an INTEREST RATE charge which is much lower than the market rate of interest for such loans. Soft loans are made available by the government to encourage investment in particular types of industrial activity or in particular regions, and by international organizations such as the INTERNATIONAL MONETARY FUND and WORLD BANK to help countries with balance-of-payments difficulties, and to assist industrial development. See INDUSTRIAL POLICY, REGIONAL POLICY, ECONOMIC AID.

**soft sell** a gentle and indirect approach to marketing a BRAND or product. This style of ADVERTISING or PERSONAL SELLING can appeal to more discerning prospective buyers who require more objective information about a product. See HARD SELL.

**software** the PROGRAMS or instructions that make a COMPUTER system perform particular data-processing tasks. Some software makes the computer system operate while other software packages like SPREADSHEETS or WORD PROCESSING provide solutions to particular business problems.

**sole proprietorship** a BUSINESS or firm which is owned and controlled by a single person. See PARTNERSHIP, JOINT-STOCK COMPANY, LIMITED LIABILITY.

**solidaristic (orientation to work)** see ORIENTATION TO WORK.

**SORP** see STATEMENTS OF RECOMMENDED PRACTICE.

**sources and uses of funds statement** or **funds-flow statement** an accounting statement that shows the sources from which a firm derives its cash and the use to which this cash is put during a trading period. The major source of funds is usually the net cash generated from sales, though this can be added to by cash raised from selling FIXED ASSETS and by raising further LOANS or new SHARE ISSUES. The major applications of funds are the purchase of new FIXED ASSETS, repayment of LOANS and payments of TAXES and DIVIDENDS. When further allowance is made for the cash-flow effect of changes in STOCKS, DEBTORS and CREDITORS, the sources and uses of funds statement shows the net inflow or outflow of cash to the firm.

Large JOINT-STOCK COMPANIES are required by law to in-

## SOURCES OF FINANCE

corporate a sources and uses of funds statement in their ANNUAL REPORT AND ACCOUNTS sent to shareholders. Fig. 80 shows a typical sources and uses of funds statement.

See PROFIT-AND-LOSS ACCOUNT, WORKING CAPITAL.

| | £ | £ | £ |
|---|---|---|---|
| *Sources of Funds* | | | |
| Net Profit before Tax | 15,000 | | |
| add Depreciation | 5,500 | | |
| FUNDS GENERATED FROM OPERATIONS | | 20,500 | |
| Funds from other Sources: | | | |
| Proceeds from sales of fixed assets | 1,000 | | |
| Long term loans raised | 1,500 | 2,500 | |
| TOTAL FUNDS GENERATED | | | 23,000 |
| *Application of Funds* | | | |
| Purchase of Fixed Assets | 16,000 | | |
| Taxation Paid | 8,000 | 24,000 | |
| Net increase (decrease) in working capital: | | | |
| increase (decrease) in stock | 4,000 | | |
| increase (decrease) in debtors | 3,000 | | |
| decrease (increase) in creditors | (5,000) | 2,000 | 26,000 |
| net inflow (outflow) of funds | | | (3,000) |

Fig. 80. **Sources and uses of funds statement.** Sources and applications of funds statement of Y Co Ltd for year ending 31 December 19xx.

**sources of finance** the provision of finance to a company to cover its short-term WORKING CAPITAL requirements and longer-term FIXED ASSETS and investments. In financing their business operations, companies typically resort to a mix of internally generated funds and external capital. The company's own RETAINED PROFIT is the primary source of internal funds. Short-term external finance is obtained largely in the form of TRADE CREDITS extended by suppliers, and BANK LOANS and OVERDRAFTS from the commercial banks. Long-term external finance takes the form principally of SHARE CAPITAL (ordinary and preference shares) subscribed by private investors, the institutional investors, merchant banks and venture capital specialists; LOAN CAPITAL (loan stock and debentures) subscribed by the above plus the commercial banks; and miscellaneous grants and loans made available by governments (see, for example, INDUSTRIAL POLICY, REGIONAL POLICY).

See also FACTORING, LEASING, LETTER OF CREDIT, FORFAITING, LOAN GUARANTEE SCHEMES, BUSINESS EXPANSION SCHEME.

**sourcing** the selection by a firm of its sources of supply – raw materials and components in the case of a manufacturer, final products in the case of a retailer. Strategically, a firm may chose to buy in a particular input (or product) from an outside supplier (outsourcing), or produce it for itself as part of a vertically integrated operation (see VERTICAL INTEGRATION, MAKE-OR-BUY DECISION). In the former case, a firm may choose to favour one or a number of suppliers, both domestic and overseas-based, depending on various cost and risk considerations. For example, relying on a single supplier may allow the firm to benefit from discounts given on bulk purchases, but on the other hand may expose the firm to great risk of supply disruptions. For this reason multiple-supplier locations may be preferred, especially in the case of MULTINATIONAL ENTERPRISES which may deploy global sourcing strategies to take advantage of differences in supply costs between countries and obtain access to new component technologies and products. See LOCAL CONTENT RULE, JUST IN TIME (JIT) SYSTEM.

**span of control** the number of people a manager has formal AUTHORITY over and is responsible for. Most ORGANIZATIONS are structured on the premise that there are practical limitations to the number of people one manager can effectively supervise without becoming overloaded or losing sight of what the subordinates are doing. CLASSICAL MANAGEMENT THEORY held that the optimum span of control was around six people. It is now generally believed that the effective width of the span is to some extent determined by the distribution of decision-making. Where this is decentralized a wider span is feasible. The span of control is often inversely related to the number of levels in the HIERARCHY of an ORGANIZATION. The more levels, the smaller the span of control, and vice versa.

**spare parts** see REPLACEMENT PARTS.

**special deposit** a 'call' by the monetary authorities for the COMMERCIAL BANKS to place a specified proportion of their liquid assets on deposit with the Bank of England as a means of controlling the MONEY SUPPLY. See MONETARY POLICY for further discussion.

**Special Drawing Right** see INTERNATIONAL MONETARY FUND.

**specialist shop** a RETAIL OUTLET which concentrates exclusively on selling either a particular type of product or a narrow range of related products: a shoe shop, a butcher's shop, an electrical goods shop, a chemist's shop etc. Specialist shops may be under a single shop ownership or run as a multiple CHAIN-STORE business. Traditionally, specialist shops have competed mainly by offering personal service and good quality products. Increasingly, however, with the appearance of SUPERMARKETS and DISCOUNT STORES, specialist shops have been forced to compete on price. In this regard, the large specialist shop chains have been able to obtain significant price discounts by BULK BUYING from manufacturers, while single shops have found it advantageous to participate in VOLUNTARY GROUP organizations to obtain similar concessions. See RETAILER, DISTRIBUTION CHANNEL.

**speciality goods** products such as designer clothes or photographic equipment which have unique characteristics and brand identification, and which particular buyers seek to purchase through specialist sales outlets.

**specialization** a form of division of labour whereby each individual or firm concentrates its productive efforts on a single or limited number of activities. By specializing on a single work task or JOB, an individual is usually more productive since familiarity and repetition improves work skills and time is not lost moving from one job to another. Labour specialization is a feature of PRODUCTION LINE or ASSEMBLY LINE operations used in mass production.

Likewise firms may choose to specialize in the production of a limited range of products (see HORIZONTAL INTEGRATION) to focus their business interests and to take advantage of economies of large-scale production. See ECONOMIES OF SCALE.

See also JOB DESIGN AND REDESIGN, PRODUCTIVITY, INTERNATIONAL TRADE.

**specific risk** or **diversifiable risk** that part of total risk (within the CAPITAL-ASSET-PRICING MODEL) uniquely attributable to the holding of a specific financial security. Unlike MARKET RISK, specific risk is independent of general market variations. Events unique to a particular security may comprise such corporate decisions as dividend policy, changes in capital structure, recruitment of top personnel and so forth. Changes in a firm's share price may be positive or negative depending upon the opinion of investors. The argument is that such specific variations occur randomly, and therefore if a sufficiently large and well-diversified PORTFOLIO of shares is held, such variations will cancel each other out. This means that investors can eliminate specific risk by diversifying their portfolio.

**specific tax** a TAX which is levied at a fixed rate per physical unit of output. Compare AD VALOREM TAX.

**speculation** the buying and selling of COMMODITIES (tea, tin etc.), FINANCIAL SECURITIES (shares etc.) and FOREIGN CURRENCIES whose market prices are characterized by substantial fluctuations over time, by individuals and firms (speculators) in the hope of making windfall profits. For example, in the STOCK MARKET and FOREIGN EXCHANGE MARKET, a speculator may take a 'bullish' view that a share price or the exchange rate of a currency will rise and may gamble on this possibility by buying that share or currency, using either his or her own money or short-term credits, and hoping to resell it at a higher price after a few days or weeks, in order to make a capital gain on the difference between the two prices. On the other hand, the speculator may take a 'bearish' view that a share price or currency value will fall and may gamble on this possibility by selling the share or currency (even though he or she does not currently own any), using the proceeds from this sale to buy at a lower price the shares or currency he or she has promised to deliver a week or two later.

Speculative activity may have a destabilizing effect on share prices or exchange rates if speculators take a collective view that prices will rise or fall, accelerating and magnifying upward or downward price movements. Because of the disruptive effects of speculation on international trade, countries' central banks often intervene in the foreign exchange markets to maintain 'orderly' exchange rates.

See ARBITRAGE, FORWARD MARKET, FLOATING EXCHANGE RATE SYSTEM, STAG, ACCOUNT PERIOD.

**speculator** see SPECULATION.

**split-shift working** see SHIFT WORK.

**spot market** a market which provides for the buying and selling of FINANCIAL SECURITIES (shares, stocks), FOREIGN CURRENCIES, and COMMODITIES (rubber, tin etc.) for immediate delivery, as opposed to a FORWARD MARKET which provides for delivery at some future point in time. Spot prices reflect current demand and supply conditions for the financial security, currency or commodity being traded. Spot prices for commodities and financial assets transacted at different locations are harmonized by ARBITRAGE dealings. See FOREIGN EXCHANGE MARKET, COMMODITY MARKET, STOCK MARKET.

**spread** the difference between the bid (buy) and offer (sell) price of a FINANCIAL SECURITY, FOREIGN CURRENCY or COMMODITY quoted by a MARKET MAKER or dealer. See BID PRICE.

**spreadsheet** a COMPUTER software program package which enables data to be analysed in columns and rows. Spreadsheets are widely used for financial analysis.

**SRO** see SELF-REGULATORY ORGANIZATION.

**SSAP** see STATEMENTS OF RECOMMENDED PRACTICE.

**stability index** see LABOUR TURNOVER.

**staff** see LINE AND STAFF.

**staff association** an association of employees of an organization formed (often by management) to pursue issues of common interest, such as the provision of recreational facilities at work. Such associations are rarely given the right to negotiate over WAGE RATES and conditions of employment. See COMPANY UNION, TRADE UNION.

**staff status** the status held by those individuals (usually 'white-collar' WORKERS) whose conditions of employment, including hours of work, holiday and pension entitlements are generally more favourable than those possessed by manual workers in an organization. It is also common for those enjoying staff status to have separate canteen arrangements. Many believe that these differences foster a 'them and us' attitude at work, and some organizations have attempted to overcome this by a process of harmonization – bringing the conditions of employment of all or most employees into line (usually towards the more favourable ones of those with staff status). See JAPANIZATION.

**stag** a person who subscribes for a new SHARE ISSUE by applying for a large number of shares in the hope that the demand for new shares exceeds the number being issued and that this will lead to an increase in the share price when they are first transacted on the STOCK MARKET. Stags are speculators who buy shares to make a quick profit rather than as long-term investors.

**stakeholder** someone having an interest or stake in the operations and performance of a firm. *Shareholders* in a company have an interest in so far as they have invested money in the company and look for a return on that investment in the form of dividends and share appreciation. *Employees* have a stake since they work in the firm and are dependent on the firm for their jobs and incomes. *Customers* have a stake since they buy products from the firm and require a stable supply of products that are safe, effective and affordable. *Suppliers* have a stake as providers of raw materials and services. Finally the broader *community* has a stake in the firm and looks to the firm to behave as a 'good citizen' who will avoid polluting the environment and will help in solving community problems such as inner city decay etc.

Until recent years managers were expected to run companies largely in the interests of shareholders; however in recent years firms have been urged to adopt broader responsibilities to *all* stakeholders.

See SOCIAL RESPONSIBILITY.

**stamp duty** a UK TAX on the value of SHARES purchased on the STOCK MARKET.

**standard cost** an estimated product cost, prepared in advance of production, that shows what a product ought to cost given reasonably efficient working. Standard cost includes the direct materials cost of the product, direct labour cost and production overheads, as well as distribution, selling and administration overheads. Overheads are charged to products using an appropriate COST RATE derived by dividing budgeted overheads by budgeted output. Fig. 81 shows a simplified standard cost for a product. Such predetermined standard costs are used to provide a basis for price fixing and for cost control through VARIANCE ANALYSIS. See also DIRECT-LABOUR COST VARIANCE, DIRECT-MATERIALS COST VARIANCE, OVERHEAD-COST VARIANCE.

**standard deviation** a measure of variation within a group of numerical observations, i.e. the square root of the average of the squared deviations of the observations from the group AVERAGE. Squaring the deviations eliminates negative signs and concentrates attention on the magnitude of the deviations and not their sign. For example, if five products had prices of £5, £4, £3, £2 and £1 then the average price is:

# STANDARD DEVIATION

|  | £ | £ |
|---|---|---|
| STANDARD DIRECT MATERIALS COST: | | |

| | | | £ | £ |
|---|---|---|---|---|
| STANDARD DIRECT MATERIALS COST: | | | | |
| Frame Wood | 5m at £4 per m | 20.00 | | |
| Spring Unit | one at £10 each | 10.00 | | |
| Upholstery | 3m² at £10 per m² | 30.00 | 60.00 | |
| STANDARD DIRECT LABOUR COST: | | | | |
| Assembling | 2hrs at £5 per hr | 10.00 | | |
| Upholstering | 1hr at £10 per hr | 10.00 | 20.00 | |
| STANDARD PRIME COST | | | 80.00 | |
| PRODUCTION OVERHEADS (£10 per unit)* | | | 10.00 | |
| STANDARD FACTORY COST | | | 90.00 | |
| SELLING, DISTRIBUTION, ADMINISTRATION OVERHEADS (30%)** | | | 27.00 | |
| STANDARD TOTAL COST | | | 117.00 | |

\* PRODUCTION OVERHEAD COST RATE:

$$\frac{\text{budgeted production overheads}}{\text{budgeted output}} = \frac{£20,000}{2,000 \text{ units}} = £10 \text{ per unit}$$

\*\* SELLING etc. OVERHEADS COST RATE:

$$\frac{\text{budgeted selling, distribution and administration overheads}}{\text{standard factory cost of total output}}$$

$$= \frac{£30,000}{£100,000} = 30\% \text{ on factory cost}$$

Fig. 81. **Standard cost.** Table showing the standard cost of an upholstered chair.

$$£\frac{5 + 4 + 3 + 2 + 1}{5} = £\frac{15}{5} = £3$$

and the extent by which the various prices depart from the average price is:

| | | | | | |
|---|---|---|---|---|---|
| £5 − 3 = | £2 | squared deviations | 2 | × 2 = | 4 |
| £4 − 3 = | £1 | | 1 | × 1 = | 1 |
| £3 − 3 = | £0 | | 0 | × 0 = | 0 |
| £2 − 3 = | −£1 | | −1 | × −1 = | 1 |
| £1 − 3 = | −£2 | | −2 | × −2 = | 4 |
| | £0 | | | | £10 |

The sum of the squared deviations in the example above is

£10 and their average is £10/5 = £2. This figure represents the variance of the group of observations. In order to compensate for squaring the deviations, the square root of the average is taken, so that in the example above the standard deviation would be $\sqrt{2}$ = £1.41.

Compare AVERAGE DEVIATION.

**Standard Industrial Classification (SIC)** a system which codifies and measures groups of economic activity at various levels of aggregation and disaggregation. In the UK, the Standard Industrial Classification comprises 10 major divisions, 60 classes, 222 groups and 334 activities. Activities, or their equivalent 'industries' (see INDUSTRY), are derived on the basis of their *supply* characteristics, in particular the use of common raw materials and processes of manufacture. Such a classification provides a useful source of information on industry structure and statistical details of employment, output and investment by the industrial sector. However, for purposes of MARKETING strategy, SIC data usually needs to be reinterpreted in order to provide more meaningful specifications of MARKETS, defined in terms of groups of products which are regarded by *buyers* as close substitute products. To illustrate, glass jars and metal cans are assigned to different industries by the SIC (Division 2, Activity 'glass containers', Division 3 'packaging products of metal', respectively), but would be regarded by a user of packaging materials such as a coffee manufacturer as substitute products. See STRUCTURE OF INDUSTRY.

**standardization 1.** the limitation of a firm's product and component range as a means of controlling production and marketing costs. By limiting the PRODUCT RANGE a firm can mass-produce each product and achieve ECONOMIES OF SCALE through long production runs, but forgoes potential sales by serving only a limited number of market segments. However it may be possible to cut production costs while maintaining product VARIETY through standardization and interchangeability of components. Standardization serves to reduce the variety of finished product stocks or materials and component stocks held, simplifying purchasing and STOCK CONTROL. Compare CUSTOMIZATION.

**2.** see ORGANIZATION.

**standard of living** the general level of economic prosperity in an economy as measured by, for example, the level of per capita income (GROSS NATIONAL PRODUCT divided by the size of the POPULATION). A country's standard of living will depend on such things as its level of economic maturity, investment and productivity and the provision by the government of various social welfare programmes. Advanced industrial countries like Japan (income per head $28,190 in 1992) and the UK (income per head $17,790 in 1992) are much more prosperous than developing countries such as the Upper Volta, Chad etc. (whose levels of income per head are less than $500). See DISTRIBUTION OF INCOME.

**standard rate** the average work rate at which an operative possessing the appropriate skill level and motivation performs a work task. For example, if the 'observed time' for an operative performing a task was 5 minutes and the operative was judged to be working at a faster work pace than the standard rate, say twice as fast, then the observed time would need to be lengthened to 10 minutes in calculating the 'basic time' which an operative working at standard rate would take to perform the task. See WORK MEASUREMENT.

**standard time** the time that it should take a motivated operative with the appropriate level of skill to complete a work task, including an ALLOWANCE for relaxation, machine breakdown and interruptions. See WORK MEASUREMENT.

**standing order** see COMMERCIAL BANK.

**statement of account** a periodic statement sent to a customer by a supplier that sets out both the money value of products supplied to the customer over a monthly or other period, and any amounts still owed by the customer for these products. A statement of account is sent by a supplier some time after an INVOICE has been sent. Compare DELIVERY NOTE.

**statements of recommended practice (SORP)** guideline documents on aspects of the accounting treatment of company finances produced jointly by the main UK professional bodies through the Accounting Standards Board. The issuing of accounting statements is usually preceded by widespread consultation, including the publication of *financial reporting exposure drafts*, before an accounting statement is finalized. Financial Reporting Statements (FRSs) superceded 'Statements of Standard Accounting Practice' (SSAPs), over 20 of which were issued covering such areas as accounting for goodwill. National FRSs are drawn up within the framework of International Accounting Standards. See HARMONIZATION OF ACCOUNTS.

**statistical inference** a process by which we infer conclusions about a statistical POPULATION from which only a SAMPLE has been drawn. For example, if one million Britons buy bicycles each year, and 200 are asked why they do so, 50% may say because it helps to keep them fit. From this sample one may infer that 50% of the total population of one million Britons buying bicycles do so for this reason. However, it is not possible to say with 100% accuracy that this is the case unless the views of all one million were obtained. Nevertheless, it is possible to say with reasonable confidence that the estimation of 50% is correct for the whole population.

**statistical quality control** an aspect of QUALITY CONTROL which involves inspecting and testing a sample of a raw material, component or product in order to make inferences about the quality of all the output of that material, component or product. Where inspection and testing involves destruction of the product, statistical quality control based on sampling is the only means of monitoring quality.

**statistics 1.** methods of collecting and analysing numerical data.

**2.** a group of data.

Businesspeople make considerable use of statistical methods such as collecting SAMPLES in order to make STATISTICAL INFERENCES in such areas as MARKETING RESEARCH and QUALITY CONTROL. They also use government economic data in monitoring changes in the business environment.

**status** see BUYER BEHAVIOUR, PSYCHOLOGICAL PRICING.

**statute law** the law laid down by government legislation (in the UK, an Act of Parliament). Examples include the FAIR TRADING ACT 1973 and the Companies Act 1989. Once such legislation is on the statute books, it is then up to the courts to interpret and enforce the provisions of this legislation. Compare COMMON LAW. See COMPANY LAW, LABOUR LAW.

**statutory ESOP** see EMPLOYEE SHARE OWNERSHIP PLAN.

**statutory formats** the formats in which the final accounts of companies (PROFIT AND LOSS ACCOUNT and BALANCE SHEET) have to be reported, which in the UK is governed by company law.

**statutory sick pay** see SICK PAY.

**sterling** the name given to the UK POUND when used in international dealings, primarily to distinguish it from other countries also using the pound as a domestic currency. Formerly, large amounts of sterling were held by members of the British Commonwealth (the so-called 'sterling area bloc') and others, as part of their INTERNATIONAL RESERVES.

**stimuli** the various components, verbal, written or visual, of an ADVERTISEMENT for a product which are designed to encourage consumers to buy the product. See ADVERTISING COPY.

**stock 1.** the part of a firm's ASSETS that are held in the form of raw materials, work in progress and finished goods. These are also known as INVENTORIES. Finished goods are held in stock to ensure that goods are available when required by customers. Raw materials and components are held in stock to prevent disruptions to production caused by lack of materials or components and to secure economies from BULK BUYING. Decisions as to what *level* of stock to hold may not be entirely in the businessman's hands. Involuntary investment may occur when demand turns out to be less than a producer's expectations. Fig. 82 shows the main components of stock. See STOCK VALUATION, STOCK CONTROL.

**2.** a FINANCIAL SECURITY issued by a JOINT-STOCK COMPANY or by the government as a means of raising long-term capital. In some countries (for example the US) stockholders are the equivalent of shareholders and are the owners of the company. In other countries (for example the UK) stock is a form of repayable, fixed-interest DEBT and stockholders are creditors of the company not shareholders. Stocks are traded on the STOCK MARKET. See SHARE CAPITAL.

**stock appreciation** the increase in the market value of STOCK held during a specific time period, generally because of INFLATION. Accountants value stock at the lower of either cost or net realizable value in the BALANCE SHEET, not at replacement cost, and when stock is sold, tax is paid on the profits arising. This gives rise to 'phantom profits' and is one reason why British firms were given stock relief in taxation calculations during the inflationary period of the 1970s. Where prices are falling, *stock depreciation* results. See also HISTORIC COST, INFLATION ACCOUNTING, STOCK VALUATION.

**stockbroker** a business which acts as a market intermediary in bringing together buyers and sellers of financial securities such

Fig. 82.. Stock. Diagram showing the main components.

Raw Materials Purchased

bin cards

Materials Requisitions

Raw Materials Issued

RAW MATERIALS STOCK

Raw Materials Store

job cards, time sheets

Finished Goods Completed

WORK IN PROGRESS STOCK

Factory

Finished Goods Sold

FINISHED GOODS STOCK

Finished Goods Warehouse

# STOCKBROKING

as STOCK, SHARES and BONDS.

See STOCK MARKET, AGENT, TRADER/DEALER, STOCKBROKING.

**stockbroking** the function of buying and selling FINANCIAL SECURITIES such as STOCKS, SHARES and BONDS through the STOCK MARKET by a dealer (*stockbroker*) who acts as an agent on behalf of clients wishing to buy or sell securities. In the UK, some dealers act solely as stockbrokers, but others combine stockbroking with JOBBING and act also as principals in 'making a market' in securities. See MARKET MAKER, SHARE PURCHASE/SALE, DUAL CAPACITY.

**stock control** the process of controlling STOCKS of finished products, work in progress and raw materials, in order to minimize warehousing and other stockholding costs, while maintaining an adequate level of stock to meet usage requirements.

The object of a stock–control procedure is to maintain records of existing stock levels, compare these with planned stock levels and place orders for new stock to make good the difference between the two. Replenishment of stock is achieved by placing outside orders for purchased raw materials or components, or by initiating further production for finished goods or components.

Fig. 83. **Stock control.** A simple stock-holding system.

Fig. 83 illustrates the general principle by depicting a simple stockholding problem where usage of stock is known in advance, rate of usage is constant and where stocks can be replenished completely once they run out. Once the firm is out of stock then it will immediately order and bring into stock fresh items to build its stock up to the maximum level M. After this the stock level will again fall as items are used. The average stock level A will depend upon the size of the orders placed and how frequently they are placed, with large orders placed at infrequent intervals necessitating high average stocks. In placing orders the firm may establish a stock *reorder level* R, placing orders for new stocks when stocks fall to the reorder level. The stock reorder level will be set to take into account usage of the stock item during the reorder period or *lead time* between placing a new order and delivery of the replacement items into stock. Operating on this principle the firm would replenish stock at order intervals between reorder points $T_1$, $T_2$ and $T_3$. The *minimum stock level*, S, is the smallest stock level which the firm is prepared to tolerate immediately prior to replenishment. This minimum stock level is usually greater than zero because the firm will wish to hold a certain amount of *safety stock* or *buffer stock* to meet unexpectedly rapid usage or delays in delivery which extend the lead time. Without a safety stock, usage and lead time variability could lead to costly 'stockouts' with disruptions to production or delivery delays to customers. The size of safety stock carried will seek to balance the extra stockholding costs such as warehousing costs and interest charges associated with safety stocks on the one hand, and the cost of stockouts on the other hand. Since the precise cost of stockouts is difficult to determine the firm may start by deciding the 'service level' or number of stockouts per period considered acceptable, then estimate the safety stock necessary to ensure this level of service.

The stock-control system depicted here is known as the reorder level system. One specific version of the reorder level system is the *two-bin* system which is frequently used where large quantities of inexpensive items are concerned, the stock being held in two bins or containers. Stock is drawn from one bin only until it is empty, at which stage a further full bin of items is ordered. Whilst this is being obtained, stock is drawn from the second bin. This is a simple and effective system which requires the minimum of clerical work and administration, since the physical division of stock into two areas (bins) makes the order decision almost automatic. The same result can be achieved by marking the reorder level on a single bin.

## STOCK DEPRECIATION

*Sealed minimum stock* systems operate along similar lines, where the reorder stock level is sealed in a bag and orders are placed when 'open' stock is exhausted and the bag must be opened.

Finally, *base stock* systems make provision to place a replenishment order every time a withdrawal is made from stock, ordering an amount which exactly replaces the amount withdrawn so as always to maintain a given level of base stock. Operation of reorder level systems requires the firm to maintain *perpetual stock* records, that is, up-to-date daily records of the stock situation of all items.

As an alternative to reorder level systems, firms may operate *reorder point* systems, placing orders for variable amounts of an item at fixed time intervals. With such reorder point or periodic review systems the stock of each item is checked at preplanned intervals and orders of varying size placed to replenish stocks. Such replenishment at fixed time intervals is administratively cheaper, allows orders for several items from a common supplier to be combined, and requires stocks to be checked only at the order point avoiding the expense of daily stock checks. One specific version of the reorder point system is the *single-bin* system where the desired maximum stock is marked on the side of a single bin and orders are placed for an amount to replenish the contents of the bin up to that mark at regular intervals.

See STOCKHOLDING MODEL, MATERIALS MANAGEMENT, MATERIALS REQUIREMENTS PLANNING, JUST-IN-TIME, STOCK–TURNOVER RATIO.

**stock depreciation** see STOCK APPRECIATION.

**stock dividend** a DIVIDEND payment whereby a SHAREHOLDER is paid a dividend in the form of additional SHARES or STOCKS in the company rather than in the form of cash. See also STOCK SPLITS.

**stock exchange** a MARKET which deals in the buying and selling of company stocks and shares and government bonds. See STOCK MARKET.

**Stock Exchange Automated Quotation System (SEAQ)** see STOCK MARKET.

**Stock Exchange Pool Nominees** see SEPON.

**stockholding model** or **economic order quantity model** a method used in STOCK CONTROL of raw materials, components or finished goods which seeks to balance stockholding costs and delivery costs for a STOCK item in order to determine the optimum order quantity for that item.

The principal objective of stock–control procedures is to maintain stocks at the lowest total cost consistent with satisfying demand. This involves balancing two sets of cost:

Fig. 84. **Stockholding model.** Stockholding cost.

(a) *stockholding costs*: the cost to firms of holding stocks of finished products and raw materials in order to provide immediate customer service or to prevent disruptions to production caused by lack of materials. Stockholding costs include costs of warehouse space, insurance, deterioration and obsolescence of stored items and interest on capital tied up in stocks. Such costs are roughly proportional to the value of the stock held, and to contain such costs, stock levels need to be kept low;

(b) *order costs*: costs for ordering and delivering goods for stock such as communicating with suppliers or the firm's own production department, accounting transactions, transport and unloading and inspecting goods. Many of these ordering and delivery costs will remain the same irrespective of the size of the order. Since many order and delivery costs are fixed costs, in order to reduce these costs the firm should place large orders at infrequent intervals, and such a policy would have the additional benefit of allowing the firm to earn price discounts for BULK BUYING. However if orders are placed at infrequent intervals then stocks, and thus stockholding costs, will be high. It is desirable to strike a balance between these two groups of costs so as to achieve the minimum stock cost, as in Fig. 84 which shows the *optimum order quantity* or *economic order quantity* which serves to minimize total stock cost. Order and delivery costs decrease as larger and less frequent deliveries are made; however, larger deliveries at less frequent intervals involve holding a larger average stock and thus entail higher carrying costs. The optimum order quantity OB corresponds to the minimum point on the total stock-cost curve.

See BATCH SIZE.

**stockist** a WHOLESALER or RETAILER who holds STOCKS of products, components and replacement parts for a particular manufacturer.

**stock market** or **capital market** a MARKET which deals in the buying and selling of company STOCKS and SHARES and government BONDS. The stock market, together with the MONEY MARKET (which deals in short-term company and government securities), are the main sources of external capital to industry and the government.

Institutions that are involved in the UK Stock Market include MARKET MAKERS (who perform JOBBING and STOCKBROKING functions), specialist stockbrokers, ISSUING HOUSES, MERCHANT BANKS, and, as general buyers and sellers of securities, the CENTRAL BANK, COMMERCIAL BANKS, PENSION FUNDS, INSURANCE COMPANIES, UNIT TRUSTS and INVESTMENT TRUST COMPANIES, together with private individuals, industrial companies and overseas investors and institutions.

The stock market performs two principal functions. It provides:

(a) a *primary* or 'new issue' market where capital for investment and other purposes can be raised by the issue of new stocks, shares and bonds (see SHARE ISSUE);

(b) a *secondary* market for dealings in existing securities, including forward dealings (see FORWARD MARKET), which facilitates the easy transferability of securities from sellers to buyers (see SHARE PURCHASE/SALE). The stock market thus occupies an important position in a country's FINANCIAL SYSTEM.

In the UK, the London stock exchange is the country's main centre for dealings in securities, supported by five provincial exchanges (Glasgow, Liverpool, Birmingham, York and Belfast).

In order to obtain a full listing or quotation on the London stock exchange for their shares, companies must satisfy various requirements, including proof of their financial standing and previous business history, and be prepared to issue at least 25% of their shares to the investing public. Additionally, smaller companies can raise capital without obtaining a full listing through the Alternative Investment Market (see UN-LISTED SECURITIES MARKET).

In recent years, stock markets worldwide, such as those based in London, New York, Tokyo, Zurich and Paris, have become increasingly interdependent with the growth of MULTI-NATIONAL ENTERPRISES whose securities are traded on a number of exchanges while financial institutions and securities firms themselves have become more internationally based. This has led to an increase in competitive pressures, which has brought about a number of important changes, particularly in the case of the UK stock market, including:

(a) the so-called *big bang* – the termination (under the prodding of the OFFICE OF FAIR TRADING) of the CARTEL arrangements for fixing minimum commissions on securities transactions and the ending of the traditional division between the stockbroking and jobbing functions;

(b) various *mergers* and joint ventures between UK securities firms and international securities and banking groups, so as to provide clients with a more diversified range of financial services and geographical spread;

(c) the *computerization* of dealing systems, using the *Stock Exchange Automated Quotation System* (SEAQ) which provides a mechanism for linking buying and selling transactions on a global basis. This has largely transferred day-to-day business from a physical presence on the stock exchange floor to telephone exchanges and the use of VDU computer terminals in dealing rooms.

In recognition of the growth in international dealings, the London stock exchange merged with the International Securities Regulatory Organization (ISRO) which represents the big international securities firms. The London stock exchange and ISRO now operate a single market for dealings in domestic and foreign securities: The 'London International Stock Exchange'.

## STOCKOUT

On the UK stock market, transactions (transfers and settlements) are processed by the TALISMAN and CREST systems using a *rolling settlement* procedure which has replaced the traditional ACCOUNT PERIOD arrangement. The UK stock market is a *Recognized Investment Exchange*, and operates under the regulatory framework laid down by the FINANCIAL SERVICES ACT 1986.

See SHARE PRICE INDEX, CITY CODE ON TAKEOVERS AND MERGERS, INSIDER DEALING, SPECULATION, DUAL CAPACITY, SINGLE CAPACITY, TRADEPOINT.

**stockout** see STOCK CONTROL.

**stockpiling** the holding of levels of STOCK which are greater than would be normally required by a person, firm or government agency. Stockpiling usually occurs at times of an actual or expected shortage of a product or in anticipation of a price rise.

**stock split** see SHARE SPLIT.

**stocktaking** the process of checking physical STOCKS of raw materials, components or finished goods against STORES records of materials quantities on BIN CARDS.

**stockturn** see STOCK TURNOVER RATIO.

**stock-turnover ratio** a measure of a firm's stockholdings that expresses the firm's SALES REVENUE as a ratio of its period-end STOCK, to show how many times stocks are turned over in sales during a period's trading. See also STOCK CONTROL, STOCKHOLDING MODEL.

**stock valuation** the placing of an appropriate money value upon a firm's STOCKS of raw materials, WORK IN PROGRESS and finished GOODS. Where INFLATION causes the price of several different batches of finished-goods stock bought during a trading period to differ, the firm has the problems of deciding (a) what money value to place upon the period-end physical stock in the BALANCE SHEET; (b) what cost to attach to the units sold in the PROFIT-AND-LOSS ACCOUNT. The second decision has a direct bearing upon the COST-OF-GOODS SOLD and so upon GROSS PROFIT.

Different formulas used to value stock can lead to variations in the balance-sheet value of stock and in the cost of goods sold. For example, the *first-in, first-out (FIFO)* method assumes that goods are withdrawn from stock in the order in which they are received so that the cost of goods sold is based on the cost of the oldest goods in stock, while the value of closing stock is based on the prices of the most recent purchases (see Fig. 85). By contrast, the *last-in, first-out (LIFO)* method assumes that the most recently purchased goods are (theoretically) withdrawn from stock first so that the cost of goods sold is based on the costs of the most recent purchases, while the value of closing stock is based on the oldest goods available (see Fig. 85). The last-in, first-out method gives a higher figure for cost-of-goods sold, i.e. one which more closely approximates to the replacement cost of goods sold, but it tends to understate the value of period-end stocks.

In the interests of prudence the firm would tend to value stocks at cost or market value, whichever was the lower, to avoid overstating profits. Generally stocks of work in progress and finished goods will include the raw materials, direct labour and OVERHEAD costs involved in manufacturing them.

See also STOCK APPRECIATION, INFLATION ACCOUNTING.

| FIFO | | LIFO | |
|---|---|---|---|
| sales (100 × £15) | £1,500 | sales (100 × £15) | £1,500 |
| cost of goods sold: | | cost of goods sold: | |
| 20 × £10 = £200 | | 100 × £12 | £1,200 |
| 80 × £12 = £960 | £1,160 | | |
| 100 | | | |
| profit | £340 | | £300 |
| closing stock (20 × £12) | £240 | closing stock (20 × £10) | £200 |

Fig. 85. **Stock valuation.** Two methods. The opening stock is 20 units, costing £10 each; the purchases are 100 units at £12 each; the sales are 100 units at £15 each; the closing stock is 20 units.

**storage cost** see HOLDING COST.

**store 1.** a secure area for the storage of raw materials or components not required immediately for production, or of finished goods not required immediately for despatch to customers.

Storekeeping procedures involve checking deliveries of materials or components against orders and receiving them into stores for safekeeping against damage or theft. Thereafter materials or components are issued to production departments in quantities authorized by MATERIALS REQUISITIONS, and appropriate entries made on BIN CARDS to maintain up-to-date records of stock in hand. Period STOCK CONTROL checks serve to ensure that stocks recorded agree with physical stocks held. When stocks fall to reorder levels new orders are placed for materials, to avoid production holdups. Accurate and systematic storekeeping procedures are needed if the raw materials and component cost of products is to be accurately ascertained.

Similar stores control procedures operate in the finished goods store to ensure that stocks are available to fulfil sales orders.

2. an alternative term for a SHOP.

**store of value** see MONEY.

**stores issue note** see MATERIALS REQUISITION.

**stores record card** or **bin card** a paper or computer record which is kept for each STOCK item held by a firm showing the balance in hand, details of stock received and issued, stock reserved to meet current production orders and the residual balance which is free for future use.

The information contained in stores record cards, when supplemented by data on the prices of stock items, forms the basis for stores ledger records.

**straight line depreciation** see DEPRECIATION.

**strategic alliance** the combining together of the resources and competencies of two or more firms in a particular activity (but who continue to function separately in all other respects). Strategic alliances can be contractually based or ownership based (with each partner putting equity into the business) and can take a number of formats, for example, co-marketing (with one firm undertaking to market the product supplied by the other firm); co-production (with one firm undertaking to manufacture a product using components supplied by the other firm); and joint research and development (cross fertilization of ideas).

Strategic alliances are often particularly effective in exploiting complementary resources and skills thereby enabling firms to supply products in a more cost-effective way and in increasing market penetration. See JOINT VENTURE, FOREIGN MARKET SERVICING STRATEGY.

**strategic analysis** see SWOT.

**strategic business unit (SBU)** a division of a multi-product firm which represents a discrete area of business. Each SBU is responsible for a group of interrelated products serving a core MARKET; for example, within Unilever margarines and fats represent one SBU while soap powders and detergents represent another. SBUs generally operate autonomously within the firm with their own chief executive, production and marketing staff etc., but are usually subject to overall control by the firm's main board of directors in such matters as capital investment.

SBUs are an attempt to decentralize responsibility for profit generation. It is believed that this will increase motivation and improve individual performance, thereby improving overall organizational performance and the achievement of strategic goals.

See PRODUCT-BASED STRUCTURE.

**strategic choice** see CONTINGENCY THEORY.

**strategic direction** deciding, as part of a firm's overall BUSINESS STRATEGY, which business activities the firm should operate in, and where. For example, the firm may decide to specialize in one particular activity (see HORIZONTAL EXPANSION) or it may decide to deepen its involvement in an industry by undertaking VERTICAL INTEGRATION; or it may wish to broaden the scope of its activities by DIVERSIFICATION into new product areas. The geographical markets in which the firm operates also require consideration. Some firms, for example, may choose to operate on a purely local/regional basis, some may establish themselves as national suppliers or as MULTINATIONAL ENTERPRISES supplying markets on a global basis. See PRODUCT-MARKET MATRIX, DIRECTIONAL MATRIX.

**strategic fit** the extent to which a new business activity undertaken by a conglomerate firm is compatible with its existing activities. In some cases, the new activity may be closely related to the firm's existing activities, thus providing scope for achieving SYNERGY gains across these activities. See DIVERSIFICATION.

**strategic group** a group of firms within a MARKET or INDUSTRY which each pursue broadly similar policies in respect of product and market coverage, pricing, vertical integration etc. Thus, an industry may comprise a number of distinct groups of firms depending upon differences in their business strategies: for example, one strategic group in an industry might consist of suppliers who offer a full product range from basic to luxury items and sell nationally; other suppliers in the same industry might concentrate solely on luxury items and sell in a limited number of local markets. See MOBILITY BARRIER.

Strategic-group analysis is used by corporate planners as a means of positioning and repositioning a firm in a market, so as to establish COMPETITIVE ADVANTAGES over rival suppliers as well as to identify possible gaps in the market which might be exploited.

See BUSINESS STRATEGY, COMPETITIVE STRATEGY.

**strategic management** see BUSINESS STRATEGY.

**strategic withdrawal** a repositioning of a firm's marketing effort involving its withdrawal from particular MARKET SEGMENTS in order to concentrate its efforts in market segments where its competitive position is stronger.

**strategy** a unified set of plans and actions designed to secure the achievement of the basic objectives of a business or of some other organization. BUSINESS OBJECTIVES represent the goals of the organization, i.e. the economic (and social) *purposes* for which the business exists; strategy is the *means* used to attain these goals. See BUSINESS STRATEGY, MARKETING STRATEGY, FOREIGN MARKET SERVICING STRATEGY.

**strengths and weaknesses** see SWOT ANALYSIS.

**strike** a stoppage of work by a group of workers as part of an INDUSTRIAL DISPUTE with the aim of bringing pressure to bear on the employer. In the UK most strikes arise out of disputes over pay and conditions of employment. In the UK strike activity is normally measured in three ways: the number of stoppages, the number of workers involved, and the number of working days lost per 1000 employees. Of these the best indicator of 'strike proneness' (i.e. how likely workers are to take industrial action) is the number of working days lost per 1000 employees, because it captures more of the intensity and extent of stoppages than the other indices. The UK is often said to be especially strike prone. However, international comparisons show the UK to be in a middling position.

However, patterns of strike activity have changed over time. In the 1960s the UK experienced a large number of short-lived strikes, often involving small numbers of workers. Often these were unofficial (or 'wildcat' in American parlance): they were unauthorized and unsanctioned by TRADE UNIONS, and occurred spontaneously in response to pressing grievances. In the 1970s the problem of unofficial strikes was lessened to some extent by the reform of INDUSTRIAL RELATIONS that took place in many organizations. The proportion of very short strikes declined during this decade. In the 1980s the number of strikes fell sharply, owing partly to the harsh economic climate in the early 1980s and partly, it is thought, to the government's programme of LABOUR LAW. (See EMPLOY-MENT ACT 1980, EMPLOYMENT ACT 1982, EMPLOYMENT ACT 1988, TRADE UNION ACT 1984.) However, major protracted strikes occurred in the public sector throughout the decade, in response to management plans to reform working practices and to financial restrictions imposed by government.

Strikes are generally both a protest and an attempt to improve pay and conditions. Their effectiveness is premised on the costs of a loss of output and the damage of relationships with suppliers, customers and employees that a stoppage of work can result in. However, strikes are costly to employees too since they usually suffer a loss of earnings for the duration of the stoppage. Employees therefore often take alternative forms of INDUSTRIAL ACTION, such as overtime bans, which are considerably cheaper. See TRADE UNION REFORM AND EMPLOY-MENT RIGHTS ACT 1993.

**strike ballots** see STRIKE, TRADE UNION ACT 1984, TRADE UNION RE-FORM AND EMPLOYMENT RIGHTS ACT 1993.

**structural unemployment** see UNEMPLOYMENT, STRUCTURE OF INDUSTRY.

**structure** the pattern of roles and relationships in a GROUP or ORGANIZATION. See also BUREAUCRACY and ORGANIZATION CHART.

**structure of industry** the productive activities of an ECONOMY classified according to broad groupings of activities by sector, or on an individual INDUSTRY basis (see STANDARD INDUSTRIAL CLASSIFICATION).

The three basic sectors of the economy are the *primary* sector (agriculture, minerals etc.), the *industrial* sector (manufacturing, construction, electricity etc.) and the *service* sector (banking, retailing etc.). The relative importance of these sectors tends to change as an economy matures: less developed countries are characterized by large primary sectors, whereas developed countries are characterized by large industrial and service sectors.

In the advanced countries, as Fig. 86 shows, there has been a relative decline in the industrial sector and a corresponding increase in the importance of the service sector. In the main this reflects a change in the pattern of final *demand* for goods and services over time, favouring services, and as such may be considered a natural development associated with a maturing economy. Despite this general tendency, *deindustrialization*, however, has aroused particular concern in the UK because it has been accompanied by slow growth in total output in the economy, high unemployment and balance of payments difficulties (i.e. the service sector has not been able to absorb all the slack created by industrial decline). The fact that deindustrialization has been more severe in the UK than elsewhere has been put down to mainly *supply-side* deficiencies: a low level of investment, higher supply costs and prices and lack of product sophistication and innovation has put the UK at a competitive disadvantage in INTERNATIONAL TRADE, resulting in imports taking up a rising share of the UK domestic market. See IMPORT PENETRATION.

| | Primary Sector | | Industrial Sector | | Service Sector | |
|---|---|---|---|---|---|---|
| | 1960 % | 1996 % | 1960 % | 1996 % | 1960 % | 1996 % |
| UK | 3 | 2 | 43 | 32 | 54 | 66 |
| USA | 4 | 2 | 38 | 26 | 58 | 72 |
| Japan | 13 | 2 | 45 | 38 | 42 | 60 |
| Germany | 6 | 2 | 53 | 37 | 41 | 61 |

Fig. 86. **Structure of Industry**. Distribution of gross domestic product, 1960 and 1996.

(Source: World Development Report, World Bank, 1997.)

**subcontractor** see CONTRACTOR.

**subcultures** see CULTURAL VALUES.

**subsidiarity** a principle enshrined in the MAASTRICHT TREATY which affirms that, wherever possible, decision-making in the EUROPEAN UNION (EU) should be 'taken as close as possible to the citizens' affected. This implies that matters affecting *all* member countries need to be resolved at an EU-wide level whereas matters affecting only an individual member country are best left to the member concerned. For example, under the EU's Merger Regulation, mergers between firms located in different countries of the EU may be investigated by the European Commission and vetoed if found to adversely reduce competition in the EU. By contrast, mergers between two firms whose activities are confined to a single member country are left to be investigated (if at all) under the member's own competition laws.

See SOCIAL CHAPTER.

**subsidiary company** a JOINT-STOCK COMPANY that is owned by another company (the HOLDING COMPANY). Specifically, a subsidiary company is one in which the holding company owns between 50% and 100% of the voting shares. The accounting results of subsidiary companies are consolidated (see CONSOLIDATED ACCOUNTS) in the annual accounts of the holding company. A subsidiary company is regarded as different from an ASSOCIATED COMPANY (where the holding company owns between 20% and 50% of its shares) which is less subject to the influence of the holding company and continues to produce its own annual accounts. A subsidiary company may continue to trade under its own name, but it is subject to control by the parent company.

**subsidy** the provision of finance and other resources by the government or a firm to support a business activity or person. Subsidies can be direct (cash grants, interest free LOANS etc.) or indirect (DEPRECIATION write-offs, RENT rebates) and can be used for a variety of purposes. They include:

(a) PRODUCTION subsidies: the subsidization of suppliers by government to encourage them to increase the output of particular products by partially offsetting their production costs or even financing losses. The objective may be to expand production at a low price of some product which is deemed to be 'essential' (for example a particular foodstuff, thereby also subsidizing consumers); or, for example, to assist in the start-up of a new firm (see BUSINESS EXPANSION SCHEME) or industry (see INDUSTRIAL POLICY), and encourage firms to locate in particular areas (see REGIONAL POLICY). Also such subsidies are used to support failing firms and declining industries to facilitate orderly restructuring. See PROTECTIONISM;

(b) EXPORT subsidies: the subsidization by the government of exports in general or of a particular product which is exported, as a means of assisting the country's balance of payments;

(c) EMPLOYMENT subsidies: the subsidization of wages by the government as an incentive to businesses to provide more job opportunities, thereby reducing the level of unemployment in the economy;

(d) INCOME subsidies: the subsidization of persons through government transfer payment systems (for example, social security benefits) in order to allow them to enjoy some minimum standard of living;

(e) *cross-subsidization*: businesses themselves regularly practise internal or cross-subsidization as a means of expanding their activities, for example, using the profits generated by established products to finance NEW-PRODUCT DEVELOPMENT and DIVERSIFICATION into new-product markets.

**suggestion scheme** a facility for employees to submit suggestions for revision of production equipment and working methods which will lead to improvements in efficiency or product quality. Rewards are generally given for those proposals adopted by management, usually in relation to the improvement in performance which is likely to be achieved. Suggestion schemes have been in vogue recently since they are widely seen as a simple, effective and cheap way of promoting employee identification with the company. However, they require careful management to ensure that the pattern of rewards is seen as fair and worthwhile. See EMPLOYEE INVOLVEMENT.

**Sunday Trading Act 1994** see SHOP ACT.

**sunk cost** the cost of durable and specific assets such as plant and machinery which cannot be used for other purposes or easily be resold. Where sunk costs represent a high proportion of a firm's total costs the firm may be 'locked in' to its existing products and markets, the sunk costs forming a BARRIER TO EXIT from the market. Since such specific assets have little alternative use they have no OPPORTUNITY COST and so naturally should not enter into management decision-making. Consequently in MAKE-OR-BUY DECISIONS the firm need not consider the sunk costs involved in making products but only the additional production costs as opposed to buying from outside suppliers.

**supermarket** a RETAILER which typically sells a wide range of products on a self-service basis. Supermarkets may be under single-shop ownership or run as multiple CHAIN-STORE businesses. The bigger supermarket chains are able to achieve significant economies in distribution both on a group basis by being able to obtain favourable price discounts from manufacturers by BULK BUYING, and at the individual store level by the use of capital-intensive methods of retailing (see EPOS). Initially, supermarkets appeared mainly in the grocery trade, but groups there have moved into a variety of non-food lines (hardware, television and radio, paint, etc.). Similar supermarket-type operations have been established for most mass-retailed products.

*Hypermarkets* or *superstores* are an extended form of supermarket, usually located on the outskirts of towns and cities where space is plentiful.

Supermarkets compete mainly by offering consumers highly competitive prices on manufacturers' prepacked branded products. However, as part of their MARKETING-MIX policies, emphasis is also placed on product range (including the provision of fresh foods – bread, cheeses, meat, etc.) and various ancillary facilities – cafeteria or restaurant, petrol station etc. The most significant development, however, has been the introduction of OWN-LABEL BRANDS selling under the retailer's own name in direct competition to manufacturers' brands.

See DISTRIBUTION CHANNEL.

**superstore** a very large RETAILER which is often located on the edge of a large town with extensive parking facilities, selling such products as groceries, furniture and do-it-yourself items.

**supervisor** an employee with RESPONSIBILITY for monitoring the work of others to ensure that they fulfil work targets generally established by middle managers. As such supervisors usually have little AUTHORITY in their own right, they often experience role uncertainty as they are neither 'proper' managers nor fully part of the group they supervise, and can thus be described as 'men (*sic*) in the middle'. With the recent trend towards devolving managerial authority, many organizations have attempted to enlarge the decision-making powers of supervisors. See MANAGEMENT.

**supplier** a producer or distributor of a GOOD or SERVICE. See also INTERNAL SUPPLIER.

**supplier certification** see CERTIFICATION.

**Supplier Trade Procedures Board** see EXPORTING.

**supply curve** see EQUILIBRIUM MARKET PRICE.

**supply-side economics** an area of economics concerned with the efficient and cost-effective supply of resources and products so as to maximize the aggregate output capabilities of the economy. Supply-side economists, in particular, focus attention on: inefficiencies in the labour market which can arise from RESTRICTIVE LABOUR PRACTICES, TAX and SOCIAL SECURITY systems which reduce the incentive to work, and TRADE UNION demands for 'excessive' wages which 'price people out of jobs'; and rigidities in product markets arising from the policies of private and public sector MONOPOLIES and CARTELS.

See ECONOMIC POLICY, COMPETITION POLICY, NATIONALIZATION VERSUS PRIVATIZATION.

**support price** see AGRICULTURAL POLICY.

**survey** a research tool which is used to elicit information about respondents' attitudes, opinions and preferences. In MARKETING RESEARCH, surveys are employed to discover more about potential consumers' views and perceptions of existing and proposed new products, and more specifically about the buying intentions of customers.

Surveys may also be used to discover employees' views on aspects of company policy and to assess employees' MOTIVATION, ORGANIZATIONAL COMMITMENT etc.

See MARKETING INTELLIGENCE.

**survey method** see SALES FORECASTING.

**SVQ** the Scottish equivalent of the NATIONAL VOCATIONAL QUALIFICATION (NVQ) found in England and Wales. See TRAINING.

**swap** the bilateral (and multilateral) exchange of a product, business asset, interest rate on a financial debt, or currency for another product, business asset, interest rate on a financial debt, or currency, respectively;

(a) *product* swaps: individual A offers potatoes to individual B in exchange for a bicycle. See BARTER;

(b) *business asset* swaps: chemical company A offers its ethylene division to chemical company B in exchange for B's paint division. This enables both companies to divest (see DIVESTMENT) parts of their business they no longer wish to retain while simultaneously entering, or strengthening their position in, another product area;

(c) INTEREST-RATE swaps on financial debts: a company that has a *variable-rate* debt, for example, may anticipate that interest rates will rise; another company with *fixed-rate* debt may anticipate that interest rates will fall. It therefore contracts to make variable interest-rate payments to the first company and in exchange is paid interest at a fixed rate. Interest-rate swaps may be undertaken simultaneously on a variety of debt instruments thereby enabling corporate treasurers to lower the company's total interest payments;

(d) *currency* swap: the simultaneous buying and selling of foreign currencies. This can take two main forms: a spot/forward swap (the simultaneous purchase or sale of a currency in the SPOT MARKET coupled with an offsetting sale or purchase of the same currency in the FORWARD MARKET); or a forward/forward swap (a pair of forward currency contracts involving a forward purchase and sale of a particular currency which mature at different future dates).

Currency swaps are used by firms which trade internationally to minimize the risk of losses arising from exchange rate changes (see EXCHANGE RATE EXPOSURE).

**'sweating' assets** the process of increasing the profits generated from a company's ASSETS where the RETURN ON CAPITAL EMPLOYED is inadequate. This could involve increasing selling prices of products; reducing unit production and selling costs; increasing sales volumes using present assets; or reducing the FIXED ASSETS and CURRENT ASSETS employed to achieve the present sales volume. Sweating assets is often a strategy employed after a company has been taken over.

**sweetheart union** see COMPANY UNION.

**SWOT analysis** a framework for identifying the *internal* strengths (S) and weaknesses (W) of a firm, and the *external* opportunities (O) open to it and the threats (T) it faces, which can be used by corporate planners in formulating the firm's COMPETITIVE STRATEGY in individual product markets and its overall BUSINESS STRATEGY.

## SWOT ANALYSIS

The internal appraisal of a firm's strengths and weaknesses involves looking at the firm's current resources: the amount and quality of these resources, how well they are being managed in terms of achieving operating economies and developing core skills, and how the firm's resources match up to the requirements of the MARKET place as identified by the external appraisal of threats and opportunities. This kind of audit typically reveals a checklist of strengths and weaknesses of the firm as seen by its incumbent management (but their perception could be endorsed or changed by employing the services of an outside team of MANAGEMENT CONSULTANTS). For example, the analysis may reveal that the firm is especially strong in PRODUCTION but that the firm's products have failed to sell well because of poor MARKETING. This can then be remedied by upgrading the marketing function with a more careful focus on understanding customer needs.

The appraisal of the firm's external environment involves looking both at the immediate threats and opportunities encountered in the firm's present markets and also at the long-term strategic possibilities open to the firm for developing its business interests in other directions (see PRODUCT-MARKET MATRIX, BOSTON MATRIX). A typical threat facing a firm in its existing market is loss of business to competitors and to new entrants (due possibly, as in our example above, to the firm's poor marketing), but for firms possessing COMPETITIVE ADVANTAGE (lower costs, superior products) over rivals, opportunities abound, particularly in expanding markets. The ultimate threat facing firms in an existing market is, of course, the danger of market obsolescence, i.e. the market itself goes into decline as new substitute products emerge. In consequence, careful attention needs to be paid to the identification of opportunities for successful DIVERSIFICATION, where, for example, the firm's core internal skills can be carried over and transferred to new markets.

Having drawn up a checklist of possible SWOT factors, caution needs to be exercised in interpreting them. For example, many feature film makers in the 1950s who made movie films for screening through cinemas (often their own vertical chains), initially saw the advent of television as a threat to their traditional business and refused TV companies permission to screen their films. The reality was and still is, of course, that television is simply another form of viewing, representing an opportunity for market development and concentric diversification, i.e. the basic materials and skills involved in film making (actors, film crews etc.) are the same irrespective of whether a film is being produced for the cinema or television; the key thing, strategically, is the perception of the true dimensions of the market which is being supplied.

**syndicated loan** a LOAN which is provided by a number of financial institutions on a collective basis, each subscribing a specified amount of money. Syndicated loans are usually put together by a 'lead' organization, for example, a commercial bank.

**synergy** the phenomenon whereby the *overall* return on a firm's resources is greater than the sum of its parts (the so-called '2 + 2 = 5 or more effect'). Synergy often results from the exploitation of complementary activities or from the carry over of management capabilities, synchronizing individual, group or organizational activities in a way which achieves a better result than any of the activities by themselves: for example, in the case of a MERGER, one firm may have a strong production organization, while the other excels in marketing; joining the two can make the combined firm more effective overall.

**synthetic time** SEE WORK MEASUREMENT.

**systems analysis** the process of analysing management problems into their constituent operations and then specifying these operations in a form suitable for COMPUTER programming.

# T

**table** a means of presenting statistical data in the form of columns and rows.

**tactical marketing decisions** decisions which have as their objective the achievement of an appropriate balance between the various elements of the MARKETING MIX.

**tacit skill** or **knowledge** see SKILL.

**takeover** or **acquisition** the acquisition by one firm of another firm. For companies listed on the STOCK MARKET this involves the *acquiring* firm either buying in the open market, or bidding for the voting SHARES in the *target* firm (See BID, TAKEOVER BID). Unlike a MERGER, which is usually arranged by mutual agreement between the two firms' management, a takeover is often resisted by the target firm's management, so that the bidder must convince shareholders that selling out to the acquirer, or taking shares in it in the case of a share exchange, is of benefit to them. Although a 51% stake in the target company would be sufficient to allow the acquiring company to exercise effective control, generally it would wish to take full control so as to be free from the interference of minority interests.

Takeovers are a form of EXTERNAL GROWTH by which firms expand in a horizontal, vertical and conglomerate direction. *Conglomerate* takeovers (the acquisition of a firm in an unrelated market) are undertaken primarily as a means of spreading business risks and to enable the firm to reorientate itself away from static or declining markets into areas offering good long-term growth and profit potential (see DIVERSIFICATION). *Vertical* takeovers (the acquisition of a firm which supplies inputs to the acquirer or which distributes its products) may enable the firm to cut its costs by, for example, linking together a series of sequentially related input assembly operations or reducing stockholding costs; vertical takeovers give the firm greater security of input supplies and access to distribution channels and the potential to put non-integrated competitors at

TAKEOVER BID

a disadvantage (see VERTICAL INTEGRATION). *Horizontal* takeovers (the acquisition of a competitor operating in the same market) may allow the firm to reduce its costs by realizing economies of scale in production and marketing, and by taking over the rival supplier the firm can increase its market share and perhaps exercise some degree of monopolistic control over the market (see HORIZONTAL INTEGRATION).

From society's point of view takeovers may be beneficial in so far as they improve efficiency and cut costs and prices, but also (potentially) harmful if they eliminate competition and create monopolies. For this reason, in the UK, takeovers and mergers which lead to, or extend, a firm's market share of a particular product beyond 25%, or where the value of assets taken over is greater than £70 million, can be referred by the OFFICE OF FAIR TRADING to the MONOPOLIES AND MERGERS COMMISSION to decide whether or not they are in the public interest.

See MARKET ENTRY, BARRIERS TO ENTRY, CITY CODE ON TAKE-OVERS AND MERGERS, BUSINESS POLICY, MANAGEMENT BUY-IN, MANAGEMENT BUY-OUT.

**takeover bid** an attempt by one or a number of companies to achieve the TAKEOVER of another company by bidding for (see BID) all or the majority of voting SHARES in the target company. A number of terms are used to describe the various tactics available to the bidding and defending firms, including:

(a) *black knight*: a firm that launches an unwelcome (contested) takeover bid for some other firm;

(b) *concert party*: a number of investors who each buy shares in a company with a view to pooling their shareholdings and acting in concert to take over the company;

(c) *dawn raid*: an attempt to buy up as many shares in a company as possible on the STOCK MARKET over a short period of time, as a prelude to making a full takeover bid for the company;

(d) *golden parachute*: any generous severance terms written into the employment contracts of the directors of a firm that makes it expensive to sack the directors if the firm is taken over;

(e) *greenmail*: a situation in which a firm' shares are being bought up by a (potential) takeover bidder, who is then headed off from making an actual bid, by that firm's directors buying these shares from him at a premium price;

(f) *leveraged bid*; a takeover that is financed primarily by the issue of LOAN CAPITAL rather than share capital, which increases the CAPITAL GEARING of the enlarged firm. (see JUNK BOND);

(g) *pac-man defence*; a situation in which the firm being bid for itself now makes a bid for the acquiring firm (see REVERSE TAKEOVER);

(h) *poison pill*; a tactic employed in a takeover bid whereby the intended victim itself takes over or merges with some other firm, in order to make itself financially or structurally less attractive to the potential acquirer;

(i) *porcupine*; any complex agreements between a firm and its suppliers, customers or creditors that make it difficult for an acquiring company to integrate this firm with its own business;

(j) *reverse takeover*; an attempt by a smaller firm to take over a larger firm. Since the smaller aggressor company has a smaller capital than the victim, it must usually issue additional shares or raise loans to finance the takeover (see pac-man defence);

(k) *shark repellents*; any measures specifically designed to discourage takeover bidders; for example, altering the company's ARTICLES OF ASSOCIATION to increase the proportion of shareholders' votes needed to approve the bid above the usual 50% mark;

(l) *white knight*; the intervention in a takeover bid of a third firm which itself takes over or merges with the intended victim firm to rescue it from its unwelcome suitor.

See also ARBITRAGEUR, MERCHANT BANK.

**Talisman (Transfer Accounting Lodgement for Investors)** the UK STOCK MARKET computerized transfer system which handles the administrative work involved in transferring STOCKS and SHARES and settling accounts through the official stock market company, SEPON. In 1994 a *rolling settlement* system was introduced in which settlement takes place ten working days after the completion of a deal. This replaces the traditional ACCOUNT PERIOD system. Settlement was cut to five working days in 1995 thus speeding up the whole process of concluding deals. See CREST.

**tall organization** an ORGANIZATION which has many managerial layers. Such an organizational structure tends to be characteristic of large firms or public utilities and government departments.

Tall organizations tend to have a number of drawbacks – excessive bureaucracy, remoteness of decision-making from ultimate customer needs and an inability to respond quickly to changes in the organization's external environment.

In recent years many larger firms have attempted to make themselves 'leaner and fitter' by reducing the size of their managerial hierarchies and by establishing more focused business divisions.

See FLAT ORGANIZATION, STRATEGIC BUSINESS UNIT, RIGHTSIZING, HIERARCHY, DE-LAYERING.

**tangible fixed assets** physical FIXED ASSETS such as land, buildings and machinery which have a money value.

**tap 1.** a FINANCIAL SECURITY such as a government STOCK which can always be obtained on demand because there is continuous supply.

**2.** the issue of TREASURY BILLS and government BONDS which are sold directly to government departments as opposed to being sold on the open market.

**target market** the MARKET or MARKET SEGMENTS which form the focus of a firm's MARKETING efforts.

**target-profit pricing** see COST-BASED PRICING.

**tariff 1.** a TAX (import duty) levied by a country on IMPORTS of products from foreign countries which *may* increase their prices in the domestic market. There are two main types of tariff;

(a) an *ad valorem* duty which is levied as a fixed percentage of the value of the product;

(b) a specific duty which is levied as a fixed sum of money per physical unit of the product.

Governments impose tariffs primarily to protect domestic industries from overseas competition, in order to maintain a local production base and to prevent job losses. Additionally, governments use tariffs to assist the BALANCE OF PAYMENTS, and also as a means of raising revenue.

Since 1950, the tariffs which were once applied at substantial rates on an extensive range of internationally traded products have been either reduced or eliminated, as a result of the work of the GENERAL AGREEMENT ON TARIFFS AND TRADE and the formation of various FREE TRADE BLOCS.

Firms facing tariff obstacles to overseas market may choose

to absorb the duties payable by lowering profit margins, or they may be able to remain price-competitive by increasing productivity and reducing their supply costs. A further option open to MULTINATIONAL ENTERPRISES is for them to replace exporting by setting up manufacturing plants in the markets concerned.

See PROTECTIONISM, DEINDUSTRIALIZATION, FOREIGN MARKET SERVICING STRATEGY, LOCAL CONTENT RULE.

**2.** a charge for the consumption of a product or service, for example a meals tariff at a restaurant, or a tariff for gas and electricity supplies. Two-part tariffs are often used in connection with the supply of gas, electricity, telephone services etc., involving a charge per unit of the good or service consumed, plus a fixed annual or quarterly charge to cover overhead costs. Two-part tariffs can be used by PUBLIC UTILITIES or firms to achieve the benefits of marginal cost pricing whilst raising sufficient revenues to cover total outlays (so avoiding a deficit). Additionally, multi-part tariffs can be utilized to reflect the different marginal costs involved in offering products such as electricity, and rail and bus services at peak and off-peak periods. See COST-BASED PRICING.

**task culture** see CULTURE.

**TAURUS (Transfer and Automated Registration of Uncertificated Stock)** the paperless settlement system which was to have been introduced by the London International Stock Exchange in 1994, but now abandoned. See CREST.

**tax** a levy imposed by the government on GOODS and SERVICES (INDIRECT TAX) and the INCOME and WEALTH of persons and businesses (DIRECT TAX). The government uses taxes for a number of purposes such as:

(a) to raise revenue to finance government spending (see BUDGET);

(b) to promote social equity by redistributing income and wealth (see DISTRIBUTION OF INCOME);

(c) to regulate the level of total spending in the economy (see FISCAL POLICY);

(d) to protect domestic producers from imports (see TARIFF).

See INCOME TAX, CORPORATION TAX, CAPITAL GAINS TAX, WEALTH TAX, INHERITANCE TAX, VALUE-ADDED TAX, CUSTOMS DUTY, EXCISE DUTY.

**taxable income** the amount of an individual's income that is subject to TAXATION once any tax allowances to which the taxpayer is entitled have been deducted.

**taxation** the government receipts from TAXES on personal and business income, expenditure and wealth. Taxes on income include personal INCOME TAX and CORPORATION TAX; taxes on expenditure include VALUE-ADDED TAX and EXCISE DUTIES. Taxes are used to finance government spending and as instruments of FISCAL POLICY in regulating the level of total spending in the economy. See INLAND REVENUE, BUDGET (GOVERNMENT).

**tax avoidance** any efforts by taxpayers to arrange their financial affairs so as to avoid paying TAX by taking maximum advantage of taxation allowances and reliefs. In this way taxpayers can legally minimize their tax burden. Compare TAX EVASION.

**tax burden** the total amount of TAXATION paid by the citizens of a country in the form of INCOME TAX, CORPORATION TAX, VALUE-ADDED TAX, etc.

**tax credit** see CORPORATION TAX, DIVIDEND.

**tax evasion** any efforts by taxpayers to evade TAX by various illegal means, such as not declaring all of their income to the tax authorities or falsely claiming reliefs to which they are not entitled. Compare TAX AVOIDANCE.

**tax haven** a country which imposes low rates of personal and corporate TAXES, and which as a consequence tends to attract wealthy individuals, MULTINATIONAL ENTERPRISES and FINANCIAL INSTITUTIONS seeking to minimize their taxation liabilities. At the present time, countries operating low-taxation systems include Bermuda, Jersey and the Cayman Islands. See also TRANSFER PRICE.

**tax point** see VALUE-ADDED TAX.

**tax return** a form which must be completed by all taxpayers and potential taxpayers for the INLAND REVENUE, giving details of their INCOME and CAPITAL GAINS and any allowances and reliefs to be set against this income.

**team** see GROUP.

**team briefing** a form of COMMUNICATION in which supervisors or managers pass information about company affairs to their subordinates (who in turn brief *their* subordinates) via the medium of a regular meeting. In this way information can be cascaded down the organization. Advocates of team briefing maintain that, as well as providing information useful to job performance, communication of this sort results in employees feeling more involved. As a result they become more committed to their organizations, with the benefit that performance may improve further. Team briefing can therefore be said to embody a HUMAN RELATIONS philosophy. The efficacy of team briefing, however, can be questioned. Mechanisms for transmitting employee recommendations *up* the organization hierarchy are generally absent, with the result that employees may soon question whether team briefing permits genuine involvement. Some also maintain that team briefing is an attempt to weaken TRADE UNIONS in the organization, by providing alternative channels of communication to those provided by SHOP STEWARDS. See EMPLOYEE INVOLVEMENT.

**TEC** see TRAINING.

**technical analysis** see CHARTISM.

**Technical and Vocational Educational Initiative (TVEI)** see TRAINING.

**Technical Help to Exporters** see EXPORTING.

**technological determinism** the belief that technology is the dominant influence on employee behaviour. See SOCIOLOGY OF WORK.

**technological forecasting** the process of predicting the direction and scope of future technological advances. With rapid advances in science and technology, shortening PRODUCT LIFE CYCLES and improving production techniques, firms need to forecast technological developments. Technological forecasting helps the firm to formulate its BUSINESS STRATEGY by identifying opportunities and threats presented by technical change, and assists in the planning of RESEARCH and DEVELOPMENT programmes by identifying new areas to explore. Technological forecasting can be done in several ways, by means of:

(a) methods which identify and extrapolate trends derived from historical data; for example, in plotting trends in data storage capacity and information processing speed over time, it is possible to identify the development of, first, valve-based computer technology, then transistor-based technology, present semiconductor (silicon chip)-based technology, and future fibre optics-based technology;

(b) methods based upon the subjective impressions of practising technologists. A single expert may write in some detail about the possible future of his own field of technology ('scenario' writing), or a consensus of expert opinion may be sought, using the Delphi approach where the experts first independently give opinions concerning the development of a scientific field, then distil these opinions to produce an overall view of likely advances.

**technology** the application of scientific principles and know-how in the development and operation of industrial processes, systems and products. See AUTOMATION, NUMERICAL CONTROL, ROBOT, COMPUTER, PRODUCTION LINE, INFORMATION TECHNOLOGY, TECHNOLOGICAL FORECASTING, NEW-PRODUCT DEVELOPMENT.

**technology transfer** the diffusion of technological know-how and expertise concerning processes, methods of manufacture and innovative products across industries, within an industry or, in the international context, from country to country. Intra-industry technology transfer occurs when, for example, an exclusive PATENT accruing to one firm expires and other firms are then free to adopt the technology concerned, or alternatively, the rate and scale of diffusion may be speeded up if the patentor firm is prepared to LICENSE the technology to other firms. Technology transfer between countries often occurs as a result of the FOREIGN MARKET SERVICING STRATEGIES adopted by MULTINATIONAL ENTERPRISES (MNES). For example, an MNE may choose to establish a manufacturing plant, incorporating innovative production techniques, in an overseas market, or grant licensing rights to local producers to use its technology.

Technology transfer effects can be important in upgrading the technical competence of an industry, giving it an advantage over international competitors. Similarly, from a host country perspective, technology transfer enables the country to acquire technological expertise otherwise unavailable domestically, as a means of establishing new industries.

More generally, new technologies may be developed which are applicable, in modified forms, to a wide range of industries. For example, information technology and computer-aided manufacturing systems. In the UK, the DEPARTMENT OF TRADE AND INDUSTRY has established Regional Technology Centres to disseminate information on new technology and assist in its application at local industry level, while the DTI's Overseas Technical Information Service provides details of developments elsewhere which may have reference and application in the UK.

See INDUSTRIAL POLICY.

**telecommunication** see COMMUNICATION.

**telephone selling** a form of DIRECT MARKETING in which a seller of a product contacts customers by telephone in order to establish an initial contact with them. Interested customers may then be visited by a SALES REPRESENTATIVE of the firm with a view to completing a sale.

**temporal flexibility** SEE LABOUR FLEXIBILITY.

**temporal method** SEE FOREIGN CURRENCY TRANSLATION.

**temporary work** employment which is of a less than permanent duration, i.e. where the employees are on fixed-term contracts or where they take jobs for a limited time. The reasons for employing temporary workers are that the job duties may themselves be temporary, or that the employer is uncertain about the future prospects of the organization and wishes to retain the flexibility to adjust employment levels downwards. Temporary work can be unsettling for those seeking long-term employment since it is difficult to plan for the future. However, some groups, for example students wanting holiday jobs, actively seek such employment. The amount of temporary work has increased substantially in recent years. In universities, for instance, a high proportion of staff are now on fixed-term contracts. See LABOUR FLEXIBILITY, PART-TIME WORK.

**tender 1.** an invitation from a buyer who requires particular goods or services to prospective suppliers of those products to put in competing price bids. The buyer will usually detail the precise specifications of the product, and will make a final decision about which supplier's bid to accept on the basis of comparative price and how well bids match up to the stated requirements. See QUOTATION, sense 1.

**2.** a means of making a SHARE ISSUE by offering shares to the general public, who are invited to make a bid for shares, subject to a minimum bid price. The issue price of the shares is determined by averaging out the bid prices offered by prospective purchasers. Anyone making a bid which is below the final issue price will not be offered any shares, whilst those making a bid at or above the price will be allotted shares in full at the final price.

Tenders may be similarly used to sell other financial securities such as TREASURY BILLS.

**terminal** a COMPUTER input/output device linked to the computer, usually comprising a KEYBOARD and VDU (visual display unit). MAINFRAME and MINICOMPUTERS are usually capable of serving several terminals simultaneously.

**terms of trade** a PRICE INDEX which shows the ratio of a country's EXPORT prices relative to its IMPORT prices. If a country's export prices rise at a faster rate than its import prices, this is an improvement in the country's terms of trade since a given amount of foreign exchange earnings from exports will now buy more imports.

**testing** the checking of raw materials, components and finished products to ensure that they meet specified performance standards. In principle all materials, components and products could be tested but in practice firms will usually only test a sample of such items.

See QUALITY CONTROL. See also ADVERTISING EFFECTIVENESS TEST, NEW PRODUCT DEVELOPMENT, TEST MARKETING.

**test marketing** a prelaunch trial run of a NEW PRODUCT involving a representative sample of prospective buyers who are given the product to try. Consumers' opinions and views about the performance of the product, its quality and the satisfaction they derive from it are compiled, often alongside consumer reaction to a range of possible prices that could be charged for the product. This data is then used by the firm to decide whether or not to go ahead and launch the product on to the market. Test-market reactions are useful not only in establishing whether actually to launch the product, but also in indicating whether changes in its attributes (quality, shape and form, styling etc.) would strengthen its appeal and which consumer perceptions about the product might usefully form the basis of advertising the product to maximize its impact on prospective buyers. See ADVERTISING COPY, ADVERTISING EFFECTIVENESS TESTS, NEW-PRODUCT DEVELOPMENT.

**T-group** see MANAGEMENT DEVELOPMENT.

**Theory X and Theory Y** two opposed philosophies of MANAGEMENT and ORGANIZATION, so named by the American social psychologist Douglas McGregor (1906–64). Theory X assumes that people dislike work and prefer to avoid responsibility. It therefore emphasizes that coercion is necessary to achieve satisfactory performance. By contrast, Theory Y believes that people can enjoy the activity of working and exercising responsibility and that if they are given the opportunity they can become committed to organizational goals. McGregor concluded from this that Theory Y could lead to superior organizational performance. See MANAGEMENT STYLE.

**Theory Z** the application to Western ORGANIZATIONS of the Japanese approach to management. Theory Z-type companies typically prioritize generating and sustaining employee commitment by EMPLOYEE PARTICIPATION and CONSULTATION. They also tend to invest heavily in training. See JAPANIZATION.

**therbligs** a coding system which breaks down the elements of a JOB into a number of discrete tasks. For example, therbligs could include 'search' (attempting to find an item manually or visually), 'grasp' (gaining control of an item by touch or grasping), 'position' (aligning an item for purposes of assembly) etc. By analysing a work task in this way, it may be possible to find ways of improving the methods used to do the job. See METHOD STUDY.

**The Securities Association (TSA)** See SECURITIES AND FUTURES AUTHORITY.

**threats and opportunities** see SWOT ANALYSIS.

**Three i's (3i's,** formerly **Investors in Industry)** a company which provides LOAN and SHARE CAPITAL for VENTURE CAPITAL projects, MANAGEMENT BUY-OUTS and other activities requiring specialized financing, particularly small project 'start-up' funding.

**three-shift working** see SHIFT WORK.

**tied aid** see ECONOMIC AID.

**tie-in sale** a business practice whereby a supplier encourages a dealer/purchaser not only to buy the GOOD or SERVICE of primary interest to him but to buy also, as part of the same transaction, some other related good or service. For example, a supplier of colour film might attempt to tie the processing of that film to himself by including an inclusive processing charge in the price paid for the colour film. The practice of tie-in sales may help the supplier to increase his total sales and also to protect BRAND LOYALTY (for example, in the case of colour film, inefficient processing by an independent processor might lead the purchaser to believe, erroneously, that poor picture reproduction is due to the poor quality of the film itself). However, if undertaken by a DOMINANT FIRM, the practice may serve to limit competition in a market by discouraging purchasers from placing their custom with rival businesses. See OFFICE OF FAIR TRADING.

**time and motion study** see WORK STUDY.

**time-based maintenance** an approach to MAINTENANCE which provides for the overhaul of machinery, plant and equipment at planned regular intervals, for example, once every three months.

**time card** see CLOCK CARD.

**time deposit** see COMMERCIAL BANK.

**time management 1.** the organization of a manager's working practices so as to make the optimum use of the manager's scarce time.

**2.** the process of reducing the amount of time taken in developing new product ideas into products and getting them on to the market. Firms which are able to shorten new product lead times can often gain a significant COMPETITIVE ADVANCE over rival suppliers. See NEW PRODUCT DEVELOPMENT, CONCURRENT ENGINEERING.

**time rate system** see PAY.

**time saved** the difference between the time allowed for completing a work task, the 'standard time' (see WORK MEASUREMENT) and the actual time taken. INCENTIVE BONUS SCHEMES often use a percentage of the time saved in their bonus calculations.

**times covered** see DIVIDEND COVER.

**time-series** see SALES FORECASTING.

**time sharing 1.** the joint use of a COMPUTER facility by two or more users in return for a rental payment.

**2.** the joint use of a holiday home by several users, each of whom contributes a share of the capital cost of the property and upkeep expenses in return for the right to use the property for specified weeks each year.

**time sheet** document completed by a worker in which he or she itemizes the work tasks undertaken and the time spent on each task. This information can be used for COSTING purposes in computing the direct labour cost of JOBS and as a basis for calculating PAY.

**times interest earned** see INTEREST COVER.

**time span of discretion** the length of time that elapses before an employee's work is checked by a supervisor. The concept was developed by the social psychologist Elliott Jacques (1917–  ) who believed it was a viable way of quantifying the level of judgment and discretion involved in a job. Jobs that involve little decision-making, such as assembly-line work, have a very short time span of discretion whereas managerial jobs, which have a much greater judgmental element, have a much longer span.

The time-span theory can be said to be an attempt objectively to incorporate the notions of responsibility and judgment into systems of WORK MEASUREMENT and JOB EVALUATION. Jacques has argued that it could form the basis of an equitable pay system, with rewards being based on the amount of discretion involved in each job.

See JOB DESIGN AND REDESIGN.

**time standards** see WORK MEASUREMENT.

**time study** see WORK STUDY.

**time value of money** see DISCOUNTED CASH FLOW.

**tolerance limit** the limits of permitted variation in the size, colour or other attribute of a component or product. See QUALITY CONTROL.

**tort** a civil wrong. The laws of tort are general laws which protect the personal rights of an individual to non-violation of his or her property, reputation and person:

(a) offences against property rights include *trespass*; *negligence* (where there is a breach of a legal duty to take care which results in unintended damage to the plaintiff); and *nuisance* (where there is an unlawful and unreasonable interference with a person's use or enjoyment of his or her property);

(b) offences against reputation include *libel*, and *slander* (making a false and malicious statement which damages another person's reputation);

(c) offences against one's person include *assault*; *battery*; *negligence*; and *intimidation* (a threat to perform an unlawful act interfering with the victim's freedom of action).

It may be noted in this context that an employer may be made liable for the torts of his employees which are committed during the course of their employment, having vicarious liability for their actions. In a tort action the plaintiff will usually be seeking either financial compensation (damages) for harm done to him or her by the defendant, or an injunction from the court ordering the defendant to discontinue harming the plaintiff.

**total assets** the combined amount of a company's FIXED ASSETS and CURRENT ASSETS as recorded in the company's BALANCE SHEET. This shows *all* the assets used by a company regardless of how they are financed. Compare NET ASSETS.

**total quality management (TQM)** a business philosophy which seeks to instil in *all* employees of a firm an *individual* as well as a *collective* responsibility for maintaining high QUALITY standards, in respect of both the products supplied by the firm and the attention paid to customer services and requirements. TQM has both an internal and an external dimension. Fundamentally, the success or failure of the firm will depend on its ability to satisfy the demands of its external customers. Product quality may well be the most important source of a firm's COMPETITIVE ADVANTAGE over rival suppliers. TQM emphasizes that the firm's ability to generate and sustain quality advantages stems from the totality of its internal operations. The firm is made up of a network of interrelated departments, each one standing in a customer or supplier relationship with others in terms of the internal flow of raw materials and components, processing and assembly operations, through to final product, stockholding and dispatch. TQM seeks to establish a unity of interests and commitment to the maintenance of the highest possible quality standards at each of these interfaces.

TQM in particular attempts to minimize the amount of time and money spent on QUALITY CONTROL by the PREVENTION of quality problems (e.g. component and product defects and waste) arising in the first instance, thus shifting the focus of quality control away from merely detecting and rectifying cases of failure and waste. Individual commitment to quality can be reinforced by the operation of QUALITY CIRCLES and various EMPLOYEE PARTICIPATION schemes.

See QUALITY ASSURANCE.

**TQM** see TOTAL QUALITY MANAGEMENT.

**trade** the exchange of goods, services and financial securities between BUYERS and SELLERS. In most cases trade takes place using MONEY as a means of exchange in buying and selling transactions, though occasionally trade can involve direct

BARTER. See MARKET SYSTEM, INTERNATIONAL TRADE.

**trade association** an organization which represents the interests of firms operating in the same INDUSTRY. Trade associations collect data on industrial production, sales and exports for circulation to member firms, provide a forum for the discussion of trade affairs, and represent the interests of members in dealings with other trade organizations or government departments. See INTERFIRM COMPARISON.

**trade credit** a deferred-payment arrangement whereby a supplier allows a customer a certain period of time (typically one to two months) after receiving the products in which to pay for them. See CREDITORS, CREDITORS RATIO, WORKING CAPITAL.

**trade creditors** see CREDITORS.

**trade cycle** see BUSINESS CYCLE.

**trade debt** a deferred-payment arrangement whereby a customer is allowed a certain period of time in which to pay for products after receiving them. See DEBTORS, DEBTORS RATIO, WORKING CAPITAL, CREDIT CONTROL, AGE ANALYSIS PROFILE FOR DEBTORS.

**Trade Descriptions Acts 1968** and **1972** a UK Act (1968) which makes it an offence to apply a false or misleading description to a GOOD or SERVICE and a false or misleading indication as to the PRICE of a good or service. The term 'trade description' is defined broadly to include, for example, quantity, size of gauge, composition, fitness for purpose, performance, strength, accuracy, method of manufacture, place and date of manufacture, etc. Offenders can be punished by a fine or imprisonment. The Act is administered by local authority WEIGHTS AND MEASURES officials, in conjunction with the DEPARTMENT OF TRADE AND INDUSTRY and the OFFICE OF FAIR TRADING, which keeps a central register of convictions.

The 1972 Act requires that certain imported products should have their country of origin clearly displayed. See CONSUMER PROTECTION, PRICE MARKING (BARGAIN OFFERS) ORDER, 1979, CONSUMER PROTECTION ACT 1987.

**trade discount** see QUANTITY DISCOUNT.

**trade dispute** see INDUSTRIAL DISPUTE, TRADE UNION IMMUNITIES.

**traded options market** a market where investors trade in the right to buy or sell shares or commodities at a predetermined price and time. OPTION prices reflect in more accentuated form movements in the prices of shares or commodities, so that prices in traded options markets are more volatile. See FOR-WARD MARKET.

**trade fair** an organized gathering of firms from different industries for the display and promotion of their goods and services to prospective customers. See TRADE SHOW, PROMOTIONAL MIX.

**trade gap** see BALANCE OF TRADE.

**trade-in** an allowance made by a supplier to a customer against the price of a good when the customer simultaneously trades in an older version of the good. As such, trade-ins are a form of price DISCOUNT offered to customers to induce them to buy.

**trade investment** the acquisition of STOCKS and SHARES in one FIRM by another firm. Trade investments may be undertaken for a variety of reasons including the profitable investment of surplus cash; the protection or advancement of an existing contractual trade relationship by a more direct involvement (for example, a supplier might buy a stake in a customer firm); the provision of a launching pad for a possible future TAKEOVER or merger. Where the trade investment involves the acquisition of a large but not controlling proportion of a company's shares then that company becomes an ASSOCIATED COMPANY. See QUOTED INVESTMENTS, UNQUOTED INVESTMENTS.

**trade mark** a symbol (a word or pictorial representation) which is used by a business as a means of identifying a particular good or service so that it may be readily distinguished by purchasers from similar goods and services supplied by other businesses. See BRAND NAME.

In the UK, under the Trade Marks Act 1938 and the Trade Marks (Amendments) Act 1984, trade marks can be registered with the PATENT OFFICE. Registration of a trade mark confers a statutory monopoly in the use of that mark in relation to the products for which it is registered, and the registered owner has the right to sue in the courts for infringement of the mark. In order to qualify for registration, a trade mark must be judged by the Patent Office to be uniquely distinctive (i.e. non-identical or confusable with symbols used by other traders).

Trade marks protect the registered owner from unfair competition through piracy and they provide consumers with a means of unambiguously identifying the products of their choice.

**Tradepoint** the UK share dealing system in which exchanges are 'order driven', with clients posting their own buy/sell instructions. Contrast 'quote-driven' exchanges – see SHARE PURCHASE/SALE (b).

**trade price** the PRICE paid by a RETAILER to a WHOLESALER or PRODUCER for products which will be resold at a higher price. See MARK-UP, DISCOUNT.

**trade promotions** the incentives given by a seller of a product to encourage WHOLESALERS and RETAILERS to stock and promote the product. Such inducements include TRADE DISCOUNTS, free merchandise and gifts etc. See PROMOTIONAL MIX.

**trader/dealer** generic terms which cover both businesses which *take title* to goods (that is, purchase goods) which they then on-sell to customers – food RETAILERS, car dealers; and businesses which act purely in an agency or brokerage capacity, bringing together buyers and sellers of a good or service – ESTATE AGENTS, INSURANCE BROKERS. Traders and dealers thus act as 'middlemen' or 'market intermediaries' in the economic system.

**trades council** an association of TRADE UNION branches, drawn from a variety of unions, with the objective of advancing their mutual interests and promoting trade unionism in a locality.

**trade show** an organized gathering of firms, usually from a particular industry, for the display and promotion of their goods and services to prospective customers. See TRADE FAIR, PROMOTIONAL MIX.

**Trades Union Congress (TUC)** the TRADE UNION federation to which most UK unions are affiliated. The TUC represents the trade union movement in dealings with government and formulates policy for the movement as a whole. Unlike some continental federations it has no direct role in COLLECTIVE BARGAINING, though on occasions TUC officials intervene in major INDUSTRIAL DISPUTES. The TUC can intervene in disputes (for example over membership between unions (see BRIDLINGTON RULES)). The TUC is governed by a General Council elected by constituent members in proportion to their membership. See NATIONAL ECONOMIC DEVELOPMENT COUNCIL.

**trade union** an organization of employees whose primary objective is to protect and advance the economic interests of its members by negotiating WAGE RATES and conditions of employment with employers or managers. There are a number of different types of union:

(a) *craft union*, a union that represents a particular group of skilled workers (for example electricians) who may work in many industries. A sub-species is the 'promotion-line union' which also represents those who, after a period of training, will join the skilled group;

(b) *enterprise union*, a union that represents all those employed in a particular organization;

(c) *general union*, a union composed of employees drawn from a variety of occupations and industries;

(d) *industrial union*, a union that aspires to represent all or most of those employed in a particular industry.

Traditionally, UK unionism has been a complex amalgam of (a), (c) and (d), with the result that managers in a given organization may have to negotiate with a number of unions (see MULTI-UNIONISM). It has been argued, however, that this classification is not helpful in the analysis of union behaviour: a better distinction is between *open* and *closed* unions. Open unions are those which respond to industrial change by broadening their membership base, whilst closed unions are those which maintain their exclusivity. Whilst a useful distinction, it perhaps does not do justice to the variety of union organization in the UK. Those mergers between unions in which small craft-based unions are incorporated into larger, more general unions can result in a union having both open and closed sections.

Enterprise unions are an important feature of the large-firm sector in Japan, whilst most union members in Germany are to be found in industrial unions. Trade unions may also be organized on political or religious lines, as in France.

A distinction can also be drawn between differing philosophies of trade unionism. In *business unionism* the union's sole objective is the improvement of the pay and conditions of its members. Such unions do not concern themselves with wider social and political issues. In this model the job of the union leader is simply to sell the labour of the membership at the highest price. By contrast, in *welfare unionism* unions seek improvements in social benefits (for example child benefit payments) through political action as well as improvements in pay and conditions. In so far as many British trade unions have concerned themselves with social and political issues, welfare unionism could be said to be the main approach in Britain. Nevertheless, improvements in pay and conditions remain their primary objective.

The basic unit of organization of trade unions is generally the union branch, composed of all members in a particular workplace or locality. In many industries, representation of members' interests in particular workplaces is undertaken not by officers of the branch but by lay officials elected separately (see SHOP STEWARDS). Union policy is determined by a periodic conference attended by delegates from the branches, whilst the running of the union is overseen by an executive committee elected by the members (see TRADE UNION ACT 1984). Day-to-day management of the union is in the hands of paid officials. Critics of trade unions have argued that the officials and activists do not adequately represent the views and interests of the ordinary member. However, the conduct of most unions is based on democratic procedures, and the union member does have the opportunity to influence union policy-making and behaviour.

Union membership and union density (i.e. the proportion of labour force in union membership) declined in most advanced industrialized countries during the 1980s. In the UK, membership fluctuated at around 45% of the labour force for much of the post war period but rose to over 50% in the 1970s as a result of governmental and managerial encouragement of union membership and the CLOSED SHOP. By the early 1990s it had fallen to below 40%. Though opinions differ as to the precise cause of this, important factors include political hostility to trade unionism, high unemployment, low levels of inflation and a structural shift in employment from strongly organized manufacturing industry to private services, where unions have often found it difficult to recruit. See COLLECTIVE BARGAINING, INDUSTRIAL RELATIONS, WHITE-COLLAR UNION, TRADE UNION REFORM AND EMPLOYMENT RIGHTS ACT 1993.

**Trade Union Act 1984** a UK statute regulating activities of TRADE UNIONS. Under the Act, unions are required to elect, by secret ballot, voting members of their ruling EXECUTIVE COMMITTEE at least every five years. The Act makes unions liable to civil action by employers where a STRIKE is authorized without a secret ballot of the members concerned. The Act also stipulates that those unions maintaining a POLITICAL FUND must ballot their members on its continuation at least every 10 years. See EMPLOYMENT ACT 1980, EMPLOYMENT ACT 1982, EMPLOYMENT ACT 1988, EMPLOYMENT ACT 1990, TRADE UNION IMMUNITIES.

**trade union immunities** legal protection from civil action for TRADE UNIONS taking lawful STRIKE action in furtherance of an INDUSTRIAL DISPUTE. Without these, employers could take legal action against unions every time they caused employees to breach their CONTRACT OF EMPLOYMENT in this way. The immunities in effect confer a negative right not to be sued for such action. For immunity to be held, it is essential that a strike be officially sanctioned by the union and that the union follows the procedures for taking strike action stipulated in recent labour laws. Immunity is restricted to trade disputes between employees and their employer concerning the terms and conditions of employment, allocation of work, discipline, union membership and facilities and INDUSTRIAL RELATIONS procedures. All forms of SECONDARY ACTION are now excluded from immunity. See EMPLOYMENT ACT 1980, EMPLOYMENT ACT 1982, EMPLOYMENT ACT 1990, TRADE UNION ACT 1984.

**Trade Union Reform and Employment Rights Act 1993** a UK statute which continued the trend of earlier legislation by restricting TRADE UNION activities. Pre-strike ballots (see TRADE UNION ACT 1984) are required to be postal ballots and the employer must be given a week's notice of the start of STRIKE action. Employees are given the right to join any trade union, thereby undermining the principles of the BRIDLINGTON RULES which govern union 'spheres of influence'. Employees are required to give written consent every three years to the deduction of union membership fees from their pay packets by their employer for transfer to their union (see CHECK-OFF AGREEMENT). The WAGES COUNCILS, which regulated pay in industries where unions tend to be weak, were abolished. The Act also responded to recent court judgements which had gone in unions' favour. Recent case law that employers could not give financial inducements to employees to sign PERSONAL CONTRACTS which excluded COLLECTIVE BARGAINING over pay and conditions was amended. The Act also extended some employee rights, partly to incorporate recent European judgements and legislation (see SOCIAL CHAPTER). MATERNITY RIGHTS were improved, and those taking action to prevent violations of health and safety rules were protected against UNFAIR DISMISSAL. See also ADVISORY, CONCILIATION AND ARBITRATION SERVICE (ACAS).

**trade war** the use by a number of countries of beggar-my-neighbour trade restrictions such as TARIFFS and QUOTAS to restrict imports, and subsidies and tax rebates to increase exports. These actions are usually self-defeating, leading to lower trade and income levels for all. See GENERAL AGREEMENT ON TARIFFS AND TRADE.

**trading account** the section of a PROFIT-AND-LOSS ACCOUNT where the COST OF SALES is deducted from SALES REVENUE to show the amount of GROSS PROFIT made.

**trading period** the period of trading between two successive sets of financial accounts. To comply with the requirements of company law and taxation authorities, companies generally adopt a one-year trading period, producing an ANNUAL REPORT AND ACCOUNTS at the end of each trading period. However, because for internal management control purposes, much more frequent results are generally required, a company may produce PROFIT AND LOSS ACCOUNTS and BALANCE SHEETS at monthly or even weekly intervals.

**trading profit** see OPERATING PROFIT.

**trading stamp** a coupon attached to a product, which purchasers can collect with a view to redeeming them for cash or gifts. See SALES PROMOTION.

**traditional authority** see AUTHORITY.

**training** the process of extending and improving the SKILLS and knowledge of people so as to improve JOB performance. A distinction can be made between *vocational* training, i.e. the acquisition of specific occupational skills, and *pre-vocational* training, i.e. the development of awareness of the world of work and employment. Education develops those basic skills such as writing and numeracy which form the bedrock for more specialized occupational skills.

To determine what training is required in an organization or economy, it is beneficial to undertake a *training needs analysis*. As a first step the main goals or priorities have to be established; then it is necessary to consider what skills are necessary to achieve these objectives. These are compared with the existing stock of skills amongst workers. Any deficiency is referred to as a *skills gap* and represents the skills that should be provided by training. A comprehensive approach to training will involve a needs analysis, a programme to close this gap and a monitoring and evaluation process to determine whether it has been successful.

Although it is generally accepted that training improves job performance, UK employers are often reluctant to provide training. The UK in fact has a poor record compared with its main competitors such as Germany. Training in the UK is widely viewed as a cost rather than an investment, and one whose potential benefits are difficult to quantify on the balance sheet. Employers fear that employees, once trained, will leave or be poached for higher paid employment.

Traditionally, training in the UK has centred on the apprenticeship. Confined to skilled occupations, this involves workers committing themselves to one employer for a period of time during which they are to acquire the skills of the trade, mainly through informal instruction by those already skilled. Once trained in this way such workers have a set of recognized skills which can, in theory, lead to employment in any organization in the industry. The apprenticeship system has been much censured because it can transmit outdated skills, because competence is defined in terms of time served rather than skills acquired, and because it serves to limit the supply of skilled labour. The employer may not recoup the costs of an apprenticeship in the long run because the apprentice, once trained, may leave for alternative employment. The long-term decline in the apprenticeship system accelerated towards the end of the 1980s as government removed many of its statutory supports, e.g. by abolishing the Industry Training Boards (established in 1964) and removing the right of those remaining to levy 'taxes' on employers to support training. However, mounting alarm about skill shortages led to the apprenticeship system being revitalized in the mid-1990s as the *modern apprenticeship*.

The pattern of training provision in the UK is often described as *voluntarist* (see VOLUNTARISM) in that there is relatively little direction by government, compared with most other European countries. Instead the onus is on employers to decide whether to train and what forms of training to provide. Unsurprisingly in this context much training provision has involved simple observation of how experienced workers perform tasks, often known as *sitting next to Nelly*. For a while government took a more pro-active approach, setting up the Industry Training Boards in the mid-1960s and the Manpower Services Commission in the mid-1970s (see TRIPARTISM). In the early 1980s government reaffirmed the voluntarist approach, arguing that market forces would lead to appropriate types and levels of training. However, it has become clear that in the absence of government support for training, the extent of training provision in the UK is insufficient for the UK to compete effectively in a number of key areas. The result has been that avowedly non-interventionist governments have been forced to take a more active role in designing a framework for training provision. In recent years the government has encouraged a national framework of vocational qualifications (see NATIONAL VOCATIONAL QUALIFICATION) and set up TRAINING AND ENTERPRISE COUNCILS to encourage training programmes locally. The government endorsed the initiative by the Confederation of British Industry to set *National Education and Training Targets (NETTS)*. These include the target that half of young people should attain NVQ Level 3 or equivalent (A-levels) by the year 2000.

The main government body is the Training Agency (see AGENCY STATUS), successor to the Manpower Services Commission and the short-lived Training Commission. Unlike its predecessors the Training Agency is not a tripartite body and it is shorn of trade union influence.

The main programmes supported by the Agency are:

(a) *Training for Work*, designed to help the long-term unemployed to find work and to improve the skills of the unemployed.

(b) *Youth Training (YT)*, a system of training for all 16–17 year olds not in education or employment. The package comprises work experience, some on-the-job training and some formal classroom training. Critics of this scheme have argued that it is primarily an attempt to reduce youth unemployment figures, that it is used by some employers as a source of cheap labour (trainees are paid at unemployment-benefit levels), that the quality of work training is often poor, and that participating colleges have found their curriculum increasingly determined by the specific needs of local industry.

On the other hand it has often provided much-needed work experience for those who might otherwise have found it difficult to secure employment;

(c) *Training Credits*. Commencing in the early 1990s, these are vouchers given to young people aged 16-17 with which to 'buy' training. It is envisaged that this credit system will replace Youth Training, and will shift the onus for initiating training from provider to recipient.

(d) *Learning for work*, designed to provide vocationally relevant education for the long-term unemployed.

(e) *Community action*, designed to provide work experience for the young unemployed in activities useful to the community.

Besides these schemes, government bodies have attempted to inculcate 'business' values in education, to advise and encourage teachers and also to develop specific vocational initiatives such as the Technical and Vocational Educational Initiative (TVEI) – an attempt to devise school curricula with a strong technical and vocational training component.

In evaluating recent approaches to training, two main questions stand out:

(a) How far should schools and colleges gear their activities to serving the needs of employers rather than the broad educational and development needs of their pupils?

(b) Can the provision of training be left to employers to undertake voluntarily, especially as there is now some compulsion on some people (i.e. the unemployed) to receive training?

See MANAGEMENT DEVELOPMENT, ACCREDITATION OF EXPERIENTIAL LEARNING, ACCREDITATION OF PRIOR LEARNING.

**Training Agency** see TRAINING.

**Training and Enterprise Council** an organization of local employers and civil servants responsible for devising and implementing TRAINING schemes relevant to their locality, and supported by the government's Training Agency. The TECs are now responsible for implementing much of the Youth Training and Employment Action programmes. In common with the philosophy of the NEW PUBLIC MANAGEMENT, the TECs purchase much of the training provision supported by them from other, private-sector organizations. The TECs are a half-way house between a voluntarist form of training provision (i.e. government leaves it to industry to provide training) and a more interventionist system. They have been criticized on the grounds that the UK experience suggests that employers are not the best people to determine training provision. For their part the TECs have complained that restrictions on government funding have made it impossible for TECs to meet their obligations e.g. to provide training places for all school leavers aged 16 and 17.

**training credit** see TRAINING.

**training needs analysis** see TRAINING.

**transaction costs** the costs associated with the activities of buying and selling in a MARKET system. For example, firms incur costs in finding satisfactory input suppliers and distributors for their products and in negotiating, concluding and monitoring CONTRACTS with other firms. In some market situations, transaction costs may be inflated by the application of monopoly surcharges by powerful suppliers. Although a firm may avoid some transaction costs by VERTICAL INTEGRATION (i.e. performing some functions internally), these may well be offset by the higher administrative, stockholding and other costs involved in running a vertically integrated business.

**transaction exposure** see EXCHANGE RATE EXPOSURE.

**Transfer Accounting Lodgement for Investors** see TALISMAN.

**Transfer and Automated Registration of Uncertificated Stock** see CREST.

**transfer deed** a document used to record the transfer of ownership of SHARES from a seller to a buyer. Transfer deeds are used to update a company's SHARE REGISTER and become the basis for cancelling old SHARE CERTIFICATES and issuing new ones.

**Transfer of Undertakings (Protection of Employment) Regulations 1981** a set of UK regulations which stipulate employee rights when the ownership of a business changes. Derived from the European Community's Acquired Rights Directive of 1977, the Regulations stipulate that an employee's CONTRACT OF EMPLOYMENT is automatically transferred to the new employer when a business changes hands, with the result that the employee's rights and duties are unchanged. These Regulations only applied to commercial ventures and hence it was supposed that large parts of the public services were not covered by them. However, a succession of recent judgements by the European Court of Justice has implied that this interpretation, upon which the government's COMPETITIVE TENDERING programme was based, infringed European law. The Regulations were therefore amended by the TRADE UNION REFORM AND EMPLOYMENT RIGHTS ACT 1993 to include public service activities.

**transfer payment** a payment made by the government out of taxation receipts such as state pensions and social security benefits, which transfers income from one group of persons (i.e. taxpayers) to another group of persons. See BUDGET (GOVERNMENT), DISTRIBUTION OF INCOME.

**transfer price** the internal PRICE at which raw materials, components and final products are transacted between the divisions or subsidiaries of a vertically integrated or conglomerate firm.

The transfer price charged may be set by reference to the prices ruling in outside markets for inputs and products (arms-length pricing). Alternatively, the transfer price may be set at a lower or higher level than the going market price, according to some internal accounting convention (for example, cost of production plus standard profit mark-up) and the desired 'profit split' between the firm's activities. Such administered transfer prices would generally be designed to achieve the firm's overall profit goals, but in transfer pricing decisions there may often be an inherent conflict between the overall goals of the firm and the goals of its subunits. For example, if one COST CENTRE is allowed to transfer components at cost of production plus a specific mark-up, then it has little incentive to minimize its production costs. Again, where a PROFIT CENTRE does not have discretion over its buying or selling prices but must buy or sell some or all of its inputs or outputs to other subunits at transfer prices established by headquarters, then the profit performance of the subunit will not depend solely upon the efforts of local managers, making it difficult to evaluate the performance of subgroup managers and motivate them to improve efficiency.

Transfer pricing gives a firm added flexibility in pricing its products. It may deploy transfer pricing to gain a competitive advantage over rival suppliers (to PRICE SQUEEZE a nonintegrated rival). In the case of a MULTINATIONAL ENTERPRISE, transfer pricing provides an opportunity to increase its profits by setting transfer prices across national frontiers in such a way that most of the firm's profits accrue in countries where company taxation rates are the lowest. In addition, inflated transfer prices for components or services may be used to remit surpluses back to the parent company from subsidiaries located in countries which limit the repatriation of profits through dividend controls or EXCHANGE CONTROLS. See INTERNALIZATION, TAX HAVEN, VERTICAL INTEGRATION, DIVERSIFICATION, SHADOW PRICE.

**translation exposure** see EXCHANGE RATE EXPOSURE.

**transnational company** see MULTINATIONAL ENTERPRISE.

**Transport and General Workers' Union** the UK's second largest TRADE UNION with nine hundred thousand members in a large number of industries. For many years it was the UK's largest trade union and at its peak had nearly two million members. It has been hard hit in recent years by high unemployment and contraction of semi-skilled and unskilled manual employment. It can be characterized as a general union, though in certain industries, such as the docks, it is in effect an industrial union.

**transportation model** a means of selecting the best way to distribute a product from a number of factories or warehouses to a number of destinations so as to minimize transportation costs while meeting customers' requirements. The transportation model uses LINEAR PROGRAMMING to analyse such PHYSICAL DISTRIBUTION management problems.

**treasury 1.** the department within a firm which is responsible for managing the firm's finances, making arrangements to collect cash speedily from debtors; profitably invest any short-term cash surpluses; and arrange with lenders to cover any short term cash shortages. In large multidivisional companies the treasury department may also arrange to transfer cash from company divisions earning surpluses to divisions experiencing liquidity problems so as to minimize external borrowings. In MULTINATIONAL ENTERPRISES the treasury department may also transfer funds between countries and convert currencies in order either to minimize the risk of losses or to take advantage of possible windfall gains from EXCHANGE RATE changes.

**2.** the Treasury, the UK government department responsible for managing the government's finances, authorizing the expenditure plans of government departments like Health and Education, and overseeing the tax-gathering work of the INLAND REVENUE and CUSTOMS AND EXCISE. In addition the Treasury advises the Chancellor of the Exchequer on the government's annual Budget.

**Treasury bill** a redeemable FINANCIAL SECURITY bearing a three-month redemption date which is issued by the Bank of England. Some Treasury bills are purchased *on tap* at undisclosed sums by government departments with temporary cash surpluses, but the vast majority are sold at periodic *tender* auctions to DISCOUNT HOUSES and overseas banks. Treasury bills bear a nominal face value which is repaid in full on redemption, but the price paid for them on issue depends on the outcome of a competitive tender, with discount houses and overseas banks bidding against each other for an allocation. The Treasury bills which are bought by the discount houses are usually then sold (rediscounted) in the DISCOUNT MARKET to other buyers, principally to COMMERCIAL BANKS which hold them as part of their 'liquidity base' to support their lending operations. Treasury bills are issued alongside BONDS both to raise finance for the government to cover BUDGET deficits and also as a means of controlling the MONEY SUPPLY and level of INTEREST RATES. See MONETARY POLICY.

**trend 1.** the direction of movement of a variable such as sales over time. See SALES FORECASTING.

**2.** a broad change in attitude and behaviour in society over time. These can serve to influence the acceptability of products by consumers with some products going out of *fashion* whilst others become more popular.

**trendsetter** see OPINION LEADERS.

**trial balance** a listing of the balances on a firm's LEDGER accounts that is prepared prior to the PROFIT-AND-LOSS ACCOUNT and BALANCE SHEET, as an initial check on the arithmetic accuracy of the ledger accounts.

If the total of all DEBIT balances in ledger accounts equals the total of all CREDIT balances in ledger accounts then this suggests (but does not guarantee) that the DOUBLE-ENTRY ACCOUNTS have been accurately recorded and that the data from them might be used to prepare the profit-and-loss account and balance sheet.

## TRIPARTISM

**Tripartism** a system of co-operation between both sides of industry and the state. Tripartite institutions typically include representatives of TRADE UNIONS, managers and owners, and government on the grounds that each has an interest in and worthwhile contribution to make to economic and industrial policy. Insofar as these organisations become *de facto* extensions of the state (i.e. they make and implement government policy) the more advanced forms of tripartism are sometimes referred to as *corporatism*. Tripartism developed in the UK from the 1960s. Examples of tripartite organizations include the now defunct NATIONAL ECONOMIC DEVELOPMENT COUNCIL and the Manpower Services Commission (see TRAINING). UK governments since 1979 have been hostile to tripartism on the grounds that trade unions have no legitimate role in the formulation and implementation of policy, and the trend since then has been to abolish tripartite bodies or to terminate union involvement. This contrasts with other European countries, such as Germany, Austria and the Scandinavian nations where tripartism continues to be viewed as a valued approach to formulating industrial policy.

**true and fair view** the opinion formed by an AUDITOR about a JOINT-STOCK COMPANY'S accounts, based upon evidence obtained from auditing the company's LEDGER accounts. The auditor is required to report to a company's shareholders about the accuracy and presentation of a firm's annual report and accounts. After undertaking the appropriate tests, usually on a sample basis, the auditor must be convinced that no material errors or omissions have occurred either in the firm's system of recording accounting transactions or in their summary and presentation. If the auditor is satisfied that no material irregularities have occurred, he or she will conclude that the financial statements present a 'true and fair view' for the period (year) under review. If irregularities are noted, the accounts may be prefaced with the qualification that 'subject to the following ... the financial statements audited ... present a true and fair view'. See also FINANCIAL ACCOUNTING.

**trust 1.** a collection of ASSETS held and managed by appointed *trustees* on behalf of an individual or group of people. Trusts are often established to minimize the amount of INCOME TAX and WEALTH TAX an individual or group is required to pay. See TRUSTEE INVESTMENTS.

**2.** see UNIT TRUST.

**3.** an alternative term for a CARTEL (most commonly used in the USA).

**trustee** see TRUST.

**trustee investments** investments made by a trustee on behalf of an individual or group through a TRUST. In the UK such investments are governed by the Trustee Investment Act of 1961, which lays down rules obliging trustees to maintain part of their portfolio in the form of Government BONDS, and restricting shareholdings to SHARES in larger quoted companies.

**TSA** see SECURITIES AND FUTURES AUTHORITY.

**TUC** see TRADES UNION CONGRESS.

**TUPE** see TRANSFER OF UNDERTAKINGS (PROTECTION OF EMPLOYMENT) REGULATIONS.

**turnkey project** a one-off major construction project such as the building of a dam, power station etc. in another country where usually a contracted foreign firm (operating either alone or as the leader of a consortium of firms) is responsible for the design and construction of the facility. See BUILD, OPERATE, TRANSFER PROJECT.

**turnover** see SALES REVENUE, LABOUR TURNOVER.

**turnover tax** see VALUE-ADDED TAX.

**turnround** a situation where a firm or a division of a firm that has been experiencing a protracted decline in profits is able to institute measures which not only halt the decline but form the basis of a *sustained* recovery in its profitability. A turnround situation reflects something more than a downturn in profits associated with the BUSINESS CYCLE which affects to a greater or lesser degree most companies operating in a particular activity. In essence it is a crisis situation which is firm-specific, reflecting various internal problems: ineffectual management (an autocratic chief executive, an unbalanced management team, lack of attention to the formulation of BUSINESS STRATEGY), poor financial structure (an inappropriate capital GEARING level), poor financial control (unsystematic allocation of overhead costs, lack of information on which products are generating cash and which ones are making losses) etc. All these factors can contribute to a lack of efficiency, higher costs, loss of competitive vigour and a failure to respond adequately to the changing needs of the market.

Recovery can only be achieved if there is a willingness and ability to identify the major sources of the firm's problems, followed by the initiation of action programmes involving managerial, administrative and financial reorganization, cost reduction and better directed marketing efforts aimed at re-establishing COMPETITIVE ADVANTAGE over rival suppliers. A tardiness or failure to implement appropriate turnround measures may well end in insolvency. However, before this point is reached the firm may well be TAKEN OVER, or in the case of a division, divested.

See DIVESTMENT, ENDGAME STRATEGY.

**twilight shift** see SHIFT WORK.

**two-bin system** see STOCK CONTROL.

**two factor theory of motivation** see MOTIVATION.

**two-part tariff** see TARIFF.

# U

**UBR** see UNIFORM BUSINESS RATE.

**U-form** see FUNCTIONAL STRUCTURE.

**ultra vires** *adj.* (of an action by a JOINT-STOCK COMPANY) exceeding its powers as defined in its MEMORANDUM OF ASSOCIATION. For example, if a company's memorandum authorizes it to trade in the motorcar business, and its directors then set up an ice-cream business, then they may be regarded as trading *ultra vires* and the company's CONTRACTS with ice-cream suppliers and customers may be regarded as void. To avoid falling foul of the *ultra vires* doctrine, companies now tend to draw up very wide-ranging business powers in the MEMORANDUM OF ASSOCIATION.

**UMA** see UNION MEMBERSHIP AGREEMENT.

**unaided recall test** see ADVERTISING EFFECTIVENESS TESTS.

**unapproved ESOP** see EMPLOYEE SHARE OWNERSHIP PLAN.

**unbundling** a colloquial term used to describe a DE-MERGER (the break-up of a company originally formed through a MERGER into two or more separate companies) or more gen-

erally the sale of a number of its business divisions by a conglomerate company (see DIVERSIFICATION).

**uncertainty and risk** the comparative unpredictability of a
firm's future business environment, bringing with it the possibility that the firm might incur losses if future economic and
market conditions turn out to be radically different from those
anticipated by the firm in, for example, pricing its products,
moving into new activities etc.

Since managers cannot foretell the future, they are forced to
guess the most likely outcome of any decision. All such estimates must, by their very nature, be subjective, though some
estimates will be better than others depending upon the
amount and availability of information.

Uncertainty arises because it is difficult to predict changes
and to estimate accurately the likelihood of events, including
possible losses. Unfortunately, many management decisions
are based on this uncertainty, since circumstances rarely repeat
themselves and there is little past data available to act as a
guide. Such market uncertainty can only be gauged by
managers, when launching a new product, through combining
the limited data available with their own judgment and experience. Managers can improve upon their subjective estimates
by collecting information from forecasts, market research,
feasibility studies, etc., but they need to balance the cost of
collecting such information against its value in improving
decisions.

The term 'risk' rather than uncertainty is used to describe
business situations where large amounts of information are
available about the extent of possible losses and the likelihood
of such losses occurring. For example, an insurance company
dealing with fire INSURANCE policies and claims from large
numbers of manufacturers will be able to compile detailed
statistics about numbers of fires and the amount of damage
done by each, and can use this information to predict the likelihood of a business experiencing a fire. This detailed statistical
information allows the insurance company to charge
manufacturers premiums for indemnifying them against fire
losses, and thereby to make a profit. By contrast, a single
manufacturer would find it very difficult to predict the likelihood of his premises being damaged by fire and the amount
of damage, since such an event would probably be a unique

experience for him. Faced with a possibility of fire, the manufacturer can either choose to bear the risk of losses resulting from a serious fire or can avoid the risk of fire damage by paying an insurance company a premium to bear the risk. Again, the manufacturer can take the risk that the prices of its main raw materials will be much higher next year, or it can contract now through a commodity FORWARD MARKET to buy raw materials supplies for future delivery at a fixed price.

See DECISION TREE, SALES FORECASTING, DISCOUNTED CASH FLOW, BUSINESS CYCLE, SENSITIVITY ANALYSIS.

**UNCTAD** see UNITED NATIONS CONFERENCE ON TRADE AND DEVELOPMENT.

**underwriting** the acceptance by a financial institution of the financial risks involved in a particular transaction, for an agreed fee. For example, INSURANCE COMPANIES underwrite INSURANCE risks such as damage to property, paying out monies to policy holders wholly or in part to cover *bona fide* claims for compensation; MERCHANT BANKS underwrite new SHARE ISSUES, guaranteeing to buy up any shares that are not sold in the open market, and BILLS OF EXCHANGE. See LLOYDS, EXPORT CREDIT GUARANTEE DEPARTMENT.

**undifferentiated marketing strategy** a MARKETING STRATEGY for a product based on the use of the *same* MARKETING MIX format right across the market (uniform pricing, advertising messages, retail outlets, etc.). Contrasted with a DIFFERENTIATED MARKETING STRATEGY or CONCENTRATED MARKETING STRATEGY which seek to exploit particular MARKET SEGMENTS, the undifferentiated approach attempts to reach all classes of buyer. This approach is best suited to a market where the product being sold is relatively standardized and buyers require little in the way of product variety. Mass marketing the product on a uniform basis is simpler to organize and manage than a fragmented approach, and may yield lower unit selling and production costs by enabling the firm to take advantage of economies of scale in advertising and production. On the debit side, undifferentiated marketing may fail to realize fully a product's sales potential because of its inability to appeal to key customer segments.

**undistributed profits** see RETAINED PROFIT.

**unearned income** see EARNED INCOME.

**unemployment** the non-utilization of part of the economy's available labour (and capital) resources. Labour unemployment is measured as a percentage of the total registered LABOUR FORCE currently without a job. Because idle resources lead to a loss of potential output to the economy and the divisive social effects of unemployment, most governments accord a high priority to the achievement of a high level of employment in formulating their ECONOMIC POLICIES.

There are a number of different types of unemployment, including *cyclical* unemployment (short-term unemployment associated with a fall in the level of business activity, see BUSINESS CYCLE); *seasonal* unemployment (short-term unemployment associated with changes in the demand for particular products at different seasons of the year); *frictional* unemployment (short-term unemployment associated with people changing jobs) and *structural* unemployment (long-term unemployment associated with the decline of particular industries and automation of production processes).

There are two basic causes of long-term unemployment:

(a) a level of total demand in the economy which is too low in relation to the supply capacity of the economy to produce goods and services. The traditional prescription for dealing with this situation is for the government to boost spending in the economy by decreasing taxes and by increasing its own expenditure (see FISCAL POLICY), and by expanding the money supply and lowering interest rates (see MONETARY POLICY);

(b) supply-side deficiencies, particularly in those countries which are heavily engaged in international trade, such as the UK. A lack of investment in plant and new products, low productivity and an inability to contain INFLATIONARY pressures may lead to a progressive displacement of domestic output by more competitive imported products, resulting in widespread job losses. Often the government's response to this situation is PROTECTIONISM, using tariffs and quotas to limit the extent of IMPORT PENETRATION into the home market, but this is not an effective long-term solution to the country's problems. Basically what is required to remove structural unemployment is an improvement in industrial efficiency and the creation of new enterprise.

See INDUSTRIAL POLICY, REGIONAL POLICY.

**unfair dismissal** the unfair termination of a person's employment by the employer. Dismissal can be held to be unfair if the employer cannot show a 'fair' reason and acted 'unreasonably' in taking the decision to dismiss. A fair reason is one where for some reason the employee is not able to carry out satisfactorily the duties associated with the employment or where the job is no longer needed because of REDUNDANCY. For instance, it would probably be considered fair to dismiss a chauffeur who had been disqualified from driving but unfair to dismiss someone on the grounds of personal dislike. To have acted reasonably the employer should have clearly informed the employee of the grounds for dismissal and given the employee the opportunity to put a personal point of view.

*Constructive dismissal* is where an employee feels forced to leave because the employer acts unlawfully, unfairly or otherwise breaches the CONTRACT OF EMPLOYMENT. A female employee who is subject to sexual harassment by her manager and who feels forced to leave her job as a result could possibly claim that she had been constructively dismissed.

An individual who believes the dismissal to be unfair may pursue a claim for reinstatement or compensation at an INDUSTRIAL TRIBUNAL. In determining whether dismissal is fair, tribunals draw on case law and an ADVISORY, CONCILIATION AND ARBITRATION SERVICE code of practice on DISCIPLINARY PROCEDURES. A very small minority of those who take unfair dismissal claims to tribunal actually achieve reinstatement. The number of claims taken to tribunal has increased in recent years and the Government recently took steps to limit them by requiring that those lodging unfair dismissal claims pay a large deposit to the tribunal. See EMPLOYMENT APPEALS TRIBUNAL.

**unfranked investment income** see FRANKED INVESTMENT INCOME.

**uniform business rate (UBR)** the annual charge made by local authorities in England and Wales on business premises, factories, warehouses, offices and shops. The UBR is fixed at a set rate throughout the country (for 1997/98 the rate has been fixed at 45.8p in the £ in England and 48.4p in Wales). Thus, for any given premises anywhere in England and Wales the rate payable is calculated simply by multiplying the above rates by the assessed rateable value of the premises. The UBR came into effect in April 1990, replacing the previous system of rating which gave individual local authorities discretion in setting the base rates payable in their particular areas. Inevitably, this created anomalies with large variations from area to area, as some authorities increased their local services and put the burden of paying a higher proportion of the bill on to businesses rather than householders. The introduction of the UBR required all business premises to be revalued at 1990 prices with further revaluations scheduled every five years.

**uniform delivered price system** see GEOGRAPHICAL PRICING.

**union branch** see TRADE UNION.

**union democracy** see TRADE UNION.

**union density** see TRADE UNION.

**union dues** TRADE UNION membership fees. See CHECK-OFF AGREEMENT.

**union membership agreement (UMA)** see CLOSED SHOP.

**Union of Shop, Distributive and Allied Workers** a UK TRADE UNION for retail employees with around 280,000 members. The UK's seventh largest union.

**UNISON** the UK's largest TRADE UNION formed from a merger of the Confederation of Health Service Employees, National Association of Local Government Officers and the National Union of Public Employees in 1993. It currently has around one million, three hundred and fifty thousand members in the health service, local government, schools and universities. It includes amongst its membership both manual workers, such as cleaners, and white collar workers such as managers and secretaries. It is notable for having a high proportion of female members.

**unitary frame of reference** see MANAGEMENT STYLE.

**unitary taxation** a system of TAXATION operated by a country that taxes a foreign-owned MULTINATIONAL ENTERPRISE on a predetermined proportion of its total worldwide income, rather than on the income which the multinational actually earned within that country. This involves the use of some rule of thumb to apportion tax liability: for example, if 10% of the total world ASSETS of a multinational are located in that country, then the country may seek to tax 10% of the multinational's world income, making no allowance for any foreign taxes paid. Countries might adopt unitary taxation to increase their taxation revenues and to counter manipulative TRANSFER PRICING by multinationals, but must bear in mind that such a taxation system is likely to discourage inward INVESTMENT.

Compare DOUBLE TAXATION.

**unit cost** see AVERAGE COST.

**United Nations** an international organization consisting of most of the world's countries whose primary objective is the maintenance of world peace and security and the promotion of social harmony and economic development. The UN operates a number of satellite agencies, including the FOOD AND AGRICULTURE ORGANIZATION, the INTERNATIONAL LABOUR ORGANIZATION and the UNITED NATIONS CONFERENCE ON TRADE AND DEVELOPMENT, and works closely with other international bodies such as the WORLD BANK and the GENERAL AGREEMENT ON TARIFFS AND TRADE (GATT).

**United Nations Conference on Trade and Development (UNCTAD)** an international institution which promotes the economic interests of DEVELOPING COUNTRIES by sponsoring INTERNATIONAL COMMODITY AGREEMENTS to improve export earnings on primary foodstuffs and minerals; by negotiating QUOTA and TARIFF reductions on developing countries' exports of manufacturers to the developed world; and by securing ECONOMIC AID packages for its members.

**unit of account** see MONEY.

**unit pricing** the practice of marking on product packs not only the PRICE per pack but the price per common unit of weight or volume, for example price per 500 grammes or price per litre. Unit pricing is generally undertaken for products like groceries which can be offered in a number of pack sizes for a particular brand, or where different brands are offered in a variety of sizes, in order to give consumers more accurate comparative price information. See WEIGHTS AND MEASURES ACT 1964.

**unit trust** a financial institution which specializes in investment in FINANCIAL SECURITIES on behalf of its 'unit' holders. Some unit trusts offer a single fund, but more usually they operate a number of funds catering for different investment requirements. Unit trusts pool together the monies of a large number of investors which they use to purchase a varied portfolio of investments, mainly UK and overseas corporate stocks and shares and government fixed-interest securities. They are ideal for smaller investors who wish to secure a wider spread of risk than they could achieve for themselves by direct investment in a limited number of securities, or who require professional management of their investments.

Unit trusts issue 'units' in their funds to buyers, and re-purchase units from sellers on the basis of a bid price (lower, for buying) and an offer price (higher, for selling). An initial management charge is required of buyers, followed by a smaller annual charge. The value of the individual units in a fund is obtained by dividing the total value of the fund investments plus cash held, by the number of units in existence every day. A fund which is growing will need to create new units, while one in decline will liquidate units on redemption. The value of the total investments of a fund is determined by the value of the securities it holds and the fund's valuation, and hence unit prices can go up or down with the ebb and flow of STOCK MARKET prices in general. Unit trusts usually offer investors a variety of funds to choose from, ranging from general funds which aim at a balance between current income and capital growth, to those specialized in achieving either capital growth or high current income.

The unit trust movement in the UK is represented by the UNIT TRUST ASSOCIATION (UTA) which provides a forum for the discussion of matters of general concern to members, and acts on behalf of members in dealings with other institutional bodies such as the Institutional Investors Committee and the government. The investment and management of funds by unit trusts are regulated by the INVESTMENT MANAGEMENT REGULATION ORGANIZATION and the PERSONAL INVESTMENT AUTHORITY in accordance with various standards of good practice laid down under the FINANCIAL SERVICES ACT 1986.

See INSTITUTIONAL INVESTORS, FINANCIAL SYSTEM, INSURANCE COMPANY.

**Unit Trust Association** the TRADE ASSOCIATION which represents the collective interests of UNIT TRUSTS in the UK.

**unity of command** the principle that an employee should receive instructions from only one superior. See CLASSICAL MANAGEMENT THEORY.

**universal management theory** see CLASSICAL MANAGEMENT THEORY.

**unlimited liability** see LIMITED LIABILITY.

**unlisted securities market (USM)** a market for corporate STOCKS and SHARES that have not obtained a full STOCK MARKET listing. An unlisted securities market was established in the

UK in 1980 in order to provide smaller companies with a means of raising new capital (see SHARE ISSUE) without the expense and the same formalities required by the main stock market. For example, such companies need only have a brief trading record to qualify and the proportion of their shares sold in the open market need only be 10% of their ISSUED CAPITAL instead of the usual 25%. The USM was phased out in 1996 and superseded by the Alternative Investment Market (AIM). AIM imposes no minimum on the percentage of a company's shares in public hands and no minimum trading record.

**unofficial strike** see STRIKE.

**unquoted investment** investments in UNQUOTED SECURITIES such as SHARES and DEBENTURES which are not quoted or traded on a STOCK MARKET. Where a company holds such unquoted investments, they will be shown in its BALANCE SHEET at their purchase price. See TRADE INVESTMENT.

**unquoted securities** SHARES or DEBENTURES in JOINT-STOCK COMPANIES which are not traded in the STOCK MARKET or for which no price is regularly quoted. It is difficult to determine the value of an unquoted security since no regular market exists for such a security.

**unsecured creditor** see CREDITORS.

**unsecured loan** money BORROWED by a company or individual without offering any COLLATERAL SECURITY to the lender.

**Unsolicited Goods and Services Acts 1971** and **1975** UK Acts which make it an offence for a person or business to make a demand for payment from persons or businesses to whom unrequested goods have been sent or delivered. See CONSUMER PROTECTION, INERTIA SELLING.

**upgrade** to replace an existing COMPUTER system (HARDWARE and/or SOFTWARE) by a more powerful model capable of processing data faster or storing larger amounts of data. When upgrading, computer users can experience problems of compatibility with existing programs and machines.

**upstream integration** see VERTICAL INTEGRATION.

**USM** see UNLISTED SECURITIES MARKET.

# V

**valence** see MOTIVATION.

**value** the money worth of a PRODUCT or ASSET. Value is measured in terms of the PRICE which buyers are prepared to pay for the product or asset. The amount which they are prepared to pay depends upon the benefits which they expect to derive from consuming or owning the item. See PRICE–QUALITY TRADE-OFF, PSYCHOLOGICAL PRICING.

**value added** the difference between the value of a firm's (or industry's) *output* (i.e. the total revenues received from selling that output) and the cost of the *input* materials, components or services bought in to produce that output. Value added focuses attention on the value that a company adds to its bought-in materials and services through its own production and marketing efforts within the company.

A firm will measure its value added as the difference between its SALES REVENUE and the cost of its bought-in materials and services. Where a firm operates at only one level of production or distribution in a VALUE-ADDED CHAIN, it will generally add less value than a vertically integrated firm which embraces several production and distribution stages.

See VERTICAL INTEGRATION, VALUE-ADDED TAX, VALUE-ADDED STATEMENT, VALUE ADDED PER EMPLOYEE.

**value-added chain** a chain of vertically linked activities which each add value (see VALUE ADDED) in producing and distributing a product. Depending on the nature of the product the value-added chain may involve a large number of vertically linked activities or only a few. Fig 87, for example, shows one particular value-added chain in the petrochemical industry. Here the value-added chain involves converting a raw material (oil) into intermediate materials (ethylene and PVC), then into a finished product (plastic kitchenware), then packaging and physically distributing this kitchenware to consumers.

Strategically, where a firm 'positions' itself in the value-added chain for an industry can have an important bearing on its profitability since different activities within the chain may (because of technical and competitive considerations) generate different levels of profitability. For example, supplying un-processed basic raw materials may yield low levels of profit compared to more skill-intensive later stage processsing activities or the supply of high-technology 'speciality' inputs.

In many cases, firms will choose to embrace a number of 'stages' in the value-added chain as part of a vertically inte-grated operation in order to reduce costs or secure 'tied' input supplies or market outlets. See VERTICAL INTEGRATION.

| Stage | Main Chain | Bought-In Items |
|---|---|---|
| Extraction | crude oil | |
| Refining | naphtha | |
| Petrochemical processing | ← | chemical additives |
| | ethylene | |
| | PVC | |
| | ← | dyestuffs |
| Manufacture of finished product | plastic kitchenware | |
| | ← | packaging |
| Distribution | Wholesaler | |
| | retailer | |
| Consumer | | |

Fig. 87. Value-added chain.

**value added per employee** a measure of a firm's value added/size relation, that expresses the firm's VALUE ADDED as a ratio of its size, measured in terms of number of employees. It is useful to compare value added per employee in a firm with the company's average employee remuneration.

**value-added statement** an ACCOUNTING statement showing the value added by a company during an accounting period and how this created wealth has been shared among employ-ees, providers of capital and others contributing towards its creation. Fig. 88 shows the typical layout of a value-added statement.

| | £ |
|---|---|
| Sales | 980,000 |
| Less materials and services purchased | 560,000 |
| VALUE ADDED | 420,000 |

Applied to meet:

| | | | |
|---|---|---|---|
| Remuneration | (to employees) | 150,000 | |
| Interest | (to lenders) | 30,000 | |
| Tax | (to government) | 80,000 | |
| Dividends | (to shareholders) | 40,000 | 300,000 |
| Retained for use in business | | | 120,000 |

Fig. 88. **Value-added statement.** Value-added statement of Y Co for year ending 31 December 19xx.

**value-added tax (VAT)** an INDIRECT TAX imposed by the government on the VALUE ADDED to a good or service. Governments use value-added taxes both as a means of raising revenue (see BUDGET) and as an instrument of FISCAL POLICY.

A value-added tax is based on the difference between the value of the OUTPUT over the value of the INPUTS used to produce that output. The final amount of tax is added on to the selling PRICE of the product and is paid by the buyer.

The 'mechanics' of a value-added tax may be illustrated as follows: producer Y sells his output for £10 per unit having spent £8 on inputs. Thus, value added is £2 per unit. If VAT is set at 10%, the selling price of the product is £11 with £1 being the amount of tax paid by the final buyer. Producer Y would then set off against the £1 VAT-output tax collected from the final buyer the 80p VAT-input tax which he has already paid on his £8 of inputs bought, and remit the difference of 20p to the CUSTOMS AND EXCISE. In the same way, supplier X (who has supplied producer Y with his input for £8 per unit) will have collected 80p VAT-output tax from producer Y, against which he will offset any VAT-input tax which he paid on his inputs, and remit the difference to the Customs and Excise. The total of all these sums remitted by firms X, Y etc. to the Customs and Excise will equal the £1 charged on the final sale to the customer.

VAT rates may be applied uniformly at a single rate across

the board, or, as in the UK, applied on a discretionary basis with some products being exempted from the tax, or zero-rated, while for others VAT is levied at different values for different groups of products.

VAT is a cumbersome tax system to operate, involving as it does thousands of 'tax points' and related paperwork. It does, however, require all the firms contributing to a taxed product to be involved in the tax collection operation, not just final sellers.

**value analysis** or **value engineering** the evaluation and review of a product's DESIGN, with the aim of reducing its material or manufacturing cost without impairing its function or performance. By examining all a product's components and their manufacture it may be possible to identify cheaper raw materials to replace expensive ones, or opportunities to reduce the degree of precision with which components are made.

**value chain** see VALUE ADDED CHAIN.

**value engineering** see VALUE ANALYSIS.

**value for money** the extent to which a government, business person or consumer gets a good deal from the money which they spend on goods or services.

**value-for-money audit** an audit of a private sector organization which looks at the extent to which the organization achieves *economy* (reducing waste and cutting costs); *efficiency* (ensuring that scarce resources are fully utilized); and *effectiveness* (achieving targets and fulfilling the objectives laid down by management).

**variable** a term that can take a range of numerical values. For example, price, sales quantity and quantity produced are all variables in so far as each can take a number of different values.

Variables can be divided into two groups:

(a) an *independent variable* which affects some other variable, for example the price of a product will influence demand for it;

(b) a *dependent variable* which is affected by some other variable, for example the demand for a product will be influenced by its price. It is conventional to place the dependent variable on the left-hand side of an EQUATION and to show it on the horizontal axis of a GRAPH.

**variable costs** any COSTS that tend to vary directly with the level of output. They represent payments made for the use of variable factor-inputs, notably raw materials and direct labour.

A firm will leave a market if in the short run it cannot earn sufficient SALES REVENUE to cover its total variable cost. If it can generate enough total revenue to cover total variable cost and make some CONTRIBUTION towards total FIXED COST then it will continue to produce in the short run even though it is still making a loss.

**variable overheads** any OVERHEADS that vary proportionately with the level of output of a product, so that variable-overhead cost per unit of output is constant. They include such items as fuel and lubricants, and salespersons' commissions. See also FIXED OVERHEADS, SEMIVARIABLE OVERHEADS.

**variance 1.** the difference between budgeted and actual results (see BUDGETING), or between STANDARD COSTS/revenues and actual costs/revenues. Variances can be:

(a) adverse or negative when actual revenues fall short of budget or standard, or when actual costs exceed budget or standard;

(b) favourable or positive when actual revenues exceed budget or standard, or when actual costs are less than budget or standard.

**2.** a measure of variation within a group of numerical observations, specifically the average of the squared deviations of the observations from the group AVERAGE.

See STANDARD DEVIATION.

**variance analysis** the breakdown of differences between the STANDARD COST (revenue) of a product and its comparable actual cost (revenue) into their constituent parts. Variance analysis highlights matters which are not proceeding to plan, enabling managers to take corrective action to deal with losses or inefficiencies. The main variances are MATERIALS-COST VARIANCE, the LABOUR-COST VARIANCE, the OVERHEAD-COST VARIANCE and the SALES-REVENUE VARIANCE. Fig. 89 (overleaf) shows the main cost variances and how they are linked.

**variance reports** tabulations which compare actual results with the BUDGET or STANDARD COST and show the VARIANCES. It is especially important that such reports highlight variances which are adverse and of a significant value. It is also important from a control point of view that all variances which are being reported and which require management

Fig. 89. **Variance analysis.** The relationship of the main cost variances.

action are supported by sufficient narrative to explain the reasons why the variances have occurred. See VARIANCE ANALYSIS.

**variety** the number of products sold by a firm as part of its PRODUCT RANGE. A firm may make many different products and many variants of each product in order to appeal to most market segments and maximize its potential sales. However, the providing of variety can be expensive if this is associated with short production runs, high stockholding costs, complex production scheduling and high marketing costs. Consequently, firms may aim to eliminate unnecessary variety in products or components by means of variety-reduction programmes and STANDARDIZATION of components.

**VAT** see VALUE-ADDED TAX.

**VCT** see COMPETITIVE TENDERING.

**VDU** see VISUAL DISPLAY UNIT.

**vendor** the seller of a good or service. The vendor can be a person (see PERSONAL SELLING) or a machine (see AUTOMATIC VENDING).

**venture capital** money subscribed in the form of SHARE CAPITAL and LOAN CAPITAL to finance new firms and activities which are considered to be of an especially risky nature and hence unable to attract finance from more conventional sources. There are a number of specialist institutions covering this sector of the capital market (see STOCK MARKET), including THREE I'S (formerly Investors in Industry) and the venture capital arms of the COMMERCIAL BANKS and MERCHANT BANKS.

Venture capital investors originally concentrated most of their funding on small start-up businesses offering innovative products, but recently a substantial proportion of their funds has been directed towards the less risky business of financing MANAGEMENT BUY-OUTS of established companies.

The British Venture Capital Association represents firms and institutions operating in this area.

**vertical disintegration** the withdrawal of a firm from a particular stage in a vertically linked production and distribution chain. A firm which is currently vertically integrated into a number of stages may decide to exit from a particular stage for cost or strategic reasons. For example, as a result of technical advances or a change in competitive conditions, it may be cheaper for the firm to buy in materials from outside suppliers than continue to self-supply (see MAKE OR BUY); or the emergence of new distribution channels for the firm's products may remove the imperative for it to own distribution outlets. See VERTICAL INTEGRATION.

**vertical integration** the combining in one firm of two or more vertically related activities, as opposed to these activities being performed separately in different firms and then being synchronized through arms-length market transactions. For example, a firm engaged in assembly operations may integrate backwards ('upstream') to produce its own components, or forwards ('downstream') to distribute its products. Vertical integration may involve ORGANIC GROWTH on the part of the firm, or firms may choose to expand by MERGER with, or TAKEOVER of, established suppliers and distributors.

Vertical integration may be advantageous to firms if it permits them to lower their operating costs by production savings arising from the linking of technically related processes (for example the linking together of casting and rolling operations in steel mills, and continuous motorcar assembly operations), and reduce STOCKHOLDING COSTS by a closer matching of inventory and production requirements. Vertical integration also enables firms to avoid various transaction costs in dealing with outside suppliers/distributors, including the costs of finding suppliers/dealers, agreeing contract terms and conditions, and ensuring that there is strict adherence to these undertakings. Additionally, vertical integration gives firms greater security of supplies and access to customers, as well as the potential for applying competitive pressure on non-integrated rivals by depriving them of supplies/outlets (FORECLOSURE) or PRIZE SQUEEZING.

Like HORIZONTAL INTEGRATION, vertical integration, however, offers only limited growth potential for the firm since firms are ultimately locked into the fortunes of the end-markets they serve. If these markets are static or declining (see PRODUCT LIFE CYCLE) firms must seek new growth opportunities through DIVERSIFICATION. Moreover, firms' ability to expand vertically, particularly by merger and takeover, may be restricted by the OFFICE OF FAIR TRADING.

See MAKE OR BUY DECISION, COMPETITIVE ADVANTAGE, BUSINESS STRATEGY, TRANSFER PRICE, VALUE ADDED, DISTRIBUTION CHANNEL, VERTICAL MARKETING SYSTEM, INTERNALIZATION, VERTICAL DISINTEGRATION, INTERNAL CUSTOMER, INTERNAL MARKET.

**vertical marketing system (VMS)** a distribution system in which a firm in a DISTRIBUTION CHANNEL undertakes as a vertically integrated operation a number of channel functions (wholesaling, retailing), or is able to control independent firms in the channel by, for example, contractual arrangements such as EXCLUSIVE DEALING and FRANCHISING.

**vertical segregation** the division of the HIERARCHY of an ORGANIZATION by sex or some other criterion. It is common for all or most jobs at high levels of the hierarchy to be performed by men and all or most jobs at lower levels to be performed by women. Women find it hard to obtain jobs at higher levels because of DISCRIMINATION. See GLASS CEILING.

**VET** see TRAINING.

**vicarious liability** see TORT.

**video conferencing** a form of interactive COMMUNICATION which involves the use of PERSONAL COMPUTERS. Desktop or personal video systems provide one-to-one video communications, ususally by adding a video camera and a plug-in video card to a personal computer attached to a digital telephone line or office network.

Video conferencing can be a time-saving and cost-effective means of communication since it reduces or eliminates the need for business travel.

See INFORMATION MANAGEMENT.

**visible export** See EXPORT, BALANCE OF PAYMENTS.

**visible import** see IMPORT, BALANCE OF PAYMENTS.

**visual display unit (VDU)** a means of displaying COMPUTER output, usually on a television-style screen or liquid crystal display unit.

**VMS** see VERTICAL MARKETING SYSTEM.

**Vocational and Educational Training** see TRAINING.

**voice messaging** a form of COMMUNICATION which involves the use of answering machines attached to fixed-wire and cordless telephones to store messages until such a time as recipients are present, or it is convenient for them to receive them. Around one-half of all business calls are for one-way communication only but they often interrupt work which is more important than the call itself.

See INFORMATION MANAGEMENT.

**voluntarism** the philosophy that the activities of organizations should be governed by their own codes of conduct rather than by the law. In INDUSTRIAL RELATIONS it refers to the widespread belief amongst both TRADE UNIONS and employers that the form and outcome of COLLECTIVE BARGAINING should be determined by themselves and not be subject to legal regulation. See LABOUR LAW.

**voluntary competitive tendering** see COMPETITIVE TENDERING.

**voluntary group** a business which operates as a WHOLESALER to a group of small RETAILERS who undertake to place a certain volume of orders with the voluntary group, in return for price concessions on the purchases they make and various backup services (promotions etc.). Voluntary groups such as SPAR in groceries and Unichem in chemists' goods are able to use their BULK-BUYING power to obtain price discounts from manufacturers, some of which are passed on to their members. See DISTRIBUTION CHANNEL.

**voluntary organization** an organization in which most of the members are not paid but give their time voluntarily because they identify with its objectives.

**voluntary redundancy** see REDUNDANCY.

**voluntary winding-up** see INSOLVENCY, LIQUIDATION.

**voting shares** the ORDINARY SHARES that allow the SHAREHOLDERS to cast a vote for each share held at a company's ANNUAL GENERAL MEETING. See also SHARE CAPITAL.

**Vredeling Directive** a draft directive of the European Commission (EC) concerning DISCLOSURE OF INFORMATION and

CONSULTATION with employees. Named after the former European Union/Community Commissioner Henk Vredeling, it proposes that employee representatives have rights to information concerning the organization's structure, its financial situation, investment plans and employment prospects. It also proposes that management plans which are likely to have serious consequences for the workforce should be the subject of meaningful consultation. This directive, originally formulated in the early 1980s, has not been adopted by the Commission, in part because of resistance by the UK Government.

# W

**wage** the money payment made to a worker, usually on a weekly basis, for the use of his or her labour. A worker's basic wage will depend on the hourly WAGE RATE and the number of hours worked. The latter is usually related to the number of hours specified as constituting the 'basic' working week, but in some cases workers may be given a GUARANTEED BASIC WAGE to protect them against loss of earnings due to *short-time working*, and in other cases workers may be able to add to their basic wage by OVERTIME earnings. In addition to PAYMENT BY TIME, workers may be paid in proportion to their output under a PAYMENT BY RESULTS scheme. See PAY, MEASURED DAY WORK.

**wage differential** see PAY DIFFERENTIAL.

**wage drift** the propensity for employees' actual earnings to rise faster than increases in their WAGE RATE. This tends to occur when there is full employment or when there are labour shortages in particular labour markets, and often results from informal bargaining between workers, their representatives (SHOP STEWARDS) and managers supplementing formal COLLECTIVE BARGAINING. It was considered to be a widespread problem in the UK in the 1960s and contributed to the decision to create a Royal Commission to investigate the state of UK INDUSTRIAL RELATIONS (See DONOVAN COMMISSION). See PRICES AND

INCOMES POLICY, PAY, PAYMENT BY RESULTS.

**wage freeze** see PRICES AND INCOMES POLICY.

**wage rate** the money payment made to a worker for each 'unit' of his or her labour input, usually measured either on an hourly time basis (see WAGES), or for each unit of output produced (see PIECEWORK). See PAY, PAYMENT BY TIME, PAYMENT BY RESULTS, WORK STUDY.

**wage restraint** see PRICES AND INCOMES POLICY.

**wage round** see PAY ROUND.

**Wages Council** a UK body which stipulates minimum levels of WAGES and conditions of employment in industries where TRADE UNION organization is too weak for conventional COLLECTIVE BARGAINING to operate effectively (for example hairdressing). Composed of union and employer representatives and independent members, their awards are set out in Wages Orders and policed by the Wages Inspectorate. Critics of wages councils have argued that they interfere with LABOUR MARKET mechanisms by maintaining wage rates at artificially high levels, thereby restricting employment levels. For this reason successive Conservative governments have considered abolishing wages councils. In the 1980s the Government narrowed their jurisdiction to the establishment of basic pay and hours of work. The Wages Concils were finally abolished in 1993 by the TRADE UNION REFORM AND EMPLOYMENT RIGHTS ACT 1993. See LOW PAY.

**wages inspectorate** see WAGES COUNCIL.

**wages order** see WAGES COUNCIL.

**wage system** see PAY.

**waiting time** see IDLE TIME.

**wants** see NEEDS.

**warehouse** business premises used by a manufacturer to store both raw materials, components etc. (materials store) and final products (finished goods store), and by WHOLESALERS and RETAILERS to store finished products in the course of distribution to buyers. See DISTRIBUTION CHANNEL.

**warehouse club** a RETAILER which sells an extensive range of products to club members only, at heavily discounted prices on a SELF SERVICE basis.

See DISCOUNT STORE, DISTRIBUTION CHANNEL.

**warrant** a FINANCIAL SECURITY issued by a company to raise capital, which gives the holder the right to purchase SHARES in the company at some specified future date at a set price. Warrants are quoted on the STOCK MARKET and thus can be bought and sold in the same way as the issuing company's shares, usually at a much lower price. In essence a warrant is similar to convertible LOAN STOCK (but without interest payments) which can be converted into equity at the appointed time. The holder of a warrant forgoes current income in the hope of making a sizable capital gain on conversion.

**warranty** see GUARANTEE.

**wastage** see LABOUR TURNOVER.

**wastage index** see LABOUR TURNOVER.

**wasting asset** FIXED ASSETS such as mines, quarries and oil wells, which are used up during their working lives. It is especially important to make adequate provision for DEPRECIATION of such assets.

**WDA** see WELSH DEVELOPMENT AGENCY.

**weaknesses and strengths** see SWOT ANALYSIS.

**wealth** the total stock of ASSETS owned by the population of a country. Wealth represents past income flows which have been used to buy such assets as houses, land, stocks and shares etc. One commonly used measure of wealth in the UK is that of 'marketable wealth', consisting of those assets which are readily saleable. Wealth in the UK, like income, (see DISTRIBUTION OF INCOME), is unevenly distributed (see Fig. 90). See WEALTH TAX.

|  | | £2,500 billion |
| Total marketable wealth | | % |
| --- | --- | --- |
| Most wealthy | 1% | 17 |
| "          " | 5% | 36 |
| "          " | 10% | 48 |
| "          " | 25% | 72 |
| "          " | 50% | 92 |

Fig. 90. **Wealth**. The distribution of marketable wealth in the UK, 1994. The total includes land and dwellings (net of mortgage debt), consumer durables, stocks and shares, bank and building society deposits and other financial assets. (Source: Social Trends, 1996.)

**wealth tax** a DIRECT TAX imposed by the government on a person's private assets when those assets are transferred to the person's beneficiaries. Wealth taxes are used by governments principally as a means of promoting social equity by reducing disparities in WEALTH holdings. In the UK INHERITANCE TAX is the current means of taxing wealth.

**wear out period** see FAILURE RATE CURVE.

**weighted average** a form of AVERAGE or mean, in which each of the items used in a calculation is given a weight to reflect the fact that not all items have the same importance. Weighted averages are frequently used in price indices to reflect the percentage of a CONSUMER'S income spent on various items to enable a more accurate, or representative, average price increase to be found. For example, a consumer purchases three typical goods, A, B and C and, over the time period in question, the three goods have increased in price by 35%, 10% and 45% respectively. The consumer spends all of his income on these goods in the proportion 20%, 50% and 30% respectively. An unweighted average would give an average mean price increase of:

$$\frac{35 + 10 + 45}{3} = 30\%$$

A weighted average on the other hand, would give:

$(20\% \times 35\%) + (50\% \times 10\%) + (30\% \times 45\%) = 25.5\%$

The weighted figure is a more representative average price increase because account has been taken not only of the price increases but also of the proportion, or weight, of the price increase.

See INDEX NUMBER.

**weight note** a document that lists the gross weight of packages, crates, etc. containing GOODS or COMMODITIES issued by the supplier to the buyer. See EXPORTING.

**Weights and Measures Act 1963** a UK Act which empowers the DEPARTMENT OF TRADE AND INDUSTRY to prescribe permitted weights and measures for the sale of certain products such as food and beverages. The act established a network of local authority officials to inspect goods sold in shops, public houses and other establishments to see if specified weights and measures are applied correctly and, on finding shortages, instigate proceedings against offenders through the courts. The OFFICE OF FAIR TRADING now acts as a coordinating body, keeping a central register of convictions under the Act. See CON-

SUMER PROTECTION, UNIT PRICING.

**Weights and Measures Act 1985** a UK Act which lays down the legal weights and measures to be used for trading and other purposes. For example, the UK 'primary standards' are the yard or metre as the unit of measurement of length, and the pound or kilogram as the unit of measurement of mass or weight.

**welfare** that aspect of management concerned with the well-being, both physical and emotional, of employees. It is an umbrella term for a range of services and activities. HEALTH AND SAFETY (the regulation of working conditions) is probably the most important but is often managed separately from other welfare functions. Other welfare activities include the provision of canteens and social clubs, sports facilities, medical officers etc. Some organizations also provide counselling services to help individuals cope with, for instance, work-related stress.

The reasoning behind employer concern with welfare suggests that a contented workforce is likely to be more productive. Some employers also feel that it is a social obligation to their employees. Welfare activities usually come under the remit of the PERSONNEL MANAGEMENT function. In fact, in the UK the origins of personnel management lie in the concern to improve employee welfare felt by certain employers in the early years of the 20th century.

See FRINGE BENEFIT, HUMAN RELATIONS.

**welfare unionism** see TRADE UNION.

**Welsh Development Agency (WDA)** an organization whose general remit is to foster the industrial regeneration of Wales as a means of creating employment and improving living standards. The WDA provides financial assistance and other support to manufacturing and service businesses, as well as supporting infrastructure projects. See REGIONAL POLICY (UK).

**whistle-blower** someone who publicizes or reports to the relevant authorities what they perceive to be unlawful or unethical practices by their employer or fellow employees. Whistle-blowing has become more prominent in recent years, in part because of the trend towards commercialization of public services (e.g. in the health service). Many CONTRACTS OF EMPLOYMENT now preclude employees from publicizing any aspect of the employing organization without prior authorization, and this has made whistle-blowing a more secretive and more dramatic activity. Those blowing the whistle, rather than those committing the unlawful or unethical act, are often those penalized by the employer. However, in some circumstances (e.g. health and safety violations) whistle-blowers now have legal protection (see TRADE UNION REFORM AND EMPLOYMENT RIGHTS ACT 1993).

**white-collar union** a TRADE UNION which largely or exclusively represents clerical, administrative and technical employees. In the past, such unions have generally been concerned to maintain for their members conditions of employment, rates of PAY, and status superior to those of manual WORKERS. With the growth of public sector employment and the gradual shift in the UK from manufacturing to services, such unions have generally achieved big increases in their membership since the 1960s. Some even maintained their membership during the decline of union membership in the 1980s.

**white-collar worker** SEE WORKER.

**white knight** SEE TAKEOVER BID.

**Whitley Councils** the COLLECTIVE BARGAINING institutions found in each department of the UK civil service and in the National Health Service. They are so called because they were established as a result of recommendations of the Whitley Committee on INDUSTRIAL RELATIONS in 1917–18. A National Whitley Council determines the pay and conditions of general civil servants, whilst Departmental Whitley Councils are concerned with the running of the department and the pay and conditions of specialist employees. There is also a Whitley Council system in the National Health Service dealing with pay and conditions of all health service staff except those professional groups whose pay levels are recommended by a PAY REVIEW BODY. In addition, some public corporations (for example British Rail) and local government are said to have a Whitley system, in that they have the comprehensive negotiation and consultation procedures recommended by Whitley even though their top-level industrial relations institutions are not actually called Whitley Councils.

**wholesaler** a business which buys products in relatively large quantities from manufacturers which it stocks and 'breaks bulk', on-selling in smaller quantities to RETAILERS. Thus, wholesalers act as *middlemen* between the PRODUCERS and retailers of a product in the DISTRIBUTION CHANNEL, obviating the need for the producers themselves to stock and distribute their goods to retailers, and likewise retailers to undertake their own warehousing.

Wholesalers typically sell to retailers by adding a MARK-UP on their buying-in prices from suppliers or by obtaining a commission from the retailer.

Traditionally, wholesalers have provided their retail customers with credit facilities and a delivery service, but in recent years CASH AND CARRY wholesaling has become a prominent feature of distribution systems both in the UK and elsewhere. Moreover, with the emergence of large CHAIN STORE retailers (for example supermarkets, and DIY groups) the wholesaling function of stocking and breaking-bulk has itself become increasingly integrated with the retailing operation, with retailers taking particular advantage of the price discounts associated with BULK BUYING directly from manufacturers.

Independent wholesalers may operate a single warehouse or a chain of warehouses giving wider regional coverage and in many cases national distribution.

See VOLUNTARY GROUP, CATEGORY DISCOUNTER.

**wholesaling** the function of buying products in relatively large quantities from manufacturers and 'breaking bulk', on-selling these products in smaller quantities to RETAILERS.

See WHOLESALER, DISTRIBUTION CHANNEL.

**wildcat strike** see STRIKE.

**Winchester** a large-capacity HARD DISK for storing data in a COMPUTER.

**windfall profit** an exceptional gain or PROFIT arising from a sudden and unexpected change in market conditions which serves to raise the price of a FINANCIAL SECURITY, FIXED ASSET or STOCK.

**winding-up** see LIQUIDATION, INSOLVENCY.

**window dressing** the use of discretion in the application of ACCOUNTING PRINCIPLES so as to report PROFIT and ASSET figures which are flattering to the company. Window dressing is a form of CREATIVE ACCOUNTING which is concerned with making modest adjustment to sales, debtors and stock items when preparing year-end ANNUAL REPORTS AND ACCOUNTS.

**withholding tax** TAX deducted at source from INTEREST or

DIVIDEND payments. Withholding taxes are often levied by a country upon interest and dividends paid by a domestic company to non-residents. It is a means of taxing cash flows from the company before such monies move out of their jurisdiction. Withholding taxes often provoke retaliatory action by the other countries affected, so that most countries end up imposing withholding taxes. To reduce the effect of withholding taxes on overseas investments, countries often negotiate DOUBLE TAXATION treaties.

**'word of mouth' recommendation** the personal endorsement of a product by a satisfied customer who creates additional sales potential by extolling the merits of the product to friends, neighbours etc.

**word processor** a COMPUTER software program package designed for the manipulation of text. Word processors have dramatically improved the speed with which business documents can be produced by making the correction of errors or rearrangement of blocks of text easier.

**work** see JOB, LABOUR, WORK ORGANIZATION, SOCIOLOGY OF WORK, HOMEWORKING, DOMESTIC LABOUR.

**work-based maintenance** an approach to MAINTENANCE which provides for the overhaul of machinery, plant and equipment at intervals, based on the usage or output of each machine.

**worker** a person employed by an organization to perform a JOB or work tasks either on a paid basis (as an employee) or on an unpaid basis (as, for example, a charity worker).

Traditionally, paid employees have been categorized into two groups of workers:

(a) *manual workers*, i.e. those working mainly with their hands. Although manual workers may be engaged in service occupations such as pavement sweeping, the dominant image of the manual worker is that of an employee engaged in production in a factory. Often these workers are referred to as *blue-collar workers* because their physical working environment is such that (blue) overalls are necessary;

(b) *non-manual workers*, i.e. those who can be said to work with their heads rather than their hands, providing administrative services rather than directly creating material goods. As with manual workers, the term is somewhat artificial: some non-manual employees, typists for example, require considerable manual dexterity. *White-collar worker* is an alternative term in common use, though it tends to be applied mainly to clerical rather than managerial or PROFESSIONAL employees. White-collar workers are so called because their apparently favourable working environment makes a light-coloured shirt or blouse practical work wear, and because smart clothing is often viewed as appropriate dress for work of this type and status. In sociology 'black-coated worker' has also been used to refer to clerical workers because a sober, dark jacket similarly has been seen as essential work wear.

Although these categorizations are somewhat imprecise in terms of the type of work performed, there is often a clear difference in the conditions of employment (see CONTRACT OF EMPLOYMENT) associated with each. Those workers classed as non-manual tend to have more favourable conditions (for example, better holiday entitlements) than manual workers (see STAFF STATUS).

The difference in working conditions between the two groups has been thought in the past to give rise to two distinct sets of attitudes. Manual workers were thought to subscribe to COLLECTIVISM and to a confrontational view of their relationship with their employer, whilst non-manual workers were thought to be more individualist (see INDIVIDUALISM) in their attitudes and to adopt a deferential approach to their managers. Though always an oversimplification, the picture has become more complex in recent years with the apparent spread of individualism amongst manual workers and the growth of highly repetitive, routinized clerical work, leading, some say, to the 'proletarianization' of white-collar work.

Probably the most widespread popular image of the worker is that of a male employee employed in factory work. However, this image is now a long way out of step with reality. Only 25% of the UK labour force are now employed in manufacturing, with a corresponding growth in services in recent years. In addition, there has been a large increase in the number of women workers, with the result that nearly half of the employed force is female. In the UK, the employment of males in full-time manufacturing jobs has been steadily replaced by the employment of females in PART-TIME, service sector jobs.

See DISCRIMINATION, ORIENTATION TO WORK, TEMPORARY WORK,

WHITE-COLLAR UNION.

**worker director** a representative of the workforce on the BOARD OF DIRECTORS. These directors may be selected by management or elected by the workforce (all those employed in an organization or all those in a TRADE UNION). Where worker directors are elected the scheme is a form of IN-DUSTRIAL DEMOCRACY. The rationales for worker directors include the practical consideration that it can promote commitment to and understanding of organizational goals; and the moral consideration that employees should be able to influence the direction of the organization of which they are a part. However, concern has been expressed in trade union circles that because worker directors are bound by collective board decisions (collective responsibility) they may on occasion have to implement policies which could be viewed as harmful to employee or union interests. If, on the other hand, these directors see their primary duty as advocates for their constituents, then they may be excluded by other directors from key decisions. Managerial anxieties about worker directors have also centred on the question of loyalty. The main fear has been that they will use their privileged access to top-level information to advance employee interests rather than those of the organization as a whole. For example, financial information might be leaked to other employee representatives to assist in a claim for a pay increase.

In the UK, interest in industrial democracy and worker directors grew in the 1970s, culminating in the BULLOCK REPORT which recommended that worker directors be elected to company boards. However, legislation to implement the report was abandoned because of the strength of opposition ranged against it. But where experimental schemes were launched, as in the Post Office, it was found that the potential problems outlined above were muted in practice, mainly because the worker directors had a restricted conception of their role and did not involve themselves in board affairs as fully as they might have done.

See CODETERMINATION, EMPLOYEE SHARE-OWNERSHIP PLAN.

**workers' collective** see WORKERS' COOPERATIVE.

**workers' control** an advanced form of INDUSTRIAL DEMOCRACY in which employees have tight control over both policy and operational activities of managers.

**workers' cooperative** an organization that is owned and controlled by those who work in it (though some in the UK have a few external shareholders). To be fully accepted as a workers' cooperative, such an organization must adhere to the general principles of the International Cooperative Alliance, including the requirement that each member has an equal vote at general meetings. Voting should not be proportional to share capital.

A critical issue that faces all cooperatives is how to organize the MANAGEMENT function: should all cooperative members be actively involved in management (as in a workers' collective), or should managerial functions be delegated to specialist managers? There is the obvious danger with the former that decision-making could be slowed down, that RESPONSIBILITY will be unclear and that many of those involved in management will not be sufficiently competent. But if specialists are employed, some of the democratic character of the cooperative will be lost. The question arising from this dilemma is whether the need to compete in markets will force cooperatives to 'degenerate' into conventional hierarchically organized firms.

Many believe that cooperatives are not a sustainable alternative to conventional business organizations. Proof that they could be comes from the Mondragon area of northern Spain. Here some 20,000 workers are employed in a large number of cooperatives in all sectors of the local economy. Critical to their success have been cooperation between cooperatives, facilitating the sharing of skills and resources, and the existence of a strong support structure, including a bank, providing finance and business skills. Such support is not as well advanced in the UK. Even so, the number of cooperatives in the UK has been growing consistently in recent years as local Cooperative Development Agencies (whose object is to foster development of cooperatives) have sprung up.

See INDUSTRIAL DEMOCRACY.

**workflow analysis** see JOB ANALYSIS.

**workforce** see LABOUR FORCE.

**work group** see GROUP.

**work-in** see INDUSTRIAL ACTION.

**working capital** or **net current assets** an accounting term denoting a firm's short-term CURRENT ASSETS which are turned over fairly quickly in the course of business. They include raw materials, work in progress and finished goods STOCKS, DEBTORS and cash, less short-term CURRENT LIABILITIES. Fig. 91 shows the major components of the working capital cycle.

Increases in the volume of company trading generally lead to increases in stocks and amounts owed by debtors, and so to an increase in working capital required (see OVERTRADING). Reductions in delays between paying for materials, converting them to products, selling them and getting cash in from customers, will tend to reduce the working capital needed. Decisions to hold larger than normal stocks to take advantage of bulk-order discounts or special prices, or in anticipation of materials scarcity, would tie up working capital. Increases in prices of materials or wage rates would also mean that extra working capital would be needed to cover INFLATION.

Fig. 91. Working capital.

**working-capital ratio** a measure of a firm's ability to pay its short-term liabilities out of CURRENT ASSETS, which expresses the firm's current assets as a ratio of CURRENT LIABILITIES. See also CURRENT RATIO, WORKING CAPITAL, CASH FLOW.

**work in progress** any goods that are still in the process of being made up into their final form. Work in progress together with raw materials and STOCKS of finished goods constitute INVENTORY INVESTMENT.

**work measurement** an aspect of WORK STUDY which involves the application of measurement techniques to establish the time it takes for a trained worker to carry out a particular JOB. The purpose of measuring the time required to complete a job is to provide management with information for PRODUCTION SCHEDULES, for PRODUCT COSTING, and to assist in the design of incentive payment systems such as PIECEWORK.

*Timestudy* is the most often used work measurement technique for recording the time it should take to complete a specified job. Time study involves a number of steps:

(a) Recording details of the job and checking that no obvious improvements in method can be made (see METHOD STUDY);

(b) Dividing up the job being done into discrete operational elements to facilitate the timing of each component element;

(c) Timing the work elements to obtain the *observed time*;

(d) Rating the performance of the worker by comparing his or her actual rate of working against the defined STANDARD RATE (the average rate of working of a skilled, motivated operative) and using this to adjust the observed time and arrive at the *basic time*;

(e) Determining the percentage *allowances* to be added to the basic time to compensate for fatigue, contingencies like machine breakdowns and interruptions, in order to establish the *standard time* for the job.

Time study is appropriate for short–cycle repetitive work. If, however, it is necessary to establish work standards in situations where irregular long–cycle work is conducted or where many different jobs are performed, these techniques may well be quite inappropriate. In such circumstances it may well be advisable to use some form of *activity sampling*, which in its simplest form consists of visual sampling and recording of activities in order to establish the proportion of time in which employees or machines are working or idle (see ACTIVITY CHART).

Time study is a *direct* work measurement technique. Alternatively, various *indirect* measures may be employed to generate standard times. One method uses data collected from previous time studies to provide a *synthetic standard time* for a job which differs only marginally from a job which has already been subject to direct time study or a new job which has not yet begun. A second method, the *predetermined motion time* system lists all motions that workers can utilize in performing tasks, together with times for these motions. From this general list of motions it is possible to select the specific motions involved in a particular job and thus compile a standard time for this particular job. Finally, *analytical estimating* can be used where there is insufficient synthetic data available to allow time standards to be established for all job elements and where the time required for these elements has to be based on knowledge and practical experience. See SIMULTANEOUS MOTION CHART, THERBLIGS.

**work organization** the distribution and coordination of work tasks, skills and authority in an ORGANIZATION. Work organization is the way that tasks are distributed amongst the individuals in an organization and the ways in which these are then coordinated to achieve the final product or service. For instance, in a school the work organization comprises those workers providing tuition, secretarial staff giving administrative support and ancillary workers, such as the caretaker, who ensure that the facilities are ready for teaching to take place. These activities are coordinated in part by staff meetings, in part by the headteachers and their assistants. An alternative form of work organization would be where teachers also undertake some secretarial and ancillary tasks.

Some modes of work organization may be more efficient in terms of labour utilization than others. The quality of work organization may thus have an important impact on the performance of the organization. Work organization may be determined by a number of factors:

(a) the nature of the technology used (in turn influenced by the nature of the product or service). Assembly-line technology, for instance, tends to discourage group working and to encourage a pattern of work organization where each worker does a single repetitive task;

(b) managerial choice. Technology may potentially be used in a number of ways (see SOCIOTECHNICAL SYSTEM) according to managerial objectives. Managerial competence is also important. Poor knowledge of production management may lead to inefficient work organization;

(c) workforce aspirations. Groups of workers are often able

to modify informally the way that work is done and the way that tasks are distributed among them. In addition TRADE UNIONS or SHOP STEWARDS may regulate the way work is organized, either unilaterally (see DEMARCATION LINE, RESTRICTIVE LABOUR PRACTICE), or jointly with management (see COLLECTIVE BARGAINING).

Many commentators believe that much of the UK's economic difficulties in recent decades are due to inefficient patterns of work organization. These are variously attributed to a failure to invest sufficiently in new technology, 'overmighty' unions, poor management etc. There is a growing recognition that the managerial approach to work organization should be more rigorous and strategic than in the past (see JAPANIZATION). Many also believe that greater task scope should be given to MANUAL WORKERS, supported by improved TRAINING. Operators of sophisticated equipment should be given the opportunity to program or maintain it. As well as improving JOB SATISFACTION this would lead to better standards of work.

See JOB DESIGN AND RE-DESIGN, SOCIOLOGY OF WORK.

**workplace bargaining** see COLLECTIVE BARGAINING.

**work sampling** see ACTIVITY SAMPLING.

**works committee** see CONSULTATION.

**works council** see CONSULTATION, CODETERMINATION.

**works manager** the manager with overall RESPONSIBILITY for the operation of a factory or plant. See MANAGEMENT.

**work station** see PRODUCTION-LINE BALANCING.

**work study** or **time and motion study** an area of PRODUCTION MANAGEMENT concerned with ensuring the best possible use of human and material resources in carrying out a specified activity. Work study embraces the techniques of METHOD STUDY, which analyses the ways JOBS are done with a view to improving these methods, and WORK MEASUREMENT, which seeks to measure the time required to perform jobs.

**work-to-rule** see INDUSTRIAL ACTION.

**World Bank (International Bank for Reconstruction and Development)** an international institution established in 1947 whose purpose is to assist countries to develop their economies by the provision of ECONOMIC AID in the form of loans and technical assistance. The World Bank supports a wide range of projects in the less developed countries including the establishment of infrastructure (roads, gas and water supplies, schools and hospitals), the modernization of traditional industries (farm mechanization and cultivation techniques) and the setting up of new industries (iron and steel, textiles etc.).

The Bank's resources are provided largely by subscriptions from the advanced countries, although it also issues its own securities to raise additional funds. Generally, the Bank lends on a commercial basis – loans are repayable and bear market-related interest charges – but it also provides low-interest ('soft') loans through its affiliate the *Industrial Development Association*, while a further affiliate, the *International Finance Corporation* invests in share capital in selected companies.

**world-class manufacturing** the ability of a firm to compete successfully against the best anywhere in the world. This requires the firm to have the right manufacturing capability to supply products at competitive prices and high levels of product quality and sophistication, depending on customers' demands. Achieving world-class status involves the firm embracing sound PRODUCTION AND OPERATIONS MANAGEMENT practices (for example, METHOD STUDY), concepts and techniques (for example, TOTAL QUALITY MANAGEMENT), systems (for example, MANUFACTURING RESOURCE PLANNING) and technologies (for example, COMPUTER-INTEGRATED MANUFACTURING).

**World Gold Council** an organization based in Geneva whose main objective is to promote the sale of GOLD bullion (bars and coins) to investors, and to widen the appeal of gold as an ornamental (jewellery) material and as an industrial base metal.

**World Trade Organization (WTO)** an international body which replaced the GENERAL AGREEMENT ON TARIFFS AND TRADE in 1995.

**write off** *v.* (*accounting*) to charge a cost item as an expense in computing a firm's profit or loss. Certain cost items which are fixed assets but which are of insignificant value may still be written off and charged as an expense in their year of purchase.

**writing down allowance** See CORPORATION TAX.

**written down value** see NET BOOK VALUE.

# Y

**yield** the return on a FINANCIAL SECURITY, expressed in money terms, related to the current market price of that security, to show the percentage return on the investment. Yield can refer to the INTEREST RATE payable on the market price of a BOND (INTEREST YIELD); or DIVIDEND rate payable on the market price of a SHARE (DIVIDEND YIELD); or company profit per share (after tax) related to the price of the share (EARNINGS YIELD). For example, a bond with a face value of £100 and a rate of interest of 10% generates a nominal return of £10 per year. If, however, the bond can be purchased for £50 on the open market, then the yield is 20%, representing 20% return on the £50 invested. The lower the purchase price of a bond or share with a given coupon rate of interest or dividend or profit, the higher its yield will be, and vice versa. There is thus an inverse relationship between the price paid for a bond or share and its yield.

The term *flat yield* or *current yield* is sometimes used to describe a yield calculation which does not take account of the redemption value of a bond. Yields which take into account not only the annual interest receivable but also any capital profit/loss on redemption of the bond are termed *redemption yields*. Where the current market price of a bond is below its specified redemption price, the potential profit on redemption must be divided by the number of years to the redemption date of the bond, and this annual profit equivalent added to the flat yield on the bond to arrive at its redemption yield. Where the current market price of the bond is above its specified redemption price the annualized potential loss on redemption must be deducted from the flat yield in calculating redemption yield. For example, a bond offering an interest payment of £10 per year and with a current market price of £50 would have a flat yield of 20%. If, in addition, the specified redemption price of the bond is £100 in five years' time, then the bond promises a potential profit of £100 − £50 = £50 which is equivalent to an annualized profit of £50 ÷ 5 = £10 per year or an additional return of £10 ÷ £50 or 10%. This would be added to the flat yield of 20% to give a redemption yield of 30%.

**yield gap** the difference between the YIELD on established undated or long dated gilt-edged BONDS and the average yield on SHARES. Before 1960, the yield on gilts was less than the yield on shares, and it was argued that such a gap was justified by the greater riskiness or variability in the return on shares. However, since about 1960, some countries like the UK have experienced a reverse yield gap with the yield on gilts exceeding the yield on shares as a result of high inflation and high interest rates.

**Youth Training (YT)** see TRAINING, TRAINING AND ENTERPRISE COUNCIL.

# Z

**zero-based budgeting** a management accounting technique that seeks to reexamine and challenge the assumptions underlying a firm's costs. Zero-based BUDGETING involves preparing from scratch a budget for each company department, starting from the basic premise that each department's budget is zero, then justifying every activity and its associated expenditure before including it in the budget. This contrasts with conventional budgeting, where departmental budgets are often based on last year's budget suitably updated. The purpose of this process is to identify and remove inefficient or obsolete activities within the firm.

**zero defects** a business philosophy which emphasizes the need to make all products 'right first time' in order to minimize QUALITY COSTS.

**zero-rated products** see VALUE-ADDED TAX.

**Z-score** a composite score, summarizing the weighted results of a number of ACCOUNTING RATIOS, that claims to predict a company's likelihood of failure. Z-scores were developed by distinguishing the values of various performance-and-liquidity ratios for companies which had gone bankrupt and for those which had prospered. Those accounting ratios which proved to discriminate effectively between failed companies and successful ones were incorporated in a standard formula to calculate an aggregate Z-score. Analysts can calculate Z-scores for particular companies, and use the results to try to predict whether companies are likely to fail.

# COLLINS DICTIONARY OF ECONOMICS

## Second Edition

*Christopher Pass, and Bryan Lowes and Leslie Davies*

The *Collins Dictionary of Economics* is an established and definitive guide to the intricate structures and forces of the economic world. The Dictionary is addressed primarily to the requirements of undergraduates and advanced school students, but will also prove an invaluable reference book for students of the subject at a wide range of levels or for anyone studying economics as part of a broader-base course such as business studies or social science.

The Dictionary has over 2,500 entries – from *ability-to-pay principle of taxation* to *zero-sum game*. There are also over 190 diagrams, plus numerous tables. Essential mathematical and statistical terms are included, as are brief biographies of major economists.

In addition to providing clear definitions of economic terms, the Dictionary summarizes the important theoretical principles behind the science of economics, and their application in such areas as competition policy, agricultural policy, fiscal policy and monetary policy.

As well as the basic definition and explanation of a particular term, the reader who requires further exposition is guided, where appropriate, through cross references to related terms and refinements of the original concept.

Dr Pass and Dr Lowes are lecturers in managerial economics at the University of Bradford's Management Centre. Dr Davies is professor of business administration at Bodø Graduate School of Business, Norway.

'The book will certainly earn its keep...Recommended.' – *Economics.*

ISBN 0 00 470372 3

# COLLINS DICTIONARY OF SOCIOLOGY

*David Jary & Julia Jary*

The *Collins Dictionary of Sociology* is an up-to-date resource for those concerned with the complex discipline of sociology. The book is primarily directed at the undergraduate market, but is sufficiently accessible in style and organization to be useful to the 'A' level student and the general reader. However, while its breadth recommends it to a wider readership, its depth of treatment of some of the more complex issues will make it a convenient reference book for academic sociologists.

The Dictionary explains a wide range of terms and concepts from every area of sociology, and a selection of those most likely to be met from associated disciplines such as psychology, economics, anthropology and political science. It also provides a useful coverage of methodological terms and research techniques.

The treatment and organization allows the reader to build comprehensive coverage of all sociological schools, or to compare perspectives. Its coverage extends from *social change* to *sexuality*, from *functionalism* to *Feyerabend*, and from *Lumpenproletariat* to *Likert scale*. There are also biographical entries on key figures in the development of sociology.

The *Collins Dictionary of Sociology* is an essential reference work for all who require a clear, balanced and comprehensive guide to sociology, or for anyone with an interest in contemporary society.

David Jary is Professor of Sociology at Staffordshire University. Julia Jary teaches psychology part-time at Staffordshire University and for the Open University. The Dictionary has been compiled with the assistance of a skilled editorial team of specialists from the main sociological fields.

ISBN 0 00 434359 X (paperback)

# COLLINS DICTIONARY OF PERSONAL COMPUTING

*Ian R. Sinclair*

Aimed primarily at those using microcomputers as a tool – whether it be at university, school or college, or in the home or office – rather than the professional computer expert, the Dictionary will also prove invaluable to anyone whose work is related in any way to computers, be they micro, mini or mainframe.

Far too many computer manuals assume that even the beginner knows the meaning of a vast array of specialized jargon, leaving the user in a state of near despair. Although not a handbook to particular machines, *Collins Dictionary of Personal Computing* contains definitions and explanations for over 2,000 of the terms that the average user is most likely to come across, from *access* to *zero compression*. Written with a clarity and precision that will be welcomed by all computer users, the entries are augmented by nearly 100 diagrams and explanatory captions.

Comprehensive without indulging in unnecessary padding, and of course completely up-to-date, the Dictionary includes such basic terms as *BASIC*, *bit* and *binary*, as well as those strange terms that computer buffs have made peculiarly their own, such as *blow*, *bomb* and bubble. Fields covered range through hardware, software, programming, computer logic, data and word processing, languages, systems, and graphics, to those areas of information technology in which computers play such a vital role.

Ian R. Sinclair, a full-time technical author, has written numerous best-selling computer books for Collins, and is also author of the *Collins Dictionary of Electronics*.

'...excellent value for money.' – *Computer Weekly*.

ISBN 0 00 434386 7

# SPECIAL MESSAGE TO READERS

**THE ULVERSCROFT FOUNDATION**
**(registered UK charity number 264873)**
was established in 1972 to provide funds for
research, diagnosis and treatment of eye diseases.
Examples of major projects funded by
the Ulverscroft Foundation are:-

- The Children's Eye Unit at Moorfields Eye Hospital, London
- The Ulverscroft Children's Eye Unit at Great Ormond Street Hospital for Sick Children
- Funding research into eye diseases and treatment at the Department of Ophthalmology, University of Leicester
- The Ulverscroft Vision Research Group, Institute of Child Health
- Twin operating theatres at the Western Ophthalmic Hospital, London
- The Chair of Ophthalmology at the Royal Australian College of Ophthalmologists

You can help further the work of the Foundation
by making a donation or leaving a legacy.
Every contribution is gratefully received. If you
would like to help support the Foundation or
require further information, please contact:

**THE ULVERSCROFT FOUNDATION**
**The Green, Bradgate Road, Anstey**
**Leicester LE7 7FU, England**
**Tel: (0116) 236 4325**

**website: www.foundation.ulverscroft.com**

Linda Howard is an award-winning *New York Times* bestselling author. She lives in Alabama with her husband and golden retriever.

You can discover more about the author at www.lindahowardbooks.com

# TROUBLEMAKER

For Morgan Yancy, a team leader in a para-military group, nothing comes before his job. But when he's ambushed and almost killed, the leader of his elite quasi-military group demands answers. Who is after the members of the squad, and why? Sent away to recover, Morgan must lie low and stay vigilant. He knows this will be his toughest task yet . . . Bo Maran finally has her life figured out. She's got friends, a dog, and a little money in the bank. Then Morgan Yancy shows up on her doorstep. Bo doesn't need a mysterious man in her life — especially a troublemaker as entic-ing and secretive as Morgan . . .

*Books by Linda Howard*
*Published by Ulverscroft:*

MR PERFECT